Marketing Essentials

Joel R. Evans
Hofstra University

Barry Berman
Hofstra University

William J. Wellington
University of Windsor

 Prentice Hall Canada Inc.
Scarborough, Ontario

Canadian Cataloguing in Publication Data

Evans, Joel R.
　　　Marketing essentials

Includes index.
ISBN 0-13-889031-5

1. Marketing. I. Berman, Barry. II. Wellington,
William Joseph Patrick. III. Title.

HF5415.E862 1998　　658.8　　C97-930770-8

 © 1998 Prentice-Hall Canada Inc., Scarborough, Ontario
A Division of Simon & Schuster/A Viacom Company

Prentice-Hall, Inc., Upper Saddle River, New Jersey
Prentice-Hall International (UK) Limited, London
Prentice-Hall of Australia, Pty. Limited, Sydney
Prentice-Hall Hispanoamericana, S.A., Mexico City
Prentice-Hall of India Private Limited, New Delhi
Prentice-Hall of Japan, Inc., Tokyo
Simon & Schuster Southeast Asia Private Limited, Singapore
Editora Prentice-Hall do Brasil, Ltda., Rio de Janeiro

ISBN 0-13-889031-5

Publisher: Patrick Ferrier
Acquisitions Editor: Mike Ryan
Senior Marketing Manager: Ann Byford
Developmental Editor: Amber Wallace
Copy Editor: Gail Copeland
Production Editor: Mary Ann McCutcheon
Production Coordinator: Deborah Starks
Permissions/Photo Research: Susan Wallace-Cox
Cover Design: Sputnik Art & Design
Cover Image: Christopher J. Boyle/Photonica
Page Layout: Michael Kelley

1 2 3 4 5　WC　02 01 00 99 98

Printed and bound in United States

Visit the Prentice Hall Canada Web site! Send us your comments, browse our
catalogues, and more. **www.phcanada.com** Or reach us through e-mail at
phcinfo_pubcanada@prenhall.com

To
Linda, Stacey, and Jennifer
Linda, Glenna, and Lisa
Christine, Roger, and Pamela

Brief Contents

v

Contents

Preface

These are very exciting times for all of us. During recent years, we have seen the true arrival of the PC age and the World Wide Web, the steady global movement toward service- rather than production-driven economies, a growing understanding and interest in customer service and customer satisfaction, greater focus on consumer diversity in the marketplace, the emergence of free-market economies in Eastern Europe, business and government grappling with such ethical issues as the consumer's right to privacy, the impact of deregulation on society, and many similar events.

The years ahead promise to be even more intriguing—as the European Union becomes more strongly unified; North American countries make their markets further accessible to one another; opportunities in other foreign countries grow; technological advances continue; and we try to cope with slow-growth economies in various parts of the globe. As we prepare for the rest of this decade and beyond, a thorough understanding and appreciation of marketing becomes critical.

We believe that a good marketing textbook must do several things in order to provide this critical understanding: It should incorporate both traditional and contemporary aspects of marketing, including the careful consideration of environmental factors; address the roles of marketing and marketing managers; and show the relevance of marketing for those who interact with or who are affected by marketing activities (such as consumers). We also believe that presentation is important: A textbook must describe marketing concepts to readers in an interesting, comprehensive, and balanced manner. As we indicate at the beginning of Chapter 1, marketing is truly "an exciting, fast-paced, and contemporary business discipline."

Although the basic, or traditional, components of marketing (such as consumer behaviour, marketing research and informations systems, and product, distribution, promotion, and price planning) form the foundation of any introductory-level marketing textbook, contemporary techniques and topics also need to be covered in depth. Among the contemporary topics that are examined in full chapter length in *Marketing Essentials* are strategic planning and marketing; final consumer behaviour; organizational consumers (including manufacturers, wholesalers, retailers, government, and nonprofit institutions); and integrating and analyzing the marketing plan. Environmental effects are noted throughout the book.

Marketing Essentials explains all major principles, defines key terms, integrates topics, and demonstrates how marketers make everyday and long-run decisions. Examples based on such diverse organizations as Andersen Consulting, Bata Shoes, Black & Decker, BMW, British Airways, Coca-Cola, Eaton's, Kodak, Lands' End, Metropolitan Life, Pizza Hut, Radio Shack, Swatch, Toyota, United Parcel Service (UPS), Visa, and Wrigley appear in each chapter. The illustrations build on the conceptual material, reveal the exciting and dynamic nature of marketing, cover a wide variety of firms, and involve students in real-life applications of marketing.

A Canadian Tradition Begins

In 1997, Prentice Hall Canada started a new Canadian tradition with the publication of *Marketing*, Canadian Edition, by Evans, Berman and Wellington. In response to instructor feedback and comments from focus groups, this essentials text was developed from the Canadian Edition of *Marketing*.

- A lively, easy-to-read writing style.
- A balanced treatment of topics (by size of firm, goods- and service-based firms, profit-oriented and nonprofit firms, final and organizational consumers, etc.).
- Comprehensive coverage of all important marketing concepts, including seven chapters on the marketing mix (product, distribution, promotion, and price planning).
- A full-colour design throughout the book, including about 60 photos and 100 figures. These visually attractive illustrations are all keyed to the text.
- Part openers that provide integrated overviews of the chapters they contain.
- Definitions of marketing terms.
- Service marketing coverage in the section on product planning (Chapter 7).
- Separate company and name and subject indexes.

    These features are contained in each chapter:

- Chapter objectives that outline the major areas to be investigated.
- An opening vignette that introduces the material through a real-world situation.
- An introductory overview to set the tone for the chapter.
- Thought-provoking boxed extracts on key marketing topics.
- Descriptive margin notes that highlight major concepts.
- Boldface key terms that identify important definitions.
- Many flowcharts that demonstrate marketing concepts; and current figures and tables that provide up-to-date information.

- Exciting and useful Internet sites appear in the margin and are easily identifiable by the Weblinks icon.
- Numerous footnotes to enable the reader to do further research.
- Chapter summaries keyed to chapter objectives. These summaries are followed by a listing of key terms with text page references.
- End-of-chapter questions divided into separate "review" and "discussion" categories.

Supplements

Marketing Essentials is accompanied by a complete set of supplemental learning and teaching aids.

For the Instructor.

Instructor's Resource Manual. This comprehensive guide contains resource material for each chapter of the text, including suggested sources of additional information and answers to discussion questions. It also includes sample syllabi, term paper topics and a listing of trade associations.

Instructor's Lecture Manual. This highly detailed lecture guide provides the following for each chapter of the text: eight to ten teaching goals; a complete overview; key terms; approximately fifteen suggested discussion topics not included in the text; a creative, high-involvement class exercise; and a set of lecture notes.

Test Item File. The test item file contains over 3000 multiple choice, true/false and essay questions and their answers. Questions are coded according to their difficulty and are organized by type (terminology/concept or applied/comprehensive/integrative).

PH Custom Test. This powerful computerized testing package uses a state-of-the-art software program that provides fast, simple and error-free test generation. Tests can be previewed on-screen before printing and can be saved to one of three word processing file formats: WordPerfect, Microsoft Word or ASCII. PH Custom Test can print multiple variations of the same test, scrambling the order of questions and multiple-choice answers.

Transparency Masters and Electronic Transparency Masters. Culled from figures in the text these transparency masters may be copied onto acetates for use in class. More than fifty of the transparency masters are provided in PowerPoint.

CBC Video Cases. Prentice Hall Canada and the CBC have worked together to bring you 22 segments from such notable CBC programs as *Venture* and *The National Magazine*. Designed specifically to complement the text, this case collection is an excellent tool for bringing students into contact with the world outside the classroom. The CBC icon and video segment title can be found at the top of the page with the relevant text. These programs have extremely high production quality, present substantial content, and have been chosen to relate directly to chapter content.

Case Book and Computer-Based Exercises. Contains 66 case studies, 22 of which have an accompanying CBC video for use in the classroom. Also includes a disk containing 18 computer-based marketing exercises designed to apply and reinforce specific marketing concepts. The exercises allow students to manipulate marketing factors and see their impact on costs, sales and profits.

Video Guide and Case Notes. This supplement contains answers to the case and video case questions as well as a video guide and case notes.

For the Student

Online Study Guide. A comprehensive self-instructional guide, the format of the study guide parallels that of the text. Each chapter contains objectives, an overview, key terms and concepts, true/false questions, completion questions, matching questions, and multiple-choice questions. Visit the online study guide at **www.prenticehall.ca/evans**.

Paintco V: A Marketing Simulation. Allows students to simulate marketing decision making for a fictional paint company. Contains an easy-to-use disk with instructions and background information.

How Marketing Is Organized

Marketing Essentials is divided into seven parts. Part 1 presents marketing in a contemporary society, describes the environment within which it operates, and discusses marketing information systems and the marketing research process. Part 2 deals with marketing's central thrust: understanding final and organizational consumers in the diverse marketplace. It examines demographics, life-style factors, consumer decision making, target market strategies, and sales forecasting.

Part 3 encompasses product planning, the product life cycle, goods versus services marketing, new products, mature products, branding, and packaging. Part 4 deals with distribution planning, channel relations, physical distribution, wholesaling, and retailing. Part 5 examines promotion planning, the channel of communication, advertising, public relations, personal selling, and sales promotion. Part 6 covers price planning, price strategies, and applications of pricing. Part 7 presents strategic planning from a marketing perspective, integrates marketing planning—including benchmarking and customer satisfaction measurement—and looks to the future.

Particular thanks are due to the following people for advising us on content in the planning stages, participating in a focus group, reviewing the manuscript and offering many useful suggestions: Wes Balderson, University of Lethbridge; Ken Burns, Cambrian College; Dwight Dyson, Centennial College; Gerard Edwards, Douglas College; Paul Garneau, Kwantlen University College; John Lille, Centennial College; Gerald Stephenson, Okanagan University College; and Keith Wright, Mount Royal College.

We hope this first offering of *Marketing Essentials* will surpass the needs of new adopters at Canadian colleges and universities. We would really like to know that we have satisfied the needs of the users and would enjoy receiving feedback, especially notes of support and encouragement.

Please feel free to communicate with us. We welcome comments regarding any aspect of *Marketing Essentials* or its package: William J. Wellington, Faculty of Business Administration, University of Windsor, 401 Sunset Ave., Windsor, Ontario, Canada, N9B 3P4, E-mail at R87@uwindsor.ca, or Joel R. Evans or Barry Berman, Department of Marketing and International Business, Hofstra University, Hempstead, N.Y., 11550-11725, E-mail at MKTJRE@HOFSTRA.EDU or MKTBXB@HOFSTRA.EDU. We promise to reply to any correspondence we receive.

Joel R. Evans
Barry Berman
William J. Wellington
1998

About the Authors

Joel R. Evans (Ph.D. in Business with majors in Marketing and Public Policy) is the RMI Distinguished Professor of Business and Professor of Marketing and International Business at Hofstra University. Previously, Dr. Evans was department chairperson for seven years. Before joining Hofstra, he worked for United Merchants and Manufacturers, owned a retail mail-order business, and taught at Bernard M. Baruch College and New York University. He has also served as a consultant for such diverse companies as PepsiCo, Nynex, and McCrory.

Dr. Evans is author or editor of numerous books and articles and is active in various professional associations. At Hofstra, he has been honored as a faculty inductee in Beta Gamma Sigma and received two Dean's Awards and the School of Business Faculty Distinguished Service Award. Dr. Evans has also been honored as Teacher of the Year by the Hofstra M.B.A. Association.

Barry Berman (Ph.D. in Business with majors in Marketing and Behavioral Science) is the Walter H. "Bud" Miller Distinguished Professor of Business and Professor of Marketing and International Business at Hofstra University. Previously, Dr. Berman was associate dean of the Hofstra School of Business for seven years. He has served as a consultant to such organizations as the Singer Company, Associated Dry Goods, the State Education Department of New York, and professional and trade groups.

Dr. Berman is author or editor of numerous books and articles and is active in various professional associations. He served as associate editor of the *Marketing Review* for many years. At Hofstra, he has been honored as a faculty inductee in Beta Gamma Sigma and received two Dean's Awards. Dr. Berman has also been honored as Teacher of the Year by the Hofstra M.B.A. Association.

William J. Wellington (Ph.D. in Business Administration) is an Associate Professor of Marketing at the University of Windsor, where he has taught graduate and undergraduate business students for over ten years. Prior to entering the academic field, Dr. Wellington was employed for three and a half years as a field sales representative for Parke-Davis Canada Ltd., a wholly-owned subsidiary of Warner-Lambert Inc. He received his Ph.D. from Michigan State University in 1989, where he majored in Marketing and Transportation. Dr. Wellington is particularly interested in marketing management, marketing strategy, and marketing education. He is an author and editor of several books in marketing and has written articles on market segmentation and the use of simulations in marketing education; he won best paper awards at the 1992 and 1997 conference of the Association for Business Simulation and Experiential Learning.

AN INTRODUCTION TO

MARKETING

In Part 1, we begin our study of marketing and discuss concepts that form the foundation for the rest of the text.

1

Marketing in Contemporary Society

Here, we show the dynamic nature of marketing, broadly define the term "marketing," and trace its evolution. We pay special attention to the marketing concept, a marketing philosophy, customer service, and customer satisfaction and relationship marketing. And we examine the importance of marketing, as well as marketing functions and performers.

2

The Environment in Which Marketing Operates

In this chapter, we look at the complex environment within which marketing functions, with an emphasis on both the factors that are controllable and those that are uncontrollable to an organization and its marketers. We demonstrate that without adequate environmental analysis, a firm may function haphazardly or be shortsighted.

3

Information for Marketing Decisions

In this chapter, we explain why marketing decisions should be based on sound information. We explain the role and importance of the marketing information system—which coordinates marketing research, continuous monitoring, and data storage and provides the basis for decision making. We also describe marketing research and the process for undertaking it. We show that marketing research may involve surveys, observation, experiments, and/or simulation.

Part 1 Vignette
The Process of Marketing Affects Us All

As we will show throughout *Marketing Essentials*, organizations come in all sizes and orientations. The diversity of those engaged in marketing is demonstrated by the examples provided throughout the text and in the descriptions of Canadian organizations found in each of the part-opening vignettes of *Marketing Essentials*. The kinds of issues facing these organizations and the forces affecting them are many and varied.

Firms like Soft Image and its mega-sized parent, Microsoft, have arisen as a result of the impact of technology on marketing. The human race spawns new technologies that are commercialized, and this leads to new needs and wants, which spawn more new products and take businesses and society in directions never anticipated. Soft Image is a computer technology firm at the cutting edge of computer animation. Using computers to create visual images for movies and television programming is one of the innovative uses that was never fully dreamed of by the originators of computers.

Historically, computers have been viewed as tools designed mainly for number crunching and statistical information storage and processing. Today, films like *Toy Story, Jurassic Park*, and *The Mask* include computer-animated visual sequences as integral parts of their production. Soft Image is transforming the notion that computers are used only for number crunching and non-creative pursuits. The computer has become an important tool and social force, and its powers are being rapidly enhanced by the software developed by firms like Soft Image and Microsoft. These kinds of forces and their impact on business is something that *Marketing Essentials* will examine.

Organizations involved with "marketing" practices come in all sizes and orientations.

Another critical force that affects marketers is competition. Canadian boot manufacturers like Greb have survived and flourished in Canada's footwear industry, while Canadian shoe manufacturers have struggled with foreign competition. Developing and marketing products that meet the needs of customers better than any competitor is one of the key factors for survival and success in today's marketplace. Canadian boot manufacturers are innovators and the best producers of quality footwear made to resist the "elements of nature." Understanding that business is almost always conducted in the face of competition is one key aspect of marketing that all would-be marketers must keep in the forefront of their planning.

Dealing with the environment, developing marketing plans and making marketing decisions cannot be undertaken without good information. Acquiring information can be performed by a business itself or may be contracted out to third party market research firms like Information Resources International and A.C. Nielsen. Consumer purchase information is particularly valuable to marketing decision makers, and these two firms are vying with one another to be the exclusive collectors and providers of this information for the Canadian market. Although IRI and A.C. Nielsen provide marketing information, they also undertake marketing of their own services. In this vein, they compete with one another, and other marketing information providers, and must undertake and understand the process of marketing, even as they themselves play a part in this process.

We hope you enjoy learning about marketing as undertaken by firms operating in Canada, a process that will be introduced in the remaining part-opening vignettes and presented throughout the fifteen chapters of *Marketing Essentials*.

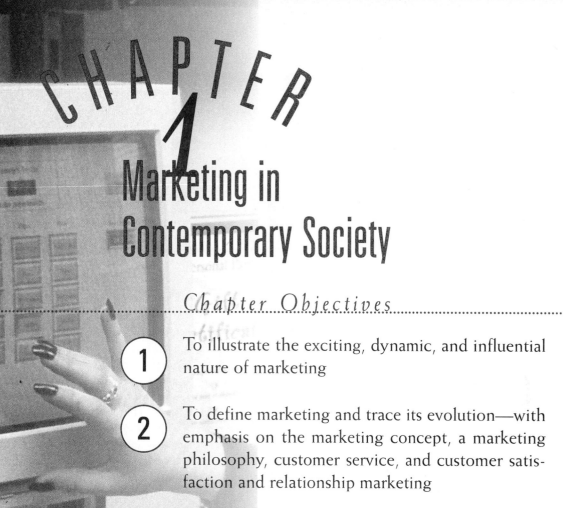

CHAPTER 1

Marketing in Contemporary Society

Chapter Objectives

1 To illustrate the exciting, dynamic, and influential nature of marketing

2 To define marketing and trace its evolution—with emphasis on the marketing concept, a marketing philosophy, customer service, and customer satisfaction and relationship marketing

3 To show the importance of marketing as a field of study

4 To describe the basic functions of marketing and those that perform these functions

{ *Marketers used to target customers; now they must learn to invite them in. Consumers have more information about products and more products to choose from than ever before. They have more ways to shop: at malls, specialty shops, and super stores; through mail-order, home shopping networks, and virtual stores on the Internet. And they are bombarded with messages from television, radio, online computer networks, the Internet, fax machines, telemarketing, and magazines and other print media.* }

Reprinted by permission.

For marketing-oriented firms, "inviting customers in" is a fundamental part of their business strategies. After all, one of the underpinnings of marketing is a strong interest in consumers—based on a belief that companies cannot succeed unless they understand and satisfy their clientele. How can firms do this in today's high-tech world? They can use information technology such as the Internet and toll-free 800 numbers to keep customers engaged in an ongoing dialogue. In contrast to traditional consumer surveys, "real-time" marketing provides continuous consumer contacts and uses consumer feedback as a critical element in developing and improving products, focuses on customer satisfaction, and refocuses the role of marketing within a firm. Let us look at how Apple Computer, Eaton's, and Federal Express use real-time marketing.

Apple Computer constantly analyzes information from its consumer hotlines for its Macintosh Performa computers. Apple's customer service personnel also use phone conversations with consumers to tell them about new products. On a weekly basis, these personnel identify the top ten consumer issues. The data are used by Apple engineers to design and improve products. For example, because of this feedback system, Apple learned about a particular problem that customers had in setting up Performa systems: Although Apple's instruction manual clearly illustrated how to set up the mouse, some people still thought it served as a foot pedal. After assessing the situation, Apple engineers devised an on-screen "welcome mat" that appears the first time people boot up their Performa computers. This mat introduces them to the basic elements of the Apple system, including the proper set-up and how the mouse functions.

Eaton's uses real-time marketing to issue new credit cards to customers. Instead of filling out long application forms, a customer need only provide a major credit-card number and some personal information to a clerk at an Eaton's sales terminal. The sales terminal then contacts a database operated by Montreal-based Equifax Canada Inc. Ninety per cent of the applicants are approved and issued an Eaton's credit card on the spot. The issued cards can contain a line of credit of up to $3000 and Eaton's promises that if the process of approval takes longer than one minute, the first credit card purchase is free (limited to $1000). As a result of this real-time marketing approach, Eaton's has noted an increase in credit-card usage rates and profitability.

Federal Express provides its larger customers with software and computer terminals to let them track their shipments. National Semiconductor, for instance, can determine if each of its customers worldwide has received the parts ordered by using the software. And a computer company seeking to order parts from National Semiconductor can look at the firm's online catalogue, order parts from Federal Express, and track parts shipping. Federal Express plans to communicate with most customers via real-time systems by the year 2000.[1]

In this chapter, we will learn more about the roles of marketing, see how marketing has evolved over the years, and look at its scope.

APPLE CANADA
www.apple.ca/

EATON'S
www.eatons.com/

EQUIFAX CANADA INC.
www.equifax.com/

NATIONAL SEMICONDUCTOR
www.nsc.com/

Overview

Marketing is a dynamic field, encompassing many activities.

Marketing is an exciting, fast-paced business discipline. We engage in marketing activities or are affected by them on a daily basis, both in our business-related roles and as consumers. Okay, but what exactly does "marketing" mean? Well, it is not just advertising or

---

[1]Regis McKenna, "Real-Time Marketing," *Harvard Business Review*, Vol. 73 (July–August 1995), pp. 87–95; Katrina Onstad, "Eaton Credit Corporation Award of Distinction for Technology," *Canadian Business* (Fall 1995 Technology Issue), p. 76.

selling goods and services, although these are aspects of marketing. And it is not just what we do as supermarket shoppers every week, although this too is part of markcting.

As formally defined in the next section, "marketing" encompasses the activities involved in anticipating, managing, and satisfying demand via the exchange process. As such, marketing encompasses all facets of buyer/seller relationships. Specific marketing activities (all discussed later in this chapter) include environmental analysis and marketing research, broadening an organization's scope, consumer analysis, product planning, distribution planning, promotion planning, price planning, and marketing management.

In a less abstract way, here are two examples of real-world marketing—one from a business perspective and one from a consumer perspective.

BUSINESS PERSPECTIVE Marie Jackson, a 1994 B.Comm. with an accounting major and CA certification, has worked for a large accounting firm since graduating from university. She is now ready to open her own practice, but must make a number of decisions: Who should her clients be? What accounting services should she offer? Where should she open her office? How will she attract her clients? What fee schedule should she set? Is it ethical to try to attract clients that she worked with from her old firm? *Each of these questions entails a business-related marketing decision.*

Let's look at some of Marie Jackson's marketing options:

- *Clients*—Marie could target small or medium businesses, nonprofit organizations such as local libraries, and/or individuals (for personal tax and estate planning).

- *Accounting services*—Marie could be a full-service accountant for her clients or specialize in a particular accounting task (such as developing customized accounting software).

- *Office location*—Marie could open an office in a professional building, a small shopping centre, or her home. She could also go on on-site visits to clients, thus making the choice of her office location less important.

- *Attracting clients*—Marie must determine if she is from the "new" school—where it is acceptable to run ads in local newspapers, send out direct-mail pieces to prospective clients, etc.—or from the "old" school—where most forms of promotion are viewed as being unprofessional.

- *Fee schedule*—Marie must rely on her own experience with her previous firm and look at what competitors are doing. Then, she could price similar to others or lower/ higher than them (depending on her desired image and a realistic reading of the marketplace).

- *Ethics*—Marie must weigh the personal dilemma of "stealing" clients from her old firm against the difficulty of starting a business from scratch without any client base.

CONSUMER PERSPECTIVE At the same time that Marie Jackson is making decisions about her new accounting practice, Albert Sampson is reappraising his status as an accounting client. He owns a small furniture repair store and has been a client of a mid-sized accounting firm for ten years. Yet he is now unhappy with the firm and feels it takes his business for granted. But before switching accountants, Albert must answer these questions: What kind of firm should he select? What accounting services should he seek? Where should the accounting firm be located? How will he learn more about possible firms? What fees should he be willing to pay? Is it ethical to show prospective firms samples of the work from his present accountant? *Each of these questions addresses a consumer-related marketing decision.*

Let's look at some of Albert Sampson's marketing options:

- *Kind of firm*—Albert could select a small, medium, or large accounting firm. Given his current dissatisfaction, he would probably avoid medium and large firms.

- *Accounting services*—Albert could continue having his accountant perform all accounting tasks for him; or he could take on some of the tasks himself (such as maintaining the ledger books and paying bills).

TECHNOLOGY & MARKETING

Windows 95: Hype or the Real Thing?

Microsoft introduced Windows 95 in August 1995. The launch was accompanied by demonstrations at convention centres, testing by 400 000 trial users, and special promotions by retailers. At its Washington headquarters, Microsoft sponsored a carnival and trade show for 2500. In total, Microsoft spent $150 million on the kickoff.

These are some of Windows 95's heralded benefits: (1) Under DOS and older Windows versions, file names were limited to eight letters, with three more after a period—for example "MKTGTEXT.DOC." In Windows 95, the same file could be "MARKETING, Canadian Edition," a more easily identifiable title. (2) Windows 95 can run up to a dozen or more programs at the same time, versus a maximum of six for the older Windows version. (3) Windows 95-compatible CD-ROMs begin playing as soon as they are inserted in a drive, without entering special commands.

However, some critics say Windows 95's benefits are overstated, and that most benefits will not be noticed unless the user buys new 32-bit versions of existing programs. Even Microsoft acknowledged that much of this software took months to be available and that consumers would have to buy software upgrades. Critics also feel that Microsoft has understated the PC hardware needed to properly run Windows 95, which requires more memory and a larger hard drive than most existing systems have. The cost of such hardware upgrades can easily exceed $900 per computer. And although Windows 95 is the most tested piece of software ever, defects and incompatibilities are still common. Furthermore, Apple has run ads commenting on how hard Windows 95 is to install, compared to easy-to-run Macintosh computers.

As a Microsoft marketing manager, how would you explain Windows 95's benefits and answer the criticisms for a cynical columnist for a newspaper?

Sources: Based on material in Don Clark, "Amid Hype and Fear, Microsoft Windows 95 Gets Ready to Roll," *Wall Street Journal* (July 14, 1995), pp. A1, A9; and Walter S. Mossberg, "Most PC Users Should Take Their Time Moving to Windows 95," *Wall Street Journal* (August 10, 1995), p. B1.

- *Office location*—Albert could look for an accountant that makes on-site visits (as his accountant does now) or seek a firm that has an office near to his store or residence.

- *Information about prospective firms*—Albert could ask prospective firms for references, check out accountants' credentials, interview candidates, and/or require firms to perform a sample task.

- *Fee schedule*—Albert knows he must get "fair" quotes, not "low ball" ones. He recognizes that you get what you pay for; and he wants better service.

- *Ethics*—Albert must determine whether he, as the client, has the right to show any old work to prospective firms—or whether there is a client/accountant relationship that he should not violate.

A MARKETING MATCH For "marketing" to operate properly, buyers and sellers need to find and satisfy each other (conduct exchanges). Do you think that Marie Jackson and Albert Sampson would make a good marketing match? We do—but only if their strategy (Marie) and expectations (Albert) are in sync.

In some way, we are all involved with or affected by marketing.

As these examples show, goods and service providers ("sellers") make marketing-related decisions like choosing who customers are, what goods and services to offer, where to sell these goods and services, the features to stress in ads, and the prices to charge. They also determine how to be ethical and socially responsible, and whether to sell products internationally (in addition to domestically). Marketing-related activities are not limited to industrial firms, large corporations, or people called "marketers." They are taken on by all types of companies and people.

As consumers ("buyers"), the marketing practices of goods and service providers affect many of the choices made by our parents, spouses, other family members, friends and associates, and/or us. For virtually every good and service we purchase, the marketing process affects whom we patronize, the assortment of models and styles offered in the marketplace, where we shop, the availability of knowledgeable sales personnel, the prices we pay, and other factors. Marketing practices are in play when we are born (which doctor our parents select, the style of baby furniture they buy); while we grow (our parents' purchase of a domestic or foreign family car or mini van, our choice of a college or university); while we conduct our everyday lives (the use of a particular brand of toothpaste, the purchase of status-related items); and when we retire (our consideration of travel options, a change in living accommodations).

The formal study of marketing requires an understanding of its definition, evolution (including the marketing concept, a marketing philosophy, and customer service), importance and scope, and functions. These principles are discussed throughout Chapter 1.

Marketing Defined

A broad, integrated definition of marketing forms the basis of this text:

> **Marketing** is the anticipation, management, and satisfaction of demand through the exchange process.

Marketing includes anticipating demand, managing demand, and satisfying demand.

It involves goods, services, organizations, people, places, and ideas.

Anticipation of demand requires that a firm do consumer research on a regular basis so it can develop and introduce offerings desired by consumers. Management of demand includes stimulation, facilitation, and regulation tasks. Stimulation motivates consumers to want a firm's offerings due to attractive product designs, distinctive promotion, fair prices, and other strategies. Facilitation is the process whereby the firm makes it easy to buy its offering by having convenient locations, accepting credit cards, using well-informed salespeople, and implementing other strategies. Regulation is needed when there are peak demand periods rather than balanced demand throughout the year or when demand is greater than the supply of the offering. Then, the goal is to spread demand throughout the year or to demarket a good or service (reduce overall demand). Satisfaction of demand involves product availability, actual performance upon purchase, safety perceptions, after-sale service, and other factors. For consumers to be satisfied, goods, services, organizations, people, places, and ideas must fulfill their expectations.

Marketing can be aimed at consumers or at publics. **Consumer demand** refers to the attributes and needs of final consumers, industrial consumers, wholesalers and retailers, government institutions, international markets, and nonprofit organizations. A firm may appeal to one or a combination of these. **Publics' demand** refers to the attributes and needs of employees, unions, shareholders, the general public, government agencies, consumer groups, and other internal and external forces that affect company operations.

Demand is affected by both **consumers** *and* **publics**.

The marketing process is not concluded until consumers and publics **exchange** their money, their promise to pay, or their support for the offering of a firm, institution, person, place, or idea. Exchanges must be done in a socially responsible way, with both the buyer and the seller being ethical and honest—and considering the impact on society and the environment.

Exchange completes the process.

A proper marketing definition should not be confined to economic goods and services. It should cover organizations (such as the Red Cross), people (for example, politicians), places (Vancouver), and ideas (the value of seat belts). A consumer orientation must be central to any definition. And from a societal perspective, a firm needs to ask whether a good or service should be sold, besides whether it can be sold. Figure 1-1 illustrates how a place (Welland, Ontario) can benefit from marketing efforts.

CANADIAN RED CROSS
www.redcross.ca/

FIGURE 1-1
Marketing Welland to Business Firms
Marketing can be used for the economic development of communities (places).

Reprinted with permission of Welland Development Commission and Canadian Tire Acceptance Limited.

The Evolution of Marketing

Marketing's evolution in an industry, country, or region of the world may be viewed as a sequence of stages: barter era → production era → sales era → marketing department era → marketing company era. In some industries, nations, and regions, marketing practices have moved through each stage and involve a good consumer orientation and high efficiency; in others, marketing practices are still in their infancy.

Marketing can be traced to the **barter era**.

Marketing's origins can be traced to people's earliest use of the exchange process: the **barter era**. With barter, people trade one resource for another—like food for animal pelts. To accommodate exchanges, trading posts, travelling salespeople, general stores, and cities evolved, along with a standardized monetary system. In the least developed nations of the world, barter is still widely practised.

The modern system of marketing begins with the industrialization of an industry, country, or region. For the world's most developed nations, this occurred with the Industrial Revolution of the late 1800s. For developing nations, efforts to industrialize are now under way. Why is industrialization so important in marketing's evolution? Unless industrialization takes place, exchanges are limited, since people do not have surplus items to trade. With the onset of mass production, better transportation, and more efficient technology, products can be made in greater volume and sold at lower prices. Improved mobility, densely populated cities, and specialization also let more people share in the exchange process: They can turn from being self-sufficient (for example, making their own clothes) to being consumers of what others produce (such as buying clothes in a store or market). In the initial stages of industrialization, output is limited and marketing is devoted to products' physical distribution. Because demand is high and competition is low, firms typically do not have to conduct consumer research, modify products, or otherwise adapt to consumer needs. The goal is to lift production to meet demand. This is the **production era** of marketing.

In the **production era**, *output increases to meet demand.*

The next stage takes place as companies expand production capabilities to keep up with consumer demand. At this point, many firms hire a sales force and some use advertising to sell their inventory. Yet, since competition is still rather low, when firms develop new products, consumer tastes or needs receive little consideration. The role of the sales force and advertising is to make consumer desires fit the features of the products offered.

FIGURE 1-2
How Marketing Evolves

For example, a shoe manufacturer might make brown wingtip shoes and use ads and personal selling to convince consumers to buy them. That firm would rarely determine consumer tastes before making shoes or adjust output to those tastes. This is the **sales era** of marketing. It still exists where competition is limited, such as in nations in the process of moving to free-market economies.

*In the **sales era**, firms sell products without first determining consumer desires.*

As competition grows, supply begins to exceed demand. Firms cannot prosper without marketing input. They create marketing departments to conduct consumer research and advise management on how to better design, distribute, promote, and price products. Unless firms react to consumer needs, competitors might better satisfy demand and leave the firms with surplus inventory and falling sales. Yet, although marketing departments share in decisions, they may be in a subordinate position to production, engineering, and sales departments. This is the **marketing department era**. It still exists where marketing has been embraced, but not as the driving force in an industry or company.

*The **marketing department era** occurs when research is used to determine consumer needs.*

Over the past forty years, firms in a growing number of industries, nations, and regions have recognized marketing's central role; marketing departments at those firms are now the equal of others. The firms make virtually all key decisions after thorough consumer analysis: Since competition is intense and sophisticated, consumers must be aggressively drawn and kept loyal to a firm's brands. Company efforts are well integrated and regularly reviewed. This is the **marketing company era**. Figure 1-2 indicates the key aspects of each era in marketing's evolution.

*The **marketing company era** integrates consumer research and analysis into all company efforts.*

The marketing concept, a marketing philosophy, customer service, and customer satisfaction and relationship marketing are the linchpins of the marketing company era. They are examined here.

The Marketing Concept

As Figure 1-3 shows, the **marketing concept** is a consumer-oriented, market-driven, value-based, integrated, goal-oriented philosophy for a firm, institution, or person.[2] Here is an illustration of the marketing concept in action:

*The **marketing concept** is consumer-oriented, market-driven, value-based, integrated, and goal-oriented.*

FIGURE 1-3
The Marketing Concept

[2]For a comprehensive analysis of the marketing concept, see Frederick E. Webster, Jr., "Defining the New Marketing Concept," *Marketing Management*, Vol. 2 (Number 2, 1994), pp. 23–31.

How does a $48-million manufacturer compete with global giant Sony? By giving dealers (its customers) what they want. Koss Corporation has been dominant in headphones since it invented "stereo phones" in 1958. Even when Sony came on the scene in the 1980s with its Walkman, which created a market for low-end headphones, Koss was able to triple its sales and stay competitive.

The simple philosophy "anything for the customer" has kept Koss in the game. In 1982, dealers requested that Koss change packaging so the headphones would be visible when hung on display. Koss responded by switching to clear packaging. In 1987, after dealers requested a bigger share of Koss's advertising dollars, the firm, which was spending the bulk of its budget on national print ads, converted most of its ad dollars to cooperative advertising. To meet dealer inventory demand, Koss began electronic data interchange (EDI) in 1989.

On a number of occasions, Koss has even gone so far as to alter product features based on one dealer's request. In 1994, Koss built a beefed-up headphone that could take customer abuse to use on store displays for one national record store chain. The store liked the headphones so much it asked Koss to also package them for sale. "We make small changes every day," says CEO Michael Koss. "Even small enhancements like changing the colour or size of packaging help keep us close to our dealers."[3]

The marketing concept's five elements are crucial to the long-term success of a good, service, organization, person, place, or idea: A *customer orientation* means examining consumer needs, not production capability, and devising a plan to satisfy them. Goods and services are seen as means to accomplish ends, not the ends themselves. A *market-driven approach* means being aware of the structure of the marketplace, especially the attributes and strategies of competing firms. A *value-based philosophy* means offering goods and services that consumers perceive to have superior value relative to their costs and the offerings of competitors. With an *integrated marketing focus*, all the activities relating to goods and services are coordinated, including finance, production, engineering, inventory control, research and development, and marketing. A *goal-oriented firm* employs marketing to achieve both short- and long-term goals—which may be profit, funding to find a cure for a disease, increased tourism, election of a political candidate, a better company image, and so on. Marketing helps attain goals by orienting a firm toward pleasing consumers and offering desired goods, services, or ideas.

These are fifteen things that managers can do to ensure that they adhere to the spirit of the marketing concept:

1. Create customer focus throughout the firm.

2. Listen to the customer.

3. Define and cultivate distinctive competencies.

4. Define marketing as market intelligence.

5. Target customers precisely.

6. Manage for profitability, not sales volume.

7. Make customer value the guiding star.

8. Let the customer define quality.

9. Measure and manage customer expectations.

10. Build customer relationships and loyalty.

11. Define the business as a service business.

12. Commit to continuous improvement and innovation.

13. Manage the company culture along with strategy and structure.

14. Grow with partners and alliances.

15. Destroy marketing bureaucracy.[4]

---

[3]Ginger Trumfio, "Anything for a Customer," *Sales & Marketing Management* (November 1995), p. 25.

[4]Frederick E. Webster, Jr., "Executing the New Marketing Concept," *Marketing Management*, Vol. 3, No. 1 (1994), pp. 9–16.

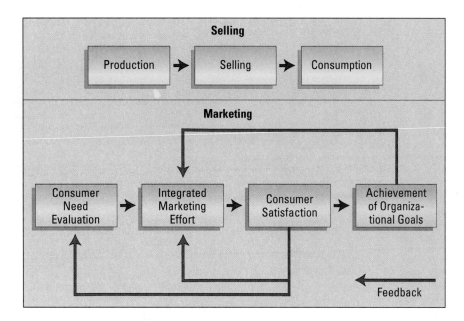

FIGURE 1-4
The Focus of Selling and Marketing Philosophies

Selling Versus Marketing Philosophies

Figure 1-4 highlights the differences between selling and marketing philosophies. The benefits of a marketing, rather than a sales, orientation are many. Marketing stresses consumer analysis and satisfaction, directs the resources of a firm to making the goods and services consumers want, and adapts to changes in consumer traits and needs. Under a marketing philosophy, selling is used to communicate with and understand consumers; consumer dissatisfaction leads to changes in policy, not a stronger or different sales pitch. Marketing looks for real differences in consumer tastes and devises offerings to satisfy them. Marketing is geared to the long run, and marketing goals reflect overall company goals. Finally, marketing views customer needs broadly rather than narrowly (for example, heating as opposed to fuel oil).

As an example, at Wahl Clipper Corporation—which makes electric shavers and hair trimmers—sales have grown at a 16 per cent annual compounded rate for twenty years. Why? According to company president Jack Wahl, "I realized the difference between sales and marketing. That's a big thing for a small company. Sales means simply presenting the product and collecting money. Marketing means stepping back and looking for the needs of the customer, and for the best way to get through to that user."[5]

Customer Service

Customer service involves the identifiable, but rather intangible, activities undertaken by a seller in conjunction with the basic goods and/or services it offers.[6] In today's highly competitive marketplace, the level of customer service a firm provides can affect its ability to attract and retain customers more than ever before.

Unless a consumer is happy with *both* the basic good (such as a new auto) or service (such as a car tuneup) offered by a seller *and* the quality of customer service (such as polite, expert sales personnel and punctual appointments), he or she is unlikely to patronize the seller—certainly not in the long run. Imagine your reaction to these situations:

Stores often tell customers that home deliveries and repairs will be made any time between 8 A.M. and 5 P.M., often effectively killing a workday. Doctors and other health professionals

With a marketing orientation, selling is used to communicate with and understand consumers.

Customer service *tends to be intangible, but quite meaningful, to many consumers.*

[5]Jerry Flint, "Father Says, 'Jump,'" *Forbes* (August 14, 1995), p. 144.
[6]Peter D. Bennett (Ed.), *Dictionary of Marketing Terms*, Second Edition (Chicago: American Marketing Association, 1995), p. 73.

International Marketing in

Why Is Customer Service at Germany's Deutsche Telekom Lagging Behind?

Customer service at Deutsche Telekom, Germany's phone monopoly, has generally been considered poor. Thus, the German government hoped to privatize the company in 1996 and to let international competitors (such as AT&T and Bell South) offer phone service in Germany as of 1998.

Experts say Deutsche Telekom has a number of customer service problems:

- It is relatively easy to tap into someone's telephone. This encourages fraud and misbilling problems.
- There are only one-quarter the number of pay phones per capita in Germany as compared to the Canadian and U.S. market.
- Although most telephone traffic in industrialized nations is switched by computer, one-half of Telekom's calls use outdated analog systems. Not only is its equipment inefficient and trouble-prone, but also it is incompatible with modern services such as call waiting.
- Deutsche Telekom is often ridiculed with regard to its customer service policies. A popular German television comedy routine, for example, shows Deutsche Telekom employees throwing complaint letters in the garbage.

Even though Deutsche Telekom executives know the firm's problems, they feel that they are due to legal factors beyond their control. For instance, German laws require phone lines to be buried underground rather than strung from poles. This increases the costs and time to service customers. German laws also require German long-distance users to subsidize local rates. Lastly, Deutsche Telekom workers are considered to be government employees; they are, thus, entitled to such benefits as annual five- to six-week paid vacations.

Despite the best intentions, some observers believe that Telekom's new competitors will aim their efforts at large industrial and commercial accounts and their entry into the market will have little impact on small residential customers.

As a Deutsche Telekom executive, what would you do to increase the quality of your customer service?

Source: Based on material in Greg Steinmetz, "Customer-Service Era Is Reaching Germany Late, Hurting Business," *Wall Street Journal* (June 1, 1995), pp. A1, A8.

DEUTSCHE TELEKOM
www.dtag.de/

frequently overbook appointments, so patients waste hours waiting to be seen. Federal, provincial, and municipal government agencies are often unreachable on the telephone.[7]

With millions of new buyers, many of them individuals and small businesses, clueless about computers, some manufacturers can't keep up with service complaints and requests for help. The result: hordes of confused and resentful—even outraged—customers.[8]

Yet, firms often have to make customer service tradeoffs. For instance, supermarkets must weigh the potential loss of business if waiting lines are too long versus the cost of opening additional checkout lines.[9]

[7]Theodore D. Kemper, "Good Service Serves the Economy, Too," *New York Times* (January 9, 1994), Section 3, p. 13.
[8]Jim Carlton, "Support Lines' Busy Signals Hurt PC Makers," *Wall Street Journal* (July 6, 1995), p. B1.
[9]Steve Weinstein, "Rethinking Customer Service," *Progressive Grocer* (May 1995), pp. 63–68.

According to one survey, most people rate the overall level of customer service of businesses as excellent or pretty good, but over 40 per cent rate service as only fair or poor. More than one-third of people say they usually purchase from a business having excellent service but higher prices, rather than a lower-priced competitor with lesser service.[10]

This is how several organizations are addressing the issue of customer service: Organizations as diverse as the Winnipeg Blue Bombers and Revenue Canada are **empowering employees**—giving workers broad leeway to satisfy customer requests, and encouraging and rewarding employees for showing initiative and imagination. The Winnipeg Blue Bombers reward their employees with success celebrations to recognize outstanding achievements, whether they are players or other personnel. Revenue Canada has also tried to improve its customer service by empowering employees. More responsibility is being granted to the regions to make decisions. For example, managers are encouraged to consult with the public; make decisions on tax cases by looking at facts rather than the letter of the law; and to consider substance instead of form when administering the Income Tax Act.[11]

To offer better customer service, some firms are **empowering employees**.

Customer service is an important "output" of a marketing system and firms are very conscious of this. McDonald's Restaurants of Canada instituted an incentive program as early as 1993 to encourage improved customer service by its employees. Employee contests for good service are held and the top performers receive prizes in merchandise or McDonald's food discounts. The contests and their results are publicized in-house using posters, newsletters, payroll stuffers, and bulletin board notices.[12]

MCDONALD'S CORP.
www.mcdonalds.com/main

No company is more comprehensive in its approach to customer service than airline giant British Airways:

> The firm tracks some 350 measures of performance, including aircraft cleanliness, punctuality, customer opinions on check-in experiences, the time it takes for a customer to get through when phoning a reservations agent, and customer satisfaction with in-flight and ground services. A monthly report goes to the chief executive officer, the managing director, the chief financial officer, and the top management team responsible for service and performance. The report usually has a section focusing on a particular problem or issue. For example, it might address in-flight food service.[13]

Customer Satisfaction and Relationship Marketing

As previously noted, **customer satisfaction** is a crucial element in successful marketing. It is the degree to which there is a match between a customer's expectations of a good or service and the actual performance of that good or service, including customer service.[14] As one expert says: "Firms that satisfy customers are ones that do their homework. They know a customer satisfaction commitment must be backed up by a complete understanding of the customer, the competition, and the marketplace—and an ability to identify and respond to areas where change is needed."[15] Figure 1-5 shows eleven representative factors that affect overall customer satisfaction.

This is how formidable it can be to keep customers satisfied:

Firms cannot usually prosper without a high level of **customer satisfaction**.

> Do smaller companies give better customer service? The clients of Roberts Express Inc. thought so. In 1983, when sales were $3 million U.S. at this multinational freight company based in Akron, Ohio, Roberts Express was specializing in emergency shipments; customers were spoiled and they enjoyed it. They spoke to service representatives on a first-name basis. Calling in, clients expected to reach a shipping agent who knew their business, even what truck size would best suit their company's products. Roberts Express rarely disappointed its small group of customers.

[10]"Many Consumers Expect Better Service—and Say They Are Willing to Pay for It," *Wall Street Journal* (November 12, 1990), pp. B1, B4.

[11]"Smart Football," *Manitoba Business*, Vol. 13, No. 2 (March 1991), p. 16; "Revenue Canada Tries to Put on a Happy Face," *Financial Post*, Vol. 5, No. 162 (November 13, 1991), p. 14.

[12] "Incentives Help to Improve Service," *Strategy*, Vol. 4, No. 11 (February 8, 1993), pp. 22–24.

[13]Steven E. Prokesch, "Competing on Service: An Interview with British Airways' Sir Colin Marshall," *Harvard Business Review*, Vol. 73 (November–December 1995), p. 108.

[14]Bennett, *Dictionary of Marketing Terms*, p. 73.

[15]Stanley Brown, "You Can Get Satisfaction," *Sales & Marketing Management* (July 1995), p. 106.

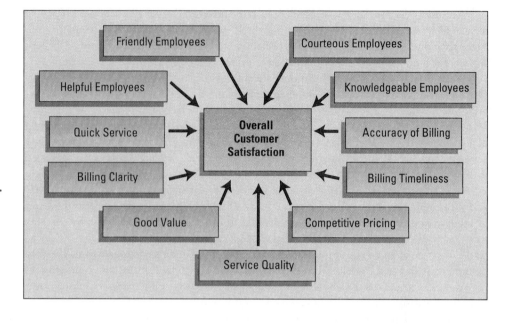

FIGURE 1-5
Factors That Affect Customer Satisfaction

Source: Steven Hokanson, "The Deeper You Analyze, the More You Satisfy Customers," *Marketing News* (January 2, 1995), p. 16. Reprinted by permission of the American Marketing Association.

But as sales doubled annually, that service started to change. Customer service reps and shipping agents who once sat side by side and solved problems by talking over a cubicle wall, now worked in separate buildings. In monthly satisfaction surveys, clients complained that the company had become too large. Customers weren't recognized anymore. "They were saying, 'I'm calling a customer service organization and one of 100 people could pick up the phone,'" recalls Bruce Simpson, president of Roberts Express.

To get back to its small-company roots, Roberts started to reorganize into teams. It now has 18 teams that give Roberts a small company feel while allowing it to grow sales. When a customer calls, the team member who picks up the phone owns the service from start to finish. The firm can give personal, immediate service because each team works as a small business for its geographic area. Today, sales are about U.S.$150 million.[16]

Companies with satisfied customers have a good opportunity to convert them into loyal customers who will purchase from them over an extended period. From a consumer perspective, when marketing activities are performed with the conscious intention of developing and managing long-term, trusting customer relations, **relationship marketing** is involved.[17] Why is this so important? According to one observer, "It's far cheaper to hold on to the [customers] you have than to acquire new ones. A happy contingent inside your tent lessens your need to beat the street for business. Loyalists may even drum up fresh prospects for you."[18]

Great Plains Software, a provider of high-end programs for accountants, is one of many firms that has mastered relationship marketing:

How's this for getting close to the customer? Great Plains codes every program in a way that blocks its use after 50 transactions. The customer must call the firm for the code that gets the program running again. At this point, the folks who answer the phones ask questions about the customer's business, computer system, and software requirements. Sound annoying? "Customers don't seem to mind a simple phone call," insists CEO Doug Bergum. Today, Great Plains has some 45 000 buyer profiles in its data bank and personally solicits those likely to upgrade. In 1993, the firm persuaded a phenomenal 42 per cent of the owners of Great Plains Accounting Version 6 to buy new Version 7.

These retention skills got dearly tested when Version 7 turned out to contain bugs. Concerned that his reputation for bug-free products would be ruined, Bergum spent $340 000 to mail new disks to every Version 7 buyer. He also wrote all 2700 Great Plains dealers, admitting that he failed to test Version 7 properly and offering cash compensation to anyone whose business suffered from the glitch. Great Plains' goof may have *enhanced* customer loyalty. More dealers wrote to praise Bergum's response than to claim redress—which amounted to $34 000,

Through **relationship marketing,** *companies try to increase long-term customer loyalty.*

GREAT PLAINS SOFTWARE
www.gps.com/

[16]Weld F. Royal, "Keep Them Coming Back," *Inc.* (September 1995), p. 51.

[17]Bennett, *Dictionary of Marketing Terms*, p. 242.

[18]Patricia Sellers, "Keeping the Buyer You Already Have," *Fortune* (Autumn–Winter 1993), p. 56.

less than 0.5 per cent of the sales from Version 7. *Accounting Today* commended Great Plains for being "a model of how problems should be handled." At "Stampede to Fargo," the firm's annual dealer conference, Bergum won the crowd by standing onstage, explaining his mistakes at length, and smashing three fresh eggs on his head.[19]

The Importance of Marketing

Because marketing stimulates demand, one of its basic tasks is to generate consumer enthusiasm for goods and services. Worldwide, about $35 trillion of goods and services are produced annually, with Canada accounting for approximately $800 billion of that sum.

A large amount of each sales dollar goes to cover the costs related to such marketing activities as product development, packaging, distribution, advertising and personal selling, price marking, and administering consumer credit programs. Some estimates place the costs of marketing as high as 50 per cent or more of sales in certain industries. Yet, it should not be assumed that the performance of some marketing tasks by consumers would automatically lead to lower prices. For example, could a small business really save money by having the owner fly to Windsor, Ontario to buy a new minivan directly from the maker rather than from a local dealer? Would a family be willing to buy clothing in bulk to reduce a retailer's transportation and storage costs?

Millions of people work in marketing-related jobs in Canada. They include those employed in the retailing, wholesaling, transportation, warehousing, and communications industries and those involved with marketing jobs for manufacturing, service, agricultural, mining, and other industries. Projections indicate future employment in marketing will remain strong.

Marketing activities also involve entire industries, such as advertising and market research. Total annual worldwide advertising expenditures exceed $480 billion. Many agencies, such as WPP Group and Cordiant of Great Britain, Interpublic Group and Omnicom Group of the United States, and Dentsu of Japan have worldwide billings of several billion dollars each. Around $11 billion worldwide is spent yearly on various types of commercial marketing research. Firms such as Nielsen, Information Resources Inc., Research International (Great Britain), and GfK (of Germany) generate yearly revenues of more than $130 million each.

All people and organizations serve as consumers for various goods and services. By understanding the role of marketing, consumers can become better informed, more selective, and more efficient. Effective channels of communication with sellers can also be established and complaints resolved more easily and favourably. Consumer groups have a major impact on sellers.

Because resources are scarce, marketing programs and systems must function at their peak. Thus, by optimizing customer service, inventory movement, advertising expenditures, product assortments, and other areas of marketing, firms will better use resources. Some industries may even require demarketing (lowering the demand for goods and services). For example, a hydroelectric utility may launch a campaign to encourage consumers to reduce their consumption of electricity.

Marketing strongly affects people's beliefs and lifestyles. In fact, it has been criticized as developing materialistic attitudes, fads, product obsolescence, a reliance on gadgets, status consciousness, and superficial product differences—and for wasting resources. Marketers reply that they merely address the desires of people and make the best goods and services they can at the prices people will pay.

Marketing has a role to play in improving our quality of life. For example, marketing personnel often encourage firms to make safer products, such as child-proof bottle caps. They create public service messages on energy conservation, AIDS prevention, driver safety, alcohol abuse, and other topics. They help new goods, ideas, and services (such as cellular phones, improved nutrition, and ATMs) to be accepted by people and organizations.

A knowledge of marketing is extremely valuable for those not directly involved in a marketing job. For example, marketing decisions must be made by:

Marketing stimulates consumers, costs a large part of sales, employs people, supports industries, affects all consumers, and plays a major role in our lives.

DENTSU (INFORMATION SERVICES INTERNATIONAL-DENTSU, LTD.)
www.dentsu.co.jp

[19]Ibid., p. 57.

Marketing awareness is invaluable for those in non-marketing jobs.

- *Doctors*—What hours are most desirable to patients?
- *Lawyers*—How can new clients be attracted?
- *Management consultants*—Should fees be higher, lower, or the same as competitors'?
- *Financial analysts*—What investments should be recommended to clients?
- *Research and development personnel*—Is there consumer demand for a potential "break-through" product?
- *Economists*—What impact will the economy have on the way various industries market their offerings?
- *Statisticians*—How should firms react to predicted demographic shifts?
- *Teachers*—How can students become better consumers?
- *City planners*—How can businesses be persuaded to relocate to the city?
- *Nonprofit institutions*—How can donor contributions be raised?

Each of these professions and organizations needs to understand and satisfy patient, client, consumer, student, taxpayer, or contributor needs. And more of them than ever before are now undertaking marketing activities such as research, advertising, and so on.

Marketing Functions and Performers

*Basic **marketing functions** range from environmental analysis to marketing management.*

There are eight basic **marketing functions**: environmental analysis and marketing research, consumer analysis, target marketing, product planning, distribution planning, promotion planning, price planning, and marketing management.

Here are brief descriptions of the functions:

- *Environmental analysis and marketing research*—Monitoring and adapting to external factors that affect success or failure, such as the economy and competition; and collecting data to resolve specific marketing issues.
- *Consumer analysis*—Examining and evaluating consumer characteristics, needs, and purchasing processes.
- *Target marketing*—Selecting the group(s) of consumers at which to aim marketing efforts.
- *Product planning (including goods, services, organizations, people, places, and ideas)*—Developing and maintaining products, product assortments, product images, brands, packaging, and optional features; and deleting faltering products.
- *Distribution planning*—Forming relations with distribution intermediaries, physical distribution, inventory management, warehousing, transportation, the allocation of goods and services, wholesaling, and retailing.
- *Promotion planning*—Communicating with customers, the general public, and others through some form of advertising, public relations, personal selling, and/or sales promotion.
- *Price planning*—Determining price levels and ranges, pricing techniques, terms of purchase, price adjustments, and the use of price as an active or passive factor.
- *Marketing management*—Planning, implementing, and controlling the marketing program (strategy) and individual marketing functions; appraising the risks and benefits in decision making; and focusing on total quality.

Generally, a firm should first study its environment and gather relevant marketing information. The firm should determine how to act in a socially responsible and ethical manner and consider whether to be domestic and/or international. At the same time, the firm should analyze potential customers to learn their needs and select the group(s) on which to focus. It should next plan product offerings, make distribution decisions, choose how to communicate with customers and others, and set proper prices. These four functions (in combination, known as the *marketing mix*) should be performed in a coordinated manner, based on environmental, societal, and consumer analysis. Through marketing management, the firm's overall marketing program would be planned and carried out in an integrated manner, with fine-tuning as necessary.

Although many marketing transactions require the performance of similar tasks, such as being ethical, analyzing consumers, and product, distribution, promotion, and price planning, these tasks can be enacted in many ways (for example, a manufacturer could choose to distribute its product via full-service retailers or self-service ones; or a financial-services firm could choose to rely on either telephone sales or in-office visits by salespeople to potential small-business clients).

Marketing performers are the organizations or individuals that undertake one or more marketing functions. They include manufacturers and service providers, wholesalers, retail-

*Usually at least one **marketing performer** must undertake each of the basic marketing functions.*

Ethics AND TODAY'S MARKETER

What Practices Do YOU Believe Are Ethical?

Ethical values in marketing can be determined by using a checklist. Here is an opportunity for YOU to assess your level of marketing ethics.

Respond to these statements on a 1 to 9 scale. For items 1-4, let "1" mean that you completely disagree and "9" mean that you completely agree. For items 5-10, use a "1" for complete agreement and a "9" for complete disagreement:

1. Business ethics and social responsibility are critical to the survival of a business enterprise.
2. Business has a social responsibility beyond making a profit.
3. Good ethics is often good business.
4. Social responsibility and profitability can be compatible.
5. If shareholders are unhappy, nothing else matters.
6. The most important concern for a firm is making a profit, even if it means bending or breaking the rules.
7. To remain competitive in a global environment, business firms will have to disregard ethics and social responsibility.
8. Efficiency is much more important to a firm than whether or not the firm is seen as ethical or socially responsible.
9. Although output quality is essential to corporate success, ethics and social responsibility are not.
10. Communication is more important to the overall effectiveness of a firm than whether it is concerned with ethics and social responsibility.

Items 1 to 4 measure a "good ethics is good business" orientation, items 5 to 8 measure a "profits are not paramount" orientation, and items 9 and 10 measure a "quality and communication" orientation. Summarize and describe your ethical nature by determining your total score, as well as your score on the three individual scales.

Source: Based on material in Anusorn Singhapakdi, Kenneth L. Kraft, Scott J. Vitell, and Kumar C. Rallapalli, "The Perceived Importance of Ethics and Social Responsibility on Organizational Effectiveness: A Survey of Marketers," *Journal of the Academy of Marketing Science,* Vol. 23 (Winter 1995), pp. 49–56.

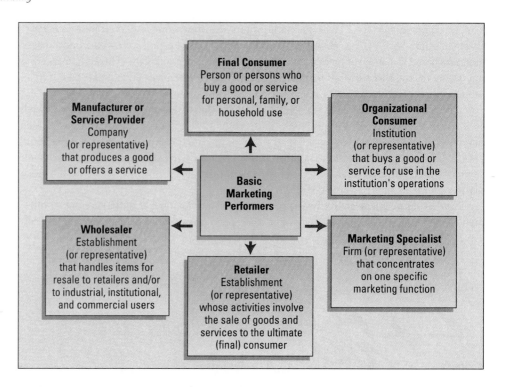

FIGURE 1-6
Who Performs Marketing Functions

ers, marketing specialists, and organizational and final consumers. As Figure 1-6 shows, each performer has a different role. Even though the responsibility for marketing tasks can be shifted and shared in various ways, basic marketing functions usually must be done by one performer or another. They cannot be omitted in many situations.

Sometimes, one marketing performer decides to carry out all—or virtually all—marketing functions (such as Boeing analyzing the marketplace, acting ethically, operating domestically and internationally, seeking various types of customers, developing aerospace and related products, distributing products directly to customers, using its own sales force and placing ads in select media, and setting prices). Yet, for these reasons, one performer often does not undertake all marketing functions:

- Many firms do not have the financial resources to sell products directly to consumers. They need intermediaries to share in the distribution process.

- Marketing directly to customers may require producers of goods and services to offer complementary products or sell the complementary products of other firms so the distribution process is carried out efficiently.

- A performer may be unable or unwilling to complete certain functions and may seek a marketing specialist to fulfil them.

- Many performers are too small to do certain functions efficiently.

- For many goods and services, established distribution methods are in force and it is difficult to set up other methods (such as bypassing independent soda distributors to sell directly to retail stores).

- Some consumers may want to buy in quantity, visit self-service outlets, pay cash, and so on, to save money.

Format of the Text

This book is divided into seven parts. The balance of Part 1 focuses on the marketing environment; and the information needed for marketing decisions. The discussion in Part 1 sets the foundation for studying the specific components of marketing.

Part 2 deals with marketing's central orientation: understanding consumers. It looks at demographics, social and psychological traits, and the decision process of final consumers; organizational consumer attributes and decision making; and developing a target market and sales forecasting. Parts 3 to 6 discuss the elements of the marketing mix (product, distribution, promotion, and price planning) and the actions needed to carry out a marketing program in depth. Part 7 considers the marketing management implications of the topics raised throughout *Marketing Essentials* and discusses how to develop marketing plans and how to integrate and analyze an overall marketing plan.

Numerous examples and illustrations of actual marketing practices by a variety of organizations and individuals are woven into our discussions. And although such topics as marketing and society, international marketing, organizational consumers, and goods versus service marketing get separate chapter coverage to highlight certain points, applications in these areas are presented throughout the text.

MARKETING IN A CHANGING WORLD
Preparing for the Year 2000 and Beyond

A daunting challenge for any organization is to examine the changing world so as to plan for the future. Thus, in each text chapter, we will look at some of the key events that are affecting or will affect marketing decision making.

Experts at Batelle, a leading research institute, feel these technologies are most apt to "bring rich rewards" to firms that are capable of developing and marketing them in the next decade:

- *Genetic mapping*—New treatments for ailments ranging from AIDS to Alzheimer Disease may be on the way.
- *Super materials*—Scientists will increasingly produce new materials with almost any desired characteristic.
- *High-density energy sources*—Batteries the size of sugar packets will bring many new, revolutionary products to life.
- *Digital HDTV*—Digital high-definition television could be the next "hot" item in the entertainment industry.
- *Miniaturization*—It will be possible to carry around a laptop computer the size of a pocket calculator. This computer will be interactive and wireless.
- *Smart manufacturing*—Factory assembly lines will more often be controlled by smart devices and systems rather than people.
- *Anti-aging goods and services*—New developments will range from aging creams that may actually work to an effective cure for baldness.
- *Medical treatments*—There will be new diagnostic tools that use extremely accurate sensors to detect diseases at very early stages.
- *Hybrid-fuel vehicles*—Research on alternative fuels will be stepped up.
- *Edutainment*—Computer software and other products will increasingly meld education and entertainment features.[20]

[20]Douglas E. Olesen, "The Top 10 Technologies for the Next 10 Years," *Futurist* (September–October 1995), pp. 9–13.

SUMMARY

In this and every chapter in the text, the summary is linked to the objectives stated at the beginning of the chapter.

1. *To illustrate marketing's exciting, dynamic, and influential nature* Marketing may be viewed from both business and consumer perspectives; and it influences us daily. As goods and service providers, we make such marketing-related decisions as choosing who customers are, what goods and services to offer, where to sell them, what to stress in promotion, what prices to charge, how to be ethical and responsible, and whether to operate internationally. As consumers, the marketing process affects whom we patronize, choices in the marketplace, where we shop, the availability of sales personnel, the prices we pay, and other factors.

2. *To define marketing and trace its evolution—with emphasis on the marketing concept, a marketing philosophy, customer service, and customer satisfaction and relationship marketing* Marketing involves anticipating, managing, and satisfying demand via the exchange process. It includes goods, services, organizations, people, places, and ideas.

The evolution of marketing can be traced to people's earliest use of barter in the exchange process (the barter era); but it has truly developed since the Industrial Revolution, as mass production and improved transportation have enabled more transactions to occur. For many firms, the evolution of modern marketing can be traced through four stages or "eras": production, sales, marketing department, and marketing company. Yet, in less-developed and developing countries, marketing practices are still in the early stages of development.

The marketing concept requires organizations or individuals to be consumer-oriented, market-driven, value-based, integrated in their efforts, and goal-oriented. A marketing philosophy means assessing and responding to consumer wants, to real differences in consumer tastes, and to long-run opportunities and threats; such a philosophy also requires coordinated decision making.

To prosper today, firms must emphasize customer service: the identifiable, rather intangible, acts performed by a seller in conjunction with the basic goods and/or services being offered. A number of firms now empower employees so as to improve the level of customer service. Customer satisfaction occurs when consumer expectations are met or exceeded; then firms have an opportunity to attract loyal customers by paying attention to relationship marketing.

3. *To show the importance of marketing as a field of study* Marketing is a crucial field for several reasons: it stimulates demand; it involves a lot of money and employs a large number of people; it involves entire industries, such as advertising and marketing research; all organizations and people are consumers in some situations; and finally, it has an impact on our beliefs and lifestyles and influences the quality of our lives. Some marketing knowledge is therefore valuable to all of us, regardless of occupation.

4. *To describe the basic functions of marketing and those that perform these functions* The major marketing functions are environmental analysis and marketing research; consumer analysis; product, distribution, promotion, and price planning; and marketing management. Responsibility for performing these tasks can be shifted and shared in several ways among manufacturers and service providers, wholesalers, retailers, marketing specialists, and consumers. Due to costs, assortment requirements, specialized abilities, company size, established distribution methods, and consumer interests, one party usually does not perform all functions.

KEY TERMS

marketing (p. 7)
consumer demand (p. 7)
publics' demand (p. 7)
exchange (p. 7)
barter era (p. 8)
production era (p. 8)

sales era (p. 9)
marketing department era (p. 9)
marketing company era (p. 9)
marketing concept (p. 9)
customer service (p. 11)
empowering employees (p. 13)

customer satisfaction (p. 13)
relationship marketing (p. 14)
marketing functions (p. 16)
marketing performers (p. 17)

Review Questions

1. How does marketing influence us daily both in our business roles and as consumers?
2. Explain the following:
   a. Anticipation of demand.
   b. Management of demand.
   c. Satisfaction of demand.
   d. Exchange process.
3. Distinguish between consumer and publics' demand.
4. Give an example of a good, service, organization, person, place, and idea that may be marketed.
5. Describe the five eras of marketing.
6. What are the five components of the marketing concept? Give an example of each component.
7. What is customer service? Why is it so important to any firm?
8. What is customer satisfaction? Why is it so important to any firm?
9. What are the basic functions performed by marketing?
10. Why do most consumers *not* buy products directly from manufacturers?

Discussion Questions

1. a. As Marie Jackson, CA, what business-related marketing decisions would you make? Why?
   b. As Albert Sampson, accounting client, what consumer-related marketing decisions would you make? Why?
   c. Develop a plan for Marie Jackson to attract Albert Sampson as a client.
2. Does the presence of a marketing department mean a firm is following the marketing concept? Explain your answer.
3. As the manager of a full-service hotel chain, how would your customer services differ from those offered by a limited-service hotel chain? Why?
4. Develop a seven-item questionnaire to assess the quality of a firm's customer satisfaction efforts.
5. Examine the technologies that the Batelle Institute experts predicted would bring rich rewards. Provide your assessment as to why these experts felt they would be so lucrative.

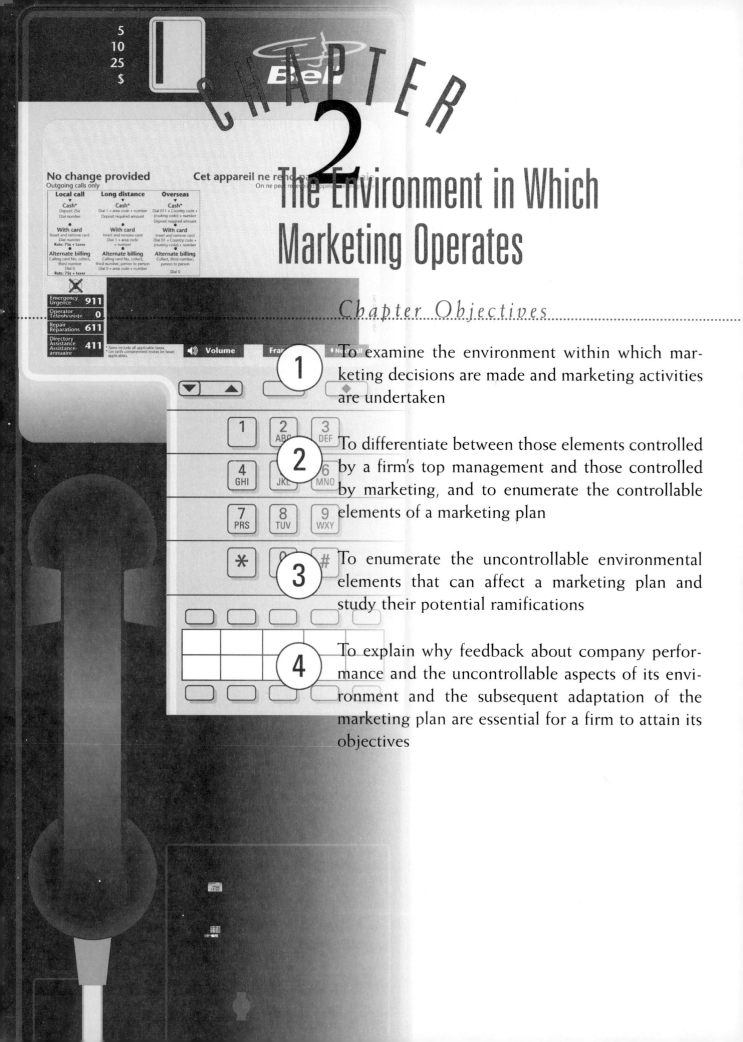

2

The Environment in Which Marketing Operates

Chapter Objectives

1 To examine the environment within which marketing decisions are made and marketing activities are undertaken

2 To differentiate between those elements controlled by a firm's top management and those controlled by marketing, and to enumerate the controllable elements of a marketing plan

3 To enumerate the uncontrollable environmental elements that can affect a marketing plan and study their potential ramifications

4 To explain why feedback about company performance and the uncontrollable aspects of its environment and the subsequent adaptation of the marketing plan are essential for a firm to attain its objectives

> *Pitches by Bell Canada, AT&T Canada, and Sprint Canada, as merciless as they are amusing, pose a challenge worthy of biblical scholars: Each claims to have the best deal offering incentives such as frequently called number discounts, U.S. rates, custom calling cards, peak-period discounts, off-peak discounts, itemized billing services, air miles, etc. Sorting through the many offers could easily cost more time than most people actually spend on the phone. But one thing rings clear to almost every viewer: That staid bastion of bureaucracy, Ma Bell, has turned into one determined competitor.*

At one time, competitors were more genteel. They would not mention a direct competitor in an ad—or even think about saying something disparaging in public. Now the rules of conduct have changed. Let's look at the new competitive tactics.

Bell Canada ads talk about sticking with a company that has always brought reliable service and quality. One ad notes how a Bell calling card's electromagnetic strip allows you to use 60 000 pay phones while the competitors' cards allow access to 0. Bell has also taken aim at its competition by showing ads where people have who have tried the "other guys" returned to Bell because they did not achieve the savings promised and have had service problems. Sprint Canada has used Candice Bergen as a spokesperson, promising that with Sprint you will "go the distance," and AT&T Canada promises to be your "True Choice." Bell, Sprint, and AT&T Canada have all engaged in telemarketing campaigns and direct mail campaigns that compare long distance savings. Bell has been particularly adept at retaining customers by using billing information to tailor custom calling plans to the actual behaviour of the individual. Sprint and AT&T Canada do the same thing to retain their existing customers, but the key to their success is in aggressively switching customers from Bell Canada.[1]

Some competition involves blatant ripoffs. The Cowichan First Nations people have been selling hand-knit sweaters since the 1880s. They use designs trademarked in Canada: the thunderbird, the whale, the eagle, and the deer. The sweaters were popular with the many Japanese tourists who visited British Columbia every year, and the Cowichans hoped to capitalize on this popularity by selling them in the Japanese market. They were stunned to find Cowichan-brand sweaters already being sold in Japan. These sweaters were imported into the Japanese market from New Zealand. The Kiwi copies are machine-made and much

BELL CANADA
www.bell.ca/

AT&T CANADA
www.attcanada.com/

SPRINT
www.sprintcanada.ca/

---

[1]"Psst, Wanna Buy Some Long-Distance?" *Canadian Business* (October 1994), p. 98, AT&T Canada Direct Mail Brochure, August 27, 1997.

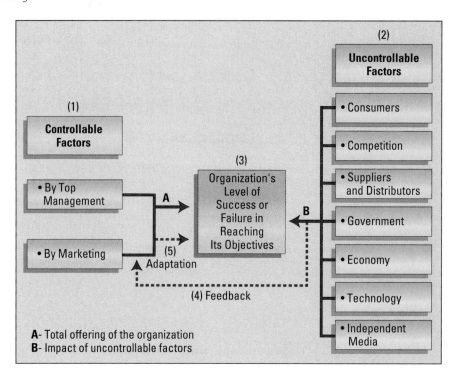

FIGURE 2-1
The Environment Within Which Marketing Operates

less expensive than the hand-made Cowichan originals. The Cowichans had not ensured international protection for their trademark. The copies have made strong inroads into the Japanese market. Now the Cowichans are fighting back by identifying their sweaters as the genuine article using tags signed by the knitters. The problem is: How do you fight a brand with the same name as yours?

In the United States firms often resort to filing law suits as a competitive tactic. Take Cyrix's feud with Intel. Although Cyrix's sales are a small fraction of Intel's (Cyrix's 1994 sales were U.S.$250 million versus Intel's sales of U.S.$11.5 billion), this has not prevented Cyrix from voluntarily running up more than U.S.$20 million in legal bills. According to Cyrix's top marketing executive, "I can't say we encourage our people to think ill of Andy Grove [Intel's chief executive], but we did put Intel's tombstone in our lobby atrium, and we make sure the flowers stay fresh."[2]

In this chapter, we will study the complex environment in which marketing decisions are made. We will see that an organization's level of success (or failure) is related not only to its marketing efforts, but also to the external environment in which it operates and its ability to adapt to environmental changes.

Overview

*The **marketing environment** consists of **controllable factors**, **uncontrollable factors**, **organizational performance**, **feedback**, and **adaptation**.*

The environment within which marketing decisions are made and enacted is depicted in Figure 2-1. **The marketing environment** consists of five parts:

1. Controllable factors.

2. Uncontrollable factors.

3. The organization's level of success or failure in reaching its objectives.

4. Feedback.

5. Adaptation.

Controllable factors are those directed by an organization and its marketers. First, several broad, fundamental decisions are made by top management. Then, marketing man-

[2]Jaclyn Fierman, "When Genteel Rivals Become Mortal Enemies," *Fortune* (May 15, 1995), pp. 90–100; "Woolly Bully," *Canadian Business* (February 1996), p. 22.

agers make specific decisions based on these guidelines. In combination, these factors result in an overall strategy or offering (A in Figure 2-1). The major **uncontrollable factors** are beyond the control of an individual organization, but they have an impact on how well an organization does (B in Figure 2-1).

The interaction of controllable factors and uncontrollable factors determines an organization's **performance**, or level of success or failure, in reaching its goals. **Feedback** occurs when a firm makes an effort to monitor uncontrollable factors and assess its strengths and weaknesses. **Adaptation** refers to the changes in a marketing plan that an organization makes to comply with the uncontrollable environment. If a firm is unwilling to consider the entire environment in a systematic manner, it will likely lack direction and may have disappointing results.

When analyzing the environment, an organization should consider it from two perspectives: the macroenvironment and the microenvironment. The **macroenvironment** refers to the broad demographic, societal, economic, political, technological, and other forces that an organization faces. The **microenvironment** refers to the forces close to an organization that have a direct impact on its ability to serve customers, including distribution intermediaries, competitors, consumer markets, and the capabilities of the organization itself.[3]

Both the **macroenvironment** *and the* **microenvironment** *must be understood.*

Throughout this chapter, the various parts of Figure 2-1 are described and drawn together so the complex environment of marketing can be understood. In Chapter 14, the concept of strategic planning is presented. Such planning establishes a formal process for developing, implementing, and evaluating marketing programs in conjunction with the goals of top management.

Controllable Factors

Controllable factors are internally directed by an organization and its marketers. Some of these factors are directed by top management; these are not controllable by marketers, who must develop plans to satisfy overall organizational goals. In situations involving small or medium-sized institutions, both broad policy and marketing decisions are often made by one person, usually the owner. Even in those cases, broad policies are typically set first and marketing plans must adjust to them. For example, a person could decide to open an office-supply store selling products to small businesses (broad policy) and stress convenient hours, a good selection of items, quantity discounts, and superior customer service (marketing plan).

The organization and its marketers can manage **controllable factors**.

Factors Controlled by Top Management

Although top management is responsible for numerous decisions, five are of extreme importance to marketers: line of business, overall objectives, the role of marketing, the role of other business functions, and corporate culture. They have an impact on all aspects of marketing. Figure 2-2 shows the types of decisions in these areas.

The **line of business** refers to the general goods/service category, functions, geographic coverage, type of ownership, and specific business of a firm. The general goods/service category is a broad definition of the industry in which a firm seeks to be involved. It may be energy, transportation, computing, or any number of others. The functions of the business outline a firm's position in the marketing system—from supplier to manufacturer to wholesaler to retailer—and the tasks it seeks to do. A firm may want to be in more than one of these positions. Geographic coverage can be a neighbourhood, city, county, or province, or it could be defined as regional, national, or international. The type of ownership can range from a sole proprietorship, partnership, or franchise to a multi-unit corporation. The specific business is a narrow definition of the firm, its functions, and its

A firm's **line of business** *refers to its business category.*

[3]Peter D. Bennett (Ed.), *Dictionary of Marketing Terms,* Second Edition (Chicago: American Marketing Association, 1995), pp. 159, 177.

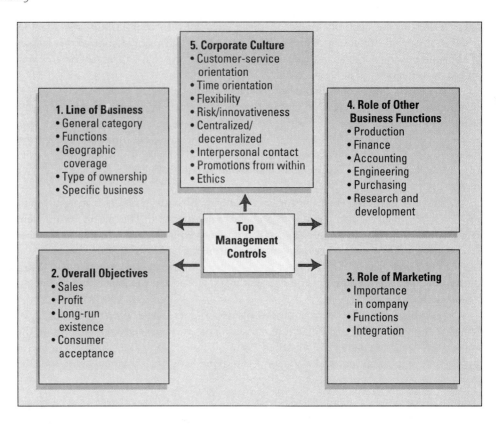

FIGURE 2-2
**Factors Controlled by Top
Management**

operations; for example, a particular dry cleaner might define itself as a local full-service dry cleaner specializing in outerwear.

Overall objectives are the broad, measurable goals set by top management. A firm's success or failure is often determined by comparing these objectives with actual performance. Usually, a combination of sales, profit, and other goals is stated by management for short-run (one year or less) and long-run (several years) periods. Most firms cite customer acceptance as a key goal with a strong effect on sales, profit, and long-run existence.

Top management determines the role of marketing by noting its importance, outlining its activities, and integrating it into a firm's overall operation. Marketing's importance is evident when marketing people have decision-making authority, the rank of the chief marketing officer is equal to that of other areas (usually vice-president), and proper resources are given. It is not considered important by a firm that gives marketing people advisory status, places marketing personnel in a subordinate position (like reporting to the production vice-president), equates marketing with sales, and withholds the funds needed for research, promotion, and other marketing tasks. The larger marketing's role, the greater the likelihood that a firm has an integrated marketing organization. The smaller its role, the greater the possibility that a firm undertakes marketing tasks on a project, crisis, or fragmented basis.

The roles of other business functions and their interrelationships with marketing need to be clearly defined to avoid overlaps, jealousy, and conflict. Production, finance, accounting, engineering, purchasing, and research and development departments each have different perspectives, orientations, and goals. This is discussed further in Chapter 3.

Top management strongly influences a firm's corporate culture: the shared values, norms, and practices communicated to and followed by those working for the firm. **Corporate culture** may be described in terms of:

Corporate culture involves
shared values, norms, and practices.

- *A customer-service orientation*—Is the commitment to customer service clearly transmitted to employees?

- *A time orientation*—Is a firm short- or long-run oriented?

- *The flexibility of the job environment*—Can employees deviate from rules? How formal are relations with subordinates? Is there a dress code?

Ethics AND TODAY'S MARKETER

How Does Corporate Culture Influence Ethical Behaviour?

Surveys of recent M.B.A. graduates found that, in many cases, they feel pressure from their companies to engage in unethical and sometimes illegal behaviour. For example, a management trainee at a consumer products company was told to make up the data to support the introduction of a new product. In another situation, a person was asked to overlook a safety defect in a product and to ship items that did not meet published specifications.

According to ethics experts, these new managers are subjected to four commandments: (1) Performance is what really counts, so make your numbers. (2) Be loyal, and show us that you are a team player. (3) Don't break the law. (4) Don't overinvest in ethical behaviour. The first three of these commandments become troublesome when combined with the fourth.

Here is how the managers responded to a series of questions involving ethical and unethical behaviour:

- Only a few believe that "sleazy" behaviour will be a drag on their career.
- Less than a third believe their firms respect or encourage "whistle blowing."
- When asked what offences would result in punishment, they rarely mention unethical behaviour. Instead, such infractions as poor performance, failure at being a team player, stealing, or drinking on the job were noted.
- Many executives fear repercussions from doing what they see as the right thing.

Although many of the managers worked in firms with formal ethics programs, in general, these programs had little effect on their behaviour or attitudes.

As an ethical compliance manager for a bank, how would you help institute a corporate culture that values high moral principles?

Source: Based on material in Joseph L. Badaracco, Jr., and Allen P. Webb, "Business Ethics: A View From the Trenches," *California Management Review*, Vol. 37 (Winter 1995), pp. 8–28.

- *The level of risk/innovation pursued*—Is risk-taking fostered?
- *The use of a centralized/decentralized management structure*—How much input into decisions do middle managers have?
- *The level of interpersonal contact*—Do employees freely communicate with one another?
- *The use of promotions from within*—Are internal personnel given preference as positions open?
- *Ethics applied*—Is the firm's conduct seen as honest and proper?

For example, IBM Canada is trying to change its corporate culture in order to get better in touch with its customers. For starters, the blue suits are out and dressing for the firm's customers is in. The elimination of IBM's dress code was an important symbol of change for both employees and customers alike. Employees are encouraged to speak their minds, and management communicates news to employees directly and provides a forum for comments and suggestions.[4]

The "ten commandments" listed below are what many experts recommend to firms that wish to foster a nurturing corporate culture:

IBM CANADA
www.can.ibm.com/

[4]Tamsen Tillson, "Be It Ever So Humble," *Canadian Business* (June 25, 1995), Special Technology Issue, pp. 26–32.

FIGURE 2-3
Factors Controlled by Marketing

1. Seek consensus—don't bark orders.
2. Set broad visions, then give people the freedom needed to carry them out.
3. Make sure people have the resources and support they need to succeed.
4. Spend more time in the field with employees than in your office.
5. Spend some time with employees off the job, too.
6. Monitor progress on projects—don't micro manage.
7. Be quick to give ambitious employees more responsibilities.
8. Make sure all employees are continuously learning and growing.
9. Reward people for reaching personal, not just financial, goals.
10. Before criticizing someone for "failing," find out why he or she fell short of expectations.[5]

After top management sets company guidelines, the marketing area begins to develop the factors under its control.

Factors Controlled by Marketing

The major factors controlled by marketing personnel are the selection of a target market, marketing objectives, the marketing organization, the marketing mix, and assessment of the marketing plan. These factors are shown in Figure 2-3.

One crucial marketing-related decision involves selecting a target market. The **target market** is the particular group(s) of customers a firm proposes to serve, or whose needs it proposes to satisfy, with a particular marketing program. When selecting a target market, a company usually engages in some form of **market segmentation**, which involves subdividing a market into clear subsets of customers that act in the same way or that have comparable needs.[6] A company can choose a large target market or concentrate on a small one, or try to appeal to both with separate marketing programs for each. Generally, these questions must be addressed before devising a marketing approach: Who are our customers? What kinds of goods and services do they want? How can we attract them to our company?

At marketing-oriented firms, the choice of a target market has an impact on all other marketing decisions. For example, a book publisher appealing to the high school science market would have a different marketing approach from one appealing to the adult fiction market. The first firm would seek an image as a prestigious, well-established publisher; spe-

A **target market** *is the customer group to which an organization appeals.* **Market segmentation** *is often used in choosing a target market.*

---

[5]Geoffrey Brewer, "The New Managers," *Performance* (March 1995), p. 32.
[6]Bennett, *Dictionary of Marketing Terms*, pp. 165–166.

cialize product offerings; make presentations to high school book-selection committees; sell in large quantities; offer durable books with many photos and line drawings that could be used for several years; and so on. The second firm would capitalize on well-known authors or publish books on hot topics to establish an image; have books on a variety of subjects; use newspaper ads and seek favourable reviews; distribute via bookstores; sell in small quantities (except if large bookstore chains are involved); de-emphasize durability, photos, and line drawings; and produce books as efficiently as possible.

Marketing objectives are more customer-oriented than those set by top management. Marketers are quite interested in the image consumers hold of a firm and its products. From a marketing perspective, sales goals will reflect a desire to foster brand loyalty (repeat purchases), encourage growth (through new product introductions), and appeal to unsatisfied market segments. Profit goals may be related to long-term customer loyalty. Most importantly, marketers seek to create **differential advantages**—the unique features in a firm's marketing program that cause consumers to patronize that firm and not its competitors. Without differential advantages, a firm would have a "me-too" philosophy and offer the consumer no reasons to select its offerings over competitors'. Differential advantages can be based on a distinctive image, new products or features, product quality, customer service, low prices, availability, and other factors. For example, Snapple is known for its offbeat beverages, Harvey's restaurants make hamburgers a beautiful thing, Zellers is known for its low prices, and the Toronto Dominion Bank's VISA credit cards are "everywhere you want to be." Figure 2-4 shows how 3M markets its differential advantages.

In any marketing situation, **ethical behaviour** based on honest and proper conduct ("what is right" and "what is wrong") should be followed. This applies both to situations involving company actions that affect the general public, employees, channel members, shareholders, and/or competitors and to situations involving company dealings with consumers. The preeminent organization for marketing in Canada and the United States is the American Marketing Association, which provides information and guidelines for managers

Differential advantages *consist of the firm's unique features that attract consumers.*

Ethical behaviour *involves honest and proper conduct.*

CODE OF ETHICS

Members of the American Marketing Association (AMA) are committed to ethical professional conduct. They have joined together in subscribing to this Code of Ethics embracing the following topics:

Responsibilities of the Marketer

Marketers must accept responsibility for the consequence of their activities and make every effort to ensure that their decisions, recommendations, and actions function to identify, serve, and satisfy all relevant publics: customers, organizations and society.

Marketers' professional conduct must be guided by:

1. The basic rule of professional ethics: not knowingly to do harm;
2. The adherence to all applicable laws and regulations;
3. The accurate representation of their education, training and experience; and
4. The active support, practice and promotion of this Code of Ethics.

Honesty and Fairness

Marketers shall uphold and advance the integrity, honor, and dignity of the marketing profession by:

1. Being honest in serving customers, clients, employees, suppliers, distributors and the public;
2. Not knowingly participating in conflict of interest without prior notice to all parties involved; and
3. Establishing equitable fee schedules including the payment or receipt of usual, customary and/or legal compensation or marketing exchanges.

Rights and Duties of Parties in the Marketing Exchange Process

Participants in the marketing exchange process should be able to expect that:

1. Products and services offered are safe and fit for their intended uses;
2. Communications about offered products and services are not deceptive;
3. All parties intend to discharge their obligations, financial and otherwise, in good faith; and
4. Appropriate internal methods exist for equitable adjustment and/or redress of grievances concerning purchases.

It is understood that the above would include, but is not limited to, the following responsiblities of the marketer:

In the area of product development and management,

• disclosure of all substantial risks associated with product or service usage;
• identification of any product component substitution that might materially change the product or impact on the buyer's purchase decision;
• identification of extra-cost added features.

In the area of promotions,

• avoidance of false and misleading advertising;
• rejection of high pressure manipulation;
• avoidance of sales promotions that use deception or manipulation.

In the area of distribution,

• not manipulating the availability of a product for purpose of exploitation;
• not using coercion in the marketing channel;

• not exerting undue influence over the reseller's choice to handle the product.

In the area of pricing,

• not engaging in price fixing;
• not practicing predatory pricing;
• disclosing the full price associated with any purchase.

In the area of marketing research,

• prohibiting selling or fund raising under the guise of conducting research;
• maintaining research integrity by avoiding misrepresentation and omission of pertinent research data;
• treating outside clients and suppliers fairly.

Organizational Relationships

Marketers should be aware of how their behavior may influence or impact on the behavior of others in organizational relationships. They should not demand, encourage or apply coercion to obtain unethical behavior in their relationships with others, such as employees, suppliers or customers:

1. Apply confidentiality and anonymity in professional relationships with regard to privileged information;
2. Meet their obligations and responsibilities in contracts and mutual agreements in a timely manner;
3. Avoid taking the work of others, in whole, or in part, and represent this work as their own or directly benefit from it without compensation or consent of the originator or owner;
4. Avoid manipulation to take advantage of situations to maximize personal welfare in a way that unfairly deprives or damages the organization of others.

Any AMA members found to be in violation of any provision of this Code of Ethics may have his or her Association membership suspended or revoked.

FIGURE 2-5
The American Marketing Association's Code of Ethics
Reprinted by permission.

who practice marketing. Figure 2-5 shows the code of ethics of the American Marketing Association.

*A **marketing organization** may be functional, product-oriented, or market-oriented.*

A **marketing organization** is the structural arrangement that directs marketing functions. It outlines authority, responsibilities, and tasks to be accomplished. An organization may be functional, with jobs assigned in terms of buying, selling, promotion, distribution, and other tasks; product-oriented, with product managers for each product category and brand managers for each brand, in addition to functional categories; or market-oriented, with jobs assigned by geographic market and customer type, in addition to functional categories. A single firm may use a combination of these forms.

*The **marketing mix** consists of four elements: product, distribution, promotion, and price.*

A **marketing mix** is the specific combination of marketing elements used to achieve objectives and satisfy the target market. Finding a satisfactory marketing mix requires that managers make decisions regarding four major variables:

• *Product decisions*—What goods, services, organizations, people, places, and/or ideas to market, the number of items to sell and their quality, the degree of innovativeness pursued, packaging, product features, warranties, when to drop existing offerings, and so on.

- *Distribution decisions*—Whether to sell via intermediaries or directly to consumers, how many outlets to sell through, how to interact with other channel members, what terms to negotiate, the functions to assign to others, supplier choice, and so on.

- *Promotion decisions*—The most appropriate combination of promotional tools (ads, public relations, personal selling, sales promotions, etc.), whether to share promotions with others, the image to pursue, the level of personal service, media choice, message content, promotion timing, and so on.

- *Price decisions*—Overall price levels, the range of prices, the relation between price and quality, the emphasis on price, how to react to competitors, when to offer discounts, how prices are computed, what billing terms to use, and so on.

When devising a marketing mix, all of these questions should be considered:

- Is the target market precisely defined?

- Does the total marketing program, as well as each element of the mix, meet the target market's needs?

- Are marketing-mix elements consistent with one another?

- Do the elements add up to form a harmonious, integrated whole?

- Is each marketing-mix element being put to its best use?

- Does the marketing mix build on the firm's cultural and tangible strengths? Does the marketing mix imply a way to correct any weaknesses?

- Does the marketing mix create a distinctive personality in the competitive marketplace?

- Is the company protected from the most obvious competitive threats?[7]

Olympus, a leading maker of cameras and other products, is an example of a firm applying the marketing-mix concept well. It has distinct marketing mixes for different target markets, such as beginners, serious amateurs, and professional photographers. For beginners, it offers very simple cameras with automatic focus and a built-in flash. The cameras are sold in all types of stores, such as discount and department stores. Ads appear on TV and in general magazines. The cameras retail for well under $100. For serious amateur photographers, Olympus has more advanced cameras with superior features and many attachments. The cameras are sold in camera stores and finer department stores. Ads appear in specialty magazines. The cameras sell for several hundred dollars. For professional photographers, Olympus has even more advanced cameras with top-of-the-line features and attachments. The cameras are quite expensive and are sold through select camera stores, with ads appearing in trade magazines. In sum, Olympus markets the right products in the right stores, promotes them in the right media, and has the right prices for its various target markets. See Figure 2-6.

The last factor directed by marketers is extremely important: Performance assessment is the monitoring and evaluation of overall and specific marketing effectiveness. Evaluations need to be done regularly, with both the external environment and internal company data being reviewed. In-depth analysis of performance should be completed at least once or twice each year. Strategy revisions need to be enacted when the external environment changes or the company encounters difficulties.

OLYMPUS
www.olympus.com/

Performance assessment involves monitoring and evaluating marketing activities.

Uncontrollable Factors

Uncontrollable factors are the external elements affecting an organization's performance that cannot be fully directed by that organization and its marketers. A marketing plan, no matter how well conceived, may fail if uncontrollable factors have too adverse an impact. Thus, the external environment must be regularly observed and its effects considered in any marketing plan. Contingency plans relating to uncontrollable variables should also be a key

Uncontrollable factors influence an organization and its marketers but are not fully directed by them.

[7]Benson P. Shapiro, "Rejuvenating the Marketing Mix," *Harvard Business Review*, Vol. 63 (September–October 1985), p. 34. See also Walter van Waterschoot and Christophe Van den Bulte, "The 4P Classification of the Marketing Mix Revisited," *Journal of Marketing*, Vol. 56 (October 1992), pp. 83–93.

FIGURE 2-6
Focused Marketing Mixes
The Olympus Stylus camera is a simple device for beginners, while the Olympus IS-3 is a sophisticated device for advanced camera buffs. A distinct marketing mix is used with each camera.
Reprinted by permission.

part of a marketing plan. Uncontrollable factors that especially bear studying are government, consumers, competition, suppliers and distributors, the economy, technology, and independent media. These factors are shown in Figure 2-7.

Government

Governmental bodies have a great impact on marketing practices by placing (or removing) restrictions on specified activities. In any country, government rulings can be on a national, provincial/state, and/or local level.

Canadian federal legislation involves international and interprovincial commerce. Each province and municipality has its own regulations as well.

In Canada there are myriad federal legislative acts affecting the practice of business and marketing, as shown in Table 2-1.

A key piece of legislation is the Competition Act, Bill C-2, which was passed in 1986. It is administered by the Director of Investigation and Research and the director's staff at the Competition Bureau, which is part of Industry Canada. Industry Canada is responsible for administering the federal legislation passed specifically for the purpose of regulating business. Currently, deceptive marketing practices covered in the Competition Act include: misleading advertising, promotional contests, bait-and-switch selling, multi-level marketing, and pyramid selling plans.

The purpose of the act is to ensure healthy competition in the Canadian marketplace by promoting the provision of information about goods and services to both consumers and businesses. Most complaints are made by consumers and handled by the marketing

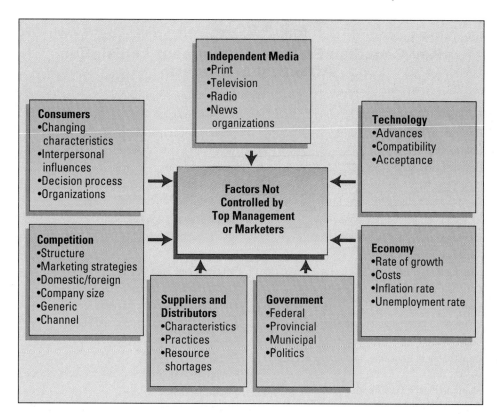

FIGURE 2-7
Uncontrollable Factors

practices branch of the Competition Bureau, but complaints from competitors are made as well and lead to actions more frequently than consumer complaints. Competitor complaints often involve detailed information and if not evaluated, could lead to widespread adoption of the marketing practice in question. Each complaint is considered by an assessment officer and then one of three options is undertaken: the file is closed if the complaint is deemed to not fall under the act or does not fall within the priorities of the marketing practices branch; the subject may be asked to provide more information about the complaint in hopes that this will stop the marketing practice; or an inquiry into the case may be undertaken.

When an inquiry is undertaken, the company whose marketing practice is called into question is contacted for an explanation. The company is able to make its case voluntarily and most companies respond by providing details. The process is designed to create a climate of cooperation and to avoid involving the courts. If it appears that an offence has been committed, then a formal inquiry may be undertaken. The cases that are pursued usually display three characteristics: there is considerable harm done in the marketplace; the case has value in terms of jurisprudence; or the resolution of the case may result in significant deterrence.[8]

In June 1995 the Competition Bureau put forward a discussion paper on issues dealing with competition policy that might call for amendments to the Competition Act. These issues include notifiable merger transactions; the protection of confidential information; mutual assistance with foreign competition law agencies; misleading advertising and deceptive marketing practices; "regular price" claims, price discrimination, and promotional allowances; prohibition orders; deceptive telemarketing solicitations; and finally, access to the Competition Tribunal.

This discussion paper generated some immediate action because Canada and the United States signed a Competition Policy agreement in August 1995 so that the two countries could cooperate to enforce laws on deceptive marketing practices and competition.

---

[8]Rachel Larabie-Lesieur, "Ottawa's Competition Act, How It Works," *Marketing Magazine* (May 1, 1995), p. 15; and Industry Canada Internet Site (http://info.ic.gc.ca) (June 1996).

T a b l e   2 – 1

Key Canadian Federal Government Legislation Affecting Marketers

Access to Information Act

Bankruptcy Act

Boards of Trade Act

Broadcasting Act

Bulk Sales Act

Canada Agricultural Products Standards Act

Canada Business Corporations Act

Canada Cooperative Association Act

Canada Corporations Act

Canada Dairy Products Act

Canadian Human Rights Act

Competition Act (Bill C-2)

Consumer Packaging and Labelling Act

Copyright Act

Department of Consumer and Corporate Affairs Act

Electricity Inspection Act

Fish Inspection Act

Food and Drugs Act

Gas Inspection Act

Gasoline Handling Act

Government Corporations Operations Act

Hazardous Products Act

Income Tax Act

Industrial Design Act

Lobbyists Registration Act

Maple Products Industry Act

Official Languages Act

Patent Act

Pension Fund Societies Act

Precious Metals Marking Act

Public Servants Invention Act

Shipping Conferences Exemption Act

Tax Rebate Discounting Act

Textile Labelling Act

Timber Marking Act

Trade Marks Act

Weights and Measures Act

Winding-Up Act

The Competition Bureau in Canada will cooperate with the U.S. Federal Trade Commission and the Antitrust division of the U.S. Department of Justice. The two countries will notify one another about investigations that involve both jurisdictions and about enforcement proceedings that might affect the interests of the other nation. The agreement also calls for sharing of investigative information and evidence and cooperation in locating witnesses.[9]

In addition to federal regulation and agencies, each province and municipal government in Canada has its own legal environment. Provincial and municipal laws may regulate where a firm is allowed to locate, the business hours, the types of items sold, if prices must be marked on every item sold, how goods must be labelled or dated, and so on. Provincial and municipal governments may also provide incentives, such as small business assistance, for firms to operate there. Examples of key provincial legislation include: the Franchises Act in Alberta, the Environmental Protection Act in Ontario, the Licensing Act in Prince Edward Island, and the Consumer Protection Act in Quebec. The latter is of particular concern for marketers because it contains a ban on all child-directed advertising. As such, marketers of products designed for children are faced with a very difficult task as they are not allowed to advertise directly to the users of their products.

The political environment often affects legislation. Should certain goods and services be prohibited from advertising on TV? Should mail-order sales to out-of-province customers be taxed? Should provincial governments become more active in handling consumer complaints? Marketing issues such as these are typically discussed via the political process before laws are enacted (or not enacted). Both firms and consumer groups may market their

---

[9]Tom Messer and James Pollock, "Canada, U.S. Agree to Share Deceptive Marketing Info," *Marketing Magazine* (August 21–28, 1995), p. 3; and Industry Canada Internet Site (June 1996).

positions on such issues to government officials. A strength of Canada's political system is its continuity, which lets organizations and individuals develop strategies for long periods of time.

One of the biggest legal and political challenges facing Canada and other countries is how to privatize organizations that were formerly run by the government:

> The obstacles to privatization are numerous. They include lack of a free-market culture; confusion over who owns the enterprises and what they're worth; poor physical infrastructure, which discourages foreign investment; the absence of a legal framework governing the conduct of business; and shortage of investment capital. After privatization, consequences can include higher prices for basic goods and services, large-scale layoffs, loss of national assets to foreign buyers, and the possible closure of vital industries.[10]

Privatization is changing the number of businesses in Canada and elsewhere.

Consumers

Although a firm has control over its selection of a target market, it cannot control the changing characteristics of its final or organizational consumers. A firm can react to, but not control, consumer trends related to age, income, marital status, occupation, race, education, place and type of residence, and the size of organizational customers. For example, health insurers who provide drug plans, out-of-province medical benefits, eyeglasses, and other special services must deal with the fact that many of their largest business customers are downsizing; thus, there are fewer employees to be insured there.

Organizations need to understand consumer trends, interpersonal influences, the decision process, and consumer groups.

Interpersonal influences on consumer behaviour need to be understood. People's purchases are affected by the corporate culture at their jobs as purchasing agents; their family, friends, and other social contacts; and the customs and taboos shaping culture and society. For instance, in some parts of Canada, liquor sales are more regulated (as to outlets, prices, other goods that can be sold, and days open) than in other parts.

People act differently in buying various types of goods and services. In the case of company cars, a purchasing agent carefully searches for information on a number of models, ranks several alternatives, selects a favourite, negotiates terms, and finally completes the purchase. On the other hand, with an inexpensive meal, a person looks at his or her watch, sees it is lunch time, and goes to a nearby fast-food outlet. Because of these differences, the consumer decision process—the steps people go through when buying products—affects the way that products are marketed.

Consumerism encompasses "the wide range of activities of government, business, and independent organizations that are designed to protect people from practices that infringe upon their rights as consumers."[11]

Consumerism *protects consumers from practices that infringe upon their rights.*

Consumerism as practised in Canada is rooted to the consumerism movement in the United States, where it has evolved through four distinct eras, and is now in a fifth. The first era was in the 1900s and focused on the need for a banking system, product purity, postal rates, antitrust, and protection against product shortages. Emphasis was on business protection against unfair practices. The second era lasted from the 1930s to the 1950s. This era's issues were product safety, bank failures, labelling, misrepresentation, stock manipulation, deceptive ads, credit, and consumer refunds. Consumer groups, such as Consumers Union and Consumers' Research, grew, as did the amount of legislation related to consumer issues. Issues were initiated but seldom resolved.

The third era began in the early 1960s and lasted to 1980. Ushering in this era was President Kennedy's **consumer bill of rights**: granting consumers the right to information, to safety, to choice in product selection, and to be heard (see Figure 2-8). These rights apply to people in any nation or economic system.

U.S. President Kennedy declared a **consumer bill of rights:** *to information, to safety, to choice, and to be heard.*

Following the American example, Canadian consumerism really took wing in this era. In fact, Canada made history when the federal government established Consumer and Corporate Affairs Canada in 1968, thereby becoming the first nation to establish a federal government agency to oversee consumer rights. Canadian consumerism has a strong expression in the electronic media from public affairs shows such as the *Fifth Estate* and *Market Place*.

---

[10]Christopher McIntosh, "To Market, to Market," *Futurist* (January–February 1994), p. 24.
[11]Bennett, *Dictionary of Marketing Terms*, p. 62.

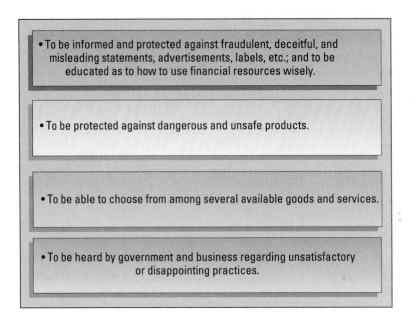

- To be informed and protected against fraudulent, deceitful, and misleading statements, advertisements, labels, etc.; and to be educated as to how to use financial resources wisely.

- To be protected against dangerous and unsafe products.

- To be able to choose from among several available goods and services.

- To be heard by government and business regarding unsatisfactory or disappointing practices.

FIGURE 2-8
Consumers' Basic Rights

The Consumers' Association of Canada gained a strong following in the 1970s, but this following waned as consumerism moved into its fourth era.

During the 1980s, consumerism entered a mature fourth era, which emphasized business deregulation and self-regulation. Nationally, no major consumer laws were enacted and budgets of federal and provincial agencies concerned with consumer issues were cut. Provincial and local governments remained active, but in general, the federal government believed that most firms took consumer issues into account when devising and applying their marketing plans. Indeed, fewer firms did ignore consumer input or publicly confront consumer groups. Cooperation between business and consumers was better, and confrontations were less likely. It was in this mature phase that what in the 1970s would have been unthinkable, happened in Canada. The Consumers' Association of Canada went broke from a lack of public support and had to be bailed out with federal government money in 1988.

In the 1990s, the federal government is still involved with consumer issues. Its goal is to balance consumer and business rights. Consumer protection derives most strongly from the Competition Act but the enforcement practices in Canada have changed in the 1990s. Instead of criminal prosecution the Competition Bureau has adopted a policy of "alternative case resolution," whereby misinformation given to consumers can be offset in one of two ways: A firm can be asked to comply with an "undertaking" or be subject to a "consent prohibition order."

An undertaking is essentially a voluntary action on the part of a business. It involves stopping the business practice in question and making sure the practice does not happen again. The process is usually completed with corrective advertising and sometimes restitution to consumers. A consent prohibition order is a much stronger response to firms that have misrepresented their products or themselves. In this circumstance a written order may be given.

In all cases where firms are involved with alternative case resolution methods, admissions of guilt to offences under the Competition Act are not assumed. Any contraventions of the Competition Act can be prosecuted by Canada's attorney general and cases that are referred for prosecution cannot be resolved under an alternative case resolution approach. Unfair business tactics, product safety, and health issues are the areas of greatest concern.

Today, consumer-rights groups speak out on behalf of consumers at public hearings, at shareholder meetings, and before the media. To avoid negative consequences brought on by active consumer groups, a firm must communicate with customers on relevant issues (such as a product recall), anticipate problems (such as delays in filling orders), respond to complaints (such as unsatisfactory customer service), and maintain good community relations (such as sponsoring neighbourhood projects).

International Marketing in

Bata Shoes: Return to the Czech Republic

Bata Ltd., a Toronto-based firm, is the world's largest shoemaker, with factories and retail stores in 65 countries around the world. The current chairman of Bata is Thomas Bata Jr., a Czechoslovakian expatriate whose family's business was nationalized by the communists in 1945. With the shift in Eastern Europe away from government run command economies to market economies, Bata was received as a hero when he visited Czechoslovakia in 1989. He has since repatriated his family business from the new government.

The deal struck by Bata involved acquiring majority ownership in a manufacturing plant and a number of retail shoe stores. There was no precedent for creating legal entities or laws governing transfers of commercial real estate when Bata began negotiations with the government, and this created some problems. The existing laws were designed to set up retail stores as separate outlets and not to allow retail chains. A further complication was that Bata management had to negotiate with American advisers who had been hired as agents for the Czech government. On December 18, 1991, a deal was signed resulting in Bata acquiring 70% of the stock in a manufacturing plant and a chain of 30 stores with head office in Zlin, Czechoslovakia, the city where the original Bata company had been founded in the late 1800s.

Today, Bata employs 1850 Czechs and produces 3800 pairs of shoes a day in its Zlin factory. The firm exports 75% of the factory's production to Western Europe and sells the remaining 25% of the output through its 52 retail stores, giving Bata a 20% share of the shoe market. However, a recent economic crisis in the Czech Republic has been causing difficulties for Bata in the Czech market. Bata has chosen to market itself as a firm that provides the best fashion, the best customer service, and the best quality for its customers at prices people can afford. Living up to this image has been difficult because of the loss of value of the Czech currency, the *koruna* or "crown."

Since the beginning of 1997 the Czech Crown has fallen 25% in value. Georg Stricker, the managing director of Czech operations, decided that as a gesture to maintain the firm's image Bata would promise to hold its prices for three months beginning in June 1997. As of August 1997, Stricker estimated that in the face of currency devaluation, increasing interest rates in the Czech Republic and inflation in Bata's costs, the move had cost the firm the equivalent of US$600,000. Stricker felt the economic crisis would resolve itself and Bata merely had to wait it out.

As a consultant to Georg Stricker, advise him on his decision to hold the line on prices given the economic crisis in the Czech Republic.

Source: Adapted from Sonja Sinclair, "The Best Revenge," *Canadian Business* (March 1994), pp. 20–31, and Normandy Madden, "Bata pays the price of return to Czech root," *Marketing Magazine* (August 11, 1997), p. 6.

Competition

The competitive environment often affects a company's marketing efforts and its success in reaching a target market. Thus, firms need to assess the following characteristics of their competitive environment:

- The industry structure.
- Their competitors' marketing strategies.

BATA LTD.
www.bata.com/

- The nationality of their competitors (domestic or foreign).
- The size of their competitors.
- Generic competition.
- Channel competition.

Monopoly, oligopoly, monopolistic competition, and pure competition are the main types of competitive structure.

A company may operate under one of four possible competitive structures: monopoly, oligopoly, monopolistic competition, or pure competition. With a **monopoly**, just one firm sells a given good or service and has a lot of control over its marketing plan. This occurs in Canada when a firm has a patent (exclusive rights to a sell a product it invented for a fixed number of years, such as new pharmaceutical products), is a public utility (such as local phone or natural gas companies), or is a Crown corporation (such as Canada Post). In an **oligopoly**, a few firms—usually large ones—account for most industry sales and tend to engage in nonprice competition. For example, General Motors, Ford, Chrysler, Honda, and Toyota account for about 95 per cent of Canadian auto sales. In **monopolistic competition**, there are several firms in an industry, each trying to offer a unique marketing mix—based on price or nonprice factors. This is the most common Canadian industry structure, followed by oligopoly. Service stations, beauty salons, stores, garment makers, computer-clone makers, and furniture makers are some firms facing monopolistic competition. In **pure competition**, many firms sell virtually identical goods or services and they are unable to create differential advantages. This rarely occurs in Canada. It is most common for selected food items and commodities (and happens if numerous small firms compete with each other).

After analyzing its industry's competitive structure, a firm needs to study the strategies of competitors. Specifically, it should look at their target markets and marketing mixes, their images, their differential advantages, which markets are saturated and which are unfulfilled, and the extent to which consumers are content with the service and quality provided by competitors.

Foreign competition is intensifying.

BANK OF MONTREAL
www.bmo.com/

MOLSON
www.molson.com/

LABATT
www.labatt.com/

INTERBREW S.A.
www.environics.ca/pr/clients/interbr.html

Both domestic and foreign competition need to be examined. For instance, in Canada, Investors Group competes with the Bank of Montreal, Canada Trust, Canada Life Insurance, and others—besides traditional brokerage firms—for financial-services business. Many Canadian, American, and West European industries are mature; the amount of domestic competition is stable. In some industries, competition is rising due to the popularity of innovations like notebook PCs. In others, domestic competition is intensifying as a result of government deregulation. For instance, witness all the companies offering long-distance telephone services in Canada.[12]

Foreign competitors play a major role in many industries in North America. In the early 1980s the Canadian brewing industry was owned and dominated by three major breweries: Molson, Labatt, and Carling-O'Keefe, who controlled over 90 per cent of the market. Now, Molson owns Carling-O'Keefe and in turn is controlled by the Miller Brewing Company of the United States. In 1995 Labatt was purchased by a Belgian firm, Interbrew S.A., leaving micro brewers as the only Canadian-owned brewing companies—and they have less than 15 per cent market share. Foreign-based firms are doing well at capturing large market shares across North America—50 per cent for steel, 65 per cent for clothing, 75 per cent for shoes, and up to 98 per cent for some consumer electronics.

At the same time, competition in foreign markets is intensifying for Canadian-based firms as rivals stress innovations, cost cutting, good distribution and promotion, and other factors. Many of the industries in which Canadian firms have international dominance are related to the harsh winter climate. For example, Canadian firms excel in the areas of snowmobiles, hockey equipment, and winter boot manufacturing. Of course, the energy and mining industries of Canada are very strong competitors too.

For many industries, there has been a trend toward larger firms because of mergers and acquisitions, as well as company sales growth. Over the last decade, mergers and acquisitions have involved telecommunications firms (AT&T acquiring Unitel, a long distance phone company), food firms (Nestlé acquiring Perrier), pharmaceuticals firms (Bristol-Myers merging with Squibb), transportation firms (Canadian Airlines joining with American Airlines), consumer-products firms (Sony buying CBS Records), retailers (Wal-

---

[12]"Psst, Wanna Buy Some Long-Distance?" p. 98.

Mart acquiring Woolco), and numerous others. Canadian sales have been growing for such firms as Potash Corp. of Saskatchewan, IPL Energy Inc., Philip Environmental, and Anderson Exploration Ltd.—each of which were among the top 10 fastest growing firms in Canada in 1996, with average sales of over 500 million dollars.[13]

For small firms, major differential advantages include personal service, a focus on under-served market segments, an entrepreneurial drive, and flexibility; cooperative ventures and franchising allow such firms to buy in quantity and operate more efficiently. Among large firms, widespread distribution, economies of scale, well-known brands, mass-media ads, and low to moderate prices are commonly used competitive tactics.

Every organization should define its competition generically, meaning as broadly as possible. Direct competitors are similar to the firm with regard to their line of business and marketing approach. Indirect competitors are different from the firm, but still compete with it for customers. Both types of competitors should be studied and accounted for in a firm's marketing plan. For instance, a movie theatre not only competes with other theatres (direct competitors), but with video stores, TV and radio shows, video games, sporting events, live music concerts, plays, amusement parks, bookstores, restaurants, and schools (indirect competitors). A theatre owner might ask, "What can I do to compete with this variety of entertainment and recreation forms in terms of movie selection, prices, hours, customer service, refreshments, and parking?"

Competition should be defined generically—as widely as possible.

A company also needs to study the competition from its channel members (resellers). Each party in the distribution process has different goals and would like to maximize its control over the marketing mix. Some wholesalers and retailers carry their own brands besides those of manufacturers.

Suppliers and Distributors

Many firms rely on their suppliers and distributors (wholesalers and retailers) to properly run their businesses. Without their ongoing support, it would be difficult, if not impossible, for a company to succeed.

Suppliers and distributors can have a dramatic impact on an organization.

Suppliers provide the goods and services that firms need to operate, as well as those that they resell to their own customers. In general, a firm is most vulnerable when there are relatively few suppliers; specific goods and services are needed to run a business or satisfy customer demand; competitors would gain if the firm had a falling out with a supplier; suppliers are better attuned to the desires of the marketplace; suppliers informally take care of maintenance and repair services; the turnaround time to switch suppliers is lengthy; or suppliers have exclusive access to scarce resources.

Firms that cannot market their products directly to consumers need distributors (wholesalers or retailers). In general, a firm is most vulnerable when there are relatively few distributors in an area; the distributors carry many brands; shelf space is tight; the firm is unknown in the marketplace; particular distributors account for a large portion of the firm's revenues; distributors help finance the firm; distributors are better attuned to the marketplace; or other competitors are waiting in the wings to stock the distributors.

Among the supplier/distributor practices that a firm should regularly study are: delivery time or requests, product availability, prices, flexibility in handling special requests, marketing support, consistency of treatment, returns policies, and other services. Unsatisfactory performance by a supplier or distributor in one or more of these areas could have a lasting impact on the firm's ability to enact its marketing plans.

Regardless of suppliers' good intentions, a firm's ability to carry out its plans can be affected by the scarcity of particular resources. Over the past twenty-five years, sporadic shortages and volatile price changes have occurred for a variety of basic commodities, such as home heating oil, other petroleum-based products, plastics, synthetic fibres, aluminum, chrome, silver, tungsten, nickel, steel, glass, grain, fertilizer, cotton, and wool. And despite efforts at conservation, some raw materials, processed materials, and component parts may remain or become scarce over the next decade.[14]

[13]"Performance 500: The Top 10," *Canadian Business* (June 1997), pp. 137–146.
[14]William B. Wagner, "Establishing Supply Service Strategy for Shortage Situations," *Industrial Marketing Management*, Vol. 23 (1994), pp. 393–401.

Resource shortages and/or rapid cost increases require one of three actions. First, substitute materials could be used in constructing products, requiring intensified research and product testing. Second, prices could be raised for products that cannot incorporate substitute materials. Third, firms could abandon products where resources are unavailable and demarket others where demand is greater than it is able to satisfy.

The Economy

The rate of growth in a nation's or region's economy can have a big impact on a firm's marketing efforts. A high growth rate means the economy is strong and the marketing potential large. Quite important to marketers are consumer perceptions—both in the business and final consumer sectors—regarding the economy. For instance, if people believe the economy will be good, they may spend more; if they believe the economy will be poor, they may cut back. In uncertain times, many organizational consumers are interested in preserving their flexibility.

Economic growth is measured by the **Gross Domestic Product**.

A country's economic growth is reflected by changes in its **Gross Domestic Product (GDP)**, which is the total annual value of goods and services produced in a country less net foreign investment. These are the 1996 GDPs (in U.S. dollars) and their percentages in real growth for ten selected nations and Canada *in order of GDP size*: United States, $6.9 trillion, 2.8%; Japan, $4.6 trillion, 3.7%; Germany, $2.4 trillion, 1.0%; France, $1.5 trillion, 1.1%; Italy, $1.1 trillion, 1.2%; Brazil, $650 billion, 2.8%; **Canada, $580 billion, 1.5%**; Russia $448 billion, -6.0%; Mexico, $328 billion, 4.3%; India, $342 billion, 6.3%; and Thailand, $186 billion, 6.7%.[15] In recent years, the yearly growth in most of these nations has been 3 per cent or less; and when certain industries, such as autos and housing, slow down, repercussions are felt in other areas, such as insurance and home furnishings. Canada is expected to have real GDP growth averaging about 2 to 4 per cent annually during the rest of the 1990s—but the rate could be lower if federal and provincial budget deficits are not reduced.

Several business costs—like raw materials, unionized labour wages, taxes, interest rates, and office (factory) rental—are generally beyond any firm's control. If costs rise by a large amount, marketing flexibility may be limited because a firm often cannot pass along all of the increase; it might have to cut back on marketing activities or accept lower profit margins. If costs are stable, marketers are better able to differentiate products and expand sales because their companies are more apt to invest in marketing activities.

Real income describes earnings adjusted for inflation. Both inflation and unemployment affect purchases.

From a marketing perspective, what happens to a consumer's real income is critical. While actual income is the amount earned by a consumer (or his/her family or household) in a given year, **real income** is the amount earned in a year adjusted by the rate of inflation. For example, if a person's actual income goes up by 4 per cent in a year (from $40 000 to $41 600) and the rate of inflation (which measures price changes for the same goods and services over time) is 4 per cent for the year, real income remains constant [($41 600) − ($41 600/1.04) = $40 000]. If actual income increases exceed the inflation rate, real income rises and people can buy more goods and services. If actual income increases are less than the inflation rate, real income falls and people must buy fewer goods and services.

A high rate of unemployment can adversely affect many firms because people who are unemployed are likely to cut back on nonessentials wherever possible. Low unemployment often means substantial sales of large-ticket items, as consumers are better off, more optimistic, and more apt to spend earnings.

Technology

Technology includes machinery, products, and processes.

Technology refers to the development and use of machinery, products, and processes. Individual firms, especially smaller ones with limited capital, must usually adapt to technological advances (rather than control them).

---

15. Bureau of Economic Analysis, http://www.bea.doc.gov/ (August 30, 1997); U.S. State Department, "1996 Country Reports on Economic Policy and Trade Practices," http://www.state.gov/ (August 30, 1997).

Many firms depend on others to develop and perfect new technology, such as computer microchips; only then can they use the new technology in their products, such as automated gas pumps at service stations, talking toys, or electronic sensors in smoke detectors for office buildings. The inventor of new technology often secures patent protection, which excludes competitors from using that technology (unless the inventor licenses rights for a fee).

In a number of areas, companies have been unable to achieve practical technological breakthroughs. For example, no firm has been able to develop and market a cure for the common cold, a good-tasting non-tobacco cigarette, a commercially acceptable electric car, or a truly effective and safe diet pill.

When new technology first emerges, it may be expensive and in short supply, both for firms using the technology in their products and for final consumers. The challenge is to mass produce and mass market the technology efficiently. In addition, some technological advances require employee training and consumer education before they can succeed. Thus, an emphasis on user-friendliness can speed up the acceptance of new technology.

Certain advances may not be compatible with goods and services already on the market or may require retooling by firms wanting to use them in products or operations. Every time an auto maker introduces a significantly new car model, it must invest hundreds of millions of dollars to retool facilities. Each time a firm buys new computer equipment to

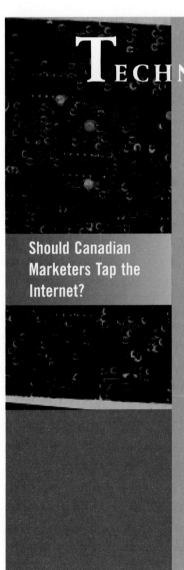

TECHNOLOGY & MARKETING

Should Canadian Marketers Tap the Internet?

In 1995 the Internet became a mainstream medium for marketers. Estimates indicate that there are 27 million North American Internet users, and that number is growing daily. Globally, the rate of adoption of Internet usage is growing 10 to 15 per cent a month!

The attraction of the Internet for both buyers and sellers is its interactive nature. Unlike the traditional media of newsprint, radio, television, magazines and outdoor advertising, which are essentially one-way communications, the Internet allows two-way communication between marketer and customer. Furthermore, the "market" access of the Internet is equal (at least so far) for all marketers. A small firm can compete with a large firm by having a good Web site, a 1-800 number (for transaction security) and a vendor's account with VISA or Mastercard. The Web site is like a store front, so its design and presentation are critical. In this regard large firms may assert an advantage by paying multimedia designers as much as $100 000 for a top-notch site. Still, do-it-your-selfers can save money and satisfy their creative fantasies by designing their own pages using packaged software. It is also pleasing to know that such software will be getting better and cheaper in the future so that updating and changing Web pages will be even easier.

It seems the wheel-of-retailing has come full circle. The new technology promises on-line catalogue shopping. These catalogues may possess sound and motion and be able to listen to their customers, but in other ways this is just catalogue shopping the way it was over 100 years ago. For the marketer, reaching customers and creating demand interactively on the Internet will present a number of new challenges, but the goods and services will still have to be physically distributed. It seems unlikely that the technology to move goods and services will be able to keep pace with the technology to move information.

How would you design an "electronic store front" for an auto dealer?

Source: Based on Angela Kryhul, "The Internet Makes the Mainstream," *Marketing Magazine* (December 18–25, 1995), p. 11; Jim McElgunn, "Smoke and Mirrors," *Marketing Magazine* (December 18–25, 1995), pp. 11–12; Tony Spencer, "Setting Up a Virtual Store," *Marketing Magazine* (December 18–25, 1995), p. 12; Christopher E. Erickson, "Copyright and New Media Marketing," *Marketing Magazine* (December 18–25, 1995), p. 14; and Tony Long, "Telecommunications and New Media Renovate the Old-Style Bazaar," *Marketing Magazine* (December 18–25, 1995), p. 15.

supplement existing hardware, it must see if the new equipment is compatible (Can it run all the computer programs used by the firm and "talk" to the firm's existing machines?).

To flourish, technological advances must be accepted by each firm in the distribution process (manufacturer/service provider, wholesaler, retailer). Should any of the firms not use a new technology, its benefits may be lost. If small retailers do not use electronic scanning equipment, cashiers will still have to ring up prices by hand even though packages are computer-coded by manufacturers.

Independent Media

Independent media affect perceptions of products and company image.

Independent media are not controlled by a firm, yet they influence government, consumer, and public perceptions of that firm's products and overall image. Media can provide positive or negative coverage when a firm produces a new product, pollutes the air, mislabels products, contributes to charity, or otherwise performs a newsworthy activity. Coverage may be by print media, TV, radio, or news organizations. To receive good coverage, a firm should willingly offer information to independent media and always try to get its position written or spoken about.

Although the media's coverage of information about a firm is beyond that firm's control, paid advertising is not. Ads may be rejected by the media, but if they are accepted, they must be presented in the time interval and form stipulated by the firm.

Attainment of Objectives, Feedback, and Adaptation

An organization's success or failure in reaching objectives depends on how well it directs its controllable factors and deals with the impact of uncontrollable factors. As shown in Figure 2-1, the interaction of an organization's total offering and its uncontrollable environment determines how well it does.

Feedback provides information that lets a firm adapt to its environment.

To optimize its marketing efforts and secure its long-run existence, a firm must get **feedback**—information about the uncontrollable environment, the organization's performance, and how well the marketing plan is received. Feedback is gained by measuring consumer satisfaction, looking at competitive trends, evaluating relationships with government agencies, studying the economy and potential resource shortages, monitoring the independent media, analyzing sales and profit trends, talking with suppliers and distributors, and utilizing other methods of acquiring and assessing information.

After evaluating feedback, a company—when necessary—needs to engage in adaptation, thereby fine-tuning its marketing plan to be responsive to the surrounding environment, while continuing to capitalize on differential advantages. A firm should look continually for new and attainable opportunities that fit its overall marketing plan and respond to potential threats by revising its marketing policies. For instance:

> In Atlantic Canada there are approximately 116 co-op food and general merchandise stores. The Price Club and Real Atlantic Superstores are opening in the Maritimes as part of the "bigger is better" trend in retailing that is sweeping across the rest of Canada. The typical victims of the bigger stores have been medium-sized food and general merchandise stores like the Atlantic co-ops.
>
> Co-ops and the Price Club operate in a similar fashion, in that fees for shopping in the outlet are often charged and some exclusivity is associated with them because a membership is required. However, the co-ops operate differently from the Price Club in a number of ways. Some co-ops use direct charges where shoppers pay weekly fees ($3 to $5) and then buy their merchandise for essentially no mark-up. Another approach to operation allows members and non-members to shop in the store and keeps pricing similar to that of the competition. However, members receive dividends based on store profits at the end of the year.
>
> The secret to success for the co-ops is their customer loyalty. The Price Club plans to charge a $40.00 annual fee to secure loyalty from its customers as well. The co-ops plan to fight back by letting their shoppers know that they are stockholders and consumers in these stores. Their advertising slogan is "It's your store for shopping," and they mean that quite literally. They

will also tell their customers that while the operating profits of the Atlantic co-ops will stay in Atlantic Canada, this will not be the case for the competition.[16]

In preparing for the future, a firm must avoid **marketing myopia**—a shortsighted, narrow-minded view of marketing and its environment. It is a "self-inflicted and avoidable harm caused to an organization due to a lack of attention to and poor implementation of marketing concepts and principles." These are some major warning signs:

Marketing myopia *is an ineffective marketing approach.*

- *We-know syndrome*—An ongoing assumption that the correct answers to crucial questions are always known.
- *Me-tooism*—Occurs when goods and services are too similar to those of competitors and there is no competitive advantage.
- *Monopricis*—Occurs when a firm's primary (or only) marketing/competitive tool is changing prices.
- *Customerphobia*—The fear of having a close relationship with and really caring about consumers and their wants.
- *Fax-me complex*—Occurs when the firm is completely dominated by tasks that require immediate attention (crises).
- *Hypermentis*—Occurs when executives devote too much of their time to thinking, studying, and planning while they take little action.
- *Global idiosis*—The lack of ability or willingness to compete in the international marketplace.
- *If it works, don't fix it*—Occurs when business is very good, but no one knows why and everyone is hesitant to make changes.
- *Interfunctionalphobia*—A lack of mutual understanding, integration, and cooperation among a firm's various functional areas.
- *Short-run fetish*—Occurs when decisions are too biased toward the short-run, thus sacrificing long-run performance.[17]

[16]Mark Higgins, "Owners and Consumers," *Marketing Magazine* (November 6, 1995), pp. 14–15.
[17]John H. Antil, "Are You Committing Marketcide?" *Journal of Services Marketing*, Vol. 6 (Spring 1992), pp. 45–53.

MARKETING IN A CHANGING WORLD

Trends That Will Affect the Future

Futurists have tried to identify environmental trends that will greatly influence how marketers do business in the world during the next several years. Here are several of them. Are we ready? Do you agree with all of these predictions?

- *Cocooning*—More people at home because they are working there, or they "cashed out," and retired early because of corporate downsizing. They are not going out as much; they are taking delivery of products rather than shopping, spending leisure time at home, focusing on home entertainment (watching videos, playing video games, surfing the Internet), and working out on home exercise equipment. This trend will produce more home renovation business and result in furniture upgrades. The home office will be fully equipped with faxes, cellular phones, computers, modems, and interactive television.

- *Consumer spending*—Recession-weary people will break out and treat themselves. The upper-income earners will buy pricey, upscale products while lower-income earners will look to warehouse stores and non-branded merchandise.

- *Staying alive*—The fitness rage of the eighties is over, but the long term, health, nutrition, fitness, stress management, meditation, holistic approach to life is here. Wellness programs, new age remedies, organic foods and longevity centres will be in demand.

- *Wildering*—People will go for more outdoor activities. Hiking boots, backpacks, and off-road vehicles should be in demand.

- *One-on-one marketing*—Customized marketing as marketers use advanced technology to get to know their customers intimately and try to establish a long-term relationship by serving as many needs as possible using this knowledge.

- *Globalnomics*—The Canadian economy will become more integrated with the international economy as international trade barriers fall. Tourism, vacationing, and travel will grow.

- *Moving targets*—Marketers will try some new target-market approaches by aiming at women with products not traditionally marketed to them, e.g. cars. Men will also be targeted with non-traditional products such as food and household products. Marketers will rediscover mass marketing by lumping the baby boomers and Generation X segments together.

- *Save our society*—Demand for ethical business practices, lifelong education, and training and environmental conservation will heat up throughout society.[18]

[18]Marvin J. Cetron, *An American Renaissance in the Year 2000* (New York: St. Martin's Press, 1994); and Jo Marney, "Towards the Next Millennium," *Marketing Magazine* (July 24, 1995), p. 17.

SUMMARY

1. *To examine the environment within which marketing decisions are made and marketing activities are undertaken* The marketing environment consists of controllable factors, uncontrollable factors, the organization's level of success or failure in reaching its objectives, feedback, and adaptation. The macroenvironment includes the broad societal and economic forces that a firm faces, while the microenvironment refers to the forces that more directly affect a firm's ability to serve its customers.

2. *To differentiate between those elements controlled by a firm's top management and those controlled by marketing, and to enumerate the controllable elements of a marketing plan* Controllable factors are the internal strategy elements directed by a firm and its marketers. Top management decides on the line of business, overall objectives, the role of marketing and other business functions, and the corporate culture. These decisions have an impact on all aspects of marketing.

The major factors directed by marketing personnel are the selection of a target market (the group(s) of customers a firm proposes to serve); marketing objectives, which are more customer-oriented than those set by top management; the marketing organization; the marketing mix, which is a specific combination of product, distribution, promotion, and price decisions; and performance assessment, which involves monitoring and evaluating marketing outcomes. It is important for marketing personnel to strive to create differential advantages—the unique features that cause consumers to patronize a firm and not its competitors.

3. *To enumerate the uncontrollable environmental elements that can affect a marketing plan and study their potential ramifications* Uncontrollable factors are the external elements affecting a company's performance that cannot be fully directed by the top management and marketers of a firm. Any marketing plan, no matter how well conceived, may fail if uncontrollable factors influence it too much.

Among the key uncontrollable variables are changing consumer traits, interpersonal influences on consumer behaviour, the consumer decision process, and consumer groups; the competitive structure of the industry in which a firm operates (monopoly, oligopoly, monopolistic competition, or pure competition) and such competitor attributes as marketing strategies, country of origin, size, generic competition, and channel competition; suppliers and distributors, their traits and practices, and resource shortages; government legislation and the political environment; the rate of economic growth (as measured by the GDP and real income), the costs of doing business, and other economic factors; technology, which refers to the development and use of machinery, products, and processes; and independent media, the communication vehicles not controlled by the firm.

4. *To explain why feedback about company performance and the uncontrollable aspects of its environment and the subsequent adaptation of the marketing plan are essential for a firm to attain its objectives* A firm's level of success or failure in reaching its goals depends on how well it directs and implements its controllable factors and the impact of uncontrollable factors on the marketing plan. When enacting a marketing strategy, a firm should obtain feedback (information about both its overall and marketing performance and the uncontrollable environment) and adapt the strategy to be responsive to the surrounding environment while continuing to exploit its differential advantages. Marketing myopia, a shortsighted view of marketing and its environment, must be avoided.

KEY TERMS

marketing environment (p. 24)
controllable factors (p .24)
uncontrollable factors (p. 24)
organizational performance (p. 25)
feedback (p. 25)
adaptation (p. 25)
macroenvironment (p. 25)
microenvironment (p. 25)
line of business (p. 25)
corporate culture (p. 26)

target market (p. 28)
market segmentation (p. 28)
differential advantages (p. 29)
ethical behaviour (p. 29)
marketing organization (p. 30)
marketing mix (p. 30)
uncontrollable factors (p. 31)
consumerism (p. 35)
consumer bill of rights (p. 35)
monopoly (p. 38)

oligopoly (p. 38)
monopolistic competition (p 38)
pure competition (p. 38)
Gross Domestic Product (GDP) (p. 40)
real income (p. 40)
technology (p. 40)
independent media (p. 42)
feedback (p. 42)
marketing myopia (p. 43)

Review Questions

1. Explain the environment within which marketing operates.
2. Differentiate between the "macroenvironment" and the "microenvironment."
3. Why are the factors controlled by top management usually considered uncontrollable by marketing personnel?
4. What criteria would you use to assess the role of marketing in a company?
5. Why should a firm select a target market before developing a specific marketing mix?
6. What is the most important marketing objective for an organization? Why?
7. Describe the four components of the marketing mix.
8. Why are suppliers an important uncontrollable factor for many companies?
9. What is the intent of the Competition Act, Bill C-2?
10. How do the independent media affect a firm's marketing practices?

Discussion Questions

1. How does a firm's corporate culture influence the performance of its personnel? Relate your answer to a small taxi service that caters to corporate accounts.
2. What are the differential advantages for each of these? Explain your answers.
   a. Your college or university.
   b. *People* magazine.
   c. A local printing service.
3. Distinguish between the marketing mixes used by Cadillac and Saturn, two car lines of General Motors.
4. Deregulation represents both opportunities and potential problems for companies. Offer several examples of both for the cable TV industry.
5. Comment on this statement: "By defining competition in generic terms, acquiring information about the uncontrollable environment, and modifying strategy when necessary, an organization will avoid marketing myopia and guarantee its long-term success."

CHAPTER 3
Information for Marketing Decisions

Chapter Objectives

1. To show why marketing information is needed

2. To explain the role and importance of marketing information systems

3. To examine a basic marketing information system, commercial databases, database marketing, and examples of MIS in action

4. To define marketing research and its components and to look at its scope

5. To describe the marketing research process

{ *At a time when growing numbers of publishing firms are racing to develop databases to market their products better, Reader's Digest Association is years ahead. Its files, started 40 years ago in much simpler form, now hold data on an astounding 100 million households worldwide (half of which are in the United States). The database is the organization's lifeblood. Virtually all company operations are connected to it. And the Association neither rents nor sells its list of names.* }

Reprinted by permission of The Reader's Digest Association, Inc.

Reader's Digest Association has one of the largest private consumer databases in the world. These files are updated continuously to reflect information about subscribers to the firm's magazines, books (both general interest and reference), interactive CDs (reference and cook books), recorded music cassettes, and videocassettes.

The main source of names for the Association's database is *Reader's Digest*, with a monthly worldwide circulation of 28 million—including 1.2 million in Canada. Two-thirds of *Reader's Digest* readers renew their subscriptions annually; and five million new subscriptions are sold throughout the world each year. *Reader's Digest* has the largest circulation among Canadian magazines (*Reader's Digest* in English and *Selection du Reader's Digest* in French) and the second largest circulation among U.S. magazines, behind only *Modern Maturity*, a magazine mailed to all members of the American Association of Retired Persons.

Reader's Digest has been expanding its global circulation. In total, the magazine publishes 45 editions in 17 different languages; and it has the largest circulation of any magazine in Britain, Finland, Germany, Mexico, and Southeast Asia. The Association publishes its general interest books and CDs in 11 languages and its condensed books in 12 languages.

In 1989, the Association began to acquire special-interest magazines. It now publishes *American Health*, *Family Handyman*, *Moneywise* (in Great Britain), *New Choices for Retirement Living*, and *Travel Holiday*. According to the company, its main goal in these acquisitions was to strengthen its database. As of 1994, three million additional names had been added to the firm's database because of the acquisitions.

Although the Association's management of its database is well respected, even this company has, on occasion, had difficulties in using it efficiently. Several years ago, for example, the firm had trouble coordinating offers from its various divisions. Thus, a *Reader's Digest* subscriber with an interest in travel might receive offers for travel books, a video on a foreign country, and a subscription to *Travel Holiday*. At that time, many people in the database felt so inundated with the direct mail offers that the firm's "hit rate" in getting new business fell off. After realizing the consumer discontent, the Association reduced its promotional mailings in the book and home entertainment business. It also became more selective in the use of its promotional mailings.[1]

In this chapter, we will look at the value of marketing information, explain the role of a marketing information system (which gathers, analyzes, disseminates, and stores relevant marketing data), and describe the marketing research process. We will also take another peek at database marketing.

Overview

Firms make better marketing decisions when they have good information.

It is essential for a firm to have appropriate information before, while, and after making (and enacting) marketing decisions if it wants to accurately assess strengths, weaknesses, opportunities, and threats; tailor its actions to the marketing environment; and maximize its performance. Good information enables marketers to:

- Gain a competitive edge.
- Reduce financial and image risks.

[1]Deirdre Carmody, "Lifeblood of Reader's Digest Is 40-Year-Old Database," *New York Times* (May 16, 1995), pp. D1, D7; Gary Hoover, Alta Campbell, and Patrick J. Spain (Eds.) *Hoover's Handbook of American Business 1995* (Austin, TX: Reference Press, 1994), pp. 910–911; and *Canadian Advertising Rates and Data* (August 1995).

- Determine consumer attitudes.
- Monitor the environment.
- Gather competitive intelligence.
- Coordinate strategy.
- Measure performance.
- Improve advertising credibility.
- Gain management support for decisions.
- Verify intuition.
- Improve effectiveness.

Relying on intuition, executive judgment, and past experience is not enough:

> In markets that are growing more slowly and are saturated with competition, businesses prosper by following two strategies. First, they learn more and more about the characteristics and location of their customers. Second, they use that knowledge to develop better goods or services and reduce unsuccessful marketing efforts.[2]

Marketing information is collected using the **scientific method**—incorporating objectivity, accuracy, and thoroughness. Objectivity means information is gathered in an open-minded way. Judgments are not reached until all data are collected and analyzed. Accuracy refers to the use of carefully constructed research tools. Each aspect of information gathering, such as the study format, the sample, interviewer training, and tabulation of responses, must be well planned and executed. Thoroughness describes the comprehensive nature of information gathering. Mistaken conclusions may be reached if probing is not intense enough.

In this chapter, two vital aspects of marketing information are covered: marketing information systems and marketing research. A marketing information system guides all of a firm's marketing-related information efforts and stores and disseminates data on a continuous basis. Marketing research involves gathering and analyzing information on specific marketing issues.

The **scientific method** *requires objectivity, accuracy, and thoroughness.*

Marketing Information Systems

The collection of marketing information should not be a rare event that occurs only when data are needed about a specific marketing topic. Research done this way exposes the firm to numerous risks:

- Opportunities may be missed.
- There may be a lack of awareness of environmental changes and competitors' actions.
- It may not be possible to analyze data over several periods.
- Marketing plans and decisions may not be properly reviewed.
- Data collection may be disjointed.
- Previous studies may not be stored in an easy-to-use format.
- Time lags may result whenever a new research study is required.
- Actions may be reactionary rather than anticipatory.

Thus, it is essential for any firm, regardless of its size or type, to devise and employ some form of marketing information system to aid decision making. A **marketing information system (MIS)** is "a set of procedures and methods designed to generate, analyze, disseminate, and store anticipated marketing decision information on a regular, continuous basis."[3]

A **marketing information system** *regularly gathers, analyzes, disseminates, and stores data.*

---

[2]Peter Francese, "Managing Market Information," *American Demographics* (September 1995), p. 59.
[3]Adapted by the authors from Robert A. Peterson, *Marketing Research*, Second Edition (Dallas: Business Publications, 1988), p. 31; and Peter D. Bennett (Ed.), *Dictionary of Marketing Terms*, Second Edition (Chicago: American Marketing Association, 1995), p. 167.

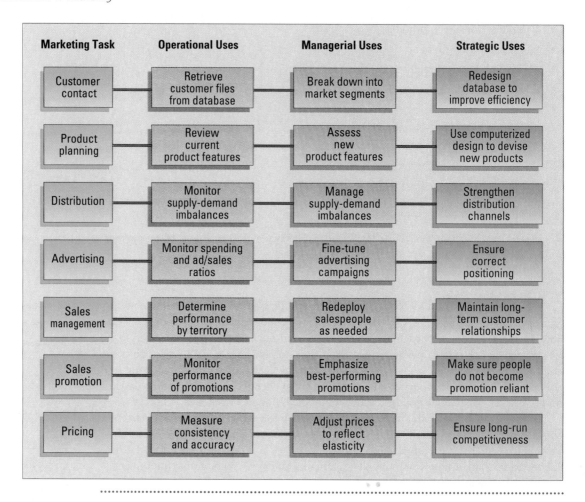

FIGURE 3-1
Uses of a Marketing Information System

Source: Adapted by the authors from Rajendra S. Sisodia, "Marketing Information and Decision Support Systems for Services," *Journal of Services Marketing*, Vol. 6 (Winter 1992), pp. 51–64.

To establish an MIS, a firm should:

- Aggressively amass data from internal company documents, existing external documents, and primary studies (when necessary).
- Analyze the data and prepare appropriate reports—in terms of the company mission, strategy, and proposed tactics.
- Disseminate the analyzed data to the right marketing decision makers in the company. They will vary on the basis of the particular topics covered.
- Store data for future use and comparisons.
- Seek out all relevant data that have either current or future marketing ramifications—not just data with specific short-term implications.
- Undertake ongoing data collection, analysis, dissemination, and storage.

Figure 3-1 shows how an information system can be used operationally, managerially, and strategically for several aspects of marketing.

In the following sections, the components of a basic marketing information system, commercial databases, database marketing, and examples of MIS in action are presented.

A Basic Marketing Information System

Figure 3-2 presents a basic marketing information system. It begins with a statement of company objectives, which provide broad guidelines. These goals are affected by environmen-

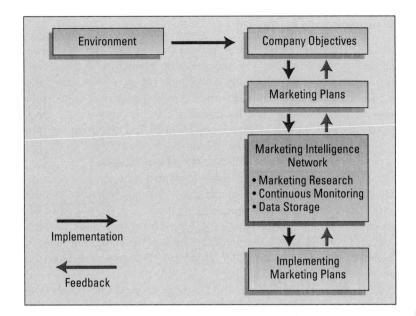

FIGURE 3-2
A Basic Marketing System

tal factors, such as competition, government, and the economy. Marketing plans involve the choice of a target market, marketing goals, the marketing organization, the marketing mix (product, distribution, promotion, and price decisions), and performance measurement.

After marketing plans are outlined, a firm's total marketing information needs can be specified and satisfied with a **marketing intelligence network**, which consists of marketing research, continuous monitoring, and data storage. **Marketing research** is used to obtain information on particular marketing issues (problems). Information may be retrieved from storage (existing company data) or acquired by collecting external secondary data and/or primary data. **Continuous monitoring** is used to regularly study a firm's external and internal environment. It can entail subscribing to trade publications, observing news reports, getting constant feedback from employees and customers, attending industry meetings, watching competitors' actions (competitive intelligence), and compiling periodic company reports. **Data storage** involves retaining all types of relevant company records (such as sales, costs, personnel performance, etc.), as well as information collected through marketing research and continuous monitoring. These data aid decision making and are kept for future reference. Marketing research should be considered as just one part of an ongoing, integrated information system.

Depending on a firm's resources and the complexity of its information needs, a marketing intelligence network may or may not be computerized. Small firms can do well without computerizing; they merely need to read industry publications, attend trade shows, observe competitors, talk with suppliers and customers, track performance, and store the results of these efforts. In any event, information needs must be stated and regularly reviewed, data sources must be identified, personnel must be given information tasks, storage and retrieval facilities must be set up, and data must be routed to decision makers. The keys to a successful MIS are consistency, completeness, and orderliness.

Marketing plans should be enacted based on information obtained from the intelligence network. For example, by continuous monitoring, a firm could ascertain that a leading competitor intends to cut prices by 7 per cent during the next month. This would give the firm time to explore its own marketing options (e.g., switch to cheaper materials, place larger orders with suppliers to get discounts, or ignore the cuts) and select one. If monitoring is not done, the firm might be caught by surprise and forced to just cut prices, without any other choice.

A basic MIS generally has many advantages: it allows the firm to organize and store data over long time periods; gain a broad perspective on their business; avoid crises; coordinate their marketing plans; make decisions more quickly; and perform cost-benefit analysis. However, forming an information system is not easy. Initial time and labour costs may be high, and setting up a sophisticated system can be complex.

A **marketing intelligence network** *includes* **marketing research, continuous monitoring,** *and* **data storage.**

Commercial Databases

Commercial databases *can provide useful ongoing information.*

Because companies need current, comprehensive, and relatively inexpensive information about the environment in which they operate, many specialized research firms offer ongoing **commercial databases** with information on population traits, the business environment, economic forecasts, industry and company performance, and other items. Databases may include newspaper and magazine articles, business and household addresses culled from Yellow Pages and other sources, industry and company news releases, government reports, conference proceedings, indexes, patent records, and so on. The research firms sell access to their databases to clients, usually for a relatively low fee.

Databases are typically available in printed form; on computer disks, CD-ROMs, or tapes; and "online" using a computer and a modem. There are commercial database firms that concentrate on tracking and clipping newspaper and magazine articles on an orderly basis; unlike computerized databases, these firms actually look for information on subjects specified by clients. They offer their services for a fee. The annual *Burwell Directory of Information Brokers* cites over 1200 information brokers in the United States, Canada and about 44 other nations.

Firms such as Pro CD Inc. and American Business Information (ABI) provide business and household addresses in CD-ROM format. ABI and Pro CD Inc. gather data from phone directories, annual reports, and government agencies; ABI makes 14 million calls per year and sends out more than 700 000 mail surveys to keep its databases current. *Canada Phone*, a $119 CD sold by Pro CD Inc., contains over 12 million Canadian phone listings including households and businesses. The *Canada Phone* CD allows users to conduct a number of database searches. ABI sells a U.S.$39.95 CD which contains data on 70 million U.S. households, while a U.S.$2500 CD has data on 10 million businesses. ABI has over 400 000 customers—from small, single-person firms to giant corporations.[4]

Many companies and libraries subscribe to one or more online computerized databases, whereby users are charged a fee based on the time spent using the database. A few of the well-known computerized database services available to Canadians are America Online, CompuServe, Prodigy, World Linx Telecommunications, WEB, UUNET Canada, and Delphi. A full list of Internet resources and Internet access providers can be found in "The 1997 Canadian Internet Directory." This directory is available from Prentice Hall Canada Inc. and lists over 300 Canadian Internet service providers along with hundreds of Canadian sources of information on the Internet. With these services, the user can do a search on a particular topic or company, generate the names and abstracts of relevant articles or reports, and then print out the information. Full articles or reports may also be accessed and printed, but doing so could be expensive.

Figure 3-3 highlights the power of information and how cheap and readily available commerical databases are for consumers and business people alike.

UUNET CANADA
www.uunet.ca/

Database Marketing

Through **database marketing**, *companies can better reach and interact with customers.*

In conjunction with their marketing information systems, growing numbers of firms are using database marketing to better identify target markets and more efficiently reach them. **Database marketing** is "an automated system to identify people—both customers and prospects—by name, and to use quantifiable information about them to define the best possible purchasers and prospects for a given offer at a given point in time."[5]

Database marketing creates a bank of information about individual customers (taken from orders, inquiries, external lists), uses it to analyze buying and inquiry patterns, and creates the ability to target goods and services more accurately to specific customers (see Figure 3-4). It may be used to promote the benefits of brand loyalty to customers at risk from competition. It can fuel sales growth by identifying customers most apt to buy new goods and services. It can increase sales effectiveness. It can support low-cost alternatives

---

[4]Jacqueline M. Graves, "Building a Fortune on Free Data," *Fortune* (February 6, 1995); American Business Information brochures; and *Canada Phone User Guide* (Danvers, Mass: ProCD Incorporated, 1995) pp.1–5.

[5]Susan K. Jones, *Creative Strategy in Direct Marketing* (Lincolnwood, Ill.: NTC Publishing, 1991), p. 5.

FIGURE 3-3
The Power of Information
Reprinted with permission of ProCD Inc.

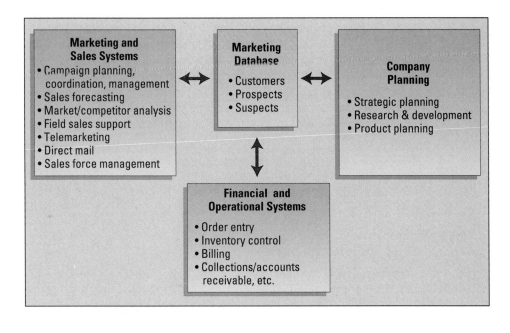

FIGURE 3-4
Fully Integrated Database Marketing
Source: Robert Shaw and Merlin Stone, *Data-Base Marketing: Strategy & Implementation* (New York, Wiley, 1990). Reprinted by permission of Gower Publishing Company Limited.

CANADIAN DIRECT MARKETING ASSOCIATION

www.westminster.ca/cdma/

Ethics AND TODAY'S MARKETER

How Can Direct Marketers Resolve the Privacy Paradox?

The growth in database-driven information has the Canadian Direct Marketing Association (CDMA) worried. So much so that it has backed away from its long-time stance in favour of industry self-regulation, and taken the unusual step of asking the federal government to legislate its discipline.

The CDMA wants the industry minister to establish minimum standards of conduct to ensure that anyone collecting or using consumer information does so in a manner that protects the privacy of individuals. In a letter to the minister, the CDMA stated: "In an age of information technology, inter-relation of databases and the amassing of transactional data, national legislation appears to be the only practical way of providing comprehensive protection to every Canadian." The CDMA has a privacy code for its member companies but only 80 per cent of the direct marketers in Canada are members of the CDMA. Canadian direct response sales were approximately $9.2 billion in 1995 but not all sectors of the industry have compulsory privacy codes.

Codes such as those developed by the Canadian Standards Association (CSA), are mainly based on guidelines from the international Organization for Economic Co-operation and Development (OECD). These guidelines indicate that firms should identify how they plan to use personal information they collect and get permission from individuals to collect, use, and disclose this information. More importantly, the consumers themselves should be able to gain access to the information which has been collected from them.

The CDMA has only one recourse in dealing with member companies that violate the voluntary code of privacy, which is to oust them. Chastisement of member organizations is not a particularly powerful deterrent and throwing paying members out is harmful to the CDMA as well as the offending firm. The CDMA sees legislation as the only way in which the conduct of marketers can be controlled effectively. What's more, non-member direct marketers who often hurt the industry would also be subject to legislative discipline.

Not all firms feel that legislation is necessary to protect privacy. American Express is an example of a firm that carefully guards its customers' right to privacy. In 1974, it was the first company that offered customers the right not to be on a mailing list. And in 1978, American Express adopted a series of privacy principles requiring employees to collect only the data absolutely needed. The firm still reviews its data-collection activities each year; and everyone with access to customer information receives customer privacy training. American Express even distributes brochures to consumers explaining how they can refuse to provide the information requested on warranty cards.

Is legislation the only way for marketers to solve the privacy paradox?

Source: Based on material in James Pollock, "Direct Marketers Want to Regulate How Consumer Data Is Used," *Marketing Magazine* (October 16, 1995), p. 12; Jeffrey Casey, "The Privacy Paradox," *Link* (May 1995), pp. 19–22; and Judith Waldrop, "The Business of Privacy," *American Demographics* (October 1994), pp. 46–54.

to traditional sales methods, including telemarketing and direct mail, which can be important in markets where margins are eroding.[6]

[6]Robert Shaw and Merlin Stone, *Data-Base Marketing: Strategy & Implementation* (New York: Wiley, 1990), p. 4. See also Mary Lou Roberts, "Expanding the Role of the Direct Marketing Database," *Journal of Direct Marketing*, Vol. 6 (Spring 1992), pp. 51–60; and Terry G. Vavra, "The Data-Base Marketing Imperative," *Marketing Management*, Vol. 2 (Number 1, 1993), pp. 47–57.

Database marketing is especially useful in the relationship marketing process. A company can identify those customers with which it would most like to have long-term relationships, learn as much as possible about them (such as demographics and purchase behaviour), tailor its marketing efforts toward them, and follow up to learn the level of customer satisfaction. A firm might even compute a "lifetime value" for specific customers, based on their purchase history with the company—and plan its marketing efforts accordingly.[7]

When setting up a database, each actual or potential customer is given an identifying code. Then, contact information (name, address, phone number, fax number, e-mail address, industry code, and demographic data) and marketing information (source and date of contacts with firm, purchase history, product interests, and responses to offers) are entered and updated for each customer. The information should be distributed to marketing decision makers in the firm and kept in the MIS, and company efforts should be coordinated so customers are not bombarded with mailings and there is a consistent image.

In practice, database marketing actually works like this:

1. You may think you're just sending in a coupon, filling out a warranty card, or entering a sweepstakes. But to a marketer, you're also volunteering information about yourself—data that gets fed into a computer, where it's combined with more information from public records.

2. Using sophisticated statistical techniques, the computer merges different sets of data into a coherent, consolidated database. Then, with powerful software, brand managers can "drill down" into the data to any level of detail they require.

3. The computer identifies a model consumer for a chosen product based on the common characteristics of high-volume users. Next, clusters of consumers who share those characteristics—interests, incomes, brand loyalties, for instance—can be identified as targets for marketing efforts.

4. The data can be used in many ways: to determine the values of coupons and who should get them; to develop new products and ensure that the appropriate consumers know about them; to tailor ad messages and aim them at the right audience.

5. Cash-register scanners provide reams of information about exactly what shoppers are buying at specific stores. Merged with the manufacturer's data, this intelligence helps to plan local promotional mailings, fine-tune shelf displays, and design store layouts.

6. The database is continually updated with information collected from product-oriented clubs, responses to coupons, calls to 800 numbers, and sweepstakes entries, as well as with new lists from outside sources.[8]

Although often associated with a computerized MIS, database marketing may also be used by small, non-computerized firms: A company might ask potential and existing customers for their names, addresses, phone and fax numbers, e-mail addresses, and product interests as they contact them, and these data could be entered on large index cards. Consumers could be enticed to provide data by means of a monthly raffle that awards a small prize to the winner. The firm would alphabetize the cards, keep them in a file cabinet, and update the records from sales receipts. Separate mailings could be sent to regular customers and to non-customers from the database.

MIS in Action

Worldwide, millions of organizations now use some form of MIS in their decision making, and the trend is expected to continue. In fact, as a result of computer networking,

Information systems are being applied today in various settings.

---

[7]See Timothy J. Keane and Paul Wang, "Applications for the Lifetime Value Model in Modern Newspaper Publishing," *Journal of Direct Marketing*, Vol. 9 (Spring 1995), pp. 59–66.

[8]Coopers & Lybrand Consulting, "Data-Base Marketing: How It Works," *Business Week* (September 5, 1994), pp. 56–57.

progressive firms (and divisions within the same firm) around the globe are transmitting and sharing their marketing information with each other—quickly and inexpensively.

One recent study on the use of MIS by large business firms discovered that:

- More than three-quarters have a marketing information system. Of those that do, over 95 per cent are computer-based.

- Nearly 80 per cent use computers to produce reports; and two-thirds store marketing data in their computers.

- All gather customer data, three-quarters are involved with competitive intelligence, and 37 per cent track government actions.

- More than 70 per cent use annual reports, sales call reports, and purchased reports to amass competitive intelligence. Just over one half hire clipping services.[9]

In Sweden, financial institutions have taken the lead in developing MIS:

> During the late 1970s, the banking community took an innovative step by organizing a business intelligence (BI) research company called Upplysnigs Centralen (UC Research). It provides fee-based BI services for banks and their major customers, such as database services consisting of public and published information on firms and individuals; proactive intelligence gathering, using participating banks' overseas offices to answer specific and time-urgent requests; and the use of some 3000 business agents around the world who can be tapped for specific expertise or information."[10]

In Japan today, almost all major firms engaged in international business have an internal intelligence unit:

> Typically, it is located in the planning or research departments. Some 10 to 20 employees are assigned responsibilities at company headquarters; but intelligence gathering is company-wide, with virtually every employee participating (from the president to salespeople). Intelligence collection and dissemination are well developed at most Japanese firms. However, it is the ability—almost culturally inherent—for sharing intelligence that makes MIS use in Japanese firms so effective.[11]

Among the specific firms with superior marketing information systems are NutraSweet, Northern Telecom, and United Cigar Stores. Each devotes considerable time and resources to its system. Here are examples of how they apply MIS.[12]

Because NutraSweet's patent protection on its aspartame-based artificial sweeteners has expired in both Europe and the United States, the company is now vulnerable to the actions of competitors. Yet, it remains, by far, the industry leader. Why? It regularly gathers competitive intelligence regarding competitors' prices, expansion plans, and advertising campaigns—and then stores this information in a computer databank. In response to its MIS findings, NutraSweet has cut costs and improved customer service.

Northern Telecom installed its first Enterprise Support System software in 1990 as part of the firm's restructuring toward a more centralized system. Now Northern Telecom has adopted a new support system to enable it to gather and utilize information along product lines and market lines. Importantly, the new system allows managers to cross-reference data along products and markets. The system currently holds information on the company's finances, personnel records, and customer satisfaction surveys. The system is set up so that

[9]Eldon Y. Li, "Marketing Information Systems in the Top U.S. Companies: A Longitudinal Analysis," *Information & Management*, Vol. 28 (January 1995), pp. 13–31.

[10]Jan P. Herring, "Business Intelligence in Japan and Sweden: Lessons for the U.S.," *Journal of Business Strategy*, Vol. 13 (March–April 1992), p. 45.

[11]Ibid., p. 47.

[12]Michael Haddigan, "Competitor Intelligence Considered More Vital Now," *Marketing News* (October 9, 1995), p. 3; Jay Finegan, "Taking Names," *Inc.* (September 1992), pp. 121–130; Robert C. Blattberg and John Deighton, "Interactive Marketing: Exploiting the Age of Addressability," *Sloan Management Review*, Vol. 33 (Fall 1991), pp. 10–11; Mark Stevenson, "He Sees All He Knows All," *Canadian Business* (Spring 1994), Special Technology Issue; and *General Host Corporation 1994 Annual Report*.

information is available to hundreds of users instead of just the firm's executives, although only the executives can access all of the information.

United Cigar Stores has installed an enterprise support system that enables senior and middle managers to "log onto the system and check sales at any of its 476 stores." For example, a marketing manager can compare weekly or monthly sales against set targets, and if there is a discrepancy, he or she

> can drill down through the data to find the division, region or district where sales are slackening.... [A manager can] cross-reference by store type or product line to see if, perhaps, it's cigarette sales at hotel locations in Ontario that are causing the problem.... [The manager] can even search by promotion, to find out, for example, if a two-pack cigarette discounting program is dragging down revenue instead of boosting it."
>
> One manager has commented "Upper management has had difficulty staying in touch, obtaining accurate, timely data. Now the information is much closer at hand."

Marketing Research Defined

Marketing research involves systematically gathering, recording, and analyzing information about specific issues related to the marketing of goods, services, organizations, people, places, and ideas. It may be done by an outside party or by the firm itself. As indicated earlier, marketing research should be one component of a firm's marketing information efforts.

Marketing research data may be obtained form different sources: the firm itself, an impartial agency (such as the government), or a research specialist working for the firm. The information thus obtained may be applied to any aspect of marketing that requires information to aid decision making. To be effective, however, marketing research must be conducted methodically, following a sequence of tasks: gathering the data, recording it, and analyzing it. Furthermore, the research findings must be communicated to the proper decision maker(s) in the firm.

A firm's decision to use marketing research does not mean it must engage in expensive projects like test marketing and national consumer attitude surveys. It may get enough data by analyzing internal sales reports or from informal meetings with customer-service personnel. Marketing research *does* require an orderly approach and adherence to the scientific method.

For each marketing issue studied, the amount and cost of research depend upon the kinds of data needed to make informed decisions, the risk involved in making those decisions, the potential consequences of the decisions, the importance of the issue to the firm, the availability of existing data, the complexity of the data-gathering process for the issue, and other factors.

Marketing research involves collecting, tabulating, and analyzing data about specific marketing issues.

The Scope of Marketing Research

Companies annually spend about U.S.$8 billion worldwide for data gathered by marketing research firms. The top 25 research firms account for more than U.S.$4 billion of that amount, with over 1000 firms responsible for the rest.[13] These amounts are in addition to research sponsored by government and other institutions and to internal research efforts of firms themselves—which also run into the billions of dollars each year.

According to the American Marketing Association's most recent Survey of Marketing Research, these are the topical areas in which companies are most apt to engage in or sponsor research efforts: industry/market characteristics and trends, product satisfaction, market-share analyses, segmentation studies, brand awareness and preference, purchase intentions, and concept development and testing. And, on average, the surveyed companies spend 1 per cent of their revenues on marketing research.[14]

Global marketing research expenditures total several billion dollars each year.

AMERICAN MARKETING ASSOCIATION
www.ama.org/

---

[13] Jack Honomichl, "The Honomichl 50," *Marketing News* (June 5, 1995), Special Section.
[14] Thomas C. Kinnear and Ann R. Root (Eds.), *1994 Survey of Marketing Research* (Chicago: American Marketing Association, 1995), pp. 38, 49.

Five aspects of marketing research merit special discussion. These involve the rapid rise in customer satisfaction studies, the use of state-of-the-art technology, the application of single-source data collection, ethical considerations, and the complexities of international marketing research.

Companies now participate in more customer satisfaction research than ever before, in keeping with the customer focus noted in Chapter 1. This form of research has more than doubled in recent years, with some firms doing their own studies and others hiring outside specialists. For instance, Whirlpool sends surveys on appliance satisfaction to 180 000 households each year. It also pays hundreds of consumers per year to "fiddle" with computer-simulated products at its Usability Lab. Whirlpool's research also extends to its European marketplace. On the other hand, the Walker Group and Maritz Marketing Research, two U.S.-based research firms, each generate worldwide revenues of several million dollars by doing customer satisfaction studies for clients. As a Maritz executive remarked, the company's success is "due to the quality movement in the country, global competitiveness, and a desire to get back to basics and make the marketing orientation more customer-driven."[15]

Over the last decade, significant technological innovations have been applied to marketing research, as these examples indicate:

INTERNATIONAL SURVEYS LTD.
www.npd.com/ww.htm

- Toronto-based Internationational Surveys Ltd. (ISL) has developed PC Meter, a system that is loaded onto home computers (by permission of the users) and is designed to monitor the activities of computer users while they "surf" on the Internet.

- Advanced Neurotechnologies has designed MindTrack, to detect emotional responses to ads and other forms of communication. MindTrack detects brainwaves using sensors attached to a headband; people are exposed to an ad campaign or a TV show and quantitative digital results appear.

- More companies are using facsimile machines to get responses to marketing surveys. In general, faxed responses are obtained quicker; response rates are higher due to the ease of return; and answer quality approximates that for other methods of transmission.[16]

Single-source data collection
is a result of high-tech advances.

Technological advances have facilitated **single-source data collection**—whereby research firms track the activities of individual consumer households from the programs they watch on TV to the products they purchase at stores. For instance, via its BehaviorScan service, Information Resources Inc. (IRI) monitors the viewing habits and shopping behaviour of thousands of households in various markets. Microcomputers are hooked to household TVs and note all programs and ads watched. Consumers shop in supermarkets and drugstores with scanning registers and present cashiers with shoppers cards (resembling credit cards). Cashiers enter each consumer's identification code, which is electronically keyed to every item bought. Via computer analysis, viewing and shopping behaviour are then matched with such information as age and income.

INFORMATION RESOURCES INC.
www.infores.com/public/prodserv/AB/
bscan.htm/

Due to the unethical practices of some firms, many potential respondents are averse to participating in marketing research projects. To turn the situation around, researchers need to avoid such practices as these:

- Unrealized promises of anonymity.
- False sponsor identification.
- Selling or fundraising under the guise of research.
- Misrepresenting research procedures.
- Observational studies without informed consent.
- Asking overly personal questions.

---

[15]Sally Solo, "How to Listen to Consumers," *Fortune* (January 11, 1993), pp. 77, 79; Laura Loro, "Customer Is Always Right," *Advertising Age* (February 10, 1992), p. 26; and "1995 Directory of Customer Satisfaction Measurement Firms," *Marketing News* (October 23, 1995), Special Section.

[16]James Pollock, "Measured Growth," *Marketing Magazine* (Jan. 15, 1996), p. 16; Kelly Shermach, "Respondents Get Hooked Up and Show Their Emotions," *Marketing News* (August 28, 1995), p. 35; and John P. Dickson and Douglas L. MacLachlan, "Fax Surveys?" *Marketing Research*, Vol. 4 (September 1992), pp. 26–30.

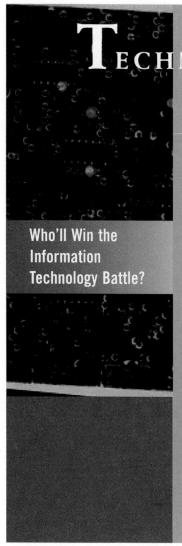

TECHNOLOGY & MARKETING

Who'll Win the Information Technology Battle?

Electronic data linkages between firms let them reduce their inventory levels and order-processing times. Companies joined by such data linkages can also eliminate duplicate functions that occur in billing and purchasing. According to the author of a book on customer-supplier alliances, 30 to 40 per cent of savings from these alliances come from improving joint processes.

With electronic linkages, firms can gather and study information as products go from raw materials to finished goods to retailer shelves. In many cases, the most influential companies in a value chain are those that have the best knowledge of the marketplace. In particular, managers need to ask three questions: What information drives our business? Who has that information? What is it worth?

MicroAge and W.W. Grainger are two examples of firms that understand the value of information. MicroAge shifted from being a wholesaler that stocked Apple, Compaq, Hewlett-Packard, and IBM computers to a producer of computers tailored to individual consumer needs. Instead of selling systems produced by single companies, MicroAge now assembles computers using parts from over 500 companies. MicroAge relies on its knowledge of customer needs, as well as the costs, features, and compatibilities of different manufacturers' products.

W.W. Grainger, which describes itself as a distributor of maintenance, repair, and operating supplies, has an average order size of U.S.$129. Unlike competitors, the firm is able to tailor its services to customer needs. Based upon the desires of individual customers, Grainger might offer electronic ordering and payment capabilities or even perform a customer's inventory management functions. According to a Grainger vice-president, "On sales calls these days, we're seldom talking about why the motor we sell is better than someone else's motor; we talk about value-added services."

As a W.W. Grainger product manager, describe how a marketing information system can be used to maximize its value-added services.

Source: Based on material in Thomas A. Stewart, "The Information Wars: What You Don't Know Will Hurt You," *Fortune* (June 12, 1995), pp. 119–120.

- Selling consumer demographic information for database use without consent.
- Misportraying research findings in ads and other communications.[17]

With more and more firms striving to expand their foreign endeavours, international marketing research is becoming increasingly important. And this can be quite challenging. The language of the survey, respondent selection, and interviewer training are among the many areas that require special consideration. Consider this example:

Firms deciding how to market to the 350 million consumers in Eastern Europe and Central Asia increasingly do marketing research there. Yet designing and conducting this research is difficult. Often, people have never been surveyed before. Communications systems, especially phone service, may be primitive by Western standards. Secondary data from government agencies and trade associations may be lacking or unavailable. Thus, companies must be adaptable.

When it did research, Kodak could not find relevant consumer data, a photography trade association, or pictures of local cameras for use in a questionnaire. So, to gather data on camera usage and preferences, Kodak took part in a multi-client survey devised by SRG International Ltd., a research firm. The survey was conducted in nine former Soviet republics; since each had its own language, nine questionnaire versions were prepared.[18]

[17]Gene R. Laczniak and Patrick E. Murphy, *Ethical Marketing Decisions: The Higher Road* (Needham Heights, Mass.: Allyn and Bacon, 1993), pp. 53–68.

[18]Lourdes Lee Valeriano, "Western Firms Poll Eastern Europeans to Discern Tastes of Nascent Consumers," *Wall Street Journal* (April 27, 1992), pp. B1–B2; Richard W. Stevenson, "Teaching the Hard Sell of Soap to Eastern Europe," *New York Times* (February 18, 1993), pp. D1, D7; and R. Craig Endicott, "European Dream Captivates Researchers," *Advertising Age* (October 18, 1993), p. S–6.

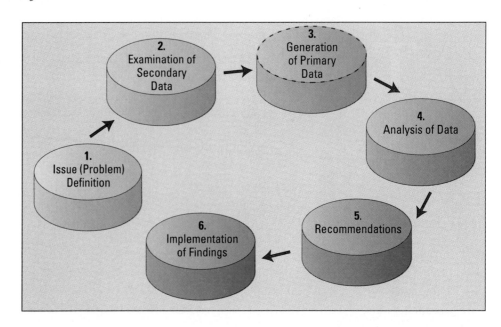

....

FIGURE 3-5
The Marketing Research Process

The Marketing Research Process

The **marketing research process** *consists of steps from issue definition to implementation of findings.*

The **marketing research process** consists of a series of activities: defining the issue or problem to be studied; examining secondary (previously collected) data; generating primary (new) data if necessary; analyzing information; making recommendations; and implementing findings.

Figure 3-5 presents the complete process. Each step is completed in order. For example, secondary data are not examined until a firm states the issue or problem to be studied, and primary data are not generated until secondary data are thoroughly reviewed. The dashed line around primary data means these data do not always have to be collected. Many times, a firm can obtain enough information internally or from published sources to make a marketing decision without gathering new data. Only when secondary data are insufficient should a firm generate primary data. The research process is described next.

Issue (Problem) Definition

Research efforts are directed by **issue definition***.*

Issue (problem) definition is a statement of the topic to be investigated. Without a focused definition of the issue or problem, irrelevant and expensive data may be gathered. A good problem definition directs the research process to collect and analyze appropriate data for the purpose of decision making.

Exploratory research looks at uncertain topics; **conclusive research** *is better defined.*

When a firm is uncertain about the precise topic to be investigated or wants to informally study an issue, exploratory research is used. The aim of **exploratory research** is to gain ideas and insights, and to break broad, vague problem statements into smaller, more precise statements.[19] Exploratory research, also called "qualitative research," may involve in-depth probing, small group discussions, and understanding underlying trends.

Once an issue is clarified, conclusive research, also called "quantitative research," is used. **Conclusive research** is the structured collection and analysis of data pertaining to a specific issue or problem. It is more focused than exploratory research, and requires larger samples, and more limited questions in order to provide the quantitative data to make decisions. Table 3-1 contrasts exploratory and conclusive research.

Secondary Data

Secondary data have been previously gathered for purposes other than the current research.

Secondary data consist of information not collected for the issue or problem at hand but for some other purpose; this information is available within a firm or externally. Whether

[19]Bennett, *Dictionary of Marketing Terms*, p. 103.

T a b l e   3 – 1

Examples of Exploratory and Conclusive Research

VAGUE RESEARCH TOPIC	EXPLORATORY RESEARCH	PRECISE RESEARCH TOPIC	CONCLUSIVE RESEARCH
1. Why are sales declining?	**1.** Discussions among key personnel to identify major cause	**1.** Why is the turnover of sales personnel so high?	**1.** Survey sales personnel and interview sales managers
2. Is advertising effective?	**2.** Discussions among key advertising personnel to define effectiveness	**2.** Do adults recall an advertisement the day after it appears?	**2.** Survey customers and non-customers to gauge advertising recall
3. Will a price reduction increase revenues?	**3.** Discussions among key personnel to determine the level of a price reduction	**3.** Will a 10 per cent price reduction have a significant impact on sales?	**3.** Run an in-store experiment to determine effects

secondary data fully resolve an issue or problem or not, their low cost and availability mean that primary data should not be collected until a thorough secondary data search is done.

ADVANTAGES AND DISADVANTAGES Secondary data have these general advantages:

- Many types are inexpensive because primary data collection is not involved.
- Data assembly can be fast, especially for published or company materials.
- There may be several sources and perspectives available.
- A source (such as the government) may obtain data a firm could not get itself.
- There is high credibility for data assembled by independent sources.
- They are helpful when exploratory research is involved.

Secondary data also have these general disadvantages:

- Available data may not suit the current research purpose because it is too general or incomplete.
- Information may be dated or obsolete.
- The methodology used in collecting the data (such as the sample size, date of the research, etc.) may be unknown.
- All the findings of a research study may not be made public.
- Conflicting results may exist.
- Because many research projects are not repeated, the reliability of data may not be proven.

SOURCES OF SECONDARY DATA There are two major sources of secondary data. Internal secondary data are available within a firm. External secondary data are available outside a firm. Most companies use both of these sources.

Internal Secondary Data Before spending time and money searching for external secondary data or collecting primary data, the information contained inside a firm should be reviewed. Internal sources include budgets, sales figures, profit-and-loss statements, customer billings, inventory records, prior research reports, and written reports.

A firm's records or past studies comprise internal secondary data.

At the beginning of the business year, most firms set detailed budgets for the next twelve months. The budgets, based on sales forecasts, outline planned expenditures for every good and service during the year. By examining the sales of each division, product line, item, geographic area, salesperson, time of day, day of week, and so on and comparing these sales with prior periods, overall performance can be measured. Through profit-and-loss statements, actual achievements can be measured against profit goals by department, salesperson, and product. Customer billings provide information on credit transactions, sales by region, peak selling seasons, sales volume, and sales by customer category. Inventory records show the levels of goods bought, manufactured, stored, shipped, and/or sold throughout the year.

Prior research reports, containing findings of past marketing research efforts, are often stored and retained for future use. When a report is used initially, it is primary data. Later reference to that report is secondary in nature because it is no longer employed for its original purpose. Written reports (ongoing data stored by a firm) may be compiled by top management, marketing executives, sales personnel, and others. Among the information attainable from such reports are typical customer complaints.

Government and nongovernment sources make available external secondary data.

External Secondary Data   If a research issue or problem is not resolved through internal secondary data, a firm may use external secondary data sources. There are government and nongovernment sources.

All levels of government in Canada distribute various types of economic and business statistics. Statistics Canada is the most important source of external secondary information in Canada. The Statistics Canada catalogue provides a listing of all the facts and figures on Canada's business, economic, and social environment. The catalogue lists sources on trade, income, employment, education, and detailed industry information, all of which have been collected by or for Statistics Canada. Aside from its regular written publications, Statistics Canada disseminates data on CD, diskettes, computer printouts, microfiche, microfilm, and magnetic tape. Direct online access is available through Statistics Canada's Internet website, which gives access to copies of "The Daily," StatsCan's newsletter, and to CANSIM, Statistics Canada's machine-readable database and retrieval system.

Industry Canada has an online Internet website called Strategis, which is billed as Canada's largest business website. This site provides access to an Industry Canada database that contains:

- 60 000 reports
- 500 000 pages of searchable text
- 2 gigabytes of statistical data
- hot links to Canadian and international business information databases.

Users of the website are told that the database can assist them with decisions such as: identifying opportunities for growth, exploring new markets, finding partners, forming alliances, finding and developing new technologies or processes, and assessing the risks of new ventures.

When using government data, particularly Census statistics, the research date must be noted. There may be a lag before government data are released.

There are three kinds of nongovernment secondary data: regular publications; books, monographs, and other nonregular publications; and commercial research houses. Regular publications contain articles on diverse aspects of marketing and are available in libraries or by subscription. Some are quite broad in scope (such as *Canadian Business*); others are more specialized (*Canadian Advertising Rates and Data*). Periodicals are published by publishing companies, as well as by professional and trade associations.

Books, monographs, and other literature are also published by conventional publishing companies, as well as by professional and trade associations. These materials deal with special topics in depth and are compiled on the basis of interest by the target audience.

Various commercial research houses conduct periodic and ongoing studies and make results available to many clients for a fee. The fee can run as high as the tens of thousands of dollars, depending on the extent of the data. That kind of research is secondary when a firm purchasing the data acts as a subscriber and does not request specific studies pertaining only to itself; in this way, commercial houses provide a number of research services more inexpensively than if data are collected for a firm's sole use. Some examples of research houses are A.C. Nielsen Canada, Canadian Facts, Dun & Bradstreet Canada, and Burke International Research.

DUN & BRADSTREET CANADA
www.dnb.com

Lists of commercial research firms and research services available in Canada can be found quickly from two sources: 1) *Marketing Magazine* annually publishes a "Guide to Market Research Services." This guide lists private research organizations in Canada, explains how to contact them, and in many cases gives a brief description of the type of information they trade in. 2) *The International Member & Marketing Services Guide* is an annual publication of the American Marketing Association in Chicago, Illinois. It contains a list of market research firms and services indexed alphabetically and geographically by country. This guide lists private research organizations throughout the world. It also provides details on how to contact these firms, and gives a brief description of the type of services they specialize in.

Primary Data

Primary data consist of information gathered to address a specific issue or problem at hand. Such data are needed when a thorough analysis of secondary data is insufficient for a proper marketing decision to be made.

Primary data *relate to a specific marketing issue.*

ADVANTAGES AND DISADVANTAGES Primary data have these general advantages:

- They are collected to fit the precise purpose of the current research topic.
- Information is current.
- The methodology of data collection is controlled and known by the firm.
- All findings are available to the firm, which can maintain their secrecy.
- There are no conflicting data from different sources.
- A study can be replicated (if desired).
- When secondary data do not resolve all questions, collecting and analyzing primary data are the only ways to acquire information.

Primary data also have these general disadvantages:

- Collection may be time consuming.
- Costs may be high.
- Some types of information cannot be collected (e.g., *Census* data).
- The company's perspective may be limited.
- The firm may be incapable of collecting primary data.

RESEARCH DESIGN If a firm decides primary data are needed, it must devise a **research design**—which outlines the procedures for collecting and analyzing data. A research design includes the following decisions.

The **research design** *outlines data collection.*

Who Collects the Data? A company can collect data itself or hire an outside research firm for a specific project. The advantages of an internal research department are its knowledge of company operations, total access to company personnel, ongoing assembly and storage of data, and high commitment. The disadvantages of an internal department are the continuous costs, narrow perspective, possible lack of expertise on the latest research techniques, and potentially excessive support for the views of top management. The strengths and weaknesses of an outside research firm are the opposite of those for an inside department.

Internal or outside personnel can be used.

What Information Should Be Collected? The kinds and amounts of data to be collected should be keyed to the issue (problem) formulated by the firm. Exploratory research requires different data collection from conclusive research.

Who or What Should Be Studied? First, the people or objects to be studied must be stated; they comprise the population. People studies generally involve customers, company personnel, and/or distribution intermediaries. Object studies usually centre on company and/or product performance.

Second, the way in which people or objects are selected must be decided. Large and/or dispersed populations usually are examined by **sampling**, which requires the analysis of selected people or objects in the designated population, rather than all of them. It saves time and money; and when used properly, the accuracy and level of representation of the sample can be measured.

The two approaches to sampling are probability and nonprobability. With a probability (random) sample, every member of the designated population has an equal or known probability of being chosen for analysis. For example, a researcher may select every fiftieth person in a phone directory. With a nonprobability sample, members of the population are chosen on the basis of convenience or judgment. For instance, an interviewer may select the first 100 residence students entering a university cafeteria. A probability sample is more accurate; but, it is more costly and difficult than a nonprobability sample.

Third, the sample size studied must be set. Generally, a large sample will yield greater accuracy and cost more than a small sample. There are methods for assessing sample size in terms of accuracy and costs, but a description of them is beyond the scope of this text.

What Technique of Data Collection Should Be Used? There are four basic primary-data collection methods: survey, observation, experiment, and simulation.

A **survey** gathers information from respondents by communicating with them. It can uncover data about attitudes, purchases, intentions, and consumer traits. However, it is subject to incorrect or biased answers. A questionnaire is used to record survey responses. A survey can be conducted in person, by phone, or by mail.

A personal survey is face-to-face and flexible, can elicit lengthy replies, and reduces ambiguity. It is relatively expensive, however, and bias is possible because the interviewer may affect results by suggesting ideas to respondents or by creating a certain mood during the interview. A phone survey is fast and relatively inexpensive, especially with the growth of discount telephone services. Responses are usually brief, and nonresponse may be a problem. It must be verified that the desired respondent is the one contacted. Some people do not have a phone, or they have unlisted numbers. The latter problem is now overcome through computerized, random digit-dialing devices.

A mail survey reaches dispersed respondents, has no interviewer bias, and is relatively inexpensive. Nonresponse, slowness of returns, and participation by incorrect respondents are the major problems. The technique chosen depends on the goals and needs of the specific research project.

A survey may be nondisguised or disguised. With a nondisguised survey, the respondent is told a study's real purpose; in a disguised survey, the person is not. The latter may be used to indirectly probe attitudes and avoid a person's answering what he or she thinks the interviewer or researcher wants to hear or read. The left side of Figure 3-6 is a nondisguised survey showing the true intent of a study on sports car attitudes and behaviour. The right side of the figure shows how the survey can be disguised: By asking about sports car owners in general, a firm may get more honest answers than with questions geared right at the respondent. The intent of the disguised study is to uncover the respondent's actual reasons for buying a sports car.

A **semantic differential** is a list of bipolar (opposite) adjective scales. It is a survey technique with rating scales instead of, or in addition to, traditional questions. It may be disguised or nondisguised, depending on whether the respondent is told a study's true purpose. Each adjective in a semantic differential is rated on a bipolar scale, and average scores for all respondents are computed. An overall company or product profile is then devised. The profile may be compared with competitors' profiles and consumers' ideal ratings. Figure 3-7 shows a completed semantic differential.

Observation is a research method whereby present behaviour or the results of past behaviour are observed and noted. People are not questioned and cooperation is unnecessary. Interviewer and question bias are minimized. Observation is often used in actual situations. The major disadvantages are that attitudes cannot be determined and observers may misinterpret behaviour.

In disguised observation, a consumer is unaware he or she is being watched. A two-way mirror, hidden camera, or other device may be used. With nondisguised observation, a participant knows he or she is being observed. Human observation is carried out by

FIGURE 3-6
Nondisguised and Disguised Surveys

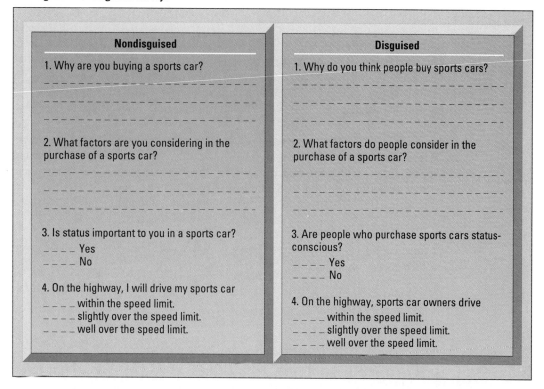

Nondisguised	Disguised
1. Why are you buying a sports car?	1. Why do you think people buy sports cars?
2. What factors are you considering in the purchase of a sports car?	2. What factors do people consider in the purchase of a sports car?
3. Is status important to you in a sports car? ____ Yes ____ No	3. Are people who purchase sports cars status-conscious? ____ Yes ____ No
4. On the highway, I will drive my sports car ____ within the speed limit. ____ slightly over the speed limit. ____ well over the speed limit.	4. On the highway, sports car owners drive ____ within the speed limit. ____ slightly over the speed limit. ____ well over the speed limit.

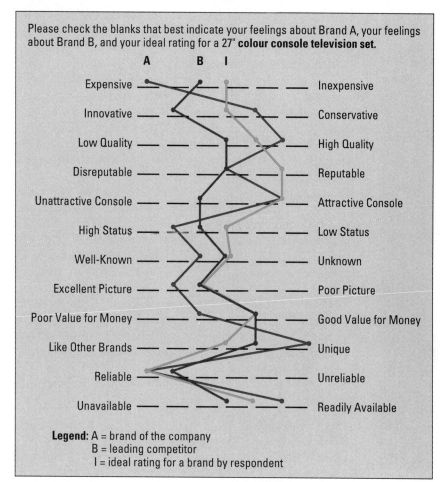

Please check the blanks that best indicate your feelings about Brand A, your feelings about Brand B, and your ideal rating for a 27" **colour console television set.**

A   B   I

Expensive	— — — — — —	Inexpensive
Innovative		Conservative
Low Quality		High Quality
Disreputable		Reputable
Unattractive Console		Attractive Console
High Status		Low Status
Well-Known		Unknown
Excellent Picture		Poor Picture
Poor Value for Money		Good Value for Money
Like Other Brands		Unique
Reliable		Unreliable
Unavailable		Readily Available

Legend: A = brand of the company
B = leading competitor
I = ideal rating for a brand by respondent

FIGURE 3-7
A Semantic Differential for a Colour Television

people; mechanical observation records behaviour through electronic or other means, such as a movie camera filming customer reactions to a sales presentation in a store.

*An **experiment** varies marketing factors under controlled conditions.*

An **experiment** is a type of research in which one or more factors are manipulated under controlled conditions. A factor may be any element of marketing from package design to advertising media. In an experiment, just the factor under study is varied; all other factors remain constant. For example, to evaluate a new package design for a product, a manufacturer could send new packages to five retail outlets and old packages to five similar outlets; all marketing factors other than packaging remain the same. After one month, sales of the new package at the test outlets are compared with sales of the old package at the similar outlets. A survey or observation is used to determine the reactions to an experiment.

An experiment's key advantage is that it can show cause and effect—such as whether a new package is the cause of increased sales. It is also methodically structured and enacted. Key disadvantages are the rather high costs, frequent use of contrived settings, and inability to control all factors in or affecting a marketing plan.

International Marketing in

Is Rummaging Through Trash in Argentina "Marketing Research?"

After evaluating its garbage-digging research technique, the Dynamics Group consulting firm decided to expand its market-surveillance activities from 400 to 1650 residences in greater metropolitan Buenos Aires, Argentina. The bulk (no pun intended) of the firm's research results come from studying disposable packaging.

As Dynamics Group's research director says, "By analyzing disposable containers, we can certify that this is real consumption and not what somebody felt like saying or what they 'thought' was right for a survey. The people in this study don't know that we are studying their garbage so the information is totally objective." Among the firm's clients are food and beverage marketers such as Coca-Cola, Argentina's largest dairy products marketer, a major pasta maker, and two big wine and meat marketers. Dynamics Group is now seeking to attract marketers of health and beauty aids, household cleaning products, and paper goods.

Dynamics Group provides clients with data on brand share gains and losses, key competitors, and customer loyalty. It can also furnish data on associated consumption (such as what food item was consumed with a specific type of beverage), the impact of advertising campaigns (measured by the amount of the advertised product in the trash), and product usage by day of week. Discarded newspapers, magazines, and cable television guides can also give marketers data on media availability by household.

As a Coca-Cola de Argentina spokesperson states, "We can get information about sales from Nielsen, but this shows us more about end consumption." For example, an analysis of garbage data suggested that people in poorer areas of Argentina consumed more expensive wines and champagnes on weekends, while the opposite pattern occurred in wealthier areas.

What types of data would you, as a brand manager for an Argentine pasta maker, want to obtain through the garbage-digging method? Why?

Source: Based on material in Mike Galetto, "Turning Trash to Research Treasure," *Advertising Age* (April 17, 1995), p. J–16.

Table 3-2

The Best Uses of Primary Data-Collection Techniques

TECHNIQUE	MOST APPROPRIATE USES
1. Survey	When determining consumer or distribution intermediary attitudes and motivations toward marketing-mix factors; measuring purchase intentions; relating consumer traits to attitudes
2. Observation	When examining actual responses to marketing factors under realistic conditions; interest in behaviour and not in attitudes
3. Experiment	When controlling the research environment is essential and establishing a cause-and-effect relationship is important
4. Simulation	When deriving and analyzing many interrelationships among variables

Simulation is a computer-based method to test the potential effects of various marketing factors using a software program rather than real-world applications. A model of the controllable and uncontrollable factors facing the firm is first constructed. Different combinations of the factors are then fed into a computer to determine their possible impact on an overall marketing strategy. Simulation requires no consumer cooperation and can handle many interrelated factors. However, it may be complex and hard to use; does not measure actual attitudes, behaviour, and intentions; and is subject to the accuracy of the assumptions made.

Simulation enables marketing factors to be analyzed using a computer model.

How Much Will the Study Cost?   Table 3-2 shows the best uses for each kind of primary data collection.

The overall and specific costs of a study must be clearly outlined. These costs may include executive time, researcher time, support-staff time, pre-testing, computer usage, respondent incentives (if any), interviewers, supplies, printing, postage or phone expenses, special equipment, and marketing expenses (such as advertising).

Research expenses range from personnel time to marketing costs.

A study's expected costs should be compared with the expected benefits to be derived. Suppose a consumer survey costing $10 000 would let a firm improve the package design of a new product. With the changes suggested by research, the firm would lift its first-year profit by $30 000. Thus, the net increase due to research is $20 000 ($30 000 profit less $10 000 in costs).

How Will the Data Be Collected?   The people needed to collect the data outlined in the research design must be determined and the attributes, skills, and training of the data-collection force specified. Too often, this important phase is improperly planned, and data are collected by unqualified people.

Data collection can be administered by research personnel or can be self-administered. With administered collection, interviewers ask questions or observers note behaviour; they record answers or behaviour and explain questions (if asked) to respondents. With self-administered collection, respondents read questions and write their answers. There is a trade-off between control and interviewer probing (administered) versus privacy and limited interviewer bias (self-administered).

Interviewers administer surveys or respondents fill them out.

How Long Will the Data-Collection Period Be?   The time frame within which data are collected must be stipulated, or else a study can drag on. Too long a time frame may lead to inconsistent responses and secrecy violations. Short time frames are easy to set for personal and phone surveys. Mail surveys, observation, and experiments often require much more time to implement; nonetheless, time limits must be defined.

When and Where Should Information Be Collected?   The day and time of data collection must be set. It must also be decided if a study will be done on or off a firm's premises. The desire for immediacy and convenience have to be weighed against the need to contact hard-to-reach respondents at the proper time.

Data analysis consists of coding, tabulation, and analysis.

DATA COLLECTION After the research design is thoroughly detailed, data are actually collected. Those engaged in data collection must be properly supervised and follow directions exactly. Responses or observations must be entered correctly.

Data Analysis

In **data analysis**, the information on questionnaires or answer forms is first coded and tabulated and then analyzed. Coding is the process by which each completed data form is numbered and response categories are labelled. Tabulation is the calculation of summary data for each response category. Analysis is the evaluation of responses, usually by statistical techniques, as they pertain to the specific issue or problem under investigation. The relationship of coding, tabulation, and analysis is shown in Figure 3-8.

Recommendations

Recommendations are suggestions for future actions that are based on marketing research findings. They are typically presented in written (sometimes, oral) form to marketing deci-

FIGURE 3-8
Data Analysis, Recommendations, and Implementation of Findings for a Study on Coffee

1. Do you drink coffee?	☐ Yes	01	300
	☐ No	02	200
2. In general, how frequently do you drink coffee? (Check only one answer.)	☐ Two or more times per day	03	142
	☐ Once per day	04	84
	☐ Several times per week	05	42
	☐ Once or twice per week	06	20
	☐ One to three times per month	07	12
	☐ Never	08	200
3. During what time of day do you drink coffee? (Check all answers that apply.)	☐ Morning	09	270
	☐ Lunch time	10	165
	☐ Afternoon	11	100
	☐ Dinner time	12	150
	☐ Evening	13	205
	☐ None	14	200

Coding: Questionnaires numbered A001 to A500. Each response is labelled 01 to 14 (e.g., Morning is 09. Evening is 13). Question 3 is a multiple-response question.

Tabulation: Total responses are shown above right.

Analysis: 60% drink coffee. About 28% drink coffee two or more times daily (representing 47% of all coffee drinkers); almost 25% of coffee drinkers (74 people) consume coffee less than once per day. 90% of coffee drinkers consume coffee in the morning; only one-third consume it in the afternoon.

Recommendations: The coffee industry and individual firms need to increase the advertising geared toward noncoffee drinkers, as well as infrequent coffee drinkers. Emphasis should also be placed on lifting coffee consumption during afternoon hours.

Implementation of findings: New, more aggressive advertising campaigns will be developed and the annual media budgets devoted to increasing overall coffee consumption will be expanded. One theme will stress coffee's value as an afternoon "pick-me-upper."

sion makers. The report must be written for the audience that reads it. Thus, technical terminology must be defined.

After recommendations are passed on to the proper decision makers, the research report should be kept in the data storage part of a firm's marketing intelligence network. It may then be retrieved in the future, as needed.

Implementation

A research report represents feedback for marketing managers, who are responsible for implementing any changes that may be necessary. If the findings are ignored, the research has little value. If decisions are based on the results, then marketing research has great value and the organization benefits in the short and long run.

Marketing managers are most apt to implement research findings if they have input into the research design, broad control over marketing decisions, and confidence that results are accurate.

MARKETING IN A CHANGING WORLD

Talking to Former Customers

In today's competitive marketplace, it may not be enough for a firm to focus its efforts on current and prospective customers. It may also be a good idea to research and try to win back various former customers. To do that, a company needs to engage in the sometimes painful task of finding out why these are "former" customers.

Yet because most company owners hate to hear harsh words about their babies, they find the hardest part of tracking lost customers is picking up the phone. Bob Ottley, president of One Step Tree and Lawn Care, hesitated for fear "the negative feedback would be impossible to deal with."

At the same time, Ottley was smart enough to know that he had to talk to former customers if his firm was to survive. Today, One Step has a weekly "cancels" report; and Ottley knows what per cent of cancellations are due to people moving, deciding to mow their own lawns, or no longer being able to afford his service—and switching to a lower-priced competitor. One Step has cut its customer attrition rate in half since it began the "cancels" report. And its leave-behind survey of current customers "puts the idea into their heads that we want to know if there's a problem."

Bruce Grench, chief executive of HDIS (a small mail-order firm that specializes in personal-care products), is another executive who has overcome his qualms. Grench uses six different approaches, from small-group gripe sessions to one-on-one telephone surveys, to gather comments from would-be, current, and former customers. He says, "We kind of look forward to it [contacting former customers], even though it's tough medicine. The hope is that we can find something we're not doing right because it offers us an opportunity." He did; that's why HDIS now offers private-label products for price-conscious customers.[20]

[20]"Where Did We Go Wrong?" *Inc.* (July 1995), p. 91.

SUMMARY

1. *To show why marketing information is needed* Marketing information lets a firm accurately assess its strengths, weaknesses, opportunities, and threats; operate properly in the marketing environment; and maximize performance. Reliance on intuition, judgment, and experience are not sufficient. The scientific method requires objectivity, accuracy, and thoroughness in research projects.

2. *To explain the role and importance of marketing information systems* Collecting marketing information should not be viewed as an infrequent occurrence. Acting in that way can have negative ramifications, especially with regard to misreading the competition and other external factors that can affect a firm's performance.

A marketing information system (MIS) is a set of procedures to generate, analyze, disseminate, and store anticipated marketing decision information on a regular, continuous basis. It can aid a company operationally, managerially, and strategically.

3. *To examine a basic marketing information system, commercial databases, database marketing, and examples of MIS in action* The key aspect of a basic MIS is the marketing intelligence network, which consists of continuous monitoring, marketing research, and data storage. The intelligence network is influenced by the environment, company goals, and marketing plans; and it affects the implementation of marketing plans. Marketing research should be considered as just one part of an ongoing, integrated information system. An MIS can be used by both small and large firms, and does not have to be computerized.

Specialized research firms offer valuable information through commercial databases that contain information on the population, the business environment, the economy, industry and company performance, and other factors. Databases are available in printed form; on computer diskettes, CD-ROMs, or tapes; and via online hookups.

An increasing number of firms are looking to database marketing to improve their interactions with customers. Database marketing involves setting up an automated system to identify and characterize customers and prospects and then using quantifiable information to better reach them.

Marketing information systems are being used by firms of every size and type.

4. *To define marketing research and its components and to look at its scope* Marketing research entails systematically gathering, recording, and analyzing data about specific issues related to the marketing of goods, services, organizations, people, places, and ideas. It may be conducted internally or externally.

Expenditures on marketing research run into the billions of dollars annually. Five key aspects of marketing research are particularly noteworthy: customer satisfaction studies, the use of advanced technology, single-source data collection, ethical considerations, and the intricacies of international research.

5. *To describe the marketing research process* It has a series of activities: defining the issue or problem to be studied, examining secondary data, generating primary data (when needed), analyzing data, making recommendations, and implementing findings. Many considerations and decisions are needed at each stage of the process.

Exploratory (qualitative) research is used to develop a clear definition of the study topic. Conclusive (quantitative) research looks at a specific issue in a structured manner. Secondary data—not gathered for the study at hand but for some other purpose—are available from internal and external (government, nongovernment, commercial) sources. Primary data—collected specifically for the purpose of the investigation at hand—are available through surveys, observation, experiments, and simulation. Primary data collection requires a research design: the framework for guiding data collection and analysis. Primary data are gathered only if secondary data are inadequate. Costs must be weighed against the benefits of research. The final stages of marketing research are data analysis—consisting of coding, tabulating, and analyzing; recommendations—suggestions for future actions based on research findings; and the implementation of findings by management.

KEY TERMS

scientific method (p. 49)
marketing information system (MIS) (p. 49)
marketing intelligence network (p. 51)
continuous monitoring (p. 51)
data storage (p. 51)
commercial databases (p. 52)
database marketing (p. 52)
marketing research (p. 57)

single-source data collection (p. 58)
marketing research process (p. 60)
issue (problem) definition (p. 60)
exploratory research (p. 60)
conclusive research (p. 60)
secondary data (p. 60)
primary data (p. 63)
research design (p. 63)

sampling (p. 64)
survey (p. 64)
semantic differential (p. 64)
observation (p. 64)
experiment (p. 66)
simulation (p. 67)
data analysis (p. 68)

Review Questions

1. Why is marketing information necessary? What may result if managers rely exclusively on intuition?
2. What is the scientific method? Must it be used each time a firm does research? Explain your answer.
3. Describe the elements of a basic marketing information system.
4. Distinguish between commercial databases and database marketing.
5. What is single-source data collection?
6. Differentiate between conclusive and exploratory research. Give an example of each.
7. What are the pros and cons of secondary data?
8. When is primary data collection necessary?
9. Outline the steps in a research design.
10. Under what circumstances should a firm use surveys to collect data? Observation? Explain your answers.

Discussion Questions

1. A small jeweller wants to get information on the average amounts that consumers spend on gold jewelry, the incomes and occupations of gold jewelry consumers, the times of year when gold jewelry purchases are heaviest and lightest, sales of the leading competitors, the criteria people use in choosing gold jewelry, and consumer satisfaction. Explain how the firm should set up and implement a marketing intelligence network. Include internal and external data sources in your answer.
2. How could a firm use a modified version of the database marketing program as shown in Figure 3-4? Apply your answer to a firm marketing expensive attaché cases to business customers via office-supply stores.
3. Pizza Hut is an internationally oriented fast-food chain. Pierre's Pizza is an independent local European fast-food restaurant. If both wanted to gather data about their respective competitors' marketing practices, how would your research design differ for each?
4. Develop a five-question disguised survey to determine attitudes toward the reputations of colleges and universities in your area. Why use a disguised survey for this topic?
5. Comment on the ethics of disguised surveys. When would you recommend that they not be used?

UNDERSTANDING AND RESPONDING TO DIVERSITY IN THE MARKETPLACE

In Part 2, we see why consumer analysis is so essential and discuss consumer characteristics, needs, profiles, and decision making—and how firms can devise marketing plans responsive to today's diverse global marketplace.

Final Consumer Behaviour

4

This chapter discusses final consumer behavior. We begin with final consumer demographics, the objective and quantifiable characteristics that describe the population. We examine population size, gender, age, location, housing, mobility, income, expenditures, occupations, education, marital status, and ethnicity/race—for Canada, the United States, and a number of other countries around the globe. Then, we investigate final consumer lifestyles and decision making, useful concepts in explaining why and how consumers act as they do. Lifestyles encompass various social and psychological factors, many of which we note here. By studying the decision process, we see how consumers move from stimulus to purchase or nonpurchase.

Organizational Consumers

5

In this chapter, we focus on the organizational consumers that purchase goods and services for further production, use in operations, or resale to other consumers. We look at how they differ from final consumers and at their individual characteristics, buying objectives, buying structures, constraints on purchases, and decision processes.

Developing a Target Market Strategy

6

We are now ready to discuss how to plan a target market strategy. Consumer-demand patterns and segmentation bases are examined; and undifferentiated marketing (mass marketing), concentrated marketing, and differentiated marketing (multiple segmentation) are explained and contrasted. The requirements for successful segmentation and the importance of positioning are also considered. We conclude with a discussion of sales forecasting.

Part 2 Vignette
The Market: The Demands of Satisfying Demand

Marketing is the anticipation, management, and satisfaction of demand through the exchange process. You must understand the reasons for, and the sources of, demand before undertaking any marketing program. The three chapters in Part 2 are designed to help us understand how to manage demand in Canada.

In Chapter 4 we will learn why it is critical for marketers to understand how consumer buying behaviour is affected by the psychology and characteristics of consumers. For example, in Canada the seniors market is very large and possesses the highest amount of disposable income, yet marketers have responded to it slowly. One reason for the lack

> *The reasons for, and the sources of, demand must be understood before any marketing program is undertaken.*

of response is that younger marketing practitioners have difficulty relating to seniors. Aging has important implications for marketers because it produces changes in the needs and wants of people and consequently in the choice of products and services used. Given that seniors represent a market of significant disposable income and absolute size, serving their needs and wants represents a tremendous business opportunity.

Another important consideration for marketers involves understanding how consumers make choices, since the philosophy of a market economy is based on having choices. One issue faced by all economic systems is whether consumers have enough choices. In North America however, some consumer advocates have observed a different phenomenon: sometimes the market economy is too responsive! For example, Baskin Robbins stocks 31 flavours of ice cream at each store, and 600 to 700 are kept in rotation. However, some flavours are much more popular than others and are always kept on hand. With 50 flavours of ice cream on hand that are completely changed once a month, it would take one year to present 600 flavours to one store's customers! Do consumers really take ice cream that seriously? Understanding how consumers make their choices when faced with brand proliferation is useful to marketers. It might help them avoid engaging in costly activities that actually impede market efficiency rather than improve it.

Chapter 5 presents you with an expanded view of the notion of "customer." Marketers must recognize that governments, businesses, manufacturers, retailers, professionals and nonprofit charities represent sources of demand that are cumulatively greater than consumer market demand. Understanding the needs, wants and buying behaviour of organizational consumers is very important. However, organizational buying behaviour often involves many individuals and a slower, much more complex buying process. Acquisition of computers by businesses is one area in which understanding organizational buying behaviour is critical to success. Given that computer technology is undergoing rapid change accompanied by cost and price reductions, computer system purchasing is a very unsettling and risky process, as is computer system development and marketing. Buyers and sellers making decisions involving large expenditures experience a great deal of stress when the marketing environment undergoes rapid and volatile changes.

Finally, Chapter 6 presents the process of target marketing—applying what we can learn about the characteristics of consumers to marketing strategy development. For example, marketing homes to Vancouver's ethnic Chinese market illustrates how target marketing drives marketing strategy. Design, development, pricing, distribution-location and promotion of homes in Vancouver are all being driven by the principle of Feng Shui. Homes constructed in adherence to Feng Shui principles are extremely important to Chinese buyers but a non-issue for others. Consequently, offering this attribute appeals to Chinese buyers yet doesn't diminish the demand of the rest of the market.

CHAPTER 4
Final Consumer Behaviour

Perhaps never before have marketers trying to reach women worldwide felt so unsure about what women want and need. Thirty years ago, even fifteen years ago, it was fairly easy. Most women did not work outside the home, and advertising featured them worrying about spotless dishes and clean floors.

Reprinted by permission.

Today, such trends as increased participation by women in the workforce, couples having fewer children, and many women's greater focus on career opportunities are having an impact around the globe. For example, research in Australia shows that only 7 per cent of families fit the "traditional" family structure of a working father, a mother at home, and two school-age children.

Here's how marketers throughout the world are responding to the changing demographics of women:

- In Spain, firms are beginning to capitalize on the shortage of time for women. Home food delivery is now a growth industry; it was practically nonexistent less than a decade ago. One firm alone, TelePizza, has annual sales of $55 million. Campofrío, a leading food marketer, uses the theme "Let Roteta cook" for its Cocina Placer line of microwaveable entrées. Roteta is a well-known Basque chef who has created many of the recipes for this food line. The concept of the ad campaign is that women can leave food preparation to a highly-regarded chef.

- When General Motors Spain introduced the Opel Corsa, the firm relied on special presentations to female journalists. It also advertised the product in such women's magazines as the Spanish *Vogue* and *Cosmopolitan*. The ads told the story of a woman going through the day, undertaking different activities, and driving her Corsa. The Corsa model became the fifth best-selling car in Spain—with 46 per cent female buyers, the highest proportion of any Opel model.

- According to the Bureau for Market Research at the University of South Africa, as of the year 2011, women will make up 42.3 per cent of the South African workforce, a significant increase from 38.6 per cent in 1991 and 21.1 per cent in 1989. As a result, the sales of convenience foods have increased and will continue to do so. And ads that once depicted women in the home now focus on other roles. More and more firms are also promoting job opportunities for women. One ad, for example, showed a young woman in coveralls and safety glasses welding machinery together. The ad, sponsored by Caltex, a gasoline retailer, described job openings for young people.

We have just looked at a few of the demographic changes occurring in Spain and South Africa—and how marketers are responding to them. In this chapter, we will focus on a number of important consumer demographic trends in Canada and elsewhere, and consider the marketing implications of these trends. We will learn more about customers than just their demographics. By understanding customers' activities and interests, companies can better pinpoint market needs, reasons for purchases, and changing lifestyles and purchase behaviour patterns. In this chapter, we will also study the way consumers live and spend time and money—as well as how they make purchase decisions.

Overview

Consumer analysis is crucial in the diverse global marketplace.

As discussed in Chapters 1 and 2, the consumer is the central focus of marketing. To devise good marketing plans, it is important to study consumer attributes and needs, lifestyles, and purchase processes and then make proper marketing-mix decisions.

The scope of consumer analysis includes the study of who buys, what they buy, why they buy, how they make decisions to buy, when they buy, where they buy, and how often they buy.[1] For example, a university student (who) purchases textbooks (what) because they are required for various classes (why). The student first looks up the book list at the school store and decides whether to purchase new or used books for each course (how).

---

[1]Adapted from Leon G. Schiffman and Leslie Lazar Kanuk, *Consumer Behaviour*, Fifth Edition (Englewood Cliffs, N.J.: Prentice-Hall, 1994), p. 7.

Then, just before the first week of classes (when), the student goes to the school store to buy the books (where). The student does this three times per year— fall, spring, and summer (how often).

An open-minded, consumer-oriented approach is imperative in today's diverse global marketplace so a firm can identify and serve its target market, minimize consumer dissatisfaction, and stay ahead of competitors. Why is this so important? As Seagate, a leader in computer data-storage products, puts it: "People buy expectations, not just things. Customer satisfaction is dependent not only on our products, but on continuously improving our way of doing business."[2]

In Chapters 4 to 6, the concepts you need to understand consumers in Canada, the United States, and other nations worldwide, to select target markets, and to relate marketing strategy to consumer behaviour are detailed. Chapter 4 examines final consumer demographics, lifestyles, and decision making. **Final consumers** buy goods and services for personal, family, or household use.

Chapter 5 centres on the characteristics and behaviour of **organizational consumers**, those buying goods and services for further production, to be used in operating the organization, or for resale to other consumers. Chapter 6 explains how to devise a target market strategy and use sales forecasts.

Final consumers *buy for personal, family, or household use;* **organizational consumers** *buy for production, operations, or resale.*

Demographics Defined and Enumerated[3]

Consumer demographics are objective and quantifiable population characteristics. They are relatively easy to identify, collect, measure, and analyze—and show diversity around the globe. The demographics covered in Chapter 4 are population size, gender, and age; location, housing, and mobility; income and expenditures; occupations and education; marital status; and ethnicity/race.

As shown in Figure 4-1, after separately examining various demographic factors a firm can form a **consumer demographic profile**—a demographic composite of a consumer group. By establishing consumer profiles, a firm can pinpoint both attractive and declining market opportunities. For example, in highly industrialized nations, the population is growing more slowly, people are older, incomes are higher, more people work in white-collar jobs, and there are smaller households than in less-developed and developing countries. Together, these factors have a great impact on the goods and services that are offered and on marketing strategies for these items.

Several secondary sources offer data on consumer demographics. For both Canadian and U.S. demographics, a key source is the *Census of Population* (undertaken by Statistics Canada in Canada), a federal government research project in both countries. Census information provides a wide range of national, provincial/state, and local data via printed reports, computer tapes, microfiche, CD-ROM diskettes, and online databases. Many marketing research firms and provincial/state data centres arrange census data by postal (zip) code, provide forecasts, and update information.

Since complete census data are gathered only once every five years in Canada, and once every decade in the U.S., they must be supplemented by Statistics Canada (U.S. Bureau of the Census) estimates and statistics from chambers of commerce, public utilities, and others. The *Canada Yearbook* and *The Market Research Handbook* (both published by Statistics Canada), along with *Canadian Markets* (published by the *Financial Post*) contain a great deal of useful information. *The Canadian Global Almanac* (published by Macmillan Canada) is also a quick reference source for demographic information.

American Demographics is a monthly magazine dealing mostly with U.S. demographic trends. The *Survey of Buying Power* (published annually by *Sales & Marketing Management*) has

Consumer demographics *are population characteristics that are easy to identify and measure.* **Demographic profiles** *may be formed.*

[2]*Seagate 1992 Annual Report*, p. 9.

[3]Unless otherwise indicated, the data presented in this chapter are all from *Market Research Handbook 1995*, Statistics Canada, Minister of Industry, Science and Technology; *The 1996 Canadian Global Almanac* (Toronto: Macmillan Canada); the U.S. Bureau of the Census (various publications); the United Nations (various publications); *International Marketing Data and Statistics 1995* (Great Britain: Euromonitor, 1995); *American Demographics* (various issues); and *World Almanac and Book of Facts 1996* (Mahwah, N.J.: World Almanac Books, 1995).

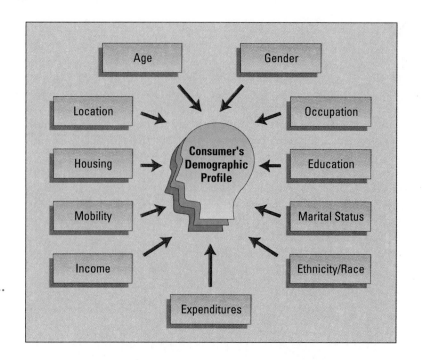

FIGURE 4-1
Factors Determining a Consumer's Demographic Profile

ORGANIZATION FOR ECONOMIC CO-OPERATION AND DEVELOPMENT (OECD)
www.oecd.org/

Relatively speaking, the Canadian population is expanding slowly. There are also many firstborns, more women than men, and a rising average age.

current Canadian and U.S. data by metropolitan area and state/province, including retail sales by merchandise category, personal disposable income, and five-year estimates. Other U.S. secondary sources are *Editor & Publisher Market Guide, Rand McNally Commercial Atlas & Market Guide, Standard Rate & Data Service*, local newspapers, and regional planning boards.

The United Nations (UN), Euromonitor, and the Organization for Economic Cooperation and Development (OECD) are sources of international demographic data. The UN publishes a *Statistical Yearbook* and a *Demographic Yearbook*. Euromonitor publishes *International Marketing Data and Statistics*. OECD issues ongoing demographic and economic reports. In highly industrialized nations, demographic data are fairly accurate because actual data are collected on a regular basis. In less-developed and developing nations, demographic data are often based on estimates rather than actual data. Throughout this chapter, information is provided on Canadian, American and worldwide demographics. A broad cross-section of country examples is provided to give the reader a good sense of the demographic diversity that exists around the globe.

Population Size, Gender, and Age

The world population is expected to grow from 5.7 billion in 1995 to 6.2 billion in 2000, an increase of 1.5 per cent annually. Over the same period, Canada's population is expected to grow from 29 million to 31 million, an annual increase of 1.4 per cent. The U.S. population is expected to grow from 263 million to 275 million, an annual increase of 1 per cent. Thus, the Canadian population will drop from .508 per cent of the world population in 1995 to .5 per cent of the world population in the year 2000. Figure 4-2 shows world population distribution by region for 1990 and 2000.

Newborns account for less than 2 per cent of the population in industrialized nations (1.3 per cent in Canada and 1.5 per cent in the United States)—compared to up to 4 per cent or more in nations such as Afghanistan, Syria, and Zaire. For industrialized countries, a large proportion of births are firstborns.

Worldwide, males and females comprise roughly equal percentages of the population (51% female in Canada in 1996, 49% male). Yet in many industrialized countries, females comprise well over one-half of the population—mostly due to differences in life expectancy. For example, the life expectancy for newborn females is 82 in Canada, 80 years in Italy, 80 in the United States, and 74 in Russia; it is 75 years for newborn males in Canada, 76 in Italy, 73 in the United States, and 64 in Russia.

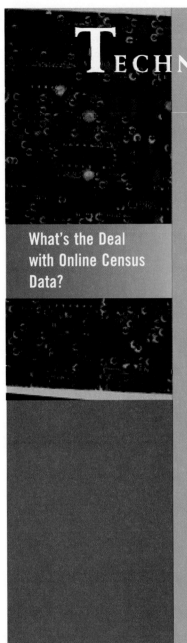

TECHNOLOGY & MARKETING

What's the Deal with Online Census Data?

Need Canadian or U.S. demographic data in a hurry? In Canada you can subscribe to *Statistics Canada Daily* by e-mail by contacting listproc@statcan.ca with the message: subscribe daily Yourfirstname Yourlastname. *The Daily* is a publication containing announcements about products and services, as well as information on new data and releases by Statistics Canada. You can also visit Statistics Canada's Home Page on the World Wide Web, which contains media releases, provides frequently requested statistics, product and service catalogues and issues of *The Daily*.

Of course, the real service comes from the Canadian Socio-Economic Information Management System (CANSIM), Statistics Canada's computerized database and information retrieval service. CANSIM is composed of three basic databases: Census Summary Data Service, Cross-Classified Database and Time Series Database. It is available online (for a fee) through modem-equipped PCs that can access Statistics Canada regional offices or one of the national data transmission networks operating in Canada.

In the United States, census statistics are now available to anyone free of charge with a computer, a modem, and a public-domain graphic interface software package called Mosaic. During its first six months of operation, over one million inquiries—an average of 5500 per day—were made to the U.S. Bureau of the Census' Internet site. And this number is expected to rise dramatically as more people learn about the service. In the near future, some Census Bureau reports will *only* be available online as the Bureau attempts to promote electronic access as a way of better serving consumers and to reduce its printing and paper costs.

Marketers interested in analyzing detailed demographic data about a specific state need only "Enter the Main Data Bank" at the initial menu and select "Statistical Abstract Summaries by States." They are then able to review data on income levels, births and deaths, business failures, and even social insurance programs. Large sets of data can be downloaded by users to their own computers for further analysis.

Another popular program offered at the Census Bureau's Internet site is County Business Patterns. This site features state- and county-based data on employment, payrolls, and establishments. Census Bureau news releases can also be accessed by both subject and date.

As a marketing researcher, how would you use online versus published Statistics Canada or U.S. Census Bureau reports?

Source: Based on material in Jackson Morton, "Census of the Internet," *American Demographics* (March 1995), pp. 52–53; and Jim Carroll and Rick Broadhead, 1996 *Canadian Internet Directory* (Toronto: Prentice Hall Canada).

The populations in industrialized nations are older than those in less-developed and developing nations. Today, the median age of the population is about 35 years in Canada, 37 years in Japan, 36 in Italy and Great Britain, 34 in the United States, 25 in China, 23 in Brazil, 20 in Mexico, and 16 in Nigeria.

Marketing Implications

Around the world, there are opportunities for marketing all types of goods and services. However, in industrialized countries, the low rate of population growth means that firms there need to focus on specific opportunities, such as firstborns, females, and expanding age groups. There will be heightened battles among firms for market share in industrialized nations.

The number of firstborns is significant because parents have many initial purchases to make, for such items as furniture, clothing, and transportation (stroller, car seat, and so on).

CANSIM

www.mun.ca/library/databases/
cansimguide.html

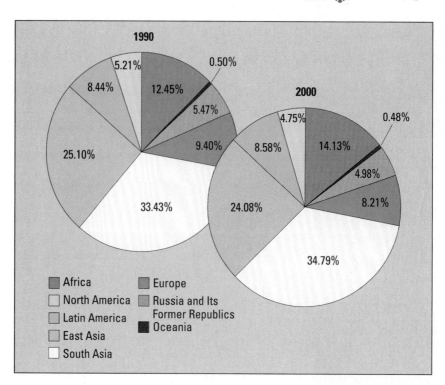

FIGURE 4-2
The World's Population Distribution, 1990 and 2000

Source: U.S. Bureau of the Census.

On average, parents in industrialized nations spend thousands of dollars (including food, clothing, furniture and bedding, toys, health care, child care, and other items) to raise a first child to just his or her first birthday, far more than on each later child. And today's parents are much more likely to bring their babies with them when they travel.

In Canada, there are 273 000 more females than males in the total population while in the United States, there are over 6 million more females than males in the total population. This has important implications for marketers of clothing, household services, appliances, cars, and other items. Accordingly, more and more companies are gearing their appeals to women. Special interest should be paid to older females, who greatly outnumber their male counterparts.

The shifting age distribution in industrialized countries brings many possibilities. For example, colleges and universities are increasing their recruitment of older, nontraditional students. Sports and recreation companies are becoming more oriented toward the over-45 age group. The over-65 age group represents a growing market for food, medical care, vacation homes, telephone services, travel, entertainment, and restaurants.

On the other hand, the much higher rate of population growth—usually across both genders and all age groups—in less-developed and developing countries means that company opportunities there will be broad-based. There will be openings for companies to substantially increase the overall sales of food, clothing, autos, communications equipment, financial services, and a host of other goods and services—rather than fight over market share or carve up very small market segments. For example, from 1990 to 2000, the total populations in China, Nigeria, and Brazil are expected to rise by 160 million, 42 million, and 28 million people, respectively.

Location, Housing, and Mobility

During this century, there has been a major move of the world population to large urban areas and their surrounding suburbs. As of 1996, over 15 cities had at least 10 million residents each—led by Tokyo/Yokohama and Mexico City. But, as Figure 4-3 shows, the level of urbanization varies greatly by country.

Today, 77 per cent of the Canadian population resides in urban areas and approximately 80 per cent of the population lives within 160 kilometres of the U.S. border. The population is

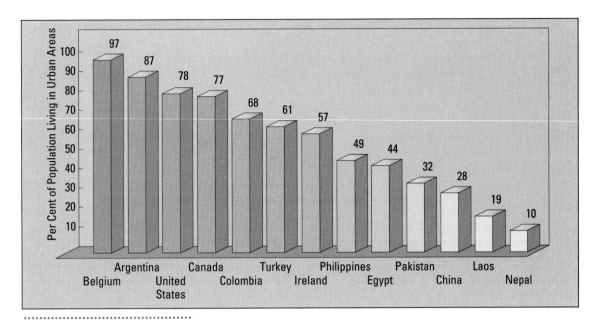

FIGURE 4-3
The Urbanization of Selected Countries
Source: United Nations

concentrated in twenty-five **Census Metropolitan Areas** or CMAs (Statistics Canada defines a CMA as a main labour-market area of an urban area with at least 100 000 people) and 115 **Census Agglomeration Areas** or CAs (Statistics Canada defines a CA as a main labour-market area of an urban area with at least 10 000 people and less than 100 000 people).

In many parts of the world, the majority of people own the homes in which they reside. Here are some examples: Canada, 63 per cent; Bangladesh, 91 per cent; Paraguay, 81 per cent; New Zealand, 74 per cent; Greece, 73 per cent; Finland, 68 per cent; United States, 65 per cent; and Sri Lanka, 61 per cent.

The worldwide mobility of the population is quite high; annually, millions of people emigrate from one nation to another and hundreds of millions move within their nations. During the last decade, more than 2 million people have legally emigrated to Canada. Among Canadian residents, 15 to 20 per cent of all people move annually. In Canada the population is moving to the west with most provinces ahaving had a net loss of inter-provincial migration in 1996 with the exceptions of British Columbia and Alberta, which have had substantial gains. While B.C. has been a net gainer of 23 460 people and Alberta 5739, Quebec (–13 217), Ontario (–5579) and Newfoundland (–7573) have had the greatest decreases.

Marketing Implications

When a nation's population is urbanized, marketing programs are more cost efficient, it is easier to offer goods and services to large groups of consumers, and mass distribution and advertising are possible. In some regions of the world, suburban shopping has been growing, leading to branch outlets in suburbs and improved transportation and delivery services.

The continuing interest in home ownership offers sales potential for such home-based items as furniture, appliances, carpeting, and insurance. Specially modified products for those occupying small homes and for apartment owners, such as space-efficient washers and dryers, are growing in importance. Because some large-ticket home purchases are greatly affected by the economy, firms need to monitor economic conditions carefully.

Population mobility offers openings for well-advertised global, national, or regional brands; retail chains and franchises; and major credit cards— among others. Their names are well known when consumers relocate and represent an assurance of quality. For example, Crest toothpaste, Heineken beer, British Airways, Honda, McDonald's, and Visa are recog-

The world is becoming more urban. Canadian urban areas are classed as **Census Metropolitan Areas** *and* **Census Agglomeration Areas**.

Globally, many people own homes and population mobility is high on a worldwide basis.

HONDA
www.honda.com/toc/

SHOPPERS DRUG MART
www.imasco.com/e/companies/
shoppers

VISA
www.visa.com/cgi-
bin/vee/vw/main.html?2+0

Country-by-country income data are hard to compare.

nized and successful worldwide, as well as throughout Canada and the United States. Shoppers Drug Mart stores do good business in Florida because a number of Canadian "Snowbirds" who winter there or have relocated there patronize them.

Companies often refocus their marketing programs as they anticipate the growth of certain geographic areas and the decline of others. For instance, in Canada, marketing efforts directed at consumers in British Columbia have risen dramatically. Still, firms should be aware of the possibility of oversaturation in these areas. Regions being abandoned by some firms, like Quebec and the Maritimes, should be reviewed by comparing population trends with competition levels.

Income and Expenditures

Consumer income and expenditure patterns are valuable demographic factors when properly studied. In examining them, these points should be kept in mind:

- Personal income is often stated as GDP per capita—the total value of goods and services produced in a nation divided by its population size. This does not report what people really earn and it inflates per-capita income if a small portion of the population is affluent. A better measure is median income—the income for those at the fiftieth percentile in a nation; it is a true midpoint. Yet median incomes are rarely reported outside Canada and the United States.

- Personal income can be expressed as family, household, and per capita. Because families are larger than households and per-capita income is on an individual basis, these units are not directly comparable. Income can also be stated in pretax or after-tax terms, which are not directly comparable.

- Since prices differ by country, a comparison of average incomes that does not take purchasing power into effect will be inaccurate.

- Economic growth is cyclical; at any given time, some countries will be performing well while others are struggling.

- Although the definition of poverty varies greatly by nation, one billion people in the world suffer from malnutrition, illiteracy, and disease.

During the 1960s and early 1970s, real income in Canada rose considerably. Growth then slowed; and from 1981 to 1983, real income fell. Between 1983 and 1990, real income rose moderately—before falling again in 1991. Since then, it has fluctuated slightly each year. Thus, in sum, real Canadian income has gone up rather little over the last twenty-five years.

The most recently released data for Canada indicates a median family income of $47 719 for 1992 and average family income of $53 676. The top 20 per cent of families had over $92 000 in average family income, the next 20 per cent had an average family income of $54 505, and the bottom 20 per cent had an average family income of $11 171.

Changes in the **cost of living** *are measured by a* **consumer price index.**

The slowdown in real Canadian income growth has occurred because income rises have been virtually offset by higher prices. This has led to a higher **cost of living**, the total amount consumers annually pay for goods and services.

Over the last twenty-five years in Canada, the greatest price increases have been for recreation, education, alcohol, and tobacco products; the smallest have been for clothing and food.

Many nations monitor their cost of living by means of a **consumer price index** (CPI), which measures monthly and yearly price changes (the rate of inflation) for a broad range of consumer goods and services. Since 1983, the overall annual rise in the Canadian CPI has been under 5 per cent (except for 1989–1992, when it rose on average by 6 per cent). In 1992, the CPI rose less than 3 per cent in Canada, and less than 5 per cent in the United States, France, Great Britain, and Germany. It went up by 10 per cent or more in many developing and less-developed countries.

Global consumption patterns have been shifting. In industrialized nations, the proportion of income that people spend on food, beverages, and tobacco has been declining.

The percentage spent on medical care, personal business, and recreation has been rising. In less-developed and developing nations, the percentage of spending devoted to food remains high. Canadians spend 15.6 per cent of income on food, beverages and tobacco and 1.9 per cent on health care. Americans spend 18 per cent of income on food, beverages, and tobacco and 16 per cent on medical care. In contrast, Argentines spend 40 per cent of income on food, beverages, and tobacco and 4 per cent on medical care, while Pakistanis spend 47 per cent of income on food, beverages, and tobacco and 5 per cent on medical care.

Disposable income is a person's, household's, or family's total after-tax income to be used for spending and/or savings. **Discretionary income** is what a person, household, or family has available to spend on luxuries, after necessities are bought. Classifying some product categories as necessities or luxuries depends on a nation's standard of living. In Canada and the United States, autos and phones are generally considered necessities; in many less-developed countries, they are typically considered luxuries.

Consumption reflects **disposable income** *and* **discretionary income***.*

Marketing Implications

Several marketing implications regarding consumer income can be drawn:

- Companies need to be quite careful in drawing conclusions about the income levels in different countries. Terms must be properly defined and purchasing power, as well as income levels, assessed.

- There is great income diversity between countries. Thus, firms' goods, services, and marketing strategies should be consistent with the income levels in the targeted nations.

- There is tremendous income diversity within countries. This means that, even in the same country, some firms can prosper by focusing on lower-income consumers while others succeed by targeting upper-income consumers.

- The cost of living affects the discretionary income that people have available to spend. For goods and services perceived as luxuries, consumers need to have discretionary income available.

U.S.-based Whirlpool is a good example of a firm that understands how to react to consumer income levels. It knows that outside Canada, the United States, and Western Europe, the middle-class consumer is quite different. A consumer has to work 40 to 45 days to afford a washing machine in Poland, 35 days in the Czech Republic, and 30 days in Hungary—versus five days in Western Europe. As a result, Whirlpool arranges for more financing in Eastern Europe.[4]

WHIRLPOOL
www.whirlpool.com/

Occupations and Education

The labour force in industrialized nations continues to move to white-collar and service occupations. In less-developed and developing nations, many jobs still involve manual work and are more often agriculture-based.

The total Canadian labour force (people over 15 who are eligible to work) is 14.9 million people. The employed labour force in Canada amounts to 13.5 million people. For the last thirty years, the per cent of Canadian workers in service-related, technical, and clerical white-collar jobs has risen; the per cent as managers, administrators, and sales workers has been relatively constant; and the per cent as unskilled workers has dropped. There are 435 000 Canadian workers who have an agriculture-related job.

The trend to white-collar and service occupations is continuing in industrialized countries.

Another change in the labour force throughout the world has been the increase in the number and percentage of working women. For example, in 1971, 3 million women comprised 34 per cent of the total Canadian labour force. Today, 6.7 million women account for 45 per cent of the labour force, and 57 per cent of adult women in Canada are working.

Women are a large and growing percentage of the worldwide labour force; they make up 45 per cent of the Canadian labour force.

[4]Rahul Jacob, "The Big Rise," *Fortune* (May 30, 1994), pp. 74–90.

Unemployment rates, which reflect the percentage of adults in the total labour force not working, vary widely by nation. For instance, during 1995, the Canadian unemployment rate was about 10 per cent but falling. In comparison, the 1995 unemployment rate in the U.S. was 6 per cent, while those in Belgium, Finland, France, Great Britain, and Italy exceeded 10 per cent; Spain's rate was 22 per cent. Some worldwide unemployment has been temporary, due to weak domestic and international economies. Other times, depending on the nation and industry, many job losses have been permanent. Unemployment is often accompanied by cutbacks in discretionary purchases.

Global education levels are going up.

Great strides are being made globally to upgrade educational attainment, but the level of education tends to be much higher in industrialized nations than in less-developed and developing ones. One measure of educational attainment is the literacy rate—the percentage of people in a country who can read and write. Canada's literacy rate is 99 per cent and in industrialized nations the literacy rate exceeds 95 per cent. Here are the rates for some less-developed and developing nations: Bolivia, 78 per cent; Cambodia, 74 per cent; Chad, 30 per cent; China, 78 per cent; Morocco, 50 per cent; and Saudi Arabia, 62 per cent.

Another measure of educational attainment is the level of schooling completed. In Canada 16.7 per cent of people ages 25 to 64 years have graduated from university. In comparison to other large industrialized nations, the United States is the most educated. A higher percentage of U.S. adults has finished high school and university than in Canada, France, Germany, Great Britain, Italy, or Japan.

The sharp increase in working women and higher educational attainment have generally contributed to the growing number of people in upper-income brackets; the rather high unemployment rates in some nations and industries and slow-growth economies have caused other families to have low incomes.

Marketing Implications

The occupations and education of the population have marketing implications. A greater number and percentage of the total population are in the labour force than before, and this workforce needs transportation, clothing, restaurants, and personal services; stores have opportunities in commercial centres; and the market for job-oriented goods and services is growing and the shift in jobs means different needs and aspirations in consumer purchases.

Because working women have less time for shopping and operating the home, they tend to be interested in convenience and customer service. They often cannot shop during weekdays and many require evening and weekend store hours, efficient store layouts, and mail-order and phone purchases. Such time-saving devices as microwave ovens and food processors, prepared foods, pre-wrapped goods, and special services (such as automatic teller machines), appeal to working women. Also, child-related services, such as daytime child care, are particularly important for them. Yet, too few firms help employees in this area, leaving a prime opening for specialized firms to market these services.

As the population's education level rises, firms need to respond in terms of better information, better product quality, better customer service, enhanced safety and environmental controls, greater accuracy in learning and meeting consumer expectations, and improved consumer-complaint departments. At the same time, companies marketing in less-developed and developing countries need to keep the literacy rates of those areas in mind and adapt products, packaging, promotion messages, and operating instructions accordingly.

Marital Status

Marriage and family remain important.

Marriage and family are powerful institutions worldwide; but in some nations they are now less dominant than they once were. Although 160 000 couples get married each year, only 60 per cent of Canadian adults are married; the percentage of married adults in many other nations is much higher. The average Canadian age at first marriage is 28 years for males and 26 years for females—up from 27.7 and 24.7 in 1960. Thus, the average Canadian family size has gone from 3.9 in 1961 to 3.0 in 1995. The male and female ages at first marriage are much lower in less-developed and developing nations; and the average family is bigger there.

A **family** is a group of two or more persons residing together who are related by blood, marriage, or adoption. A **household** is a person or group of persons occupying a housing unit, whether related or unrelated. In many nations, average household size has been dropping. Canada's has fallen from an average of 2.73 persons per household in 1985 to 2.56 in 1995. Of the 11.2 million Canadian households in 1995, 23 per cent are one-person units, with family households accounting for 73 per cent.

*A **family** has related persons residing together. A **household** has one or more persons who may not be related.*

Marketing Implications

Despite changes over the last thirty or so years, marriage and family are still vital institutions around the world and in Canada. This creates opportunities for industries associated with weddings (such as caterers and travel agents), family life (such as financial services and full-sized cars), and divorce (such as attorneys). When marriages occur later in individuals' lives, those people have better financial resources and two-income families are more prevalent. This presents opportunities for firms involved with clothing, furniture, entertainment, and recreation.

The growth of single-person households provides opportunities for home and home furnishings industries and those that produce specialized products. These implications also apply to divorced and widowed persons. For example, smaller households have a demand for smaller homes, appropriate-sized furnishings and appliances, and single-serving food packages.

Ethnicity/Race

From a demographics perspective, **ethnicity/race** is studied to determine the existence of diversity among and within nations in terms of language and country of origin or race.

Worldwide, there are over 200 different languages spoken by at least 1 million people each—and twelve of those are spoken by 100+ million people each (including Mandarin, English, Hindi, and Spanish). Thus, there are vast linguistic differences among nations. Even within nations, there is often linguistic diversity. For example, Canada (English and French), Chad (French and Arabic), India (Hindi and English), and Peru (Spanish and Quechua) all have two official languages. One of the issues facing the European Community in its unification drive is the multiplicity of languages spoken in the fifteen member nations.

*Demographically, **ethnicity/race** is one measure of a population's diversity with regard to language, country of origin, or race.*

Most nations consist of people representing different ethnic and racial backgrounds. For instance, among those living in the Philippines are Malays, Chinese, Americans, and Spaniards. Sometimes, the people in various groups continue to speak in the languages of their countries of origin, even though they may have resided in their current nations for one or two generations.

Canada is comprised of people from virtually every ethnic group in the world. Statistics Canada measures ethnic origin, which is defined as the ethnic or cultural group to which the respondent or the respondent's ancestors belonged on first coming to North America. The 1996 Census in Canada was the first time that "race" was measured as a census category. The 1993 Canadian population was 20.8 per cent British, 22.8 per cent French, 3.4 per cent German, 2.8 per cent Italian and 1.7 per cent aboriginal people.

Marketing Implications

The ethnic/racial diversity of the world's population means firms must be careful not to generalize or stereotype—either in dealing with multiple nations or in marketing to different ethnic/racial groups within the same nation. Companies marketing goods and services in Canada might miss some prime opportunities if they do not research and adapt to the racial/ethnic characteristics of the marketplace:

- Marketers can reach specific ethnic groups in Canada with specialized media. Figure 4-4 shows an ad for one such medium. *Marketing Magazine's* "1995 Guide to Ethnic Marketing Services" lists the following marketing-service providers that specialize in ethnic marketing services in Canada: eight advertising agencies, three consultant

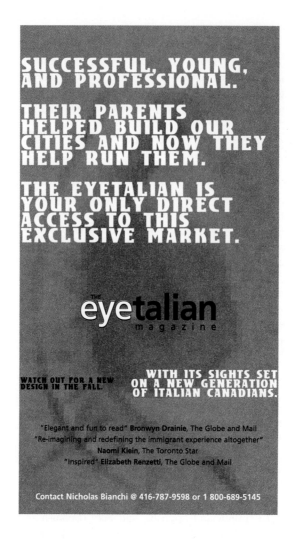

services, three creative services, one direct mail service, three magazines, two media brokers, two market research firms, seven newspapers, five radio stations, seven television services and one translation service.[5]

• Vancouver, Toronto, and Montreal are home to over 80 per cent of Canada's ethnic population (about 2.1 million people). Italian and Chinese people represent over half of this market.

• The purchasing power and population growth rate of ethnic markets are expected to be greater than those for the Canadian market as a whole by the year 2000. For example, population growth among Italian, Chinese, East Indian, Portuguese, Greek, and Polish ethnic groups is expected to be 33 per cent, growing from 2.1 million in 1995 to 2.8 million people by the year 2000.[6]

• "For those approaching target marketing correctly, the benefits are there. One of Canada's major banks showed a 400 per cent increase over five years in its Chinese business when it took an aggressive marketing approach. Besides showing Chinese in their mass marketing material, they also developed Chinese-language ads, direct-mail and in-branch materials, and took a highly visible role supporting community events. Another advertiser, an automaker, saw a 25 per cent boost in sales to the Chinese market due to an integrated ethnic-marketing approach."[7]

---

[5]"Guide to Ethnic Marketing Services," *Marketing Magazine* (July 3/10 1995), pp. 12–14.
[6]Charles Laughlin, "Speaking in Tongues," *Link* (October 1993), p. 15; "The Economics of Growing Communities," *Marketing Magazine*, (July 3/10, 1995), p. 11.
[7]Jennifer Lynn, "Approaching Diversity," *Marketing Magazine* (July 3/10, 1995), p. 11.

Uses of Demographic Data

As we noted at the beginning of the chapter, after studying individual demographics a firm can form consumer demographic profiles to better focus marketing efforts. Here, three examples of demographic profiles are presented.

Profiles of the Canadian, American, and Mexican populations can be contrasted:

	CANADA	UNITED STATES	MEXICO
Annual population growth (%)	1.4	1.0	1.9
Life expectancy (years)	78	77	74
Median age (years)	35	34	20
Urban population (%)	78	80	71
Income ratio of top fifth of population to bottom fifth	8.3	15	14
Working women as part of total labour force (%)	45	46	37
Literacy rate (%)	99	96	90
Average household size	2.5	2.7	5.6

One of the best indicators of consumer buying trends and the underlying interplay of needs, tastes, and desires is the rate at which people buy certain household goods and appliances. It comes as no surprise that 98 per cent of households in Canada have a colour television. That figure drops to 81.5 per cent for microwave ovens and to 79 per cent for VCRs. In the have-not category are automatic dishwashers (46 per cent), compact disk players (41 per cent) and home computers (29 per cent). Households with children are more likely to have a video camera (27 per cent versus 4 per cent), a home computer (40 per cent versus 28 per cent) and, of course, a mortgage (55 per cent versus 27 per cent).[8]

Limitations of Demographics

In applying demographic data, these limitations should be noted:

- Information may be old. In Canada, a full census is done only once every five years and there are time lags before data are released.

- Data on various demographics may be unavailable in some nations, especially less-developed and developing ones.

- Summary data may be too broad and hide opportunities and risks in small markets or specialized product categories.

- Single demographics may not be useful. A demographic profile may be needed.

- The psychological or social factors influencing people are not considered.

- The purchase-making process is not explained.

- Demographics do not provide insights into what motivates people to make purchase decisions. Why do people with similar demographic profiles buy different products or brands?

Demographic data may be dated, unavailable, or too general, may require profile analysis, and may not consider reasons for behaviour.

To overcome these limitations, marketers, in increasing numbers, are going beyond just demographics in studying final consumers. They are using demographic data in conjunction with and as part of consumer lifestyle and decision-making analysis. The latter two topics are the focus of the rest of this chapter.

A **lifestyle** represents the way in which a person lives and spends time and money. It is based on the social and psychological factors that have been internalized by that person—as well as his or her demographic background.[9] These factors overlap and complement each

*Consumer **lifestyles** describe how people live. In making purchases, people use a decision process with several stages.*

---

[8]George Vasic, "Why Today's Luxuries Are Tomorrow's Necessities," *Canadian Business* (June 1995), p. 159 and Statistic Canada, "Household facilities by income and other characteristics, 1995," *The Daily*, Sat. 12, 1996.
[9]Peter D. Bennett (Ed.), *Dictionary of Marketing Terms*, Second Edition (Chicago: American Marketing Association, 1994), p. 154.

other; they are not independent or exclusive of one another. The consumer's decision process involves the steps a person uses in buying goods and services: stimulus, problem awareness, information search, evaluation of alternatives, purchase, and post-purchase behaviour. Demographics, social factors, and psychological factors all affect the process.

Consumer Lifestyles

The social and psychological characteristics that help form final consumer lifestyles are described next.

Social Characteristics of Consumers

The social profile of a final consumer is based on a combination of culture, social class, social performance, reference groups, opinion leaders, family life cycle, and time expenditures (activities). See Figure 4-5.

Each **culture** *transmits socially acceptable behaviour and attitudes.*

A **culture** comprises a group of people who share a distinctive heritage, such as Canadians or Americans. People learn about socially proper behaviour and beliefs through their culture. As a nation, Canada was founded upon the principles of "Law, Order, and Good Government," in contrast to the United States, which enshrined "life, liberty and the pursuit of happiness" in their constitution. Canadians' culture can be characterized as follows: support collective responsibility; have confidence in social institutions such as education, health care, and the police; place importance on consensus; willing to accept difference and diversity; health conscious; pessimistic and skeptical; value driven; frugal; seeking personalization; brand disloyal; informed buyers.[10] However, slower economic growth, the strong influence of American culture, the rising tide of foreign immigration, and a maturing Canadian population may be signalling changes in some of these values.

From a cultural perspective, consumers often have a difficult time when there are dramatic changes in their way of living. This is exemplified by the current situation in eastern Germany.

> People have been propelled into a new consumer society and have had to learn its ways quickly. They remain confused by the huge product choice that has been available to them since the 1990 reunification. Many express the need to relearn consumption and feel inadequate for the task. Not that they get much help; stores may still be poorly laid out, and distribution problems still cause some basics to be out of stock. Sales assistants generally are not equipped to advise consumers, and product literature is absent at the point of sale. Yet, the desire to own Western products and luxury items is strong. People are optimistic they will learn to cope with modern consumer society. Yet, they also feel the old way of life, with basic necessities subsidized by the state, had positive points, too.[11]

Social class *separates society into divisions.*

Social class systems reflect a "status hierarchy by which groups and individuals are classified on the basis of esteem and prestige."[12] They exist virtually everywhere and separate society into divisions, informally or formally grouping those with similar values and lifestyles. Such systems in industrialized nations have a larger middle class, greater interchange among classes, and less rigidly defined classes than those in less-developed and developing nations. Social classes are based on income, occupation, education, and type of dwelling. Each social class may represent a distinct target market for a firm. Table 4-1 shows an informal social class structure.

---

[10]Elliott Ettenberg, "Les blokes Canadiens," *Marketing Magazine* (March 13, 1995), p. 8; Graham Watt, "History and the Canadian Way," *Marketing Magazine* (May 1, 1995), p. 8; Shirley Roberts, "New Consumer Attitudes," *Strategy* (April 14, 1994), p. 4; "A Common Border Does Not Mean Shared Values," *Marketing Magazine*, (January 25, 1993), p 3.

[11]Carla Millar and Christine Restall, "The Embryonic Consumer of Eastern Europe," *Marketing Management*, Vol. 1 (Spring 1992), pp. 48–49.

[12]Bennett, *Dictionary of Marketing Terms*, p. 265. See also Chip Walker, "The Global Middle Class," *American Demographics* (September 1995), pp. 40–46.

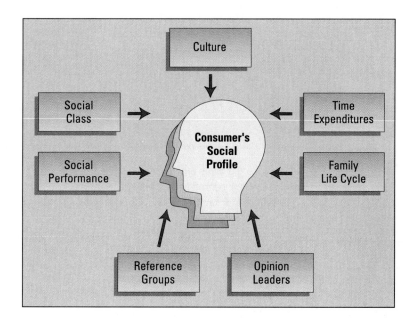

FIGURE 4-5
Factors Determining a Consumer's Social Profile

Table 4-1
The Informal Social Class Structure

CLASS	SIZE	CHARACTERISTICS
Upper Class		*each can be a target market.*
Upper-upper	0.3%	Social elite; inherited wealth; exclusive neighbourhoods; summer homes; children attend best schools; money unimportant in purchases; secure in status; spending with good taste
Lower-upper	1.2%	Highest incomes; earned wealth; often business leaders and professionals; college or university educated; seek best for children; active socially; insecure; conspicuous consumption; money unimportant in purchases
Upper-middle	12.5%	Career-oriented; executives and professionals earning well over $50 000 yearly; status tied to occupations and earnings; most educated, but not from prestige schools; demanding of children; quality products purchased; attractive homes; socially involved; gracious living
Middle Class		
Middle	32%	Typical Canadians; average-earning white-collar workers and the top group of blue-collar workers; many university educated; respectable; conscientious; try to do the right thing; home ownership sought; do-it-yourselfers; family focus
Working	38%	Remaining white-collar workers and most blue-collar workers; working class lifestyles; some job monotony; job security sought more than advancement; usually high school education; close-knit families; brand loyal and interested in name brands; not status-oriented
Lower Class		
Upper-lower	9%	Employed, mostly in unskilled or semiskilled jobs; poorly educated; low incomes; rather difficult to move up the social class ladder; protective against lower-lower class; standard of living at or just above poverty; live in affordable housing
Lower-lower	7%	Unemployed or most menial jobs; poorest income, education, and housing; the bottom layer; present-oriented; impulsive as shoppers; overpay; use credit

Sources: This information is derived from Richard P. Coleman, "The Continuing Significance of Social Class in Marketing," *Journal of Consumer Research*, Vol. 10 (December 1983), pp. 265–280; James F. Engel, Roger D. Blackwell, and Paul W. Miniard, *Consumer Behaviour*, Seventh Edition (Hinsdale, Ill.: Dryden, 1993), pp. 117–119; and William L. Wilkie, *Consumer Behaviour*, Third Edition (New York: Wiley, 1994), pp. 344–351.

Social performance refers to how a person carries out his or her roles as a worker, family member, citizen, and friend. One person may be an executive, have a happy family life, be

Social performance *describes how people fulfil roles.*

Ethics AND TODAY'S MARKETER

What Should Be Done with Unethical Consumers?

Although we often dwell on the unethical practices of business people, consumers can also engage in unethical activities. For example, in a retail setting, there are many opportunities for unethical behaviour by consumers. These include deliberately misrepresenting where an item was bought in order to get an exchange at a local store, returning merchandise beyond a store's posted return period, misrepresenting a price at another store as a bargaining tactic, buying an item (such as a notebook PC to be used during an out-of-town vacation) with the intention of returning it, offering to pay a retailer in cash to avoid payment of sales taxes, and shoplifting. In Canada it is estimated that retailers lose about $3 billion in goods to shoplifting and bookkeeping errors (about 1.5 per cent of sales) with about one-half of this amount accounted for by customers, about one-quarter by employees and the other quarter due to book-keeping errors and other causes.

Many consumers try to rationalize their unethical practices as a way of reducing self-blame or to make the activities appear more socially acceptable. Let's look at how people typically seek to rationalize the act of shoplifting:

- *Denial of responsibility*—"It's not my fault, I had no other choice."
- *Denial of injury*—"What's the big deal? Nobody will miss it."
- *Denial of victim*—"It's their fault; if they had been fair with me, I would not have done it."
- *Condemning the condemners*—"It's a joke they should find fault with me, after the ripoffs they have engineered."
- *Appealing to higher loyalties*—"To some, what I did may appear wrong, but I did it for my family."

These excuses can also be used to rationalize other unethical practices. For instance, denial of injury can be used to suggest that stores plan for consumer shoplifting in setting their original prices.

As vice-president of operations for a retail chain, how would you try to get shoppers to understand that they too have a responsibility to be ethical?

Source: Based on material in David Strutton, Scott J. Vitell, and Lou E. Pelton, "How Consumers May Justify Inappropriate Behaviour in Market Settings: An Application on the Techniques of Neutralization," *Journal of Business Research*, Vol. 30 (July 1994), pp. 253–260; "Retail Council of Canada's Annual Survey," *Globe & Mail*, Metro Edition (April 11, 1995), p. B13 ; "Retailers Get Upper Hand on Five-Finger Discounts," *Globe & Mail*, Metro Edition (April 19, 1994), p. B7.

active in the community, and have many friends. Another may never go higher than assistant manager, be divorced, not partake in community affairs, and have few friends. Many combinations of social performance are possible—such as vice-president and divorced.

Reference groups influence thoughts and behaviour.

A **reference group** is one that influences a person's thoughts or actions. For many goods and services, these groups have a large impact on purchases. Face-to-face reference groups, such as family and friends, have the most effect. Yet, other—more general—groups also affect behaviour and may be cited in marketing products. Ads showing goods and services being used by college students, successful professionals, and pet owners often ask viewers to join the "group" and make similar purchases. By pinpointing reference groups that most sway consumers, firms can better aim their strategies.[13]

[13]See Basil G. Englis and Michael R. Solomon, "To Be *and* Not to Be: Lifestyle Imagery, Reference Groups," *Journal of Advertising*, Vol. 24 (Spring 1995), pp. 13–28.

Table 4-2
The Traditional Family Life Cycle

STAGE IN CYCLE	CHARACTERISTICS	MARKETING OPPORTUNITIES
Bachelor, male or female	Independent; young; early in career; low earnings, low discretionary income	Clothing; auto; stereo; travel; restaurants; entertainment; status appeals
Newly married	Two incomes; relative independence; present- and future-oriented	Apartment furnishings; travel; clothing; durables; appeal to enjoyment and togetherness
Full nest I	Youngest child under 6; one to one-and-a-half incomes; limited independence; future-oriented	Goods and services for the child, home, and family; durability and safety; pharmaceuticals; day care; appeal to economy
Full nest II	Youngest child over 6, but dependent ; one-and-a-half to two incomes; at least one spouse set in career; future-oriented	Savings; home; education; family vacations; child-oriented products; some luxuries; appeal to comfort and long-term enjoyment
Full nest III	Youngest child living at home, but independent; highest income level; thoughts of future retirement	Education; expensive durables for children; replacement and improvement of parents' durables; appeal to comfort and luxury
Empty nest I	No children at home; independent; good income; thoughts of self and retirement	Vacation home; travel; clothing; entertainment; luxuries; appeal to self-gratification
Empty nest II	Retirement; less income and expenses; present-oriented	Travel; recreation; new home; health-related items; less interest in luxuries; appeal to comfort at a low price
Sole survivor I	Only one spouse alive; actively employed; present-oriented; good income	Immersion in job and friends; interest in travel, clothing, health, and recreation areas; appeal to productive citizen
Sole survivor II	Only one spouse alive; retired; some feeling of futility; less income	Travel; recreation; pharmaceuticals; security; appeal to economy and social activity

Firms want to know which persons in reference groups are **opinion leaders**. These are people to whom other consumers turn for advice and information via face-to-face communication. They tend to be expert about a product category, socially accepted, long-standing members of the community, gregarious, active, and trusted; and they tend to seek approval from others. They normally have an impact over a narrow product range and are perceived as more believable than company-sponsored information.

The **family life cycle** describes how a family evolves through various stages from bachelorhood to solitary retirement. At each stage, needs, experience, income, family composition, and the use of **joint decision making**—the process whereby two or more people have input into purchases—change. The number of people in different life-cycle stages can be obtained from demographic data. Table 4-2 shows the traditional family life cycle and its marketing relevance. The cycle's stages apply to families in all types of nations—both industrialized and less-developed/developing—but the marketing opportunities in Table 4-2 are most applicable for industrialized countries.

When using life-cycle analysis, the people who do not follow a traditional pattern because they do not marry, do not have children, become divorced, have families with two working spouses (even if there are very small children), and so on, should be noted. They are not adequately reflected in Table 4-2, but may represent good marketing opportunities.

Opinion leaders *affect others through face-to-face contact.*

The **family life cycle** *describes life stages, which often use* **joint decision making.** *The* **household life cycle** *includes family and nonfamily units.*

T a b l e 4 - 3

The Current Status of Canadian Family and Nonfamily Households

HOUSEHOLD STATUS	PERCENTAGE OF ALL CANADIAN HOUSEHOLDS	
Total Husband and Wife Families	77.1	
Married couples, no children		29.3
Married couples, with children		47.8
Total Families of Common-law Couples	9.9	
Unmarried couples, no children		5.8
Unmarried couples, with children		4.1
Total Lone-Parent Families	13	
Female Parent		10.7
Male parent		2.3

Source: Computed by the authors from Statistics Canada, *Marketing Research Handbook, 1995,* p. 156.

Time expenditures *reflect time allocated to the work week, to family care, and to leisure.*

For that reason, the concept of the **household life cycle**—which incorporates the life stages of both family and nonfamily households—is taking on greater significance.[14] Table 4-3 shows the current status of Canadian households.

Time expenditures refer to the activities in which a person participates and the time allocated to them. Such activities include work, commuting, personal care, home maintenance, food preparation and consumption, childrearing, social interactions, reading, shopping, self-improvement, recreation, entertainment, vacations, and so on. Although the average work week for an individual's primary job has stabilized at 35 to 40 hours weekly, more people are working at two jobs. Canadians enjoy TV, phone conversations, pleasure driving, swimming, sightseeing, walking, bicycling, attending spectator events, reading, and playing outdoor games and sports.

Psychological Characteristics of Consumers

The psychological profile of a final consumer involves his or her personality, attitudes (opinions), class consciousness, motivation, perceived risk, and innovativeness, as well as the importance of the purchase. See Figure 4-6.

A **personality** *describes a person's composite internal, enduring, psychological traits.*

A **personality** is the sum total of the enduring internal psychological traits that make a person unique. Self-confidence, dominance, autonomy, sociability, defensiveness, adaptability, and emotional stability are selected personality traits. Personality has a strong impact on an individual's behaviour. For example, a self-confident and sociable person often will not purchase the same goods and services as an inhibited and aloof person. It is necessary to remember that a personality is made up of many traits operating in association with one another.

Attitudes *can be positive, negative, or neutral.*

Attitudes (opinions) are an individual's positive, neutral, or negative feelings about goods, services, firms, people, issues, and/or institutions. They are shaped by demographics, social factors, and other psychological characteristics. One role of marketing is to generate favourable attitudes; given the intensive competition in many industries, a firm cannot normally succeed without positive consumer attitudes. When studying attitudes, two concepts should often be measured—the attitude itself and the purchase intention toward a firm's brand. For example: (1) Do you like brand A? Would you buy brand A in the future? (2) How does brand A compare with other brands? Would you buy brand A if it were priced higher than other brands?

[14]Robert E. Wilkes, "Household Life-Cycle Stages, Transitions, and Product Expenditures," *Journal of Consumer Research,* Vol. 22 (June 1995), pp. 27–42.

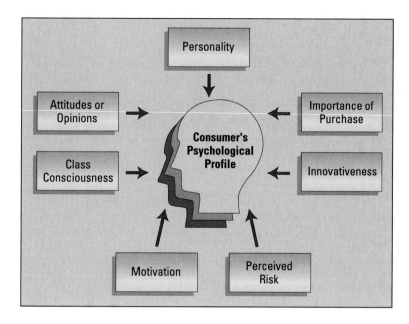

FIGURE 4-6
Factors Determining a Consumer's Psychological Profile

Class consciousness is the extent to which a person seeks social status. It helps determine his or her interest in social-class mobility, use of reference groups, and the importance of prestige purchases. Inner-directed people want to please themselves and are generally attracted by products that perform well functionally. They are not concerned with social mobility, rely on their own judgment, and do not value prestige items. Outer-directed people want to please the people around them. Upward social mobility, reference group approval, and ownership of prestige items are sought. These people are generally attracted by products providing social visibility, well-known brands, and uniqueness. Functional performance may be less important.

Class consciousness *is low for inner-directed persons and high for outer-directed ones.*

Motivation involves the positive or negative needs, goals, and desires that impel a person to or away from certain actions, objects, or situations.[15] By identifying and appealing to people's **motives**—the reasons for behaviour—a firm can produce positive motivation. For example:

Motivation *is a drive-impelling action; it is caused by* **motives**.

MOTIVES	MARKETING ACTIONS THAT MOTIVATE
Hunger reduction	Television and radio ads just before mealtimes
Safety	Smoke detector demonstrations in stores
Sociability	Perfume ads showing social success due to products
Achievement	Use of consumer endorsements in ads specifying how much knowledge can be gained from an encyclopedia
Economy	Newspaper coupons advertising sales
Social responsibility	Package labels that emphasize how easy it is to recycle products

Each person has distinct motives for purchases, and these change by situation and over time. Consumers often combine economic (price, durability) and emotional (social acceptance, self-esteem) motives when making purchases.

Perceived risk is the level of uncertainty a consumer believes exists as to the outcome of a purchase decision; this belief may or may not be correct. Perceived risk can be divided into six major types:

Perceived risk *is the uncertainty felt by the consumer.*

1. *Functional*—risk that a product will not perform adequately.
2. *Physical*—risk that a product will be harmful.
3. *Financial*—risk that a product will not be worth its cost.

[15] Bennett, *Dictionary of Marketing Terms*, pp. 179–180.

4. *Social*—risk that a product will cause embarrassment before others.

5. *Psychological*—risk that one's ego will be bruised.

6. *Time*—risk that the time spent making a purchase will be wasted if the product does not perform as expected.[16]

Because high perceived risk can dampen customer motivation, companies must deal with it even if people have incorrect beliefs. Firms can lower perceived risk by giving more information, having a reputation for superior quality, offering money-back guarantees, avoiding controversial ingredients, and so on.

Innovativeness is trying a new product others see as risky.

A person willing to try a new good or service that others perceive as risky exhibits **innovativeness**. An innovator is apt to be young and well educated, and to have above-average income for his or her social class. He or she is also likely to be interested in change, achievement-oriented, open-minded, status-conscious, mobile, and venturesome. Firms need to identify and appeal to innovators when introducing a new good or service.

*The **importance of a purchase** determines the time, effort, and money spent.*

The **importance of a purchase** affects the time and effort a person spends shopping for a product—and the money allotted. An important purchase means careful decision making, high perceived risk, and often a large amount of money. An unimportant purchase means less decision time (an item may be avoided altogether) and low perceived risk, and it is probably inexpensive.

Selected Consumer Lifestyles

Many distinct consumer lifestyles are expected to continue, including: family values, voluntary simplicity, getting by, "me" generation, blurring of gender roles, poverty of time, and component lifestyles.

*In some households, **family values** have a great impact.*

A **family values** lifestyle emphasizes marriage, children, and home life. It encourages people to focus on children and their education; family autos, vacations, and entertainment; and home-oriented products. Yet, as previously noted, the traditional family is becoming less representative of Canadian households. Thus, firms need to be careful in targeting those who say they follow this lifestyle. They should also keep in mind that a family values lifestyle remains the leading one in many nations outside of Canada. For instance, in Italy, less than one-third of women are in the labour force and the divorce rate is about one-sixth that of Canada.

Voluntary simplicity is based on ecological awareness and self-reliance.

Voluntary simplicity is a lifestyle in which people have an ecological awareness, seek product durability, strive for self-reliance, and buy simple products. People with this lifestyle are cautious, conservative, and thrifty shoppers. They do not buy expensive cars and clothing, hold on to products for long periods, and rarely eat out or go on pre-packaged vacations. They like going to a park or taking a vacation by car, are more concerned with product toughness than appearance, and believe in conservation. They tend to be attracted to rational appeals and no-frills retailing.

*When economic circumstances are tough, people place more emphasis on **getting by**.*

Getting by is a frugal lifestyle pursued by people because of economic circumstances. Those who are getting by seek product durability, self-reliance, and simple products. But unlike voluntary simplicity, they do so because they must. In less-developed and developing nations, most people have this lifestyle; a much smaller proportion do in industrialized countries. Getting by consumers are attracted to well-known brands (to reduce perceived risk), do not try new goods and services, rarely go out, and take few vacations. They look for bargains and tend to patronize local stores. They rarely believe they have any significant discretionary income.

The "me" generation stresses self-fulfillment.

A **"me" generation** lifestyle stresses being good to oneself, self-fulfillment, and self-expression. It involves less pressure to conform, as well as greater diversity; there is also less interest in responsibilities and loyalties. Consumers with this lifestyle want to take care of themselves. They stress nutrition, exercise, and grooming. And they buy expensive cars and apparel, and visit full-service stores. These people are more concerned with product appearance than durability, and some place below-average value on conservation if it will have a negative effect on their lifestyle.

[16]Leon G. Schiffman and Leslie Lazar Kanuk, *Consumer Behaviour*, Fifth Edition (Englewood Cliffs, N.J.: Prentice-Hall, 1994), pp. 562–564.

Because many women are working, more men are assuming the once-traditional roles of their wives, and vice versa, thus **blurring gender roles**: "Men are doing more shopping and housework, but only because women are making them change. Knowing how men are changing—and how they aren't—is the key to targeting them. Meanwhile, more women are learning how to buy cars, program VCRs, and use power tools."[17]

The prevalence of working women, the long distances between home and work, and the large number of people working at second jobs contribute to a **poverty-of-time** lifestyle in many households. For them, the quest for financial security means less free time. This lifestyle leads people to greater use of time-saving goods and services. Included are convenience foods, quick-oil-change services, microwave ovens, fast-food restaurants, mail-order retailers, one-hour film processing, and professional lawn and household care.

Today, more people are turning to a **component lifestyle**, whereby their attitudes and behaviour depend on particular situations rather than an overall lifestyle philosophy. For example, consumers may take their children with them on vacations (family values), engage in trash recycling programs (voluntary simplicity), look for sales to save money (getting by), take exercise classes ("me" generation), share food-shopping chores (blurring gender roles), and eat out on busy nights (poverty of time). As the Roper Organization, a research firm, has noted:

> Consumer behaviour is becoming more individualistic and less defined by reference to easily identified social groups. People are piecing together "component lifestyles" for themselves, choosing goods and services that best express their growing sense of uniqueness. A consumer may own a BMW but fill it with self-service gas. Buy take-out fast food for lunch but good wine for dinner. Own expensive photo equipment and low-priced home stereo equipment.[18]

Marketing Implications of Lifestyle Analysis

Over the years, analysis of the social and psychological characteristics of final consumers has increased dramatically. In this section, we present both general and specific applications of lifestyle analysis in marketing.

Several organizations are involved with defining and measuring consumer lifestyles. They sell this information to client firms, who use it to improve their marketing efforts. Here are some well-known North American services:

- *VALS (Values and Lifestyles)* is a research program sponsored by SRI International. SRI's VALS 2 classification categorizes consumers into eight basic lifestyle groups: actualizers, fulfilleds, believers, achievers, strivers, experiencers, makers, and strugglers.

- *PRIZM (Potential Rating Index by Zip Market)* is a program that relies on census data and examines consumer lifestyles by postal code. It uses about sixty different neighbourhood designations, such as blue blood ("old money"), to describe lifestyles.

These services have been used by companies marketing financial instruments, cars, health-care products, appliances, women's girdles, liquor, food, and other items.

Studies of consumer lifestyles around Canada have been conducted.

- *The Bureau of Broadcast Measurement* (BBM) conducts a Radio Product Measurement study of several thousand respondents on a regular basis in Vancouver, Toronto, and Montreal, with occasional measurements in Winnipeg, Edmonton, and Calgary. The surveys measure lifestyles and shopping behaviour. Lifestyles are categorized as: active, traditional, insecure, and career-driven while shopping behaviour is categorized as: impulse, pro-advertising, early adopter, and uninvolved.[19]

- *Target Mail* of Toronto has a database of more than 200 000 consumers from across Canada, entitled Target Lifestyle Changes. The consumers are surveyed and asked to report whether they or a family member have undergone a major lifestyle change in the past six months or will be undergoing one in the upcoming year.[20]

[17]Diane Crispell, "The Brave New World of Men," *American Demographics* (January 1992), pp. 38, 43.
[18]"Thirty-One Major Trends Shaping the Future of American Business," *Public Pulse*, Vol. 2, No. 1 (1988), p. 1.
[19]"RPM Adds to Radio's Sales Arsenal," *Marketing Magazine* (May 4, 1992), p. 2.
[20]"Harvesting the Power of Synchrographics," *Marketing Magazine* (November 30, 1992), p 10.

Blurring gender roles *involves men and women undertaking nontraditional duties.*

A **poverty of time** *exists when a quest for financial security means less free time.*

With a **component lifestyle**, *consumer attitudes and behaviour vary by situation.*

Here are some findings for firms to consider when planning their marketing mixes:

- Although North American men go to shopping centres somewhat more often than women, the latter spend nearly 25 per cent more time in a shopping centre per visit (and stop at more stores). Two-thirds of North American women make apparel decisions on their own, compared with 48 per cent of men.

Limitations of Lifestyle Analysis

Social and psychological factors can be difficult to measure.

Unlike demographics, many of the social and psychological aspects of final consumer lifestyles are difficult to measure, somewhat subjective, usually based on the self-reports of consumers, and sometimes hidden from view (to avoid embarrassment, protect privacy, convey an image, and other reasons). In addition, there are still some ongoing disputes over terminology, misuse of data, and reliability.

The Final Consumer's Decision Process

*The **final consumer's decision process** has many stages and various factors affect it.*

The **final consumer's decision process** is the way in which people gather and assess information and choose among alternative goods, services, organizations, people, places, and ideas. It consists of the process itself and factors affecting it. The process has six stages: stimulus, problem awareness, information search, evaluation of alternatives, purchase, and post-purchase behaviour. Demographic, social, and psychological factors affect the process. Figure 4-7 shows the total consumer decision-making process.

When a consumer buys a good or service, decides to vote for a political candidate or donate to a charity, and so on, he or she goes through a decision process. Sometimes, all six stages in the process are used; other times, only a few steps are necessary. For example, the purchase of an expensive stereo requires more decision making than the purchase of a new music video.

At any point in the decision process, a person may decide not to buy, vote, or donate—and, thereby, end the process. A good or service may turn out to be unneeded, unsatisfactory, or too expensive.

A. The Decision Process

Stimulus → Problem Awareness → Information Search → Evaluation of Alternatives → Purchase → Post-Purchase Behaviour

B. Factors Affecting the Process

Demographics → Social and Psychological Factors
(a)
(b)

Arrows connect all the elements in the decision process and show the impact of demographics, social factors, and psychological factors upon the process.

Arrows show feedback.
(a) Shows the impact of social and psychological factors on certain demographics such as family size, occupation, and marital status.
(b) Shows the impact of a purchase on social and psychological factors such as social class, social performance, and attitudes.

FIGURE 4-7
The Final Consumer's Decision Process

International Marketing in Action

A Moving Target: Understanding Consumer Behaviour in Eastern Europe

A North American pet food producer presented a new cat food to former communist Eastern Europeans in an ad showing a Persian cat with a jewelled collar eating cat food off of fine china. The reaction was strong and negative: Western pets eat better than Eastern Europeans. Understanding consumer behaviour in international markets is difficult enough due to cultural and social differences, but when cultural and social change is occurring rapidly it becomes nearly impossible. When formerly communist Eastern European markets first opened up in the early 1990s marketers merely had to translate their product packaging and get the products on the retail shelf to enjoy record sales.

A market that had lots of demand and few products to satisfy it was a new experience to western marketers—as new as having products to fill demand was to Eastern European consumers. Now formerly communist Eastern Europeans are faced with a wide variety of products to fill their demand and are faced with something they have not experienced before: choice.

The nature of consumer behaviour and the approach to influencing consumers used in the West is much different from what is required in Eastern Europe. Western consumers have been inundated with product choice and variety and have come to accept these as a natural condition. Promotional efforts in western markets feature puffery and persuasive advertising efforts to convince people to try new products. Formerly communist Eastern European consumers are not used to choice but are used to receiving persuasive messages about making choices, the choices the government wanted them to make! Consequently, the approach to promotion employed by Western marketers needs to be adjusted.

Interestingly, the old approach is what appears to work for these new consumers. Eastern Europeans are responding to a consumer education approach to product marketing, not the usual propaganda approach, which is reminiscent of the former communist government. Post-communist European society bears some similarity to post-World War II North American society: couples marry at young ages, divorce rates are low, women work at home and raise families, and children live with their parents until they marry. And a simple, honest approach to promoting products (reminiscent of North American advertising in the 1950s) seems to work.

As for research on consumer behaviour, it has its own unique problems. Because of past conditioning, consumers tell researchers in Poland what they (the consumers) believe the researchers want to hear, as opposed to what they really feel. Therefore, researchers have to adjust their approach to questioning so they get honest responses and not socially-expected responses.

One thing marketers discovered early on was that Eastern Europeans were very responsive to sales promotions that involved giveaways. However, response rates have been falling as Eastern Europeans, like their North American brethren, have discovered that you generally get what you pay for.

As a marketing manager for a Canadian firm considering marketing a packaged-good product in Slovenia, what approach would you take to keep up with the changes in consumer behaviour?

Source: Based on material in Normandy Madden, "Former Eastern Bloc Consumers Now Savvy To Marketing Wiles," *Marketing Magazine* (May 29, 1995), p. 6.

Stimulus

*A **stimulus** is a cue or drive intended to motivate a consumer.*

A **stimulus** is a cue (social, commercial, or noncommercial) or a drive (physical) meant to motivate a person to act.

A *social cue* occurs when someone talks with friends, family members, co-workers, or another interpersonal source not affiliated with a seller. A *commercial cue* is a message sponsored by a seller—such as that shown in Figure 4-8—to interest a person in a particular good, service, organization, person, place, or idea. Ads, personal selling, and sales promotions are commercial cues. They are less regarded than social cues because people know they are seller-controlled. A *noncommercial cue* is a message from an impartial source, such as Consumer Reports or the government. It has high believability because it is not affiliated with the seller. A *physical drive* occurs when a person's physical senses are affected. Thirst, hunger, and fear cause physical drives.

A person may be exposed to any or all of these stimuli. If sufficiently stimulated, he or she will go to the next step in the decision process. If not, the person will ignore the cue and delay or terminate the decision process for the given good, service, organization, person, place, or idea.

Problem Awareness

Problem awareness *entails recognition of a shortage or an unfulfilled desire.*

At the **problem awareness** stage, a consumer recognizes that the good, service, organization, person, place, or idea under consideration may solve a problem of shortage or unfulfilled desire.

Recognition of shortage occurs when a consumer realizes a repurchase is needed. A suit may wear out. A man or woman may run out of razor blades. An eye examination may be needed. A popular political candidate may be up for re-election. It may be time for a charity's annual fund-raising campaign. In each case, the consumer recognizes a need to repurchase.

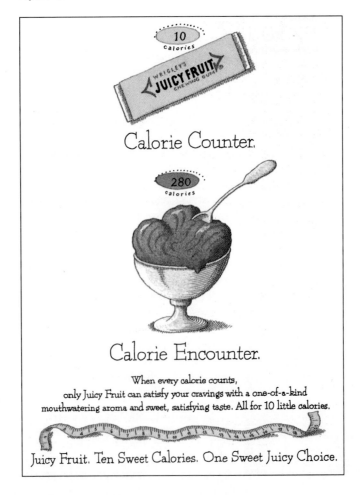

FIGURE 4-8
A Manufacturer-Sponsored Commercial Stimulus

Reprinted by permission of Wm. Wrigley Jr. Company.

Recognition of unfulfilled desire occurs when a consumer becomes aware of a good, service, organization, person, place, or idea that has not been patronized before. Such an item may improve status, appearance, living conditions, or knowledge in a manner not tried before (luxury auto, cosmetic surgery, proposed zoning law, encyclopedia), or it may offer new performance features not previously available (laser surgery, tobacco-free cigarettes). Either way, a consumer is aroused by a desire to try something new.

Many consumers hesitate to act on unfulfilled desires due to the greater risk entailed. It is easier to replace a known product. Whether a consumer becomes aware of a problem of shortage or of unfulfilled desire, he or she will act only if the problem is perceived as worth solving.

Information Search

Next, an **information search** requires listing the alternatives that will solve the problem at hand and determining their characteristics.

*An **information search** determines alternatives and their characteristics.*

A list of alternatives does not have to be written. It can be a group of items a consumer thinks about. With an internal search, a person has experience in the area being considered and uses a memory search to list choices. A person with minimal experience will do an external search to list alternatives; this can involve commercial sources, noncommercial sources, and/or social sources. Often, once there is a list of choices, items (brands, companies, and so on) not on it do not receive further consideration.

The second phase of information search deals with the attributes of each alternative. This information can also be generated internally or externally, depending on the expertise of the consumer and the level of perceived risk. As risk increases, the information sought increases.

Once an information search is completed, the consumer must determine whether the shortage or unfulfilled desire can be satisfied by any alternative. If one or more choices are satisfactory, the consumer moves to the next decision. The process is delayed or discontinued when no alternative provides satisfaction.

Evaluation of Alternatives

There is now enough information for a consumer to select one alternative from the list of choices. This is easy when one option is clearly the best across all attributes: A product with excellent quality and a low price will be a sure choice over an average-quality, expensive one. The choice is usually not that simple, and a consumer must carefully engage in an **evaluation of alternatives** before making a decision. If two or more alternatives seem attractive, the individual needs to determine which criteria to evaluate and their relative importance. Alternatives are then ranked and a choice made.

Evaluating alternatives consists of weighing features and selecting the most desired product.

Decision criteria are the features a person deems relevant—such as price, style, quality, safety, durability, status, and warranty. A consumer sets standards for various features and forms an attitude toward each alternative according to its ability to meet the standards. In addition, each criterion's importance is set because the multiple attributes of a given product are usually of varying weight. For example, a consumer may consider shoe prices to be more important than style and select inexpensive, nondistinctive shoes.

A consumer now ranks alternatives from most to least desirable and selects one. Ranking is sometimes hard because alternatives may have technical differences or be poorly labelled, new, or intangible (as is the case when evaluating two political candidates). On these occasions, options may be ranked on the basis of brand name or price, which is used to indicate overall quality.

In situations where no alternative is satisfactory, a decision to delay or not make a purchase is made.

Purchase

After choosing the best alternative, a person is ready for the **purchase act**: an exchange of money, a promise to pay or support in return for ownership of a specific good, the perfor-

*The **purchase act** includes deciding where to buy, agreeing to terms, and seeing if the item is available.*

mance of a specific service, and so on. Three considerations remain: place of purchase, terms, and availability.

Although most items are bought at stores, some are bought at school, work, and home. The place of purchase is picked in the same way as a product. Choices are noted, attributes detailed, and a ranking done. The best locale is chosen.

Purchase terms involve the price and method of payment. Generally, a price is the amount (including interest, tax, and other fees) a person pays to gain the ownership or use of a good or service. It may also be a person's vote, time investment, and so on. The payment method is the way a price is paid (cash, short-term credit, or long-term credit).

Availability refers to the timeliness with which a consumer receives a product that he or she buys. It depends on stock on hand (or service capacity) and delivery. Stock on hand relates to a seller's ability to provide a good or service when requested. For items requiring delivery, the period from when an order is placed by a consumer until it is received and the ease with which an item is transported to its place of use are crucial.

A consumer will make a purchase if these elements are acceptable. However, dissatisfaction with any one may cause a consumer to delay or not buy, even though there is no problem with the good or service itself.

Post-Purchase Behaviour

Post-purchase behaviour often embodies further buying and/or re-evaluation. **Cognitive dissonance** *can be reduced by proper consumer after-care.*

Once a purchase is made, a person may engage in **post-purchase behaviour**, in the form of further purchases and/or re-evaluation of the original purchase. Many times, one purchase leads to others: A house purchase leads to the acquisition of fire insurance, a PC purchase leads to the acquisition of computer software.

A person may also re-evaluate a purchase after making it: Does performance match expectations? Satisfaction usually leads to a repurchase when a good or service wears out, another contribution when a charity holds a fund-raising campaign, and so on, and leads to positive communication with other people interested in the same item. Dissatisfaction can lead to brand switching and negative communication.

Dissatisfaction is often due to **cognitive dissonance**—doubt that a correct decision has been made. A person may regret a purchase or wish another choice was made. To overcome dissonance, a firm must realize the process does not end with the purchase. Follow-up calls, extended warranties, and ads aimed at purchasers can reassure people.

Factors Affecting the Final Consumer's Decision Process

The decision process is affected by demographic, social, and psychological factors.

Demographic, social, and psychological factors affect the way final consumers make choices and can help a firm understand how people use the decision process. For example, an affluent consumer would move through the process more quickly than a middle-income one because he or she faces less financial risk. An insecure consumer would spend more time making a decision than a secure one.

By knowing how these factors influence decisions, a firm can fine-tune its marketing strategies to cater to the target market and its purchase behaviour, and answer these questions: Why do two or more people use the decision process in the same way? Why do two or more people use it differently?

Types of Decision Processes

Final consumer decision making can be categorized as **extended**, **limited**, *or* **routine**.

Each time a person buys a good or service, donates to a charity, and so on, he or she uses the decision process. This may be done subconsciously, without the person being aware of it. Some situations allow a person to move through the process quickly and de-emphasize or skip certain steps; others may require a thorough use of each step. A consumer may use extended, limited, or routine decision making—based on the degree of search, level of experience, frequency of purchase, amount of perceived risk, and time pressure. See Figure 4-9.

Extended consumer decision making occurs when a person fully uses the decision process. Much effort is spent on information search and evaluation of alternatives for

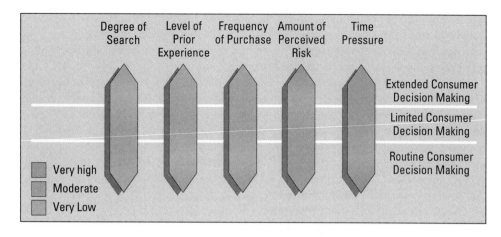

FIGURE 4-9
The Three Types of Final Consumer Decision Processes

expensive, complex items with which a person has little or no experience. Purchases are made infrequently. Perceived risk is high, and the purchase is important. A person has time available to make a choice. Purchase delays often occur. Demographic, social, and psychological factors have their greatest impact. Extended decision making is often involved in picking a college, a house, a first car, or a location for a wedding.

Limited consumer decision making occurs when a person uses every step in the purchase process but does not spend a great deal of time on some of them. The person has previously bought a given good or service, but makes a fresh decision when it comes under current purchase consideration—due to the relative infrequency of purchase, the introduction of new models, or an interest in variety. Perceived risk is moderate, and a person is willing to spend some time shopping. The thoroughness with which the process is used depends on the amount of prior experience, the importance of the purchase, and the time pressure facing the consumer. Emphasis is on evaluating a list of known choices, although an information search may be done. Factors affecting the decision process have some impact. A second car, clothing, gifts, home furnishings, and an annual vacation typically need limited decision making.

Routine consumer decision making occurs when a person buys out of habit and skips steps in the process. He or she spends little time shopping and often rebuys the same brands (or brands bought before). In this category are items with which a person has much experience. They are bought regularly, have little or no perceived risk, and are relatively low in price. Once a person realizes a good or service is depleted, a repurchase is made. The time pressure to buy is high. Information search, evaluation of alternatives, and postpurchase behaviour are normally omitted, as long as a person is satisfied. Factors affecting the process have little impact because problem awareness typically leads to a purchase. Examples of items routinely purchased are the daily newspaper, a haircut by a regular stylist, and weekly grocery items.

There are several differences between consumers in industrialized nations and those in less-developed and developing ones. In general, consumers in less-developed and developing countries:

The way the decision process is used varies by country.

- Are exposed to fewer commercial and noncommercial cues.
- Have access to less information.
- Have fewer goods and services from which to choose.
- Are more apt to buy a second choice if the first one is not available.
- Have fewer places of purchase and may have to wait in long lines.
- Are more apt to find that stores are out of stock.
- Have less purchase experience for many kinds of goods and services.
- Are less educated and have lower incomes.
- Are more apt to rebuy items with which they are only moderately satisfied (due to the lack of choices).

Low-involvement purchasing
is often used when buying unimportant products.

Brand loyalty *involves consistent repurchases of and preference for specific brands.*

Because many consumers—in both industrialized nations and less-developed nations—want to reduce shopping time, the use of complex decision making, and risk, most purchases are made using routine or limited decision making. Thus, consumers often rely on low-involvement purchasing and/or brand loyalty.

With **low-involvement purchasing**, a consumer minimizes the time and effort expended in both making decisions about and shopping for those goods and services he or she views as unimportant. Included are "those situations where the consumer simply does not care and is not concerned about brands or choices and makes the decision in the most cognitively miserly manner possible. Most likely, low involvement is situation-based and the degree of importance and involvement may vary with the individual and with the situation."[21] In these situations, consumers feel little perceived risk, are passive about getting information, act fast, and may assess products after (rather than before) buying.

Firms can adapt to low-involvement purchasing by using repetitive ads to create awareness and familiarity, stressing the practical nature of goods and services, having informed salespeople, setting low prices, using attractive in-store displays, selling in all types of outlets, and offering coupons and free samples. Table 4-4 compares the traditional high-involvement view of consumer behaviour with the newer low-involvement view.[22]

Once a consumer tries one or more brands of a good or service, **brand loyalty**—the consistent repurchase of and preference for a particular brand—may develop. Brand loyalty allows the consumer to reduce the amount of time, thought, and risk required when buying a given good or service. Brand loyalty can develop for simple items such as gasoline (due to low-involvement purchasing) and for complex items like autos (to minimize the risk of switching brands).

Canadians are less brand loyal than they used to be. A recent survey indicated that 57 per cent of shoppers would buy a product on sale rather than their favourite brand. In comparison, only 45 per cent of shoppers felt this way in 1989. Approximately 56 per cent of Canadian shoppers think generics are as good as national brands, compared to 52 per cent in 1989.[23]

How can companies generate and sustain customer loyalty? Here is the way Zellers and the Royal Bank of Canada have tackled this issue:

> Zellers offers all its customers a Club Z card, which entitles them to build up points on all merchandise purchases at Zellers. These points can be redeemed in merchandise selected from the retailers Club Z catalogue. Part of the secret of the success of Club Z is that merchandise purchases are credited no matter how they are paid for (cash, Zellers Card, VISA, Master Card, etc.). The Club Z approach rewards store loyalty without constraining purchase behaviour. Most other frequent-purchase programs require the use of a credit card.
>
> Another example is the Royal Bank's VISA Classic II card. Launched in the spring of 1996, the card targets value-conscious consumers, such as young families and students. The idea is for participating retailers to give customers savings discounts of up to 25 per cent and other bonuses when they use the card to make purchases. Participating retailers include: Radio Shack, Music World, Cotton Ginny, and Domino's Pizza, among others. Of course, the VISA card is good at nonparticipating retailers as well, and any card usage allows customers to build up points which can be exchanged for gift certificates on merchandise from Radio Shack or Eaton's.[24]

Marketing Implications of the Final Consumer's Decision Process

Over the years, the marketing implications of the final consumer's decision process have been studied in many settings, as these present-day illustrations indicate:

- When acquiring information for a car purchase, people read articles in newspapers and magazines, talk to friends and relatives, and consider their previous experience. On average, men spend fourteen weeks thinking about a new-car purchase; and 32 per cent visit a closed showroom so they can look at models and learn about sticker prices.

RADIO SHACK
www.tandy.com/

ROYAL BANK
www.royalbank.com/

---

[21]Bennett, *Dictionary of Marketing Terms*, p. 157.
[22]See also Stephen L. Vargo, "Consumer Involvement: An Historical Perspective and Partial Synthesis," in Barbara B. Stern and George M. Zinkham (Eds.), *1995 AMA Educators' Proceedings* (Chicago: American Marketing Association, 1995), pp. 139–145.
[23]"Brand Loyalty Declining, Study Shows," *Marketing Magazine* (April 27, 1992), p 2.
[24]Lara Mills, "Royal Bank Rolls Out New Customer Loyalty Card," *Marketing Magazine* (May 13, 1996), p. 4.

Table 4-4

High-Involvement View of Active Consumers Versus Low-Involvement View of Passive Consumers

TRADITIONAL HIGH-INVOLVEMENT VIEW OF ACTIVE CONSUMERS	NEWER LOW-INVOLVEMENT VIEW OF PASSIVE CONSUMERS
1. Consumers are information processors.	**1.** Consumers learn information at random.
2. Consumers are information seekers.	**2.** Consumers are information gatherers.
3. Consumers are an active audience for ads and the effect of ads on them is *weak*.	**3.** Consumers are a passive audience for ads and the effect of ads on them is *strong*.
4. Consumers evaluate brands before buying.	**4.** Consumers buy first. If they do evaluate brands, it is done after the purchase.
5. Consumers seek to maximize satisfaction. They compare brands to see which provide the most *benefits* and buy based on detailed comparisons.	**5.** Consumers seek an acceptable level of satisfaction. They choose the brand least apt to have *problems* and buy based on few factors. Familiarity is key.
6. Lifestyle characteristics are related to consumer behaviour because the product is closely tied to a consumer's identity and belief system.	**6.** Lifestyle characteristics are not related to consumer behaviour because the product is not closely tied to a consumer's identity and belief system.
7. Reference groups influence behaviour because of the product's importance to group norms.	**7.** Reference groups have little effect on behaviour because the product is unlikely to be related to group norms.

Source: Henry Assael, *Consumer Behaviour and Marketing Action*, Fourth Edition (Boston: PWS-Kent, 1992), p. 104. Reprinted by permission of Wadsworth, Inc.

Once the actual "hunt" starts, men average fourteen shopping days to buy a car and visit five dealers. Two-thirds of men say they have a good time when buying a new car.

- For several reasons, "substantial time often elapses between the time people recognize the need for a product and the time they actually purchase it." People may believe they do not have enough time to devote to the decision. They may feel shopping is an unpleasant experience. They may experience perceived risk. They may need advice from others that is not readily available. They may not know how to gather adequate information about products and their attributes. They may expect prices to fall or improved products to be introduced later.

- Satisfied consumers discuss their experiences with far fewer people than dissatisfied ones. Yet, according to one auto-industry consultant, "It costs you five times as much to get a new customer as to keep an old one."[25]

Limitations of the Final Consumer's Decision Process

The limitations of the final consumer's decision process for marketers lie in the hidden (unexpressed) nature of many elements of the process; the consumer's subconscious performance of the process or a number of its components; the impact of demographic, social, and psychological factors on the process; and the differences in decision making among consumers in different countries.

Much of purchase behaviour is hidden or subconscious.

[25]"How Men Buy Cars," *Ad Week* (September 18, 1995), p. 21; and "How Guys Buy Cars," *Advertising Age* (September 18, 1995), p. 3; Raymond Serafin and Cleveland Horton, "Auto Makers Focus on Service," *Advertising Age* (July 6, 1992), pp. 3, 33; Eric A. Greenleaf and Donald R. Lehmann, "Reasons for Substantial Delay in Consumer Decision Making," *Journal of Consumer Research*, Vol. 22 (September 1995), pp. 186–199.

MARKETING IN A CHANGING WORLD

From Boomers to Xers

Two of the key age groups that today's marketers must continually strive to understand and satisfy are *Baby Boomers* and *Generation Xers*. In some cases, the first group includes the parents of the second group.

Baby boomers are people born between 1947 and 1965 (with the peak birth rate occurring in 1959), in the aftermath of World War II. They are generally divided into two groups: older and younger boomers. By the year 2000, the 7 million Canadian and 77 million U.S. baby boomers will range in age from 35 to 54, be in their peak earnings years, and dominate consumer spending.

The older baby boomers grew up with the "Vietnam War, the Civil Rights Movement, and economic expansion." The younger group of boomers grew up with stagflation, wage-and-price controls, and government spending freezes. Overall, baby boomers are "well-educated, high-tech parents who suffer from a lack of leisure time. Despite their financial worries, most can expect a healthy, active, and fun-filled retirement."[26]

Generation Xers—a term coined by marketers and disliked by most in this group (don't YOU dislike this name?)—are people born between 1965 and 1976, a period also known as the "baby bust." By the year 2000, Generation Xers will range in age from 24 to 35 and be embarking on major life changes: getting married, having children, and moving along career ladders. In contrast to baby boomers, Generation Xers "are more apt to have participated in household chores at an earlier age, so they are more knowledgeable about products at a comparable age. They are more apt to seek a balance of work and leisure activities. They are more diverse and more accepting of diversity, whether it be defined by ethnicity or by sexual preference. And while they are not anti-advertising, they are repulsed by insincerity—and they are experts at spotting it."[27]

SUMMARY

1. *To show the importance and scope of consumer analysis* By analyzing consumers, a firm is better able to determine the most appropriate audience to which to appeal and the combination of marketing factors that will satisfy this audience. This is a critical task given the diversity in today's global marketplace. The scope of consumer analysis includes who, what, why, how, when, where, and how often.

2. *To define and enumerate important consumer demographics for the Canadian population and other countries* Consumer demographics are objective and quantifiable population statistics. They include size, gender, and age; location, housing, and mobility; income and expenditures; occupations and education; marital status; and ethnicity/race.

3. *To examine trends and projections for these important demographics and study their marketing implications* The world population is 5.7 billion people and rising by 1.5 per cent annually. Canada's population is 29 million people and increasing by 1.4 per cent each year. In many nations, a large proportion of births are firstborns. Worldwide, the number of men and women is roughly equal. However, women generally live longer than men; and the average age of populations in industrialized nations is higher than in less-developed and developing countries.

There has been a significant movement of the world population to large urban areas. The level of urbanization does vary by country, with 78 per cent of Canadians living in urban areas. In many countries, the majority of people own the home in which they live, with almost two-thirds of the Canadian population residing in homes they own. Each year, millions of people emigrate from one country to another and hundreds of millions move within their countries. About 240 000 people move to Canada from abroad every year; and about 15 to 20 per cent of the Canadian population moves annually.

For several reasons, comparing countries' personal income data can be rather difficult. The 1992 Canadian after-tax median family income was $47 719—with the top one-fifth of families having after-tax incomes averaging $92 000 and the bottom one-fifth having after-tax incomes averaging $11 171. Many nations measure their cost of living and rate of inflation using a consumer price index. There are differences in consumption patterns between people in industrialized nations and in less-developed and developing countries. When assessing consumption patterns, the distinction between disposable-income spending and discretionary-income expenditures should be kept in mind.

[26]Patricia Braus, "The Baby Boom at Mid-Decade," *American Demographics* (April 1995), pp. 40–45; Harvey Schachter, "Power Shift," *Canadian Business* (August 1995), p. 21.

[27]Karen Ritchie, "Marketing to Generation X," *American Demographics* (April 1995), pp. 34–39.

In industrialized nations, the labour force is continuing its movement to white-collar and service occupations; many more jobs in less-developed and developing nations still entail manual work and are agriculture-based. The total employed Canadian civilian labour force is 13.5 million people. Throughout the world, women comprise a significant portion of the labour force (45 per cent in Canada). Unemployment rates vary widely among nations, based on economic conditions and industry shifts. Globally, educational attainment has gone up—though there are great variations among countries. In Canada, a much larger percentage of the population is now graduating high school and attending college or university than did thirty years ago.

Marriage and family are powerful institutions, although less dominant than in the past for some nations. Three-fifths of Canadian adults are married, with couples waiting until they are older for marriage and having fewer children than in prior decades. A family consists of relatives living together. A household consists of a person or persons occupying a housing unit, related or not. In many nations, both family and household size have declined, due to the growth in single-person households and other factors.

Demographically, ethnicity/race is important as it pertains to the diversity of people among and within nations. Globally, over 200 languages are spoken by at least 1 million people; and some nations have two or more official languages. Most countries have populations representing different ethnic and racial groups. Statistics Canada measures ethnic origin, which is defined as the ethnic or cultural group to which the respondent or the respondent's ancestors belonged on first coming to North America. The 1993 Canadian population was 20.8 per cent British, 22.8 per cent French, 3.4 per cent German, 2.8 per cent Italian and 1.7 per cent aboriginal people.

Each of these demographics has marketing implications, which are discussed in the chapter.

4. *To define and describe consumer lifestyles and their characteristics, examine selected lifestyles, and present marketing implications of lifestyle analysis* A final consumer's lifestyle is the way in which a person lives and spends time and money. It is a function of the social and psychological factors internalized by that person, along with his or her demographic background. Consumer social profiles are made up of several elements, including culture, social class, social performance, reference groups, opin-

ion leaders, the family life cycle, and time expenditures. Psychological profiles are based on a combination of personality, attitudes (opinions), the level of class consciousness, motivation, perceived risk, innovativeness, and purchase importance.

These seven lifestyle types are expected to continue, with their popularity often differing by country. A family values lifestyle emphasizes marriage, children, and home life. With voluntary simplicity, people have an ecological awareness, seek material simplicity, strive for self-reliance, and buy inexpensive product versions. Getting by is a frugal lifestyle brought on because of economic circumstances. The "me" generation stresses being good to oneself, self-expression, and the acceptance of diversity. With blurring gender roles, more husbands are assuming the once traditional roles of their wives, and vice versa. A poverty of time occurs for some consumers because the quest for financial security means less free time as the alternatives competing for time expand. In a component lifestyle, consumer attitudes and behaviour depend on particular situations, rather than on an overall lifestyle philosophy. The various marketing implications of these consumer lifestyles are discussed further in the text.

5. *To define and describe the final consumer's decision process and present marketing implications* The final consumer's decision process is the procedure by which those consumers collect and analyze information and make choices among alternatives. It consists of the process itself and the factors affecting it (demographic, social, and psychological). It can be delayed or terminated by the consumer at any point.

The process has six steps: stimulus, problem awareness, information search, evaluation of alternatives, purchase, and post-purchase behaviour. There are three types of process: extended, limited, and routine. The way people make decisions varies widely between industrialized nations and less-developed and developing nations. Consumers often reduce shopping time, thought, and risk through low-involvement purchasing (for goods and services viewed as unimportant) and brand loyalty (the consistent repurchase of and preference toward a brand).

The marketing implications of the final consumer's decision process have been detailed for years. Several current applications are discussed in the text.

KEY TERMS

final consumers (p. 77)

organizational consumers (p. 77)

consumer demographics (p. 77)

consumer demographic profile (p. 77)

Census Metropolitan Area (CMA) (p. 81)

Census Agglomeration Area (CA) (p. 81)

cost of living (p. 82)

consumer price index (CPI) (p. 82)

disposable income (p. 83)

discretionary income (p. 83)

family (p. 85)

household (p. 85)

ethnicity/race (p. 85)

lifestyle (p. 87)

culture (p. 88)

social class (p. 88)

social performance (p. 89)

reference group (p. 90)

opinion leaders (p. 91)

family life cycle (p. 91)

joint decision making (p. 91)

household life cycle (p. 91)

time expenditures (p. 92)

personality (p. 92)

attitudes (opinions) (p. 92)

class consciousness (p. 93)

motivation (p. 93)

motives (p. 93)
perceived risk (p. 93)
innovativeness (p. 94)
importance of a purchase (p.94)
family values (p. 94)
voluntary simplicity (p. 94)
getting by (p. 94)
"me" generation (p. 94)

blurring gender roles (p. 95)
poverty of time (p. 95)
component lifestyle (p. 95)
final consumer's decision process (p. 96)
stimulus (p. 98)
problem awareness (p. 98)
information search (p. 99)
evaluation of alternatives (p. 99)

purchase act (p. 99)
post-purchase behaviour (p. 100)
cognitive dissonance (p. 100)
extended consumer decision making (p. 100)
limited consumer decision making (p. 100)
routine consumer decision making (p. 100)
low-involvement purchasing (p. 102)
brand loyalty (p. 102)

Review Questions

1. How does the use of consumer demographics aid marketing decision making?

2. In Canada, how does a Census Metropolitan Area (CMA) differ from a Census Agglomeration Area (CA)?

3. Distinguish between the terms "cost of living" and "consumer price index."

4. Describe the major limitations of demographics.

5. Distinguish between the traditional family life cycle and the household life cycle.

6. How does class consciousness differ for inner-directed and outer-directed people? What does this signify for marketers?

7. Differentiate among social, commercial, and noncommercial stimuli. Provide specific examples of each.

8. What causes cognitive dissonance? How can it be reduced?

9. Draw a flowchart showing the steps in routine purchase behaviour.

10. Define low-involvement purchasing and explain its use by consumers. Give an example.

Discussion Questions

1. The biggest CMA in Canada is Toronto, with 4.3 million people. What are the pros and cons of marketing products there? Recommend a marketing approach for a local bank.

2. Using the *Census of Population*, develop a demographic profile of the people residing in the CA or CMA nearest to where you live. What are the marketing overtones of this profile?

3. As the owner-operator of a prospective camera store in Canada, what demographic factors would you study? Describe the demographic profile of your ideal consumer.

4. Canadian culture emphasizes collective responsibility, confidence in social institutions such as education, health care, and the police, consensus, willingness to accept difference and diversity, health consciousness, pessimism, and skepticism; Canadian consumers are value-driven, frugal, seeking personalization, brand disloyal, and informed buyers. What

are the implications of this for firms marketing the following goods and services?
  a. Motorcycles.
  b. Tanning salons.
  c. Adult education.
  d. Vacation travel.

5. A large cereal manufacturer has hired you as a marketing consultant. It is particularly interested in learning more about the concept of a component lifestyle and developing an appropriate strategy.
  a. Explain the relevance of the component lifestyle concept for the cereal industry.
  b. Suggest various ways in which the cereal manufacturer can appeal to component lifestyles.

CHAPTER 5
Organizational Consumers

Harbil RA-80
Retail Automatic
Dispenser

Chapter Objectives

1 To introduce the concept of industrial marketing

2 To differentiate between organizational consumers and final consumers and look at organizational consumers from an international perspective

3 To describe the different types of organizational consumers and their buying objectives, buying structure, and purchase constraints

4 To explain the organizational consumer's decision process

5 To consider the marketing implications of appealing to organizational consumers

> *In 1989, Fred Brunk, vice-president of sales at Fluid Management, a supplier of display shelving for paint, wanted to grow the company's domestic sales. What was missing from his portfolio were the big retailers such as Wal-Mart, which would bring him larger volumes. Six years later, Brunk got his wish—domestic sales doubled, from $20 million to $40 million, thanks to an increase in volume to the mass merchants. But what Brunk did not count on were the tremendous expectations of these companies.*

Reprinted by permission.

For many small firms, large retailers represent a great opportunity, but selling to them is often more complicated than expected. As Fluid Management's Fred Brunk says, "Even when the details are in place, such as the specific needs of the company and negotiated prices, you have to constantly watch when new stores are opening. There must always be a salesperson ready at a moment's notice to make a trip to the retailer's headquarters." And while Fluid Management's eight-member sales force may not be able to visit each of Wal-Mart's thousands of stores, the firm's chief executive officer is willing to go to Wal-Mart's Bentonville, Arkansas, headquarters as often as needed.

Here are some other complexities in selling to big accounts like Wal-Mart:

WAL-MART
www.wal-mart.com/

- Wal-Mart does not purchase from wholesalers. Thus, small firms must service the firm directly. This could be especially tough for a small supplier selling a narrow product line.
- Most small manufacturers do not have the resources to set up offices near to Wal-Mart stores.
- Some large retailers require that suppliers take back excess inventories, seek extended payment policies, and even ask that suppliers handle data collection responsibilities. Other demands may include requiring rebates on purchases, adhering to an automatic return policy, and dictating that a supplier give donations to the retailers' favourite charities. A number of small manufacturers say the demands that large retailers place on them are so great that they would lose money selling to those retailers.
- A small supplier's current customers may resent it selling to firms that are viewed as direct competitors, such as Wal-Mart.
- The loss of a key account could drive a small supplier into bankruptcy.

So, why bother? There are major benefits for a small firm selling to a large retailer. First, there is the huge sales potential. For example, after Wal-Mart began to upgrade the paint departments in its stores, Fluid Management received more business from Wal-Mart in two months than the firm otherwise received in an entire year. Second, small suppliers can use their contracts with large buyers as a means of getting increased financing or better terms from banks. Third, it may be less costly to sell to large retailers based on their high average sales and the delivery of big orders to a single distribution centre instead of to a number of small stores.[1]

In this chapter, we will study much more about the characteristics and behaviour of organizational consumers such as Wal-Mart. We will also discuss the different types of organizational customers, their buying objectives, buying structure, and purchase constraints.

Overview

As defined in Chapter 4, organizational consumers purchase goods and services for further production, use in operations, or resale to others. In contrast, final consumers buy for personal, family, or household use. Organizational consumers are manufacturers, wholesalers, retailers, and government and other nonprofit institutions. When firms deal with organizational consumers, they engage in **industrial marketing**, as shown in these examples.

Purchasing executives around the world spend trillions of dollars annually for the goods and services their companies require. According to one estimate, "On average, manufacturers shell out 55 cents of each dollar of revenues on goods and services, from raw materials to overnight mail. By contrast, labour seldom exceeds 6 per cent of sales, overhead 3 per cent."[2]

Although purchasing executives at large corporations often deal with major suppliers, in North America over 100 000 small businesses sell goods and services to these big companies. As one purchasing director noted, "We've discovered that smallness just equates with quality. A tiny company just tends to pay more attention. After all, it's risking everything on a small output. Sloppiness can be ruinous." One-third of the largest North American companies use formal programs for seeking out small suppliers. Why then do only a little over 100 000 of the millions of small North American firms sell to big corporations? Many feel there is a "nightmare of paperwork, pre-qualifying inspections, mazes to find the right contact, and the time involved before the contract is signed."[3]

For a long time, Polaroid Corporation earned its reputation (and considerable profits) by making and marketing self-developing cameras for final consumers. But in recent years, due to the popularity of inexpensive 35-mm cameras and the growth of one-hour photo developing labs, Polaroid has reduced its focus on final consumers. Today, Polaroid places greater emphasis on products for organizational consumers, including digital scanners, medical imaging systems, photo ID systems, and security systems.[4] And as Figure 5-1 shows, Polaroid now advertises some of its cameras to such organizational consumers as real-estate brokers.

Bombardier Inc. of Montreal "is an international powerhouse in transportation equipment" and had sales of about $7.9 billion in 1996. Most Canadians think of Bombardier as making snowmobiles and Sea-Doo water craft. However, Bombardier also designs and manufactures mass-transit vehicles, rail cars, and just happens to be the leading executive jet manufacturer in the world. Bombardier owns Canadair, Learjet Inc., Short Brothers PLC and de Havilland Inc. The market for the products of these jet and turboprop manufacturers is small passenger commuter airlines, business jet operators, national heads of state, and a handful of entrepreneurs. In the age of the Internet, which allows executives to communicate online, why is Bombardier expecting to make any sales at all? Because in the increasingly global economy, people will still have to travel on business, especially if it is big

Firms involved with organizational consumers use **industrial marketing**.

POLAROID
www.polaroid.com/

---

[1] Allison Lucas, "Can You Sell to Wal-Mart?" *Sales & Marketing Management* (August 1995), p. 14.

[2] Shawn Tully, "Purchasing's New Muscle," *Fortune* (February 20, 1995), pp. 75–76.

[3] Arthur Bragg, "How to Sell in the Big Time," *Sales & Marketing Management* (February 1990), pp. 42–44; and Michael Selz, "Some Suppliers Rethink Their Reliance on Big Business," *Wall Street Journal* (March 29, 1993), p. B2.

[4] Gary Hoover, Alta Campbell, and Patrick J. Spain, *Hoover's Handbook of American Business 1995* (Austin, Texas: Reference Press, 1994), pp. 880–881.

FIGURE 5-1
At Polaroid: A Heightened Emphasis on Industrial Marketing
As Polaroid's core consumer photography business has stagnated, it has turned to imaginative approaches to industrial marketing.
Reprinted by permission.

GENERAL ELECTRIC
www.ge.com/

business. And big businesses are more likely to need the travelling flexibility and the office in the sky facilities of computers, fax machines and satellite communication links afforded by corporate jets.[5] See Figure 5-2.

Andersen Consulting, a division of Arthur Andersen & Co., has annual revenues of $3.5 billion and nearly 30 000 consultants in about 50 countries. Its specialties are technical consulting—with which it first became involved in 1954 when helping General Electric install its initial computer—and strategic planning. Its Method/1 approach is a widely-used process for teaching clients how to handle any type of computer project in a systematic and cost-efficient manner.[6]

In this chapter, organizational consumers are distinguished from final consumers and an international perspective is provided. The various types of organizational consumers are described. Key factors in organizational consumer behaviour are presented. The organizational consumer's decision process is outlined, and marketing implications are offered.

The Characteristics of Organizational Consumers

Organizational consumers differ from final consumers in several key ways. As shown in Table 5-1, these differences are due to the nature of their purchases and the nature of the market. Organizational consumer characteristics also vary by nation.

---

[5]Daniel Stoffman, "Bombardier's Billion-Dollar Space Race," *Canadian Business* (June 1994) pp. 90–101.
[6]Lee Berton, "Big Six's Shift to Consulting Services," *Wall Street Journal* (September 21, 1995), pp. B1, B4.

FIGURE 5-2
Industrial Marketing for Corporate Jets
Reprinted with permission of Bombardier Aerospace.

Table 5-1

Major Differences Between Organizational and Final Consumers

DIFFERENCES IN PURCHASES

Organizational consumers

1. Buy for further production, use in operations, or resale to others. Final consumers buy only for personal, family, or household use.
2. Commonly purchase installations, raw materials, and semifinished materials. Final consumers rarely purchase these goods.
3. Often buy on the basis of specifications and technical data. Final consumers frequently buy based on description, fashion, and style.
4. Utilize multiple-buying and team-based decisions more often than final consumers.
5. Are more apt to apply formal value and vendor analysis.
6. More commonly lease equipment.
7. More frequently employ competitive bidding and negotiation.

DIFFERENCES IN THE MARKET

Organizational consumers

1. Derive their demand from that of final consumers.
2. Have demand states that are more subject to cyclical fluctuations than final consumer demand.
3. Are fewer in number and more geographically concentrated than final consumers.
4. Often employ buying specialists.
5. Require a shorter distribution channel than do final consumers.
6. May require special relationships with sellers.
7. Are more likely than final consumers to be able to make goods and undertake services as alternatives to purchasing them.

The Nature of Organizational Consumer Purchases

Organizational and final consumers vary in the way they use goods and services and in the items they buy. Organizational consumers purchase capital equipment, raw materials, semifinished goods, and other products for use in further production or operations or for resale to others. Final consumers, by contrast, usually acquire finished items (and are not involved with million-dollar purchases of plant and equipment) for personal, family, or household use. As a result, organizational consumers are more apt to use specifications, multiple-buying decisions, value and vendor analysis, leased equipment, and competitive bidding and negotiation than are final consumers.

Many organizational consumers rely on product specifications in purchase decisions and do not consider alternatives unless they meet minimum standards, such as engineering and architectural guidelines, purity, horsepower, voltage, type of construction, and construction materials. Final consumers more often purchase on the basis of description, style, and colour.

Organizational consumers often use **multiple-buying responsibility**, whereby two or more employees formally participate in complex or expensive purchase decisions. For example, a decision to buy computerized cash registers may involve input from computer personnel, marketing personnel, the operations manager, a systems consultant, and the controller. The firm's president might make the final choice about the system's characteristics and the supplier. Though final consumers use multiple-buying responsibility (joint decision-making), they employ it less frequently and less formally.

A lot of organizational consumers use value analysis and vendor analysis. In **value analysis**, organizational consumers thoroughly compare the costs and benefits of alternative materials, components, designs, or processes so as to reduce the cost/benefit ratio of purchases.[7] They seek to answer such questions as: What is the purpose of each good or service under purchase consideration? What are the short-run and long-run costs of each alternative? Is this purchase necessary? Are there substitute goods or services that could perform more efficiently? How long will a good or service last before it must be replaced? Can uniform standards be set to ease reordering?

In **vendor analysis**, organizational consumers thoroughly assess the strengths and weaknesses of current or new suppliers in terms of quality, customer service, reliability, and price.[8] Satisfaction with current vendors often means customer loyalty. Figures 5-3 and 5-4 illustrate value analysis and vendor analysis.

Multiple-buying responsibility *may be shared by two or more employees.*

Value analysis *reduces costs;* **vendor analysis** *rates suppliers.*

FIGURE 5-3
Value Analysis by a Purchaser of an Electrical Pump

[7]Peter D. Bennett (Ed.), *Dictionary of Marketing Terms*, Second Edition (Chicago: American Marketing Association, 1995), pp. 297–298.
[8]Ibid., p. 299. See also Stephanie Gruner, "The Smart Vendor-Audit Checklist," *Inc.* (April 1995), pp. 93–95.

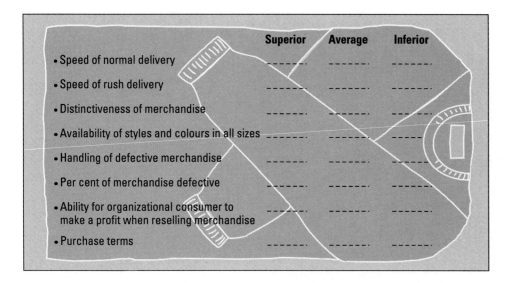

	Superior	Average	Inferior
• Speed of normal delivery	-------	-------	-------
• Speed of rush delivery	-------	-------	-------
• Distinctiveness of merchandise	-------	-------	-------
• Availability of styles and colours in all sizes	-------	-------	-------
• Handling of defective merchandise	-------	-------	-------
• Per cent of merchandise defective	-------	-------	-------
• Ability for organizational consumer to make a profit when reselling merchandise	-------	-------	-------
• Purchase terms	-------	-------	-------

FIGURE 5-4
Vendor Analysis of a Sweater Supplier by a Purchaser

Organizational consumers of all sizes frequently lease major equipment. Each year, Canadian firms spend between $50–60 billion in leasing equipment (measured by the original cost of the equipment). Commonly leased equipment include aircraft, computers, office machinery, and trucks and trailers. The worldwide use of commercial leasing is rising rapidly. Final consumers are less involved with leasing; it is most common in apartment and auto leasing.

Organizational consumers often use competitive bidding and negotiation. In **competitive bidding**, two or more sellers submit independent price quotes for specific goods and/or services to a buyer, who chooses the best offer. In **negotiation**, a buyer uses bargaining ability and order size to get sellers' best possible prices. Bidding and negotiation are mostly used for complex, custom-made goods and services.

In **competitive bidding,** *sellers submit price bids; in* **negotiation,** *the buyer bargains to set prices.*

The Nature of the Organizational Consumer Market

Derived demand occurs for organizational consumers because the quantity of the items they purchase is often based on the anticipated level of demand by their subsequent customers for specific goods and services. For example, the demand for the precision rivets used in cruise ships is derived from the demand for new cruise ships, which ultimately is derived from the demand for cruises. Firms know that unless demand is generated at the end-user level, distribution pipelines become clogged and resellers will not buy fresh goods and services. Organizational consumers' price sensitivity depends on end-user demand. If end users are willing to pay higher prices, organizational consumers will not object to increases. However, if end-user demand is low, organizational consumers will reduce purchases, even if suppliers lower their prices. Figure 5-5 illustrates derived demand for major household appliances.

Organizational consumers **derive demand** *from their own customers. With the* **accelerator principle,** *final consumer demand impacts on many organizational consumers.*

Organizational consumers' demand tends to be more volatile than final consumers'. A small change in the final demand for highly processed goods and services can yield a large change in organizational consumers' demand. This is a due to the **accelerator principle**, whereby final consumer demand affects many layers of organizational consumers. For example, a drop in auto demand by final consumers reduces dealer demand for cars, auto maker demand for steel, and steel maker demand for iron ore. In addition, capital purchases by organizational consumers are highly influenced by the economy.

Organizational consumers are fewer in number than final consumers. In Canada, there are about 35 000 manufacturing establishments, 65 000 wholesaling establishments (including manufacturer-owned facilities), and 206 000 retailing establishments, as compared with 11 million final consumer households. In some industries, large organizational consumers dominate, and their size and importance give them bargaining power in dealing with sellers.

FIGURE 5-5
Derived Demand for Major Appliances

XEROX
www.xerox.com/

Organizational consumers tend to be large and geographically concentrated.

Over the last several years a number of global firms have exercised this bargaining power. For example, Xerox has gone from dealing with 5000 suppliers to 500, Motorola from 10 000 to 3000, Ford from 10 000 to 2300, and Texas Instruments from 22 000 to 14 000. And Allied Signal has gone from buying valves, pipes, and fittings from more than 400 suppliers to just one. This practice has severely affected those dropped, causing some to go out of business and others to invest considerable amounts to upgrade their facilities and products. Furthermore, the suppliers that are kept are expected to meet the highest levels of quality and customer service—while holding prices down.[9]

Organizational consumers tend to be geographically concentrated. For instance, two provinces (Ontario and Quebec) contain 70 per cent of the nation's manufacturing plants. Some industries (such as steel, wood, petroleum, rubber, auto, and tobacco) are even more geographically concentrated.

Because of their size and the types of purchases they make, many organizational consumers use buying specialists. These people often have technical backgrounds and are trained in supplier analysis and negotiating. Their full-time jobs are to purchase goods and services and analyze purchases. Expertise is high.

Inasmuch as many organizational consumers are large and geographically concentrated, purchase complex and custom-made goods and services, and use buying specialists, distribution channels tend to be shorter than those for final consumers. For example, a laser-printer maker would deal directly with a firm buying 100 printers; a salesperson from the manufacturer would call on the firm's purchasing agent. A company marketing printers to final consumers would distribute them through retail stores and expect final consumers to visit those stores.

Organizational consumers may require special relationships. They may expect to be consulted while new products are developed; want extra customer services, such as extended warranties, liberal returns, and free credit; and want close communications with vendors. Systems selling and reciprocity are two specific tactics used in industrial marketing. In **systems selling**, a combination of goods and services is provided to a buyer by one vendor. This gives a buyer one firm with which to negotiate and an assurance of consistency among various parts and components. For example, Hewlett-Packard uses systems selling for its laser printers, personal computers, and servicing.

Systems selling *offers single-source accountability.*

[9]John R. Emshwiller, "Suppliers Struggle to Improve Quality as Big Firms Slash Their Vendor Rolls," *Wall Street Journal* (August 16, 1991), pp. B1–B2; Kathleen Kerwin and Bill Vlasic, "A Shrinking Supply of Suppliers," *Business Week* (January 8, 1996), p. 83; Tully, "Purchasing's New Muscle," p. 79; and *Market Research Handbook 1995*, Statistics Canada (Ottawa: Minister of Industry, Science, and Technology).

Reciprocity is a procedure by which organizational consumers select suppliers that agree to purchase goods and services, as well as sell them. In Canada, the Competition Bureau monitors reciprocity because of its potential lessening of competition. However, in international marketing efforts, sellers may sometimes have to enter into reciprocal agreements (in this case, known as countertrade). For instance, in 1973, because of currency restrictions in the then Soviet Union, PepsiCo began trading soft-drink syrup concentrate for Stolichnaya vodka. Since then, it has exchanged syrup concentrate for more than a million cases of vodka and two Russian-built ships. Its countertrade in today's Russia remains high.[10]

In **reciprocity***, suppliers purchase as well as sell.*

PEPSI
www.pepsi.com/

Finally, organizational consumers may produce goods and services themselves, if they find purchase terms, the way they are treated, or available choices unacceptable. They may sometimes suggest to suppliers that they will make their own goods or perform services as a way of improving their bargaining positions.

An International Perspective

As with final consumers, many dissimilarities exist among organizational consumers around the world, and sellers must understand and respond to them. In this section, several topics are discussed: attitudes toward foreign firms as suppliers, the effects of culture on negotiating styles and decision making, the impact of a nation's stage of economic development, the need for an adaptation strategy, and the opportunities available due to new technology.

Foreign organizational consumers must be carefully studied.

Firms doing business in foreign markets need to know how organizational consumers in those markets perceive the goods and services of firms from different countries. The attitudes of purchasing agents in foreign nations to Canadian products are often quite positive, especially with regard to high-technology items, professional services, raw materials, and industrial machinery. Likewise, many Canadian firms believe the product quality and/or prices for some foreign goods and services are better than those of Canadian suppliers. That is why Bombardier's Canadair subsidiary is having Sextant Avionique of France supply the flight-control systems for its new Global Express Airplane.

National culture has a large impact on the way organizational consumers negotiate and reach decisions. Here is an illustration:

> The Chinese believe that one should build the relationship and, if successful, transactions will follow. Westerners build transactions and, if they are successful, a relationship will follow. This difference underlies many negotiating failures.
>
> In China, negotiating responses may be riddled with contradictions. Westerners will see illogical behaviour, evasion, deviousness perhaps, where none may be intended. Disentangling these communications supplies much of the challenge that is China. The deadline-driven, transcontinental executive may find it hard to slow down to the pace required to share "a loaf of bread, a jug of wine, and Tao," but marketing in China requires the patient building of relationships. Not that China is slow. The pace can simultaneously be fast and slow. Those involved in negotiations know how long they can drag when the Chinese side is consulting internally or has other reasons for delay, and yet how swiftly they move on other occasions.[11]

The stage of economic development in foreign countries affects the types of goods and services purchased by organizational consumers there. Many less-developed and developing nations do not yet have the infrastructure (electricity, roads, transportation systems, skilled workers) to properly use state-of-the-art machinery and equipment. In addition, such machinery and equipment may be too expensive for customers in those markets to afford. On the other hand, there is substantial long-term growth potential in those nations due to the scarcity of industrial goods and services. Firms marketing to less-developed and developing nations need to be patient and flexible in dealing with organizational consumers.

When marketing goods and services to organizational consumers in foreign markets, firms have to consider how much to adapt their strategies to address the unique charac-

---

[10]Nathaniel Gilbert, "The Case for Countertrade," *Across the Board* (May 1992), p. 44. See also Peter W. Liesch, "Government-Mandated Countertrade in Australia," *Industrial Marketing Management*, Vol. 23 (October 1994), pp. 299–305.

[11]Tim Ambler, "Reflections in China: Re-Orienting Images of Marketing," *Marketing Management* (Summer 1995), pp. 24, 25–26.

International Marketing in *Action*

Does Country of Origin Affect Industrial Buyers?

In the past, most country-of-origin studies looked at the impact of where a product was made on industrial buyers' quality perceptions. But a more recent study assessed country-of-origin effects by distinguishing between where a good was designed and where it was assembled. That study investigated the perceptions of members of the Canadian Association of Purchasing Managers.

The study suggests that, in general, products designed and assembled in industrialized countries have higher evaluations than those designed and assembled in developing and less-developed nations. Among seven industrialized nations, Japan, Germany, the United States, and Canada rank highest as countries of origin for design and assembly. France, Italy, and Belgium have lower ratings on these two criteria. South Korea, a rapidly industrializing nation, rates almost as highly as France and Italy as a country of assembly and was slightly higher than Belgium.

Country of design is a more important cue to purchasing managers than country of assembly for all three product categories evaluated: computer systems, fax machines, and ballpoint pens. It appears that purchasing managers perceive a large difference in design and assembly capabilities based on a country's stage of economic development. And this perceived difference is greater in design than assembly capabilities.

Although brand name has a significant impact in terms of perceived quality and perceived value for both computer systems and fax machines, it has much less impact than both country-of-origin cues. Brand name has no impact on the evaluation of ballpoint pens. In summary, according to this study, brand name plays a limited role as a predictor of quality or purchase value.

As a consultant to a South Korean-based maker of electronic components, how would you incorporate the results of this study into your recommended marketing plan?

Source: Based on material in Sadrudin A. Ahmed, Alain d'Astous, and Mostafa El Adraoui, "Country-of-Origin Effects on Purchasing Managers' Product Perceptions," *Industrial Marketing Management*, Vol. 23 (October 1994), pp. 323–332.

---

teristics and needs of those customers. Because large organizational consumers can account for a significant part of any firm's overall revenues, selling firms are often quite willing to be responsive to customers' desires—by employing personnel who fluently speak the language of the foreign markets, utilizing the most appropriate negotiating styles, and adapting product features and customer service as requested. In general, it is more likely that selling firms will engage in meaningful adaptation of their marketing efforts if a potential customer order is big, the good or service being marketed is complex, and the business cultures and stage of economic development in their domestic and foreign markets are dissimilar.

With the new technology now available, there are more opportunities to market to international organizational consumers than ever before. For example, the Internet, e-mail, fax machines, satellite TV, and video conferencing all facilitate buyer-seller communications—and tear down the barriers caused by weak transportation infrastructures, differences in time zones, and the inability for both parties to see each other in regular phone calls. See Figure 5-6.

FIGURE 5-6
All the World's a Stage—for Business
From *Canadian Business* 1996 Performance 500,
p. 176. *Reprinted by permission of ADCOM Inc.*

Types of Organizational Consumers

In devising a marketing plan aimed at organizational consumers, it is necessary to research their attributes: areas of specialization, size and resources, location, and goods and services purchased. As shown in Figure 5-7, organizational consumers can be placed into five broad major categories: manufacturers, wholesalers, retailers, government, and nonprofit.

The Canadian **Standard Industrial Classification (SIC)** for Companies and Enterprises contains information about most organizational consumers. The 1980 Canadian SIC, compiled by Statistics Canada, assigns organizations to eighteen sector classifications: (A) food, beverage, and tobacco; (B) wood and paper; (C) energy; (D) chemicals, chemical products, and textiles; (E) metallic minerals and metal products; (F) machinery and equipment (except electrical machinery); (G) transportation equipment; (H) electrical and electronic products; (I) construction and related activities; (J) transportation services; (K) communications; (L) finance and insurance; (M) general services to business; (N) government services; (O) education, health, and social services; (P) accommodation, restaurants, and recreation services; (Q) food retailing; and (R) consumer goods and services. Within these groups, there are over 1000 more specific industry classifications, such as computer programming and system services, tea and coffee processing, and automobile recyclers. Canadian data by SIC code are available from Statistics Canada, and various provincial government and commercial publications.

With the advent of NAFTA, Canada, Mexico and the United States are cooperating to harmonize the SIC code systems of the three nations into a North American Industrial

The **Standard Industrial Classification (SIC)** *provides information on Canadian and foreign organizational consumers.*

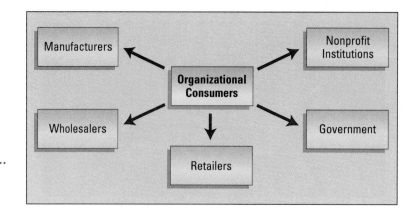

FIGURE 5-7
Types of Organizational Consumers

Classification System (NAICS). Considerable data on industrial activity and companies in other nations are also available in the context of the SIC code. Dun & Bradstreet's yearly *Principal International Businesses* directory lists 50 000 firms in 140 different nations. *Predicasts F&S Index Europe* annually cites articles with industry and company data by nation for Western and Eastern Europe, and Russia and the former Soviet republics. *Dun's Latin America's Top* 25 000 annually provides data on companies in thirty-five countries. The U.S. Department of Commerce's *Global Trade and Economic Outlook* has information on a number of international industries.

*With **end-use analysis**, a seller studies sales made in different industries.*

End-use analysis, by which a seller determines the proportion of sales made to organizational consumers in different industries, is one way in which SIC data can be employed. Table 5-2 shows end-use analysis for a glue manufacturer (in this example, the seller). First, the firm ascertains the current relative importance of various categories of its customers—5-2(A). It then applies end-use analysis to make an overall sales forecast by estimating the expected growth of each customer category in its geographic area—5-2(B).

Next, several characteristics of manufacturers, wholesalers, retailers, government, and nonprofit organizations as consumers are described.

Manufacturers as Consumers

Manufacturers make items for resale to others.*

Manufacturers produce products for resale to other consumers. The *Canadian Standard Industrial Classification Manual* lists twenty-nine major two-digit industry segments that manufacture goods. Each may be divided into three-digit groups and then into four-digit subgroupings. Thus, SIC 16 includes textile products; 162, textile products manufacturing; and 1621, carpets, mats, and rugs manufacturing.

In Canada, 60 per cent of manufacturers have twenty or more workers. The annual costs of their materials are $209 billion. Their expenditures for plant and equipment (from trucks to generator sets) are billions of dollars each year. They annually use billions of BTUs of energy and their annual net sales (including shipments between firms in the same industry category) exceed $330 billion.

By knowing where different industries are located, a firm can concentrate its efforts and not worry about covering geographically dispersed markets. Because manufacturers' purchasing decisions tend to be made centrally at headquarters or at divisional offices, the seller must identify the location of the proper decision makers.

As consumers, manufacturers buy a variety of goods and services, including land, capital equipment, machinery, raw materials, component parts, trade publications, accounting services, supplies, insurance, advertising, and delivery services. For example, Boeing has long- and short-term contracts with suppliers that total $56 billion; and it buys equipment, raw materials, component parts, finished materials, and services from thousands of different subcontractors and other businesses.[12]

[12]Jeff Cole, "Boeing's Bid to Avoid Swings in Business Falls Short of Hopes," *Wall Street Journal* (February 16, 1993), pp. A1, A12.

T a b l e 5 - 2

End-Use Analysis for a Regional Glue Manufacturer

(A) SIMPLE END-USE ANALYSIS

SIC Code	Industry Classification of Customers	Current Total Sales (in Per Cent)[a]
07	Wood and wood products	25
08	Wood and paper products	13
15	Plastic and rubber	15
55	Printing and publishing	17
85	Apparel	10
86	Household furniture and other consumer goods	20
	Total	100

(B) APPLYING END-USE ANALYSIS TO SALES FORECASTING

SIC Code	Industry Classification of Customers	Per Cent of Current Total Sales	Estimated Annual Percentage Growth Rate of Industry[b]	Overall Sales Growth Percentage for Glue Manufacturer[c]
07	Wood and wood products	25	+1.8	+0.45
08	Wood and paper products	13	+2.0	+0.26
15	Plastic and rubber	15	+3.0	+0.45
55	Printing and publishing	17	+1.9	+0.32
85	Apparel	10	-2.0	-0.20
86	Household furniture and other consumer goods	20	+3.2	+0.64
	Total estimated sales increase			+1.92

[a] Firm examines its sales receipts and categorizes them by SIC group.

[b] Firm estimates growth rate of each category of customer (in its geographic area) on the basis of trade-association and government data.

[c] Firm multiplies per cent of current sales in each SIC group by expected growth rate in each industry to derive its own expected sales for the coming year. It expects sales to increase by 1.92 per cent during the next year.

Wholesalers as Consumers

Wholesalers buy or handle merchandise and its subsequent resale to organizational users, retailers, and other wholesalers. They do not sell significant volume to final users but are involved when services are marketed to organizational consumers. Chapter 10 has a broad discussion of wholesaling.

Canadian wholesalers are most prominent in Ontario and Quebec. Annual wholesaling and related sales (excluding manufacturer wholesaling) exceed $248 billion. Sales are largest for food products ($44 billion); coal and petroleum products ($32 billion); motor vehicles and accessories ($22.8 billion); machinery and equipment ($21 billion); electrical machinery ($19.4 billion); lumber and building materials ($17.4 billion); and farm products ($14.8 billion).

As consumers, wholesalers buy or handle many goods and services, including warehouse facilities, trucks, finished products, insurance, refrigeration and other equipment, trade publications, accounting services, supplies, and spare parts. A major task in dealing with wholesalers is getting them to carry the selling firm's product line for further resale, thereby placing items into the distribution system. For new sellers or those with new products, gaining cooperation may be difficult. Even well-established manufacturers may have

Wholesalers *buy or handle merchandise and its resale to nonfinal consumers.*

problems with their wholesalers because of the competitive nature of the marketplace, wholesalers' perceptions that they are not being serviced properly, or wholesalers' lack of faith in the manufacturers' products.

Retailers as Consumers

Retailers *sell to the final consumer.*

Retailers buy or handle goods and services for sale (resale) to the final (ultimate) consumer. They usually obtain goods and services from both manufacturers and wholesalers. Chapter 10 has a broad discussion of retailing.

Annual Canadian retail sales exceed $200 billion. Chains operate about 20 per cent of all retail stores, accounting for about 40 per cent of total retail sales. A large amount of retailing involves auto dealers, food stores, general merchandise stores, eating and drinking places, gas stations, furniture and home furnishings stores, and apparel stores.

As consumers, retailers buy or handle a variety of goods and services, including store locations, facilities, interior design, advertising, resale items, insurance, and trucks. Unlike wholesalers, they are usually concerned about both product resale and the composition of their physical facilities (stores). This is because final consumers usually shop at stores, whereas wholesalers frequently call on customers. Thus, retailers often buy fixtures, displays, and services to decorate and redecorate stores.

Getting retailers to stock new items or continue handling current ones can be difficult because store and catalogue space is limited and retailers have their own goals. Many retail chains have evolved into large and powerful customers, not just "shelf stockers." Some are so powerful that they may even charge *slotting fees* just to carry manufacturers' products in their stores. For instance:

> Nowadays, most supermarket-savvy manufacturers chalk them up as a cost of doing business. But if fees for shelf-space had been around in the 1980s, products like granola, herbal tea, and yogurt might never have made it into stores and kitchens. These so-called slotting fees [charged by retailers for providing shelf-space] can often exceed $40 000 per retail chain per item, which adds up to millions of dollars for national distribution.[13]

Retailers (and wholesalers) sometimes insist that suppliers make items under the retailers' (or wholesalers') names. For private-label manufacturers, the continued orders of these customers are essential. If a large retailer or wholesaler stops doing business with a private-label manufacturer, then that firm has to establish its own identity with consumers—and it may even go out of business due to its lack of marketplace recognition.

Government as Consumer

Government *purchases and uses a variety of routine and complex products.*

Government consumes goods and services in performing its duties and responsibilities. Federal (1), provincial (10), territorial (2), and municipal (6006) units together account for the greatest volume of purchases of any consumer group in Canada with total expenditures of $153 billion on goods and services each year. The federal government accounts for 22 per cent of this, the provincial governments for 33 per cent and the territorial and local governments for the remaining 45 per cent. The biggest budget shares (including employee wages) go for operations, capital outlays, military services, postal services, education, highways, public welfare, health care, police, fire protection, sanitation, and natural resources.[14]

Governmental consumers buy a wide range of goods and services, including food, military equipment, office buildings, subway cars, office supplies, clothing, and vehicles. Some purchases involve standard products offered to traditional consumers; others, such as highways, are specially made for a government customer. Bombardier is one of the large Canadian firms that has its own marketing specialists dedicated to making government sales.

---

[13]Bernice Kanner, "Shelf Control," *New York* (January 22, 1990), p. 22.

[14]Statistics Canada, *Market Research Handbook 1995* (Ottawa: Minister of Industry Science and Technology); and Statistics Canada, *1991 Census Dictionary* (Ottawa: Minister of Industry Science and Technology), Catalogue 92-301E; and Statistics Canada, *Canadian Standard Industrial Classification For Companies And Enterprises 1980* (Ottawa: Minister of Supply and Services Canada, 1986).

Some firms are unaccustomed to the bureaucracy, barriers, political sensitivities, and financial constraints of selling to government consumers. To aid them, the federal government publishes the *Weekly Bulletin of Business Opportunities*, which contains opportunities for businesses to sell to government. As noted earlier, the major government organization in Canada that undertakes buying is the federal agency, Supply and Services Canada. Each government unit (federal, provincial, and municipal) and division typically has a purchasing department. Every one of these purchasing departments will gladly divulge their procurement policies to anyone who wishes to supply goods and services.

The size of the government market in Canada is further enlarged by the fact that the federal, provincial, and local governments own some of the nation's largest corporations. There are 48 federal crown corporations with assets of over $57 billion. In fact, thirty-seven of the top 500 Canadian corporations are government owned. These thirty-seven corporations had combined sales of $58 billion in 1996, and combined net income of $15.5 billion. Referred to as "Crown" corporations, some of these companies include: Petro-Canada, Canadian Mortagage and Housing Corp., Export Development Corp., Royal Canadian Mint, Canada Post, Canadian Broadcasting Corporation, Canadian Commercial Corporation, Atomic Energy of Canada Ltd., (all owned by the federal government), Ontario Hydro, Ontario Lottery Corporation, Liquor Control Board of Ontario (all owned by the province of Ontario), and Hydro-Québec.[15]

CBC
www.cbc.ca/

The buying behaviour of these corporations is very much like that of privately owned corporations; however, large contracts are awarded in a fashion very similar to government bid purchasing. Further, political considerations affect the decision-making behaviour of these organizations more often than for privately owned corporations.

Nonprofit Institutions as Consumers

Nonprofit institutions act in the public interest or to foster a cause, and do not seek financial profits. Hospitals, charitable organizations, museums, universities, political parties, civic organizations, and parks are nonprofit institutions. They buy goods and services in order to run their organizations and also buy items for resale to generate additional revenues to off-set costs.

Nonprofit institutions function in the public interest.

There are many national and international nonprofit institutions, such as the Canadian Cancer Society; the Liberal, Progressive Conservative, New Democratic, Bloc Québécois and Reform parties; the Boy Scouts and Girl Guides; chambers of commerce; and the Red Cross. Hospitals, museums, and universities, due to fixed sites, tend to be local nonprofit institutions.

Key Factors in Organizational Consumer Behaviour

Organizational consumer behaviour depends on buying objectives, buying structure, and purchase constraints.

Buying Objectives

Organizational consumers have several distinct goals in purchasing goods and services. Generally, these organizational buying objectives are important: availability of items, reliability of sellers, consistency of quality, delivery, price, and customer service. See Figure 5-8.

Organizational buying objectives relate to availability, reliability, consistency, delivery, price, and service.

Availability means a buyer can obtain items when needed. An organizational consumer's production or resales may be inhibited if products are unavailable at the proper times. Seller reliability is based on its fairness in allotting items in high demand, nonadversarial relationships, honesty in reporting bills and shipping orders, and reputation. Consistency of quality refers to buyers' interest in purchasing items of appropriate quality on a regular basis. For example, drill bits should have the same degree of hardness each

[15]"Performance 500," *Canadian Business* (June 1997), pp. 150–175.

FIGURE 5-8
Goals of Organizational Consumers

time they are bought. Delivery goals include minimizing the length of time from order placement to the receipt of items, minimizing the order size required by the supplier, having the seller responsible for shipments, minimizing costs, and adhering to an agreed-on schedule. Price considerations involve purchase prices and the flexibility of payment terms. Customer service entails the seller's ability or willingness to satisfy special requests, to have staff ready to field questions when needed, to promptly address problems, and to have an ongoing dialogue with customers.

Industrial marketers must recognize that price is only one of several considerations for organizational consumers; and it may be lower in importance than availability, quality, service, and other factors:

> Cutting purchasing costs has surprisingly little to do with browbeating suppliers. Purchasers at companies like Moore Business forms and Chrysler aim to reduce the total cost—not just the price—of each part or service they buy. They form enduring partnerships with suppliers that let them chip away at key costs year after year. Purchasing companies are also packing once-fragmented purchases of goods and services into companywide contracts for each.[16]

With regard to more specific goals, manufacturers are concerned about quality standards for raw materials, component parts, and equipment. Some like dealing with many suppliers to protect against shortages, foster price and service competition, and be exposed to new products. Others have been reducing the number of suppliers from which they buy, to foster better relationships, cut ordering inefficiencies, and have more clout with each supplier.[17]

Salability and exclusivity are keys for wholesalers and retailers.

Wholesalers and retailers consider further salability (their customers' demand) to be the highest priority. If possible, they seek buying arrangements whereby the number of distribution intermediaries that can carry goods and services in a geographic area is limited. They also seek manufacturers' advertising, transportation, and warehousing support.

Government consumers frequently set exact specifications for some products they buy; as large-volume buyers, they can secure them. Government consumers may sometimes consider the economic conditions in the geographic areas of potential sellers. Contracts may be awarded to the firms with the higher unemployment in their surrounding communities.

Nonprofit consumers stress price, availability, and reliability. They may seek special terms in recognition of their nonprofit status.

Buying Structure

The organization's buying structure depends on its attributes.

The buying structure of an organization refers to the formality and specialization used in the purchase process. It depends on the organization's size, resources, diversity, and format.

---

[16]Tully, "Purchasing's New Muscle," p. 76; Shona McKay, "A Paper Tiger in the Paperless World," *Canadian Business* (April 1996), pp. 25–29.
[17]See Cathy Owens Swift, "Preferences for Single Sourcing and Supplier Selection Criteria," *Journal of Business Research*, Vol. 32 (February 1995), pp. 105–111.

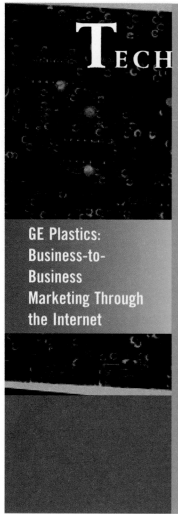

TECHNOLOGY & MARKETING

GE Plastics: Business-to-Business Marketing Through the Internet

One of the key uses of the Internet is for customer support. Because a firm can use the Internet to communicate with thousands (millions) of current and potential users of a product with a small customer support staff, it is a very cost-effective way of disseminating product information to customers.

GE Plastics is ideally suited to the Internet since almost all of its customers have PCs with modems. Although the firm will not divulge the costs in setting up its Internet site, one analyst estimated them at up to $150 000.

GE Plastics was the first *Fortune 500* firm to use the Internet in a major marketing effort. Its Internet site provides its engineer, designer, and scientist customers with instant access to crucial product and technical information, design guidelines, and graphics. Customers can also communicate and exchange ideas within five newsgroup forums (automotive, building and construction, computers, design, and plastics) that collect information from a variety of sources. This information is updated on a weekly basis.

GE Plastics went online in October 1994. It first had to digitize roughly 1500 pages of technical literature. An additional challenge it faced was that Internet standards at the time did not allow for a variety of page layouts. So, it had to find other ways of making documents look good. GE Plastics also hired a software developer to simplify the commands relating to accessing, searching, retrieving, and saving data on the Internet. According to the software developer, "The steps GE took to ease user access to the Internet are highly unusual. Most of the businesses establishing a presence on the Internet leave it up to users to find their own way."

As the customer support manager for GE Plastics, develop specific criteria to evaluate the success of the firm's Internet site.

Source: Based on material in Thayer C. Taylor, "Marketing: The New Generation," *Sales & Marketing Management* (February 1995), pp. 43–44.

The structure is apt to be formal (i.e., separate department) for a large, corporate, resourceful, diversified, and departmentalized organization. It will be less formal for a small, independently owned, financially limited, focused, and non-departmentalized organization.

Large manufacturers normally have specialized purchasing agents who work with the firms' engineers or production department. Large wholesalers tend to have a single purchasing department or a general manager in charge of operations. Large retailers tend to be quite specialized and have buyers for each narrow product category. Small manufacturers, wholesalers, and retailers often have their buying functions completed by the owner-operator.

As mentioned previously, each government unit (federal, provincial, and municipal) and division typically has a purchasing department. Supply and Services Canada is the federal office responsible for centralized procurement and coordination of purchases. In a nonprofit organization, there is usually one purchasing department, or a member of the operations staff performs buying functions.

Constraints on Purchases

For manufacturers, wholesalers, and retailers, derived demand is the major constraint on purchase behaviour. Without the demand of consumers, production halts and sales drop as the backward chain of demand comes into play (final consumers → retailers → wholesalers → manufacturers).

Manufacturers also are constrained by the availability of raw materials and their ability to pay for large-ticket items. Wholesalers and retailers are limited by the finances avail-

Derived demand is the key constraint on organizational purchases.

able to make purchases, as well as by the level of risk they are willing to take. In this case, risk refers to the probability that wholesalers or retailers will be able to sell the products they buy in a reasonable time and at a satisfactory profit. Products like fashion clothing have higher risks than such staple items as vitamins and disposable diapers.

Government consumers are constrained by the budgeting process. Approval for categories of purchases must normally be secured well in advance, and deviations must be explained. Budgets must be certified by legislative bodies. For many nonprofit consumers, cash flow (the timing of the money they have coming in versus the money they spend) is the major concern.

The Organizational Consumer's Decision Process

*An **organizational consumer's decision process** is like a final consumer's.*

Organizational consumers use a decision-making procedure in much the same way as final consumers. Figure 5-9 shows the **organizational consumer's decision process**, with its four components: expectations, buying process, conflict resolution, and situational factors.[18]

Expectations

Expectations are based on buyers' backgrounds, information, perceptions, and experience.

Purchasing agents, engineers, and users bring a set of organizational consumer expectations to any buying situation: "These expectations refer to the perceived potential of alternative suppliers and brands to satisfy a number of explicit and implicit objectives."[19]

For purchases to be made, buyers must have positive expectations of such supplier attributes as product availability and quality, vendor reliability, delivery time, price, and customer service. Expectations are based on the backgrounds of those participating in the buying process, the information received, perceptions, and satisfaction with past purchases.

Buying Process

Autonomous or joint decision making is based on product and company buying factors.

During the buying process, a decision as to whether to consider making a purchase is initiated, information gathered, alternative suppliers evaluated, and conflicts among the dif-

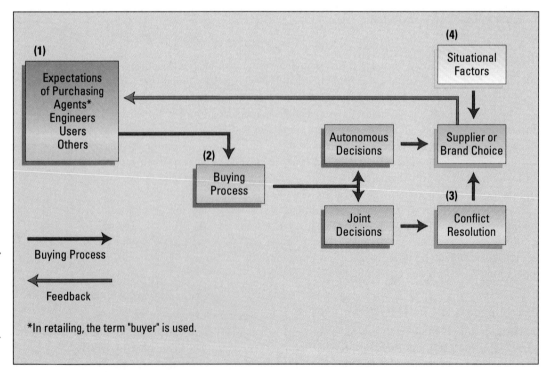

FIGURE 5-9
The Organizational Consumer's Decision Process

Source: Adapted from Jagdish N. Sheth, "A Model of Industrial Buyer Behaviour," *Journal of Marketing*, Vol. 37 (October 1973), pp. 50–56.

---

[18]The material in this section is drawn from Jagdish N. Sheth, "A Model of Industrial Buyer Behaviour," *Journal of Marketing*, Vol. 37 (October 1973), pp. 50–56.

[19]Ibid., p. 52.

ferent representatives of the buyer resolved. The process itself is similar to the final consumer buying process in Figure 4-7.

The buying process may involve autonomous (independent) or joint decisions based on product-specific and company-specific factors. *Product-specific buying factors* include perceived risk, purchase frequency, and time pressure. Autonomous decisions most often occur with low perceived risk, routine products, and high time pressure. Joint ones are more apt to be undertaken when dealing with high perceived risk, seldom-bought products, and low time pressure. *Company-specific buying factors* are an organization's basic orientation, size, and level of decision-making centralization. Autonomous decisions most often occur when the buyer has a high technology or production orientation, is small, or is highly centralized. Joint ones are more likely with a low technology or production orientation, large organization, and little centralization in decision making.

As noted earlier in the chapter, competitive bidding is often used with organizational consumers: Potential sellers specify in writing all terms and conditions of a purchase in addition to the product attributes they offer; the buyer then selects the best bid. With *open bidding*, proposals can be seen by competing sellers. With *closed bidding*, contract terms are kept secret and sellers are asked to make their best presentation in their first bids. Bidding is used in government purchases to avoid charges of bias or unfair negotiations, and bids for government purchases tend to be closed.

Conflict Resolution

Joint decision making may lead to conflicts due to the diverse backgrounds and perspectives of purchasing agents, engineers, and users. **Conflict resolution** is then needed to make a decision. Four methods of resolution are possible: problem solving, persuasion, bargaining, and politicking.

Problem solving occurs when members of a purchasing team decide to acquire further information before making a decision. This is the best procedure. Persuasion takes place when each member of a team presents his or her reasons why a particular supplier or brand should be selected. In theory, the most logical presentation should be chosen. However, the most dynamic (or powerful) person may persuade others to follow his or her lead.

Under bargaining, team members agree to support each other in different situations, with less attention paid to the merits of a purchase. One member may select the supplier of the current item; in return, another member would choose a vendor the next time. The last, and least desired, method of conflict resolution is politicking. With it, team members try to persuade outside parties and superiors to back their positions, and seek to win at power plays.

Problem solving, persuasion, bargaining, and politicking lead to **conflict resolution**.

Situational Factors

A number of **situational factors** can interrupt the decision process and the actual selection of a supplier or brand. These include "temporary economic conditions such as price controls, recession, or foreign trade; internal strikes, walkouts, machine breakdowns, and other production-related events; organizational changes such as merger or acquisition; and *ad hoc* changes in the marketplace, such as promotional efforts, new-product introduction, price changes, and so on, in the supplier industries."[20]

Situational factors *affect organizational consumer decisions.*

Purchase and Feedback

After the decision process is completed and situational factors are taken into account, a purchase is made (or the process terminated) and a product is used or experienced. The level of satisfaction with a purchase is then fed back to a purchasing agent or team, and the data are stored for future use.

To maintain customer satisfaction and ensure continued purchases, regular service and follow-up calls by sellers are essential. As one study concluded: "Industrial salespeople today are generally younger, better educated, and more professional in their handling of

[20]Ibid., p. 56.

business activities than in the past. That higher level of education is something that both purchasers and sales professionals benefit from. Both sides appear to be more sensitive to the other's responsibilities. Among purchasers and suppliers interested in developing partnerships, it's not unusual to see sales professionals attending purchasing courses, purchasing agents attending sales courses, and even purchasers and suppliers attending seminars together."[21]

Types of Purchases

Organizational buyers use a new-task process for unique items, modified rebuys for infrequent purchases, and straight rebuys for regular purchases.

A **new-task purchase process** is needed for expensive products an organizational consumer has not bought before. A lot of decision making is undertaken, and perceived risk is high. This is similar to extended decision making for a final consumer. A **modified-rebuy purchase process** is employed for medium-priced products an organizational consumer has bought infrequently before. Moderate decision making is needed. This type of purchase is similar to limited decision making for a final consumer. A **straight-rebuy purchase process** is used for inexpensive items bought regularly. Reordering, not decision making, is applied because perceived risk is very low. This process is like a routine purchase for a final consumer.

Research on the Organizational Consumer's Decision Process

Throughout the world, the organizational consumer's decision process has been heavily researched. Here is a sampling of the findings:

- There are significant differences in the way that decisions are made by Russian purchasing managers who are 40 years of age or less and those who are over 40. The younger managers see entrepreneurs, flexibility, and autonomy rising; their older counterparts do not.[22]

- Nigerian purchasers of capital equipment rely mostly on salesperson visits and manufacturers' catalogues for information; joint decision making is used during all stages of the decision process; and dissatisfaction with existing suppliers is a key reason a detailed decision process is triggered.[23]

- Some Eastern European purchasing agents, due to their lack of experience in a free-market economy, are having a tough time adjusting to situations in which they have more autonomy and a greater voice in decisions.[24]

Marketing Implications

There are many similarities, as well as differences, between organizational and final consumers.

Although organizational and final consumers have substantial differences (as mentioned earlier), they also have similarities. Both can be described demographically; statistical and descriptive data can be gathered and analyzed. Both have different categories of buyers, each with separate needs and requirements. Both can be defined by using social and psychological factors, such as operating style, buying structure, purchase use, expectations, perceived risk, and conflict resolution. Both use a decision process, employ joint decision making, and face various kinds of purchase situations.

Industrial marketers must develop plans that reflect the similarities, as well as the differences, between organizational and final consumers. In their roles as sellers, manufacturers and wholesalers may also need two marketing plans—one for intermediate buyers and another for final consumers.

---

[21]Derrick C. Schnebelt, "Turning the Tables," *Sales & Marketing Management* (January 1993), p. 23.

[22]John F. Veiga and John N. Yanouzas, "Emerging Cultural Values Among Russian Managers: What Will Tomorrow Bring?" *Business Horizons*, Vol. 38 (July–August 1995), pp. 20–27.

[23]E. D. Bamgboye, "Equipment Buying in Nigeria," *Industrial Marketing Management*, Vol. 21 (August 1992), pp. 181–185.

[24]Johan Roos, Ellen Veie, and Lawrence S. Welch, "A Case Study of Equipment Purchasing in Czechoslovakia," *Industrial Marketing Management*, Vol. 21 (August 1922), pp. 257–263; and Dale A. Lunsford and Bradley C. Fussell, "Marketing Business Services in Central Europe," *Journal of Services Marketing*, Vol. 7 (Number 1, 1993), pp. 13–21.

Ethics AND TODAY'S MARKETER

Is Environmental Impact an Issue for Purchasing Agents?

How important is social responsibility—a concern for the environmental impact associated with an industrial good or service—to purchasing managers? According to one study, organizations can be placed into four categories:

- *Type I (Founder's Ideals)*—Social responsibility is an extension of the founder's ideals and values. A social mission for such firms is clearly articulated. This mission often acts as a second "bottom line" by which the firm would be evaluated. For example, "What we're trying to do is to suspend the standard rules in purchasing, which are to get the job done as quickly as possible and as cheaply as possible."
- *Type II (Symbolism)*—Socially responsible buying is indirectly tied to company success. Firms in this group want to discourage further government regulation. For example, "Now that we buy socially responsible products, people perceive us as green. This is important in getting the company name to where we want it to be."
- *Type III (Opportune)*—Socially responsible purchasing is seen as a way to lower costs or to increase sales. In one such firm, the purchase of a socially responsible product reduced costs by 70 per cent. Thus, "We do not buy socially irresponsible products, but it isn't as you say for a moral reason. It's for hassle avoidance more than anything else."
- *Type IV (Restraint)*—There is no deliberate plan as to socially responsible purchasing. And there are negligible "bottom-line" benefits to buying socially responsible products. For example, "If a supplier that we've worked with for twenty years before all the environmental concerns came up didn't share our views, it was hard. I feel much more like an extension of the supplier."

As a product manager for recycled paper, how would you use the preceding typology in marketing to book publishers?

Source: Based on material in Minette E. Drumwight, "Socially Responsible Organizational Buying: Environmental Concern as a Noneconomic Buying Criterion," *Journal of Marketing*, Vol. 58 (July 1994), pp. 1–9.

Finally, it must be recognized that purchasing agents or buyers have personal goals, as well as organizational goals. They seek status, approval, promotions, bonuses, and other rewards. And as noted in Figure 5-9, they bring distinct expectations to each buying situation, just as final consumers do.

One leading consultant offers these suggestions for industrial marketers:

- Understand how your customers run their business.
- Show how your good or service fits into your customer's business.
- Make sure the benefits you sell stay current.
- Know how customers buy and fit your selling to their buying process.
- When selling, reach everyone on the customer's side involved in the buying decision.
- Communicate to each decider the message that will address his or her chief concerns.
- Be the person or firm with whom your customers prefer to have a relationship.

Industrial marketing strategies should be insightful.

- Be sure everything you do is consistent with your chosen level of quality, service, price, and performance.

- Understand your competitors' strengths and weaknesses.

- Strive to dominate your niche.

- Train your people in each aspect of your business and your customers'.

- Have a distribution system that meets your needs and your customers'.

- Seek new markets and new applications for your existing products.

- Enhance your products with customer service.

- Have your goals clearly in mind.[25]

MARKETING IN A CHANGING WORLD

The Quest for Purchasing Partnerships[26]

In an era when so many purchasing companies are cutting down on the number of suppliers from which they will buy, industrial marketers must be sure they have a strong appreciation of what makes good "purchasing partnerships"—and they must do so from the buyer's point of view.

Purchasing partnerships are "informal or formal agreements between sellers and buyers, in which buyers receive quality products per customer requirements and sellers become primary suppliers. Through such arrangements, partners are able to plan requirements on a mutually beneficial time schedule with mutually satisfactory pricing."

According to a recent study, organizational consumers want to achieve these specific benefits (in the order listed) from purchasing partnerships: better communication, better prices, better quality products, better delivery schedules, development of trust with suppliers, and better forecasting and planning. With regard to communication, organizational consumers expect that purchasing partnerships will result in "more attention" and vendors who "know our business."

Here's what two study participants remarked:

In business, a relationship is worth a great deal. It is invaluable because the companies can grow together, share information for good planning, and stabilize the pricing environment. We then enter a trust relationship.

Suppliers with ongoing partnerships feel more secure about future business. Consequently, they don't build in contingency costs, and this reduces the cost of our materials. A good working relationship allows for better parts design, standardization, and packaging.

To measure their suppliers' performance, organizational consumers review the quality of the products; on-time delivery; competitive pricing; personnel responsiveness; how well needs, technology, and design are understood; and the ability to resolve problems.

---

[25]F. Michael Hruby, "Seventeen Tips (Not Just) for Industrial Marketers," *Sales & Marketing Management* (May 1990), pp. 68–76.

[26]The material in this section is based on Eugene H. Fram, "Purchasing Partnerships: The Buyer's View," *Marketing Management* (Summer 1995), pp. 49–55.

SUMMARY

1. *To introduce the concept of industrial marketing* When firms market goods and services to manufacturers, wholesalers, retailers, and government and other nonprofit institutions, industrial marketing is used.

2. *To differentiate between organizational consumers and final consumers and look at organizational consumers from an international perspective* Organizational consumers buy goods and services for further production, use in operations, or resale to others; they buy installations, raw materials, and semifinished materials. They often buy on the basis of specifications, use joint decision making, apply formal value and vendor analysis, lease equipment, and use bidding and negotiation. Their demand is generally derived from that of their consumers and can be cyclical. They are fewer in number and more geographically concentrated. They may employ buying specialists, expect sellers to visit them, require special relationships, and make goods and undertake services rather than buy them.

There are distinctions among organizational consumers around the globe.

3. *To describe the different types of organizational consumers and their buying objectives, buying structure, and purchase constraints* Organizational consumers may be classified by area of specialization, size and resources, location, and goods and services purchased. The major types of organizational consumers are manufacturers, wholesalers, retailers, government, and nonprofit organizations. The SIC system provides information on organizational consumers in Canada and the rest of the world.

These consumers have general buying goals, such as product availability, seller reliability, consistent quality, prompt delivery, good prices, and superior customer service.

They may also have more specific goals, depending on the type of firm involved. An organization's buying structure refers to its level of formality and specialization in the purchase process. Derived demand, availability, further salability, and resources are the leading purchase constraints.

4. *To explain the organizational consumer's decision process* The process involves buyer expectations, the buying process, conflict resolution, and situational factors. Of prime importance is whether an organization uses joint decision making and, if so, how. Some form of bidding may be used with organizational consumers (most often with government).

If conflicts arise in joint decisions, firms may use problem solving, persuasion, bargaining, or politicking to arrive at a resolution. Situational factors can intervene between a decision to buy and an actual purchase. Such factors include strikes, economic conditions, and organizational changes.

New task, modified rebuy, and straight rebuy are the different purchase situations facing organizational consumers.

5. *To consider the marketing implications of appealing to organizational consumers* Organizational consumers and final consumers have many similarities and differences. Industrial marketers must understand them and adapt marketing plans accordingly. Dual marketing campaigns may be necessary for manufacturers and wholesalers that sell to intermediate buyers and have their products resold to final consumers.

Purchasing agents and buyers have personal goals, such as status, promotions, and bonuses; these may have a large impact on decision making.

KEY TERMS

industrial marketing (p. 109)
multiple-buying responsibility (p. 112)
value analysis (p. 112)
vendor analysis (p. 112)
competitive bidding (p. 113)
negotiation (p. 113)
derived demand (p. 113)
accelerator principle (p. 113)

systems selling (p. 114)
reciprocity (p. 115)
Standard Industrial Classification (SIC) (p. 117)
end-use analysis (p. 118)
manufacturers (p. 118)
wholesalers (p. 119)
retailers (p. 120)
government (p. 120)

nonprofit institutions (p. 121)
organizational consumer's decision process (p. 124)
conflict resolution (p. 125)
situational factors (p. 125)
new-task purchase process (p. 126)
modified-rebuy purchase process (p. 126)
straight-rebuy purchase process (p. 126)

Review Questions

1. Describe five of the most important differences between organizational and final consumers.
2. Distinguish between vendor analysis and value analysis.
3. What is the relationship between derived demand and the accelerator principle?
4. How is the Standard Industrial Classification a useful marketing tool?
5. What are the most important general organizational consumer buying objectives?
6. For manufacturers, wholesalers, and retailers, what is the major constraint on their purchase behaviour? Why?
7. On what basis are organizational consumer expectations formed?
8. How do product-specific and company-specific buying factors affect the use of autonomous or joint decision making?
9. Which is the worst form of conflict resolution? The best? Explain your answers.
10. Cite several suggestions that industrial marketers should keep in mind when developing and enacting their strategies.

Discussion Questions

1. As a university's purchasing agent, what would you have to do to get useful competitive bids from suppliers of new dormitory furniture?
2. As a chemical manufacturer's liaison to China, how would you handle the cultural relationships that would be necessary to win over prospective Chinese business clients?
3. A packaging firm knows its current sales are allocated as follows: 15 per cent to wine manufacturers (SIC code 0223), 20 per cent to sugar and chocolate confectionery manufacturing (SIC code 0173), 30 per cent to soft drink manufacturers (SIC code 0211), 25 per cent to tea and coffee processors (SIC code 0174), and 10 per cent to fish and other seafood processing (SIC code 0112). The firm expects next year's industry sales growth in these categories to rise as follows: wine manufacturing, 5 per cent; sugar and chocolate confectionery manufacturing, 2 per cent; soft drinks, 3 per cent; tea and coffee, 0 per cent; and seafood processing, –5 per cent. According to end-use analysis, by how much should the packaging firm's sales increase next year? Explain your answer.
4. Describe a floral arranger's decision process in choosing a transportation firm to use to ship its products to retailers. Does this process entail a new task, modified rebuy, or straight rebuy? Explain your answer.
5. "It must be understood that organizational purchasing agents or buyers have personal as well as company goals." Comment on this statement.

CHAPTER 6

Developing a Target Market Strategy

Chapter Objectives

1. To describe the process of planning a target market strategy

2. To examine alternative demand patterns and segmentation bases for both final and organizational consumers

3. To explain and contrast undifferentiated marketing (mass marketing), concentrated marketing, and differentiated marketing (multiple segmentation)

4. To show the importance of positioning in developing a marketing strategy

5. To discuss sales forecasting and its role in target marketing

{ *"As the world becomes closer due to technological advances in transportation and telecommunications, and with multinational companies expanding worldwide, increasingly there is a great interest in whether individuals in different parts of the world are more alike than different,"* says Thomas A. W. Miller, senior vice-president of Roper Starch Worldwide. }

Reprinted by permission.

Roper Starch Worldwide (a marketing research firm) recently conducted a series of studies on global trends. In all, it surveyed nearly 40 000 adults. According to this research, four major shopping styles of consumers are found throughout the world: deal makers, price seekers, brand loyalists, and luxury innovators. And the shopping styles of consumers are heavily influenced by where they live.

Let's look at these four consumer segments and their characteristics.

- *Deal makers*—They enjoy the buying process. This is an educated group, with a median age of 32 years and average affluence and employment. Deal makers make up 29 per cent of all consumers.

- *Price seekers*—They place major emphasis on the product. This group has the highest per cent of retirees, the lowest education level, and an average level of affluence. Price seekers constitute 27 per cent of all consumers.

- *Brand loyalists*—They agree that a brand gives good value for the money. This is the least affluent group and is mostly male. Brand loyalists have a median age of 36 and hold average education and employment. They make up 23 per cent of all consumers.

- *Luxury innovators*—They seek brands that are prestigious and new. This is the most affluent and educated group, with the highest proportion of executives and other professionals. Luxury innovators are mostly male and have a median age of 32. They constitute 21 per cent of all consumers.

The above segment percentages are global figures that vary greatly by country. For example, in Mexico, 35 per cent of consumers are deal makers, 23 per cent are price seekers, 20 per cent are luxury innovators, and 19 per cent are brand loyalists. In the United States, 37 per cent of consumers are deal makers, 36 per cent are price seekers, 17 per cent are luxury innovators, and 11 per cent are brand loyalists. In Saudi Arabia, 40 per cent of consumers are deal makers, 34 per cent are luxury innovators, 15 per cent are brand loyalists, and 9 per cent are price seekers. In the Czech Republic, 27 per cent of consumers are price seekers, 26 per cent are luxury innovators, 24 per cent are brand loyalists, and 23 per cent are deal makers. As Thomas Miller notes:

> Price seekers exist more in competitive, developed markets, where shoppers generally cannot haggle or negotiate. Deal makers are more often in developing markets that have less brand competition and a tradition of open-air markets, where the process is half the fun. America straddles the two styles because of our more heterogeneous culture and also because shoppers can bargain at many retail outlets and even large category-killer stores.[1]

In this chapter, we will examine each step involved in planning a target market strategy and the related topic of sales forecasting. Lifestyle segmentation is only one of the ways in which a company may appeal to a target market.

Overview

After gathering data on consumer traits, desires, and decision making; company and industry attributes; and environmental factors, a firm is ready to select the target market(s) to

[1]Kelly Shermach, "Portrait of the World," *Marketing News* (August 28, 1995), pp. 20–21; and Leah Rickard, "Ex-Soviet States Lead World in Ad Cynicism," *Advertising Age* (June 5, 1995), p. 3.

FIGURE 6-1
The Steps in Planning a Target Market Strategy

which it will appeal and for which it will develop a suitable strategy. The total **market** for a particular good or service consists of all the people and/or organizations who desire (or potentially desire) that good or service, have sufficient resources to make purchases, and are willing and able to buy. Firms often use **market segmentation**—dividing the market into distinct subsets of customers that behave in the same way or have similar needs. Each subset could possibly be a target market.

Developing a **target market strategy** consists of three general phases: analyzing consumer demand, targeting the market, and developing the marketing strategy. These phases break down into the seven specific steps shown in Figure 6-1 and described throughout this chapter. First, a firm determines the demand patterns for a given good or service, establishes bases of segmentation, and identifies potential market segments. For example, do prospective consumers have similar or dissimilar needs and desires? What consumer characteristics, desires, and behaviour types can be best used to describe market segments?

Second, a firm chooses its approach and selects its target market(s). It can use **undifferentiated marketing** (mass marketing)—targeting the whole market with a single basic marketing strategy intended to have mass appeal; **concentrated marketing**—targeting one well-defined market segment with one tailored marketing strategy; or **differentiated marketing** (multiple segmentation)—targeting two or more well-defined market segments with a marketing strategy tailored to each segment.[2]

Third, a firm positions its offering relative to competitors and outlines the proper marketing mix(es). Of particular importance here is attaining **product differentiation**, whereby "a product offering is perceived by the consumer to differ from its competition on any physical or nonphysical product characteristic, including price." When differentiation is favourable, it yields a differential advantage. A firm may be able to achieve a key differential advantage by simply emphasizing how its offering satisfies existing consumer desires and needs better than do competitors' products. However, sometimes demand patterns may have to be modified for consumers to perceive a firm's product differentiation as worthwhile. Thus, Tylenol is promoted as an alternative to aspirin for persons who cannot take aspirin (appealing to existing consumer needs), whereas Dove is marketed as a nonsoap bar cleanser with moisturizing qualities (modifying consumer perceptions of soap's role). If targeted consumers do not believe that moisturizing is a meaningful product attribute, then they will probably not buy Dove—no matter how much better a job of moisturizing it does

A **market** *is all possible consumers for a good or service. Through* **market segmentation**, *it can be subdivided.*

In a **target market strategy**, *a firm first studies demand.*

Targeting approaches are **undifferentiated, concentrated,** *and* **differentiated marketing**.

The marketing strategy is then actually developed, with emphasis on **product differentiation**.

[2]Peter D. Bennett (Ed.), *Dictionary of Marketing Terms*, Second Edition (Chicago: American Marketing Association, 1995), p. 166.

compared to competing soaps. Given the fact that Dove is the industry leader, moisturizing is clearly a desirable attribute.[3]

In this chapter, the steps in a target market strategy are detailed—as they pertain to both final and organizational consumers. Sales forecasting and its role in developing a target market strategy are also examined.

Analyzing Consumer Demand

The initial phase in planning a target market strategy (analyzing consumer demand) consists of three steps: determining demand patterns, establishing possible bases of segmentation, and identifying potential market segments.

Determining Demand Patterns

Demand patterns *show if consumer desires are similar for a good or service. People may demonstrate* **homogeneous, clustered,** *or* **diffused demand.**

UPS
www.ups.com/about/story.html

A firm must first determine the **demand patterns**—the uniformity or diversity of consumer needs and desires for particular categories of goods and services—it faces in the marketplace. A firm faces one of the three alternative demand patterns shown in Figure 6-2 and described here for each good or service category it markets.

With **homogeneous demand,** consumers have rather uniform needs and desires for a good or service category. A firm's marketing tasks are straightforward—to identify and satisfy the basic needs of consumers in a superior way. For instance, business customers in the express mail-delivery market are most interested in rapid, reliable delivery and reasonable prices. A firm such as United Parcel Service (UPS) appeals to customers by convincing them it is better than competitors in these areas. As competition picks up, firms may try to modify consumer demand patterns so new-product features become desirable and homogeneous demand turns to clustered demand, with only one or a few firms marketing the new features.

With **clustered demand,** consumer needs and desires for a good or service category can be divided into two or more clusters (segments), each having distinct purchase criteria. A firm's marketing efforts must be geared toward identifying and satisfying the needs and desires of a particular cluster (or clusters) in a superior way. For example, in the auto market, people can be grouped by their interest in price, car size, performance, styling, handling, sportiness, and other factors. Thus, auto makers offer luxury cars, economy cars, full-sized family cars, high-performance vehicles, and sports cars—each appealing to a particular cluster of consumer needs and desires. Clustered demand is the most prevalent demand pattern.

With **diffused demand,** consumer needs and desires for a good or service category are so diverse that clear clusters (segments) cannot be identified. A firm's marketing efforts are complex because product features are harder to communicate and more product versions may be offered. For example, consumers have diverse preferences for lipstick colours; even

FIGURE 6-2
Alternative Consumer Demand Patterns for a Good or Service Category

[3]Peter R. Dickson and James L. Ginter, "Market Segmentation, Product Differentiation, and Marketing Strategy," *Journal of Marketing*, Vol. 51 (April 1987), pp. 1–10; and "Superbrands '96: Category Charts," *Superbrands 1996: Brandweek's Marketers of the Year* (October 6, 1995), p. 129.

the same person may desire several colours, to use on different occasions or just for variety. Thus, cosmetics firms offer an array of lipstick colours. It would be nearly impossible for a firm to succeed with one colour or a handful of colours. To make marketing strategies more efficient, firms generally try to modify diffused consumer demand so clusters of at least moderate size appear.

Firms today often try to perform a balancing act with regard to consumer demand patterns. Just as the world marketplace is now getting closer due to more open borders and enhanced communications, there is also more information available on the diversity of the marketplace through customer databases, point-of-sale scanning in supermarkets, and other emerging data-collection techniques. On the one hand, some firms are looking for demand patterns that let them standardize (perhaps even globalize) their marketing mixes as much as possible—to maximize efficiency, generate a well-known image, and use mass media. On the other hand, some companies are searching for demand patterns that let them pinpoint more specific market segments—to better address the consumer needs in those segments.

Establishing Possible Bases of Segmentation

Next, a company studies possible bases for segmenting the market for each of its products or product lines. Some of these are shown in Table 6-1. The firm must decide which of these segmentation bases are most relevant for its particular situation.

GEOGRAPHIC DEMOGRAPHICS Geographic demographics are basic identifiable characteristics of towns, cities, provinces or states, regions, and countries. A company may use one or a combination of the geographic demographics cited in Table 6-1 to describe its final or organizational consumers.

Geographic demographics
describe towns, cities, provinces, regions, and countries

T a b l e   6 - 1
Possible Bases of Segmentation

BASES	EXAMPLES OF POSSIBLE SEGMENTS
Geographic Demographics	
Population (people or organizations)	
Location	Maritimes, Quebec, Ontario, Western Canada; domestic, international
Size	Small, medium, large
Density	Urban, suburban, rural
Transportation network	Mass transit, vehicular, pedestrian
Climate	Warm, cold
Type of commerce	Tourist, local worker, resident; SIC codes
Retail establishments	Downtown shopping district, shopping mall
Media	Local, regional, national
Competition	Underdeveloped, saturated
Growth pattern	Stable, negative, positive
Legislation	Stringent, lax
Cost of living/operations	Low, moderate, high

PERSONAL DEMOGRAPHICS

A. Final Consumers

Age	Child, young adult, adult, older adult
Gender	Male, female
Education	Less than high school, high school, college, university
Mobility	Same residence for 2 years, moved in last 2 years

Table   6 - 1   (Cont.)

Income	Low, middle, high
Occupation	Blue-collar, white-collar, professional
Marital status	Single, married, divorced, widowed
Household size	1, 2, 3, 4, 5, 6, or more
Ethnicity	Anglophone, Francophone, European, Asian

B. Organizational Consumers

Industry designation	SIC codes; end-use analysis
Product use	Further production, use in operations, resale to others
Institutional designation	Manufacturer, wholesaler, retailer, government, nonprofit
Company size	Small, medium, large
Industry growth pattern	Slow, moderate, high
Company growth pattern	Slow, moderate, high
Age of company	New, 5 years old, 10 years old or more
Language used	English, French, Chinese

CONSUMER LIFESTYLES

Social class (final consumers)	Lower-lower to upper-upper
Family life cycle (final consumers)	Bachelor to solitary survivor
Buying structure	Informal to formal, autonomous to joint
Usage rate	Light, medium, heavy
Usage experience	None, some, extensive
Brand loyalty	None, some, total
Personality	Introverted-extroverted, persuasible-nonpersuasible
Attitudes	Neutral, positive, negative
Class consciousness	Inner-directed, outer-directed
Motives	Benefit segmentation
Perceived risk	Low, moderate, high
Innovativeness	Innovator, laggard
Opinion leadership	None, some, a lot
Importance of purchase	Little, a great deal

A segmentation strategy could be geared to geographic differences. For example, among Canada's twenty-five Census Metropolitan Areas (CMAs), annual per-household expenditures on food are highest in Toronto, Ontario ($6457), and lowest in Saskatoon, Saskatchewan ($4348); annual household expenditures on furnishings are highest in Edmonton, Alberta, at $1562 compared to only $1032 in Winnipeg, Manitoba; the best-dressed Canadians appear to be in Thunder Bay, Ontario, where annual household expenditures on clothing were $2637, while the people in Saskatoon, Saskatchewan, were most likely to make the worst-dressed list with expenditures of only $1780; those well-dressed people in Thunder Bay, Ontario, are also voracious readers, spending $338 on reading material, while another hotbed of readers can be found in Ottawa-Hull where household expenditures are $309 annually; as for consuming hedonistic products, annual expenditures on tobacco and alcohol are highest in Halifax, Nova Scotia ($1751), while the people of Saskatoon spend the least with only $1131 annual household expenditures on these products. Figure 6-3 shows a demographic map of Canada.[4]

Personal demographics describe people and organizations. They should be used in studying final and organizational consumers.

PERSONAL DEMOGRAPHICS Personal demographics are basic identifiable characteristics of individual final consumers and organizational consumers and of groups of

[4]Statistics Canada, *1995 Market Research Handbook,* (Ottawa: Minister of Industry Science and Technology), pp. 243–473.

final consumers and organizational consumers. They are often used as a segmentation base because groups of people or organizations with similar demographics may have similar needs and desires that are distinct from those with different backgrounds. Personal demographics may be viewed singly or in combinations.

Final Consumers As noted in Table 6-1, several personal demographics for final consumers may be used in planning a segmentation strategy.

Applications of personal demographic segmentation are plentiful. In Latin America, 14 per cent of all urban households are headed by an "emerging professional elite," people with professional and executive professions. More than one-half of this group is university educated. The "emerging professional elite" represents a strong market for major appliances, credit card services, consumer electronics, and cars.[5]

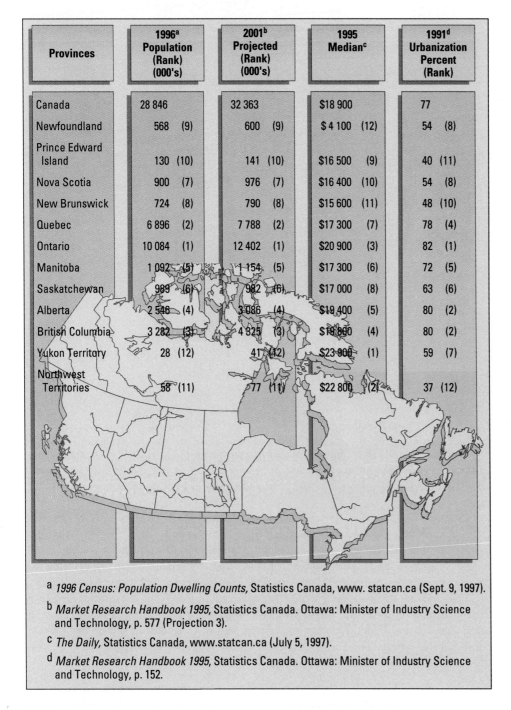

Provinces	1996[a] Population (Rank) (000's)	2001[b] Projected (Rank) (000's)	1995 Median[c]	1991[d] Urbanization Percent (Rank)
Canada	28 846	32 363	$18 900	77
Newfoundland	568 (9)	600 (9)	$ 4 100 (12)	54 (8)
Prince Edward Island	130 (10)	141 (10)	$16 500 (9)	40 (11)
Nova Scotia	900 (7)	976 (7)	$16 400 (10)	54 (8)
New Brunswick	724 (8)	790 (8)	$15 600 (11)	48 (10)
Quebec	6 896 (2)	7 788 (2)	$17 300 (7)	78 (4)
Ontario	10 084 (1)	12 402 (1)	$20 900 (3)	82 (1)
Manitoba	1 092 (5)	1 154 (5)	$17 300 (6)	72 (5)
Saskatchewan	989 (6)	982 (6)	$17 000 (8)	63 (6)
Alberta	2 546 (4)	3 086 (4)	$19 400 (5)	80 (2)
British Columbia	3 282 (3)	4 325 (3)	$19 800 (4)	80 (2)
Yukon Territory	28 (12)	41 (12)	$23 900 (1)	59 (7)
Northwest Territories	58 (11)	77 (11)	$22 800 (2)	37 (12)

[a] *1996 Census: Population Dwelling Counts*, Statistics Canada, www. statcan.ca (Sept. 9, 1997).

[b] *Market Research Handbook 1995*, Statistics Canada. Ottawa: Minister of Industry Science and Technology, p. 577 (Projection 3).

[c] *The Daily*, Statistics Canada, www.statcan.ca (July 5, 1997).

[d] *Market Research Handbook 1995*, Statistics Canada. Ottawa: Minister of Industry Science and Technology, p. 152.

FIGURE 6-3
Demographic Map of Canada

[5]Jeffrey D. Zbar, "Gallup Offers New Take on Latin America," *Advertising Age* (November 13, 1995), p. 21.

TECHNOLOGY & MARKETING

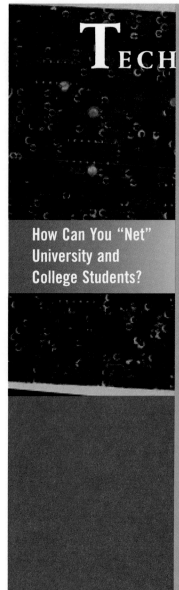

How Can You "Net" University and College Students?

The Internet is a particularly effective medium for providing information and promotions targeting university and college students. Unlike other populations, a very large proportion of students are computer literate. And currently, more than 35 per cent of full-time university and college students own PCs. At many American universities, such as the University of Wisconsin-Madison, students can access the Internet directly from their dormitory rooms simply by hooking up their PC to a special phone jack. Students at York University's Calumet College residence in Toronto are part of a trial project called Intercom Ontario, which involves direct network communications including Internet access for an entire community. The students will have access to Apple computers in the common areas of the residence as well as have hand-held remote-control Newton Message Pads to tap into the World Wide Web. Intercom is specifically interested in measuring actual levels of usage (particularly among students). Before expanding and pricing their services, Intercom might well refer to a survey by Roper College Track, which shows that Internet use among college students doubled between 1994 and 1995 alone.

One important Internet site aimed at the university market is *Link* magazine's *Digital Campus.* Introduced in fall 1995, *Digital Campus* already has a circulation of one million plus. *Digital Campus* shows a rendering of a university campus—complete with a library, a bookstore, a student union, and an athletic stadium. Each building in the *Digital Campus* represents an information and service site. For example, students who browse through the bookstore can view flight schedules for Northwest Airlines, apply for an AT&T Universal credit card, order Paco Rabanne men's fragrance, and request free samples of many products.

By clicking on the "Specialized Bicycles" icon in the bookstore, students can enter a sweepstakes to win an $800 RockHopper bike, download a screen saver for their computer, and correspond with the manufacturer (via e-mail) about mountain biking. Students can even use a ZIP code-based locator service that lists the nearest authorized Specialized Bicycles' dealer. Specialized Bicycles' marketing director say this about *Digital Campus,* "If you want to play the game, you've got to speak the language."

As the promotion manager for a magazine subscription service, assess the pros and cons of using *Digital Campus* as a vehicle for reaching the university market.

Source: Based on material in "Hot Wiring the College Crowd," *Promo* (July 1995), pp. 62–63; and Saul Chernos, "Intercom tries to figure what consumers really want," *Marketing Magazine,* (April 24, 1995), p. 18.

In Canada, the United States and other western nations, Clairol and many other companies are now placing greater emphasis on wooing consumers in the early stages of middle age. This group is quite large and particularly interested in slowing the aging process. See Figure 6-4.

Procter & Gamble marketed specially designed Luvs Deluxe Diapers for Boys and Luvs Deluxe Diapers for Girls. Radio Station EZ Rock FM 97.3 in Toronto, Ontario, is targeting the 329 000 women ages 35–44 (8.5 per cent of the population) who live in the area.[6]

At "A Buck or Two," a discount store chain, value-conscious consumers are attracted by low prices: many items are $5 or less. The firm locates in mall locations, sells many irregulars and factory overruns, and has few employees in each store. In contrast, American Express attracts upper-income consumers with its platinum card. These consumers pay an annual fee of a few hundred dollars and charge tens of thousands of dollars per year; in return, they get special services (such as a worldwide valet service to help them shop, plan trips, and so on) and a high credit line.

[6]Maria Mallory, Dan McGraw, Jill Jordan Siedler, and David Fischer, "Women on a Fast Track," *U.S. News & World Report* (November 6, 1995), pp. 60–72; and Jim McElgunn, "Where the Girls Are," *Marketing Magazine* (February 26, 1996), pp. 11–12.

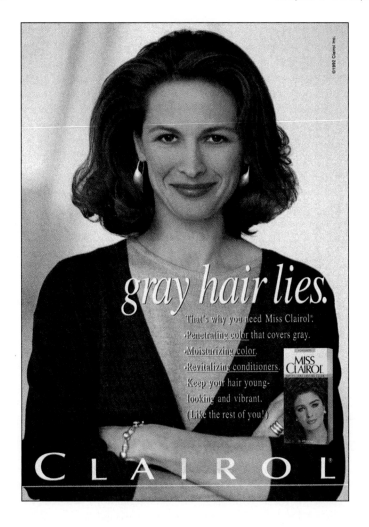

FIGURE 6-4
Wooing Consumers in Early Middle Age
Reprinted by permission.

There are approximately 600 000 Chinese in Canada and the market is expected to grow to 1.3 million by 2001. This segment represents a lot of buying power with personal income of $27 675 compared to $24 329 for an average Canadian. Marketers have responded with specialized goods and services—including the Toronto Dominion Bank's Chinese information phone lines and *Maclean's* Magazine Chinese edition.[7]

Organizational Consumers Table 6-1 also shows several personal demographics for organizational consumers that may be used in planning a segmentation strategy.

The easiest way to segment organizational consumers is by their industry designation. As an illustration, if a firm studies the information-services industry, it would learn it has over 26 000 North American businesses, with a total of one million employees, and that global information-services revenues are divided as follows: North America, 48 per cent; Europe, 33 per cent; Asia/Pacific, 17 per cent; Latin America, 1.5 per cent; and Middle East/Africa, 0.5 per cent. The businesses offer electronic information, systems integration, data processing, network services, programming, and consulting and training.[8]

To access potential organizational consumers by institutional type, some sellers rely on trade directories—such as the *Canadian Trade Index* with 15 000 Canadian manufacturers, *Hoover's Masterlist of Major Latin American Companies* with 1250 businesses, *ABC Europ Production* with 100 000 European manufacturers, and *Scott's Directories* with 53 800 Canadian manufacturers. Mailing lists of organizational consumers are also available. *Canadian Business*

---

[7]James Pollock, "Opening Doors of Opportunity," *Marketing Magazine* (September 18, 1995), pp. 17–18; James Pollock, "A Burgeoning Segment," *Marketing Magazine* (September 18, 1995) p. 18; and James Pollock, "Nailing the Niche," *Marketing Magazine* (September 18, 1995), p. 20.
[8]*U.S. Industrial Outlook 1994* (Washington, D.C.: U.S. Department of Commerce, 1994), pp. 25-1–25-8.

Information lists 1.08 million Canadian businesses, including 21 883 big businesses (more than fifty employees), 1 028 079 small businesses (less than fifty employees), 144 657 professionals, and 75 847 business services. And American Business Lists' U.S. lists cite hundreds of thousands of manufacturers and wholesalers, over one million retailers, one million professional service businesses, and 450 000 membership organizations.

Organizational consumers may be divided into small, medium, and large categories. Some companies prosper by marketing goods and services to smaller customers, while others focus on medium and/or large accounts. For example, Panasonic has a line of inexpensive fax machines for small customers that cost a few hundred dollars, while Pitney Bowes markets fax machines that cost up to $5000 and can handle 1200 pages of text and store 1000 phone numbers. In Canada 97.9 per cent of business locations have under 50 employees, 2 per cent have 50 to 499 employees, and 0.1 per cent have 500 or more employees. Fifty per cent of Canadian business locations have annual revenues of less than $500 000, 18 per cent have annual revenues between $500 000 and $999 999, 22 per cent have annual revenues of $1 million or more and the revenues for the remaining 10 per cent are unknown.[9]

Growth patterns in various industries may give an indication of a firm's future success in marketing to businesses in those industries and provide a good segmentation base. According to the International Trade Administration of the U.S. Department of Commerce, which makes forecasts for North American industries, electronic information services, health services, pre-recorded music, semiconductors, and surgical and medical instruments are fast-growing industries. Aircraft, paper industries machinery, personal leather goods, farm machinery, and newspapers are slow-growing industries.

CONSUMER LIFESTYLES Lifestyles are the ways in which people live and spend time and money; and many lifestyle factors can be applied to both final and organizational consumers. Table 6-1 listed a number of lifestyle segmentation bases; except where indicated, these factors are relevant when segmenting either final or organizational consumer markets.

Final consumers may be segmented by social class and stage in the family life cycle. In North America, the posh Four Seasons hotel chain appeals to upper-middle-class and upper-class guests with luxurious accommodations, whereas the Choice Hotels (formerly Journey's End) chain appeals to middle-class and lower-middle-class consumers with reasonable rates and limited services (such as no restaurant). To attract families with children, various Club Med resorts have day-camp programs.

Final and organizational consumer market segments may be based on their usage rate—the amount of a product they consume. People or organizations can use very little, some, or a great deal. A **heavy-usage segment** (at times known as the **heavy half**) is a consumer group that accounts for a large proportion of a good's or service's sales relative to the size of the market. For instance, women buy 85 per cent of all greeting cards. Heavy yogurt consumers eat nearly double the amount consumed by average yogurt consumers. Manufacturers, wholesalers, and retailers account for over 90 per cent of all equipment leasing, while government and nonprofit organizations make less than 10 per cent of equipment leases.[10] Sometimes, a heavy-usage segment may be attractive because of the volume it consumes; other times, the competition for consumers in that segment may make other opportunities more attractive.

Consumer motives may be used to establish benefit segments. **Benefit segmentation** groups people into segments on the basis of the different benefits they seek from a product. It was first popularized in the late 1960s when Russell Haley divided the toothpaste market

Final consumer and organizational consumer segments each can be described on the basis of lifestyle factors.

CLUB MED
www.clubmed.com

A **heavy-usage segment** *has a rather large share of sales.*

Benefit segmentation *groups consumers based on their reasons for using products.*

---

[9]*Statistical Abstract of the United States 1995* (Washington, D.C.: U.S. Department of Commerce, 1995), various pages; Karen Maru File, "Is There a Trillion-Dollar Family Business Market?" *Industrial Marketing Management*, Vol. 24 (August 1995), pp. 247–255; and "A Catalogue of Sales Leads," *Canadian Business Information* (March 1996), pp. 24–29.

[10]Gerri Hirshey, "Happy [ ] Day to You," *New York Times Magazine* (July 2, 1995), p. 27; Henry Assael and David F. Poltrack, "Can Demographic Profiles of Heavy Users Serve as a Surrogate for Purchase Behavior in Selecting TV Programs?" *Journal of Advertising Research*, Vol. 34 (January–February 1994), pp. 11–17; "Brewing Up a Storm," *Advertising Age* (May 15, 1995), pp. I–3; *Statistical Abstract of the United States 1995*, various pages; and *U.S. Industrial Outlook 1994*, various pages.

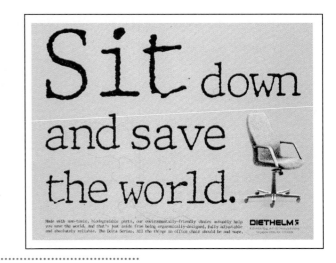

FIGURE 6-5
Applying Benefit Segmentation to Office Furniture
The ad on the left targets people who are interested in comfort, while the one on the right targets people who are attracted to environmentally friendly products.
Reprinted by permission.

into four segments: sensory—people wanting flavour and product appearance; sociable—people wanting bright teeth; worrier—people wanting decay prevention; and independent—people wanting low prices. Since then, benefit segmentation has been applied in many final and organizational consumer settings.[11] Figure 6-5 shows how benefit segmentation is used to market office furniture.

BLENDING DEMOGRAPHIC AND LIFESTYLE FACTORS It is generally advisable to use a mix of demographic and lifestyle factors to set up possible bases of segmentation. A better analysis then takes place. Two broad classification systems are the **VALS (Values and Lifestyles) program**, which divides final consumers into lifestyle categories; and the **Social Styles model**, which divides the personnel representing organizational consumers into lifestyle categories.

VALS and the **Social Styles** model *describe market segments in terms of a broad range of factors.*

In North America, the current VALS 2 typology, shown in Figure 6-6, seeks to explain why and how people make purchase decisions, and places them into segments based on self-orientation and resources. Principle-oriented people are guided by their beliefs; status-oriented people are influenced by others; and action-oriented people are guided by a desire for activity, variety, and risk taking. People's resources include their education, income, self-confidence, health, eagerness to buy, intelligence, and energy level; and resources rise from youth to middle age and fall with old age. Here are descriptions of the basic VALS 2 segments (in terms of adult characteristics):

- *Actualizers*—Highest resources. Successful, sophisticated. Can indulge in any self-orientations. Have a taste for the finer things in life. Comprise 8 per cent of population. Ninety-five per cent have at least some university education. Median age of 43.

- *Fulfilleds*—Principle-oriented, abundant resources. Mature, satisfied, comfortable, and reflective. Mostly professional and well educated. As consumers, concerned with functionality, value, and durability. Comprise 11 per cent of population. Eighty-one per cent have at least some university education. Median age of 48.

[11]Russell I. Haley, "Benefit Segmentation: A Decision-Oriented Research Tool," *Journal of Marketing*, Vol. 32 (July 1968), pp. 30–35; Russell I. Haley, "Benefit Segments: Backwards and Forwards," *Journal of Advertising Research*, Vol. 24 (February–March 1984), pp. 19–25; James W. Harvey, "Benefit Segmentation for Fund Raisers," *Journal of the Academy of Marketing Science*, Vol. 18 (Winter 1990), pp. 77–86; P. J. O'Connor and Gary L. Sullivan, "Market Segmentation: A Comparison of Benefits/Attributes Desired and Brand Preference," *Psychology & Marketing*, Vol. 12 (October 1995), pp. 613–635; and Chatrathi P. Rao and Zhengyuan Wang, "Evaluating Alternative Segmentation Strategies in Standard Industrial Markets," *European Journal of Marketing*, Vol. 29 (Number 2, 1995), pp. 58–75.

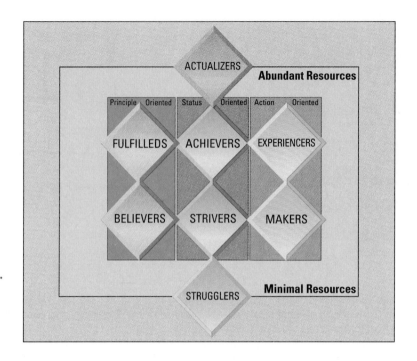

FIGURE 6-6
The VALS 2 Network
Reprinted by permission of SRI International, Menlo Park, California.

- *Believers*—Principle-oriented, lower resources. Follow routines organized around homes, families, and social or religious organizations. Want domestic products and known brands. Resources sufficient for needs. Comprise 16 per cent of population. Six per cent have at least some university education. Median age of 58.

- *Achievers*—Status-oriented, second-highest resources. Committed to jobs and families, and satisfied with them. Like to be in control. Favour established products that demonstrate their success to peers. Comprise 13 per cent of population. Seventy-seven per cent have at least some university education. Median age of 36.

- *Strivers*—Status-oriented, lower resources. Values similar to achievers but fewer resources. Unsure of themselves. Concerned about approval from others. Most-desired goods and services generally beyond reach. Comprise 13 per cent of population. Twenty-three per cent have at least some university education. Median age of 34.

- *Experiencers*—Action-oriented, acquiring resources. Young, enthusiastic, and rebellious. Seek variety and excitement. Spend much of income on clothing, fast food, music, movies, and videos. Comprise 12 per cent of population. Forty-one per cent have at least some university education. Median age of 26.

- *Makers*—Action-oriented, lower resources. Live in a traditional context of family, work, and physical recreation. Unimpressed by possessions. Like do-it-yourself projects. Comprise 13 per cent of population. Twenty-four per cent have at least some university education. Median age of 30.

- *Strugglers*—Lowest resources (too few to include in any self-orientation). Chronically poor, ill-educated, older, and low in skills. Concerned about health, safety, and security. Brand loyal and cautious. Comprise 14 per cent of population. Three per cent have at least some university education. Median age of 61.[12]

In conjunction with SRI International (VALS' developer), Market Statistics has devised a high-tech way to use the VALS 2 model—called GeoVALS. Through GeoVALS, the eight VALS 2 market segments can be broken down by metropolitan area, city, and postal code.[13]

The VALS system is so popular that it is also being applied in Japan, and tailored to people there. For example, ryoshiki ("socially intelligent") innovators are career-oriented,

---

[12]SRI International, Menlo Park, California.
[13]"The Best 100 Sources for Marketing Information," *American Demographics* (January 1995), p. 29.

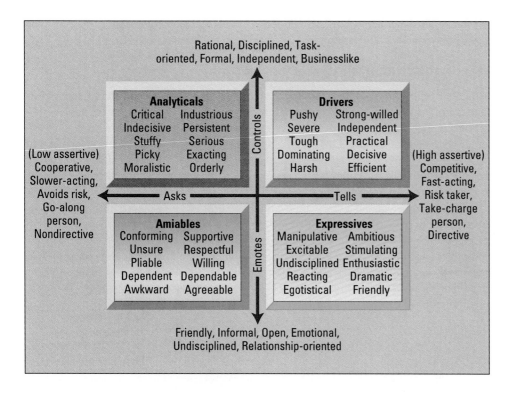

FIGURE 6-7
The Social Styles Model for Organizational Consumers

Sources: Wilson Learning Corporation and Tracom Corporation, Reprinted by permission of Crain Communications Inc., from Tom Eisenhart, "How to Really Excite Your Prospects," *Business Marketing* (July 1988).

middle-aged innovators; ryoshiki adapters are shy and look to ryoshiki innovators; tradition adapters are young and affluent; and the low pragmatic are attitudinally negative and oriented to inexpensive products.[14]

According to the Social Styles model, highlighted in Figure 6-7, social styles affect how people react to various stimuli on and off the job. This model looks at two traits—assertiveness and responsiveness—and divides organizational personnel into "analyticals," "drivers," "amiables," and "expressives." Assertiveness is the degree to which a person states views with assurance, confidence, and force, and the extent to which he or she tries to direct others' actions. Responsiveness is the extent to which a person is affected by appeals, influence, or stimulation and how his or her feelings, emotions, or impressions are shown to others:

- *Analyticals*—Low in both assertiveness and responsiveness. Like facts and details. Money- and numbers-oriented. Work well alone. Stay under control. Interested in processes. Risk avoiders.

- *Expressives*—High in both assertiveness and responsiveness. Personality opposites of analyticals. Use hunches to make decisions. Need to be with people. Focus on generalities. Thrive on freedom from outside control. Risk takers, but seek approval for themselves and their firms.

- *Drivers*—Low in responsiveness and high in assertiveness. Get right to the point. Limited time. "Hard chargers." Self-motivated and impatient. Work well alone. Risk takers. Success-oriented.

- *Amiables*—Low in assertiveness and high in responsiveness. Team players. Like to build relationships. Friendly and loyal. Need support from others. Careful. Less time-oriented. Can be indecisive. Risk avoiders.[15]

The Social Styles model has been used to classify personnel within industries—including banking, computers and precision instruments, chemicals, pharmaceuticals,

[14]Lewis C. Winters, "International Psychographics," *Marketing Research*, Vol. 4 (September 1992), pp. 48–49.
[15]Tom Eisenhart, "How to Really Excite Your Prospects," *Business Marketing* (July 1988), pp. 44–45 ff.; and Raymond E. Taylor, Lorraine A. Krajewksi, and John R. Darling, "Social Style Application to Enhance Direct Mail Response," *Journal of Direct Marketing*, Vol. 7 (Autumn 1993), pp. 42–53.

telecommunications, aerospace, utilities, and industrial and farm equipment. In all cases, the analyticals segment is the largest.

Identifying Potential Market Segments

Consumer profiles are used in identifying market segments.

After establishing possible bases of segmentation, a firm is ready to construct specific consumer profiles—which identify potential market segments for that firm by aggregating consumers with similar characteristics and needs and separating them from those with different characteristics and needs. For example, a supermarket could segment female and male shoppers in terms of their in-store behaviour. In general, on each visit, women spend more time shopping, buy more items, are more apt to bring children, and more often use a shopping list than men; and they are equally apt to shop in the evening.

A photocopier manufacturer could group the office-copier market into benefit segments, such as: basic copying (satisfied with simple, inexpensive machines that make up to 99 black-and-white copies of a single page at a time); extensive copying (satisfied with mid-priced machines that make up to 100 or more one- or two-sided copies of multiple pages and then collate them); and desktop publishing (satisfied with expensive, sophisticated machines that make high-quality colour copies in large quantities). Both domestic and international prospects for each segment are bright.

International Marketing in *Action*

How Do Americans, Argentines, and Venezuelans Spend Their Money?

*R*oper Reports Americas tracks people's activities in the United States and leading Latin American markets, including Argentina and Venezuela. The data it compiles help to highlight target market opportunities in these markets. The data reported below refer to urban adults aged 18 and older.

In a typical month, people in Argentina and Venezuela are more likely than those in the United States to perform job-related duties at home (32 per cent Argentina, 28 per cent Venezuela, and 25 per cent U.S.), make an international phone call (11 per cent Argentina, 14 per cent Venezuela, and 8 per cent U.S.), and take a vacation for four or more days (14 per cent Argentina, 10 per cent Venezuela, and 6 per cent U.S.).

On the other hand, in a given month, people in Argentina and Venezuela are less likely than those in the United States to buy clothing for themselves (38 per cent Argentina, 41 per cent Venezuela, and 48 per cent U.S.), use a credit card (21 per cent Argentina, 17 per cent Venezuela, and 44 per cent U.S.), and send or receive a fax at work (7 per cent Argentina, 7 per cent Venezuela, and 15 per cent U.S.).

There are also significant differences between Argentine and Venezuelan consumers. Consumers in Argentina are more apt to buy recorded music (23 per cent in Argentina versus 10 per cent in Venezuela). In contrast, consumers in Argentina are less apt than their Venezuelan counterparts to go away for a weekend (15 per cent in Argentina versus 21 per cent in Venezuela).

As a marketing consultant who works with small Canadian companies that want to market products in the United States, Argentina, and Venezuela, how would you use these findings?

Source: Based on material in Ignacio Galceran and Jon Berry, "A New World of Consumers," *American Demographics* (March 1995), pp. 26–33.

Targeting the Market

The second phase in planning a target market strategy consists of choosing the proper approach and selecting the target market(s).

Choosing a Target Market Approach

A firm now decides upon undifferentiated marketing (mass marketing), concentrated marketing, or differentiated marketing (multiple segmentation). These options are shown in Table 6-2, and are discussed next.

With undifferentiated marketing, a firm appeals to a broad range of consumers with one basic marketing plan.

UNDIFFERENTIATED MARKETING (MASS MARKETING) An undifferentiated marketing (mass marketing) approach aims at a large, broad consumer market using one basic marketing plan. With this approach, a firm believes consumers have very similar desires regarding product attributes or opts to ignore differences among segments. An early practitioner of mass marketing was Henry Ford, who sold one standard car at a reasonable price to many people. The original Model T had no options and came only in black.

Mass marketing was popular when large-scale production started, but the number of firms using a pure undifferentiated marketing approach has declined in recent years. Competition has grown, and firms need to stimulate consumer demand by appealing to specific segments. In addition, improved marketing research can better pinpoint different segments' desires, and total production and marketing costs can be reduced by segmentation.

Before engaging in undifferentiated marketing, a firm must weigh several factors. Large total resources are needed to mass produce, mass distribute, and mass advertise. At the same time, per-unit production and marketing costs may be lower, because a limited product line is offered and different brand names are not employed. These savings may allow low competitive prices.

A major goal of undifferentiated marketing is to maximize sales—that is, a firm tries to sell as many units of an item as possible. Regional, national, and/or international goals are set. Diversification is not undertaken.

Table 6-2

Contrasting Target Market Approaches

STRATEGIC FACTORS	APPROACHES		
	Undifferentiated Marketing	*Concentrated Marketing*	*Differentiated Marketing*
Target market	Broad range of consumers	One well-defined consumer group	Two or more well-defined consumer groups
Product	Limited number of products under one brand for many types of consumers	One brand tailored to one consumer group	Distinct brand or version for each consumer group
Distribution	All possible outlets	All suitable outlets	All suitable outlets—differs by segment
Promotion	Mass media	All suitable media	All suitable media—differs by segment
Price	One "popular" price range	One price range tailored to the consumer group	Distinct price range for each consumer group
Strategy emphasis	Appeal to a large number of consumers with a uniform, broad-based marketing program	Appeal to one specific consumer group with a highly specialized but uniform marketing program	Appeal to two or more distinct market segments with different marketing plans catering to each segment

For pure mass marketing to succeed, a large group of consumers must have a desire for the same product attributes (homogeneous demand), so a firm can use one basic marketing program. Or, demand must be so diffused that it is not worthwhile for a firm to aim marketing plans at specific segments; the firm would try to make demand more homogeneous. Under undifferentiated marketing, different consumer groups are not identified and sought. For example, if all consumers buy Windsor salt for its freshness, quality, storability, availability, and fair price, a pure mass-marketing strategy is then proper. However, if various consumers want attractive decanters, low-sodium content, larger crystals, and smaller-sized packages (as they now do), Windsor would be unable to appeal to all consumers using one basic marketing mix.

With undifferentiated marketing, a firm sells through all possible outlets. Some resellers may be displeased if a brand is sold at nearby locations and insist on carrying additional brands to fill out their product lines. It may be hard to persuade them not to carry competing brands. The shelf space a firm gets is based on its brand's popularity and the promotion support it provides.

An undifferentiated marketing strategy should take both total and long-run profits into account. Firms sometimes become too involved with revenues and lose sight of profits. For example, for several years, A&P's sales rose as it competed with Safeway for leadership in North American supermarket sales. A&P incurred large losses during that period. Only when it began to close some unprofitable stores and stop pursuing sales at any cost did it regain profitability.

A firm and/or its products can ensure a consistent, well-known image with a mass marketing approach. Consumers have only one image when thinking of a firm (or a brand), and it is retained for a number of years.

TV Guide is an example of undifferentiated marketing in action. It is a magazine with television program listings, descriptions, and evaluations, as well as current events and articles on personalities, shows, and the industry. Each week, 14 million copies are sold in North America (down from 18 million a decade ago). It is advertised on TV and in newspapers and stores. It is inexpensive and available through subscription or at a number of stores and newsstands. The concept of the product, a TV listing magazine, is the same throughout North America. In the U.S., the only regional differences are in program listings (program descriptions, articles, and features remain the same). Canada has its own edition of *TV Guide*, which has uniquely Canadian articles and features, but as in the U.S. these remain the same in all regions of the country.

To be more competitive, *TV Guide* now includes cable-TV listings and VCR-Plus codes (for easy taping), and it has moved all feature stories to the front of the magazine. *TV Guide* is recognized as the standard in the field. Consumers of varying backgrounds and lifestyles buy it for the completeness of its listings and the interesting stories.

With concentrated marketing, a firm appeals to one segment using a tailored marketing plan.

CONCENTRATED MARKETING By means of a concentrated-marketing approach, a firm aims at a narrow, specific consumer segment with one specialized marketing plan catering to the needs of that segment. Concentrated marketing is often appropriate if demand is clustered or if diffused demand can be clustered by offering a unique marketing mix.

Concentrated marketing has become more popular, especially for smaller firms, because the firm does not have to mass produce, mass distribute, or mass advertise. It can succeed with limited resources and abilities by focusing efforts. This method does not usually maximize sales; the goal is efficiency—attracting a large portion of one segment at controlled costs. The firm wants recognition as a specialist and does not diversify.

A firm using concentrated marketing must do better than its competitors in tailoring a strategy for its segment. Areas of competitor strength should be avoided and weaknesses exploited. For instance, a new vendor selling standard office stationery would have a harder time distinguishing itself from competitors than a new vendor that provides customers with free recycling services for the office stationery it sells.

When there are two or more attractive market segments from which a firm may choose, it should select the one with the greatest opportunity—while being alert to these two factors:

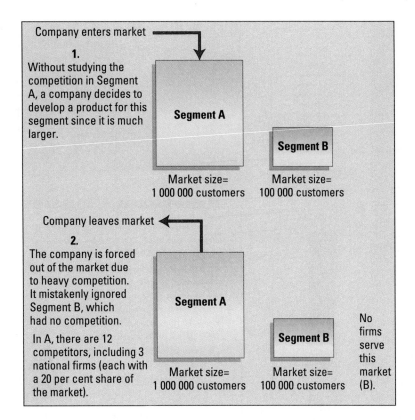

Company enters market

1.
Without studying the competition in Segment A, a company decides to develop a product for this segment since it is much larger.

Segment A

Segment B

Market size=
1 000 000 customers

Market size=
100 000 customers

Company leaves market

2.
The company is forced out of the market due to heavy competition. It mistakenly ignored Segment B, which had no competition.

In A, there are 12 competitors, including 3 national firms (each with a 20 per cent share of the market).

Segment A

Segment B

No firms serve this market (B).

Market size=
1 000 000 customers

Market size=
100 000 customers

FIGURE 6-8
How the Majority Fallacy Occurs

1. The largest segment may not be the best option, due to heavy competition or high consumer satisfaction with competitor offerings. A firm entering this segment may regret it due to the **majority fallacy**, which causes some firms to fail if they go after the largest market segment because competition is intense (see Figure 6-8).

2. A potentially profitable segment may be one ignored by other firms. As an example, in the United States, Frank Perdue is very successful in the poultry business. This is due to its being the first chicken processor to see a market segment desiring superior quality, an identifiable brand name, and a guarantee—and with a willingness to pay premium prices. Previously, chicken was sold as an unbranded commodity.

To avoid the **majority fallacy,** *a company can enter a smaller, but untapped, market segment.*

Concentrated marketing can enable a firm to maximize per-unit profits, but not total profits, because only one segment is sought. It also allows a firm with low resources to vie effectively for specialized markets. There are many local and regional firms that do not have the finances to compete nationally or internationally but that profitably compete in their own markets with national and international companies. However, minor shifts in population or consumer tastes can sharply affect a firm engaging in concentrated marketing.

By carving out a distinct niche through concentrated marketing, a firm may foster a high degree of brand loyalty for a current offering and also be able to develop a product line under a popular name. As long as the firm stays within its perceived area of expertise, the image of one product will rub off on another: Even though it makes several car models, Porsche aims only at the upscale segment of the market—people interested in styling, handling, acceleration, and, of course, status.

DIFFERENTIATED MARKETING (MULTIPLE SEGMENTATION) In differentiated marketing (multiple segmentation), a firm appeals to two or more distinct market segments, with a different marketing plan for each. This approach combines the best aspects of undifferentiated marketing and concentrated marketing: A broad range of consumers can be sought and efforts focused on satisfying identifiable consumer segments. Differentiated marketing is appropriate to consider if there are two or more significant demand clusters, or if diffused demand can be clustered into two or more segments and satisfied by offering unique marketing mixes to each one.

In differentiated marketing, two or more marketing plans are tailored to two or more consumer segments.

FIGURE 6-9
Differentiated Marketing in Action: Targeting Final Consumers
These two watch brands are both marketed by SMH, but they are targeted at different market segments.
Reprinted by permission.

Some firms appeal to each segment in the market and achieve the same market coverage as with mass marketing. Mita markets photocopiers ranging from the simple and inexpensive to the sophisticated and expensive, thus separately appealing to small and large businesses. Other firms appeal to two or more, but not all, market segments. Dylex Limited operates several different apparel outlets: Fairweather and Braemar for women, Tip Top for men, and Biway and Thrifty's for families, thus aiming at several—but not all—apparel segments. And Switzerland's SMH markets Swatch watches for teenagers and young adults, Hamilton watches for adults attracted by classic styles, and upscale Blancpain, Omega, and Tissot brands. See Figure 6-9.

Firms may use both mass marketing and concentrated marketing in their multiple segmentation strategies. They could have one or more major brands aimed at a wide range of consumers (the mass market) and secondary brands for specific segments. Maclean Hunter publishes *Maclean's* magazine for general audiences, *Chatelaine* for women, and *Pharmacist News* and *Marketing Magazine* for more specialized segments.

Multiple segmentation requires thorough analysis. The company must have the resources and abilities to produce and market two or more different sizes, brands, or product lines. This can be costly, especially with high-technology products. However, if a firm sells similar products under its own and retailer brands, added costs are small.

Differentiated marketing lets a firm reach many goals. For one thing, it can maximize sales: Procter & Gamble is the world leader in laundry products—with such brands as Tide, Bold, Dash, Cheer, Gain, Oxydol, Era, Ivory Snow, and Ariel; and Boeing leads in the global commercial aircraft business, offering planes with different sizes and configurations (including the 737, 747, 757, 767, and 777). Recognition as a specialist can continue if the firm has separate brands for items aimed at separate segments or has a narrow product line: Whirlpool has a clear image under its own label; few people know it also makes products for Sears under the latter's Kenmore brand. Multiple segmentation lets a firm diversify and minimize risks because all emphasis is not placed on one segment: Honda's motorcycles and small engines (for lawn mowers and outboard motors) provide an excellent hedge against a drop in the sales of its cars.

Differentiated marketing does not mean a firm has to enter segments where competitors are strongest and be subjected to the majority fallacy. Its goals, strengths, and weaknesses must be measured against its competitors. A firm should target only those segments it can handle. And the majority fallacy can work in reverse. If a firm enters a segment before a competitor, it may prevent the latter from successfully entering that segment in the future.

Differentiated marketing requires the existence of at least two consumer segments (with distinct desires by each), and the more potential segments that exist, the better the opportunity for multiple segmentation. Firms that start with concentrated marketing often turn to multiple segmentation and pursue other segments after they become established in one segment.

Wholesalers and retailers usually find differentiated marketing by their suppliers to be attractive. It lets them reach multiple segments, offers some brand exclusivity, allows orders to be placed with fewer suppliers, and may enable them to carry their own private brands. For the selling firm, several distribution benefits exist. Items can be placed with competing resellers under different brands; shelf space is given to display various sizes, packages, and/or brands; price differentials among brands can be maintained; and competitors may be discouraged from entering a distribution channel. Overall, differentiated marketing places the seller in a good bargaining position.

Multiple segmentation can be profitable because total profits should rise as a firm increases the number of segments it services. Per-unit profits should also be high if a firm does a good job of creating a unique marketing plan for each segment. Consumers in each segment would then be willing to pay a premium price for the tailor-made offering.

Even though serving diverse segments lessens the risks from a decline in any one segment, extra costs may be incurred by making product variations, selling in more channels, and promoting more brands. The firm must weigh the revenues gained from selling to multiple segments against the costs.

A company must be careful to maintain product distinctiveness for each market segment and guard its overall image. Many consumers still perceive various General Motors' divisions as having "look-alike" cars, and IBM's image has been affected by its past weak performance in the home PC segment.

Selecting the Target Market(s)

At this point, a firm must decide which segment(s) offer the best opportunities and how many segments it should pursue. In evaluating market segments, a firm must review its goals and strengths, competition, segment size and growth potential, distribution requirements, necessary expenditures, profit potential, company image, and ability to create and sustain differential advantages, as well as any other factors that are relevant.

A company now chooses which and how many segments to target.

Based on the target market approach chosen, the firm then decides whether to pursue one or more segments (or the mass market). For example, due to the high costs of entering the office PC market and the existence of several well-defined demand clusters, it is most likely that a firm new to that industry would start with a concentrated marketing effort. On the other hand, a new sweater maker could easily use differentiated marketing to target boys, girls, men, and women with its products.

REQUIREMENTS FOR SUCCESSFUL SEGMENTATION For concentrated marketing or differentiated marketing plans to succeed, the selected market segment(s) have to meet five criteria:

Effectiveness requires segments that are distinct, homogeneous, measurable, large enough, and reachable.

1. There must be *differences* among consumers, or mass marketing would be the appropriate strategy.

2. Within each segment, there must be enough consumer *similarities* to develop an appropriate marketing plan for that segment.

3. A firm must be able to *measure* consumer attributes and needs in order to form groups. This may be hard for some lifestyle attributes.

4. A segment must be *large enough* to produce sales and cover costs.

5. The members of a segment must be *reachable* in an efficient way. For example, young women can be reached via *Teen* magazine. It is efficient because males and older women do not read the magazine.

The shortcomings of segmentation need to be considered.

LIMITATIONS OF SEGMENTATION Although segmentation is often a consumer-oriented, efficient, and profitable marketing technique, it should not be abused. Firms could fall into one or more traps. For example, companies may:

- Appeal to segments that are too small.
- Misread consumer similarities and differences.
- Become cost inefficient.
- Spin off too many imitations of their original products or brands.
- Become short-run instead of long-run oriented.
- Be unable to use certain media (due to the small size of individual segments).
- Compete in too many segments.
- Confuse people.
- Get locked into a declining segment.
- Be too slow to seek innovative possibilities for new products.

Developing the Marketing Strategy

The third phase in planning a target market strategy includes two steps: positioning the company's offering relative to competitors and outlining the appropriate marketing mix(es).

Positioning the Company's Offering

A good or service must be carefully positioned against competitors.

Once a firm selects its target market(s), it must identify the attributes and images of each competitor and select a position for its own offering.

For example, a firm considering entry into the office PC market could describe the key strengths of some of the major competitors as follows:

- *IBM*—Reliability, service, range of software applications, product variety.
- *Apple*—Ease of use, graphics, desktop publishing, innovativeness.
- *Compaq*—Innovativeness, construction, monitor quality, competitive pricing.
- *Dell*—Low prices, range of accessories carried, direct marketing experience.

In positioning itself against these competitors, the firm would need to present a combination of customer benefits that are not being offered elsewhere and that are desired by a target market. Customers must be persuaded that there are clear reasons for buying the new firm's computers. It is not a good idea for the firm to go head-on against big, well-known competitors.

As one alternative, the firm could focus on small businesses that have not yet bought a computer and that need a personal touch during both the purchase process and the initial use of the product. It could thus market fully configured PC systems, featuring IBM clones that are installed by the seller (complete with software libraries and customized programs), in-office training of employees, and a single price for a total system. The positioning emphasis would be "to provide the best ongoing, personalized customer service possible to an underdeveloped market segment, small-business owners."

A fuller discussion of product positioning appears in Chapter 7.

Ethics AND TODAY'S MARKETER

Wheelchair Advertising: Targeting Your Market With Billboard Bob's

Bob Gerrie offers marketers a unique specific targeting vehicle—vehicle as in wheelchair with a billboard on it. Disabled in a car crash, Bob has turned his handicap into a business opportunity. Based in Toronto, Bob has a 50 cm by 75 cm weatherproof sign board on the back of his wheelchair. He rents this space at a rate of $295 for seven days of exposure. He goes further than simply displaying an ad, however. Bob will hand out coupons and flyers and talk up his client's business too. This unique personal selling touch is certainly a rare commodity in advertising. As for targeting, although Bob may not be ambulatory, he is certainly very mobile. He takes his wheelchair to where the crowds are to provide maximum exposure for his client's message. Local businesses have been the ones who have utilized his services so far. However, Bob is looking for other people in wheelchairs to join his company and expand his business. He has also given some thought to having wheelchairs with corporate logos to supplement the advertising business.

One concern that Bob has had to deal with is the notion that people are responding to his promotional efforts out of sympathy. His position is very professional: he is selling advertising, period. In addition, Bob gets a lot of exposure for his clients but not in a typical fashion. Although it is not considered polite, it is human nature to stare at people in wheelchairs, and Bob is capitalizing on this.

Despite these issues, the advertisers who have hired Bob report that feedback has been very positive and effective. Representatives of organizations for people with disabilities also feel Bob's business is an excellent idea. It shows the public that a wheelchair is a useful tool and shows the person in the wheelchair engaged in meaningful and useful work. Certainly advertisers feel good about supporting Bob while targeting their message to the people living in the areas where they do business. It seems like a winning approach for everyone concerned.

As the marketing manager for a local food store, discuss how you might use Bob Gerrie's services and discuss the possible concerns associated with their use.

Source: Based on material in Peter Kenter, "How Bob Gerrie Used His Wheelchair to Create a Vehicle for Advertising," *Marketing Magazine* (March 11, 1996), p. 6.

Outlining the Appropriate Marketing Mix(es)

The last step in the target marketing process is for a firm to outline a marketing-mix plan for each customer group it is targeting. Marketing decisions relate to product, distribution, promotion, and price factors.

The marketing mix must be attractive to the target market.

Here is a logical marketing-mix plan for a firm entering the office PC market and concentrating on small-business owners:

- *Product*—Good-quality, Pentium-based IBM clone with expansion capability; very user-friendly, with a simple keyboard layout; high-resolution colour monitor; four-speed CD-ROM player and suitable speakers; one gigabyte hard drive; basic software library; customized software; and more.

- *Distribution*—Direct calls and installations at customers' places of business; follow-up service calls.

- *Promotion*—Emphasis on personal selling and direct mail; hands-on, on-site training programs; customer referrals.
- *Price*—Average to above-average; customers presented with nonprice reasons for purchase; positioning linked to high value for the price relationship; price of computer, software, and service bundled together.

Sales Forecasting

*A **sales forecast** predicts company sales over a specified period.*

As a firm plans a target market strategy, it should forecast its short-run and long-run sales to that market. A **sales forecast** outlines expected company sales for a specific good or service to a specific consumer group over a specific period of time under a specific marketing program. By accurately projecting sales, a firm can better set a marketing budget, allot resources, measure success, analyze sales productivity, monitor the environment and competition, and modify marketing efforts.[16]

A firm should first study industry forecasts; they can strongly affect any company's sales. Next, analysis of the sales potential for the product outlines the upper limit for the firm, based on its marketing and production capacity. A sales forecast then enumerates a firm's realistic sales. The forecast is also based on the expected environment and company performance. Figure 6-10 shows this sales-forecasting process.

A sales forecast should take into account demographics (such as per-capita income), the economy (such as the inflation rate), the competitive environment (such as promotion levels), current and prior sales, and other factors. When devising a forecast, precision is required. A forecast should break sales down by good or service (model 1, 2, 3, etc.), consumer group (for example, adult female), time period (July through September), and type of marketing plan (intensive advertising).

Data Sources

Several external secondary sources may be consulted to obtain some of the data needed for a sales forecast. Government agencies provide data on global, national, regional, and local demographic trends; past sales by industry and product; and the economy. Trade associations publish various statistics and often have libraries for member firms. General and specialized media, such as *The Financial Post* and *Ward's Automotive Reports*, do regular forecasts.

A firm can also obtain data from present and future customers, executives, salespeople, research studies and market tests, and internal records. These data will usually centre on company rather than industry predictions.

FIGURE 6-10
Developing a Sales Forecast

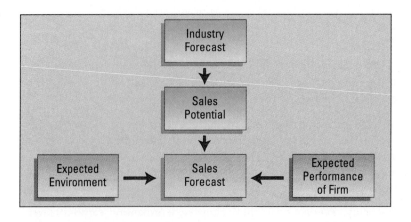

[16]See Paul A. Herbig, John Milewicz, and James E. Golden, "The Do's and Don'ts of Sales Forecasting," *Industrial Marketing Management*, Vol. 22 (February 1993), pp. 49–57; Theodore Modis, "Life Cycles: Forecasting the Rise and Fall of Almost Anything," *Futurist* (September–October 1995), pp. 20–25; and John B. Mahaffie, "Why Forecasts Fail," *American Demographics* (March 1995), pp. 34–40.

Table 6-3
Applying Sales Forecasting Techniques

TECHNIQUE	ILLUSTRATION	SELECTED POTENTIAL SHORTCOMINGS
Simple trend analysis	This year's sales = $2 million; company trend is 5% growth per year; sales forecast = $2 100 000.	Industry decline not considered.
Market-share analysis	Current market share = 18%; company seeks stable market share; industry forecast = $10 000 000; company sales forecast = $1 800 000.	New competitors and greater marketing by current ones not considered.
Jury of executive opinion	Three executives see strong growth and three see limited growth; they agree on a 6% rise in this year's sales of $11 million; sales forecast = $11 680 000.	Change in consumer attitudes not uncovered.
Jury of expert opinion	Groups of wholesalers, retailers, and suppliers meet. Each group makes a forecast; top management utilizes each forecast in forming one projection.	Different beliefs by groups about industry growth.
Sales-force survey	Sales personnel report a competitor's price drop of 10% will cause company sales to decline 3% from this year's $7 million; sales forecast = $6 790 000.	Sales force unaware a competitor's price cut will be temporary.
Consumer survey	85% of current customers indicate they will repurchase next year and spend an average of $1000 with the firm; 3% of competitors' customers indicate they will buy from the firm next year and spend an average of $800; sales forecast = $460 000.	Consumer intentions possibly not reflecting real behaviour.
Chain-ratio method	Unit sales forecast for introductory marketing text = (number of students) $\times$ (% annually enrolled in marketing) $\times$ (% buying a new book) $\times$ (expected market share) = (500 000) $\times$ (0.07) $\times$ (0.87) $\times$ (0.11) = 3350.	
Market buildup method	Total sales forecast = region 1 forecast + region 2 forecast + region 3 forecast = $2 000 000 + $7 000 000 + $13 000 000 = $22 000 000.	Incorrect assumption that areas will behave similarly in future.
Test marketing	Total sales forecast = (sales in test market A + sales in test market B) $\times$ (25) = ($1 000 000 + $1 200 000) $\times$ (25) = $55 000 000.	Test areas not representative of all locations.
Detailed statistical analyses	Simulation, complex trend analysis, regression, and correlation.	Lack of understanding by management; all factors not quantifiable.

Methods of Sales Forecasting

Sales forecasting methods range from simple to sophisticated. Among the simple ones are trend analysis, market-share analysis, jury of executive or expert opinion, sales-force surveys, and consumer surveys. Among the more complex ones are the chain-ratio technique, market buildup method, and statistical analyses. Table 6-3 illustrates each. By combining two or more techniques, a firm can have a better forecast and minimize the weaknesses in any one method.

With simple trend analysis, a firm forecasts sales on the basis of recent or current performance. For example, if sales have risen an average of 10 per cent annually over the last five years, it will forecast next year's sales to be 10 per cent higher than the present year's. Although the technique is easy to use, the problems are that sales fluctuations, changing consumer tastes, changing competition, the economy, and market saturation are not considered. A firm's growth may be affected by these factors.

Market-share analysis is similar to simple trend analysis, except that a company bases its forecast on the assumption that its share of industry sales will remain constant. However, all firms in an industry do not progress at the same rate. Market-share analysis has the same weaknesses as simple trend analysis, but relies more on industry data—and it would let an aggressive or declining firm adjust its forecast and marketing efforts.

A **jury of executive or expert opinion** is used if the management of a firm or other well-informed persons meet, discuss the future, and set sales estimates based on the group's experience and interaction. By itself, this method relies too much on informal analysis. In conjunction with other methods, it is effective because it enables experts to directly interpret and respond to concrete data. Because management lays out goals, sets priorities, and guides a firm's destiny, its input is crucial.

The employees most in touch with consumers and the environment are sales personnel. A sales-force survey allows a firm to obtain input in a structured way. Salespeople are often able to pinpoint trends, strengths and weaknesses in a firm's offering, competitive strategies, customer resistance, and the traits of heavy users. They can break sales forecasts down by product, customer type, and area. However, they can have a limited perspective, offer biased replies, and misinterpret consumer desires.

Many marketers feel the best indicators of future sales are consumer attitudes. By conducting a consumer survey, a firm can obtain information on purchase intentions, future expectations, consumption rates, brand switching, time between purchases, and reasons for purchases. However, consumers may not reply to surveys and may act differently from what they say.

In the **chain-ratio method**, a firm starts with general market information and then computes a series of more specific information. These combined data yield a sales forecast. For instance, a maker of women's casual shoes could first look at a trade association report to learn the industry sales estimate for shoes, the percentage of sales from women's shoes, and the percentage of women's shoe sales from casual shoes. It would then project its own sales of casual women's shoes to its target market. This method is only as accurate as the data plugged in for each market factor. It is useful, since it gets management to think through a forecast and obtain different information.

Opposite to the chain-ratio method is the **market buildup method**, by which a firm gathers data from small, separate market segments and aggregates them. For example, the market buildup method lets a company operating in four urban areas develop a forecast by first estimating sales in each area and then adding the areas. With this method, a firm must note that consumer tastes, competition, population growth, and media differ by geographic area. Segments of equal size may present dissimilar sales opportunities; they should not be lumped together without careful study.

Test marketing is a form of market buildup analysis in which a firm projects a new product's sales based on short-run, geographically limited tests. The company usually introduces a new product into one or a few markets for a short time and carries out a full marketing campaign there. Overall sales are then forecast from test-market sales. However, test areas may not be representative of all locales; and test-market enthusiasm may not carry into national distribution. Test marketing is discussed further in Chapter 8.

There are a number of detailed statistical methods for sales forecasting. Simulation allows a firm to enter market data into a computer-based model and forecast under varying conditions and marketing plans. With complex trend analysis, the firm includes past sales fluctuations, cyclical factors (such as economic conditions), and other factors when looking at sales trends. Regression and correlation techniques explore mathematical links between future sales and market factors, such as annual family income or derived demand. These methods depend on reliable data and the ability to use them correctly. A deeper discussion is beyond the scope of this text.

Additional Considerations

The method and accuracy of sales forecasting depend on the newness of a firm's offering. A forecast for a continuing good or service could be based on trend analysis, market-share analysis, executive and expert opinion, and sales-force surveys. Barring major alterations in the economy, industry, competition, or consumer tastes, the forecast should be relatively accurate.

A forecast for an item new to the firm but that already has a track record in the industry could be based on trade data, executive or expert opinion, sales-force and consumer surveys, and test marketing. The first year's forecast should be somewhat accurate, the ensuing years more so. It is hard to project first-year sales precisely, since consumer interest and competition may be tough to gauge.

A forecast for a good or service new to both the firm and the industry should rely on sales-force and consumer surveys, test marketing, executive and expert opinion, and simulation. The forecast for the early years may be highly inaccurate, since the speed of consumer acceptance cannot be closely determined in advance. Later forecasts will be more accurate. While an initial forecast may be imprecise, it is still needed for setting marketing plans, budgeting, monitoring the environment and competition, and measuring success.

A company must consider **sales penetration**—the degree to which a firm is meeting its sales potential—in forecasting sales. It is expressed as:

$$\text{Sales penetration} = \text{Actual sales/Sales potential}$$

A firm with high sales penetration needs to realize that **diminishing returns** may occur if it seeks to convert remaining nonconsumers because the costs of attracting them may outweigh revenues. Other products or segments may offer better potential.

A company must always keep in mind that factors such as economic conditions, industry conditions, company performance, competition, and consumer tastes may change and lead to an inaccurate forecast unless the forecast is revised.

Sales penetration *shows whether a firm has reached its potential.* **Diminishing returns** *may result if it seeks nonconsumers.*

MARKETING IN A CHANGING WORLD

Targeting the Interactive Marketplace[17]

As companies look ahead to further advances in interactive technology—and the fascinating new marketing opportunities that will accompany such advances—they also need to think about the alternative target market approaches they could pursue. After all, just like other consumer markets, the interactive marketplace will encompass all sorts of potential segments.

With this in mind, Arbitron's NewMedia Pathfinder Study recently examined the U.S. interactive marketplace. Arbitron surveyed thousands of American adults and included 612 variables related to demographics, lifestyles, current media experiences, and expectations. What did it find? Well, the research firm did come up with some catchy segment names, as well as a lot of implications for marketers. There are fast laners (14 per cent of all respondents), diverse strivers (5 per cent), savvy sophisticates (11 per cent), family-focused (15 per cent), bystanders (16 per cent), sports fanatics (11 per cent), moral Americans (11 percent), and the settled set (17 per cent).

Let's highlight a few of these segments:

- *Fast laners* are mostly Generation Xers and teens. They are more open to new technology.
- *Savvy sophisticates* are high-income, well-educated baby boomers. They are confident and innovative. More own and use PCs than any other group.
- *Family-focused* consumers are mostly price-oriented women with average income and below-average involvement with PCs and technology.
- *Bystanders* are lowest in confidence and innovativeness. They tend to be baby boomers with an above-average number of children living at home.

As summarized in the *Marketing News*, "Home shopping channels appeal most to fast laners, diverse strivers, family-focused, and bystanders. Infomercials have only average appeal among family-focused and well below-average appeal among bystanders. Savvy sophisticates show the heaviest involvement with online and print catalogues. They do not see TV as a purchasing medium." Furthermore, "Internet shoppers are pioneers more in the way they shop than in what they buy."

---

[17]The material in this section is based on Kelly Shermach, "Study Identifies Types of Interactive Shoppers," *Marketing News* (September 25, 1995), p. 22.

S U M M A R Y

1. *To describe the process of planning a target market strategy* After collecting information on consumers and environmental factors, a firm is ready to select the target market(s) to which it will appeal. A potential market contains people with similar needs, adequate resources, and a willingness and ability to buy.

Developing a target market strategy consists of three general phases, comprising seven specific steps: analyzing consumer demand—determining demand patterns (1), establishing bases of segmentation (2), and identifying potential market segments (3); targeting the market—choosing a target market approach (4) and selecting the target market(s) (5); and developing the marketing strategy—positioning the company's offering relative to competitors (6) and outlining the appropriate marketing mix(es) (7). Of particular importance is product differentiation, whereby a product offering is perceived by the consumer to differ from its competition on any physical or nonphysical product characteristic, including price.

2. *To examine alternative demand patterns and segmentation bases for both final and organizational consumers* Demand patterns indicate the uniformity or diversity of consumer needs and desires for particular categories of goods and services. With homogeneous demand, consumers have relatively uniform needs and desires. With clustered demand, consumer needs and desires can be classified into two or more identifiable clusters (segments), with each having distinct purchase requirements. With diffused demand, consumer needs and desires are so diverse that clear clusters (segments) cannot be identified.

The possible bases for segmenting the market fall into three categories: geographic demographics—basic identifiable characteristics of towns, cities, provinces, regions, and countries; personal demographics— basic identifiable characteristics of individual final consumers and organizational consumers and groups of final consumers and organizational consumers; and lifestyles—patterns by which people (final consumers and those representing organizational consumers) live and spend time and money. It is generally advisable to use a combination of demographic and lifestyle factors to form possible segmentation bases. Although the distinctions between final and organizational consumers should be kept in mind, the three broad segmentation bases could be used in both cases.

After establishing possible segmentation bases, a firm is ready to develop consumer profiles. Such profiles identify potential market segments by aggregating consumers with similar characteristics and needs.

3. *To explain and contrast undifferentiated marketing (mass marketing), concentrated marketing, and differentiated marketing (multiple segmenta-*tion) Undifferentiated marketing aims at a large, broad consumer market using one basic marketing plan. In concentrated marketing, a firm aims at a narrow, specific consumer group with one specialized marketing plan catering to the needs of that segment. With differentiated marketing, a firm appeals to two or more distinct market segments, with a different marketing plan for each. When segmenting, a firm must understand the majority fallacy: The largest consumer segment may not offer the best opportunity since it often has the greatest number of competitors.

In selecting its target market(s), a firm should consider its goals and strengths, competition, segment size and growth potential, distribution needs, required expenditures, profit potential, company image, and ability to develop and sustain a differential advantage.

Successful segmentation requires differences among and similarities within segments, measurable consumer traits and needs, large enough segments, and efficiency in reaching segments. It should not be abused by appealing to overly small groups, using marketing inefficiently, placing too much emphasis on imitations of original company products or brands, confusing consumers, and so on.

4. *To show the importance of positioning in developing a marketing strategy* In positioning its offering against competitors, a firm needs to present a combination of customer benefits that are not being provided by others and that are desirable by a target market. Customers must be persuaded that there are clear reasons for buying the firm's products rather than those of its competitors.

The last step in the target marketing process is for a firm to develop a marketing mix for each customer group to which it wants to appeal.

5. *To discuss sales forecasting and its role in target marketing* Short- and long-run sales should be forecast in developing a target market strategy. This helps a firm compute budgets, allocate resources, measure success, analyze productivity, monitor the environment and competition, and adjust marketing plans. A sales forecast describes the expected company sales of a specific good or service to a specific consumer group over a specific time period under a specific marketing program.

A firm can obtain sales-forecasting data from a variety of internal and external sources. Forecasting methods range from simple trend analysis to detailed statistical analyses. The best results are obtained when methods and forecasts are combined. A sales forecast should consider the newness of a firm's offering, sales penetration, diminishing returns, and the changing nature of many factors.

KEY TERMS

market (p. 133)
market segmentation (p. 133)
target market strategy (p.133)
undifferentiated marketing (mass marketing) (p. 133)
concentrated marketing (p. 133)
differentiated marketing (multiple segmentation) (p. 133)
product differentiation (p. 133)
demand patterns (p. 134)

homogeneous demand (p. 134)
clustered demand (p. 134)
diffused demand (p. 134)
geographic demographics (p. 135)
personal demographics (p. 136)
heavy-usage segment (heavy half) (p. 140)
benefit segmentation (p. 140)
VALS (Values and Lifestyles) program (p. 141)

Social Styles model (p. 141)
majority fallacy (p. 147)
sales forecast (p. 152)
jury of executive or expert opinion (p. 154)
chain-ratio method (p. 154)
market buildup method (p. 154)
sales penetration (p. 155)
diminishing returns (p. 155)

Review Questions

1. Distinguish between the terms "market" and "market segmentation."

2. What are the three general phases in planning a target market strategy?

3. Explain this comment: "Sometimes a firm can achieve a key differential advantage by simply emphasizing how its offering satisfies existing consumer desires and needs better than its competitors' products do. Sometimes demand patterns must be modified for consumers to perceive a firm's product differentiation as worthwhile."

4. Differentiate among homogeneous, clustered, and diffused consumer demand. What are the marketing implications?

5. Describe five personal demographics pertaining to organizational consumers.

6. What is the majority fallacy? How can a firm avoid it?

7. Cite the five key requirements for successful segmentation.

8. Why is sales forecasting important when developing a target market strategy?

9. Contrast the jury of executive opinion and the chain-ratio methods of sales forecasting.

10. Why are long-run sales forecasts for new products more accurate than short-run forecasts?

Discussion Questions

1. How could an international manufacturer of personal beepers apply geographic-demographic segmentation?

2. Develop a personal-demographic profile of the students in your marketing class. For what goods and services would the class be a good market segment? A poor segment?

3. Describe several potential benefit segments for a firm marketing maintenance services to business clients.

4. Develop a marketing strategy for a utility-vehicle manufacturer that wants to appeal to experiencers (as described in VALS 2). How should the strategy differ if the target market is strivers?

5. If a firm has a sales potential of $4 000 000 and attains actual sales of $2 400 000, what does this signify? What should the firm do next?

PRODUCT

PART 3

PLANNING

To adhere to the marketing concept, a firm needs to devise, enact, and monitor a systematic marketing plan. This plan centres on the four elements of the marketing mix: product, distribution, promotion, and price. We present these elements in Parts 3 to 6, with Part 3 concentrating on product planning.

7 Basic Concepts in Product Planning

Here, we define tangible, augmented, and generic products and distinguish among different types of consumer and industrial products (both goods and services). Then, we study the special considerations in the marketing of services. We examine how nonprofit organizations can be classified, as well as the role of nonprofit marketing in the economy. We look at product mix strategies and product management organizations in detail. We also study product positioning and the product life cycle in depth. The chapter concludes with a look at the international dimensions of product planning.

8 Conceiving, Developing, and Managing Products

In this chapter, we look at products from their inception to their deletion. We discuss the types of new products, reasons for new-product failures, and the new product planning process. We look at the branding decisions that centre on corporate symbols, the branding philosophy, the choice of brand names, and the use of trademarks. We also consider the six basic functions of packaging: containment, usage, communication, market segmentation, channel cooperation, and new-product planning. We explain the growth of products in terms of the adoption and diffusion processes, and note several methods for extending the lives of mature products. We also offer product deletion strategies.

Part 3 Vignette
Products: Satisfying Customer Needs and Wants

Designing products to satisfy customers' demands is the focus of Chapters 7 and 8. Canadian entrepreneur Jim Scharf has a keen eye for product innovation. His approach to marketing involves product orientation. Finding unmet needs and wants—and developing goods and services to satisfy them—is central to product orientation. However, he also realizes the importance of the other aspects of the marketing mix. Therefore, when he developed his E-ZEEWRAP plastic wrap dispenser, it was designed as a way to sell plastic wrap. Designed to overcome the problems of tangling, snarling and uneven tearing associated with most plastic wraps and their dispensers, E-ZEEWRAP was satisfying an incompletely met need.

Chapter 7 also introduces us to services that account for two-thirds of Canada's GDP. For example, Canada Trust offers credit card services with its MasterCard. Credit services available to the mass market via credit cards have been one of the most significant marketing innovations of this century—each Canadian holds an average of two major credit cards. The "product" concept associated with credit cards is very sophisticated. The basic concept of delayed payment combined with "instant" buying power has been enhanced by a variety of other features, including consumer protection services for card purchases, insurance services, frequent usage rewards and enhanced ability to make non-personal transactions.

> *Marketers offer products to satisfy customer needs and wants in exchange for the customer's money or products.*

Chapter 8 raises the topics of new-product development, branding, and packaging. When it comes to product development, marketing managers must be prepared to cope with failure more often than success. Marketers wishing to avoid past mistakes can visit The New Product Showcase and Learning Centre in Ithaca, New York. Curator Robert McMath is an excellent source of information and a consultant for new-product development. The museum contains examples of over 80 000 commercialized ventures, most of which offer a "lesson" of failure. Products fail for a variety of reasons: poor product concepts, good product concepts that were not technically feasible, poor packaging, inappropriate branding, and bad timing.

Branding is one of the most powerful concepts of modern product marketing. In the most basic sense, brand names identify products just as branding cattle was used to identify ownership in the Old West to prevent cattle rustling. Its modern equivalent, counterfeit branding, is much more lucrative because branding has more power than mere identification. The world's number one brand is Coca-Cola, but Microsoft wants to become number one.

Why is this recognition so important? The brand is the bridge between target market, product positioning, and product concept. Brands are personalized images and are often entities unto themselves. In fact, for many products the brand name defines the product category. For example, one uses an IBM or a Mac computer with a DOS, Windows 95, or Mac operating system. Each of these terms refers to trademarked product identifiers. An established brand name provides a key boost for new products associated with it. Hence, Microsoft launched Windows 95 as an upgrade replacement for its earlier Windows version. In cases such as this, the new product must be able to live up to, or surpass, the previous image of the brand. In its most basic sense, branding allows consumers to purchase goods holistically and efficiently. In the absence of branding, every purchase transaction would require intensive product inspection. If every transaction in our society involved this, it could take an entire day just to complete the weekly grocery shopping!

CHAPTER 7

Basic Concepts in Product

Planning

Chapter Objectives

1 To define product planning and differentiate among tangible, augmented, and generic products

2 To examine the scope of goods and services, and explain how goods and services may be categorized

3 To look at the use of marketing by goods versus services firms and provide illustrations of service marketing

4 To describe nonprofit marketing organizations and the role of nonprofit marketing in society

5 To examine the various types of products, product mixes, and product management organization forms from which a firm may select

6 To discuss product positioning and its usefulness for marketers

7 To study the different types of product life cycles that a firm may encounter and the stages of the traditional product life cycle (introduction, growth, maturity, and decline)

> *Upon his appointment as General Motors' (GM's) head of marketing, Ronald L. Zarrella stated that although GM had some of the most recognized car names in the world—from the Buick Roadmaster to the Cadillac Fleetwood—it had failed to keep many of the models up-to-date enough to be competitive with rivals. "We have too many models and vehicle lines," he said, adding that he counted as many as seventy-seven different car and light-truck varieties in GM's lineup. Zarrella also said a GM survey found that 35 per cent of people shopping for cars didn't even consider a GM model.*

GENERAL MOTORS OF CANADA
www.gm.com/index.htm

Reprinted by permission.

Because of GM's weak product positioning strategy, Ronald Zarrella was hired away from Bausch & Lomb and given the job of revamping General Motors' marketing approach. No longer would the company's various divisions be so muddled in consumers' minds.

Zarrella announced that the company's seven vehicle divisions would each become more focused and consistent: "We can't escape the fact that the way our vehicle products have been targeted in the past, many are right on top of one another." To accomplish this, he planned to recruit more marketers to sharpen GM's strategy and to serve as brand managers for the divisions. And to provide inducement for change, each divisional marketing manager will have greater profit-and-loss responsibility.

Here is Zarrella's product-positioning vision for GM's vehicle divisions:

- *Chevrolet*—This is GM's high-volume and light-truck division. Chevrolet should offer dependability, reliability, and the widest range of models.
- *Pontiac*—This is GM's sportiest brand. Pontiac should represent youthfulness and spirit and feature "in-your-face styling."
- *Saturn*—It should target import buyers and younger buyers. Saturn needs to stand for "dependability, intelligence, and friendliness." Saturn needs also to retain its "overall shopping, buying, and ownership experience."
- *Oldsmobile*—It should represent the logical trade-up alternative for Saturn owners as they become more affluent and want larger cars. Oldsmobile should compete for market share with Audi, Acura, and entry-level Infiniti and Lexus purchasers.
- *Buick*—It should represent GM's "premium American car." Buick should offer products that are "substantial, distinctive, powerful, mature." Buick needs to target baby boomers in their 50s.

- *Cadillac*—GM's luxury car division. Cadillac should represent "sophisticated, highly perfected cars." Cadillac needs to compete against Mercedes, BMW, Jaguar, and Lexus "in all of the markets of the world." Cadillac is especially seen as attracting foreign buyers willing to pay for a large, luxury automobile.
- *GMC*—This is GM's "premium truck brand with differentiated products from Chevrolet." High-end sports-utility vehicles are in the domain of GMC. These vehicles need to be differentiated from Chevrolet's mainstream truck business.

Ronald Zarrella also sees Saturn, Chevrolet, and Cadillac as global divisions that should sell more cars and light trucks outside of North America. And he intends to convey brand identities through easy-to-remember ads, like those used by consumer products manufacturers such as Procter & Gamble.[1]

In this chapter, we will look at several basic product-planning decisions a firm must make, including those involving product management organizations and product positioning.

Overview

Product planning is systematic decision making relating to all aspects of the development and management of a firm's products, including branding and packaging. Each **product** consists of a bundle of attributes (features, functions, benefits, and uses) capable of exchange or use, usually in a mix of tangible and intangible forms. Thus, a product may be an idea, a physical entity (a good), a service, or any combination of the three. It exists for the purpose of exchange in the satisfaction of individual and organizational objectives.[2]

A well-structured product plan lets a company pinpoint opportunities, develop appropriate marketing programs, coordinate a mix of products, maintain successful products as long as possible, reappraise faltering products, and delete undesirable products.

A firm should define its products in three distinct ways: tangible, augmented, and generic. By considering all three definitions, the company is better able to identify consumer needs, competitive offerings, and distinctive product attributes. This is illustrated in Figure 7-1.

Product planning means devising and managing products that satisfy consumers.

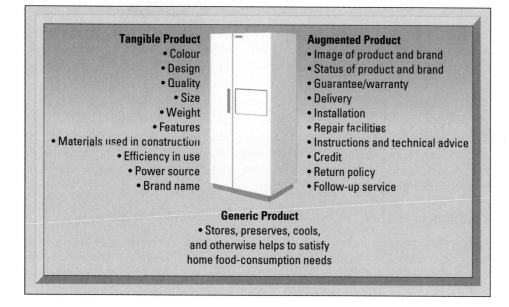

Tangible Product
- Colour
- Design
- Quality
- Size
- Weight
- Features
- Materials used in construction
- Efficiency in use
- Power source
- Brand name

Augmented Product
- Image of product and brand
- Status of product and brand
- Guarantee/warranty
- Delivery
- Installation
- Repair facilities
- Instructions and technical advice
- Credit
- Return policy
- Follow-up service

Generic Product
- Stores, preserves, cools, and otherwise helps to satisfy home food-consumption needs

[1]Gabriella Stern, "GM's New Marketing Chief Seeks Clarity Amid Muddle of Overlapping Car Lines," *Wall Street Journal* (May 1, 1995), pp. A3, A5.

[2]Peter D. Bennett (Ed.), *Dictionary of Marketing Terms*, Second Edition (Chicago: American Marketing Association, 1995), p. 219.

*A **tangible product** has precise specifications, while an **augmented product** includes image and service features.*

A **tangible product** is a basic physical entity, service, or idea; it has precise specifications and is offered under a given description or model number. Windows 95 software, a Caterpillar diesel engine, *Canadian Business* magazine, a seven-day Caribbean cruise on the QE2 (Queen Elizabeth 2), and a proposal to cut provincial income taxes by 15 per cent are examples of tangible products. Colour, style, size, weight, durability, quality of construction, price, and efficiency in use are some tangible product features.

An **augmented product** includes not only the tangible elements of a product, but also the accompanying cluster of image and service features. For example, one political candidate may receive more votes than another because of charisma (augmented product), despite identical party platform issues (tangible product). Rolex watches are popular chiefly due to the image of luxury and status they convey. At Cummins Engine, offering augmented products means "helping our customers be successful, not simply supplying them with quality engines. Increasingly, the value we bring to customers can be described as *smart power*, which is a value-added package of products, information systems, and support services that provides improved performance and business solutions to our customers."[3]

*A **generic product** centres on consumer benefits.*

A **generic product** focuses on what a product means to the customer, not the seller. It is the broadest definition and is consistent with the marketing concept:

- "In the factory we make cosmetics, and in the drugstore we sell hope." (Charles Revson, founder of Revlon)
- "We know our customers come to us to buy more than bearings and steel. They come to us looking for solutions." (Timken Company)

When applying the generic product concept, several points should be kept in mind. First, because a generic product is a consumer view of what a product represents, a firm should learn what the product means to the consumer before further product planning—as shown in Figure 7-2. Second, inasmuch as people in various nations may perceive the same product (such as a car) in different generic terms (such as basic transportation versus comfortable driving), a firm should consider the impact of this on a possible global strategy.

This chapter provides an overview of product planning. It examines the basic areas in which a firm must make decisions: product type(s), product mix, product management organization, and product positioning. It also covers the product life cycle and its marketing relevance, and presents considerations for international marketers. Finally, the planning involved in marketing goods versus services is presented. Chapter 8 presents an in-depth discussion of how to manage products over their lives, from finding new product ideas to deleting faltering products. Chapter 8 concludes with a presentation of two specialized aspects of product planning: branding and packaging.

Types of Products

The initial product-planning decision is choosing the type(s) of products to offer. Products can be categorized as goods or services and as consumer or industrial. Categorization is important because it highlights the differences in the characteristics of products and the resulting marketing implications.

Fundamental Distinctions Between Goods and Services

*Goods marketing involves the sale of **durable** and **nondurable** goods.*

Goods marketing entails the sale of physical products. **Durable goods** are physical products that are used over an extended period of time, such as furniture and heavy machinery. **Nondurable goods** are physical products made from materials other than metals, hard plastics, and wood; they are more quickly consumed or worn out; or they become dated, unfashionable, or otherwise unpopular. Examples are food and office supplies.

*Service marketing covers **rented-goods**, **owned-goods**, and **non-goods services**.*

Service marketing includes the rental of goods, the alteration, maintenance, or repair of goods owned by consumers, and personal services. **Rented-goods services** involve the

---

[3]*Cummins Engine Company 1994 Annual Report.*

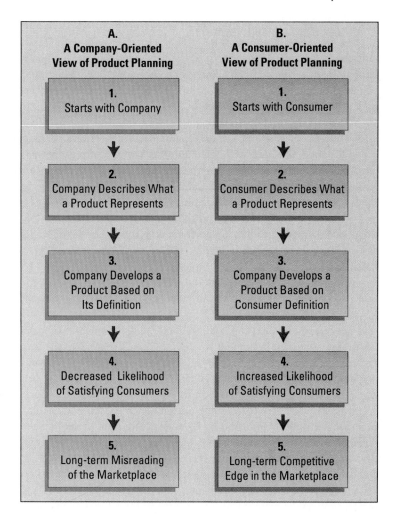

FIGURE 7-2
Applying the Generic Product Concept
In A, the firm is not properly employing the generic product concept and does not understand its customers' needs. In B, the firm is properly using the generic product concept and is successful with its customers.

Source: Adapted by the authors from Leon G. Schiffman and Elaine Sherman, "Value Orientations of New-Age Elderly: The Coming of an Ageless Market," *Journal of Business Research,* Vol. 22 (March 1991), p. 193.

leasing of goods for a specified period of time—such as auto, hotel-room, office-building, and tuxedo rentals. **Owned-goods services** involve alterations to, or maintenance or repair of, goods owned by consumers, such as house painting, clothing alterations, lawn care, equipment maintenance, and machinery repair. **Nongoods services** involve personal service on the part of the seller, such as accounting, legal, consulting, and tutoring services; they do not involve goods.

Four attributes generally distinguish services from goods: intangibility, perishability, inseparability from the service provider, and variability in quality. Their impact is greatest for personal services, which are usually more intangible, more perishable, more dependent on the skills of the service provider (inseparability), and have more quality variations than rented- or owned-goods services.

The sales of goods and services are frequently connected. For instance, a tractor manufacturer may provide—for an extra fee—extended warranties, customer training, insurance, and financing. In goods marketing, goods dominate the overall offering and services augment them. In service marketing, services dominate the overall offering and goods augment them.

Overall, the value of manufacturers' shipments of Canadian-made nondurable goods slightly exceeds that of durable goods. The leading durable products are transportation equipment, electronic and electrical equipment, machinery, and fabricated metal products. Among Canadian final consumers, 52 per cent of expenditures are on services, 26 per cent are on nondurables led by food products, and 22 per cent are on durable and semi-durable goods. Because nondurables are bought more often and consumed more quickly, sales are more influenced by ads and sales promotions.

In industrialized nations, services generally account for well over one-half of the GDP. In developing and less-developed nations, services account for a lower share of GDP; goods

Service marketing is huge in industrialized nations, and accounts for two-thirds of the total output of the Canadian economy.

production (including agricultural items and extracted resources) is more dominant. Yet, even in these countries, the role of services is growing rapidly. In Canada services-producing industries account for 66 per cent of the total output of the economy, at $360 billion. The United States is the world's leading service economy: services account for U.S.$ 4.5 trillion in annual output, or 60 per cent of the GDP. On an international level, the United States is by far the leading service exporter.

Three-quarters of the spending on services in Canada is by the business sector in such areas as transportation and storage; communications; wholesale trade; retail trade; finance; insurance and real estate; and community, business, and personal services. In contrast, the non-business sector accounts for the remaining quarter of service expenditures in categories such as government services and community and personal services. Among the leading Canadian service industries are finance; insurance and real estate; community, business, and personal services; and transportation and storage services. More than 78 per cent of the private-sector Canadian labour force is in service jobs. Among the other nations with at least 50 per cent of their labour forces in service jobs are Australia, Great Britain, France, Japan, Germany and the United States.[4]

These reasons have been cited for the worldwide growth of final consumer services: the rising living standard of the population; the complex goods that require specialized installation and repair; consumers' lack of technical skills; the high purchase prices of items that can be rented rather than bought; and the greater need for health care, child care, and educational services. In the industrial sector, here are some of the services experiencing the greatest growth: computer repair and training, management consulting, engineering, and equipment leasing. There are 612 000 people in Canada working in business services and these services are worth $68 billion to the nation's economy.[5]

The **hidden service sector** *refers to services offered by goods-oriented firms.*

AIR CANADA
www.aircanada.ca/

The scope of services is sometimes underestimated because services may be lumped together with goods in assigning revenues. The **hidden service sector** encompasses the delivery, installation, maintenance, training, repair, and other services provided by firms that emphasize goods sales. For instance, although IBM is a manufacturer, its Integrated Systems Solutions division now generates billions of dollars in revenues. Through outsourcing, IBM "takes back a company's data-processing operations and then sells back computing services, or simply runs the operation for a fixed annual fee." In 1994 Air Canada signed an agreement for $800 million in contracts over a seven-year period with Advantis Canada. Advantis is a subsidiary of IBM Canada and will be composed of employees who formerly worked for IBM Canada, Air Canada, and the Gemini airline reservation system. Advantis will operate in conjunction with ISM Information Systems Management, IBM's outsourcing company.[6]

Categorizing Goods and Services

Goods and services can be categorized in two ways. They can be located on a goods/services continuum; and they can be placed into separate classification systems.

With a **goods/services continuum**, *products are positioned from pure goods to pure services.*

A GOODS/SERVICES CONTINUUM A **goods/services continuum** categorizes products along a scale from pure goods to pure services. With pure goods, the seller offers the consumer only physical goods without any accompanying services. With pure services, the seller offers the consumer only nongoods services without any accompanying physical goods. Between the two extremes, the seller would offer a combination of goods and services to the consumer.

Figure 7-3 shows a goods/services continuum with four different examples. In each one, a pure good is depicted on the far left and a pure service is depicted on the far right. Moving from left to right within each example, the combined good/service offerings

---

[4]Bureau of Economic Analysis, U.S. Commerce Department; and *Statistical Abstract of the United States 1995* (Washington, D.C.: U.S. Department of Commerce, 1995), various pages. See also Fanglan Du, Paula Mergenhagen, and Marlene Lee, "The Future of Services," *American Demographics* (November 1995), pp. 30–47; Statistics Canada, *The Daily* (April 30, 1996); and Statistics Canada, *The Daily* (January 29, 1996).

[5]Statistics Canada, *The Daily* (January 29, 1996).

[6]"Advantis Takes Over Air Canada IS," *Computing Canada* (September 1, 1994), pp. 1,4; and Ira Sager, "The View from IBM," *Business Week* (October 30, 1995), p. 145.

Please note: The above continuum should be viewed from left to right. Within each row, there is a consistent pattern from pure good to pure service. When comparing different rows, there is somewhat less consistency due to the diversity of the examples shown.

FIGURE 7-3
Illustrating the Goods/Services Continuum

become more service-oriented. For example, a computer diskette is usually marketed as a pure good—a product free from defects. With most computer software, there is a telephone hotline to answer questions. A PC is typically set up (configured) by the seller, preloaded with software, and accompanied by on-site servicing. Computer programming involves labour-intensive service on a physical good. Systems design entails professional consultation regarding a client's information system needs; the seller provides a pure service and does not sell or service goods.

Several things can be learned from a goods/services continuum. First, it applies to both final consumer and organizational consumer products. Second, most products embody goods/services combinations; the selling firm must keep this in mind. Third, each position along the continuum represents a marketing opportunity. Fourth, the bond between a goods provider and its customers becomes closer as the firm moves away from marketing pure goods. Fifth, a firm must decide if it is to be perceived as goods- or services-oriented.[7]

Whether it is goods- or services-oriented, a company needs to specify which are its core services and which are peripheral—and then decide what level of peripheral services to offer. **Core services** are the basic services that firms must provide to their customers to be competitive. At Casio, core services include prompt delivery, credit, advertising support, and returns handling for the retailers that carry its watches in 150 nations around the globe. At Federal Express, core services involve taking phone orders, picking up packages, tracking them, shipping them overnight, and delivering them the next morning or afternoon.

Peripheral services are supplementary (extra) services that firms provide to customers. Casio's peripheral services are extended credit terms and advice on how to set up displays for its retailers, and a toll-free phone number for consumer inquiries. Federal Express' peripheral services include giving shipping advice to customers, making address labels and special packaging materials available, and tracing packages in transit. Although these services may increase a firm's costs, require added employee and management skills, and be time-consuming, they may also help a company create and sustain a competitive advantage.[8]

By adding **peripheral services** *to their* **core services**, *firms can create a competitive advantage.*

FEDERAL EXPRESS
www.fedex.com/

---

[7]See Ralph W. Jackson, Lester A. Neidell, and Dale Lunsford, "An Empirical Investigation of the Differences in Goods and Services as Perceived by Organizational Buyers," *Industrial Marketing Management*, Vol. 24 (March 1995), pp. 99–108.

[8]See James C. Anderson and James A. Narus, "Capturing the Value of Supplementary Services," *Harvard Business Review*, Vol. 73 (January–February 1995), pp. 75–83.

Goods may be classified as to market, durability, value added, goals, regulation, distribution channel, and customer contact.

GOODS AND SERVICES CLASSIFICATION SYSTEMS   In selecting a market segment, a goods seller should remember that final and organizational consumers have similarities and differences. The same good may be offered to each segment. The major distinctions between the segments are the reasons for purchases, the amount bought, and the features desired.

Durable-goods marketers have a particular challenge. On the one hand, they want to emphasize the defect-free, long-running nature of their products. On the other hand, inasmuch as they need to generate repeat business from current customers, they must continually strive to add unique features and enhance the performance of new models—and then convince people to buy again while the durable goods they own are still functional. For nondurable goods marketers, the key task is to engender brand loyalty, so consumers rebuy the same brands.

High value-added goods are those where manufacturers convert raw materials or components into distinctive products. The more value firms add to the goods they sell, the better the chance for a goods-based differential advantage. Low value-added goods are those where manufacturers do little to enhance the raw materials or components they extract or buy. These firms often must compete on price, since their goods may be seen as commodities. Superior customer service can be a major differential advantage and enable marketers of low value-added goods to avoid commodity status.

For the most part, goods-oriented firms are profit-oriented. Sometimes goods are marketed by nonprofit organizations—usually as a way of generating revenues to support their activities. Nonprofit marketing is discussed in later in this chapter.

Goods may be grouped by the extent of government regulation. Some items, such as those related to the health and safety of people and the environment, are highly regulated. Others, generally those not requiring special health and safety rules, are subject to less regulation.

Distribution channel length refers to the number of intermediaries between goods producers and consumers. Final consumer goods tend to have more intermediaries than organizational consumer goods due to the size and importance of the latter. Furthermore, goods that are complex, expensive, bulky, and perishable are more apt to have shorter channels.

Goods may be classified by the degree of customer contact between sellers and buyers. Contact is greater for sophisticated equipment, items requiring some training, and custom-made goods. In these instances, proper employee training is needed. Low customer contact is required for goods that consumers are able to buy and use with little assistance from sellers.

A good would normally be classified on a combination of factors. *Chatelaine* magazine appeals to final consumers, is nondurable, has a high added value, is profit-oriented, is subject to few regulations, is sold through newsstands (long channel) and home delivery (short channel), and has low customer contact.

As with goods, final and organizational consumers have similarities and differences in their use of services. Both groups can counter high prices or poor service by doing some tasks themselves. The major differences between the segments are the reasons for the service, the quantity of service required, and the complexity of the service performed.

In general, the less tangible a service, the less services marketing resembles goods marketing. For nongoods services, second performance can only be judged after the service is completed. Rentals and owned-goods services involve physical goods and may be marketed in a manner somewhat similar to goods.

Services may be provided by persons of greatly varying skills. For services requiring high skill levels, customers are quite selective in picking a provider. That is why professionals often achieve customer loyalty. For services requiring low levels of skill, the range of acceptable substitutes is usually much greater.

Service firms may be profit- or nonprofit-oriented. Nonprofit service marketing may be undertaken by government or private organizations. The major distinctions between profit- and nonprofit-oriented marketing are noted later in this chapter.

Services may be classed by the extent of government regulation. Some firms, such as insurance companies, are highly regulated. Others, such as caterers and house painters, are subject to limited regulation.

The traditional view of services has been that they are performed by one person for another. However, this view is too narrow. Services do differ in labour intensity—for example, automated versus teller-oriented bank services. Labour intensity rises if highly skilled personnel are involved or services must be provided at the customer's home or business. Some labour-intensive services may be done by do-it-yourself consumers—for example, home repair.

Services may be grouped by their degree of customer contact. If contact is high, training personnel in interpersonal skills is essential, in addition to the technical schooling needed to perform a service properly. An appliance repair person or a car mechanic may be the only contact a person has with a firm. If contact is low, technical skills are most essential.

A service would typically be classified using a combination of factors. A firm tutoring students for graduate school entrance examinations appeals to final consumers, has an intangible service, requires skill by the service provider, is profit-oriented, is not regulated, has many trainers, and has high customer contact. A company may also operate in more than one part of a category (this also applies to goods marketers): A CA (chartered accountant) may have both final and organizational consumer clients.

Consumer Products

Consumer products are goods and services destined for the final consumer for personal, family, or household use. The use of a good or service designates it as a consumer product. For example, a calculator, dinner at a restaurant, phone service, and an electric pencil sharpener are consumer products only if purchased for personal, family, or household use.

Consumer products *are final consumer goods and services.*

Consumer products may be classed as convenience, shopping, or specialty products, based on shoppers' awareness of alternative products and their characteristics prior to a shopping trip and how extensively people will search for the product. Thus, which class a product belongs in depends on shopper behaviour. See Table 7-1.

Convenience products are those bought with a minimum of effort because a consumer has knowledge of product attributes prior to shopping and/or is pressed for time. The person does not want to search for much information and will accept a substitute (Libby's instead of Green Giant corn) rather than visit more than one store. Marketing tasks centre on distribution at all available outlets, convenient store locations and hours, the use of mass advertising and in-store displays, well-designed store layouts, and self-service to minimize purchase time. Resellers often carry many brands.

Convenience products *are purchased with minimum effort and are categorized as staples, impulse products, and emergency products.*

Convenience products can be subdivided into staples, impulse products, and emergency products. Staples are low-priced and routinely purchased on a regular basis, such as detergent, mass transit, and cereal. Impulse products are items or brands a person does not plan to buy on a specific store trip, such as candy, magazines, or lottery tickets. According to a recent study, 70 per cent of brand decisions at supermarkets are made in the stores.[9] Emergency products are bought out of urgent need—such as an umbrella in a rainstorm and aspirin for a headache.

Shopping products are those for which consumers feel they lack sufficient information about product alternatives and their attributes (or prices), and therefore must acquire further knowledge in order to make a purchase decision. People will exert effort searching for information because shopping products are bought infrequently, have large purchase prices, or require comparisons. The marketing emphasis is on full assortments (such as many colours, sizes, and options), the availability of sales personnel, the communication of competitive advantages, informative ads, well-known brands (or stores), distributor enthusiasm, and customer warranties and follow-up service to reduce perceived risk.

Shopping products *require an information search.*

[9]"POPAI's 1995 Study: 'More Purchase Decisions Made In-Store,'" *Promo* (October 1995), p. 15.

T a b l e   7 - 1

Characteristics of Consumer Products

CONSUMER CHARACTERISTICS	TYPE OF PRODUCT		
	Convenience	*Shopping*	*Specialty*
Knowledge prior to purchase	High	Low	High
Effort expended to acquire product	Minimal	Moderate to high	As much as needed
Willingness to accept substitutes	High	Moderate	None
Frequency of purchase	High	Moderate or low	Varies
Information search	Low	High	Low
Major desire	Availability without effort	Comparison shopping to determine best choice	Brand loyalty regardless of price and availability
Examples	(a) Staple: cereal	(a) Attribute-based: name-brand clothes	Hellmann's mayonnaise
	(b) Impulse: candy	(b) Price-based: budget hotel	
	(c) Emergency: tire repair		

SONY CANADA
www.bccc.com/partners/Sony.html

Consumers are loyal to **specialty** **products***.*

JOHNSON & JOHNSON
www.jnj.com/homepage.htm

Industrial products *are organi-* *zational consumer goods and services.*

Shopping centres and downtown business districts ease shopping behaviour by having many adjacent stores.

Shopping products may be attribute- or price-based. With attribute-based shopping products, consumers get information on product features, performance, and other factors. Items with the best combination of attributes are bought. Sony electronics and Calvin Klein clothes are marketed as attribute-based shopping products. With price-based shopping products, people feel the choices are relatively similar and shop for the best prices. Budget hotels and low-end electronics are marketed as price-based shopping products.

Specialty products are particular brands, stores, and persons to which consumers are loyal. People are fully aware of these products and their attributes prior to making a purchase decision. They will make a significant effort to acquire the brand desired and will pay an above-average price. They will not buy if their choice is unavailable: Substitutes are unacceptable. The marketing emphasis is on maintaining the attributes that make the products so unique to loyal consumers, reminder ads, proper distribution (Hellmann's mayonnaise and *Canadian Business* require different distribution to loyal customers: supermarkets versus home subscriptions), brand extension to related products (such as Hellmann's tartar sauce), product improvements, ongoing customer contact (such as *Nintendo Power* magazine for owners of Nintendo game consoles), and monitoring reseller performance.

Because many people may view the same products differently, the preceding classification is excellent for segmentation. For example, Tylenol pain reliever may be a convenience product for some people (who will buy another brand if Tylenol is unavailable), a shopping product for others (who read ingredient labels), and a specialty product for still others (who insist on Tylenol). Johnson & Johnson, maker of Tylenol, must understand how Tylenol fits into the various categories and plan its marketing strategy accordingly.

Industrial Products

Industrial products are goods and services purchased for use in the production of other goods or services, in the operation of a business, or for resale to other consumers. A cus-

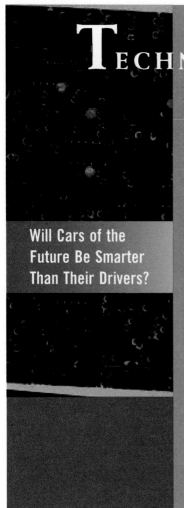

TECHNOLOGY & MARKETING

Will Cars of the Future Be Smarter Than Their Drivers?

Passenger car makers have come up with many new optional features that add convenience, safety, and comfort for drivers and their passengers. Let's look at some of these innovations.

Several car makers have begun to market devices based on satellite-linked navigational systems. GM's system, Guidestar, uses a voice synthesizer that provides directions to lost motorists. Guidestar is currently available on some Oldsmobile models as a $2000 option. Volvo's Dynaguide Info System is similar to Guidestar, but also includes specific traffic report information. Not to be outdone, Lincoln's Remote Emergency Satellite Cellular Unit (RESCU) will notify the nearest police department, fire department, medical unit, and tow truck in the event of an emergency. The unit dials 911 and then uses satellite information to tell the rescuing unit your car's exact location. RESCU is available as an option on the Lincoln Continental.

Another safety-related option would properly adjust driver and passenger headrests every time the car is started. The option, in final development by Lear Seating, uses ultrasonic sensors that determine the proper positions and adjust each headrest automatically. Improperly positioned headrests provide little protection from whiplash.

Other options are designed to ease the tasks of driving. The Mitsubishi Galant LS and Infinity I30, for example, include a single transmitter that controls a garage door, car doors, and windows. Robert Bosch Corporation, a major parts supplier, has devised an electronic rain sensor that automatically turns the windshield wipers on and closes the sunroof at the first sign of rain or snow. The sensor then continually adjusts the windshield wiper speed based on weather conditions.

As a marketing consultant to Oldsmobile, develop a brief report on how Guidestar and other options can be used as part of a product life-cycle strategy.

Source: Based on material in Kathleen Kerwin, "The Smart Cars Ahead," *Business Week* (May 1, 1995), p. 158 E-6.

tomer may be a manufacturer, wholesaler, retailer, or government or other nonprofit organization.

Industrial products may be categorized by the degree of decision making involved in a purchase, costs, consumption rapidity, the role in production, and the change in form. Since industrial-product sellers tend to visit customers, store shopping behaviour is often not a factor. Installations, accessory equipment, raw materials, component materials, fabricated parts, business supplies, and business services are types of industrial products—as shown in Table 7-2.

Installations and **accessory equipment** are capital goods. They are used in the production process and do not become part of the final product. Installations are nonportable, involve considerable consumer decision making (usually by upper-level executives), are very expensive, last many years, and do not change form. The key marketing tasks are direct selling from producer to purchaser, lengthy negotiations on features and terms, having complementary services such as maintenance and repair, tailoring products to buyers' desires, and offering technical expertise and team selling (in which various salespeople have different areas of expertise). Examples are buildings, assembly lines, major equipment, large machine tools, and printing presses.

Accessory equipment consists of movable goods that require moderate consumer decision making, are less costly than installations, last many years, and do not become part of the final product or change form. The key marketing tasks are tying sales to those of installations; providing various choices in price, size, and capacity; having a strong distribution

Installations *and* **accessory equipment** *are expensive and do not become part of the final product.*

Table 7-2

Characteristics of Industrial Products

CHARACTER-ISTICS	TYPE OF PRODUCT						
	Installa-tions	*Accessory Equipment*	*Raw Materials*	*Component Materials*	*Fabricated Parts*	*Supplies*	*Services*
Degree of consumer decision making	High	Moderate	Low	Low	Low	Very low	Low to high
Per-unit costs	High	Moderate	Low	Low	Low	Very low	Low to moderate
Rapidity of consumption	Very low	Low	High	High	High	High	Low to high
Item becomes part of final product	No	No	Sometimes	Yes	Yes	No	Sometimes
Item undergoes changes in form	No	No	Yes	Yes	No	No	Sometimes
Major consumer desire	Long-term facilities	Modern equipment	Continuous, low-cost, graded materials	Continuous, low-cost, specified materials	Continuous, low-cost, fabricated materials	Continuous, low-cost, efficient supplies	Efficient, expert services
Examples	Production plant	Forklift truck	Coal	Steel	Thermostat	Light bulb	Machinery repair, accounting

channel or sales force; stressing durability and efficiency; and having maintenance and technical support. Examples are drill presses, trucks, vans, and lathes.

Raw materials, component materials, and **fabricated parts** are consumed in production.

Raw materials, component materials, and fabricated parts are used up in production or become part of final products. They are expense rather than capital items. They require limited consumer decision making, are low cost on a per-unit basis, and are rapidly consumed. Raw materials are unprocessed primary materials from extractive and agricultural industries—minerals, coal, and crops, for example. Component materials are semimanufactured goods that undergo further changes in form—steel, textiles, and basic chemicals, for example. Fabricated parts are placed in products without changes in form—electric motors, thermostats, and microprocessors, for example. The major marketing tasks for materials and parts are to ensure consistent quality, continuity in shipments, and prompt delivery; pursue reorders; have competitive prices; seek long-term contracts; use assertive distributors or sales personnel; and meet buyer specifications.

Industrial supplies are used daily, and **industrial services** are classified as maintenance and repair, and business advisory.

Industrial supplies are convenience goods used in a firm's daily operations. They can be maintenance supplies, such as light bulbs, cleaning materials, and paint; repair supplies, such as rivets, nuts, and bolts; or operating supplies, such as stationery, pens, and business cards. They require little consumer decision making, are very low cost on a per-unit basis, are rapidly consumed, and do not become part of the finished product. Marketing emphasis is on availability, promptness, and ease of ordering.

Industrial services involve maintenance and repair services, and business advisory services. Maintenance and repair services (such as janitorial services and machinery repair) usually involve little consumer decision making, are rather inexpensive, and are consumed quickly. They may become part of a final product (for example, keeping for-sale equipment in good working condition) or involve a change in form (for example, janitorial services converting a dirty office into a clean one). The key marketing thrust is on consistent, efficient service at a reasonable price. Business advisory services (such as accounting and legal services) may involve a moderate to high level of consumer decision making when these services are first purchased. Ongoing costs tend to be low to moderate, while benefits may be long-lasting. These services do not become part of the final product. The major marketing task is to present an image of expertise and convey the reasons for a client to use the service.

Special Considerations in the Marketing of Services

As noted earlier, services have four attributes that typically distinguish them from goods: higher intangibility, greater perishability, inseparability of the service from the service provider, and greater variability in quality. Their effect is greatest for personal services.

Services differ from goods in terms of **intangibility, perishability, inseparability,** *and* **variability.**

The **intangibility of services** means they often cannot be displayed, transported, stored, packaged, or inspected before buying. This occurs for repair services and personal services; only the benefits to be derived from the service can be described. The **perishability of services** means many of them cannot be stored for future sale. If a painter who needs eight hours to paint a single house is idle on Monday, he or she will not be able to paint two houses on Tuesday; Monday's idle time is lost. A service supplier must try to manage consumer usage so there is consistent demand over various parts of the week, month, and/or year.

The **inseparability of services** means a service provider and his or her services may be inseparable. When this occurs, the service provider is virtually indispensable, and customer contact is often considered an integral part of the service experience. The quality of machinery repair depends on a mechanic's skill and the quality of legal services depends on a lawyer's ability. **Variability in service quality**—differing service performance from one purchase occasion to another—often occurs even if services are completed by the same person. This may be due to a service firm's difficulty in problem diagnosis (for repairs), customer inability to verbalize service needs, and the lack of standardization and mass production for many services.

In planning its marketing strategy, a service firm needs to consider how intangible its offering is, how perishable its services are, how inseparable performance is from specific service providers, and the potential variability of service quality. Its goal would be to prepare and enact a marketing strategy that lets consumers perceive its offering in a more tangible manner, makes its services less perishable, encourages consumers to seek it out but enables multiple employees to be viewed as competent, and makes service performance as efficient and consistent as possible.

Service intangibility can make positioning harder. Unlike goods positioning, which stresses tangible factors and consumer analysis (such as touching and tasting) prior to a purchase, much service positioning must rely on performance promises (such as how well a truck handles after a tune-up), which can only be measured once a purchase is made. But, there are ways to use positioning to help consumers perceive a service more tangibly. A firm can:

Service intangibility makes positioning decisions more complex.

- Associate an intangible service with tangible objects better understood by the customer.

- Focus on the relationship between the company and its customers. It can sell the competence, skill, and concern of its employees.

- Popularize the company name.

- Offer tangible benefits, such as Scudder Funds of Canada promoting specific reasons for people to buy mutual funds from it. See Figure 7-4.

- Establish a unique product position, such as 24-hour, on-site service for the repair of office equipment.[10]

---

[10]Gordon H. G. McDougall and Douglas W. Snetsinger, "The Intangibility of Services: Measurement and Competitive Perspectives," *Journal of Services Marketing*, Vol. 4 (Fall 1990), pp. 27–40.

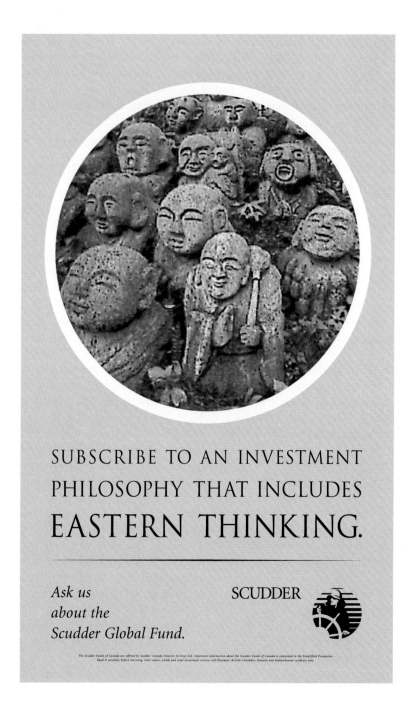

FIGURE 7-4
Scudder Funds of Canada: Offering Tangible Benefits

Reprinted with permission of Scudder Canada Investor Services.

Services often cannot be stored for later sale, so demand must be carefully matched with supply.

Service intangibility may be magnified if only a small portion of the provided service is visible to the consumer. For example, in-shop repairs are normally not seen by consumers. Although a repair person may spend two hours on a facsimile machine and insert two parts priced at $35, when the consumer sees a bill for $145, he or she may not appreciate the service time involved. Thus, a firm must explain how much time is needed to render each aspect of service—and the tasks performed—to make that service more tangible to customers.

Because of service perishability, a service firm needs to match demand and supply patterns as well as it can. Thus, it might have to alter the timing of consumer demand and/or exert better control over the supply of its service offering. It should try to avoid situations in which excess demand goes unsatisfied and cases in which excess capacity causes an unproductive use of resources. To better match demand with supply, a firm can:

- Market similar services to segments having different demand patterns.
- Market new services with different demand patterns from existing services.

- Market new services that complement existing ones.
- Market service "extras" during nonpeak periods.
- Market new services not affected by existing capacity constraints.
- Train personnel to perform multiple tasks.
- Hire part-time employees during peak periods.
- Educate consumers to use services during nonpeak periods.
- Offer incentives and price reductions in nonpeak periods.[11]

The existence of a close relationship between service provider and consumer makes employee interpersonal skills important. The workforce must be trained to interact well with people in such diverse situations as selling and performing services, handling payments, and delivering repaired goods. Generally, more personal involvement, personal contact, and customer input are needed to market services than to market goods. Thus, employee empowerment can be quite beneficial. Those who participate in the marketing of complex services often act as *relationship managers*. As such, the quality of the relationship between a firm's employees and its customers "determines the probability of continued interchange between those parties in the future." Greyhound Courier Express, the courier division of Greyhound Lines of Canada, is trying to build customer loyalty through a one-to-one relationship with shippers and decision makers. Greyhound had the names of the companies they have dealt with in their database, but not the names of the shippers or decision makers of these firms. Using a $3.6 million sweepstakes promotion Greyhound encouraged shippers to register their names to build a database so these individuals could be contacted personally along with their companies.[12]

Many customers of personal service firms become loyal to a particular employee rather than the company. If that person leaves the firm, he or she may take some customers too. That is why it is important for a firm to show its customers that multiple employees are equally capable of providing excellent service.

By their nature, many services have the potential for great variability in their quality. It is hard for lawn care firms to mow lawns in exactly the same way each week, for marketing consultants to make sales forecasts for clients that are always accurate, and for each airline flight to arrive on time. But what service firms can do is strive to make their performance as efficient and consistent as possible. One solution to the issue of high costs (inefficiency) and low reliability (performance variability) is the **industrialization of services** by using hard, soft, and hybrid technologies.[13] Service reliability can also be improved by setting high-level standards and by tying employee pay and promotions to performance levels.

Hard technologies substitute machinery for people. An example is the implementation of an electronic credit authorization system to replace manual credit checks. Hard technologies cannot be as readily applied to services requiring extensive personal skill and contact, such as medical, legal, and hairstyling services. *Soft technologies* substitute pre-planned systems for individual services. For example, travel agents sell pre-packaged vacation tours to standardize transportation, accommodations, food, and sightseeing. *Hybrid technologies* combine both hard and soft technologies. Examples include muffler repair and quick oil-change shops.

Interpersonal skills are crucial for service businesses.

GREYHOUND COURIER EXPRESS
www.greyhound.ca/courier.html

The **industrialization of services** *can lower inefficiency and excessive variability using hard technologies, soft technologies, or hybrid technologies.*

---

[11]Leonard L. Berry, A. Parasuraman, and Valarie A. Zeithaml, "Synchronizing Demand and Supply in Service Businesses," *Business*, Vol. 34 (October–December 1984), pp. 36–37; James L. Heskett, W. Earl Sasser, Jr., and Christopher W. L. Hart, *Service Breakthroughs* (New York: Free Press, 1990), pp. 135–158; and Donald J. Shemwell, Jr. and J. Joseph Cronin, Jr., "Services Marketing Strategies for Coping with Demand/Supply Imbalances," *Journal of Services Marketing*, Vol. 8 (Number 4, 1994), pp. 14–24.

[12]Lawrence A. Crosby, Kenneth R. Evans, and Deborah Cowles, "Relationship Quality in Services Selling: An Interpersonal Influence Perspective," *Journal of Marketing*, Vol. 54 (July 1990), p. 68; and "Greyhound: A Plan To Hold Its Ground," *Strategy* (September 6, 1993) p. 15. See also David E. Bowen and Edward E. Lawler III, "Empowering Service Employees," *Sloan Management Review*, Vol. 36 (Summer 1995), pp. 73–84.

[13]Theodore Levitt, *The Marketing Imagination* (New York: Free Press, 1983), pp. 50–71; and James S. Hensel, "Service Quality Improvement and Control: A Customer-Based Approach," *Journal of Business Research*, Vol. 20 (January 1990), pp. 43–54. See also Myron Magnet, "Good News for the Service Economy," *Fortune* (May 3, 1993), pp. 46–52.

BANK OF NOVA SCOTIA
www.scotiabank.ca/

A **service blueprint** *enhances productivity.* **Service gaps** *must be reduced.*

This is how the Bank of Nova Scotia industrialized its services to improve the Customer Service Centre that supports its VISA card and banking services for customers and branches. In 1990 the Centre began receiving so many customer inquiries by mail and telephone that the paper-based system of responding was overwhelmed. The bank decided to use technology to help solve the problem, so a computer system using IBM's ImagePlus imaging technology, running on an AS/400 minicomputer linked to fifty networked PCs was put in place. The bank set up a pilot team of eight people doing day-to-day work in the VISA centre to enable a hands-on system development approach. The system evolved and was customized as a result of this development approach, resulting in improvements in: customer service, operating efficiency, employee morale, and productivity. Other imaging applications for Scotiabank include: VISA sales draft processing, mortgage discharging, automated draft retrievals, and processing of chargebacks.[14]

To industrialize their services better, many firms use a **service blueprint**, which is a visual portrayal of the service process: "It displays each subprocess (or step) in the service system, linking the various steps in the sequence in which they appear. A service blueprint is essentially a detailed map or flowchart of the service process."[15]

While planning their marketing strategies, it is also important for firms to understand service quality from the perspective of their customers. They must try to minimize any possible **service gaps**—the difference between customer expectations and actual service performance. Consumer expectations regarding service companies cover these ten areas:

1. *Tangibles*—facilities, equipment, personnel, communication materials.
2. *Reliability*—ability to perform a desired service dependably and accurately.
3. *Responsiveness*—willingness to provide prompt service and assist customers.
4. *Competence*—possession of the necessary skills and knowledge.
5. *Courtesy*—respect, politeness, and friendliness of personnel.
6. *Credibility*—honesty, trustworthiness, and believability of service performers.
7. *Security*—freedom from risk, doubt, or danger.
8. *Access*—ease of contact.
9. *Communication*—keeping customers informed and listening to comments.
10. *Understanding the customer*—knowing the customer's needs.[16]

The Use of Marketing by Goods and Services Firms

Goods and services firms have differed in their use of marketing, but service firms are now better adapting to their special circumstances than in the past.

The low use of marketing for services has been due to small firm size, an emphasis on technical expertise, limited competition, negative attitudes, and other factors.

A Transition in the Marketing of Services

Service firms have tended to lag behind manufacturers in the use of marketing for several reasons.

1. Many service firms are so small that marketing specialists cannot be afforded.
2. Because manufacturers often have a larger geographic market, they can more efficiently advertise.
3. A lot of service firms are staffed by people with technical expertise in their fields but limited marketing experience.

[14]"Using People to Drive Success (How One of Canada's Leading Banks Built a Successful Imaging Application)," *I.T. Magazine* (September 1993), pp. 18–22.

[15]Valarie A. Zeithaml, A. Parasuraman, and Leonard L. Berry, *Delivering Quality Service* (New York: Free Press, 1990), p. 158. See also Susan J. Devlin and H. K. Dong, "Service Quality from the Customers' Perspective," *Marketing Research* (Winter 1994), pp. 5–13.

[16]Zeithaml, Parasuraman, and Berry, *Delivering Quality Service*, pp. 18–22.

4. Strict licensing provisions sometimes limit competition among service firms and therefore the need for marketing; in most industries, manufacturers have faced intense competition for years.

5. Consumers have held some service professionals, such as doctors and lawyers, in such high esteem that marketing has not been needed.

6. In the past, some professional associations banned advertising by members; this was changed by various court rulings that now permit it.

7. There are still service professionals who dislike marketing, do not understand it, or question the use of marketing practices, such as advertising, in their fields.

8. Many manufacturers have only recently set up services as profit centres.

Over the next few years, the use of marketing for services will continue to rise, due to a better understanding of the role of customer service in gaining and retaining consumers; worldwide service opportunities; deregulation in the banking, transportation, and communication industries; competition among service providers; consumer interest in renting/leasing rather than buying; the aggressive marketing of services by firms that once focused on manufacturing (such as IBM); the advent of high-technology services (such as video conferencing); the growing number of do-it-yourselfers because of high service costs; and the number of service professionals with formal business training.

Service providers' use of marketing practices is expected to continue increasing in the future.

Nonprofit Marketing

Nonprofit marketing is conducted by organizations and individuals that operate in the public interest or that foster a cause and do not seek financial profits. It may involve organizations (Crown corporations, charities, unions, trade associations), people (political candidates), places (resorts, convention centres, industrial sites), and ideas ("stop smoking"), as well as goods and services. See Figure 7-5.

Nonprofit marketing *serves the public interest and does not seek financial profits.*

FIGURE 7-5
Nonprofit Marketing in Action
Nonprofit marketing is very broad in scope and growing in stature. In this leaflet, the Sandwich Community Health Centre in Windsor, Ontario, promotes its "Healthy Mothers: Healthy Babies" prenatal program.
Reprinted with permission of Sandwich Community Health Centre Inc.

Although nonprofit organizations conduct exchanges, they do not have to be in the form of dollars for goods and services. Politicians request votes in exchange for promises of better government services. Canada Post wants greater use of postal codes in exchange for improved service and lower rate hikes. The Canadian Red Cross seeks funds to help victims of all kinds of disasters.

Prices charged by nonprofit organizations often have no relation to the cost or value of their services. The Brownies and Girl Guides of Canada sell cookies to raise funds; only part of the price goes to pay for the cookies. In contrast, the price of a chest X-ray at an overseas health clinic may be below cost or free.

Due to its unique attributes, marketing by nonprofit organizations rates a discussion from a product-planning perspective. In the following sections, nonprofit marketing is compared with profit-oriented marketing, a classification system is given for nonprofit marketing, and the extent of nonprofit marketing in the economy is examined.

Nonprofit Versus Profit-Oriented Marketing

Nonprofit marketing has both similarities with and distinctions from profit-oriented marketing.

There are a number of marketing similarities between nonprofit and profit-oriented firms. In today's uncertain and competitive arena, nonprofit organizations must apply appropriate marketing concepts and strategies if they are to generate adequate support, financial or otherwise.

With both nonprofit and profit-oriented organizations, people usually can choose among competing entities; the benefits provided by competitors differ; consumer segments may have distinct reasons for their choices; people are lured by the most desirable product positioning; and they are either satisfied or dissatisfied with performance.

There are also some basic differences in marketing between nonprofit and profit-oriented organizations. They are highlighted in Table 7-3 and described in the following paragraphs.

Nonprofit marketing includes organizations, people, places, and ideas, as well as goods and services. It is much more apt to be involved with social programs and ideas than is profit-oriented marketing. Examples include AIDS prevention, recycling, highway safety, family

Table 7-3

The Basic Differences Between Nonprofit and Profit-Oriented Marketing

NONPROFIT MARKETING	PROFIT-ORIENTED MARKETING
1. Nonprofit marketing is concerned with organizations, people, places, and ideas, as well as goods and services.	1. Profit-oriented marketing is largely concerned with goods and services.
2. Exchanges may be nonmonetary or monetary.	2. Exchanges are generally monetary.
3. Objectives are more complex because success or failure cannot be measured strictly in financial terms.	3. Objectives are typically stated in terms of sales, profits, and recovery of cash.
4. The benefits of nonprofit services are often not related to consumer payments.	4. The benefits of profit-oriented marketing are usually related to consumer payments.
5. Nonprofit organizations may be expected or required to serve economically unfeasible market segments.	5. Profit-oriented organizations seek to serve only those market segments that are profitable.
6. Nonprofit organizations typically have two key target markets: clients and donors.	6. Profit-oriented organizations typically have one key target market: clients.

planning, gun control, and energy conservation. The use of marketing to increase the acceptability of social ideas is referred to as **social marketing**.[17]

Nonprofit marketing is broad in scope and frequently involved with **social marketing**.

The nonprofit exchange process can include nonmonetary and monetary transactions. Nonmonetary transactions can be votes, volunteers' time, blood donations, and so forth. Monetary transactions can be donations, magazine subscriptions, tuition, and so on. Sometimes, nonprofit marketing does not generate revenues in day-to-day exchanges; instead, it may rely on infrequent fund-raising efforts. In addition, a successful marketing campaign may actually lose money if services or goods are provided at less than cost. Thus, operating budgets must be large enough to serve the number of anticipated clients, so none are poorly treated or turned away.

Goals may be complex because success or failure cannot be measured in purely financial terms. A nonprofit organization might have this combination of goals: raise $250 000 from government grants, increase client usage, find a cure for a disease, change public attitudes, and raise $750 000 from private donors. Goals must include the number of clients to be served, the amount of service to be rendered, and the quality of service to be provided.

The benefits of nonprofit organizations may not be allotted on the basis of consumer payments. Only a small portion of the population contracts a disease, requires humanitarian services, visits a museum, uses a public library, or goes to a health clinic in a given year; yet the general public pays to find cures, support fellow citizens, or otherwise assist nonprofit organizations. Many times, the people who would benefit most from a nonprofit organization's activities may be the ones least apt to seek or use them. This occurs for libraries, health clinics, remedial programs, and others. With profit-oriented organizations, benefits are usually distributed equitably, based on consumers' direct payments in exchange for goods or services.

Consumer benefits may not be related to their payments.

Crown corporations fall generally within the terms of reference of nonprofit organizations. They are owned and operated by the government in the public interest and they are often expected, or required, to serve markets that profit-oriented firms find uneconomical. For example, Canada Post must have rural post offices. Crown corporations are given the same tax treatment as profit organizations but because they serve in the public interest they are usually only marginally profitable at best. This usually gives profit-oriented, privately owned firms an edge; they can concentrate on the most lucrative market segments.

CANADIAN NATIONAL
www.cn.ca/

Profit-oriented firms have one major target market—clients (customers)—to whom they offer goods and services and from whom they receive payment; a typical nonprofit organization has two: **clients**, to whom it offers membership, elected officials, locations, ideas, goods, and services, and **donors**, from whom it receives resources (which may be time from volunteers or money from foundations and individuals). There may be little overlap between clients and donors.

Nonprofit organizations must satisfy **clients** *and* **donors**.

Private nonprofit organizations have been granted many legal advantages. These include tax-deductible contributions, exemptions from most sales and real-estate taxes, and reduced postal rates. Profit-oriented firms often feel they are harmed competitively by these legal provisions.[18]

Classifying Nonprofit Marketing

As shown in Figure 7-6, nonprofit organizations may be classified in terms of tangibility, structure, objectives, and constituency. An organization would be classed by a combination of factors. For example, postage stamps for collectors are tangible, distributed by Canada Post (a Crown corporation), intended to reduce Canada Post's usual operating losses, and aimed at the general public.

The classification of nonprofit marketing may be based on tangibility, structure, goal, and constituency.

[17]See Alan R. Andreasen, "Social Marketing: Its Definition and Domain," *Journal of Public Policy & Marketing*, Vol. 13 (Spring 1994), pp. 108–114; and Patricia Braus, "Selling Good Behavior," *American Demographics* (November 1995), pp. 60–64.

[18]Edward T. Pound, Gary Cohen, and Penny Loeb, "Tax Exempt!" *U.S. News & World Report* (October 2, 1995), pp. 36–51; and John R. Emshwiller, "More Small Firms Complain About Tax-Exempt Rivals," *Wall Street Journal* (August 8, 1995), pp. B1–B2.

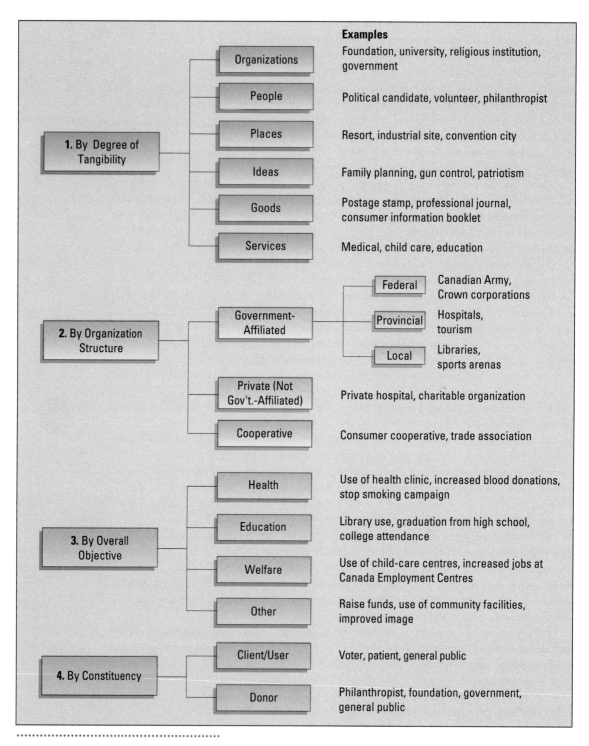

Examples

Organizations		Foundation, university, religious institution, government
People		Political candidate, volunteer, philanthropist
Places		Resort, industrial site, convention city
Ideas		Family planning, gun control, patriotism
Goods		Postage stamp, professional journal, consumer information booklet
Services		Medical, child care, education

FIGURE 7-6
A Classification System for Nonprofit Marketing

As already noted, nonprofit marketing may involve organizations, people, places, ideas, goods, and services. Organizations include foundations, universities, religious institutions, and government; people include politicians and volunteers; places include resorts and industrial centres; ideas include family planning and multiculturalism; goods include postage stamps and professional journals; and services include medical care and education.

Nonprofit organizations may have a government-affiliated, private, or cooperative structure. The federal government markets military service to recruits, and owns and operates Crown corporations (such as Canadian National Railways, Canada Post, and Atomic Energy of Canada), and other goods and services; provincial governments market tourism and hospitals; local governments market libraries and sports arenas. Government marketing is also used to secure support for tax increases, programs, and legislative initiatives. Private organizations market religions, charities, social services, and other goods and services. They also use marketing to increase membership and donations. Cooperative organizations (such as the Better Business Bureau) aid consumers and businesses; their success depends on securing a large membership base and performing their function efficiently.

Overall nonprofit marketing objectives may be divided into health (increase the number of nonsmokers), education (increase usage of the local library), welfare (list more job openings at the Canada Employment Centre office), and other (finding leaders for Scouts Canada) components.

Nonprofit organizations usually require the support of both clients/users and donors. Clients/users are interested in the direct benefits they get by participating in an organization, such as their improved health, education, or welfare. Donors are concerned about the efficiency of operations, success rates, the availability of goods and services, and the recognition of their contributions. For each constituency, an organization must pinpoint its target market. For example, the Easter Seal Society would focus on households with direct mail during the Easter campaign season and seek funds from corporate donors during the rest of the year.

The Extent of Nonprofit Marketing in the Economy

Worldwide, millions of organizations and people engage in nonprofit marketing. In 1994, individual Canadian tax filers claimed $3.39 billion in charitable donations on their taxes. This represented a 1 per cent increase in donations over 1993. A total of 5 344 480 tax filers reported charitable donations, but this number was down 3 per cent from 1993 donations. The most generous Canadians are over 65 years of age, giving an average of $890 to charity in comparison to the national average of $634 for all of Canada. The most generous donors live in Alberta, where the average donation was $812 per taxfiler. By definition, charitable donations can only be claimed if they are made to nonprofit organizations.

Employment in Canadian nonprofit sectors such as health and social services, education, and public administration was 2.8 million people in 1995, which represented 25 per cent of industrial employees.[19]

These examples further demonstrate the scope of nonprofit marketing:

- The Canadian Council on Smoking and Health annually sponsors National Non-Smoking Week, a key part of a national public education campaign that has these five objectives: to educate Canadians about the dangers of tobacco use; to prevent people from becoming addicted to tobacco; to help smokers quit; to ensure a smoke-free environment for non-smokers; and to help Canada become a smoke-free society.

  The week was founded in 1977 and is held annually during the third week of January. The Wednesday of this week is designated as Weedless Wednesday, when people are encouraged to stop smoking for one day (in the hope that they will quit for life).[20]

- Universities are seeking to retain their student populations longer by encouraging growth of their graduate programs. *Canadian Business Magazine* routinely carries advertising for executive MBA programs offered by Queen's University and the University of Western Ontario. The University of Windsor has a Co-op MBA program targeted specifically at students with nonbusiness degrees and no work experience and has produced posters, ads, and brochures based on the theme "Earn As You Learn." (See Figure 7-7.) Simon Fraser University goes after mature students with its Harbour Centre Campus in downtown Vancouver. The target is well-educated, mid-career adults who want courses specifically tailored to their workplace requirements. At the Harbour

There are millions of nonprofit organizations in the world and their use of marketing is increasing.

---

[19]Statistics Canada, *The Daily* (December 13, 1995); Statistics Canada, *The Daily* (April 30, 1996).

[20]Jim Carroll and Rick Broadhead, *1996 Canadian Internet Directory*, (Scarborough: Prentice Hall Canada), p. 252; "National Non-Smoking Week 1996," *Canadian Council on Smoking and Health Home Page* (www.ccsh.ca).

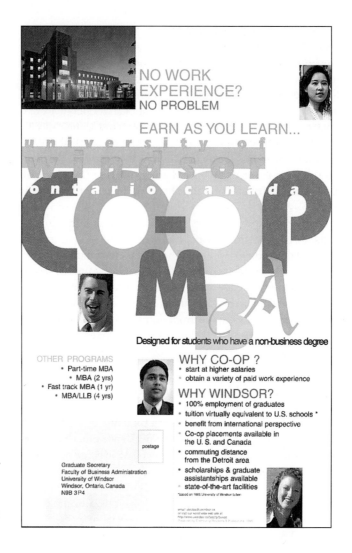

FIGURE 7-7
The Marketing of Higher Education
Reprinted with permission of University of Windsor, graphic design by Steve Daigle.

Centre, the executive MBA is marketed by direct mail and newspaper ads, and large companies like BC Hydro and CP Rail have been approached with degree programs designed for their employees.[21]

Elements of a Product Mix

*A **product item** is a specific model; a **product line** has related items; a **product mix** is all a firm's lines.*

After determining the type(s) of products to offer, a firm needs to outline the variety and assortment of those products. A **product item** is a specific model, brand, or size of a product that a company sells, such as a college course on the principles of marketing, a General Motors truck, or Sony 3.5-inch diskettes for PCs. Usually a firm sells a group of closely related product items as part of a **product line**. In each product line, the items have some common characteristics, customers, and/or uses; they may also share technologies, distribution channels, prices, related services, and so on.[22] As an example, Revlon markets lipstick, eye makeup, and other cosmetics. Caterpillar makes several different tractor models. Prentice Hall Canada publishes a number of college and university textbooks on marketing. Many local lawn-service firms offer lawn mowing, landscaping, and tree-trimming services.

The **product mix** consists of all the different product lines a firm offers. For instance, Heinz markets ketchup, tuna fish, low-calorie foods, frozen french fries, soup, pet food, and various other food products in over 200 countries around the globe. Metropolitan Life operates North America's largest life insurer (MetLife), as well as its biggest franchised real-

PRENTICE HALL CANADA
www.phcanada.com

---

[21]Terry Bullick, "Recruitment 101," *Marketing Magazine* (March 11, 1996), p. 8.
[22]Bennett, *Dictionary of Marketing Terms*, p. 222.

estate broker (Century 21). The Seagram Company Ltd. is a global multinational with two major product lines: wines and spirits with brand names such as Crown Royal whisky and Chivas Regal scotch, and beverages such as Tropicana juices and Seagram's coolers and mixers.[23]

A product mix can be described in terms of its width, depth, and consistency. The width of a product mix is based on the number of different product lines a company offers. A wide mix lets a firm diversify products, appeal to different consumer needs, and encourage one-stop shopping. A narrow mix requires lower resource investments and does not call for expertise in different product categories.

A product mix has levels of width, depth, and consistency.

The depth of a product mix is based on the number of product items within each product line. A deep mix can satisfy the needs of several consumer segments for the same product, maximize shelf space, discourage competitors, cover a range of prices, and sustain dealer support. A shallow mix imposes lower costs for inventory, product alterations, and order processing; and there are no overlapping product items.

The consistency of a product mix is based on the relationship among product lines in terms of their sharing a common end-use, distribution outlets, consumer group(s), and price range. A consistent mix is generally easier to manage than an inconsistent one. It allows a firm to concentrate on marketing and production expertise, create a strong image, and generate solid distribution relations. However, excessive consistency may leave the firm vulnerable to environmental threats, sales fluctuations, or decreased growth potential, since emphasis is on a limited product assortment. Figure 7-8 shows product mix alternatives in terms of width and depth. Figure 7-9 displays Jergens' deep product line of hand soaps.

Product-mix decisions can have both positive and negative effects on companies,[24] as these examples demonstrate:

- Bombardier Corporation is booming because of its product-mix diversification strategy. The firm began in the 1960s as the maker of Ski-Doo snowmobiles. Now, Bombardier manufactures aircraft for commuter airlines and corporate air fleets, railroad and subway cars, and Sea-Doo personal watercraft—as well as Ski-Doo snowmobiles. Its annual revenues have gone from $11 million in 1964 to $7.1 billion today.[25]

Width of Product Mix

	Narrow	Wide
Shallow	Few models in one or a few product lines	Few models in each of several different product lines
Deep	Many models in one or a few product lines	Many models in each of several different product lines

Depth of Product Mix

FIGURE 7-8
Product Mix Alternatives

[23]Mark Stevenson, "Can This Marriage Survive?" *Canadian Business* (October 1994), p. 26.

[24]See John A. Quelch and David Kenny, "Extend Profits, Not Product Lines," *Harvard Business Review*, Vol. 72 (September–October 1994), pp. 153–160.

[25]Patrick J. Spain and James R. Talbot (Eds.), *Hoover's Handbook of World Business 1995-1996* (Austin, Texas: Reference Press, 1995), pp. 138–139.

- H.J. Heinz Co. of Canada dominates the Canadian jarred baby-food market, worth about $110 million, with an 80 per cent market share. The company recently launched a new niche product branded Heinz Toddler, which was designed for children one to two years old. The new product line has ten meals, a cereal, and three desserts, and it is hoped it will dominate this niche market, estimated to have $1.5 million in sales potential. The new product line replaces the less successful Good 'n Chunky line of canned baby foods, which never really caught on. The action is being taken in response to Gerber Canada (which controls the other 20 per cent of the market), who was first into this market niche with a microwaveable product line called Gerber Graduates.[26]

[26]"Heinz Food for Toddlers," *Strategy* (June 28, 1993), p. 4.

Product Management Organizations

A firm may select from among several organizational forms of product management, including: marketing manager, product manager, product planning committee, new-product manager, and venture team.[27]

Under a **marketing manager system**, an executive is responsible for overseeing a wide range of marketing functions (such as research, target marketing, planning for existing and new products, distribution, promotion, pricing, and customer service) and for coordinating with other departments that perform marketing-related activities (such as warehousing, order filling, shipping, credit, and purchasing). It works well for firms with a line of similar products or one dominant product line, and for smaller firms that want centralized control of marketing tasks. It may be less successful if there are several product lines and they require different marketing mixes—unless there are category marketing managers, with each responsible for a broad product line.

One person is directly in charge of a host of marketing tasks, including product planning, with a **marketing manager system**.

Ontario Lottery Corporation, Pepsi Cola, and Christie Brown (maker of Oreo cookies and Ritz crackers, among others) have used some form of marketing manager system.[28]

With a **product (brand) manager system**, there is a level of middle managers, each of whom is responsible for planning, coordinating, and monitoring the performance of a single product (brand) or a small group of products (brands). The managers handle both new and existing products and are involved with all the marketing activities related to their product or group of products. The system lets all products or brands get adequate attention. It works well when there are many distinct products or brands, each needing special marketing attention. But, it has two potential shortcomings: lack of authority for the product manager and inadequate attention to new products. Labatt Breweries, Procter & Gamble, and Black & Decker have used product managers.[29]

Middle managers handle new and existing products in a category in the **product manager system**.

A **product planning committee** is staffed by high-level executives from various functional areas in a firm, such as marketing, production, engineering, finance, and research and development. It handles product approval, evaluation, and development on a part-time basis. Once a product is introduced, the committee usually turns to other opportunities and completely gives that product over to a product manager. This system lets management have strong input into product decisions; but, because the committee meets irregularly and must pass projects on to line managers, this method functions best as a supplement to other methods. It is utilized by many large and small firms.

A **product planning committee** *has top executives involved part time.*

A **new-product manager system** has product managers to supervise existing products and new-product managers to develop new ones. It ensures enough time, resources, enthusiasm, and expertise for new-product planning. Once a product is introduced, it is given to a product manager who oversees the existing products in that line (or brand). The system can be costly, incur conflicts, and cause discontinuity when an item is introduced. Kraft General Foods, General Electric, and Johnson & Johnson have used new-product managers.

A **new-product manager system** *has separate middle managers for new and existing products.*

A **venture team** is a small, independent department comprised of a broad range of specialists, drawn from the marketing, finance, engineering, and other functional departments, who are involved with a specific new product's entire development process. Team members work on the team full time and act in a relatively autonomous manner. The team disbands when its new product is introduced, and the product is then managed within the firm's regular management structure. A venture team ensures there are proper resources, a flexible environment, expertise, and continuity in new-product planning. It is valuable if a firm wants to be more far-sighted, reach out for truly new ideas, and foster creativity. It is also expensive to establish and operate. Xerox, Ault Foods, Campbell Soup, and 3M have used venture teams.

A **venture team** *is an autonomous new-product department.*

The correct organization for a particular firm depends on the diversity of its offerings, the number of new products it introduces, its level of innovativeness, company resources, management expertise, and other factors. A combination organization may be highly desirable; among larger firms, this is particularly common.

---

[27]The definitions in this section are drawn from Bennett, *Dictionary of Marketing Terms*, various pages.

[28]See "The Dynamics of Category Management," *Promo/Progressive Grocer Special Report* (December 1994); "Interview with Tom Dawley, Marketing Director of Online Products Ontario Lottery Corp," *Strategy* (June 27, 1994), p. 9; and "Mr Christie gives Teddy a Canadian Ad Flavour," *Marketing Magazine* (January 21, 1991), p. 3.

[29]"Career Labatt Man Set to Fill New VP Slot," *Marketing Magazine* (December 21–28, 1992), p 2.

Product Positioning

Distinctive and desirable product features must be communicated to the marketplace.

Product positioning *maps out consumer perceptions of product attributes.* **Ideal points** *show the most preferred attributes.*

Both competitive and company product positioning are important.

Critical to a firm's product-planning efforts is how the items in its product mix are perceived in the marketplace. The firm must work hard to make sure that each of its products is perceived as providing some combination of unique features (product differentiation) and that these features are desired by the target market (thereby converting product differentiation to a differential advantage).

When a product is new, a company must clearly communicate its attributes: What is it? What does it do? How is it better than the competition? Who should buy it? The goal is to have consumers perceive product attributes as the firm intends. When a product has an established niche in the market, a company must regularly reinforce its image and communicate the reasons for its success. Once consumer perceptions are formed, they may be hard to alter. And it may also be tough later to change a product's niche in the market (for instance, from low price, low quality, to high price, high quality).

Through **product positioning**, a firm can map each of its products in terms of consumer perceptions and desires, competition, other company products, and environmental changes. Consumer perceptions are the images of products, both a firm's and competitors', in people's minds. Consumer desires refer to the attributes that people would most like products to have—their **ideal points**. If a group of people has a distinctive "ideal" for a product category, that group is a potential market segment. A firm will do well if its products' attributes are perceived by consumers as being close to their ideal.

Competitive product positioning refers to people's perceptions of a firm relative to competitors. The goal is for the firm's products to be perceived as "more ideal" than competitors'. *Company product positioning* shows a firm how consumers perceive that firm's different brands (items) within the same product line and the relationship of those brands (items) to each other. The goal is for each of the firm's brands to be positioned near an ideal point, yet not too close to one another in the consumer's mind—the brands should appeal to different ideal points (market segments).

A firm must monitor the environmental changes that may alter the way its products are perceived. Such changes could include new technology, shifts in consumer lifestyles, new offerings by competitors, and negative publicity.

Product positioning is illustrated in Figure 7-10, which depicts the ice cream marketplace in terms of the consumer desires regarding two key ice cream attributes: price and

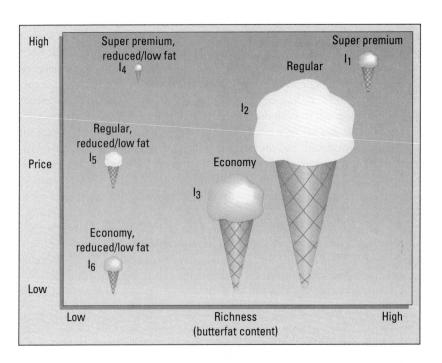

FIGURE 7-10
The Product Positioning of Ice Cream

Ethics AND TODAY'S MARKETER

Old Dutch Potato Chips Expands Their Product Market to Ontario and Finds a "Chippy" Response from Hostess Frito-Lay

Faced with a maturing market for potato chips in Western Canada, Winnipeg-based Old Dutch Foods Ltd. decided to head east to the Ontario market. At the time, Old Dutch was the market leader in Western Canada with sales of $115 million and market shares of nearly 60 per cent in Manitoba, Saskatchewan, and Alberta respectively and 40 per cent in British Columbia. However, the Canadian chip market is worth over $1 billion in annual sales, with a great majority of these sales to be found in the large and lucrative, but fairly mature, Ontario chip market. Hostess Frito-Lay of Toronto and Humpty-Dumpty Foods Ltd. of Montreal were comfortably in control of Eastern Canada with 45 per cent of the market each, and were not too pleased to discover Old Dutch was planning to move in.

Old Dutch expected a bit of a battle, maybe price cutting, promotional contests, in-store promotional displays, trade incentives, trade inventory loading, the usual. However, the tactic Hostess Frito-Lay chose came as a complete surprise to Old Dutch: the sales representatives from Hostess Frito-Lay went to all of the retailers who had purchased Old Dutch potato chips and bought up their inventory! Since Old Dutch was trying to supply Ontario from its Winnipeg base and did not have an extensive truck fleet, they could not replenish chip supplies quickly enough. The power of the tactic was that Old Dutch had been promoting its product to Ontario consumers and creating demand, but because there was no shelf-stock, consumers could not try the product and became dismayed and disenchanted. Dismay was also the reaction of Old Dutch, because the purchase of their stocks from some eighty-two retailers was rumoured to have occurred as a result of coercion on the part of Hostess Frito-Lay.

The activity was clearly anti-competitive and Old Dutch complained to the Federal Competition Bureau. At this point, Hostess Frito-Lay ceased buying up the product. When the Competition Bureau investigated they concluded that since the tactic was no longer being employed, they did not need to take action and the issue was closed. Curiously, Old Dutch was accused of employing this same tactic when Miss Vickie's, a small Ontario potato chip manufacturer, attempted to penetrate the Western market.

As the marketing manager of Old Dutch potato chips, how would you proceed now?

Source. Based on "Crunch Time," *Report on Business Magazine*, Vol. 8 (December 1991), pp. 48–52; "Chipping Away for More Share," *Playback Strategy*, Vol. 2 (July 15, 1991), pp. 1–2; "Hostess on Buying Binge of Rival's Potato Chips: Consumers Blocked from Product, Old Dutch Manager Says," *Globe & Mail*, Metro edition (July 3, 1991), p. B3; "Bureau Checking Chips," *Globe & Mail*, Metro edition (July 13, 1991), p. B4.

richness (level of butterfat content). In this figure, there are six ideal points (target markets)—I1–I6, each associated with a specific type of ice cream. Here is a brief description of the six categories:

- I_1—*super premium*. The creamiest, richest ice cream (butterfat content of 15 to 18 per cent) with the highest price. Häagen-Dazs, Mövenpick's, Richard D's, Laura Secord, and Ben & Jerry's are in this grouping. This segment is the fastest growing and represents about 3 per cent of Canadian ice cream sales.

- I_2—*regular.* A creamy, rich ice cream (butterfat content of 10 to 12 per cent) with an average to slightly above-average price. Sealtest, Breyers, Natrel, and Baskin Robbins are positioned here.

- I_3—*economy.* An average ice cream (butterfat content of 10 per cent) at a below-average price. Private-label brands fit here.

- I_4—*super premium, reduced or low fat.* A flavourful ice cream with a high price for moderately health-conscious consumers (butterfat content of 5 to 10 per cent). The reduced-fat versions of the leading super premiums go here.

- I_5—*regular, reduced or low fat.* A good-quality ice cream for more health-conscious consumers (butterfat content of less than 8 per cent) at an average price. Weight Watcher's, Light n' Lively, and Sealtest Parlour 1% are positioned here.

- I_6—*economy, reduced or low fat.* An average ice cream for more health-conscious consumers (butterfat content of 4 to 8 per cent) at a below-average price. Private-label brands fit here.

FRITO-LAY
www.fritolay.com/

An examination of competitive product positioning reveals that there are competing products in each market niche. In some instances, the marketplace is saturated. Nonetheless, the companies in the industry have done a good job in addressing the needs of the various consumer segments and in differentiating the products offered to each segment.

Breyers, Sealtest, and Light n' Lively are all marketed by Unilever. From an analysis of company product positioning, it is clear that Unilever serves the customers in its markets well. However, it must continue to differentiate carefully between Breyers (the "all natural" ice cream) and Sealtest (the "ice cream parlor" ice cream).

By undertaking product-positioning analysis, a company can learn a great deal and plan its marketing efforts accordingly, as these examples show:

- Wrigley is always on the lookout for positioning opportunities for its chewing gums. Because of the negative attention placed on cigarette smoking, Wrigley recently embarked on a very creative marketing strategy for Wrigley's Spearmint gum—positioning it with the phrase, "When you can't smoke, enjoy pure chewing satisfaction."

- Air Canada believes numerous travellers perceive airlines as indifferent and impersonal. To remedy this, it is emphasizing the quality of its service—depicted in ads by the worldwide symbol for outstanding service, the red carpet. See Figure 7-11.

The Product Life Cycle

The **product life cycle** *describes each stage in a product's life.*

The **product life cycle** is a concept that attempts to describe a product's sales, competitors, profits, customers, and marketing emphasis from its inception until it is removed from the market.

From a product-planning perspective, there is interest in the product life cycle for several reasons.

1. Some product lives are shorter than before.

2. New products often require high marketing and other investments.

3. An understanding of the concept lets a firm anticipate changes in consumer tastes, competition, and support from resellers and adjust its marketing plan accordingly.

4. The concept enables a firm to consider the product mix it should offer; many firms seek a **balanced product portfolio**, whereby a combination of new, growing, and mature products is maintained.

Companies often desire a **balanced product portfolio.**

The life-cycle concept can be applied to a product class (watches), a product form (quartz watches), or a brand (Seiko quartz watches). Product forms generally follow the traditional life cycle more faithfully than product classes or brands.

Product life cycles may be traditional, boom, fad, extended fad, seasonal, revival, or bust.

As Figure 7-12 shows, product life cycles vary greatly, in both duration and shape. A *traditional cycle* has distinct periods of introduction, growth, maturity, and decline. A *boom*

FIGURE 7-11
Air Canada: A Customer-Service Positioning Approach
Reprinted by permission.

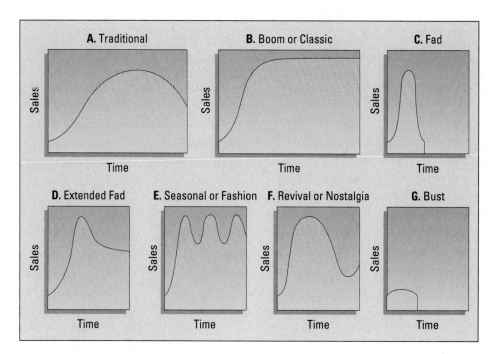

FIGURE 7-12
Selected Product Life-Cycle Patterns

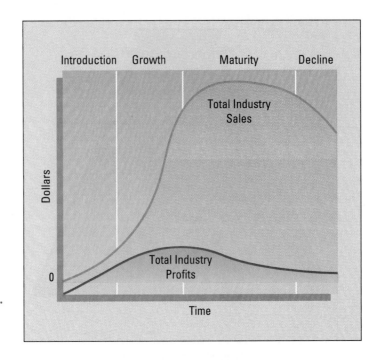

FIGURE 7-13
The Traditional Product Life Cycle

or *classic cycle* describes a very popular product that sells well for a long time. A *fad* cycle represents a product with quick popularity and a sudden decline. An *extended fad* is like a fad, but residual sales continue at a lower level than earlier sales. A *seasonal* or *fashion cycle* results if a product sells well in nonconsecutive periods. With a *revival* or *nostalgia cycle*, a seemingly obsolete product achieves new popularity. A *bust cycle* occurs for a product that fails.

T a b l e   7 - 4

The Characteristics of the Traditional Product Life Cycle

	STAGE IN LIFE CYCLE			
CHARACTERISTICS	*Introduction*	*Growth*	*Maturity*	*Decline*
Marketing goal	Attract innovators and opinion leaders to new product	Expand distribution and product line	Maintain differential advantage as long as possible	(a) Cut back, (b) revive, or (c) terminate
Industry sales	Increasing	Rapidly increasing	Stable	Decreasing
Competition	None or small	Some	Substantial	Limited
Industry profits	Negative	Increasing	Decreasing	Decreasing
Customers	Innovators	Resourceful mass market	Mass market	Laggards
Product mix	One or a few basic models	Expanding line	Full product line	Best-sellers
Distribution	Depends on product	Rising number of outlets/ distributors	Greatest number of outlets/ distributors	Decreasing number of outlets/ distributors
Promotion	Informative	Persuasive	Competitive	Informative
Pricing	Depends on product	Greater range of prices	Full line of prices	Selected prices

Stages of the Traditional Product Life Cycle

The stages and characteristics of the traditional product life cycle are shown in Figure 7-13 and Table 7-4, which both refer to total industry performance during the cycle. The performance of an individual firm may vary from that of the industry, depending on its specific goals, resources, marketing plans, location, competitive environment, level of success, and stage of entry.

During the **introduction stage of the product life cycle**, a new product is introduced to the marketplace and the goal is to generate customer interest. The rate of sales growth depends on a product's newness, as well as its desirability. Generally, a product modification gains sales faster than a major innovation. Only one or two firms have entered the market, and competition is minimal. There are losses due to high production and marketing costs; and cash flow is poor. Initial customers are innovators who are willing to take risks, can afford to take them, and like the status of buying first. Because one or two firms dominate and costs are high, only one or a few basic product models are sold. For a routine item like a new cereal, distribution is extensive. For a luxury item like a new boat, distribution is limited. Promotion must be informative, and free samples may be desirable. Depending on the product and choice of consumer market, a firm may start with a high status price or low mass-market price.

*In the **introduction stage**, the goal is to establish a consumer market.*

Over the **growth stage of the product life cycle**, a new product gains wider consumer acceptance, and the marketing goal is to expand distribution and the range of available product alternatives. Industry sales increase rapidly as a few more firms enter a highly profitable market that has substantial potential. Total and unit profits are high because an affluent (resourceful) mass market buys distinctive products from a limited group of firms and is willing to pay for them. To accommodate the growing market, modified versions of basic models are offered, distribution is expanded, persuasive mass advertising is utilized, and a range of prices is available.

*During the **growth stage**, firms enlarge the market and offer alternatives.*

During the **maturity stage of the product life cycle**, a product's sales growth levels off and firms try to maintain a differential advantage (such as a lower price, improved features, or extended warranty) for as long as possible. Industry sales stabilize as the market becomes saturated and many firms enter to capitalize on the still sizable demand. Competition is at its highest. Thus, total industry and unit profits drop because discounting is popular. The average-income mass market makes purchases. A full product line is made available at many outlets (or through many distributors) and many prices. Promotion becomes very competitive.

*In the **maturity stage**, companies work hard to sustain a differential advantage.*

In the **decline stage of the product life cycle**, a product's sales fall as substitutes enter the market or consumers lose interest. Firms have three options. They can cut back on marketing, thus reducing the number of product items they make, the outlets they sell through, and the promotion used; they can revive a product by repositioning, repackaging, or otherwise remarketing it; or they can drop the product. As industry sales decline, many firms exit the market since customers are fewer and they have less money to spend. The product mix focuses on best-sellers, selected outlets (distributors) and prices, and promotion that stresses informatively—availability and price.

*In the **decline stage**, firms reduce marketing, revive a product, or end it.*

The bulky, electric-powered portable calculator is a good example of a product form that moved through the life cycle. It went from an exclusive, expensive item to a widespread, moderately priced item to a mass-marketed, inexpensive item to obsolescence. Today, earlier versions of the portable calculator have been replaced by technologically advanced product forms—such as credit card-sized, solar-powered calculators.

Evaluating the Product Life-Cycle Concept

The product life cycle provides a good framework for product planning; but, it has not proven very useful in forecasting. In using the product life-cycle concept, these key points should be kept in mind:

1. The stages, the time span, and the shape of the cycle (such as flat, erratic, or sharply inclined) vary by product.

2. Such external factors as the economy, inflation, and consumer lifestyles may shorten or lengthen a product's life cycle.

3. A firm may do better or worse than the industry "average" at any stage in the cycle. Just because an industry is in the growth stage for a product does not mean every firm that enters the market will succeed, nor does the decline stage mean lower sales for every firm.

4. A firm may not only be able to manage a product life cycle, it may also be able to extend it or reverse a decline. Effective marketing may lure a new market segment, find a new product use, or foster better reseller support.

5. As Figure 7-14 illustrates, firms may engage in a **self-fulfilling prophecy**, whereby they predict falling sales and then ensure this by reducing or removing marketing support. With proper marketing, some products might not fail.

*A **self-fulfilling prophecy** may occur when a firm anticipates declining sales and reduces marketing efforts.*

The International Dimensions of Product Planning

When an international product plan is being devised, the following points should be kept in mind:

- Although a firm may offer the same products in countries around the globe, these products can have distinct generic meanings in different countries.
- In developing and less-developed countries, product "frills" are often less important than in industrialized countries.
- Due to their intangibility, perishability, inseparability, and variability, international marketing efforts for services are often more complex than those for goods.
- The concept of convenience, shopping, and specialty products is less valid in markets where distribution is limited or consumers have few choices.
- Installations and accessory equipment may be hard to ship overseas.
- Marketing all of the items in a wide and/or deep product mix may not be appropriate, or economically feasible, on an international basis.
- The diversity of international markets may necessitate a decentralized product management organization, with some executives permanently assigned to foreign countries.

FIGURE 7-14
A Self-Fulfilling Prophecy

- For many products, there are differences in product positioning and consumer ideal points by country or region. Simple positioning messages travel better than more complicated ones.

- Some products are in different stages of their life cycles in developing and less-developed countries than in industrialized countries.

- Expectations regarding goods/services combinations may differ by country.

- A product modification or minor innovation in a home market may be a major innovation internationally, necessitating different marketing approaches.

- The characteristics of the market segments—innovators, early adopters, early majority, late majority, and laggards—in the diffusion process (covered in Chapter 8) often differ by country.

- Even though global branding and packaging may be desirable, various nations may have special needs or requirements.

International Marketing in

Are the Positioning Factors Used by MBA Students Universal?

As consumers, how do MBA students decide upon a product's positioning? To answer this question, a marketing research study was conducted to evaluate the importance of brand name, price, physical appearance, and retailer reputation as indicators of product quality for consumer electronics. A questionnaire was completed by 640 beginning MBA students from thirty-eight mostly western industrialized countries and Japan. The respondents were matched on such factors as age, education, professional goals, and income; and they were separated into four cultural groups: North American countries (Canada and the U.S.), EU member countries, European countries not belonging to the EU, and others.

The researchers found that brand-name cues are more important than price or physical appearance—regardless of cultural group. And price and physical appearance are more important than a retailer's reputation in positioning a product's overall quality. The findings support the notion that the value of certain product positioning cues does not vary by culture.

The study's authors suggest that culture or country boundaries are less important in product positioning than these five factors:

- The more consumers rely on a particular quality cue, the more they also want information from other sources.
- Consumers who are willing to accept certain forms of risk also tend to use positioning cues the most.
- Brand-prone consumers are less price sensitive.
- The use of brand and price as signals increases when people have a greater intention to buy a product or when they perceive product benefits as high.
- The use of specific positioning cues decreases as a consumer's education increases and when the consumer is more technologically oriented.

As a Sony Discman marketing manager responsible for the Canadian and the U.S. markets, how would you use these results in catering to educated young adults?

Source: Based on material in Niraj Dawar and Philip Parker, "Marketing Universals: Consumers' Use of Brand Name, Price, Physical Appearance, and Retailer Reputation as Signals of Product Quality," *Journal of Marketing*, Vol. 58 (April 1994), pp. 81–95.

MARKETING IN A CHANGING WORLD

Even Toyota's Not Infallible[30]

With its stable of Toyota and Lexus vehicles, Toyota has been one of the most respected manufacturers in the world for decades. Toyota is admired for its ability to read the market, its deep product mix, the quality of its vehicles, its ability to position its models in the marketplace (especially the upscale Lexus brand), and its strong customer following. And lest we forget, Toyota's annual sales exceed U.S.$100 billion and it is very profitable.

Yet, despite its prowess, this manufacturing dynamo recently had a major stumble in its home Japanese market with the redesigned Corolla. What does this signify? Careful product planning turns into successful product planning only if the consumer says so.

TOYOTA
www.toyota.com/

For years, Japanese car makers built base models that were luxurious by other makers' standards. The Toyota Corolla was Japan's best-selling car for twenty-six years. Thus, when Toyota—worried that sticker prices had grown too steep—did a full remodelling and stripped features from the Corollas it sells in Japan, consumers rebelled. Toyota responded by restoring some of the removed features in a mid-year replacement model.

Before the remodelling, a basic Toyota Corolla sold for U.S.$10 700 in Japan. Standard features included an AM-FM stereo, self-adjusting air-conditioning, and bumpers painted so they matched the car's colour. The remodelled Corolla sold for U.S.$9750 due to a simplified engine, an AM mono radio, partially vinyl seats, black bumpers, and manual-control air-conditioning. Said one dealer, the car "looked cheaper" and "the interior was much poorer."

Once Toyota saw the consumer reaction to the redesign, it had a revamped Corolla at dealer showrooms within five months. The remodelled U.S.$10 400 basic Corolla included full-fabric seats, power windows, automatic door locks, and a driver's airbag (which is not legally mandated in Japan). As Toyota learned, "cutting costs too much—or too obviously—can backfire, turning [the] consumer off," even if prices are cut, too.

S U M M A R Y

1. To define product planning and differentiate among tangible, augmented, and generic products Product planning systematically allows a firm to pinpoint opportunities, develop marketing programs, coordinate a product mix, maintain successful products, reappraise faltering ones, and delete undesirable products.

Products should be defined in a combination of ways. A tangible product is a basic physical entity, service, or idea with precise specifications; it is offered under a given description or model number. An augmented product includes not only tangible elements, but also the accompanying cluster of image and service features. A generic product focuses on the benefits a buyer desires; this concept looks at what a product means to the consumer rather than the seller.

2. To examine the scope of goods and services, and explain how goods and services may be categorized Goods marketing encompasses

the sales of durable and nondurable physical products; service marketing involves goods rental, goods alteration, maintenance, or repair, and personal services. In Canada, consumer expenditures on nondurable goods are slightly higher than those for durable goods. Services account for a very large share of the GDP in industrialized nations, 66 per cent of Canada's GDP, and a smaller share in developing and less-developed nations. Both final consumer and business services have seen significant growth in recent years. The scope of services is sometimes underestimated due to the hidden service sector.

With a goods/services continuum, products can be positioned on a scale from pure goods to goods/services combinations to pure services. Much can be learned by studying this continuum, including its use for final and organizational consumer products, the presence of unique marketing opportunities, and the changing relationship between sellers

---

[30]The material in this section is based on Andrew Pollack, "The Risks of Cutting Too Far," *New York Times* (December 21, 1995), pp. D1, D8.

and buyers as pure goods become goods/services combinations. Both goods- and services-oriented firms need to identify core and peripheral services.

Goods can be classed by market, product durability, value added, company goal, degree of regulation, distribution channel length, and extent of customer contact. Services can be classed by market, level of tangibility, service provider skill, service provider goals, degree of regulation, labour intensiveness, and amount of customer contact. A firm would be categorized on the basis of a combination of these factors. Services are generally less tangible, more perishable, less separable from their provider, and more variable in quality than goods that are sold.

3. *To look at the use of marketing by goods versus services firms and provide illustrations of service marketing* Many service firms have lagged behind manufacturers in the use of marketing because of their small size, the larger geographic coverage of goods-oriented companies, their technical emphasis, less competition and the lack of need for marketing, the high esteem of consumers for certain service providers, past bans on advertising, a dislike of marketing by some service professionals, and the reluctance of some manufacturers to view services as profit centres. Yet, for a number of reasons, this has been changing and the marketing of services is now expanding greatly.

4. *To describe nonprofit marketing and the role of nonprofit marketing in society* Nonprofit marketing is conducted by organizations and people that operate for the public good or to foster a cause and not for financial profits. Nonprofit organizations can be classed on the basis of tangibility, organization structure, objectives, and constituency. A nonprofit organization would be categorized by a combination of these factors. Worldwide, there are millions of organizations and people engaged in nonprofit marketing. Nonprofit organizations play a key roll in the Canadian economy, employing 25 per cent of industrial employees. Funding for nonprofits comes from corporations, government, and individuals. In 1994, 5.3 million individual Canadian tax filers claimed $3.39 billion in charitable donations on their taxes.

5. *To examine the various types of products, product mixes, and product management organization forms from which a firm may select* Goods marketing entails the sale of physical products. Service marketing includes goods rental, servicing goods owned by consumers, and personal services. Goods and services often differ in terms of intangibility, perishability, inseparability from the service provider, and variability in quality.

Consumer products are goods and services for the final consumer. They can be classified as convenience, shopping, and specialty items. These products are differentiated on the basis of consumer awareness of alternatives prior to the shopping trip and the degree of search and time spent shopping. Industrial products are goods and services used in the production of other goods or services, in the operation of a business, or for resale. They include installations, accessory equipment, raw materials, component materials, fabricated parts, business supplies, and business services. They are distinguished on the basis of decision making, costs, consumption, the role in production, and the change in form.

A product item is a specific model, brand, or size of a product sold by a firm. A product line is a group of closely related items sold by a firm. A product mix consists of all the different product lines a firm offers. The width, depth, and consistency of the product mix are important.

A firm may choose from or combine several product management structures, including: marketing manager system, product (brand) manager, product planning committee, new-product manager system, and venture team. Each has particular strengths and best uses.

6. *To discuss product positioning and its usefulness for marketers* A firm must ensure that each of its products is perceived as providing some combination of unique features and that they are desired by the target market. Through product positioning, a firm can map its offerings with regard to consumer perceptions, consumer desires, competition, its own products in the same line, and the changing environment. Competitive positioning, company positioning, and consumers' ideal points are key concepts.

7. *To study the different types of product life cycles that a firm may encounter and the stages of the traditional product life cycle* The product life cycle seeks to describe a product's sales, competitors, profits, customers, and marketing emphasis from its inception until its removal from the market. Many firms desire a balanced product portfolio, with products in various stages of the life cycle. The product life cycle has several derivations, ranging from traditional to fad to bust. The traditional cycle consists of four stages: introduction, growth, maturity, and decline. During each stage, the marketing objective, industry sales, competition, industry profits, customers, and the marketing mix change. While the life cycle is useful in planning, it should not be used as a forecasting tool.

KEY TERMS

product planning (p. 163)
product (p. 163)
tangible product (p. 164)
augmented product (p. 164)
generic product (p. 164)
goods marketing (p. 164)
durable goods (p. 164)
nondurable goods (p. 164)
service marketing (p. 164)
rented-goods services (p. 164)
owned-goods services (p. 164)
nongoods services (p. 164)
hidden service sector (p. 166)
goods/services continuum (p. 166)
core services (p. 167)
peripheral services (p. 167)
consumer products (p. 169)
convenience products (p. 169)
shopping products (p. 169)

specialty products (p. 170)
industrial products (p. 170)
installations (p. 171)
accessory equipment (p. 171)
raw materials (p. 172)
component materials (p. 172)
fabricated parts (p. 172)
industrial supplies (p. 172)
industrial services (p. 172)
intangibility of services (p. 173)
perishability of services (p. 173)
inseparability of services (p. 173)
variability in service quality (p. 173)
industrialization of services (p. 175)
service blueprint (p. 176)
service gap (p. 176)
nonprofit marketing (p. 177)
social marketing (p. 179)
clients (p. 179)

donors (p. 179)
product item (p. 182)
product line (p. 182)
product mix (p. 182)
marketing manager system (p. 185)
product (brand) manager system (p. 185)
product planning committee (p. 185)
new-product manager system (p. 185)
venture team (p. 185)
product positioning (p. 186)
ideal points (p. 186)
product life cycle (p. 188)
balanced product portfolio (p. 188)
introduction stage of the product life cycle (p. 191)
growth stage of the product life cycle (p. 191)
maturity stage of the product life cycle (p. 191)
decline stage of the product life cycle (p. 191)
self-fulfilling prophecy (p. 192)

Review Questions

1. Why is it so important to understand the concept of a generic product?

2. Distinguish between a consumer product and an industrial product.

3. How can the same product be a convenience, shopping, and a specialty product? What does this mean to marketers?

4. What is a goods/services continuum? Why should firms be aware of this concept?

5. How can a service be positioned more tangibly?

6. Discuss the factors that may be used to classify nonprofit marketing.

7. What is a wide/shallow product mix? State the advantages and disadvantages of such a mix.

8. Under what circumstances is a product manager system appropriate? A new-product manager system?

9. What is the role of product positioning for a new product? A continuing product?

10. Explain the basic premise of the product life cycle. What is the value of this concept?

Discussion Questions

1. For each of the following, describe the tangible, augmented, and generic product:
   a. A review course for the Graduate Management Aptitude Test (GMAT).
   b. A computer mouse.
   c. A *Tragically Hip* CD.
   d. Highway paving materials.

2. Identify, describe, and differentiate between two product lines offered by the Pepsi Cola company. Refer to the definition of "product line" offered in the chapter to support your answer.

3. Present a goods/services continuum related to entertainment. Discuss the implications of this continuum for a firm interested in developing a marketing plan in the entertainment field.

4. What product management organization would you recommend for a large firm that makes, installs, and services home security systems? The firm is thinking about getting involved with auto alarms, fire detectors, and/or television satellite dishes. Explain your answer.

5. How has the positioning of the cellular telephone changed since the product has been on the market? Why?

8
Conceiving, Developing, and Managing Products

Chapter Objectives

(1) To detail the importance of new products and describe why new products fail

(2) To present the stages in the new-product planning process

(3) To define and distinguish among branding terms, to examine the importance of branding, and to study the key branding decisions that must be made

(4) To define and distinguish among packaging terms and to examine the importance of packaging

(5) To analyze the growth and maturity of products, including the adoption process, the diffusion process, and extension strategies, and to examine product deletion decisions and strategies

Ask just about any company these days to give up its facsimile machine and you're in for a fight. For most businesspeople today, it's difficult to remember what life was like before fax machines made it possible to send documents easily and cheaply across the country or around the world. Final consumers are also finding uses for the fax machine. They order take-out food, request a song on the radio, and make mail-order purchases via fax.

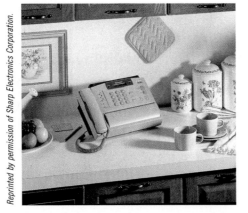

Reprinted by permission of Sharp Electronics Corporation.

According to a recent survey, two-thirds of North American adults have either received or sent a fax message at some point (usually at work). Yet, even though PC sales have successfully made the transition from office to home, just 7 per cent of North American households now own a freestanding fax machine. In contrast, 28.8 per cent of Canadian households own PCs and 42 per cent of these computers have a modem.

The survey just cited also indicates that fax machine manufacturers will have to work awfully hard to increase their market penetration in the home market. Seventy-one per cent of North American adults feel there is no benefit to being able to send and receive faxes at home. Of the 28 per cent who believe there are benefits to having a fax machine at home, only 11 per cent (equal to 3 per cent of all North American adults) think there is a great benefit. Among the key benefits to home faxes are ease of use, flexibility (they allow individuals to work at home), convenience (not having to leave home to send a fax), and speed (compared to mail or express carriers).

According to the survey, among people who would purchase fax equipment for home use, one-half of them would prefer a fax machine built into their home computer. (Note: While a built-in computer fax modem can generally be bought for less than $100, it cannot be used to send documents that are not part of a computer file—but a fax modem can receive noncomputerized documents). One-quarter would buy a freestanding machine and 25 per cent do not know what type of machine they would purchase.

Many consumers are also uncertain about the cost of a freestanding fax machine, where they would buy it, and the name of a good brand. On average, consumers expect to pay $640 for a freestanding machine—double today's real "street prices." Price expectations vary with the person's previous experience with fax machines. More experienced shoppers plan to pay less (an average price of $540) than nonusers (an average price of $860). The place to shop for a freestanding fax machine that people mention most is electronics stores (35 per cent of respondents), followed by office supply stores (15 per cent), and then mail-order catalogues (12 per cent). Most people do not know the name of a good brand of fax machine; some even mention names of firms that do not produce free-standing fax machines.[1]

In this chapter, we will study how new products are developed, the factors causing rapid or slow growth for new products, how to manage mature products, and what to do when existing products falter. In addition, the various types of brand designations, key branding decisions, the basic functions of packaging, key packaging decisions, and selected criticisms of packaging are discussed. As our home fax discussion illustrates, it takes a lot of work—and persistence—to stay ahead.

Overview

While any product combines tangible and intangible features to satisfy consumer needs, a **new product** involves a modification of an existing product or an innovation the consumer perceives as meaningful. To succeed, a new product must have desirable attributes, be unique, and have its features communicated to consumers. Marketing support is therefore necessary.[2]

*Product planning involves **new products** and existing products.*

Modifications are alterations in or extensions of a firm's existing products and include new models, styles, colours, features, and brands. **Minor innovations** are items not previously marketed by a firm that have been marketed by others. For example, the Toronto Dominion Bank introduced a Visa TD Gold Travel Card that is not affiliated with any major airline or other travel service. Instead, cardholders create their own travel package with points built up on the basis of their dollar purchases.[3]

*New products may be **modifications**, **minor innovations**, or **major innovations**.*

Major innovations are items not previously sold by any firm (like the first cellular telephone). If a firm works with major innovations, the costs, risks, and time required for profitability all rise. Overall, most new products are modifications; few are major innovations.

New products may be conceived of and developed by a company itself or purchased from another firm. A company may buy a firm, buy a specific product, or sign a licensing agreement (whereby it pays an inventor a royalty fee based on sales). Acquisitions may reduce risks and time demands, but they rely on outsiders for innovations and may require large investments.

Early in a product's life, there is usually strong sales growth, as more people purchase and repurchase. This is an exciting time; and if a product is popular, it can last for quite a while. Later, the market becomes more saturated and competition intensifies. At that point, a firm can maintain high sales by adding features that provide convenience and durability, using new materials in construction, offering a range of models, stressing new packaging, and/or adding customer services. It can also reposition a product, enter untapped geographic markets, demonstrate new uses, offer new brands, set lower prices, use new media, and/or appeal to new segments. At some point, however, firms must decide whether these items have outlived their usefulness and should be dropped.

When conceiving, developing, and managing its products, a firm needs to make and enact a variety of decisions regarding the brand and package used with each item. A **brand** is a name, term, design, symbol, or any other feature that distinguishes the goods and services of one seller from those of other sellers. A **package** is a container used to protect, promote, transport, and/or identify a product.[4] It may consist of a product's physical container, an outer label, and/or inserts.

Brands identify a firm's products; packages are product containers that serve many functions.

[1]Susan Reda, "Home Faxes Fail to Strike," *Stores* (April 1995), pp. 28–29; and Statistics Canada, *The Daily* (Friday, January 12, 1996).

[2]See Roger J. Calantone, C. Anthony Di Benedetto, and Ted Haggbloom, "Principles of New Product Management: Exploring the Beliefs of Product Practitioners," *Journal of Product Innovation Management*, Vol. 12 (June 1995), pp. 235–247.

[3]Andrea Haman, "TD Piles on Features in New Travel Card," *Marketing Magazine* (June 5, 1995), p. 4.

[4]Peter D. Bennett (Ed.), *Dictionary of Marketing Terms*, Second Edition (Chicago: American Marketing Association, 1995), pp. 27, 201.

The Importance of New Products

A firm's product policy should be future-oriented and recognize that products, no matter how successful, tend to be mortal—they usually cannot sustain a peak level of sales and profits indefinitely. "Innovation can give a company a competitive advantage and profits, but nothing lasts forever. Success brings on imitators, who respond with superior features, lower prices, or some other new way to draw customers. Time ultimately renders nearly all advantages obsolete."[5] So, replacements should be constantly planned and a balanced product portfolio pursued—by both small and large firms.

New products offer differential advantages.

Introducing new products is important for several reasons. Desirable differential advantages can be attained. For example, the Seiko Kinetic Quartz watch is the first quartz watch that does not require a battery or have to be wound. It is advertised as "No more batteries. No more winding. No more hassles." Goodyear's "smart tire" for trucks is embedded with a computer chip allowing drivers to easily see the wear and air pressure of tires; this improves tire life and fuel efficiency.

New products lead to sales growth or stability.

New products may be needed for continued growth. That is why Quaker Oats has a new line of rice cakes; due to their poor taste, earlier Quaker Rice Cakes did not attain company goals—as Quaker admits in Figure 8-1. At Timken, a nearly 100-year-old U.S.-based maker of industrial roller bearings, "Today's bearing is a dramatically different product than it was ten years ago, and we would be very surprised if the 2005 version is anything like we're making today." By thinking like this, Timken still holds a one-third share of the world market for tapered roller bearings.[6]

QUAKER OATS COMPANY
www.quakeroats.com/

BLACK & DECKER
www.blackanddecker.com/

New products can take time.

For firms with cyclical or seasonal sales, new products can stabilize revenues and costs. Union Carbide manufactures medical-testing equipment, to reduce its dependence on cyclical chemicals. Black & Decker has cut back on lawn mowers and looks for new opportunities in less seasonal products (such as power tools for the home).

Planning for growth must take into consideration the time it takes for a new product to move from idea stage to commercialization. For instance, in 1983, Canadian Brian Maxwell came up with the idea for a food bar for exercise enthusiasts that would let them fuel up for long workouts while circumventing the stomach problems that often accompany eating while exercising. He immediately began experimenting with various recipes; it took three years and 800 experimental recipes to find one that worked: "For three years, people would say the texture wasn't right, the bar was upsetting their stomachs, or there was something wrong with the taste." At that point, Maxwell and his partner, Jennifer Biddulph, invested their life savings to contract for a 50 000-bar production run and start a mail-order business. In 1989, they opened their first plant. And in 1993, Powerfood Inc. became a Price/Costco vendor. Today, the maker of PowerBar has annual revenues of more than $30 million and does business in thirty countries.[7]

New products can increase profits and control.

New products can lead to larger profits and give a company better control over a marketing strategy. For example, the new Lincoln line of cars is quite popular, so the cars have been selling at close to the sticker price, with dealers earning gross profits of up to $10 000 on each car sold. Because there are fewer Lincoln dealers relative to lower-priced cars, they do not use much price discounting and have firm command over their marketing efforts.

Risk may be lessened through diversity.

To limit risk, many firms seek to reduce dependence on one product or product line. That is why many movie theatres converted to multiplexes; their revenues are not tied to any one film's performance. Hewlett-Packard makes electronic components and test equipment, medical electronic equipment, and analytical instrumentation—in addition to its core computing and printing products; and it regularly adds new products. Turtle Wax, the world's leader in car care products, now makes shoe polish, household cleaners, and fabric protectors.

New products may improve distribution.

Firms may try to improve the efficiency of their established distribution systems by placing new products in them. They can then spread advertising, sales, and distribution

[5]Jeffrey R. Williams, "How Sustainable Is Your Competitive Advantage?" *California Management Review*, Vol. 34 (Spring 1992), p. 29.
[6]Eric S. Hardy, "The Soul of an Old Company," *Forbes* (March 13, 1995), pp. 70–71.
[7]Tod Jones, "The Power of Persistence," *Price Costco Connection* (June 1995), p. 15.

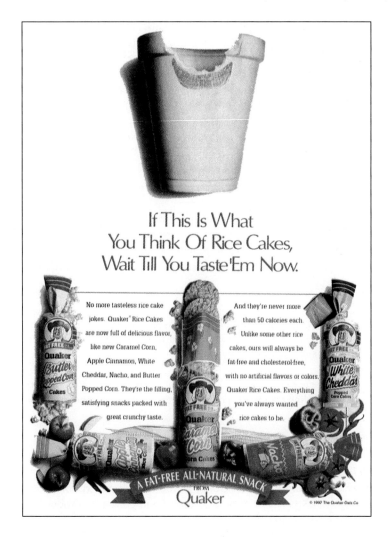

FIGURE 8-1
Better-Tasting Rice Cakes from Quaker Oats
Reprinted by permission.

costs among several products, gain dealer support, and discourage other companies from entering the market. Manufacturers like Neilsen-Cadbury's, Unilever, and Revlon can place new products in many outlets quickly. Service firms, such as banks, also can efficiently add new products (financial services) into their distribution networks.

Firms often seek technological breakthroughs. For instance, Kodak has developed a line of digital cameras that create electronic images, and which promise to revolutionize the photodeveloping business. This may well mean the demise of traditional film-based cameras—and the core of Kodak's business. To remain viable, Kodak has chosen to embrace digital technology, as it did with VCRs and camcorders, which replaced "film based" movie cameras in the 1980s. Kodak is now a leading producer of videotapes.[8]

Sometimes, firms want to find uses for waste materials from existing products—to aid productivity or be responsive to environmental concerns. Just over a decade ago, the chicken industry found that "we have four billion broilers, and the consumer generally doesn't want the necks and backs. What do we do? We grind them into baloney and hot dogs."[9] The sales of these products have skyrocketed since then. For environmental and cost reasons, Johnson Controls makes auto batteries from recycled lead and plastic; Reynolds Metals uses recycled paperboard in foil and wax paper packaging; and Scotch-Brite steel wool pads are made from recycled bottles and packaged in recycled paper.

Companies may bring out new products to respond to changing consumer demographics and lifestyles. For example, Royal Plastics markets a basic 500-square-foot plastic house targeted at underdeveloped nations. At a cost of U.S.$30 a square foot for con-

Technology can be exploited.

KODAK
www.kodak.com/

Waste materials can be used.

JOHNSON CONTROLS
www.johnsoncontrols.com/

New products respond to consumer needs.

[8]Deborah McKay-Stokes, "Old Products and New Processes," *Marketing Magazine* (April 24, 1995), p. 15.
[9]R. Kleinfield, "America Goes Chicken Crazy," *New York Times* (December 9, 1984), Section 3, p. 9.

struction, it is priced right for these markets. Added to the fact that many of the homes are built in tropical climates where termites and dampness are very hard on wood-frame construction, it is a product well positioned to meet people's needs.[10]

Government mandates are addressed.

New products are sometimes developed in response to government mandates. In 1990, the Ontario provincial government mandated that all new cars sold in the province be equipped with daytime running lights. Prior to this, North American manufacturers had no experience with this type of feature on automobiles. They had to scramble to come up with technologies to deal with this requirement. As a result of the Ontario legislation, foreign manufacturers have essentially equipped all automobiles for the Canadian market with daytime running lights. And General Motors has been selling automobiles in the United States with daytime running lights, promoting this as a safety feature, even though it is not required there by law.

Good long-run new-product planning requires systematic research and development, matching the requirements of new-product opportunities against company abilities, emphasizing consumer desires, properly spending time and money, and defensive—as well as offensive—planning. A firm must accept that some new products may fail; a progressive firm will take risks:

> Innovation is a risky business, and failure is commonplace. Rewarding success is easy, but rewarding intelligent failure is more important. Don't judge people strictly by results; try to judge them by the quality of their efforts. People should take intelligent business risks without also risking their compensation or their careers.[11]

And there has been some criticism of the negative effects of many Canadian firms' short-run, bottom-line orientation on their level of innovativeness (and willingness to take risks).

Why New Products Fail

Despite better product-planning practices today than ever before, the failure rate for new products is quite high. According to the consulting firm of Booz, Allen, & Hamilton, an average of 35 per cent of new industrial and consumer products fail. Others say the rate may be even greater.[12]

With **absolute product failure**, *costs are not regained. With* **relative product failure**, *goals are not met.*

Product failure can be defined in both absolute and relative terms. **Absolute product failure** occurs if a firm is unable to regain its production and marketing costs. It incurs a financial loss. **Relative product failure** occurs if a firm makes a profit on an item but that product does not reach profit goals and/or adversely affects a firm's image. In computing profits and losses, the impact of the new product on the sales of other company items must be measured.

Even firms with good new-product records have had failures along the way. These include "light" pizza (Pizza Hut), Crystal Pepsi (PepsiCo), Bic perfume, McLean Deluxe (McDonald's), "new" Coke (Coca-Cola), Premier smokeless cigarettes (R.J. Reynolds) and *Junior* (the Universal movie starring Arnold Schwarzenegger, Danny DeVito, and Emma Thompson).

[10]Katrina Onstad, "The Midas Touch," *Canadian Business* (December 1995), p. 40.

[11]"How Can Big Companies Keep the Entrepreneurial Spirit Alive?" *Harvard Business Review*, Vol. 73 (November–December 1995), p. 190.

[12]See Cyndee Miller, "Survey: New Product Failure Is Top Management's Fault," *Marketing News* (February 1, 1993), p. 2; Erik Jan Hultink and Henry S. J. Robben, "Measuring New Product Success: The Difference That Time Perspective Makes," *Journal of Product Innovation Management*, Vol. 12 (November 1995), pp. 392–405; James Dao, "From a Collector of Turkeys, A Tour of a Supermarket Zoo," *New York Times* (September 24, 1995), Section C, p. 12; and Ulrike de Brentani, "New Industrial Service Development: Scenarios for Success and Failure," *Journal of Business Research*, Vol. 32 (February 1995), pp. 93–103.

Numerous factors may cause new-product failure. The key ones are lack of a differential advantage, poor planning, poor timing, and excessive enthusiasm by the sponsor. Illustrations of poor performance due to those factors follow.

Vancouver's Harvard Capital Corporation thought they had a sure winner with the "Spud Stop," a french fry vending machine, till they filed for bankruptcy in October 1994. The concept of bringing french fries to the masses in every location where there are vending machines is very alluring. The differential advantage of delivering a desired product with the convenience of a vending machine was very appealing to investors. The problem is that fast food outlets are easy to access too and very good at making french fries.

The "Spud Stop" machines were designed to deliver fries in 50 seconds by mixing dehydrated potato powder with water, producing thirty-two potato strands, dipping the strands in oil and then putting them in a box. But the machines could not deliver on their potential. For example, a "Spud Stop" machine was tested in Sedgewick Hall at the University of British Columbia. The students found that the machine would often begin smoking, the quality of the fries dispensed was often less than acceptable, and there were sanitation problems as well. In one instance the fire department was called and this resulted in the removal of the machine. Despite investments of over $10 million, Harvard Capital was unable to make a product that was able to deliver on its promise.[13]

Thermalux was the only North American maker of aerogels, "special substances that look like glass, feel like styrofoam, and are as light as a feather. They are great insulators." Despite the apparent potential of the product, after two years of poor planning, Thermalux had no customers; its aerogels remained "a solution looking for a problem." At first, it thought refrigerator makers would be the best market since they were under pressure to avoid using insulation materials made from certain fluorocarbons and to cut energy use. But the company underestimated competition from other insulation-materials firms. It also had a tough time setting the prices of its aerogels; and when aerogel insulation was tested in refrigerators, it did not show the benefits expected. Finally, Thermalux could not produce aerogels in sufficient quantity.[14]

Poor timing led to the failure of Zap Mail by Federal Express. When it was introduced, Federal Express expected its Zap Mail (which was essentially a facsimile machine service) to change the way business customers sent documents. With it, a customer could send a copy of a document almost anywhere in Canada or the United States in under two hours. The sender called a Federal Express operator, who had a courier pick up a document and take it to a Zap Mail office, which forwarded a copy to a receiving site. The copy was delivered by courier. Yet, within three years, Zap Mail was off the market. Although Federal Express felt Zap Mail would be successful, it failed for three reasons: computer modems let customers communicate instantly and without a delivery firm; many clients did not believe two-hour service (at a high price) was better than overnight service; and as Zap Mail started, inexpensive fax machines began to flood the market.[15]

Excessive enthusiasm caused RCA to overinvest in its videodisc player, causing a loss of nearly $600 million before the product was dropped. RCA felt the player's superior picture quality and low price would lead to success with the mass market. It underestimated consumer interest in recording programs (which the videodisc player could not do, but a VCR could). Firms with more focused goals, such as Hitachi, have done well marketing videodisc players to business customers as aids in sales training and point-of-purchase displays. Pioneer has laser videodisc players that "marry the superb sound of audio compact discs with crisp pictures." Philips has interactive players.[16]

Leading to failure are lack of an advantage, poor planning and timing, and excess enthusiasm.

[13]David Baines, "The Frying Game," *Canadian Business* (September 1994), pp. 32–36; and "Harvard Flunks Out," (editorial) *Canadian Business* (December 1994), p. 22.

[14]John R. Emschwiller, "Thermalux Seeks Customers for a New Technology," *Wall Street Journal* (February 15, 1991), p. B2.

[15]Federal Express Corporation reports.

[16]Sandra Salmans, "RCA Defends Timing of Videodisc Canceling," *New York Times* (April 6, 1984), pp. D1, D15; Marcia Watson, Jeff Kemph, and Judith Steele, "Marketing Muscle and the Videodisc," *Business Marketing* (June 1985), pp. 130–140; Brian O'Reilly, "Pioneer's Bright Picture," *Fortune* (August 13, 1990), p. 89; and "How to Sell Yourself on a CD-Interactive Player from Philips," *Wall Street Journal* (May 1, 1992), p. A13.

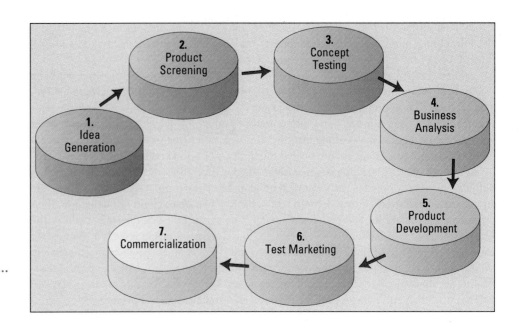

FIGURE 8-2
The New-Product Planning Process

New-Product Planning

*The **new-product planning** process moves goods and services from ideas to commercialization.*

The **new-product planning process** involves a series of steps from idea generation to commercialization. See Figure 8-2. During the process, a firm generates ideas, evaluates them, weeds out poor ones, obtains consumer feedback, develops the product, tests it, and brings it to market. An idea can be terminated at any time, and costs rise as the process goes on. The process could be used by firms of any size or type, and applies to goods and services.

Booz, Allen, & Hamilton says it generally takes a firm an average of seven well-defined ideas to yield one commercially successful new product. But this number can be much higher. A study of new-product managers found that it took nearly seventy-five ideas to yield one successful new product. In the pharmaceuticals industry, it may take up to 10 000 compounds to come up with one drug that is approved by government regulators.[17]

During the new-product planning process, a firm tries to balance such competing goals as these:

- A systematic process should be followed; however, there must be flexibility to adapt to each unique new-product opportunity.
- The process should be thorough, yet not unduly slow down introductions.
- True innovations should be pursued, yet fiscal constraints must be considered.
- An early reading of consumer acceptance should be sought, but the firm must not give away too much information to potential competitors.
- There should be an interest in short-run profitability, but not at the expense of long-run growth.[18]

Figure 8-3 highlights 3M's perspective on new-product planning: The "unique 3M culture, passed on from generation to generation, has resulted in more than 60 000 small miracles that make our lives safer, easier, better."

[17]Miller, "Survey: New Product Failure Is Top Management's Fault," p. 2; T. Erickson and L. Brenkus, *Healthcare R & D: Tools and Tactics* (Cambridge, Mass.: Arthur D. Little, October 1986), meeting notes; Laura Jereski, "Block That Innovation!" *Forbes* (January 18, 1993), p. 48; and Lara Mills, "The New Rx for Drug Marketing," *Marketing Magazine* (September 11, 1995), p. 15.

[18]See Robert G. Cooper and Elko J. Kleinschmidt, "Benchmarking the Firm's Success Factors in New Product Development," *Journal of Product Innovation Management*, Vol. 12 (November 1995), pp. 374–391; and James M. Higgins, "Innovate or Evaporate," *Futurist* (September–October 1995), pp. 42–48.

FIGURE 8-3
The 3M Approach to New-Product Planning
Reprinted by permission.

Idea Generation

Idea generation is a continuous, systematic search for new product opportunities. It involves new-idea sources and ways to generate ideas.

Sources of ideas may be employees, channel members, competitors, outside inventors, customers, government, and others. *Market-oriented sources* identify opportunities based on consumer needs and wants; laboratory research is used to satisfy them. Light beer, many ice cream flavours, and easy-to-open soda cans have evolved from market-oriented sources. *Laboratory-oriented sources* identify opportunities based on pure research (which seeks to gain knowledge and indirectly leads to specific new-product ideas) or applied research (which uses existing scientific techniques to develop new-product ideas). Penicillin, antifreeze, and synthetic fibres have evolved from laboratory sources.

Methods for generating ideas include brainstorming (small-group sessions to come up with a variety of ideas), analyzing current products, reading trade publications, visiting suppliers and dealers, and doing surveys. An open perspective is key: different people should be consulted; many ideas should be offered; and ideas should not be criticized, no matter how offbeat:

> Think of the *worst* possible idea you can for a new soup. How about a soup with rocks in it? Or a soup made of green slime? Terrible ideas, right? Maybe not. Thinking about a soup with rocks in it could inspire you to invent a new, extra-chunky brand of soup. Thinking about green slime soup could lead you to create a new $100-million line of "Slime Soups" for young boys, who we know like anything and everything that's "gross."[19]

Product Screening

Once a firm spots potential products, it must screen them. In **product screening**, poor, unsuitable, or otherwise unattractive ideas are weeded out. Today, many firms use a new-

Idea generation *is the search for opportunities.*

Product screening *weeds out undesirable ideas.*

[19]Bryan W. Mattimore, "Eureka! How to Invent a New Product," *Futurist* (March–April 1995), p. 34.

General Characteristics of New Products	Rating
Profit potential	_ _ _ _ _ _
Existing competition	_ _ _ _ _ _
Potential competition	_ _ _ _ _ _
Size of market	_ _ _ _ _ _
Level of investment	_ _ _ _ _ _
Patentability	_ _ _ _ _ _
Level of risk	_ _ _ _ _ _
Marketing Characteristics of New Products	
Fit with marketing capabilities	_ _ _ _ _ _
Effect on existing products (brands)	_ _ _ _ _ _
Appeal to current consumer markets	_ _ _ _ _ _
Potential length of product life cycle	_ _ _ _ _ _
Existence of differential advantage	_ _ _ _ _ _
Impact on image	_ _ _ _ _ _
Resistance to seasonal factors	_ _ _ _ _ _
Production Characteristics of New Products	
Fit with production capabilities	_ _ _ _ _ _
Length of time to commercialization	_ _ _ _ _ _
Ease of production	_ _ _ _ _ _
Availability of labour and material resources	_ _ _ _ _ _
Ability to produce at competitive prices	_ _ _ _ _ _

FIGURE 8-4
A New-Product Screening Checklist

product screening checklist for preliminary analysis. In it, they list the attributes deemed most important and rate each idea on those attributes. The checklist is standardized and allows ideas to be compared.

Figure 8-4 shows a new-product screening checklist with three major categories: general characteristics, marketing characteristics, and production characteristics (which can be applied to both goods and services). In each category, there are several product attributes to assess. They are scored from 1 (outstanding) to 10 (very poor) for each product idea. In addition, the attributes would be weighted because they vary in their impact on new product success. The checklist yields an overall score for every idea. Here is an example of how a firm could develop overall ratings for two product ideas. Remember, in this example, the best rating is 1 (so, 3 is worse than 2):

1. Product idea A gets an average rating of 2.5 on general characteristics, 2.9 on marketing characteristics, and 1.4 on production characteristics. Product idea B gets ratings of 2.8, 1.4, and 1.8, respectively.

2. The firm assigns an importance weight of 4 to general characteristics, 5 to marketing characteristics, and 3 to production characteristics. The best overall rating is 12 [(1 × 4) + (1 × 5) + (1 × 3)]. The poorest possible overall average rating is 120 [(10 × 4) + (10 × 5) + (10 × 3)].

3. Idea A gets an overall rating of 28.7 [(2.5 × 4) + (2.9 × 5) + (1.4 × 3)]. B gets an overall rating of 23.6 [(2.8 × 4) + (1.4 × 5) + (1.8 × 3)].

4. Idea B's overall rating is better than A's because of its better marketing evaluation (the characteristics judged most important by the firm).

A **patent** *gives exclusive selling rights to an inventor.*

In screening, patentability must often be determined. A **patent** grants an inventor of a useful product or process exclusive selling rights for a fixed period. An invention may be patented if it is a "useful, novel, and nonobvious process, machine, manufacture, or composition of matter" and not patented by anyone else. Separate applications are needed for protection in foreign markets. Many nations have simplified matters by signing patent cooperation treaties; however, some do not honour such treaties. Today, Canada and the other members of the World Trade Organization grant patents that last for twenty years from the date that applications are filed. In 1992–93, 26 865 patent applications were filed in Canada and 17 247 were granted. Only 12 per cent of the patent applications were filed by Canadians and only 7 per cent of the applications that were granted went to Canadians. The remaining 88 per cent of applications and 93 per cent of patents granted involved foreign nationals (mainly U.S., European, and Japanese) of which 50 per cent were from the U.S.[20]

A company should answer several questions regarding patents during the screening stage. For example:

- Can the proposed new product be patented by the firm?
- Are competitive items patented?
- When do competitors' patents expire?
- Are patents on competing items available under a licensing agreement?
- Would the firm be free of patent liability (infringement) if it introduced the proposed new product?

Concept Testing

Next, a firm needs consumer feedback about the new-product ideas that pass through screening. **Concept testing** presents the consumer with a proposed product and measures attitudes and intentions at an early stage of the new-product planning process.

Concept testing is a quick, inexpensive way to assess consumer enthusiasm. It asks potential consumers to react to a picture, written statement, or oral product description. This lets a firm learn initial attitudes prior to undertaking costly, time-consuming product development. Heinz, Kodak, Sony, and Sunbeam are among those using concept testing.

Concept testing generally asks consumers these types of questions:

- Is the idea easy to understand?
- Would this product meet a real need?
- Do you see distinct benefits for this product over those on the market?
- Do you find the claims about this product believable?
- Would you buy the product?
- How much would you pay for it?
- Would you replace your current brand with this new product?
- What improvements can you suggest in various attributes of the concept?
- How frequently would you buy the product?
- Who would use the product?[21]

Concept testing *determines customer attitudes before product development.*

Business Analysis

At this point, a firm does business analysis for the new-product concepts that have thus far been deemed attractive. **Business analysis** involves the detailed review, projection, and evaluation of such factors as consumer demand, production costs, marketing costs, break-even points, competition, capital investments, and profitability for each proposed new product. It is much more detailed than product screening.

Business analysis *looks at demand, costs, competition, etc.*

---

[20]Teresa Riordan, "Patents," *New York Times* (June 12, 1995), p. D2; Neil Gross, "New Patent Office Pending," *Business Week* (October 23, 1995), p. 130; Masaaki Kotabe, "A Study of Japanese Patent Systems," *Journal of International Business Studies*, Vol. 23 (First Quarter 1992), pp. 147–168; and "Patents," in *Resource Book For Science and Technology Consultations, Volume I*, Secretariat for Science and Technology Review, Industry Canada (June 1994), Internet Download.

[21]Adapted from Philip Kotler, *Marketing Management: Analysis, Planning, Implementation, and Control*, Eighth Edition (Englewood Cliffs, N.J.: Prentice-Hall, 1994), p. 331.

Here are some of the considerations at this planning stage:

CRITERIA	SELECTED CONSIDERATIONS
Demand projections	Short- and long-run sales potential; speed of sales growth; price/sales relationship; seasonality; rate of repurchases
Production cost projections	Total and per-unit costs; startup vs. continuing costs; estimates of raw materials and other costs; economies of scale; break-even points
Marketing cost projections	Product planning (patent search, product development, testing); promotion; distribution; marketing research; break-even points
Competitive projections	Short-run and long-run market shares of company and competitors; competitors' strengths and weaknesses; potential competitors; likely strategies by competitors in response to firm
Capital investment projections	Need for new equipment and facilities vs. use of existing facilities and resources
Profitability projections	Time to recoup initial costs; short- and long-run total and per-unit profits; reseller needs; control over price; return on investment; risk

Because the next step is expensive and time-consuming, critical use of business analysis is essential to eliminate marginal items.

Product Development

*Product development **focuses** on devising an actual product and a broad marketing strategy.*

During **product development**, an idea for a new product is converted into a tangible form and a basic marketing strategy is identified. Depending on the product involved, this stage in the planning process encompasses product construction, packaging, branding, positioning, and consumer attitude and usage testing.

Product construction decisions include the type and quality of materials comprising the product, the method of production, production time, production capacity, the assortment to be offered, and the time needed to move from development to commercialization. Packaging decisions include the materials used, the functions performed, and alternative sizes and colours. Branding decisions include the choice of a name, trademark protection, and the image sought. Product positioning involves selecting a target market and positioning the new good or service against competitors and other company offerings. Consumer testing studies perceptions of and satisfaction with the new product.

If a modification is involved, product-development costs may be relatively low. However, an innovation may be costly (up to several million dollars or more) and time-consuming (up to four years for a new car). And this is true of services, as well as goods:

> AlphaNet Telecom of Toronto supplies in-room hotel fax services and has a near monopoly on this market. In 1994 it supplied 8400 fax machines to 120 major North American hotels including chains such as Hyatt, Westin, Hilton, Loews, and Fairmont. AlphaNet Telecom also has arrangements to serve Hong Kong, Singapore, Japan, Indonesia, Australia, and New Zealand, with more countries under negotiation. Fax machines are installed in the hotels at cost but AlphaNet Telecom receives much of the usage revenue. AlphaNet is building its installed customer base and has added such services as FollowFax, which gives subscribers a permanent fax number.[22]

Besides being costly and time consuming, product development can be complicated. For example:

> Boeing's traditional method for designing new aircraft has three phases. First, engineers design a plane's shape and components. Then, they hand blueprints to manufacturing experts, who plan the production of components and final assembly. Finally, the manufacturing plan goes to tooling specialists who design specialized production machinery. Since the phases are completed in sequence, they take a long time and the system forces each group to turn out reams of corrections, consuming millions of hours a year in engineering time.
>
> Once final drawings are ready, carpenters and artisans go to work. They build a full-scale mock-up of the plane incorporating replicas of every part. Converted for the first time from drawings to three-dimensional reality, parts don't necessarily fit. Electricians stringing mock

ALPHANET TELECOM
www.alphanet.net/about/about.htm

---

[22]"AlphaNet Delivers Room Service (In-Room Hotel Fax Service)," *Financial Times of Canada*, (June 11–17, 1994), pp. 4–5.

instrument wires through the model, for instance, may discover that a structural beam gets in the way. Result: more expensive changes, as engineers redesign the beam so it has a hole in the centre and tool makers reconfigure machines to accommodate the fix. Similar mistakes inevitably plague construction of the first few planes. And since subsequent planes must be tailored to the customer, Boeing goes through a minor version of the same tortuous process with each order.[23]

Test Marketing

Test marketing involves placing a fully developed new product (a good or service) in one or more selected areas and observing its actual performance under a proposed marketing plan. The purpose is to evaluate the product and pre-test marketing efforts in a real setting prior to a full-scale introduction. Rather than just study intentions, test marketing lets a firm monitor actual consumer behaviour, competitor reactions, and reseller interest. After testing, the firm could decide to go ahead, modify the product and then go ahead, modify the marketing plan and then go ahead, or drop the product.

Test marketing *occurs in selected areas and observes real performance.*

Many companies routinely use test marketing to help introduce new products and refine their marketing strategies. McDonald's, in particular, tests new products regularly by bringing out "special" offerings and gauging consumer response. Consumer products firms are much more apt to engage in test marketing than industrial products firms:

> In consumer products, test marketing is a science dominated by marketing consultants, database collection firms, and electronic test marketing services. The business is so sophisticated that Information Resources Inc. of Chicago, which runs several electronic test markets, not only measures what every member of its participating households buys but also identifies exactly which television ads propelled them into stores.
>
> By contrast, the test marketing of business-to-business products has only recently become a widespread practice. In the past, a manufacturer created a product, ran it by a few executives, and hoped customers would buy it. Thus, manufacturers often spent huge sums on parts and labour to fix any problems that cropped up after installation. Now, a growing number of manufacturers in such diverse industries as computers, electronics, industrial chemicals, cleaning equipment, maintenance products, and insurance have begun intensive on-site tests of new products. In most cases, these tests are conducted with anywhere from five to fifty clients and last from two to six months.[24]

The test-marketing process requires several decisions: when to test, where to test, how long to test, what test information to acquire, and how to apply test results. Figure 8-5 shows the criteria to weigh in making the choices.

Although test marketing has been beneficial in many cases, some firms now question its effectiveness and downplay or skip this stage in new-product planning. Their dissatisfaction arises from test marketing's cost, the time delay required before full introduction, the fact that it may provide information to competitors, the inability to predict national (global) results based on limited test-market areas, and the impact of such external factors as the economy and competition on test results. Test marketing can even allow nontesting competitors to catch up with an innovative firm by the time a product is ready for a full rollout.

Commercialization

When testing goes well, a firm is ready to introduce a new product to its full target market. This involves **commercialization** and corresponds to the introductory stage of the product life cycle. During commercialization, the firm enacts a total marketing plan and works toward production capacity. Among the factors to be considered are the speed of acceptance by consumers and distribution intermediaries, the intensity of distribution (how many outlets), production capabilities, the promotion mix, prices, competition, the time until profitability, and commercialization costs.

Commercialization *involves a major marketing commitment.*

---

[23]Shawn Tully, "Can Boeing Reinvent Itself?" *Fortune* (March 8, 1993), p. 72. See also Alex Taylor III, "Boeing Sleepy in Seattle," *Fortune* (August 7, 1995), pp. 92–98.

[24]Aimee L. Stern, "Testing Goes Industrial," *Sales & Marketing Management* (March 1991), p. 30. See also Steve Blount, "It's Just a Matter of Time," *Sales & Marketing Management* (March 1992), pp. 32–43.

FIGURE 8-5
Test-Marketing Decisions

Commercialization may require large outlays and a long-term commitment. For example, manufacturers may spend an average of $5 million for a national rollout in both Canadian and U.S. supermarkets—nearly half on consumer promotion and the rest on product costs, market research costs, and promotions for supermarkets. Yet, commercialization costs can go much higher. When Coca-Cola Canada launched PowerAde, a new sports drink, in Canada, it paid $1 million for its promotional campaign alone (which included TV and print ads, coupons, and in-store promotions).[25]

The commercialization of a new product sometimes must overcome consumer and reseller reluctance because of ineffective prior company offerings. Diet Coke's test marketing of new sweeteners in Canada encountered consumer resistance because of the failure of New Coke.[26] The same thing happened to Texas Instruments, which encountered resistance in the business computer market after it bowed out of the home computer market.

Branding

An important part of product planning is *branding*, the procedure a firm follows in researching, developing, and implementing its brand(s). As noted at the beginning of the chapter, a brand is a name, term, design, or symbol (or combination of these) that identifies the products of a seller or group of sellers. By establishing well-known brands, firms gain acceptance, distributor cooperation, and above-average prices.

There are four types of brand designation:

Branding involves **brand names,** **brand marks, trade characters,** *and* **trademarks**.

1. A **brand name** is a word, letter (number), group of words, or letters (numbers) that can be spoken. Examples are Labatt's Blue, Windows 95, and Lipton Cup-a-Soup.

2. A **brand mark** is a symbol, design, or distinctive colouring or lettering that cannot be spoken. Examples are Lexus' stylized L crest, Ralston Purina's checkerboard, and Prudential's rock.

3. A **trade character** is a brand mark that is personified. Examples are Qantas Airlines' koala bear, McDonald's Ronald McDonald, and the Pillsbury Doughboy.

COCA-COLA CANADA
www.cocacola.com/

[25]Douglas Faulkner, "The Coca-Cola Kid," *Marketing Magazine* (August 14, 1995), p. 24.
[26]"Coke Quietly Tests New Diet Sweetener," *Marketing Magazine* (June 12, 1995), p. 7.

4. A **trademark** is a brand name, brand mark, or trade character or combination thereof that is given legal protection. When it is used, a registered trademark is followed by ®. Examples are Scotch Brand® tape and MasterCard®.

Brand names, brand marks, and trade characters do not offer legal protection against use by competitors, unless registered as trademarks. Trademarks ensure exclusivity for trademark owners or those securing their permission and provide legal remedies against firms using "confusingly similar" names, designs, or symbols. With the exception of Labatt's Blue, all of the previous examples are registered trademarks. Trademarks are discussed more fully later in the chapter.

Branding started during the Middle Ages, when craft and merchant guilds required producers to mark goods so output could be restricted and inferior goods traced to their producer. The marks also served as standards for quality when items were sold outside the local markets in which the guilds operated. The earliest and most aggressive promoters of brands in North America were patent medicine manufacturers. Examples of current well-known brands that started more than 100 years ago are Vaseline Petroleum Jelly and Pillsbury's Best Flour. The best known Canadian brand names in the world in 1995 were Molson's and Seagram's.[27]

Worldwide, there are now millions of brand names in circulation. Each year, Canadian advertisers spend over $13.3 billion advertising their brands.[28] Permanent media expenditures (such as company logos, stationery, brochures, business forms and cards, and vehicular and building signs) for brands are another large marketing cost. For instance, when Allied-Signal decided to remove its hyphen and become AlliedSignal, it cost U.S.$500 000 for new stationery, signs, and so forth.

A key goal of firms is to develop brand loyalty, which allows them to maximize sales and maintain a strong brand image. As one expert noted:

> Brands work by facilitating and making more effective the customer's choice process. Every day an individual makes hundreds of consumer decisions. He or she is besieged by countless products and messages competing for attention. To make life bearable and to simplify this decision-making process, the individual looks for shortcuts. The most important of these is to rely on habit—buy brands that have proved satisfactory in the past.[29]

Sometimes, brands do so well that they gain "power" status—they are both well known and highly esteemed. At present, according to a survey of 25 300 people in sixteen nations, the world's ten most powerful brands are (in order) Coca-Cola, Kodak, Sony, Mercedes-Benz, Pepsi-Cola, Nestlé, Gillette, Colgate, Adidas, and Volkswagen. The ten brands with the greatest "vitality"—global growth potential—are Coca-Cola, Nike, Adidas, Sony, Ferrari, Reebok, Disney, Porsche, Pepsi-Cola, and Mercedes-Benz.[30] See Figure 8-6.

Brand rankings do differ by region. Thus, in China, six of the top ten brands are from Japan, led by Hitachi; three are from the United States— Coca-Cola, Mickey Mouse, and Marlboro; and one is from China—Tsing Tao (beer).[31] Europeans favour such brands as BMW, Porsche, and Rolls-Royce. Sony is the most powerful brand for Japanese consumers. In North America, the top brands include Coca-Cola, Campbell, Disney, Pepsi-Cola, Kodak, NBC, Black & Decker, Kellogg, McDonald's, and Hershey.

The use of popular brands can also speed up public acceptance and gain reseller cooperation for new products. For instance, here's a product that gained quick public approval and dealer enthusiasm:

[27]World Line, "Coke, Marlboro Still the World's Top Brands," *Marketing Magazine* (July 24, 1995), p. 5.

[28]Editorial, "Electronic Indicators," *Marketing Magazine* (June 9, 1997), p. 23.

[29]Peter Doyle, "Building Successful Brands: The Strategic Options," *Journal of Consumer Marketing*, Vol. 7 (Spring 1990), p. 7.

[30]Laurel Wentz, "Upstart Brands Steal Spotlight from Perennials," *Advertising Age* (September 19, 1994), pp. I-13–I-14.

[31]Kevin Goldman, "U.S. Brands Lag Behind Japanese in Name Recognition by Chinese," *Wall Street Journal* (February 16, 1995), p. B8.

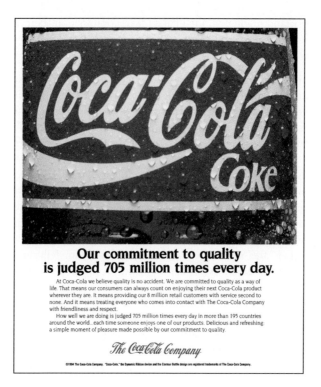

FIGURE 8-6
The Most Popular and Powerful Brand in the World
Reprinted by permission.

In mid-1992, Gillette Company unveiled its Sensor for Women razor. Within six months, the stout green-and-white gadgets—designed to give women a better shave in the shower, had a 36 per cent dollar share of the total North American women's razor market. Gillette followed this up by launching SensorExcel for Women in 1996. The SensorExcel represents Gillette's best effort yet to pitch shavers to women. Although Gillette also sells such products as Oral-B toothbrushes and Soft & Dri deodorant, to many consumers, its name is synonymous with razors and blades.[32]

Today, annual sales of Sensor for Women exceed U.S.$50 million. And it is by far the leading product in its category—with foreign revenues growing rapidly.

Gaining and maintaining brand recognition is a top priority for all kinds of firms. As an example, the national TV networks in Canada (CBC and CTV) and the U.S. (ABC, CBS, Fox, and NBC) "are facing increasing competition and are very conscious of the need to get their brands out there. As more choices are given to consumers, networks have to make sure their viewers understand who they are and what they offer. That can mean anything from a logo subtly popping up in the corner of the viewer's TV screen to a major cross-promotion with some big-name packaged-goods marketers."[33]

Brand equity *represents a brand's worth.*

In recent years, a new branding concept—which more concretely recognizes the worth of brands—has emerged. It is known as **brand equity** and measures the "financial impact associated with an increase in a product's value accounted for by its brand name above and beyond the level justified by its quality (as determined by its configuration of brand attributes, product features, or physical characteristics)."[34] As one expert noted:

> In a general sense, brand equity is defined in terms of the marketing effects uniquely attributable to the brand—for example, when certain outcomes result from the marketing of a good or service because of its brand name that would not occur if the same good or service did not have

[32]Kathleen Deveny, "Sensor Gets Big Edge in Women's Razors," *Wall Street Journal* (December 17, 1992), pp. B1, B10. See also Laurie Freeman, "Sensor Still Helping Gillette Fend Off Razor Challenges," *Advertising Age* (September 28, 1994), p. 21; and Barbara Carton, "Gillette Looks Beyond Whiskers to Big Hair and Stretchy Floss," *Wall Street Journal* (December 14, 1994), pp. B1, B4.

[33]Cyndee Miller, "Stay Tuned for TV Networks as Brands," *Marketing News* (October 9, 1995), pp. 1, 10; and Canadian Media Directors' Council, *23rd Annual Media Digest* (Toronto: Marketing Magazine, 1995), p. 8.

[34]Morris B. Holbrook, "Product Quality, Attributes, and Brand Names as Determinants of Price: The Case of Consumer Electronics," *Marketing Letters*, Vol. 1 (1992), p. 72.

that name. A brand is said to have positive (negative) customer-based brand equity if consumers react more (less) favourably to the product, price, promotion, or distribution of the brand than they do the same marketing-mix element when it is attributed to a fictitiously named or unnamed version of the good or service.[35]

According to *Financial World*, the fifteen most valuable brands in the world—based on sales, profitability, and growth potential—are Coca-Cola, Marlboro, IBM, Motorola, Hewlett-Packard, Microsoft, Kodak, Budweiser, Kellogg, Nescafé, Intel, Gillette, Pepsi-Cola, GE, and Levi's.[36]

Branding creates identities, assures quality, and performs other functions.

Here is an example of how the brand equity concept can be applied. When Cadbury Schweppes acquired the Hires and Crush soda lines from Procter & Gamble, it paid U.S.$220 million. Twenty million dollars of that amount was for physical assets and the balance was for "brand value."[37] Brand equity is even higher when licensing royalties can be generated from other firms' use of the brand, such as occurs with trade characters like Walt Disney's Mickey Mouse. Nonetheless, there are no widely approved techniques for assessing overall brand equity.

These reasons summarize why branding is important:

- Product identification is eased. A customer can order a product by name instead of description.

- Customers are assured that a good or service has a certain level of quality and that they will obtain comparable quality if the same brand is reordered.

- The firm responsible for the product is known. The producer of unbranded items cannot be as directly identified.

- Price comparisons are reduced when customers perceive distinct brands. This is most likely if special attributes are linked to different brands.

- A firm can advertise (position) its products and associate each brand and its characteristics in the buyer's mind. This aids the consumer in forming a **brand image**, which is the perception a person has of a particular brand. It is "a mirror reflection (though perhaps inaccurate) of the brand personality or product being. It is what people believe about a brand—their thoughts, feelings, expectations."[38]

Brand images *are the perceptions that consumers have of particular brands.*

- Branding helps segment markets by creating tailored images. Multiple market segments can be attracted by using two or more brands.

- For socially visible goods and services, a product's prestige is enhanced by a strong brand name.

- People feel less risk when buying a brand with which they are familiar and toward which they have a favourable attitude. This is why brand loyalty occurs.

- Cooperation from resellers is greater for well-known brands. A strong brand also may let its producer exert more control in the distribution channel.

- A brand may help sell an entire line of products, as with Kellogg cereals.

- A brand may help a company enter a new product category, like Reese's peanut butter.

- "A product is something made in a factory [or offered by a service firm]; a brand is something bought by a customer. A product can be copied by a competitor; a brand is unique. A product can be quickly outdated; a successful brand is timeless."[39]

[35]Kevin Lane Keller, "Conceptualizing, Measuring, and Managing Customer-Based Brand Equity," *Journal of Marketing*, Vol. 57 (January 1993), pp. 1, 8. See also David A. Aaker, *Managing Brand Equity* (New York: Free Press, 1991); and David C. Bello and Morris B. Holbrook, "Does an Absence of Brand Equity Generalize Across Product Categories?" *Journal of Business Research*, Vol. 34 (October 1995), pp. 125–131.

[36]"Coke Is Still It," *Advertising Age* (July 17, 1995), p. 8.

[37]Peter H. Farquhar, Julia Y. Han, and Yuji Ijiri, "Brands on the Balance Sheet," *Marketing Management*, Vol. 1 (Winter 1992), pp. 16–22.

[38]Bennett, *Dictionary of Marketing Terms*, p. 28. See also Ernest Dichter, "What's in an Image," *Journal of Product & Brand Management*, Vol. 1 (Spring 1992), pp. 54–60.

[39]Stephen King, WPP Group, London, as quoted in Aaker, *Managing Brand Equity*, p. 1.

There are four basic branding decisions firms must make: choosing their corporate symbols, creating their branding philosophy, selecting a brand name, and deciding whether or not to use trademarks.

Corporate Symbols

Corporate symbols *help establish a companywide image.*

Corporate symbols are a firm's name (and/or divisional names), logo(s), and trade characters. They are significant parts of an overall company image. If a firm begins a business; merges with another company; reduces or expands product lines; seeks new geographic markets; or finds its name to be unwieldy, nondistinctive, or confusing, it needs to evaluate and possibly change its corporate symbols. Here are examples of each situation.

Fifteen years ago, a new PC maker hired a consultant to devise a company name. It wanted a name that "would be memorable and at the same time take command of the idea of portableness; something that would distinguish it from all other IBM PC compatibles." The consultant recommended a name combining two syllables representing "communications" and "small but important." Today, Compaq is one of the 100 largest firms in North America.[40]

In 1995, Nike acquired Canstar Sports, a Canadian company which is well known for making hockey equipment. Canstar had been making hockey equipment under the Lange, Micron, Cooper and Bauer brand names. A decision was made to change the firm's name to Bauer and consolidate all of the firm's brand names under the Bauer brand because Bauer was the best known hockey brand and had the strongest image in Canada. After this, Nike planned to launch skates using the Nike name, which would become a competing brand for Bauer. Rather than launch the new Nike skates right away, Nike waited until January 1997 because they wanted time to build an association of their brand with hockey. They built this association in 1996 by getting their trademarked swoosh symbol on the hockey jerseys of NHL teams and the World Cup winning Team USA hockey team.

Federal Express now promotes the FedEx name, since it is easier to say. United Telecommunications converted its nondistinctive name to Sprint, in recognition of its leading brand. When Corel software of Ottawa acquired the rights to WordPerfect, a leading word processing product from Novell of Orem, Utah, in January 1996, they wanted to link their corporate name with this new brand. WordPerfect is now marketed as Corel WordPerfect, linking the product and its producer together.[41]

COREL
www.corel.com/

Branding Philosophy

While developing a brand strategy, a firm needs to determine its branding philosophy. This philosophy outlines the use of manufacturer, private, and/or generic brands, as well as the use of family and/or individual branding.

Manufacturer brands *are well known and heavily promoted.*

MANUFACTURER, PRIVATE, AND GENERIC BRANDS[42] **Manufacturer brands** use the names of their makers. They generate the vast majority of North American revenues for most product categories: over 85 per cent of food, all autos, 75 per cent of major appliances, and over 80 per cent of gasoline. They appeal to a wide range of people who desire low risk of poor product performance, good quality, routine purchases, status, and convenience shopping. The brands are often well known and trusted because quality control is strictly maintained. They are identifiable and present distinctive images. Producers may have a number of product alternatives under their brands.

[40]Robert A. Mamis, "Name-Calling," *Inc.* (July 1984), pp. 67–74; and "Fortune 500," *Fortune* (May 15, 1995), pp. F-3–F-4.

[41]"Canstar Consolidates Brand-Name Lineup," *Marketing Magazine* (December 11, 1995), p. 5; Lara Mills and Anita Lahey, "Power Play," *Marketing Magazine* (December 2, 1996), p. 11; James Pollock, "Nike Launches Skates with Offbeat Posters," *Marketing Magazine* (February 3, 1997), p. 4; and Sean Eckford, "Corel Plans Big Marketing Relaunch for WordPerfect," *Marketing Magazine* (February 19, 1996), p. 5.

[42]For a good overview of this topic, see John A. Quelch and David Harding, "Brands Versus Private Labels," *Harvard Business Review*, Vol. 74 (January–February 1996), pp. 99–109; Marcia Mogelonsky, "When Stores Become Brands," *American Demographics* (February 1995), pp. 32–38; and "Special Report: Brand Power," *Progressive Grocer* (October 1994), supplement.

Manufacturers have better channel control over their own brands, which may be sold through many competing intermediaries. Yet individual resellers can have lower investments if the brands' pre-sold nature makes turnover high—and if manufacturers spend large sums promoting their brands and sponsor cooperative ads with resellers (so costs are shared). Prices are the highest of the three brands, with the bulk going to the manufacturer (which also has the greatest profit). The marketing goal is to attract and retain loyal consumers for these brands, and for their makers to direct the marketing effort for the brands.

Private (dealer) brands use names designated by their resellers, usually wholesalers or retailers—including service providers. They account for sizable North American revenues in many categories: 50 per cent of shoes, one-third of tires, 14 per cent of food items, and one-quarter of major appliances. And unit market shares are even higher. Some firms, such as Bata Shoes and McDonald's, derive most revenues from their own brands. Private brands account for 20 per cent of unit food sales in supermarkets. In the Canadian grocery-store soft drink market (worth about $1.6 billion per year), private brands have captured 25 per cent of the market. The dominant manufacturer is Cott Corporation, which makes 90 per cent of the private label sodas; and Cott is expanding its efforts into the United States where they have agreements with the Wal-Mart and Safeway chains as well as many others. Private-brand foods are more popular in Europe than in North America but the North American market is catching up fast, with Canada leading the way. In Europe, private labels generate 28 per cent of revenues in British grocery stores and about 20 to 24 per cent in French and German ones.[43]

Private brands appeal to price-conscious people who buy them if they feel the brands offer good quality at a lower price. In the past, Canadians used to accept some risk with regards to quality, but brands like President's Choice from Loblaws, Master Choice from A&P, Our Best from Sobey's and Life Brand from Shoppers Drug Mart have caused people to view the private brands as comparable to national brands. In some cases, such as President's Choice Decadent Chocolate Chip Cookies, private brands are even considered superior. Private brands are usually presented as of similar quality to manufacturer brands, with less emphasis on packaging, and are often made to dealer specifications. In the past, brand assortments were smaller and the reseller's private brand was unknown to people who did not shop there. However, the President's Choice brand has transcended this case. It is closely associated with Loblaw's in Canada but it is also being carried by competing retailers and is being sold in the United States as a manufacturer's brand.

Resellers have more exclusive rights for these brands, and are more responsible for distribution and larger purchases. Inventory turnover may be lower than for manufacturer brands; and promotion and pricing are the reseller's job. Due to lower per-unit packaging and promotion costs, resellers can sell private brands at lower prices and still have better per-unit profits (due to their higher share of the selling price). The marketing goal is to attract people who become loyal to the reseller and for that firm to exert control over marketing. Large resellers advertise their brands widely and essentially every major Canadian retailer sells some type of private brand. Loblaw's President Choice brand is even more popular than some manufacturer brands; and in Loblaw's stores, private-label products represent a remarkable 33 per cent of the products purchased by customers.[44]

Generic brands emphasize the names of the products themselves and not manufacturer or reseller names. They started in the drug industry as low-cost alternatives to expensive manufacturer brands. Today, generics have expanded into cigarettes, batteries, motor oil, and other products. In Canada, the pharmaceutical industry is worth $5.9 billion and

Private brands *enable channel members to gain loyal customers.*

Generic brands *are low-priced items with little advertising.*

[43]Chad Rubel, "Price, Quality Important for Private Label Goods," *Marketing News* (January 2, 1995), p. 24; E. S. Browning, "Europeans Witness Proliferation of Private Labels," *Wall Street Journal* (October 20, 1992), pp. B1, B5; Laurel Wentz, "Private Labels March in Europe Too," *Advertising Age* (May 9, 1994), p. 53; Tara Parker-Pope, "U.K. Grocer Aims to Bag U.S. Customers," *Wall Street Journal* (May 16, 1995), p. A14; Mark Stevenson, "The Hired Hand Waves Goodbye," *Canadian Business* (August 1994), pp. 12–22; and Laura Medcalf, "Club Monaco Cola Highlights New Trend in Private-Label Pop," *Marketing Magazine* (March 18, 1996), p. 4.

[44]Mark Stevenson, "The Hired Hand Waves Goodbye," *Canadian Business* (August 1994), pp. 12–22; Laura Medcalf, "Club Monaco Cola Highlights New Trend in Private-Label Pop," *Marketing Magazine* (March 18, 1996), p. 4; Donalee Moulton, "Sobeys Launches Premium House Brand," *Marketing Magazine* (December 11, 1995), p. 4; James Pollock, "A&P Expands No-Frills Food Basics Division," *Marketing Magazine* (November 27, 1995), p. 2.

T a b l e 8 - 1

Manufacturer, Private, and Generic Brands

CHARACTERISTIC	MANUFACTURER BRAND	PRIVATE BRAND	GENERIC BRAND
Target market	Risk avoider, quality conscious, brand loyal, status conscious, quick shopper	Price conscious, comparison shopper, quality conscious, moderate risk taker, dealer loyal	Price conscious, careful shopper, willing to accept lower quality, large family or organization
Product	Well known, trusted, best quality control, clearly identifiable, deep product line	Same overall quality as manufacturer, less emphasis on packaging, less assortment, not known to nonshoppers of the dealer	Usually less overall quality than manufacturer, little emphasis on packaging, very limited assortment, not well known
Distribution	Often sold at many competing dealers	Usually only available from a particular dealer in the area	Varies
Promotion	Manufacturer-sponsored ads, cooperative ads	Dealer-sponsored ads	Few ads, secondary shelf space
Price	Highest, usually suggested by manufacturer	Moderate, usually controlled by dealer	Lowest, usually controlled by dealer
Marketing	To generate brand loyalty and manufacturer control	To generate dealer loyalty and control	To offer a low-priced, lesser-quality item to those desiring it

the generic manufacturers have about 10 per cent of this market. However, the prescription volume for generic drugs is closer to 40 per cent; the low prices of the drugs results in significantly lower dollar volume. Virtually all of Canada's supermarkets stock some generic products but they only account for about 1 per cent of supermarket revenues. Generics appeal to price-conscious, careful shoppers, who perceive them as being a very good value, are sometimes willing to accept lower quality, and often purchase for large families or large organizations.

Generics are seldom advertised and receive poor shelf locations; consumers must search them out. Prices are lower than those of other brands by anywhere from 10 to 50 per cent, due to quality, packaging, assortment, distribution, and promotion economies. The major marketing goal is to offer low-priced, lower-quality items to consumers interested in price savings. Table 8-1 compares the three types of brands.

A mixed-brand strategy combines brand types.

Many companies—including service firms—use a **mixed-brand strategy**. This strategy involves producing products that are sold under both manufacturer and private brands (and maybe generic brands). For example, apple juice producers often put many different brand labels on their juice cans. Mixed branding benefits manufacturers and resellers: it gives the firm associated with the brand name a chance to gain a customer franchise. Multiple segments may be targeted. Loyalty to manufacturers and loyalty to dealers can be fostered separately. In addition, mixed branding means a producer firm is given more shelf space (under different brand names), gets more cooperation in the distribution channel (when they supply products branded in the reseller's cheaper juice), and allows producers to offer a wider assortment (sweeter apple juice, cheaper juice). Selling more means producing more, which stabilizes production and uses excess capacity. As such, sales are maximized for manufacturing firms and profits are shared more equitably between producers and resellers. Planning is better too. For example, in Japan, Kodak markets its own brand of film and COOP private-brand film (for the 2500-store Japanese Consumer Cooperative Union). By doing this, it hopes to make a dent in Fuji's 75 per cent share of the Japanese market.[45]

Manufacturer, private, and generic brands also repeatedly engage in a **battle of the brands**, in which each strives to gain a greater share of the consumer's dollar, control over marketing strategy, consumer loyalty, product distinctiveness, maximum shelf space and locations, and a large share of profits. In recent years, this battle has been intensifying:

> You know the old joke: Just because you're paranoid doesn't mean that they're not out to get you. In a nutshell, that describes how manufacturers of brand-name products react to competition from private labels. On one hand, manufacturers have the right to be concerned: There are more private labels on the market than ever before. Collectively, private labels in North America command higher unit shares than the strongest national brands in 77 of 250 supermarket product categories. But on the other hand, many manufacturers have overreacted to the threat posed by private labels without fully recognizing two essential points. First, private-label strength generally varies with economic conditions. Second, through their actions, manufacturers of brand-name products can temper the challenge posed by private labels.[46]

FAMILY AND MULTIPLE BRANDING In **family (blanket) branding**, one name is used for two or more individual products. Many firms selling industrial goods and services (such as Boeing and IBM), as well as those selling consumer services (such as Bell Canada), use some form of family branding for all or most of their products. Other companies employ a family brand for each category of products. For example, Sears has Kenmore appliances and Craftsman tools and Canadian Tire Corporation has Mastercraft tools and parts. Family branding can be applied to both manufacturer and private brands, and to both domestic and international (global) brands.

Family branding is best for specialized firms or those with narrow product lines. Companies capitalize on a uniform, well-known image and promote the same name regularly—keeping promotion costs down. The major disadvantages to family branding are that differentiated marketing opportunities may be low (if only one brand is used to target all of a firm's customers), company image may be adversely affected if vastly different products (such as men's and women's cologne) carry one name, and innovativeness may not be projected to consumers.

Brand extension, whereby an established name is applied to new products, is an effective use of family branding. It is a way of gaining quick customer acceptance, since people are familiar with existing products having the same name. Figure 8-7 shows how Campbell has applied brand extension to its chicken noodle soup line. Keep in mind that brand extension may have a negative effect if people do not see some link between the original product and a new one. Most new products now use some form of brand extension.

These are seven situations in which brand extension could be effective:

1. The same product is produced in a different form—for example, Jell-O Pudding Pops.

2. A distinctive taste/ingredient/component is presented in a new item—for example, Arm & Hammer detergent.

3. A new companion product is introduced—for example, Colgate Plus toothbrush.

4. A different product is offered to the same target market—for example, Visa travellers cheques aimed at Visa credit card customers.

5. A brand's perceived expertise is conferred on a new product—for example, Canon bubble-jet printers.

6. An existing benefit/attribute/feature is conferred on a new product—for example, Ivory shampoo (which connotes mildness).

In a **battle of the brands**, *the three brand types compete.*

Family branding *uses a single name for many products.*

CANADIAN TIRE CORPORATION
www.canadiantire.com

Brand extension *gains quick acceptance.*

[45]Lara Mills, "The New Rx for Drug Marketing," *Marketing Magazine* (September 11, 1995), p. 15; Rob McKenzie, "A Hard Pill To Swallow," *Canadian Business* (February 1994), pp. 44–50; and Wendy Bounds, "Kodak Pursues a Greater Market Share in Japan with New Private-Label Film," *Wall Street Journal* (March 7, 1995), p. B9.
[46]Quelch and Harding, "Brands Versus Private Labels," pp. 99–100.

FIGURE 8-7
How Campbell's Soup Stays on Top Through Brand Extension
Reprinted by permission of Campbell Soup Company.

7. A designer image/status is conveyed to a new product—for example, Pierre Cardin sunglasses.[47]

Individual branding *uses distinct brands.*

With **individual (multiple) branding**, separate brands are used for different items or product lines sold by a firm.

[47]Edward M. Tauber, "Brand Leverage: Strategy for Growth in a Cost-Controlled World," *Journal of Advertising Research*, Vol. 28 (August–September 1988), pp. 26–30.

Through individual branding, a firm can create multiple product positions (separate brand images), attract various market segments, increase sales and marketing control, and offer both premium and low-priced brands. Individual branding also lets manufacturers secure greater shelf space in retail stores.

However, each brand incurs its own promotion costs and there is no positive brand-image rub-off. Economies from mass production may be lessened and new products may not benefit from an established identity. And there may be some cannibalization among company brands. Consumer products firms are more likely than industrial products firms to engage in individual branding.

To gain the benefits of family and individual branding, many firms combine the approaches, perhaps by having a flagship brand and other secondary brands. For example, one-third of Heinz's products have the Heinz name; the rest have names like StarKist, 9-Lives, Ore-Ida, and Weight Watchers. Or, a family brand could be used together with individual brands: Honda markets the upscale Acura and mainstream Honda auto lines. The Honda line includes the Honda Accord, Honda Civic, Honda Del Sol, Honda Odyssey, and Honda Prelude. It has an overall image and targets a specific market. New models gain from the Honda name, and there is a relationship among models. Individual brands are used with each model so differences can be highlighted.

Choosing a Brand Name

A firm may choose a brand name from several potential sources. Under brand extension, an existing name is employed with a new product (Kid Fresh Flushable Wipes from Baby Fresh Wipes, Hewlett-Packard Deskjet printers). For a private brand, the reseller specifies the name (BayCrest—a traditional clothing and soft goods brand name of The Bay).

If a new name is sought, these alternatives are available:

- Initials (YTV, A&W).
- Invented name (Kleenex, Compaq).
- Numbers (Boeing 777, Century 21).
- Mythological character (Atlas tires, Samsonite luggage).
- Personal name (Labatt, Ford).
- Geographical name (Texas Instruments, Air Canada).
- Dictionary word (Close-Up toothpaste, Airlift water-based release agents—Air Products and Chemicals, Inc.'s way for its industrial customers to reduce or eliminate solvent emissions).
- Foreign word (Nestlé, Lux).
- Combination of words, initials, numbers, etc. (General Foods International Coffee, Head & Shoulders shampoo).

Under a **licensing agreement**, a company pays a fee to use a name or logo whose trademark rights are held by another firm. Due to the high consumer recognition of many popular trademarks, sales for a product may be increased by paying a royalty fee to use one. Examples of names used in licensing are Coca-Cola, Montreal Canadiens, and Anne of Green Gables. Two hundred Coca-Cola licensees make and market 3000 products in thirty nations. Annually, sports merchandise licensing generates a total of U.S.$12 billion in worldwide retail sales alone.[48]

In **co-branding**, two or more brand names are used with the same product to gain from the brand images of each. Typically, a company uses one of its own brand names in conjunction with another firm's—often under a licensing agreement. For instance, credit card companies have embraced this idea, and there are now Canadian Tire MasterCards and GM-Visa cards; and Zeller's and the Canadian Imperial Bank of Commerce have launched

*Brand sources range from existing names to **licensing agreements** and **co-branding**.*

[48]Carolyn Shea, "Taking License," *Promo* (June 1995), pp. 33–34; Donalee Moulton, "Green Gables Grows Greener," *Marketing Magazine* (November 6, 1995), pp. 14–16; and Lara Mills, "From Boxer Shorts to Beach Towels," *Marketing Magazine* (November 6, 1995), p. 11.

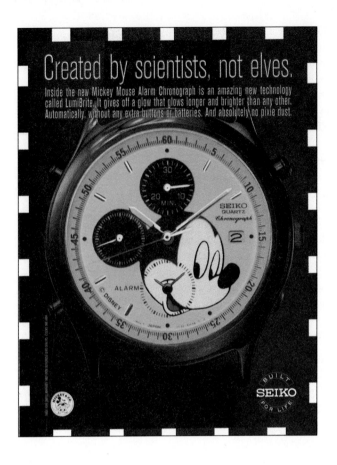

FIGURE 8-8
Co-Branding: The Seiko Mickey Mouse Alarm Chronograph

Reprinted by permission.

a Club Z Visa Card. Other examples of co-branding include the Pillsbury Deluxe Bar with M&M's, and the Seiko Mickey Mouse Alarm Chronograph. See Figure 8-8.

Brand names should be suggestive, easy to remember, and flexible.

A good brand name has several attributes, depending on the situation. It suggests something about a product's use or attributes (Sleep-Eze, Wash 'n Dry); is easy to spell and remember and is pronounceable in only one way (Bic, Tang); can be applied to a whole line of products (Deere tractors, Calvin Klein clothing); is capable of legal protection from use by others (Perrier, Equal artificial sweetener); has a pleasant or at least neutral meaning internationally (Esso, Kodak); and conveys a differential advantage (Pert Plus, Acutrim).

As firms expand globally, branding takes on special significance. Regardless of whether brands are "global" or tailored to particular markets, their meanings must not have negative connotations or violate cultural taboos. To avoid this, specialized firms such as NameLab (which can devise names that are acceptable around the world) can be hired. But brands must also reflect cultural and societal differences. This example illustrates why:

> The Lewis Woolf Griptight company makes infant and toddler products such as pacifiers. These products are sold in Great Britain, and the United States. When it talked to parents in Great Britain about the Griptight brand name being used before a new line was launched, the company discovered that it was 'the most un-user-friendly name.' People thought it was a carpet glue, a denture fixative, a kind of tire. The brand name became Kiddiwinks, a British word for children. In the United States, however, recognition of the name Binky was high, with some consumers using it as a generic term for pacifiers— hence, the name Binkykids.[49]

*The **consumer's brand decision process** moves from nonrecognition to insistence (or aversion).*

When branding, a firm should plan for the stages in the **consumer's brand decision process**, as displayed in Figure 8-9. For a new brand, a consumer begins with nonrecognition of the name, and the seller must make the person aware of it. He or she then moves

[49]Cyndee Miller, "Kiddi Just Fine in the U.K., But Here It's Binky," *Marketing News* (August 28, 1995), p. 8. See also Martin S. Roth, "The Effects of Culture and Socioeconomics on the Performance of Global Brand Image Strategies," *Journal of Marketing Research*, Vol. 32 (May 1995), pp. 163–175.

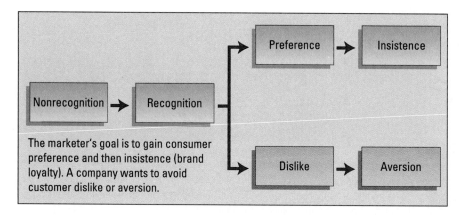

The marketer's goal is to gain consumer preference and then insistence (brand loyalty). A company wants to avoid customer dislike or aversion.

FIGURE 8-9
The Consumer's Brand Decision Process

to recognition, wherein the brand and its attributes are known, and the seller stresses persuasion. Next, the person develops a preference (or dislike) for a brand and buys it (or opts not to buy); the seller's task is to gain brand loyalty. Last, some people show a brand insistence (or aversion) and become loyal (or never buy); the seller's role is to maintain loyalty. Often times, people form preferences toward several brands but do not buy or insist upon one brand exclusively.

Using brand extension, a new product begins at the recognition, preference, or insistence stage of the brand decision process because of the carryover effect of the established name. However, consumers who dislike the existing product line would be unlikely to try a new product under the same name; but they might try another company product under a different brand.

The Use of Trademarks

Finally, a firm must decide whether to seek trademark protection.[50] In Canada, the Canadian Trademarks Act is administered by Industry Canada through the Competition Bureau. Trademarking gives a firm the exclusive use of a word, name, symbol, combination of letters or numbers, or other devices—such as distinctive packaging—to identify the goods and services of that firm and distinguish them from others for as long as they are marketed. Both trademarks (for goods) and service marks (for services) are covered by trademark law.

Trademarks are voluntary and require registration and implementation procedures that can be time-consuming and expensive (challenging a competitor may mean high legal fees and many years in court). A multinational firm must register trademarks in every nation in which it operates; even then, trademark rights may not be enforceable. For a trademark to be legally protected in Canada, it must have a distinct meaning that does not describe an entire product category, be used in interprovincial commerce (for federal protection), not be confusingly similar to other trademarks, and not imply attributes a product does not possess. A surname by itself cannot be registered because any person can generally do business under his or her name; it can be registered if used to describe a specific business (for example, McDonald's restaurants).

When U.S. retailer Wal-Mart entered Canada in 1994 it became embroiled in a couple of trademark disputes. One of the issues involved Wal-Mart putting up "Canada Proud" signs in their stores. Tom Shaw, President of Canada Proud Inc. was not amused and Wal-Mart was forced to remove these signs. However, Wal-Mart faced a more serious trademark issue. Wool-mart Inc. of Nepean took Wal-Mart to court over trademark infringement. Wool-mart registered its trade name in 1990, before Wal-Mart came to Canada. Wool-mart's owner, Teresa de Vries, offered to change the name if Wal-Mart would give her a fee of $1 million. Wal-Mart refused, believing this to be a situation of trademark piracy and, recognizing that Wool-mart is a very small firm (annual sales of $1 million versus Wal-Mart's annual sales of U.S.$82 billion) that might not be able to afford

Trademark protection grants exclusive use of a brand or mark for as long as it is marketed.

[50]See Dorothy Cohen, *Legal Issues in Marketing Decision Making* (Cincinnati: South-Western, 1995), pp. 111–136.

Ethics AND TODAY'S MARKETER

Controversial Brand Names On Not-So-Controversial Products

Sometimes it seems that the marketplace is plagued by products with controversial brand names on products that are accepted in society. Products like beer and perfume could certainly be consumed in front of children and their usage explained fairly easily. But having to explain the meanings behind brands like Nude Beer, Lakeport Truly Naked Beer, Opium perfume, and Sexual perfume could present a lot more difficulty. Although many people feel that these brand names are in questionable taste, and most people would agree that a name alone does not really make a product, the fact is that many of these brands sell very well.

Lakeport brewing company is having success with Truly Naked beer; the beer's name ostensibly comes from the fact that it is a filtered beer and thus pure, or "naked." The beer has nothing to hide and is pioneering a new category of beers. One has to wonder though, if it is merely a coincidence that the brand has a "sexy" name and is being targeted at young males, 18–25 years old.

It is usually the case that the consumers of these brands with controversial names use them because of their shock value. Once this wears off, the brands tend to fade away.

Branding is one of the key strategic marketing decisions that relates to the target market. A sexy or risqué name is selected with the express intent of appealing to a certain type of customer. Contrary to popular belief, offending people is not necessarily something marketers wish to avoid. Market experience with controversial brands clearly proves this. Of course, for products with broad appeal, like Pepsi-Cola, offending people is of great concern. This is why Pepsi-Cola quickly stopped running ads featuring Madonna and Mike Tyson when some consumers responded very negatively to the images of these celebrities.

When a brand presents an unwholesome image, like Death Cigarettes (shocking name but it clearly reflects the actual nature of the product) or Nude Beer (which featured women on its containers who became nude when the containers got wet with condensation), and Opium perfume (which would be addictive to your lover), then it is clear that some segments will be offended. Have marketers crossed the line of decency in these cases? It is not simply a matter of selling "smut" (a product in itself) or being shocking, which falls under freedom of speech, but a matter of using "smut" or shock value to sell a product which is, of itself, not particularly smutty or shocking.

Beer, cigarettes, and perfumes can be branded and promoted on the basis of their own inherent benefits and characteristics. However, a large number of sexual appeals are associated with the products, even if the brand names themselves are not "sexy." For example, Molson Canadian Beer, Alfred Sung's Sung Perfume, and Virginia Slim's cigarettes are not brand names that bring to mind anything particularly controversial. Yet advertising associated with these brands has featured prominent sexual appeals. Perhaps, the overt appeals presented by brand names like Sexual perfume, Death cigarettes, and Truly Naked beer are simply more honest.

Research and identify some "controversial" brand names associated with noncontroversial products and try to determine how long these "brands" have lasted. Discuss the advantages and disadvantages of controversial branding for a firm's product strategy.

Source: Based on material in "The Naked and the Dinosaur in Brewing," *Marketing* (September 4, 1995), p. 3; Gail Chiasson, "Canadian Sexual Goes National," *Marketing* (May 22, 1995), p. 4.

a long legal battle. In a preliminary hearing the Federal Court of Canada refused to give Wool-Mart an interlocutory injunction that would have forced Wal-Mart to stop using the Wal-Mart name and would have cost them an estimated $3 million dollars to change their store signs and stationary. This decision allows Wal-Mart to operate under their current trade name until the case is resolved in a trial. For its part, Wool-Mart has filed for damages of $105 million and although the Federal Court ruling allows them to go to trial it is questionable whether Wool-Mart will go to trial since its sales have actually increased since Wal-Mart came on the scene.[51]

When brands become too popular or descriptive of a product category, they run the risk of becoming public property. A firm then loses its trademark position. Brands fighting to remain exclusive trademarks include L'eggs, Rollerblade, Xerox, Levi's, Plexiglas, Formica, Kleenex, and Teflon. Former trademarks that are now considered generic—and, thus, public property—are cellophane, aspirin, shredded wheat, cola, linoleum, monopoly, and lite beer.

Trademark rulings can have wide implications. For example, a ruling in Ontario on a trademark infringement case involving Orkin pest control affected a ruling in India on a trademark case involving Calvin Klein. In the Ontario situation, Orkin of America tried to force an Ontario company named Orkin to change its name. Orkin was an unregistered foreign trademark in Canada. If the trademark is unregistered, a firm needs a local reputation acquired through doing business locally to gain protection. The problem was that Orkin of America had no history of doing business in Canada under the name Orkin. The court ruled, however, that Orkin of America did have a local reputation acquired by virtue of "spillover" advertising and by the fact that millions of Canadians were exposed to the brand in the Southern U.S. when they travelled there. Consequently, the Ontario Court ruled in favour of Orkin of America.

A similar situation cropped up in India where International Apparel Syndicate (IAS) sought to market "Calvin Klein" brand jeans in India. The real Calvin Klein company did not have a distribution relationship with IAS, had not registered its trademark in India, and was not selling any jeans there at the time. However, Calvin Klein sought trademark protection from IAS. The justice of the High Court of Calcutta looked for legal precedents for the case in jurisdictions throughout the British Commonwealth and came upon the Orkin decision in Ontario. As a result, a ruling was made in favour of Calvin Klein and trademark protection in India was granted.

Packaging

Packaging is the part of product planning where a firm researches, designs, and produces packages. As noted at the beginning of the chapter, a package consists of a product's physical container, label, and/or inserts.

Packaging *involves decisions as to a product's physical container, label, and inserts.*

The physical container may be a cardboard, metal, plastic, or wooden box; a cellophane, waxpaper, or cloth wrapper; a glass, aluminium, or plastic jar or can; a paper bag; styrofoam; some other material; or a combination of these. Products may have more than one container: Cereal is individually packaged in small cardboard boxes, with inner waxpaper wrapping, and shipped in large corrugated boxes; and watches are usually covered with cloth linings and shipped in plastic boxes. The label indicates a product's brand name, the company logo, ingredients, promotional messages, inventory codes, and/or instructions for use. Inserts are (1) instructions and safety information placed in drug, toy, and other packages or (2) coupons, prizes, or recipe booklets. They are used as appropriate.

Prior to the advent of the modern supermarket and department store, manufacturers commonly shipped merchandise in bulk containers such as: cracker barrels, sugar sacks, and butter tubs. Retail merchants repackaged the contents into smaller, more convenient

[51]Brian Banks and David North, "Ticked off: Wal-Mart's Infuriating Ways," *Canadian Business* (January 1996), pp. 23–24; Eric Swetsky, "Wool-Mart Versus Wal-Mart," *Marketing Magazine* (June 24, 1996), p. 20; Eric Swetsky, "Corporate Reputations," *Marketing Magazine* (October 2, 1995), p. 24; and "Wal-Mart Unravels Wool-Mart," Cassels Brock and Blackwell, Marketing Low Group Newsletter (March 1996) www.nstn.cainternetdownload.

FIGURE 8-10
The Package as the Product
Reprinted by permission.

units to meet customer needs. With the growth of mass merchants and self-service, manufacturers came to realize the value of packaging as a marketing tool. Today, it is a vital part of a firm's product development strategy; a package may even be the product itself (such as the Reynolds Wrap shown in Figure 8-10) or an integral part of the product (such as the aerosol can for shaving cream).

Packaging plays a key role in helping consumers form perceptions about a product (brand). As one packaging expert noted, "Our experience, supported by research, indicates that the consumer does not conceptually strip away the packaging and consider the actual product when making a buying decision. For instance, in the case of food and beverages, the package communicates a promise of quality, taste, and enjoyment, and the consumer expects the product inside to measure up. If it does not, or if the package fails to deliver on the product's promise, another product failure is the likely result."[52]

About 10 per cent of a typical product's final selling price goes for its packaging. The amount is higher for such products as cosmetics (up to 40 per cent and more). The complete package redesign of a major product might cost millions of dollars for machinery and production. Packaging decisions must serve both resellers and consumers. Plans are often made in conjunction with production, logistics, and legal personnel. Errors in packaging can be costly.

Package redesign may occur when a firm's current packaging receives a poor response from channel members and customers or becomes too expensive; the firm seeks a new market segment, reformulates a product, or changes or updates its product positioning; or new technology becomes available. For instance:

When Hostess Frito-Lay "reinvented" their flat potato chip they wanted to inform consumers in a unique and interesting way. They approached the Thomas Pigeon Design Group which specializes in packaging design. Thomas Pigeon is somewhat biased in his view, but he is a believer in the power and importance of packaging on brand identification and sales. Hostess

---

[52]Primo Angeli, "Thinking Out of the Box: A New Approach to Product Development," *Business Horizons*, Vol. 38 (May–June 1995), p. 18.

Frito-Lay asked Pigeon's company to "redesign" their potato chip package so it would reflect the "redesign" of the chips inside. What Pigeon's company came up with was a "newspaper bag." The initial idea was to run a short-term trial of the "newspaper bag" to announce the change in the Hostess brand chips. The initial results of the packaging change were a 200 per cent increase in sales in a number of regions. The group product manager of potato chips at Hostess Frito-Lay, Rob Carscadden, gives a lot of credit to the package design as he states "the relaunch of Hostess Potato Chips has become the most successful made-in-Canada marketing project Hostess Frito-Lay has ever undertaken." [53]

The basic functions of packaging, factors considered when making packaging decisions, and criticisms of packaging are described next.

Basic Packaging Functions

The basic **packaging functions** are containment and protection, usage, communication, segmentation, channel cooperation, and new-product planning:

Packaging functions range from containment and protection to product planning.

- *Containment and protection*—Packaging enables liquid, granular, and other divisible products to be contained in a given quantity and form. It also protects a product while it is shipped, stored, and handled.

- *Usage*—Packaging lets a product be easily used and re-stored. It may even be reusable after a product is depleted. Packaging must also be safe to all who use it, from the youngest child to the oldest senior.

- *Communication*—Packaging communicates a brand image, provides ingredients and directions, and displays the product. It is a major promotion tool.

- *Segmentation*—Packaging can be tailor-made for a specific market group. If a firm offers two or more package shapes, sizes, colours, or designs, it may employ differentiated marketing.

- *Channel cooperation*—Packaging can address wholesaler and retailer needs with regard to shipping, storing, promotion, and so on.

- *New-product planning*—New packaging can be a meaningful innovation for a firm and stimulate its sales.

Factors Considered in Packaging Decisions

Several factors must be weighed in making packaging decisions. Colour, shape, and material all influence consumer perceptions. For example:

What image is sought?

> After 115 years, Listerine Antiseptic changed from glass to plastic in its most popular bottle sizes, as well as redesigned the classic barbell-shaped package that signified amber mouthwash—and 'medicine-y' taste to generations of consumers. The product inside is the same. But, we wanted to update and modernize it from the package in your grandmother's medicine cabinet.[54]

In family packaging, a firm uses a common element on each package in a product line. This approach parallels family branding. Campbell has virtually identical packages for its traditional soups, distinguished only by flavour or content identification. Procter & Gamble, the maker of Head & Shoulders and Pert Shampoo, does not use family packaging with the two brands; they have distinct packages to attract different segments.

Should family packaging be used?

An international firm must determine if a standardized package can be used worldwide (with only a language change on the label). Standardization boosts global recognition. Thus, Coke and Pepsi have standard packages when possible. Yet some colours, symbols, and shapes have negative meanings in some nations. For example, white can mean purity or mourning, two vastly different images.

Should standard packages be used worldwide?

Package costs must be considered on both a total and per-unit basis. As noted earlier, total costs can run into the millions of dollars; and per-unit costs can go as high as 40 per cent of a product's selling price—depending on the purpose and extent of the packaging.

What should costs be?

---

[53]Thomas Pigeon, "Read All About It," *Marketing Magazine* (May 6, 1996), p. 10; and Rob Carscadden, "Trash the Flash," *Marketing Magazine* (May 6, 1996), p. 12.

[54]Glenn Collins, "New Looks for Two Staples of the Medicine Cabinet," *New York Times* (July 19, 1994), p. D4.

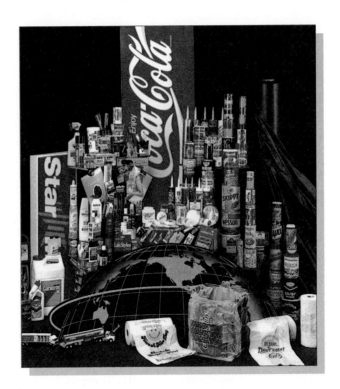

FIGURE 8-11
Innovative Packaging from Sonoco
Sonoco's consumer packaging operations are known around the world for innovative packaging solutions. These products include composite canisters, plastic tennis ball containers, capseals, plastic and fibre caulk cartridges, carry-out plastic bags for supermarkets and high volume retail stores, plastic produce roll bags, agricultural film, pressure-sensitive labels, promotional coupons, screen process printing for vending machine graphics, screen printing for fleet graphics, flexible packaging, specialty folding cartons, coasters, and glass covers.
Reprinted by permission.

What materials and innovations are right?

What features should the packaging incorporate?

What size(s), colour(s), and shape(s) are used?

How should the label and inserts appear?

Should multiple packaging be used?

A firm has many packaging materials from which to select, such as paperboard, plastic, metal, glass, styrofoam, and cellophane. In making the choice, trade-offs are often needed: cellophane allows products to be attractively displayed, but it is highly susceptible to tearing; paperboard is relatively inexpensive, but it is hard to open. A firm must also decide how innovative it wants its packaging to be. Figure 8-11 displays some of the innovative packaging from Sonoco.

There is a wide range of package features from which to choose, depending on the product. These features include pour spouts, hinged lids, screw-on tops, pop-tops, see-through bags, tuck- or seal-end cartons, carry handles, product testers (for items like batteries), and freshness dating. They may provide a firm with a differential advantage.

A firm has to select the specific size(s), colour(s), and shape(s) of its packages. In picking a package size, shelf life (how long a product stays fresh), convenience, tradition, and competition must be considered. In the food industry, new and larger sizes have captured high sales. The choice of package colour depends on the image sought. Mello Yello, a citrus soft drink by Coca-Cola, has a label with bright orange and green lettering on a lemon-yellow background. Package shape also affects a product's image. Hanes created a mystique for L'eggs pantyhose by packaging them in an egg-shaped package. The number of packages used with any one product depends on competition and the firm's use of differentiated marketing. By selling small, medium, and large sizes, a firm may ensure maximum shelf space, appeal to different consumers, and make it difficult and expensive for a new company to gain channel access.

The placement, content, size, and prominence of the label must be determined. Both company and brand names (if appropriate) need to appear on the label. The existence of package inserts and other useful information (some of which may be required by law) should be noted on the label. Sometimes, a redesigned label may be confusing to customers and hurt a product's sales. As one analyst noted, "Marketers are always trying to improve things, and they may end up causing problems for themselves."[55]

Multiple packaging couples two or more product items in one container. It may involve the same product (such as razor blades) or combine different ones (such as a comb and a brush or a first-aid kit). The goal is to increase usage (hoarding may be a problem), get people to buy an assortment of items, or have people try a new item (such as a new

[55]Stuart Elliott, "Advertising," *New York Times* (January 28, 1993), p. D20.

toothpaste packaged with an established toothbrush brand). Many multiple packs, like cereal, are versatile—they can be sold as shipped or broken into single units.

Individually wrapping portions of a divisible product may offer a competitive advantage. This may be weighed against the fact that it is often costly and contributes to environmental waste. Kraft has done well with its individually wrapped cheese slices. Alka-Seltzer sells tablets in individually wrapped tin-foil containers, as well as in a bottle without wrapping.

Should items be individually wrapped?

For certain items (such as shirts, magazines, watches, and candy), some resellers want pre-printed prices. They then have the option of charging those prices or adhering their own labels. Some resellers prefer only a space for the price on the package and insert their own price labels automatically. Because of the growing use of computer technology by resellers in monitoring their inventory levels, more of them are insisting on pre-marked inventory codes on packages. The **Universal Product Code (UPC)**, is a voluntary marking standard used by retailers and manufacturers in Canada and the United States. Using the UPC, manufacturers pre-mark items with a series of thick and thin vertical lines. Price and inventory data codes are represented by these lines, which appear on outer package labels— but are not readable by employees and customers. The lines are "read" by computerized optical scanning equipment at the checkout counter. The cashier does not have to ring up a transaction manually and inventory data are instantly transmitted to the main computer of the retailer (or the manufacturer). In the UPC system, human-readable prices must still be marked on items, either by the manufacturer or the reseller.[56]

*Should a package have a pre-printed price and use the **Universal Product Code**?*

The Product Code Council of Canada, located at 885 Don Mills Rd., Ste. #301, Don Mills, Ontario, M3C 1V9, is responsible for assigning and administering Universal Product Codes in Canada. In 1995, the Product Code Council of Canada would assign a six-digit manufacturer's code number for a sum of $321.

Last, a firm must be sure the package design fits in with the rest of its marketing mix. A well-known perfume brand may be extravagantly packaged, distributed in select stores, advertised in upscale magazines, and sold at a high price. In contrast, a firm making perfumes that imitate leading brands has more basic packaging, distributes in discount stores, does not advertise, and uses low prices. The two perfume brands may cost an identical amount to make, but the imitator would spend only a fraction as much on packaging.

How does the package interrelate with other marketing variables?

Criticisms of Packaging

The packaging practices of some industries and firms have been heavily criticized and regulated in recent years due to their impact (or potential impact) on the environment and scarce resources, the high expenditures on packaging, questions about the honesty of labels and the confusion caused by inconsistent designations of package sizes (such as large, family, super), and critics' perceptions of inadequate package safety.

Packaging is faulted for waste, misleading labels, etc.

Yet, consumers—as well as business—must bear part of the responsibility for the negative results of packaging. Throwaway bottles (highly preferred by consumers) use almost three times the energy of returnable ones. Shoplifting annually adds to packaging costs because firms must add security tags and otherwise alter packages.

In planning their packaging programs, firms need to weigh the short-term and long-term benefits and costs of providing environmentally safer ("green"), less confusing, and more tamper-resistant packages. Generally, firms are responding quite positively to the criticisms raised here.

Growing Products

Once a new product is commercialized, the goal is for consumer acceptance and company sales to rise rapidly. This occurs in some cases; in others, it may take a long while. The growth rate and total sales level of new products rely heavily on two related consumer

---

[56]See Barry Berman and Joel R. Evans, *Retail Management: A Strategic Approach*, Sixth Edition (New York: Prentice Hall, 1995), pp. 232–234; and *U.P.C. Guidelines Manual* (Don Mills, Ontario: Product Code Council of Canada), pp. 1–4.

TECHNOLOGY & MARKETING

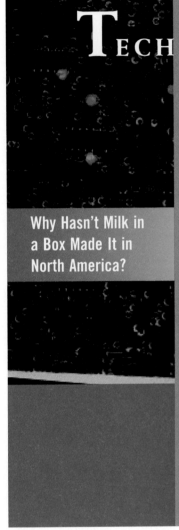

Why Hasn't Milk in a Box Made It in North America?

Several years ago, Parmalat (Italy's largest milk producer) developed a superheated milk product that is packaged in special aseptic cartons (also known as drink boxes). The major advantage of Parmalat's processed milk is that it can be kept without refrigeration for at least six months. As a result, Parmalat milk accounts for 70 per cent of the total fresh milk consumed by Europeans; and annual sales are almost U.S.$2 billion. In contrast, the product accounts for less than 1 per cent of North American fresh milk sales.

Parmalat has learned that North Americans like to purchase their milk fresh and cold. This means they are suspicious of Parmalat milk. Many consumers think the milk is irradiated or produced from specially treated cows. And Parmalat's higher price (20 per cent more than regular milk) may also reduce consumer demand. Although North American consumers may be suspicious of the taste, a test by a noted food critic found only subtle differences between Parmalat and regular whole milk.

To broaden its appeal in the North American market, Parmalat has given out leaflets explaining that it uses heat (not radiation) to preserve the milk, its process does not destroy nutrition, and its milk tastes the same as traditional milk. To underscore the point, some Parmalat packages even contain the wording "Not Irradiated" and "No Preservatives" in large letters.

Parmalat has spent millions of dollars to promote its product to North American consumers. Its TV ads highlight the convenience of nonrefrigerated milk and stress the ease of children handling the package. It has distributed discount coupons and free samples. Parmalat even added a two-quart carton to appeal to the larger-sized refrigerators and kitchen cabinets found in North American homes. To date, none of these strategies has significantly increased sales.

As a branding and packaging consultant to Parmalat, develop a marketing strategy to increase its market penetration in the Canadian market.

Sources: Based on material in John Tagliabue, "Unchilled Milk: Not Cool Yet," *New York Times* (June 10, 1995), pp. 33–34, and Carolyn Shea, "Parmalat Pours It On," *Promo* (October 1995), pp. 94–99.

---

behaviour concepts: the adoption process and the diffusion process. In managing growing products, a firm must understand these concepts and plan its marketing efforts accordingly.

*The **adoption process** explains the new-product purchase behaviour of individual consumers.*

The **adoption process** is the mental and behavioural procedure an individual consumer goes through when learning about and purchasing a new product. It consists of these stages:

1. *Knowledge*—A person (organization) learns of a product's existence and gains some understanding of how it functions.

2. *Persuasion*—A person (organization) forms a favourable or unfavourable attitude about a product.

3. *Decision*—A person (organization) engages in actions that lead to a choice to adopt or reject a product.

4. *Implementation*—A person (organization) uses a product.

5. *Confirmation*—A person (organization) seeks reinforcement and may reverse a decision if exposed to conflicting messages.[57]

The rate (speed) of adoption depends on consumer traits, the product, and the firm's marketing effort. Adoption is faster if consumers have high discretionary income and are willing to try new offerings; the product has low perceived risk; the product has an advantage over other items on the market; the product is a modification and not an innovation;

[57]Everett M. Rogers, *Diffusion of Innovations*, Third Edition (New York: Free Press, 1982), pp. 164–175.

the product is compatible with current consumer lifestyles or ways of operating a business; product attributes can be easily communicated; product importance is low; the product can be tested before a purchase; the product is consumed quickly; the product is easy to use; mass advertising and distribution are used; and the marketing mix adjusts as the person (organization) moves through the adoption process.

The **diffusion process** describes the manner in which different members of the target market often accept and purchase a product. It spans the time from product introduction through market saturation and affects the total sales level of a product as it moves through the life cycle:

*The **diffusion process** describes when different segments are likely to purchase.*

1. Innovators are the first to try a new product. They are venturesome, willing to accept risk, socially aggressive, communicative, and worldly. It must be determined which innovators are opinion leaders—those who influence others. This group is about 2.5 per cent of the market.

2. Early adopters are the next to buy a new product. They enjoy the prestige, leadership, and respect that early purchases bring—and tend to be opinion leaders. They adopt new ideas but use discretion. This group is about 13.5 per cent of the market.

3. The early majority is the initial part of the mass market to buy a product. They have status among peers and are outgoing, communicative, and attentive to information. This group is about 34 per cent of the market.

4. The late majority is the second part of the mass market to buy. They are less cosmopolitan and responsive to change, and include people (firms) with lower economic and social status, those past middle age (or set in their jobs), and skeptics. This group is about 34 per cent of the market.

5. Laggards purchase last, if at all. They are price-conscious, suspicious of change, low in income and status, tradition bound, and conservative. They do not adopt a product until it reaches maturity. Some sellers ignore them because it can be hard to market a product to laggards. Thus, concentrated marketing may do well by focusing on products for laggards. This group is about 16 per cent of the market.[58]

Growth for a major innovation often starts slowly because there is an extended adoption process and the early majority may be hesitant to buy. Sales may then rise quickly. As an illustration, the PC was first marketed in 1977; yet, by the end of 1981, less than 10 per cent of North American businesses and under 2 per cent of North American households owned one. Consumers were hesitant to make a purchase due to high initial prices, the perceived difficulty of mastering the PC, its early image as a game console, and the limited software. Sales then grew dramatically, going from 1.1 million units in 1981 to over 7.5 million in 1984; inexpensive models entered the market, PCs became more user-friendly, the product lost its game image, and software became widely available.

By 1995, North American businesses owned about 40 million PCs and North American households nearly 40 million. In contrast, at that time, a total of 40 million PCs were owned by organizational and final consumers in the European Union and fewer than 20 million PCs were owned by organizational and final consumers in Japan. Why has ownership been so low in Japan? It is due to skepticism about the benefits of PCs among Japanese businesspeople; limited office and household space; and rather high prices (compared to North America).[59]

For minor innovations or product modifications, growth is usually much faster. Therefore, marketers often prefer to launch these kinds of products as opposed to developing "innovations." As an example, in the spring of 1996, Gillette introduced SensorExcel™ for women with a $2.5 million multi-media rollout. The SensorExcel is a premium adaptation from the Sensor line of razors for men.[60] See Figure 8-12.

[58]Ibid, pp. 246–261.
[59]*Industrial Outlook 1994* (Washington, D.C.: U.S. Department of Commerce, 1993), pp. 26-16–26-21; Jim Carlton, "Foreign Markets Give PC Makers a Hearty Hello," *Wall Street Journal* (September 15, 1995), pp. B1, B4; and authors' estimates.
[60]"Gillette Readies Launch Of Women's Razor," *Marketing Magazine*, (December 11, 1995), p. 5.

FIGURE 8-12
**Introducing the New SensorExcel™
for Women**
Reprinted with permission of Gillette Canada.

These products are among those now in the growth stage of the product life cycle. They represent good opportunities for firms: CD-ROM software, cellular phones and related phone services, anti-lock car brakes, men's hair-colouring products, solar-powered products, generic drugs, plain-paper fax machines, stereo TVs, international financial services, adult education, rechargeable batteries, subnotebook PCs, and business-to-business video conferencing.

Mature Products

Proper marketing can let mature products maintain high sales.

Products are in the maturity stage of the life cycle when they reach the late majority and laggard markets. Goals turn from growth to maintenance. Because new products are so costly and risky, more firms are placing marketing emphasis on mature products with steady sales and profits, and minimal risk.

In managing mature products, a firm should examine the size, attributes, and needs of the current market; untapped market segments; competition; the potential for product modifications; the likelihood of new company products replacing mature ones; profit margins; the marketing effort required for each sale; reseller attitudes; the promotion mix; the impact of specific products on the overall product line; each product's effect on company image; the number of years remaining for the products; and the management effort needed.

Having a popular brand in a mature product category has many benefits. First, the life cycle may be extended almost indefinitely. Budweiser beer, Coke Classic soft drink, Goodyear tires, Ivory soap, Lipton tea, Maxwell House coffee, Life Savers mints, Sherwin-Williams paints, and Quaker Oats oatmeal are among the leaders in their product categories; each is well over seventy-five years old. Second, the brand attracts a loyal customer group and has a stable, profitable position in the market. Third, the likelihood of future low demand is greatly reduced; this is a real risk for new products. Fourth, a firm's overall image is enhanced, allowing the firm to extend a popular name to other products. Fifth, it allows for more control over marketing efforts and more precision in sales forecasting. Sixth, mature products can be used as cash cows to support spending on new products. However, some marketing support must be continued if a mature product is to remain popular.

Popular mature brands offer several benefits for companies.

Successful industries and companies market products that stay in maturity for long periods, as the following illustrate:

- The paper clip was invented in 1899 by Norwegian Johan Vaaler. Since then, "several hundred inventors have patented paper clips in every conceivable shape—square, round, oval, triangular, teardrop, and arrowhead." Today, it is more popular than ever due to its ease of use, flexible applications, and large customer following. It seems that after nearly 100 years, there is still nothing to match a paper clip. Twenty billion are sold yearly.[61]

- "Whether clothes are lean or loose, short or long, there's a common thread running through much of today's fashion: Lycra—DuPont's trademark for spandex fibre that started out in the 1950s as a substitute for rubber in girdles." After sales stagnated for a while, the fibre gained attention in the 1980s with the advent of cycling pants and leggings, and technological advances that let Lycra fibres be used in sheer hosiery. Lycra is now "in everything from long, willowy cotton and linen sheaths by Liz Claiborne's Lizsport to crewneck bodysuits from Anne Klein II and tank dresses from designer Donna Karan's DKNY division." In certain parts of Europe, the Lycra name has a consumer recognition rate of 98 per cent; and expansion in Latin America and the Far East are under way.[62]

There are many options available for extending the mature stage of the product life cycle. Table 8-2 shows seven strategies and gives examples of each.

Not all mature products can be revived or extended. Consumer needs may disappear, as when frozen juice replaced juice squeezers. Lifestyle changes may lead to less interest in products, such as teller services in banks. Better and more convenient products may be devised, such as when CD players replaced record players. The market may be saturated and further marketing efforts may be unable to garner enough sales to justify time and costs, which is why Japan's NEC has a diminished role in consumer electronics.

Product Deletion

Products should be deleted from a firm's offerings if they offer limited sales and profit potential, reflect poorly on the firm, tie up resources that could be used for other opportunities, involve large amounts of management time, create reseller dissatisfaction due to low inventory turnover, and divert attention from long-term goals.

Products need to be deleted if they have consistently poor sales, tie up resources, and cannot be revived.

However, there are many points to weigh before deleting a product: As a product matures, it blends in with existing items and becomes part of the total product line (mix). Customers and distribution intermediaries may be hurt if an item is dropped. A firm may not want competitors to have the only product for customers. Poor sales and profits may be only temporary. Or the marketing strategy, not the product, may be the cause of poor results. Thus, a systematic procedure should be used to handle faltering products.

[61]Amal Kumar Naj, "Hey, Get a Grip! Your Basic Paper Clip Is Like a Mousetrap," *Wall Street Journal* (July 24, 1995), pp. A1, A5.
[62]Pat Sloan, "Lycra Stretches Fashion Appeal," *Advertising Age* (November 2, 1992), pp. 3, 36.

T a b l e　8 - 2

Selected Strategies for Extending the Mature Stage of the Product Life Cycle

STRATEGY	EXAMPLES
1. Develop new uses for products	Jell-O used in garden salads WD-40 used in the maintenance of kitchen appliances
2. Develop new product features and refinements	Zoom lenses for 35mm cameras Battery-powered televisions
3. Increase the market	Bell Canada's 1-800 & 1-888 phone services for small businesses International editions of major magazines
4. Find new classes of consumers for present products	Nylon carpeting for institutional markets Johnson & Johnson's baby shampoo used by adults
5. Find new classes of consumers for modified products	Industrial power tools altered for do-it-yourself market Inexpensive copy machines for home offices
6. Increase product usage among current users	Multiple packages for soda and beer Discounts given for making more long distance phone calls
7. Change marketing strategy	Greeting cards sold in supermarkets Office furniture promoted in mail-order catalogues

As these examples show, low-profit or rapidly declining products are often dropped or de-emphasized:

- After seven years on the market, the Cadillac Allante, a U.S.$62 000 General Motors' two-seat luxury roadster, was discontinued due to weak sales. Although the car was profitable, only 2000 units were sold during its last year. And the Allante was very complicated to build, with undercarriages made in Detroit and bodies and interiors made in Italy.
- The Scott Paper Company decided to drop the White Swan brand of facial tissues and paper towels in Atlantic Canada and Quebec because they could not see significant product differentiation in the facial tissue and paper towel markets. The reduction in the number of products would allow Scott Paper to focus its efforts on building national and international brands, like Scotties facial tissues and Scott towels.[63]
- "If business is a jungle, then the rise and fall of the typewriter is one of its more cherishable demonstrations of evolution, of the little creature that could. As Smith Corona filed for bankruptcy protection last week [July 1995], one of the final signals in the triumph of PCs and software over the typewriter [originally patented in 1868] was at hand."[64]

During deletion, customer and distributor needs must be considered.

In discontinuing a product, a firm must take replacement parts, the notification time for customers and resellers, and the honouring of warranties/ guarantees into account. For example, a company planning to delete its line of office telephones must resolve these questions: Who will make replacement parts? How long will they be made? How soon before the actual deletion will an announcement be made? Will distributors be alerted early enough so they can line up other suppliers? How will warranties be honoured? After they expire, how will repairs be handled?

[63]"Scott Trims White Swan Product Line," *Marketing Magazine* (September 25, 1995), p. 1.
[64]Francis X. Clines, "An Ode to the Typewriter," *New York Times* (July 10, 1995), p. D5.

International Marketing in

Why Did Unilever Lose the Power?

Dutch-British Unilever is one of the world's global giants, with annual sales of nearly U.S.$50 billion—including U.S.$11 billion from laundry detergents alone. Yet the firm recently suffered a major embarrassment with its new Power detergent, which featured a "patented, stain-annihilating, manganese-based catalyst" known as Accelerator. Just months after it was introduced, Power had to be pulled from the market because it damaged clothes. "It's the greatest marketing setback we've seen," said Sir Michael Perry, Unilever's chairperson.

Why did this happen? According to one expert, "The [U.S.]$300 million Power introduction is a cautionary tale highlighting the pressure multinational firms face to come up with winning products that work internationally—and roll them out faster. With only half of [Procter & Gamble's] detergent sales, Unilever was desperate to parlay its technology breakthrough into a greater market share."

Specifically, here's what Unilever did:

- It ignored a pre-introduction warning from arch-rival Procter & Gamble that Power could damage clothes.
- It was so enthusiastic that it skipped test marketing and placed Power into full commercialization right after product development.
- It was a victim of its own efficiency. Until recently, it took Unilever up to three years to roll out a new product in sixteen European countries. Today, such a roll-out is done in a few months, leaving no real chance to catch product errors early in commercialization.
- It decided not to create a strong new brand and "piggybacked" Power onto two of its existing brands, hence Omo Power and Persil Power.
- It underestimated the marketing blitz that P&G would use to call public attention to Power's potentially damaging effect on clothing.

As Unilever's laundry detergent manager, how would you avoid such errors, while still being an aggressive competitor?

Source: Laurel Wentz, "Unilever's Power Failure a Wasteful Use of Haste," *Advertising Age* (March 6, 1995), p. 42.

MARKETING IN A CHANGING WORLD

Marketers Aren't Only Building Brands, They're Branding Buildings!

The task of building up a firm's brand name image is often thought of as monumental. However, a number of firms have chosen to make their brand names literally monumental, by sponsoring buildings. At first thought, this might not seem like a particularly new idea, since most large companies do have a corporate headquarters named after the company. And benefactors have been getting their names on university buildings for years in response to generous donations.

However, the new trend now emerging in Canada and the United States is to brand public sports and entertainment venues in response to major donations by corporations. Examples include Vancouver's GM Place, the Canadian Airlines Saddle Dome in Calgary, the United Centre in Chicago (United Airlines is the sponsor), the Corel Centre in Ottawa (formerly the Palladium), the Molson Centre in Montreal, and the Air Canada Toronto Raptors stadium. The hockey teams located in the Corel Centre and the Molson Centre are owned by their corporate sponsors, although they are not the main businesses of their owners. But this is not always the case: Ford has its name on performing arts centres in both Toronto and Vancouver.

What possible advantages accrue to these companies by virtue of "branding" these buildings? For starters, the exposure of the firm's name is linked with the entertainment taking place at the venue—not just the 17 000 to 22 000 fans who pack the various arenas and concert halls, but the millions who watch on TV and the millions more who see the sports highlights later or read about the event in the newspaper the next day. This "free" publicity goes on game-in, game-out, year-after-year. The degree of exposure is also extremely high. Whereas thousands may use your university building or visit your corporate headquarters, millions hear about the events that occurred in your sports arena.

A couple of possible problems with branding a building are that the teams using your venue may be losers, and over time the building may begin to look disreputable. Both of these reflect negatively on the sponsor. In the case of Molson and Corel some of the disaffection for the team's performance and the sponsor might be justified because of the ownership relation. However, it is doubtful that anyone will blame Canadian Airlines for an early playoff exit by the Calgary Flames. As for the second problem, one can remove sponsorship, make it conditional on the structure being maintained, or even ante up to renovate and rebuild, thus garnering more positive public relations.[65]

SUMMARY

1. *To detail the importance of new products and describe why new products fail* New products are important because they may foster differential advantages, sustain sales growth, require a lot of time for development, generate large profits, enable a firm to diversify, make distribution more efficient, lead to technological breakthroughs, allow waste products to be used, respond to changing consumers, and address government mandates.

When a firm suffers a financial loss, a product is an absolute failure. When it makes a profit but does not attain its goals, a product is a relative failure. Failures occur because of such factors as a lack of a significant differential advantage, poor planning, poor timing, and excessive enthusiasm by the product sponsor.

2. *To study the stages in the new-product planning process* New-product planning involves a comprehensive, seven-step process. During idea generation, new opportunities are sought. In product screening, unattractive ideas are weeded out using a new-product screening checklist. At concept testing, the consumer reacts to a proposed idea. Business analysis requires a detailed evaluation of demand, costs, competition, investments, and profits. Product development converts an idea into a tangible form and outlines a marketing strategy. Test marketing, a much-debated technique, involves placing a product for sale in selected areas and observing performance under actual conditions. Commercialization is the sale of a product to the full target market. A new product can be terminated or modified at any point in the process.

3. *To define and distinguish among branding terms, to examine the importance of branding, and to study the key branding decisions that must be made* Branding is the procedure a firm follows in planning and marketing its brand(s). A brand is a name, term, design, or symbol (or combination) that identifies a good or service. A brand name is a word, letter (number), or group of

---

[65]Nimisha Raja, "Branded Buildings," *Marketing Magazine* (May 27, 1966), p. 20.

words or letters (numbers) that can be spoken. A brand mark is a symbol, design, or distinctive colouring or lettering. A trade character is a personified brand mark. A trademark is a brand name, brand mark, or trade character given legal protection.

There are millions of brand names in circulation worldwide. Ad spending on them is many billions of dollars annually. Through strong brands, brand loyalty can be secured. Popular brands also speed up the acceptance of new products. Gaining and keeping brand recognition is a top priority, as are the development of brand equity and a brand image. Branding benefits all parties: manufacturers, distribution intermediaries, and consumers.

Four fundamental decisions are necessary in branding. First, corporate symbols are determined and, if applicable, revised. The company's name (and/or divisional names), logo(s), and trade characters set its overall image. Second, a branding philosophy is set, which includes the proper use of manufacturer, private, and/or generic brands, as well as family and/or individual branding. At this stage, a mixed-brand strategy, the battle of the brands, and brand extension (a popular approach) are also assessed.

Third, a brand name is chosen from one of several sources, including brand extension from existing names, private brands, licensing a name from another firm, and co-branding. With a new brand, the consumer's brand decision process moves from nonrecognition to recognition to preference (or dislike) to insistence (or aversion). With a continuing name applied to a new product, the brand decision process would begin at recognition, preference (or dislike), or insistence (or aversion). Fourth, the use of trademarks is evaluated and planned.

4. *To define and distinguish among packaging terms and to examine the importance of packaging* Packaging is the procedure a firm follows in planning and marketing their product package(s). A package consists of a physical container, label, and/or inserts. Today, packaging is an integral part of a firm's new-product planning strategy.

Ten per cent of a typical product's final selling price goes for packaging. Package redesign can be quite expensive. Both channel member and final consumer needs must be taken into consideration. Errors can be quite costly.

5. *To analyze the growth and maturity of products, including the adoption process, the diffusion process, and extension strategies, and to examine product deletion decisions and strategies* Once a new product is commercialized, the firm's goal is consumer acceptance and for company sales to rise as rapidly as possible. However, the growth rate and sales level for a new product are dependent on the adoption process—which describes how a single consumer learns about and purchases a product—and the diffusion process—which describes how different members of the target market learn about and purchase a product. These processes are faster for certain consumers, products, and marketing strategies.

When products mature, company goals turn from growth to maintenance. Mature products can provide stable sales and profits and loyal consumers. They do not require the risks and costs of new products. There are several factors to consider and alternative strategies from which to choose when planning to sustain mature products. It may not be possible to retain aging products if consumer needs disappear, lifestyles change, new products make them obsolete, or the market becomes too saturated.

At some point, a firm may have to determine whether to continue a faltering product. Product deletion may be difficult because of the interrelation of products, the impact on customers and resellers, and other factors. It should be done in a structured manner; and replacement parts, notification time, and warranties should all be considered in a deletion plan.

KEY TERMS

new product (p. 199)
modifications (p. 199)
minor innovations (p. 199)
major innovations (p. 199)
brand (p. 199)
package (p. 199)
absolute product failure (p. 202)
relative product failure (p. 202)
new-product planning process (p. 204)
idea generation (p. 205)
product screening (p. 205)
patent (p. 206)
concept testing (p. 207)
business analysis (p. 207)

product development (p. 208)
test marketing (p. 209)
commercialization (p. 209)
brand name (p. 210)
brand mark (p. 210)
trade character (p. 210)
trademark (p. 210)
brand equity (p. 212)
brand image (p. 213)
corporate symbols (p. 214)
manufacturer brands (p. 214)
private (dealer) brands (p. 215)
generic brands (p. 215)
mixed-brand strategy (p. 216)

battle of the brands (p. 217)
family (blanket) branding (p. 217)
brand extension (p. 217)
individual (multiple) branding (p. 218)
licensing agreement (p. 219)
co-branding (p. 219)
consumer's brand decision process (p. 220)
packaging (p. 223)
packaging functions (p. 225)
Universal Product Code (UPC) (p. 227)
adoption process (p. 228)
diffusion process (p. 229)

Review Questions

1. Distinguish among a product modification, a minor innovation, and a major innovation. Present an example of each for a hospital.
2. Give four reasons why new products are important to a company.
3. What are the pros and cons of test marketing?
4. Differentiate among these terms: brand, brand mark, trade character, brand name, and trademark.
5. Why do manufacturer brands have such a large percentage of sales in so many product categories? Will private brands and generic brands eventually displace manufacturer brands? Explain your answer.
6. In which circumstances is brand extension most effective? Least effective?
7. Describe the six major functions of packaging. Give an example of each.
8. How does the Universal Product Code (UPC) assist channel members, such as wholesalers and retailers?
9. Cite five ways in which a firm could extend the mature stage of the product life cycle. Provide an example of each.
10. Why is a product deletion decision so difficult?

Discussion Questions

1. Comment on the following statement: "We never worry about relative product failures because we make a profit on them. We only worry about absolute product failures."
2. Differentiate between the commercialization strategies for a product modification and a major innovation. Relate your answers to the adoption process and the diffusion process.
3. An office-supply company, Horizon Paper Corporation, recently changed its name to Horizon Products Corporation. Why do you think this name change was necessary? Do you think this is a good name? Explain your answer.
4. Comment on this statement: "In planning packaging programs, firms need to weigh the short-term and long-term benefits and costs of environmentally safer, less confusing, and more tamper-resistant packages."
5. Select a product that has been in existence for twenty or more years and explain why it has been successful for so long.

DISTRIBUTION

PLANNING

PART 4

Part 4 deals with the second major element of the marketing mix, distribution.

9 Considerations in Distribution Planning and Physical Distribution

Here, we broadly study distribution planning, which involves the physical movement and transfer of ownership of a product from producer to consumer. We explore the functions of distribution, types of channels, supplier/distribution intermediary contracts, channel cooperation and conflict, the industrial channel, and international distribution. We also look at physical distribution, in particular at transportation and inventory management issues.

10 Retailing and Wholesaling

Here, we present retailing, which consists of those business activities involved with the sale of goods and services to the final consumer. We show the impact of retailing on the economy, its functions in distribution, and its relationship with suppliers. We categorize retailers by ownership, store strategy mix, and nonstore operations. We also describe several retail planning considerations and note recent trends in retailing.

Next, we examine wholesaling, which entails buying and/or handling goods and services and their subsequent resale to organizational users, retailers, and/or other wholesalers. We show the impact of wholesaling on the economy, its functions, and its relationships with suppliers and customers. We describe the major types of company-owned and independent wholesalers and note recent trends in wholesaling.

Part 4 Vignette
Goods and Services Distribution

The exchange process of marketing requires a physical transfer from producer to consumer of both goods and services and the transaction requirements associated with the transfer. Transaction requirements usually involve the title to goods or rights to services. In Part 4 you will encounter two chapters describing goods and services distribution in Canada.

Chapter 9 presents distribution planning and physical distribution. The physical distribution of goods is an important issue for Canadian firms because Canada is such a large country with a relatively small and widely dispersed population. Insight into the importance of physical distribution in Canada is illustrated by the operations of Canada's busiest shipping port. The Port of Vancouver is a hub of intermodal transportation activity, which, on a daily basis, receives containers full of imported products from visiting ships. These containers are then transported to Ontario and Quebec via truck, train, or aircraft. Containers of finished products from Canadian factories also await loading for shipment overseas. The true nature of Canada's foreign trade relationships are illustrated by the fact that the majority of goods exported through the port are made up of softwood lumber, wood pulp, grain, coal, potash, and sulphur.

Chapter 10 presents the retailing and wholesaling institutions used by marketers to reach their customers. The Canadian retail landscape has been undergoing a number of fundamental shifts. A major story in Canadian retailing is the entry of Wal-Mart into Canada as part of a modern retail revolution. Canada is an attractive new market for American retailers because of its close geographic proximity and the fact that cross-border shopping, combined with the powerful spillover effect of advertising, have made Canadians familiar with, and well disposed to, U.S. retailers. For these reasons, it was only natural that Wal-Mart, the world's largest retailer, selected Canada as its first major site for international expansion. Wal-Mart's entry was seen as a major threat by Canadian retailers. Understanding your competitors and customers and then responding appropriately to them both is the key to survival in retailing. Wal-Mart recognizes that it is involved in face-to-face contact with customers. As a marketing organization, it sees itself as the leader in the channel of distribution and it works for its customers backwards through the channel of distribution to the producers to lower costs and raise quality. This constant interaction with suppliers helps Wal-Mart build relationships and lower costs, to the detriment of its competitors and the satisfaction of its customers.

Chapter 10 also presents a characteristically Canadian form of distribution, the producer co-op. Cooperative enterprises were founded on the pioneer spirit and are managed on the principle of democracy, with members voting on important decisions. The Saskatchewan Wheat Pool is one of the largest and most successful cooperative enterprises in Canada; it has 57 000 farmer-members and is a publicly traded company on the Toronto Stock Exchange. Like most producer cooperatives, it handles all distribution and product marketing for its members. It operates grain storage elevators, fish farms, a donut chain, a flour mill, and twenty-seven farm service centres. The Saskatchewan Wheat Pool markets livestock, wheat and other grains, publishes a newspaper for farmers, and acts as a lobby interest group to the provincial and federal governments on behalf of its farmer-members. The marketplace is fast-paced and more volatile than ever, requiring faster decision making of enterprises. Cooperatives are threatened in this environment because democracy is a slow decision-making process. The Saskatchewan Wheat Pool is viewed as the model cooperative adapting best to marketplace volatility.

> *Distribution is part of the exchange process of marketing and involves the physical transfer of goods and services from producer to consumer.*

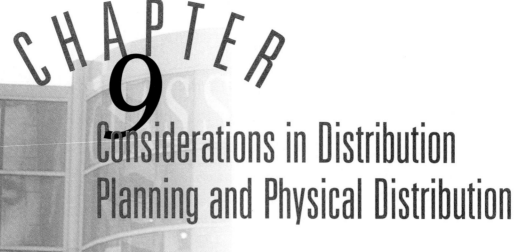

CHAPTER 9

Considerations in Distribution Planning and Physical Distribution

Chapter Objectives

1 To define distribution planning and to examine its importance, distribution functions, the factors used in selecting a distribution channel, and the different types of distribution channels

2 To describe the nature of supplier/distribution intermediary contracts, and cooperation and conflict in a channel of distribution

3 To examine the special aspects relating to a distribution channel for industrial products and to international distribution

4 To define physical distribution and to demonstrate its importance

5 To discuss transportation alternatives and inventory management issues

> *A pivotal battle in the war over the distribution of recorded music is taking place in Canada and it is being fuelled by changes in technology and demographics. The following statement sums up the situation: "Nowhere in the world is music retailing more brutally competitive than Canada."*

Photo by Bob Carroll

Traditional music retailers like Music World, HMV Records, and Sam the Record Man are in a life-and-death struggle with the record clubs such as BMG and Columbia House, who sell ten CDs for a penny. It's not just music clubs who are bothering these retailers. Now hardware retailers of stereos and computers, like Future Shop and A&B Sound, are selling music. In addition, Tower Records/Video of Sacramento, California, opened up a record store in Toronto in December 1995 and Virgin Records, part of a Beverly Hills, California, conglomerate, opened a megastore on Robson Street in Vancouver in 1997. Both retail outlets represent the front-end entry of these retail chains and these stores promise to appeal to customers by their unusual presentation and display of the merchandise.

The distribution channels for recorded music are undergoing a rapid change and the future promises more of the same. Currently, the major Canadian music retailers are: HMV Canada (19 per cent market share), Music World (17 per cent market share), Sam the Record Man (12 per cent market share), BMG and Columbia House music clubs (25 per cent market share) with the remainder of the market going to an assortment of: independent record retailers, department stores (like the Bay, Eaton's, Sears, Kmart, Zellers, and Wal-Mart), and sound equipment outlets like the Future Shop and A&B Sound. However, these players are about to be blind sided.

The dominant medium for music these days is the compact disc (CD). People can carry personal CD players, play them in their cars, play them in multi-CD players in a home stereo, and in CD-equipped home computers. Technology for "recordable" CDs is still very expensive, but it is only a matter of time before the costs fall dramatically. The existence of copyright piracy has always been a thorn in the side of the recording industry, and the thorn is getting sharper. The CD's utility as a storage medium combined with its link to the computer has opened up the potential for another channel of distribution: direct from producer (the musician) to the consumer.

John Parry Barlow, a co-founder of the Electronic Frontier Foundation, believes that in the future, copyright and intellectual property will not exist. Recordings, technology designs, video games, books, and videos will be "free." He claims that the interchange of information and technology brought about by the computer's ability to copy and transfer digital images will mean that enforcing copyright and intellectual property rights will be impossible and this will mean that collecting royalties and fees will be impossible too. Barlow sees a world in which people will browse through an online catalogue and then download the music or entertainment they see to their computers. From there, they may permanently record the entertainment (music, video, game, computer software, etc.) on a recordable CD or on their mega-megabyte hard drives.

If you think Barlow is just speculating, think again. CDnow! is a commercial service with an online catalogue (look out music clubs) that allows browsers to sample the products from their computers, place a mail order, and even download items for a fee. Cerberus Sound + Vision in Britain has a licence to sell music online. Meanwhile, Cyberspace Promotions in Los Altos, California, offers "Virtual Radio." Bands can pay to have their demo music played on virtual radio, which is accessed through the Internet. Listeners can download the music free of charge. According to Barlow, it is only a matter of time before the artists will be selling music directly to the listeners, bypassing the record companies and their distributors. At the moment, Internet music products are only half CD quality. However, this technological issue will likely be resolved in the future. From the marketing standpoint, reaching out directly to the customer is the key. If the customer wants "full CD" quality now, they will order an actual CD through their computer and get it in the mail.

HMV Canada uses the HMV Toronto Superstore as part of an internet marketing approach for their products. Users can sample and order products by computer but still receive conventional media (CDs, music cassettes, videos, and computer software) through mail order. The music clubs BMG (started up in 1995) and Columbia House (in business since 1955) have depended primarily on mail order for their operations but direct ordering on the Internet is a natural extension for them.

HMV
www.hmv.ca

Will there be a growth in Internet purchases and a fall-off in music store buying? The demographics appear to say yes. Apparently the older crowd, people in their late 20s up through their 40s (a crowd that is getting older and represents the largest market potential) is not buying as much music as they once did. The most likely reason is that they have been mostly ignored by the music industry in favour of the younger crowd. They do not feel at home in music stores, which play "alternative" music and prominently display and feature price the artists targeted at the teenage group. This older 20- to 40-year-old segment also represents the Internet types who just might be more likely to respond to mail order and Internet appeals and shun music stores. The future of distribution in the music industry will be interesting to watch. As for predicting the winners and losers, one winner has already emerged: the consumers.[1]

In this chapter, we will learn more about the decisions made in distribution planning and the activities involved in physical distribution, including quick response inventory systems.

Overview

Distribution planning is systematic decision making regarding the physical movement of goods and services from producer to consumer, as well as the related transfer of ownership (or rental) of them. It encompasses such diverse functions as transportation, inventory management, and customer transactions.

Functions are carried out via a **channel of distribution**, which is comprised of all the organizations or people involved in the distribution process. Those organizations or people are known as **channel members** and may include manufacturers, service providers, wholesalers, retailers, marketing specialists, and/or consumers. When the term **distribution intermediaries** is used, it refers to wholesalers, retailers, and marketing specialists (such as transportation firms) that act as facilitators (links) between manufacturers/service providers and consumers.

This chapter presents an in-depth look at distribution planning and looks at the role of physical distribution. Chapter 10 covers retailing's and wholesaling's role in the distribution process.

Distribution planning *involves movement and ownership in a* **channel of distribution***. It consists of* **channel members***.*

Distribution intermediaries *often have a channel role.*

[1]Christian Allard, "Loony Tunes," *Canadian Business* (August 1995), pp. 73–74; Michael McCullough, "The Changing Sounds of Music Marketing," *Marketing Magazine* (June 19, 1995), p. 20; James Pollock, "Luckhurst Rising Fast on HMV's Charts," *Marketing Magazine* (February 5, 1996), p. 7; James Pollock, "Tower Entry Stokes up TO Record Market," *Marketing Magazine* (January 22, 1996), p. 5; Michael McCullough, "Virgin Awaits Approval for First Canadian Store," *Marketing Magazine* (February 19, 1996), p. 5; Laura Medcalf, "Music Industry Tests Ways to Reach Grown-Up Consumers," *Marketing Magazine* (August 21–28, 1995), p. 3; and Eva Lazarus, " That's Robson, not Rodeo," *Marketing Magazine* (April 21, 1997), p. 7.

Distribution Planning

Distribution arrangements vary widely.

A channel of distribution can be simple or complex. It can be based on a handshake agreement between a small manufacturer and a local reseller or require detailed written contracts among numerous manufacturers, wholesalers, and retailers. Some firms seek widespread distribution and need independent wholesalers and/or retailers to carry their merchandise and improve cash flow. Others want direct customer contact and do not use independent resellers. Industrial channels usually have more direct contact between manufacturers/ service providers and customers than final consumer channels. International channels also have special needs.

The importance of distribution planning, the range of tasks performed in the distribution process, the criteria to consider in picking a distribution channel, supplier/distribution intermediary contracts, channel cooperation and conflict, the industrial channel of distribution, and international distribution are discussed next.

The Importance of Distribution Planning

Distribution decisions have a great impact on a company's marketing efforts. Because intermediaries can perform a host of functions, a firm's marketing plan will differ if it sells direct rather than through intermediaries; and a decision to sell in stores rather than through the mail or the World Wide Web requires a different marketing orientation and tasks.

The choice of a distribution channel is one of the most critical decisions a firm will make. Close ties with intermediaries and/or customers may take time to develop; if there are existing bonds among channel members, it may be hard for a new firm to enter. Once channel alliances are achieved, suitable new products can be put into distribution more easily. Channel members need to act in a coordinated way. Strong resellers enhance manufacturers' marketing abilities. Consumers like to buy products the same way over time.

Through relationship marketing, companies strive for ongoing ties with suppliers, intermediaries, and customers.

Today, more companies recognize the value of having good relationships throughout the distribution channel. As a result, many firms now engage in relationship marketing, whereby they seek to develop and maintain continuous long-term ties with suppliers, distribution intermediaries, and customers. By doing so, these firms ensure a more consistent flow of goods and services from suppliers, encourage intermediaries to act more as partners than adversaries, and increase the likelihood of having loyal customers. They improve employee morale by empowering them to respond positively to reasonable requests—in the employees' judgment—from suppliers, intermediaries, and/or customers. They get earlier and better data on prospective new products and the best strategies for continuing ones. They also lower operating and marketing costs, thus improving efficiency. As one expert noted, with relationship marketing, it is "traumatic to leave someone who you believe is responsive to your personal needs. We don't change doctors, lawyers, or accountants at the drop of a hat. Firms want to build the same relationships with suppliers, distribution intermediaries, and customers so they won't leave every time they get a better offer."[2] See Figure 9-1.

These are several recommendations as to how effective relationship marketing in a distribution channel may be achieved:

- Relationship marketing should be conducted as a continuous and systematic process that incorporates both buyer and seller needs.

- Relationship marketing needs top management support; and its principles should permeate a firm's corporate culture.

---

[2]Aimee L. Stern, "Courting Consumer Loyalty with the Feel-Good Bond," *New York Times* (January 17, 1993), Section 3, p. 10. For further information on relationship marketing, see Barry Berman, *Marketing Channels* (New York: Wiley, 1996), pp. 201–239; "Special Issue on Relationship Marketing," *Journal of the Academy of Marketing Science*, Vol. 23 (Fall 1995); Robert M. Morgan and Shelby D. Hunt, "The Commitment-Trust Theory of Relationship Marketing," *Journal of Marketing*, Vol. 58 (July 1994), pp. 20–38; Robert D. Buzzell and Gwen Ortmeyer, "Channel Partnerships Streamline Distribution," *Sloan Management Review*, Vol. 36 (Spring 1995), pp. 85–96; and Gregory T. Gundlach, Ravi S. Achrol, and John T. Mentzer, "The Structure of Commitment in Exchange," *Journal of Marketing*, Vol. 59 (January 1995), pp. 78–92.

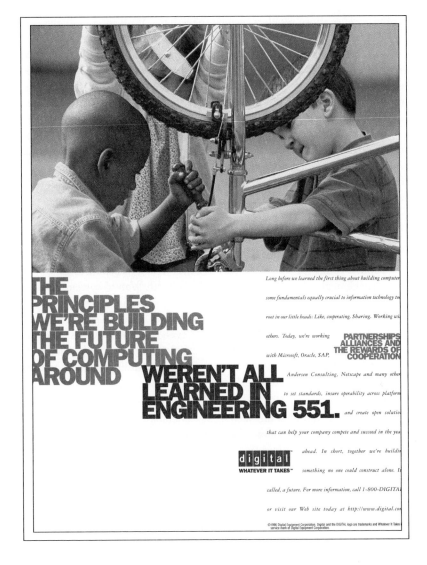

FIGURE 9-1
Relationship Marketing and Digital Equipment
To illustrate its commitment to relationship marketing, Digital Equipment Corporation discusses its partnerships and willingness to cooperate. Firms are encouraged to phone or visit Digital's Web site.

Reprinted with permission of Digital Equipment Corporation.

- At a minimum, relationship marketing means understanding consumer expectations, building service partnerships, empowering employees, and total quality management (from buyer and seller perspectives).

- Suppliers, intermediaries, and customers should be surveyed—by category—to determine the aspects of relationship marketing to be emphasized for them.

- Although increased profitability is a desirable result from relationship marketing, other important measures of success are customer satisfaction, customer loyalty, and product quality.

- Both positive and negative feedback (going far beyond just passively receiving customer complaints) can provide meaningful information.

- Sellers need to communicate to their customers that relationship marketing involves responsibilities, as well as benefits, for both parties.

- Mutually agreeable (by buyers and sellers) contingency plans should be devised in case anything goes awry.[3]

Costs, as well as profits, are affected by the selection of a particular type of distribution channel. A firm doing all functions must pay for them itself; in return, it reaps all profits. A firm using intermediaries reduces per-unit distribution costs; it also reduces per-unit

---

[3]Joel R. Evans and Richard L. Laskin, "The Relationship Marketing Process: A Conceptualization and Application," *Industrial Marketing Management*, Vol. 23 (December 1994), p. 451.

profits because those resellers receive their share. With intermediaries, a firm's total profits would rise if there are far higher sales than the firm could attain itself.

Distribution formats are long-standing in some industries. For example, in the beverage and food industry, manufacturers often sell through wholesalers that then deal with retailers. Auto makers sell through franchised dealers. Mail-order firms line up suppliers, print catalogues, and sell to consumers. So, firms must frequently conform to the channel patterns in their industries.

A firm's market coverage is often influenced by the location and number, market penetration, image, product selection, services, and marketing plans of the wholesalers, retailers, and/or marketing specialists with which it deals. In weighing options, a firm should note that the more intermediaries it uses, the less customer contact it has and the lower its control over marketing.

These examples show the scope of distribution planning:

- Shoppers Drug Mart is Canada's largest drugstore chain with 850 stores and $4 billion in annual sales. Shoppers doesn't just distribute and sell prescription and over-the-counter drugs (as well as numerous other items). It also distributes customized health management information through the "Health Watch" system. Each prescription customer is given a detailed fact sheet on their prescription medications, which provides warnings to both pharmacists and customers about the dangers of drug interactions with other drugs, food, beverages, and even types of activities. The information is produced by linking the customer information database with a large drug information database and then having a computer print out the details on the medicines, the customer, and their physicians.[4]

- Shoppers Advantage is a member-based shopping service that operates exclusively through the World Wide Web. It has a database of 250 000 brand-name products that are offered at a discount. Shoppers Advantage "acts as an online broker, displaying wares and taking orders and payment. Orders are passed on to distributors, manufacturers, and vendors, which ship products to, or book reservations for, customers."[5]

- Century 21 is the world's largest residential real estate broker. It relies on 6000 franchisee-operated offices in eleven countries.[6]

McAFEE ASSOCIATES

www50.dt.navy.mil/code521/Virus/
McAfee.html

Intermediaries can perform **channel functions** *and reduce costs, provide expertise, open markets, and lower risks.*

Channel Functions and the Role of Distribution Intermediaries

For most goods and services, the **channel functions** shown in Figure 9-2 and described here must be undertaken somewhere in the distribution channel and responsibility for them assigned.

Distribution intermediaries can play a vital role in marketing research. Due to their closeness to the market, they generally have good insights into the characteristics and needs of customers.

In buying products, intermediaries sometimes pay as items are received; other times, they accept items on consignment and do not pay until after sales are made. Purchase terms for intermediaries may range from net cash (payment due at once) to net sixty days (payment not due for sixty days) or longer. If intermediaries do not pay until after resale, manufacturers risk poor cash flow, high product returns, obsolescence and spoilage, multiple transactions with the intermediaries, and potentially low sales to customers.

Manufacturers and service firms like H&R Block often take care of national (and international) ads when assigning promotion roles. Wholesalers may help coordinate regional promotions among retailers and may motivate and train retail salespeople. Most retailers use local ads, personal selling, and special events as forms of promotion.

Customer services include delivery, credit, in-office and in-home purchases, training programs, warranties, and return privileges. Again, these services can be provided by one channel member or a combination of them.

---

[4]Lara Mills, "Drug Retail Rumble," *Marketing Magazine* (March 4, 1996), p. 11.
[5]Peter H. Lewis, "Online Middleman Opens for Business," *Wall Street Journal* (October 2, 1995), p. D5.
[6]Suzanne Woolley, "I Want My Century 21!" *Business Week* (January 15, 1996), pp. 72–73.

Ethics AND TODAY'S MARKETER

Can New Firms Use an Honour System to Gain Distribution?

McAfee Associates markets two computer software packages: VirusScan, which protects PCs from viruses, and Netshield, which monitors security in local area networks. The firm's annual sales revenues exceed US$30 million.

Unlike many other similar firms, both of McAfee's products are shareware. Thus, these programs can be downloaded from electronic bulletin boards by anyone with a modem and a personal computer. In theory, consumers are given a sixty-day trial period. Those who wish to continue using the products are expected to pay a US$100 fee for access to technical support and for future upgrades. However, in practice, most consumers do not pay the fee, realizing that it is quite difficult for any shareware provider to enforce payment.

About 100 000 potential customers download McAfee's software packages each month. Of this group, about 20 per cent eventually remit the US$100 fee. In some cases, McAfee's technical support people have fielded questions from nonpaying users. Why? The firm is careful not to offend nonpayers, hoping they will pay for the programs they use. McAfee also realizes that many of these "freeloaders" are responsible for publicizing its software within their firms.

Unlike hobbyists, almost all corporate users are quick to pay for the shareware they use. As a result, the majority of McAfee's actual sales are from corporate users. Ford Motor Company, for instance, has a licence for 52 000 users and Mobil Corporation has one for over 36 000 computers.

Shareware is typically marketed by small software firms that cannot afford to get distribution through traditional channels. These companies typically concentrate on the hobbyist market. In many cases, shareware authors also do not have the resources to properly test and refine their products.

As a channels manager for McAfee, evaluate the pros and cons of the firm's continued use of shareware. What would you do next? Why?

Source: Based on material in Julie Pitta, "Honour System," *Forbes* (October 24, 1994), pp. 258–260.

Distribution intermediaries can contribute to product planning in several ways. They often provide advice on new and existing products; test marketing requires their cooperation; and intermediaries can be helpful in positioning products against competitors and suggesting which products to drop.

Wholesalers and retailers often have strong input into pricing decisions. They state their required markups and then price-mark products or specify how they should be marked. Court rulings limit manufacturers' control over final prices. Intermediaries thus have great flexibility in setting prices.

Distribution incorporates three major factors: transportation, inventory management, and customer contact. Goods must be shipped from a manufacturer to consumers; intermediaries often provide this service. Because production capabilities and customer demand frequently differ, inventory levels must be properly managed (and items may require storage in a warehouse before being sold). Consumer transactions may require a store or other selling location, long hours of operation, and store fixtures (such as dressing rooms).

Manufacturers typically like to make a limited variety of items in large quantities and have as few transactions as possible to sell their entire output. On the other hand, consumers tend to want a variety of brands, colours, sizes, and qualities from which to select—

FIGURE 9-2
Channel Functions

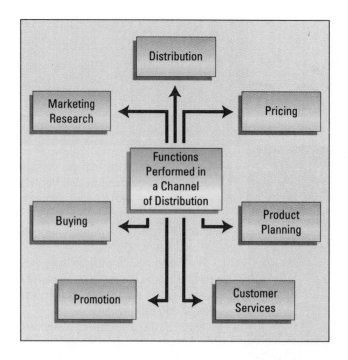

and opt to buy a small amount at a time. Manufacturers might also prefer to sell products from the factory, have nine to five hours and spartan fixtures, and use a limited sales force. Yet organizational consumers may want salespeople to come to their offices and final consumers may want to shop at nearby locations and visit attractive, well-staffed stores on weekends and evenings.

The sorting process coordinates manufacturer and consumer goals.

To resolve these differences, intermediaries can be used in the **sorting process**, which consists of four distribution functions: accumulation, allocation, sorting, and assorting. Accumulation is collecting small shipments from several firms so shipping costs are lower. Allocation is apportioning items to various consumer markets. Sorting is separating products into grades, colours, and so forth. Assorting is offering a broad range of products so the consumer has many choices.

Selecting a Channel of Distribution

In choosing a distribution channel, several key factors must be considered:

Channel choice depends on consumers, the company, the product, competition, existing channels, and legalities.

- *The consumer.*
  Characteristics—number, concentration, average purchase size.
  Needs—shopping locations and hours, assortment, sales help, credit.
  Segments—size, purchase behaviour.
- *The company.*
  Goals—control, sales, profit, timing.
  Resources—level, flexibility, service needs.
  Expertise—functions, specialization, efficiency.
  Experience—distribution methods, channel relationships.
- *The product.*
  Value—price per unit.
  Complexity—technical nature.
  Perishability—shelf life, frequency of shipments.
  Bulk—weight per unit, divisibility.
- *The competition.*
  Characteristics—number, concentration, assortment, customers.
  Tactics—distribution methods, channel relationships.

- *Distribution channels.*

    Alternatives—direct, indirect.

    Characteristics—number of intermediaries, functions performed, tradition.

    Availability—exclusive arrangements, territorial restrictions.

- *Legalities*—current laws, pending laws.

While assessing the preceding factors, a firm would make decisions about the type of channel used, contractual arrangements or administered channels, channel length and width, channel intensity, and whether to use dual channels.

There are two basic types of channels: direct and indirect. A **direct channel of distribution** involves the movement of goods and services from producer to consumers without the use of independent intermediaries. An **indirect channel of distribution** involves the movement of goods and services from producer to independent intermediaries to consumers. Figure 9-3 shows the transactions necessary for the sale of 200 000 men's umbrellas under direct and indirect channels. Figure 9-4 shows the most common indirect channels for final consumer and organizational consumer products.

In a **direct channel** *one firm performs all tasks. An* **indirect channel** *has multiple firms.*

If a manufacturer or service provider sells to consumers via company-owned outlets (for example, Imperial Oil's Esso gas stations), this is a direct channel. In an indirect channel, a manufacturer may employ several layers of independent wholesalers (for example, regional, provincial, and local) and sell through different kinds of retailers (such as discount, department, and specialty stores). A direct channel is most used by firms that want control over their entire marketing programs, desire close customer contact, and have limited markets. An indirect channel is most used by firms that want to enlarge their markets, raise sales volume, and give up distribution functions and costs, and that are willing to surrender some channel control and customer contact.

Because an indirect channel has independent members, marketing responsibilities may be assigned in different ways. With a *contractual channel arrangement*, all the terms regarding distribution tasks, prices, and other factors are stated in writing for each member. A manufacturer and a retailer could sign an agreement citing promotion support, delivery and payment dates, and product handling, marking, and displays. In an *administered channel arrangement*, the dominant firm in the distribution process plans the marketing program and itemizes and coordinates each member's duties. Depending on their relative strength, a manufacturer/service provider, wholesaler, or retailer could be a channel leader. Accordingly, a manufacturer with a strong brand could set its image, price range, and selling method.

Channel length refers to the levels of independent members along a distribution channel. In Figure 9-3, *A* is a short channel and *B* is a long channel. Sometimes, a firm shortens its channel by acquiring a company at another stage, as when a manufacturer merges with a wholesaler. Doing so allows the firm to be more self-sufficient, ensure supply, control channel members, lower distribution costs, and coordinate timing throughout the channel. However, it may also limit competition and foster inefficiency, and may not result in lower consumer prices.

Channel length *describes the number of levels of independent members.*

Channel width refers to the number of independent members at any stage of distribution. In a narrow channel, a manufacturer or service provider sells through few wholesalers or retailers; in a wide channel, it sells through many. If a firm wants to enhance its position at its stage of the channel, it may buy other companies like itself, such as one janitorial-services firm buying another. This lets a firm increase its size and share of the market, improve bargaining power with other channel members, enlarge its market, and utilize mass promotion and distribution techniques more efficiently.

Channel width *refers to the independent members at one level.*

In selecting a distribution channel, a firm must decide on the intensity of its coverage. Under **exclusive distribution**, a firm severely limits the number of resellers utilized in a geographic area, perhaps having only one or two within a specific shopping location. It seeks a prestige image, channel control, and high profit margins, and accepts lower total sales than it would attain using another type of distribution. With **selective distribution**, a firm employs a moderate number of resellers. It tries to combine some channel control and a solid image with good sales volume and profits. A firm uses a large number of resellers in **intensive distribution**. Its goals are to have wide market coverage, channel acceptance, and high total sales and profits. Per-unit profits are low. It is a strategy aimed at the greatest number of consumers. See Table 9-1.

Exclusive, selective, and **intensive distribution** depend on goals, sellers, customers, and marketing.

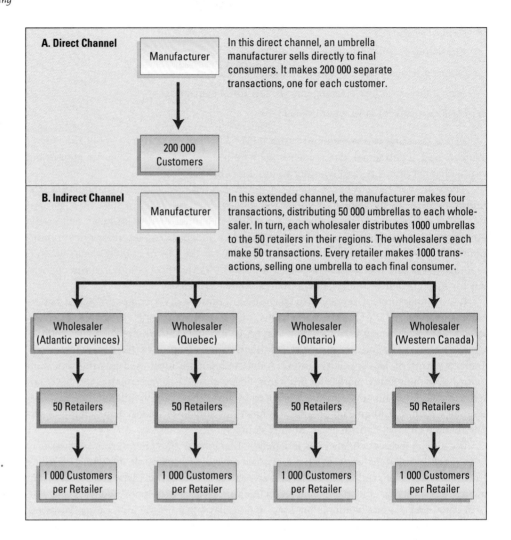

FIGURE 9-3
Transactions in a Direct Versus an Indirect Channel

A. Direct Channel

Manufacturer

200 000 Customers

In this direct channel, an umbrella manufacturer sells directly to final consumers. It makes 200 000 separate transactions, one for each customer.

B. Indirect Channel

Manufacturer

In this extended channel, the manufacturer makes four transactions, distributing 50 000 umbrellas to each wholesaler. In turn, each wholesaler distributes 1000 umbrellas to the 50 retailers in their regions. The wholesalers each make 50 transactions. Every retailer makes 1000 transactions, selling one umbrella to each final consumer.

Wholesaler (Atlantic provinces)	Wholesaler (Quebec)	Wholesaler (Ontario)	Wholesaler (Western Canada)
50 Retailers	50 Retailers	50 Retailers	50 Retailers
1 000 Customers per Retailer	1 000 Customers per Retailer	1 000 Customers per Retailer	1 000 Customers per Retailer

FIGURE 9-4
Typical Indirect Channels of Distribution

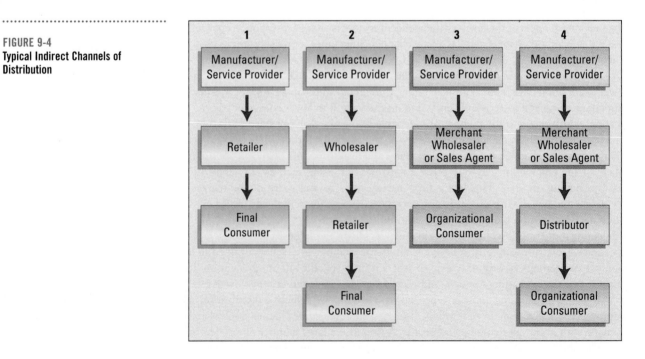

	1	2	3	4
	Manufacturer/ Service Provider	Manufacturer/ Service Provider	Manufacturer/ Service Provider	Manufacturer/ Service Provider
	Retailer	Wholesaler	Merchant Wholesaler or Sales Agent	Merchant Wholesaler or Sales Agent
	Final Consumer	Retailer	Organizational Consumer	Distributor
		Final Consumer		Organizational Consumer

T a b l e   9 - 1
Intensity of Channel Coverage

ATTRIBUTES	EXCLUSIVE DISTRIBUTION	SELECTIVE DISTRIBUTION	INTENSIVE DISTRIBUTION
Objectives	Prestige image, channel control and loyalty, price stability and high profit margins	Moderate market coverage, solid image, some channel control and loyalty, good sales and profits	Widespread market coverage, channel acceptance, volume sales and profits
Resellers	Few in number, well-established, reputable firms (outlets)	Moderate in number, well-established, better firms (outlets)	Many in number, all types of firms (outlets)
Customers	Final consumers: fewer in number, trend setters, willing to travel to store, brand loyal. Organizational consumers: focus on major accounts, service expected from manufacturer	Final consumers: moderate in number, brand conscious, somewhat willing to travel to store. Organizational consumers: focus on many types of accounts, service expected from manufacturer or intermediary	Final consumers: many in number, convenience-oriented. Organizational consumers: focus on all types of accounts, service expected from intermediary
Marketing	Final consumers: personal selling, pleasant shopping conditions, good service. Organizational consumers: availability, regular communications, superior service	Final consumers: promotional mix, pleasant shopping conditions, good service. Organizational consumers: availability, regular communications, superior service	Final consumers: mass advertising nearby location, items in stock. Organizational consumers: availability, regular communications, superior service
Major weakness	Limited sales potential	May be difficult to carve out a niche	Limited channel control
Examples	Autos, designer clothes, capital equipment, complex services	Furniture, clothing, mechanics' tools, industrialized services	Household products, groceries, office supplies, routine services

Some additional factors are noteworthy in selecting a channel. First, a firm may use a **dual channel of distribution**, which allows it to appeal to different market segments or diversify business by selling through two or more separate channels. A company could use selective distribution for a prestige brand of watches and intensive distribution for a discount brand, or use both direct and indirect channels (such as an insurance firm selling group health insurance directly to large businesses and individual life insurance indirectly to final consumers via independent agents). Kodak uses a three-tiered distribution approach for microfilm, supplies, and imaging systems and software: (1) Kodak's own sales representatives concentrate on complex document-imaging systems. (2) Well-trained brokers market such Kodak equipment as reader-printers and other stand-alone components; they must be certified to sell and service each product line carried. (3) Other intermediaries handle film sales, film processing, and delivery to all business clients in their territories.

> A **dual channel** lets a company reach different segments or diversify.

Second, a firm may go from exclusive to selective to intensive distribution as a product passes through its life cycle. However, it would be hard to go in the opposite direction, from intensive to selective to exclusive distribution. For example, designer jeans rapidly moved from prestige stores to better stores to all types of outlets. This process would not have worked in reverse. Third, a firm may distribute products in a new way and achieve great success. The sale of women's hosiery was revolutionized when L'eggs products were placed in supermarkets.

Supplier/Distribution Intermediary Contracts

Supplier/distribution intermediary contracts cover prices, sale conditions, territories, commitments, timing, and termination.

Supplier/distribution intermediary contracts focus on price policies, conditions of sale, territorial rights, the services/responsibility mix, and contract length and conditions of termination. The highlights of a basic contract follow.

Price policies largely deal with the discounts given to intermediaries for their functions, quantity purchases, and cash payments, and with commission rates. Functional discounts are deductions from list prices given to intermediaries for performing storage, shipping, and other jobs. Quantity discounts are deductions for volume purchases. Cash discounts are deductions for early payment. Some intermediaries are paid commissions for their tasks.

Conditions of sale cover price and quality guarantees, payment and shipping terms, reimbursement for unsold items, and return allowances. A guarantee against a price decline protects one intermediary from paying a high price for an item that is then offered to others at a lower price; if prices are reduced, the original buyer receives a rebate so its product costs are like competitors'. Otherwise, it could not meet the prices that competitors charge customers. Suppliers sometimes employ full-line forcing, whereby intermediaries are required to carry an entire line of products. This is legal if they are not prevented from also buying items from other suppliers.

Territorial rights outline the geographic areas (such as greater Paris) in which resellers may operate and/or the target markets (such as small-business accounts) they may contact. In some cases, they have exclusive territories, as with McDonald's franchisees; in others, many firms are granted territorial rights for the same areas, as with retailers selling Sharp calculators.

The services/responsibility mix describes the role of each channel member. It outlines such factors as who delivers products, stores inventory, trains salespeople, writes ad copy, and sets up displays; and it sets performance standards. If included, a hold-harmless clause specifies that manufacturers or service providers—and not resellers—are accountable for lawsuits arising from poor product design or negligence in production.

Contract length and conditions of termination protect an intermediary against a manufacturer or service provider prematurely bypassing it after a territory has been built up. The manufacturer or service provider is shielded by limiting contract duration and stating the factors that may lead to termination.

Not all relationships among channel members are so formal. Some firms rely on handshake agreements. However, without a contract, the danger exists that there will be misunderstandings regarding goals, compensation, tasks to be performed, and the length of the agreement. The one constraint of a written contract may be its inflexibility under changing market conditions.

Channel Cooperation and Conflict

Channel member goals need to be balanced.

All firms in a distribution channel have similar general goals: profitability, access to goods and services, efficient distribution, and customer loyalty. Yet, the way these and other goals are achieved often leads to differing views, even if the parties engage in relationship marketing. For example, how are profits allocated along a channel? How can manufacturers sell products through many competing resellers and expect the resellers not to carry other brands? Which party coordinates channel decisions? To whom are consumers loyal—manufacturers/service providers, wholesalers, or retailers?

There are natural differences among the firms in a distribution channel by virtue of their channel positions, the tasks performed, and the desire of each firm to raise its profits and control its strategy. A successful channel will maximize cooperation and minimize conflict. Table 9-2 cites causes of channel conflict. Table 9-3 shows how channel cooperation can reduce these conflicts.

In the past, manufacturers dominated channels because they had the best market coverage and recognition; resellers were small and localized. Now, with the growth of large national (and international) wholesalers and retailers, the volume accounted for by them, and the popularity of private brands, the balance of power has shifted more to resellers. As one expert said:

Table 9-2

Potential Causes of Channel Conflict

FACTOR	MANUFACTURER'S/ SERVICE PROVIDER'S GOAL	DISTRIBUTION INTERMEDIARY'S GOAL
Pricing	To establish final price consistent with product image	To establish final price consistent with the intermediary's image
Purchase terms	To ensure prompt, accurate payments and minimize discounts	To defer payments as long as possible and secure discounts
Shelf space	To obtain plentiful shelf space with good visibility so as to maximize brand sales	To allocate shelf space among multiple brands so as to maximize total product sales
Exclusivity	To hold down the number of competing brands each intermediary stocks while selling through many intermediaries	To hold down the number of competing intermediaries carrying the same brands while selling different brands itself
Delivery	To receive adequate notice before deliveries are required	To obtain quick service
Advertising support	To secure ad support from intermediaries	To secure ad support from manufacturers/service providers
Profitability	To have adequate profit margins	To have adequate profit margins
Continuity	To receive orders on a regular basis	To receive shipments on a regular basis
Order size	To maximize order size	To have order size conform with consumer demand to minimize inventory investment
Assortment	To offer a limited variety	To secure a full variety
Risk	To have intermediaries assume risks	To have manufacturers/service providers assume risks
Branding	To sell products under the manufacturer's/ service provider's name	To sell products under private brands as well as manufacturers'/service providers' brands
Channel access	To distribute products wherever desired by the manufacturer/service provider	To carry only those items desired by intermediaries
Importance of account	To not allow any one intermediary to dominate	To not allow any one manufacturer/service provider to dominate
Consumer	To have consumers loyal to the manufacturer/service provider	To have consumers loyal to the intermediary
Channel control	To make key channel decisions	To make key channel decisions

Table 9-3

Methods of Channel Cooperation

FACTOR	MANUFACTURER'S/SERVICE PROVIDER'S ACTIONS	DISTRIBUTION INTERMEDIARY'S ACTIONS
New-product introduction	Thorough testing, adequate promotional support	Good shelf location and space, enthusiasm for product, assistance in test marketing
Delivery	Prompt filling of orders, adherence to scheduled dates	Proper time allowed for delivery, shipments immediately checked for accuracy
Marketing research	Data provided to resellers	Data provided to manufacturers/service providers
Pricing	Prices to intermediaries let them gain reasonable profits, intermediary flexibility encouraged	Infrequent sales from regular prices, maintaining proper image
Promotion	Training reseller's salespeople, sales force incentives, developing appropriate ad campaign, cooperative ad programs	Attractive store displays, knowledgeable salespeople, participation in cooperative programs
Financing	Liberal financial terms	Adherence to financial terms
Product quality	Product guarantees	Proper installation and servicing of products for customers
Channel control	Shared and specified decision making	Shared and specified decision making

In highly competitive markets, with so many manufacturers competing for the same customers, distributors and dealers can afford to be choosy about which firms' products they will push. Getting them to push your products is what motivation in marketing channels is all about. With so many [North American] manufacturers interested in marketing products overseas, and needing foreign dealers and distributors to do so, the motivation of channel partners needs to be addressed from an international perspective, as well as a domestic one.[7]

If conflicts are not resolved cooperatively, confrontations may occur. A manufacturer or service provider may then ship late, refuse to deal with certain resellers, limit financing, withdraw promotional support, or use other tactics. Similarly, a reseller may make late payments, give poor shelf space, refuse to carry items, return many products, and apply other tactics. A channel cannot function well in a confrontational framework. Here is an example of channel conflict:

> In March 1996, 100 members of the Retail Music Association of Canada boycotted the 1996 Juno awards. They refused to put up posters promoting the awards, would not distribute ballots so fans could vote on entertainer of the year and refused to sponsor or be represented at the awards. The only major retailer not to comply was Sam the Record Man, which has incurred the disapproval of other retailers for breaking ranks.
> Why would music retailers boycott the big show that promotes the performers whose products they sell? Because Columbia House, a mail-order record club, was the main sponsor of the event and the music stores did not want to be involved in anything that allied them with one of their most hated competitors. Record clubs used to get delayed music releases, products that had already been selling in music stores for a few months. It was a concession the large record companies made to the traditional music retailers. This concession is no longer given, and music clubs now have the newest music releases, which they sell as loss leaders (ten CDs for a penny). Music stores cannot compete with this and they are rebelling against the industry.[8]

A thriving existing manufacturer or service provider can often secure reseller support and enthusiasm when introducing new products and continuing popular ones. This occurs because resellers know the manufacturer's or service provider's past track record, the promotion support that will be provided, and the manufacturer's or service provider's reliability in future deliveries. Thus, a **pushing strategy** is used, whereby the various firms in a distribution channel cooperate in marketing a product. With this approach, a manufacturer or service provider uses relationship marketing.

*In a **pushing strategy**, there is cooperation among channel members. With **pulling**, a firm generates demand before receiving channel support.*

As a rule, it is harder for a new manufacturer or service provider to break into an existing channel. Resellers are unfamiliar with the firm, not able to gauge its sales potential, and wonder about its support and future deliveries. So, a new firm would need a **pulling strategy**, whereby it first stimulates consumer demand and then gains dealer support. This means heavy promotion expenses, fully paid by the manufacturer or service provider; it must often offer guarantees of minimum sales or profits to resellers, and make up shortfalls. Figure 9-5 contrasts pushing and pulling strategies.

FIGURE 9-5
Pushing Versus Pulling Strategies

---

[7]Bert Rosenbloom, "Motivating Your International Channel Partners," *Business Horizons*, Vol. 33 (March–April 1990), p. 53.

[8]Anita Lahey, "Music Retailers Boycott Junos Over Club Sponsorship," *Marketing Magazine* (March 4, 1996), p. 2.

In today's competitive environment, with so many new domestic and foreign products being introduced each year, even market-leading firms must sometimes use pulling strategies. They have to convince resellers that consumer demand exists for their products, before the resellers agree to tie up shelf space.

The Industrial Channel of Distribution

The distribution channel for industrial products differs from that for consumer products in the following key ways:

An industrial channel has unique characteristics.

1. Retailers are typically not utilized.
2. Direct channels are more readily employed.
3. Transactions are fewer and orders are larger.
4. Specification selling is more prevalent.
5. Intermediaries are more knowledgeable.
6. Team selling (two or more salespeople) may be necessary.
7. Distinct intermediaries specialize in industrial products.[9]
8. Leasing, rather than selling, is more likely.
9. Customer information needs are more technical.
10. Activities like shipping and warehousing may be shared.

International Distribution Planning

When devising an international distribution plan, a number of factors should be kept in mind. Here are several of them.

International distribution requires particular planning.

Channel length often depends on a nation's stage of economic development and consumer behaviour patterns. Less-developed and developing nations tend to use shorter, more direct channels than industrialized ones. They have many small firms marketing goods and services to nearby consumers; and the more limited transportation and communications networks encourage local shopping. At the same time, cultural norms in nations—both developing and industrialized—affect the expected interactions between sellers and consumers. For instance, in Japan, people treasure personal attention when making purchases, especially of expensive products. Unlike North American shoppers, Japanese consumers are not used to making purchases by telephone.

Distribution practices and formats vary by nation, as these examples show:

- Some Mexican supermarkets shut off their electricity overnight to hold down costs. Thus, items such as dairy products have a much shorter shelf life and must be more frequently delivered than in Canada.

- Large Japanese firms often set up *keiretsus*. A vertical keiretsu is an integrated network of suppliers, manufacturers, and resellers. A horizontal keiretsu typically consists of a money-centre bank, an insurance company, a trust banking company, a trading company, and several major manufacturers. North American firms have some channels that resemble vertical keiretsus, but they do not have networks that emulate horizontal keiretsus.[10]

- Although it has about three times as many people as both Canada and the United States, India has roughly the same number of retail establishments; just one-quarter of them are in metropolitan areas. "Pan-bidi" are the popular neighbourhood grocery and general stores that offer very low prices.[11]

---

[9]See Kris Frieswick, "Surviving the Mass Merchant Diagnosis," *Industrial Distribution* (September 1995), pp. 28–35.

[10]Roy L. Simerly, "Should U.S. Companies Establish Keiretsus?" *Journal of Business Strategy*, Vol. 13 (November–December 1992), pp. 58–61.

[11]Janet Zhang, "Asia: Opportunities Large and Small," *Chain Store Age Executive* (January 1995), Section 3, p. 7.

International Marketing in

How Do Mexican Distributors Rate Foreign Manufacturers?

To answer this question, a survey was mailed to Mexican distributors in four industries: industrial machinery, parts and components, chemicals and allied products, and office equipment. A total of one hundred distributors responded. By using distributor *importance* ratings for several attributes, as well as ratings of manufacturer *performance* on these same attributes, the study researchers developed performance "gap" measures.

Respondents were first asked to evaluate the importance of eleven types of support that manufacturers typically provide to distributors. Two of the eleven items related to distributors' terms: adequacy of profit margins and territorial exclusivity. The others related to the manufacturer support provided (such as financial assistance, sales force training, and advertising assistance). According to study results, "quick responses to requests for information" and "adequate profit margins" were the most important factors.

The distributors then assessed the manufacturers on each of the eleven factors and gap measures were generated by subtracting the performance ratings from the importance ratings. Where importance ratings were higher than performance ratings, manufacturers were deemed "underperforming." The opposite results would be categorized as "overperforming." For items rated as important, manufacturers should have high performance ratings. Very high ratings on items viewed as less important indicated that resources could be allocated to other support activities.

In the study, all performance ratings were lower than their importance ratings. This indicates underperformance by manufacturers. Items of high importance with large performance gaps included: "quick responses to requests for information," "training for your salespeople," "materials to assist your salespeople," "advertising to your customers," and "exclusive territories."

As a sales manager for a firm selling products through Mexican distributors, integrate these findings into your overall distributors' sales strategy.

Source: Based on material in Lance Leuthesser, Douglas W. LaBahn, and Katrin R. Harich, "Assessing Cross-National Business Relationships," *Industrial Marketing Management*, Vol. 24 (January 1995), pp. 61–68.

If a firm enters a foreign market for the first time, it must resolve various questions, including: Should products be made domestically and shipped to the foreign market or made in the foreign market? If products are made domestically, what form of transportation is best? What kind of distribution intermediaries should be used? Which specific intermediaries should be used?

Industry Canada and the Department of Foreign Affairs and International Trade are only too willing to help Canadian businesses that wish to distribute products internationally. They have set up a a network of Canada Business Service Centres in each province in Canada, with the Northwest Territories being served out of Manitoba and the Yukon Territory being served out of Alberta. Currently, each centre can be contacted by toll-free number or fax. The purpose of these centres is to provide small businesses with one-stop-shopping convenience for information on provincial and federal government programs and services, as well as private programs and services. Canada Business Service Centres offer their users: Business Information Systems (a database of information on programs and services offered by federal, provincial, and private-sector organizations), pathfinders (which describe services and programs by topic), toll-free telephone information and referral services, and leading-edge business products (such as videos, how-to manuals, CD-ROM products, and external database access).[12]

Through these centres, or through a personal computer with an Internet feed, you can access *Strategis*, Industry Canada's and the Department of Foreign Affairs and International Trade's online database and information system. *Strategis* has computerized market data on industries in many foreign nations and names of contacts in many of these industries as well. Legal requirements regarding distribution differ by country—and some have strict laws as to hours, methods of operation, and sites. In France, there are severe limits on Sunday retail hours. In Germany, there are strict limits on store size and Sunday hours. And many nations have complex procedures for foreign firms wishing to distribute products there. Thus, firms interested in standardized (global) distribution may be stymied in their efforts.

What is likely to cause a company to be more or less satisfied with its international distribution channel? According to one study:

- The better a firm's domestic channel performs relative to its international channel, the lower its satisfaction with the international channel.

- The more experience a firm has in foreign markets, the greater its satisfaction with its existing international channel.

- A firm is more satisfied with an existing international channel if it believes it has the ability to change channels.

- A firm has less satisfaction with its existing international channel if environmental uncertainty is high.

- A firm is less satisfied with its existing international channel if it is difficult to monitor the behaviour of channel members.[13]

Physical Distribution

Physical distribution (also known as **logistics**) encompasses the broad range of activities concerned with efficiently delivering raw materials, parts, semifinished items, and finished products to designated places, at designated times, and in proper condition. It may be undertaken by any member of a channel, from producer to consumer.

Physical distribution involves such functions as customer service; shipping; warehousing; inventory control; private trucking-fleet operations; packaging; receiving; materials handling; and plant, warehouse, and store location planning. The physical distribution activities involved in a typical **order cycle**—the period of time from when the customer places an order to its receipt—are illustrated in Figure 9-6.

Physical distribution involves the location, timing, and condition of deliveries. An **order cycle** *covers many activities.*

FIGURE 9-6 ✳
Selected Physical Distribution Activities Involved in a Typical Order Cycle

[12]Industry Canada & Department of Foreign Affairs and International Trade, "Canada Business Service Centre Network," Industry Canada *Strategis* Web site (1996).

[13]Saul Klein and Victor J. Roth, "Satisfaction with International Marketing Channels," *Journal of the Academy of Marketing Science*, Vol. 21 (Winter 1993), pp. 39–44.

The Importance of Physical Distribution

Physical distribution is important for a number of reasons: its costs, the value of customer service, and its relationship with other functional areas.

Cost control is a major goal.

COSTS Physical distribution costs amount to 10 to 12 per cent of the Canadian GDP, with transportation (freight) and storage accounting for almost one-half of that total. To contain costs, firms have been working hard to improve efficiency. Today, physical distribution tasks are completed faster, more accurately, and with fewer people than twenty years ago. Due to computerization and improved transportation, firms have reduced their inventory levels by hundreds of millions of dollars, thus saving on warehousing and interest expenses.

Distribution costs vary widely by industry and company type. At individual firms, total physical distribution costs depend on such factors as the nature of the business, the geographic area covered, the tasks done by other channel members, and the weight/value ratio of the items involved. For example, while many retailers spend 2 to 3 per cent of their revenues on transportation from vendors and receiving, marking, storing, and distributing goods, petroleum refiners spend almost one-quarter of their sales just on inbound and outbound transportation. And whenever Canada Post raises rates, shipping costs are dramatically affected for all kinds of firms.

Firms must identify the symptoms of poor distribution systems and strive to be more efficient. Up to one-fifth of the perishable items carried by Canadian grocers, like fish and dairy items, are lost to spoilage due to breakdowns in shipping or too much time on store shelves. To reduce losses, many grocers now insist on smaller, more frequent deliveries and have upgraded their storage facilities. Table 9-4 shows several cost ramifications of poor distribution.

CUSTOMER SERVICE A major concern in planning a firm's physical distribution program is the level of customer service it should provide. Decisions involve delivery frequency, speed, and consistency; emergency shipments; whether to accept small orders; warehousing; coordinating assortments; whether to provide order progress reports; and other factors. Weak performance may lose customers.

Accordingly, distribution standards—clear and measurable goals as to service levels in physical distribution—must be devised. Examples are filling 90 per cent of orders from

Table 9-4

Selected Symptoms of a Poor Physical Distribution System

SYMPTOM	COST RAMIFICATIONS
1. Slow-turning and/or too-high inventory	Excessive capital is tied up in inventory. The firm has high insurance costs, interest expenses, and high risks of pilferage and product obsolescence. Merchandise may be stale.
2. Inefficient customer service	Costs are high relative to the value of shipments; warehouses are poorly situated; inventory levels are not tied to customer demand.
3. A large number of interwarehouse shipments	Merchandise transfers raise physical distribution cost because items must be handled and verified at each warehouse.
4. Frequent use of emergency shipments	Extra charges add significantly to physical distribution costs.
5. Peripheral hauls and/or limited backhauling	The firm uses its own trucking facilities; but many hauls are too spread out and trucks may only be full one way.
6. A large number of small orders	Small orders often are unprofitable. Many distribution costs are fixed.

existing inventory, responding to customer requests for order information within two hours, filling orders with 99 per cent accuracy, and limiting goods damaged in transit to 2 per cent or less.

One way to set the proper customer service level is the **total-cost approach**, whereby the distribution service level with the lowest total costs—including freight (shipping), warehousing, and lost business—is the best service level. An ideal system seeks a balance between low expenditures on distribution and high opportunities for sales. Seldom will that be at the lowest level of distribution spending; lost sales will be too great. Figure 9-7 illustrates the total-cost approach.

By offering superior customer service, a firm may establish a significant competitive advantage. The opposite is also true: "Customers increasingly demand on-time delivery from their suppliers. If they don't get it, they go elsewhere. The standard delivery window in supermarkets used to be four hours. Now, top suppliers deliver within an hour of their promised times, sometimes within fifteen minutes. The trend toward more reliable delivery times reaches across all industries."[14]

*The **total-cost approach** considers both costs and opportunities.*

PHYSICAL DISTRIBUTION AND OTHER FUNCTIONAL AREAS There is an interaction between physical distribution and every aspect of marketing, as well as other functional areas in the firm, as the following indicate.

Physical distribution must be coordinated with other areas.

Product variations in colour, size, features, quality, and style impose a burden on a firm's distribution facilities. Greater variety means lower volume per item, which increases unit shipping and warehousing costs. Stocking a broader range of replacement parts also becomes necessary.

Physical distribution is related to an overall channel strategy. A firm seeking extensive distribution needs dispersed warehouses. One involved with perishables needs to be sure that most of a product's selling life is not spent in transit.

Because promotion campaigns are often planned well in advance, it is essential that distribution to resellers be done at the proper times to ensure ample stocks of goods. Resellers may get consumer complaints for not having sufficient quantities of the items they advertise, even if the manufacturer is at fault. Some new products fail due to poor initial distribution.

Physical distribution also plays a key part in pricing. A firm with fast, reliable delivery and an ample supply of replacement parts—that ships small orders and provides emergency shipments—may be able to charge higher prices than one providing less service.

A distribution strategy has a link with production and finance functions. High freight costs inspire firms to put plants closer to markets. Low average inventories in stock allow firms to reduce finance charges. Warehouse receipts may be used as collateral for loans.

Overall, there are many decisions to be made and coordinated in planning a physical distribution strategy: the transportation form(s) used, inventory levels and warehouse form(s), and the number and sites of plants, warehouses, and shopping facilities. A strategy can be simple. A firm can have one plant, focus on one geographic market, and ship to resellers or customers without the use of decentralized warehouses. On the other hand,

Carrier				
Air	$1.5 mill.	$100 000 / $1.6 mill.		Annual freight costs
Rail	$300 000 / $800 000 / $300 000	$1.4 mill.		Annual warehousing costs
Truck	$500 000 / $500 000	$200 000 / $1.2 mill.		Annual costs of lost sales due to being out of stock
		Costs		

FIGURE 9-7
An Illustration of the Total-Cost
Approach in Distribution

[14]Anil Kumar and Graham Sharman, "We Love Your Product, But Where Is It?" *Sloan Management Review*, Vol. 33 (Winter 1992), p. 92. See also Ronald Henkoff, "Delivering the Goods," *Fortune* (November 28, 1994), pp. 64–78.

a strategy can include multiple plants, assembly and/or warehouse locations in each market, thousands of customer locations, and several transportation forms.

The rest of this chapter looks at two central aspects of a physical distribution strategy: transportation and inventory management.

Transportation

Transportation is rated on speed, availability, dependability, capability, frequency, losses, and cost.

There are five basic transportation forms: railroads, motor carriers, waterways, pipelines, and airways. Table 9-5 ranks them on seven operating characteristics. Because the range of products that can be shipped by pipeline is so restricted, business firms typically ship products using one or a combination of railroads, motor carriers, waterways, and airways. Table 9-6 shows the share of Canadian cargo tonnage and revenue for these four most commonly employed forms of transportation. Each transportation form and three transport services will now be presented.

Railroads *ship mostly heavy items over long distances.*

RAILROADS **Railroads** usually carry heavy, bulky items that are low in value (relative to weight) over long distances. They ship items too heavy for trucks. Canada has 146 444 kilometres of railway connecting the nation from coast to coast. Because of the fact that Canada's economy is commodity-based, railways will always have a unique position as a transportation mode. Despite this, railroads have had various problems. Canadian Pacific lost $823 million in 1995 although they have rebounded with net income of $82.4 million for the first six months of 1997. Canadian National lost over $1 billion on their operations in 1995 but have had a modest turnaround with earnings of $124 million in 1996. Railway operations are risky because fixed costs are high due to investments in facilities. Shippers face rail car shortages in high-demand months for agricultural goods. Some tracks and rail cars are in serious need of repair. Trucks are faster, more flexible, and are more easily packed. In response to these problems, railroads are relying on new shipping techniques and operating flexibility to improve efficiency.[15]

CANADIAN PACIFIC RAILWAYS
www.cprailway.com/

CANADIAN NATIONAL RAILWAYS
www.cn.ca

Table 9-5

The Relative Operating Characteristics of Five Transportation Forms

OPERATING CHARACTERISTICS	RANKING BY TRANSPORTATION FORM[a]				
	Railroads	*Motor Carriers*	*Waterways*	*Pipelines*	*Airways*
Delivery speed	3	2	5	4	1
Number of locations served	2	1	4	5	3
On-time dependability[b]	3	2	4	1	5
Range of products carried	1	2	3	5	4
Frequency of shipments	4	2	5	1	3
Losses and damages	5	4	2	1	3
Cost per tonne-mile	3	4	1	2	5

[a]1 = highest ranking.

[b]Relative variation from anticipated delivery time.

Sources: Adapted by the authors from Donald J. Bowersox and David J. Closs, *Logistical Management: The Integrated Supply Chain Process* (New York: McGraw-Hill, 1996); Ronald H. Ballou, *Business Logistics Management: Planning and Control,* Third Edition (Englewood Cliffs, N.J.: Prentice Hall, 1992); and James C. Johnson and Donald F. Wood, *Contemporary Logistics,* Fourth Edition (New York: Macmillan, 1990).

[15]John Robert Colombo, *The 1996 Canadian Global Almanac* (Toronto: Macmillan Canada, 1996); Performance 500, "Biggest Money Losers," *Canadian Business* (June 1996), p. 151; and *Canadian National Annual Report 1996.*

T a b l e 9 - 6

The Relative Share of Canadian Cargo Tonnage and Revenue by Transportation Form

TRANSPORTATION FORM	% SHARE OF TONNAGE SHIPPED	% SHARE OF SHIPPING REVENUE
Railroads	22.42	13.11
Motor carriers	47.58	73.35
Waterways	29.96	12.67
Airways	.04	00.87

Sources: Adapted by the authors from Bernd Zechel, "Transportation Industries—Overview," *Industry Canada, Strategis Web site* (1996), http://strategis.ic.gc.ca; Statistics Canada, "For-Hire Motor Carriers of Freight, All Carriers, First and Second Quarters 1995," *The Daily* (Thursday, June 6, 1996); Statistics Canada, "Port Activity 1995," *The Daily* (Thursday, June 4, 1996); "Air Canada Reports Record Operating Income for Second Consecutive Year, Earnings of $52 Million For 1995," *Canada NewsWire* (February 23, 1996), http://www.newswire.ca; and John Robert Colombo, *The 1996 Canadian Global Almanac* (Toronto: Macmillan Canada, 1996).

MOTOR CARRIERS **Motor carriers** predominantly transport small shipments over short distances. They handle about 80 per cent of Canadian shipments weighing less than 500 kilograms. Seventy per cent of all motor carriers are used for local deliveries and two-thirds of total truck miles are local. For these reasons, motor carriers account for a large share of shipping revenue. Motor carriers are more flexible than rail because they can pick up packages at a factory or warehouse and deliver them to the customer's door. They are often used to supplement rail, air, and other forms of transportation that cannot deliver direct to customers. In addition, trucks are faster than rail for short distances. In Canada, statistics for for-hire motor carriers are reported by Statistics Canada but the majority of truck freight is hauled by private carriers (business firms have their own truck fleets that carry their own goods and raw materials). It is estimated that private motor carriers have an economic value of $20 billion per year and they carry 227 million tonnes of merchandise, compared to 173 million tonnes by for-hire carriers who take in about $13 billion in revenues. In the for-hire carrier motor transport segment, carriers had an operating ratio of .97 in 1997 (the ratio of operating expenses divided by revenues). A ratio of .95 is considered a sign of a healthy industry. Ratios near 1 indicate problems while ratios over 1 mean the industry is losing money.[16]

Motor carriers handle small shipments for short distances.

WATERWAYS In Canada, **waterways** involve the movement of goods on barges via inland rivers and on tankers and general-merchandise freighters through the Great Lakes, intercoastal shipping, and the St. Lawrence Seaway. They are used primarily for transporting low-value, high-bulk freight (such as coal, iron ore, gravel, grain, and cement). Waterways are slow, and may be closed by ice in winter, but rates are quite low. Various improvements in vessel design have occurred over the last several years. For example, many "supervessels" now operate on the Great Lakes and other waterways. Their conveyor systems are twice as efficient as the ones on older boats. Navigation is computer-controlled.

Waterways specialize in low-value, high-bulk items.

In 1996 Canada's 200 ports handled a total of 357.9 million tonnes of goods (260.3 million tonnes of foreign goods and 97.7 million tonnes of domestic goods). Canada's ports employ 30 000 people. The busiest port is Vancouver, which handled about 26 per cent of all the foreign tonnage.[17]

[16]Bernd Zechel, "Transportation Industries: Overview," Industry Canada, *Strategis* Web site (1996); and Statistics Canada, "For-Hire Motor Carriers of Freight, All Carriers, First Quarter 1997," *The Daily* (Thursday, June 12, 1997).

[17]Statistics Canada, "Port Activity 1996," *The Daily* (June 4, 1997).

Pipelines *centre on liquids, gases, and semiliquids.*

TRANS CANADA PIPELINES
www.transcanada.com

Airways *handle valuable, perishable, and emergency items.*

CANADIAN AIRLINES INTERNATIONAL
www.cdnair.ca/

These transportation service companies ship packages: government parcel post, private parcel, and express.

PUROLATOR COURIER LTD.
www.purolator.com/

Containerization *and* **freight forwarding** *simplify intermodal shipping.*

PIPELINES Within **pipelines**, there is continuous movement and there are no interruptions, inventories (except those held by a carrier), and intermediate storage sites. Handling and labour costs are minimized. Although pipelines are very reliable, only certain commodities can be moved through them. In the past, emphasis was on gas and petroleum-based products. Pipelines have now been modified to accept coal and wood chips, which are sent as semiliquids. Still, the lack of flexibility limits their potential. Some pipelines carry enormous volumes of products. For example, TransCanada Pipelines is a leading transporter of natural gas in North America. In the first three months of 1997, its main line in Canada delivered 1268 billion cubic feet of natural gas. In addition, TransCanada moved 105.8 million barrels of crude oil through its oil pipeline holdings in the first three months of 1997.[18]

AIRWAYS **Airways** are the fastest, most expensive transportation form. High-value, perishable, and emergency goods dominate air shipments. For example, flowers from the Caribbean can be flown north to Canada during the winter; electronics parts and emergency repair items or high-fashion clothing items might also be shipped airfreight. Although air transit is costly, it may lower other costs, such as the need for outlying or even regional warehouses. The costs of packing, unpacking, and preparing goods for shipment are lower than for other transportation forms. Modern communications and sorting equipment have also been added to airfreight operations to improve their efficiency. Firms specializing in air shipments have done well by stressing speedy, guaranteed service at acceptable prices. In 1994, Canadian Airlines transported 395 000 tonnes of goods. However, in terms of volume, air freight represents a minuscule amount of goods shipped.[19]

TRANSPORTATION SERVICES Transportation service companies are marketing specialists that chiefly handle the shipments of small and moderate-sized packages. Some pick up at the sender's office and deliver direct to the addressee. Others require packages to be brought to a service company outlet. The major kinds of transportation service firms are parcel post (Canada Post's service), private parcel, and express.

Canada Post's parcel post service operates out of post offices and has rates based on shipping weight and distance shipped. Parcel post can be insured or sent COD (collect on delivery). Regular service is completed in a few days. Special handling is available to expedite shipments. Priority Post mail is available at post offices for next-day service between major Canadian cities.

Private parcel services specialize in small-package delivery, usually less than twenty-kilogram shipments. Most shipments go from businesses to their customers. Regular service usually takes two to three days. More expensive next-day service is also available from many carriers. The largest private firm is United Parcel Service (UPS), a multibillion-dollar, international company.

Specialized express companies, such as Federal Express and Purolator (majority-owned by Canada Post), typically provide guaranteed nationwide delivery of small packages for the morning after pickup. The average express delivery is under four kilograms.

COORDINATING TRANSPORTATION Because a single shipment may involve a combination of transportation forms—a practice known as *intermodal shipping*—coordination is needed. A firm can enhance its ability to coordinate shipments by using containerization and freight forwarding.

With **containerization**, goods are placed in sturdy containers that can be loaded on trains, trucks, ships, or planes. The marked containers are sealed until delivered, thereby reducing damage and pilferage. Their progress and destination are monitored. The containers are mobile warehouses that can be moved from manufacturing plants to receiving docks, where they remain until the contents are needed.

In **freight forwarding**, specialized firms (freight forwarders) collect small shipments (usually less than 200 kilograms each) from several companies. They pick up merchandise

[18]"TransCanada Earnings Up 9.6 Per Cent in First Half of 1997," *Canada NewsWire* (July 22, 1997),.
[19]Colombo, *The 1996 Canadian Global Almanac.*

TECHNOLOGY & MARKETING

How Are Carriers Weblike in Tracking Shipments?

According to experts, the role of the Internet has gone from being a library of data (phase one) to a provider of important customer services (phase two). In its third phase, the Internet will enable customers to better handle financial transactions. Evidence of the transition from phase one to phase two is the use of the Internet's World Wide Web by business customers to track packages shipped by Federal Express and United Parcel Service (UPS).

Since November 1994, all Federal Express customers have been able to log on to the FedEx home page on the World Wide Web and enter their bill-tracking numbers into online package-tracking forms. Within minutes, the Internet server connects with Federal Express' main computer and returns reports to customers on the locations of their packages. As packages move through the FedEx distribution system, the data passed on to clients are constantly updated by Federal Express personnel.

Although Federal Express had to design special software and contract with an Internet provider, the overall costs of implementing its system have been very low. In addition, the FedEx site—which receives over 4500 inquiries per day—saves money by reducing the need for customer service personnel. All customers have access to this Internet-based service, but larger ones can also access the firm's private network. According to a Federal Express spokesperson, 60 per cent of all package tracking is now done through automated procedures.

Likewise, UPS has begun to offer package tracking on the Internet. As with Federal Express, UPS's site was not started to save money for the firm, but is less costly than other package tracking methods.

As a customer service supervisor for Federal Express, outline the pros and cons of using the World Wide Web to automate package tracking.

Source: Based on material in Laurie Flynn, "Companies Use Web Hoping to Save Millions," *New York Times* (July 17, 1995), p. D5.

at each shipper's place of business and arrange for delivery at buyers' doors. Freight forwarders prosper because less-than-carload (lcl) shipping rates are sharply higher than carload (cl) rates. They also provide traffic management services, such as selecting the best transportation form at the most reasonable rate.

Inventory Management

The intent of **inventory management** is to provide a continuous flow of goods and to match the quantity of goods kept in inventory as closely as possible with customer demand. When production or consumption is seasonal or erratic, this can be particularly difficult.

Inventory management deals with the flow and allocation of products.

Inventory management has broad implications: A manufacturer or service firm cannot afford to run out of a crucial part that could put a halt to its business. Yet inventory on hand should not be too large because the costs of storing raw materials, parts, and/or finished products can be substantial. If models change yearly, as with autos, large inventories can adversely affect new-product sales or rentals. Excessive stock may also lead to stale goods, cause a firm to mark down prices, and tie up funds.

To improve their inventory management, a lot of companies are now applying either or both of two complementary concepts: a just-in-time inventory system and electronic data interchange. With a **just-in-time (JIT) inventory system**, a purchasing firm reduces the amount of inventory it keeps on hand by ordering more often and in lower quantity. This requires better planning and information on the part of the purchaser, geographic-

JIT *and* **QR inventory systems** *closely monitor inventory levels.*

ally closer sellers, improved buyer–seller relationships, and better production and distribution facilities. To retailers, a JIT system is known as a **quick response (QR) inventory system**—a cooperative effort between retailers and suppliers to reduce retail inventory while providing a merchandise supply that more closely addresses the actual buying patterns of consumers.[20]

JIT and QR systems are being used by auto makers, Hewlett-Packard, Canon, DuPont, Ryder, Whirlpool, Levi Strauss, Wal-Mart, Motorola, General Electric, Deere, Black & Decker, Boeing, and many other large and small firms. For example, Raymond Industrial Equipment, a forklift truck manufacturer in Brantford, Ontario, implemented a JIT system to replace their batch production system. They benefited by reducing their inventory by 60 per cent, they released warehouse space, and they reduced the manufacturing time to make a forklift truck from fifteen days to only four.[21]

*With **EDI**, computers are used to exchange information between suppliers and their customers.*

Through **electronic data interchange** (EDI), suppliers and their manufacturers/service providers, wholesalers, and/or retailers exchange data through computer linkups. This lets firms maximize revenues, reduce markdowns, and lower inventory carrying costs by speeding the flow of data and products. For EDI to work well, each firm in a distribution channel must use the Universal Product Code (UPC) and electronically exchange data. Although all major food makers use the UPC, many makers of general merchandise do not. However, the number of general merchandise manufacturers using the UPC on their products has been rising; and more will begin using the UPC in the near future.

Four specific aspects of inventory management are examined next: stock turnover, when to reorder, how much to reorder, and warehousing.

Stock turnover *shows the ratio between sales and average inventory.*

STOCK TURNOVER Stock turnover—the number of times during a stated period (usually one year) that average inventory on hand is sold—shows the relationship between a firm's sales and the inventory level it maintains. It is calculated in units or dollars (in selling price or at cost):

$$\text{Annual rate of stock turnover} = \frac{\text{Number of units sold during year}}{\text{Average inventory on hand (in units)}}$$

or

$$= \frac{\text{Net yearly sales}}{\text{Average inventory on hand (valued in sales dollars)}}$$

or

$$= \frac{\text{Cost of goods sold}}{\text{Average inventory on hand (valued at cost)}}$$

For example, in retailing, average annual stock turnover ranges from less than three in jewellery stores to more than thirty in gasoline service stations.

A high stock turnover rate has many advantages: inventory investments are productive, items are fresh, losses from style changes are reduced, and inventory costs (such as insurance, breakage, warehousing, and credit) are lower. Turnover can be improved by reducing assortments, dropping slow-selling items, keeping only small amounts of some items, and buying from suppliers that deliver on time. On the other hand, too high a turnover rate may have adverse effects: small purchases may cause a loss of volume discounts, low product assortment may reduce sales volume if consumers do not have enough choice or related items are not carried, discounts may be needed to lift sales volume, and

[20]See Jitendra Chhikara and Elliott N. Weiss, "JIT Savings—Myth or Reality?" *Business Horizons*, Vol. 38 (May–June 1995), pp. 73–78; Susan R. Helper and Mari Sako, "Supplier Relations in Japan and the United States: Are They Converging?" *Sloan Management Review*, Vol. 36 (Spring 1995), pp. 77–84; Lisa Phillips and Cornelia Drîge, "Quick Response: A Theoretical Framework," in David W. Stewart and Naufel J. Vilcassim (Eds.), *1995 AMA Winter Educators' Proceedings* (Chicago: American Marketing Association, 1995), pp. 295–302; Paul F. Christ and Jack Gault, "The Benefits, Costs, and Strategic Implications of Quick Response Systems," in Barbara B. Stern and George M. Zinkham (Eds.), *1995 AMA Educators' Proceedings* (Chicago: American Marketing Association, 1995), pp. 485–491; and "The Next Industrial Revolution: Canada's Manufacturers Are Hard at Work Turning Today's Factories Into Tomorrow's Success Stories," *Canadian Business* (June, 1992), pp. 96–101.

[21]Marcia Berss, "Watizzit?" *Forbes* (August 28, 1995), p. 100.

FIGURE 9-8
What Happens When a Firm Has Stock Shortages

chances of running out of stock go up when average inventory size is low. Figure 9-8 shows how people can act should a firm run out of stock.

Knowing when to reorder merchandise helps protect against stockouts while minimizing inventory investments.

WHEN TO REORDER INVENTORY By having a clear reorder point for each of its products (or raw materials or parts), a firm sets the inventory levels for new orders. A **reorder point** depends on order lead time, the usage rate, and safety stock. Order lead time is the period from the date an order is placed until the date items are ready to sell or use (received, checked, and altered, if needed). Usage rate is the average unit sales (for a reseller) or the rate at which a product is used in production (for a manufacturer). Safety stock is extra inventory kept to guard against being out of stock due to unexpectedly high demand or production and delivery delays.

The reorder point formula is:

Reorder point = (Order lead time × Usage rate) + (Safety stock).

For instance, a wholesaler that needs four days for its purchase orders to be placed and received, sells ten items per day, and wants to have ten extra items on hand in case of a supplier's delivery delay of one day, has a reorder point of fifty [(4 × 10) + (10)]. Without safety stock, the firm would lose ten sales if it orders when inventory is forty items and the items are received in five days.

*The **reorder point** is based on lead time, usage, and safety stock.*

HOW MUCH TO REORDER A firm must decide its order size—the right amount of products, parts, and so on, to buy at one time. Order size depends on volume discounts, the firm's resources, the stock turnover rate, the costs of processing each order, and the costs of holding goods in inventory. If a firm places large orders, quantity discounts are usually available, a large part of its finances are tied up in inventory, its stock turnover rate is relatively low, per-order processing costs are low, and inventory costs are generally high. The firm is also less apt to run out of goods. The opposite is true for small orders.

Many companies seek to balance their order-processing costs (filling out forms, computer time, and product handling) and their inventory-holding costs (warehouse expenses, interest charges, insurance, deterioration, and theft). Processing costs per unit fall as orders get bigger, but inventory costs rise. The **economic order quantity (EOQ)** is the order volume corresponding to the lowest sum of order-processing and inventory-holding costs.

EOQ balances ordering and inventory costs.

Table 9-7 demonstrates three ways to compute EOQ. In this illustration, a firm has an annual demand of 3000 units for a product; the cost of each unit is $1; order-processing costs are $3 per order; and inventory-holding costs equal 20 per cent of each item's cost. As shown in the table, the economic order quantity is 300 units. Thus, the firm should place orders of 300 units and have 10 orders per year.

WAREHOUSING Warehousing involves the physical facilities used to store, identify, and sort goods in expectation of their sale and transfer within a distribution channel. Warehouses can be used to store goods, prepare goods for shipment, coordinate shipments, send orders, and aid in product recalls.

Warehousing *involves storing and dispatching goods.*

Table 9-7

Computing an Economic Order Quantity

A.

AVERAGE ORDER QUANTITY (UNITS)	INVENTORY MAINTAINED (UNITS)[a]	ANNUAL INVENTORY-HOLDING COSTS[b]	ANNUAL ORDER-PROCESSING COSTS[c]	ANNUAL TOTAL COSTS
100	50	$10	$90	$100
200	100	20	45	65
EOQ ⟶ 300	150	30	30	60
400	200	40	24	64
500	250	50	18	68

B.

C.

$$EOQ = \sqrt{\frac{2DS}{IC}} = \sqrt{\frac{2\,(3,000)\,(\$3)}{0.20\,(\$1)}} = 300$$

where EOQ = Order quantity (units)　　　I = Annual holding costs (as a % of unit costs)

　　　　D = Annual demand (units)　　　C = Unit cost of an item ($)

　　　　S = Costs to place an order ($)

[a]The average inventory on hand = ½ × Order quantity.

[b]Inventory-holding costs = Annual holding costs as a per cent of unit cost × Unit cost × Average inventory.

[c]Order-processing costs = Number of annual orders × Costs to place an order. Number of orders = Annual demand/Order quantity.

Private warehouses are owned and operated by firms that store and distribute their own products. They are most likely to be used by those with stable inventory levels and long-run plans to serve the same geographic areas.

Public warehouses provide storage and related distribution services to any interested firm or individual on a rental basis. They are used by small firms that do not have the resources or desire to have their own facilities, larger firms that need more storage space (because their own warehouses are full), or any size of firm entering new geographic areas. Public warehouses offer shipping economies for users by receiving carload shipments from factories or distribution centres, and then allowing short-distance, smaller shipments to be made from these warehouses to customers. Firms can also reduce their investments in facilities and maximize flexibility by using public warehouses. If products must be recalled, these warehouses can be used as collection points, where items are separated, disposed of, and/or salvaged. There are hundreds of public warehouses in Canada.

Public warehouses can accommodate both bonded warehousing and field warehousing. In bonded warehousing, imported or taxable goods are stored and can be released for sale only after applicable taxes are paid. This enables firms to postpone tax payments until they are ready to make deliveries to customers. Cigarettes and liquor are often stored in bonded warehouses. In field warehousing, a receipt is issued by a public warehouse for goods stored in a private warehouse or in transit to consumers. The goods are put in a special area, and the field warehouser is responsible for them. A firm may use field warehousing because a warehouse receipt serves as collateral for a loan.

MARKETING IN A CHANGING WORLD

Being Aware of the Problem of Export Diversion[22]

As companies expand globally, they face a greater chance of dealing with unscrupulous foreign distributors. Why? There are two major reasons: One, it is difficult to do the proper background checks on such distributors—and less is known about them than about domestic distributors. Two, it is hard to monitor distributor performance in distant markets.

A particularly troublesome distribution practice for North American manufacturers is known as "export diversion." This hypothetical example shows how it works:

1. A North American manufacturer sells 100 000 widgets to European-based ABC Distributors for $10 each (half the wholesale price) so as to gain access to Kazakhstan.
2. The manufacturer ships the widgets to Rotterdam, while ABC secretly pre-sells them to Canadian or U.S. supermarket chains and wholesalers for $15 apiece. In Rotterdam, the widgets are repackaged and sent back to Canada or the U.S. duty-free as "goods returned."
3. ABC earns $500 000—the difference between the manufacturer's export price and the price paid by the Canadian or U.S. supermarkets and wholesalers.
4. The returned widgets are sold in North America, and the manufacturer cannot understand why some of its supermarket customers are no longer buying from it.

Johnson & Johnson, a very sophisticated U.S.-based manufacturer, recently learned that export diversion is not just "hypothetical":

> It seemed like the perfect opportunity to break into an important emerging market. At least that's what LifeScan Inc., a Johnson & Johnson subsidiary, thought when it agreed to sell U.S.$400 000 worth of glucose test strips at half its wholesale price. The buyer, Swiss-based Anglo-American Foundation, promised to distribute LifeScan's devices to needy diabetics in the former Soviet Union. But the deal was costly—particularly when LifeScan discovered that its strips never even left U.S. shores. Instead, they allegedly were diverted by Anglo-American to a New Jersey warehouse and then resold to local wholesalers for a tidy profit.

Because of export diversion, international companies now have one more illegal and unethical business practice to worry about—and to police.

SUMMARY

1. To define distribution planning and to examine its importance, distribution functions, the factors used in selecting a distribution channel, and the different types of distribution channels Distribution planning is systematic decision making as to the physical movement of goods and services from producer to consumer, as well as the related transfer of ownership (or rental). A channel of distribution consists of the organizations or people—known as channel members or distribution intermediaries—involved in the distribution process.

Distribution decisions often affect a firm's marketing plans. For many firms, the choice of a distribution channel is one of the most important decisions they make. More companies now realize the value of relationship marketing and work for long-term relations with suppliers, intermediaries, and customers. Both costs and profits are affected by the channel chosen. Firms may have to conform to existing

channel patterns; and their markets' size and nature are also influenced by the channel employed.

No matter who does them, channel functions include research, buying, promotion, customer services, product planning, pricing, and distribution. Intermediaries can play a key role by doing various tasks and resolving differences in manufacturer and consumer goals through the sorting process.

In selecting a method of distribution, these factors must be considered: the consumer, the company, the product, the competition, the distribution channels themselves, and legal requirements.

A direct channel requires that one party do all distribution tasks; in an indirect channel, tasks are done by multiple parties. In comparing methods, a firm must weight its costs and abilities against control and total sales. An indirect

[22]The material in this section is based on Amy Borrus, "Exports That Aren't Going Anywhere," *Business Week* (December 4, 1995), pp. 121, 124.

channel may use a contractual or an administered agreement. A long channel has many levels of independent firms; a wide one has many firms at any stage. A channel may be exclusive, selective, or intensive, based on company goals, resellers, customers, and marketing. A dual channel lets a company use two or more distribution methods.

2. *To describe the nature of supplier/distribution intermediary contracts, and cooperation and conflict in a channel of distribution* In contracts between suppliers and distribution intermediaries, price policies, sale conditions, territorial rights, the services/responsibility mix, and contract length and termination conditions are specified.

Cooperation and conflict may both occur in a distribution channel. Conflicts must be settled fairly because confrontation can cause hostility and negative acts by all parties. Frequently, a pushing strategy—based on channel cooperation—can be employed by established firms. But a pulling strategy—based on proving that consumer demand exists prior to gaining intermediary support or acceptance—must be used by many new companies.

3. *To examine the special aspects relating to a distribution channel for industrial products and to international distribution* An industrial channel normally does not use retailers; it is more direct, entails fewer transactions and larger orders, requires specification selling and knowing resellers, uses team selling and special intermediaries, includes more leasing, provides more technical data, and embraces shared activities.

Channel length depends on a nation's stage of economic development and consumer behaviour. Distribution practices and structures differ by nation. International decisions must be made as to shipping and intermediaries. Each country has distinct legal provisions pertaining to distribution.

4. *To define physical distribution and to demonstrate its importance* Physical distribution (logistics) involves efficiently delivering products to designated places, at designated times, and in proper condition. It may be undertaken by any member of a channel, from producer to consumer.

There are various reasons for studying physical distribution: its costs, the value of customer service, and its relationship with other functional areas in a firm. With the total-cost approach, the service level with the lowest total cost (including freight, warehousing, and lost business) is the best one. In a physical distribution strategy, decisions are made as to transportation, inventory levels, warehousing, and facility locations.

5. *To discuss transportation alternatives and inventory management issues* Railroads typically carry bulky goods for long distances. Motor carriers dominate small shipments over short distances. Waterways primarily ship low-value freight. Pipelines provide ongoing movement of liquid, gaseous, and semiliquid products. Airways offer fast, expensive movement of perishables and high-value items. Transportation service firms are specialists that mostly handle small and medium-sized packages. Coordination can be improved through containerization and freight forwarding.

Inventory management is needed to provide a continuous flow of goods and to match the stock kept in inventory as closely as possible with demand. In a JIT or QR system, the purchasing firm reduces the stock it keeps on hand by ordering more often and in lower quantity. With electronic data interchange, channel members exchange information via computer linkages.

The interplay between a firm's sales and the inventory level it keeps is expressed by its stock turnover. A reorder point shows the inventory level when goods must be reordered. The economic order quantity is the optimal amount of goods to order based on order-processing and inventory-holding costs. Warehousing decisions include selecting a private or public warehouse and examining the availability of public warehouse services.

KEY TERMS

distribution planning (p. 241)
channel of distribution (p. 241)
channel members (p. 241)
distribution intermediaries (p. 241)
channel functions (p. 244)
sorting process (p. 246)
direct channel of distribution (p. 247)
indirect channel of distribution (p. 247)
channel length (p. 247)
channel width (p. 247)
exclusive distribution (p. 247)
selective distribution (p. 247)

intensive distribution (p. 247)
dual channel of distribution (p. 249)
pushing strategy (p. 252)
pulling strategy (p. 252)
physical distribution (logistics) (p. 255)
order cycle (p. 255)
total-cost approach (p. 257)
railroads (p. 258)
motor carriers (p. 259)
waterways (p. 259)
pipelines (p. 260)

airways (p. 260)
containerization (p. 260)
freight forwarding (p. 260)
inventory management (p. 261)
just-in-time (JIT) inventory system (p. 261)
quick response (QR) inventory system (p. 261)
electronic data interchange (EDI) (p. 262)
stock turnover (p. 262)
reorder point (p. 263)
economic order quantity (EOQ) (p. 263)
warehousing (p. 263)

Review Questions

1. What is relationship marketing?
2. Explain the sorting process. Provide an example in your answer.
3. Which factors influence the selection of a distribution channel?
4. Under what circumstances should a company engage in direct distribution? Indirect distribution?
5. What is meant by a short, narrow channel of distribution?
6. Explain how a product could move from exclusive to selective to intensive distribution.
7. Compare motor carrier and waterway deliveries on the basis of the total-cost approach.
8. The average stock turnover rate in jewellery stores is less than three. What does this mean? How could a jewellery store raise its turnover rate?
9. Two wholesalers sell identical merchandise. Yet, one plans a safety stock equal to 20 per cent of expected sales, while the other plans no safety stock. Comment on this difference.
10. Why would a firm use both private and public warehouses?

Discussion Questions

1. What distribution decisions would a new firm that rents vans to small, seasonal businesses have to make?
2. Devise distribution channels for the sale of a daily newspaper, pianos, and cellular phones. Explain your choices.
3. Present a checklist that a firm could use in making international distribution decisions on a country-by-country basis.
4. Develop a list of distribution standards for a firm delivering fresh fruit to supermarkets.
5. Are there any disadvantages to a JIT or QR system? Explain your answer.

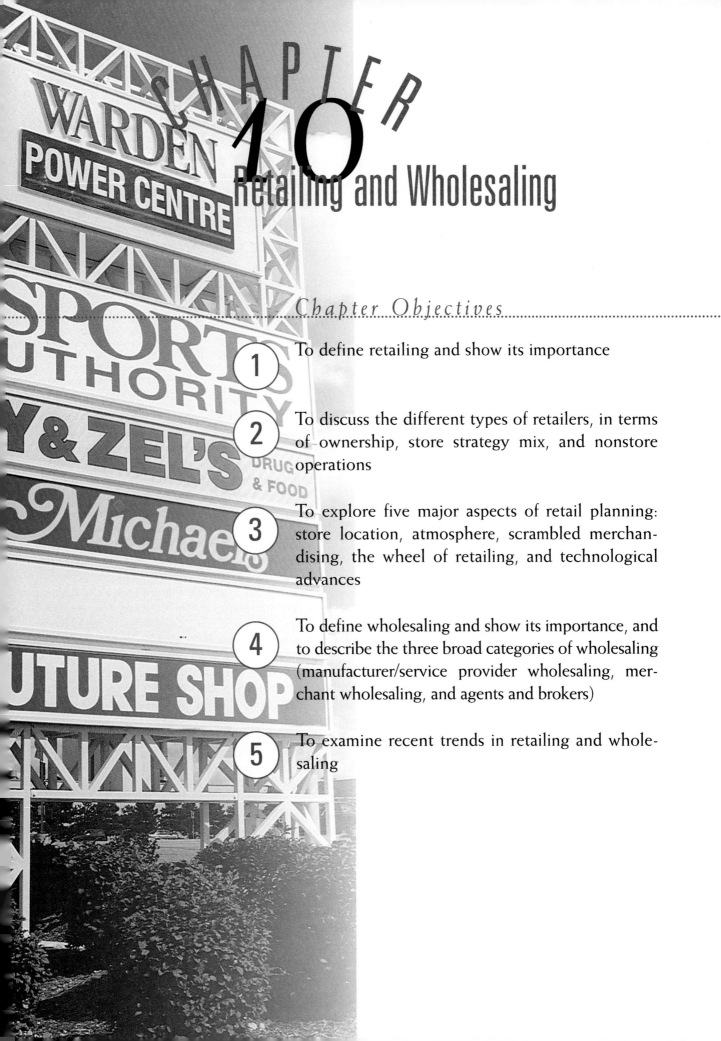

CHAPTER 10
Retailing and Wholesaling

> *Retailing in Canada in the 1990s is undergoing a revolution. One sign of this revolution is the widespread advent of so-called "category killer" stores, which are locating close to one another in groups, to create "power malls." A power mall is created when large product-specific retail stores such as Toys "Я" Us and The Home Depot (referred to as category killers) locate near stores like Wal-Mart or a Price Club/Costco warehouse (referred to as big box stores).*

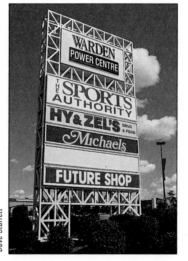

Dave Starrett

In early 1995, retail estimates indicated that the U.S. market had about 250 power malls while Canada had between fifteen and twenty with more on the way. So far, these large competitors have chosen to locate in large metropolitan areas such as Metro Toronto, Montreal, Vancouver, and Ottawa. However, all of Canada's twenty-five CMAs (census metropolitan areas) represent potential markets for power malls. For example, in Moncton, New Brunswick, Price Club/Costco opened up a 120 000-square-foot warehouse in late 1995 as part of a power mall. This mall also includes a 100 000-square-foot Kent Building supply warehouse, a 110 000-square-foot oversized K mart store, and a 60 000-square-foot Real Atlantic Superstore (owned by Loblaws).

These new power malls are threatening the existence of one of the traditional mainstays of retailing, the shopping mall. The regional and super-regional malls (like the West Edmonton Mall) are particularly at risk. Says Carl Steidtmann, director of research at Management Horizons, a retail consulting division of Price Waterhouse: "Regional malls clearly have a life cycle, and a lot of them are in their last throes."

Those that survive will have to reinvent themselves somehow. They will have to become primary destinations once again, catering to a consumer generation no longer willing to drift through loads of boutiques while slowly annihilating the family budget. Ironically, the malls that are falling victim may respond by taking on category killers as allies. In Toronto, the Warden Woods shopping centre was in deep trouble. It had lost half of its tenants and was losing one of its anchor stores, the Bay. The response: create a power mall with some category killer stores. Warden Woods attracted the Sports Authority, Michaels (a craft store), Petstuff, and the Future Shop. In addition, a six-screen Odeon movie theatre was put in and there is room for sixty other stores as well.

Offering shoppers on-premises entertainment is another way shopping malls are hoping to entice customers. Many centres have added movie theatres, video arcades, and fancy restaurants to enhance the shopping experience. Even some factory outlet malls now offer festivals, concerts, and book signings as a means of attracting greater consumer traffic. As one real estate executive says, "The idea is to give people multiple reasons to come to your centre."

Cambridge Shopping Centres of Toronto, owners and operators of a large number of Canadian malls, has certainly not surrendered to the power malls. In 1995 they committed to spending $500 million to renovate their forty-five Canadian malls, adding two million square feet of retail space to their existing 28.5 million square feet of mall space. They recognize that big box stores and category killers that combine to form power malls are going to have an impact, but traditional malls have a loyal customer base that they can serve. New malls are probably not going to arise very often but the existing ones plan to stay.[1]

In this chapter, we will examine various aspects of retailing—including trends affecting shopping centres—and consider their ramifications. We will study wholesalers and their relationships with their suppliers and customers. We will also examine the different types of firms that perform wholesaling activities and the strategies they use to compete in the marketplace.

Overview

Retailing encompasses those business activities involved with the sale of goods and services to the final consumer for personal, family, or household use. It is the final stage in a channel of distribution. Manufacturers, importers, and wholesalers act as retailers when they sell products directly to the final consumer.

Retailing, *the last channel stage, entails selling to final consumers.*

Surveys undertaken for the Food and Consumer Products Manufacturers of Canada indicated the following about Canadian shoppers: The average spending on groceries by individual shoppers was about $85/week. The shoppers were mostly female (85 per cent) and 80 per cent of the shoppers bought brands with which they were familiar. Only 6 per cent were familiar with the Internet. Methods of payment were cash (55 per cent), debit card (29 per cent), and cheque (13 per cent). Studies of shopping behaviour in North America indicate that the average retail sale per shopping trip is small, about $40 for department stores and $50 for specialty stores. Convenience stores, such as 7-Eleven, have average sales of just a few dollars (not including gasoline).

Chain supermarkets average about $25 per customer transaction.[2] Accordingly, retailers try to increase their sales volume by using one-stop shopping appeals, broadening merchandise and service assortments, increasing customer shopping frequency, and encouraging more family members to go shopping. Inventory controls, automated merchandise handling, and electronic cash registers enable retailers to reduce their transaction costs.

Despite the low average size of customer transactions, about one-half of sales for such retailers as department stores involve some form of customer credit. This means these retailers must pay a percentage of each transaction to a bank or other credit card service company or absorb the costs of their own credit programs—in return for increased sales.[3] For example, The Bay and Eaton's each have millions of holders of their own credit cards; these people buy hundreds of millions of dollars in goods and services every year.

Whereas salespeople regularly visit organizational consumers to initiate and conclude transactions, most final consumers patronize stores. This makes the location of the store, product assortment, store hours, store fixtures, sales personnel, delivery, customer service, and other factors critical tools in drawing customers.

Final consumers make many unplanned purchases. In contrast, those that buy for resale or use in production (or operating a business) are more systematic in their purchasing. Therefore, retailers need to place impulse items in high-traffic locations, organize store layout, train sales personnel in suggestion selling, place related items next to each other, and sponsor special events to stimulate consumers.

[1]Kenneth Labich, "What It Will Take to Keep People Hanging Out at the Mall," *Fortune* (May 29, 1995), pp. 102–106; James Pollock, "Attack of the Killer Malls!" *Marketing Magazine* (February 20, 1995), p. 11; James Pollock, "Cambridge Investment a Sign of Mall Revival," *Marketing Magazine* (July 24, 1995), p. 5; Mark Higgins, "Price Club Opens Two Atlantic Warehouse Stores," *Marketing Magazine* (November 6, 1995), p. 15.

[2]"Retailing: Basic Analysis," *Standard & Poor's Industry Surveys* (June 15, 1995), p. R82; Jo Marney, "North American Shoppers," *Marketing Magazine* (April 24, 1995), p. 41; and "Canadian Council of Grocery Distributors: Supermarket Loyalty Up, Switching Down—Trends in Canada Survey," *Canada NewsWire* (July 18, 1995), http://www.newswire.ca:80; "Issues," *Canadian Grocer* (March 1997); "New Study Looks at Shopper's Attitudes Toward Grocery Home Delivery," *Canadian Grocer* (November 1996), www.mhbizlink.com/grocer.

[3]"Survey of Retail Payment Systems," *Chain Store Age* (January 1996), Section Two.

In the first part of this chapter, the importance of retailing, the various types of retailers, considerations in retail planning, and recent trends in retailing are all discussed.

Wholesaling *is the buying/ handling of products and their resale to organizational buyers.*

Wholesaling encompasses the buying and/or handling of goods and services and their subsequent resale to organizational users, retailers, and/or other wholesalers—but not the sale of significant volume to final consumers. Wholesaling undertakes many vital functions in a channel of distribution, particularly those in the sorting process.

Manufacturers and service providers sometimes are their own wholesalers; other times, independent firms are employed. Independents may or may not take title to or possession of products, depending on the type of wholesaling. Some independents have limited tasks; others perform a wide range of functions.

Industrial, commercial, and government institutions are wholesalers' leading customers, followed closely by retailers. Sales from one wholesaler to another also represent a significant proportion of wholesaling activity.

In the second part of this chapter, the importance of wholesaling, the different types of wholesaling, and recent trends in wholesaling are all discussed.

The Importance of Retailing

Retailing is a significant aspect of distribution because of its impact on the economy, its functions in the distribution channel, and its relationships with suppliers.

Retailing's Impact on the Economy

Retailing embodies high annual sales, employment, and costs.

LOBLAWS
www.loblaw.com

SEARS CANADA INC.
www.sears.ca

Retail sales and employment account for substantial amounts of sales and employment. In 1997 Canadian retail-store sales volume was expected to be $230 billion. This figure does not include nonstore retail activities such as vending machines, mail order, electronic shopping, and other forms of direct selling. In 1996, Canada's ten largest retail organizations were George Weston Ltd. ($12.7 billion in sales), Loblaws Cos. Ltd. ($9.8 billion in sales), Oshawa Group Ltd. ($6.3 billion in sales), Hudson's Bay Co. ($6.0 billion in sales), Provigo Inc. ($5.8 billion in sales), Canada Safeway Ltd. ($4.7 billion in sales), Sears Canada Inc. ($3.9 billion in sales), Canadian Tire Corporation Ltd. ($3.9 billion in sales) Zellers Inc. ($3.6 billion in sales) and Westfair Foods Ltd. ($3.3 billion in sales). Globally, the world's top 100 retailers generate U.S.$1.3 trillion in total annual revenues and include firms from fourteen different nations. The largest retailer on the planet, by far, is U.S.-based Wal-Mart—with annual sales approaching U.S.$100 billion (more than 95 per cent in the United States), nearly 3000 stores, and multiple store formats (such as Wal-Mart and Sam's Clubs).[4]

The retailing sector employed 1 415 000 Canadians in 1996, which is approximately 10 per cent of all working Canadians. Within the Canadian market and around the globe, a wide range of retailing career opportunities are available, including store management, merchandising, and owning one's own retail business.[5]

From a cost perspective, retailing is a significant field in North America. For example, on average, 38 to 40 cents of every dollar a consumer spends in a department or specialty store pays for the functions it performs. The corresponding figure is 22 cents for a supermarket. This compensation—known as gross margin—is for rent, taxes, fuel, advertising, management, personnel, and other retail costs, as well as profits. One of the reasons Wal-Mart is the world's leading retailer is that its operating costs are so low (16 per cent of sales) compared to its close competitors like K mart, whose operating costs are 22 per cent.[6]

[4]Statistics Canada, "Retail Sales, by Trade Group, and Total Retail Sales, Canada, The Provinces And Territories," CANSIM matrix 2400 (Ottawa: Minister of Supply Services Canada); "Performance 500," *Canadian Business* (June 1997), pp. 150–152; "State of the Industry," *Chain Store Age* (August 1995), Section Two; "The Shopping Spree That Wasn't," *Wall Street Journal* (January 5, 1996), p. B1; and Coopers & Lybrand, "Global Powers of Retailing," *Chain Store Age* (December 1995).

[5]A discussion of careers in retailing can be found in Barry Berman and Joel R. Evans, *Retail Management: A Strategic Approach*, Sixth Edition (New York: Prentice Hall, 1995), pp. A1–A13; and Statistics Canada, "Employment, Earning and Hours," *The Daily* (May 28, 1996).

[6]*Stores*, various issues; "Progressive Grocer Annual Report," *Progressive Grocer* (April 1996); and Mary Kuntz, et al., "Reinventing the Store," *Business Week* (November 27, 1995), p. 92.

Retailing Functions in Distribution

Retailers generally perform four distinct functions. They:

Retailers undertake four key functions.

- Engage in the sorting process by assembling an assortment of goods and services from a variety of suppliers and offering them for sale. The width and depth of assortment depend on the individual retailer's strategy.

- Provide information to consumers via ads, displays and signs, and sales personnel. And marketing research support (feedback) is given to other channel members.

- Store products, mark prices, place items on the selling floor, and otherwise handle products. Retailers usually pay for items before selling them to final consumers.

- Facilitate and complete transactions by having appropriate locations and hours, credit policies, and other services (like delivery).

The Relationship of Retailers and Suppliers

Retailers deal with two broad supplier categories: those selling goods or services for use by the retailers and those selling goods or services that are resold by the retailers. Examples of goods and services purchased by retailers for their use are store fixtures, computer equipment, management consulting, and insurance. Resale purchases depend on the lines sold by the retailer.

Suppliers must have knowledge of their retailers' goals, strategies, and methods of business operation to sell and service accounts effectively. Retailers and their suppliers may have divergent viewpoints, which must be reconciled. For example:

> Current and former Reebok insiders say the toughest fight with Nike is being waged at Woolworth Corporation's Foot Locker unit—and Reebok is losing. With little fanfare, the shoe retailer has grown into a behemoth: Its 2800 outlets chalk up about 23 per cent of North American sneaker sales. When a retailer achieves such dominance in a product category, it expects to get preferred terms from manufacturers, early looks at new models, and speedy shipments. Nike has been playing the game. Reebok has not. Thus, in 1995, Foot Locker's Nike sales were U.S.$750 million, while Reebok's were only U.S.$172 million.[7]

Types of Retailers[8]

Retailers can be categorized by ownership, store strategy mix, and nonstore operations. See Figure 10-1. The categories overlap; that is, a firm can be correctly placed in more than

FIGURE 10-1
Categorizing Retailers

---

[7]Joseph Pereira, "In Reebok-Nike War, Big Woolworth Chain Is a Major Battlefield," *Wall Street Journal* (September 22, 1995), p. A1.

[8]Unless otherwise indicated, the statistics in these subsections are the authors' current projections, based on data from Statistics Canada, "Retail Sales, by Trade Group, and Total Retail Sales, Canada, The Provinces And Territories," CANSIM matrix 2400 (Ottawa: Minister of Supply and Services Canada); Leonard Kubas, "Navigating the New Retail Landscape," *Marketing Magazine* (July 31/August 7, 1995) pp. 11–12; *1992 Census of Retail Trade* (Washington, D.C.: U.S. Bureau of the Census); *Stores; Progressive Grocer; Discount Store News; Inc.; Vending Times Census of the Industry* (1995); *Direct Marketing;* and Berman and Evans, *Retail Management: A Strategic Approach.*

Ethics AND TODAY'S MARKETER

Green Products: Retailing's Endangered Species

In the late 1980s and early 1990s store shelves were awash with "green" products. Retailers were actively promoting the availability and the importance of using products that were environmentally friendly. At the time many environmentalists chalked up the responses of marketers to this trend as commercialism. They may have been right because now finding products promoted and labelled as "green" is almost as difficult as it was before they were hyped. In Canada, one of the leaders of the "green" product revolution was Loblaws, which brought more than 100 "Green" products to market alone. But consumers are no longer willing to pay a premium price for a "green" product and with sales slowing, many of these products have been removed from the shelves.

A lot of "product greening" revolved around the way products were being packaged and how the packaging was disposed of. Many retailers and their suppliers say that the "green" revolution really changed the way they do things in this regard. For them, the concept of "green" is now engendered in their products in terms of packaging, recycling, and environmental impact. They have found that concentrating marketing effort on "green" does not have the appeal to consumers it once did. People will not pay more for "green" but they will select "green" products over others if the price and quality are comparable and the only point of difference is "green" or not.

Patrick Carson of Loblaws was one of the main proponents behind Green products and their success. He sees "green" as an attitude not a label. Any products or services that contribute to a society or healthier humans can be considered "green" and do not necessarily have to carry that label. Therefore, low cholesterol and low-fat foods could be considered "green" products. Since many producers and retailers have embraced the ideals brought about by the "green" revolution, they are still "green" even if they do not say so.

However, the original charge by environmentalists that environmental friendliness was a guise for crass commercialism remains valid. When asked about the future of green products, Carson replied, "Environmental initiatives are normally economic issues for us." Still, Loblaws is committed to its Green products, which have had a steady level of sales at 0.3 per cent of the chain's total revenues. It seems clear that what it takes to "survive" in the intensely competitive environment of retailing is often at odds with what it takes to survive in the natural environment.

Develop a definition of a "green" product, and on your next visit to a food store try to find three different product categories of labelled "green" products. Identify some brands in the same product category that are not labelled as "green." Compare the labelled "green" products and the brands not labelled as "green" to see if they meet your definition and discuss why.

Source: Based on material in James Pollock, "The Green Devolution," *Marketing Magazine* (April 15, 1996), p. 9.

one grouping. For example, 7-Eleven is a chain, a franchise, and a convenience store. The study of retailers by group provides data on their traits and orientation, and the impact of environmental factors.

Ownership

An **independent retailer** operates only one outlet and offers personal service, a convenient location, and close customer contact. Nearly 80 per cent of North American retail establishments (including those staffed solely by the owners and their families)—and an even higher percentage in some foreign nations—are operated by independents, including many dry cleaners, beauty salons, furniture stores, gas stations, and neighbourhood stores. This large number is due to the ease of entry because various kinds of retailing require low investments and little technical knowledge. Therefore, competition is plentiful. Numerous retailers do not succeed because of the ease of entry, poor management skills, and inadequate resources. About one-third of new retailers do not last one full year and two-thirds do not make it past the first three years.

*An **independent retailer** has one store, while a **retail chain** has multiple outlets.*

A **retail chain** involves common ownership of multiple outlets. It usually has central purchasing and decision making. Although independents have simple organizations, chains tend to rely on specialization, standardization, and elaborate control systems. Chains can serve a large, dispersed target market and have a well-known company name. There are approximately 1200 chains in Canada operating about 38 000 stores. They represent 17 per cent of Canadian retail establishments and account for 40 per cent of all retail store sales. Chains are common for department stores, supermarkets, and fast-food outlets, among others. Examples of chains are The Bay, Loblaws, Wal-Mart, and Foot Locker.

Retail franchising is a contractual arrangement between a franchiser (a manufacturer, wholesaler, or service sponsor) and a retail franchisee, which allows the latter to run a certain form of business under an established name and according to specific rules. It is a form of chain retailing that lets a small-business person benefit from the experience, buying abilities, and name of a large multi-unit retailer. Many times, the franchisee gets management training and engages in cooperative buying and advertising. The franchiser benefits by obtaining franchise fees and royalties, faster payments, strict operating controls, consistency among outlets, and motivated owner-operators. There are an estimated 25 000 franchise outlets in Canada. The total sales statistics for Canadian franchises are not accurately known but estimates range from a low of $13 billion[9] up to $90 billion.[10] Franchising is popular for auto and truck dealers, gasoline stations, donut shops, fast-food outlets, hotels and motels, service firms, and convenience-foods stores. Examples of retail franchises include: Chevrolet dealers, Petro-Canada Service Stations, Tim Hortons Donuts, Pizza Hut, and H&R Block. See Figure 10-2.

Retail franchising *uses an established name and operates under certain rules.*

A **leased department** is a section of a retail store rented to an outside party. The lessee operates a department—under the store's rules—and pays a percentage of sales as rent. Lessors gain from the reduced risk and inventory investment, expertise of lessees, lucrative lease terms, increased store traffic, and appeal to one-stop shopping. Lessees gain from the location in established stores, lessor name awareness, overall store traffic, one-stop customers attracted to stores, and whatever services (such as ads) lessors provide. Leased departments are popular for beauty salons, jewellery, photo studios, shoes and shoe repairs, cosmetics and food service. Radio Shack and AT&T Canada plan to set up AT&T stores inside of Radio Shack's 450 Canadian outlets. The idea of this alliance is to provide one stop shopping for telecommunications services and products.[11]

*A **leased department** is one rented to an outside party.*

With a **retail cooperative**, independent retailers share purchases, storage and shipping facilities, advertising, planning, and other tasks. Individual stores remain independent—

*With a **retail cooperative**, stores organize to share costs.*

[9]Donna Jean MacKinnon, "Franchising Shrugs Off Recession," *The Toronto Star* (November 19, 1992), pp. B1, B3.

[10]Canadian Franchise Association, "Franchising Has Come of Age," Advertising Supplement to *Canadian Business* (January, 1994), pp. 79–84.

[11]News Line, "AT&T Connects with Radio Shack," *Marketing Magazine* (September 15, 1997), p. 3.

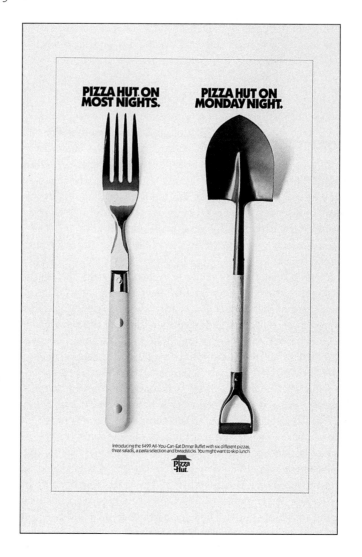

but agree on broad, common policies. Cooperatives are growing due to chains' domination of independents. They are popular for pharmacies, hardware stores, and grocery stores. An example of a well-known retail cooperative is IDA Pharmacies (Independent Druggists Association). *Retail cooperative* and *retailer-owned wholesale cooperative* are synonymous terms.

Table 10-1 compares the various forms of retail ownership.

Store Strategy Mix

*A **retail store strategy mix** combines the hours and products, etc. offered.*

Firms can be classed by the store strategy mix they choose. A typical **retail store strategy mix** consists of an integrated combination of hours, location, assortment, service, advertising, prices, and other factors retailers employ. Store strategy mixes vary widely, as the following indicate.

*A **convenience store** stresses fill-in items.*

A **convenience store** is usually a well-situated, food-oriented store with long hours and a limited number of items. In Canada, these stores have annual sales of $4.1 billion, including gasoline, and account for about 7.5 per cent of total grocery sales. The average store has yearly sales that are a fraction of those of a conventional supermarket. Consumers use a convenience store for fill-in merchandise, often at off-hours. Gasoline, milk, groceries, newspapers, soda, cigarettes, beer, and fast food are popular items. 7-Eleven and Beckers operate convenience stores.

*A **conventional supermarket** is a large, self-service food store.*

A **conventional supermarket** is a departmentalized food store with minimum annual sales of $2 million; it emphasizes a wide range of food and related products—general merchandise sales are limited. It originated in the 1930s, when food retailers realized a large-scale operation would let them combine volume sales, self-service, low prices,

Table 10-1

Key Characteristics of Retail Ownership Forms

OWNERSHIP FORM	CHARACTERISTICS		
	Distinguishing Features	*Major Advantages*	*Major Disadvantages*
Independent	Operates one outlet, easy entry	Personal service, convenient location, customer contact	Much competition, poor management skills, limited resources
Retail chain	Common ownership of multiple units	Central purchasing, strong management, specialization of tasks, larger market	Inflexibility, high investment costs, less entrepreneurial
Retail franchising	Contractual arrangement between central management (franchiser) and independent business persons (franchisees) to operate a specified form of business	To franchiser: investments from franchisees, faster growth, entrepreneurial spirit of franchisees To franchisee: established name, training, experience of franchiser, cooperative ads	To franchiser: some loss of control, franchisees not employees, harder to maintain uniformity To franchisee: strict rules, limited decision-making ability, payments to franchisers
Leased department	Space in a store leased to an outside operator	To lessor: expertise of lessee, little risk, diversification To lessee: lower investment in store fixtures, customer traffic, store image	To lessor: some loss of control, poor performance reflects on store To lessee: strict rules, limited decision-making ability, payments to store
Retail cooperative	Purchases, advertising, planning, and other functions shared by independent retailers	Independence maintained, efficiency improved, enhances competitiveness with chains	Different goals of participants, hard to control members, some autonomy lost

impulse buying, and one-stop grocery shopping. The car and refrigerator aided the supermarket's success by lowering travel costs and adding to perishables' life spans. Loblaws, A&P, Provigo, Sobey's and Safeway are among the large chains operating conventional supermarkets.

A **food-based superstore** is a diversified supermarket that sells a broad range of food and nonfood items. A food-based superstore typically has greeting cards, floral products, VCR tapes, garden supplies, some apparel, film developing, and small household appliances—besides a full line of supermarket items. A food-based superstore typically has about twice the floor space of a conventional supermarket and generates about $16 million in average sales.

*A **food-based superstore** stocks food and other products for one-stop shoppers.*

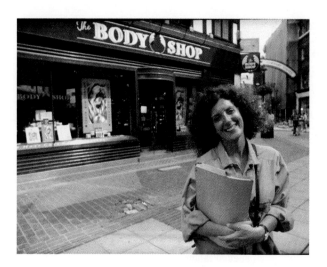

*A **combination store** offers a large assortment of general merchandise, as well as food. One type is a **supercentre**.*

*A **specialty store** emphasizes one kind of product, with a **category killer** store being a large version.*

*A **variety store** sells an assortment of lower-priced items.*

Several factors have caused many conventional supermarkets to switch to superstores: consumer interest in one-stop shopping, the levelling of food sales due to population stability and competition from fast-food stores and restaurants, and higher margins on general merchandise (double those of food items). For large food chains, the superstore is now the preferred supermarket format.

A **combination store** unites food/grocery and general merchandise sales in one facility, with general merchandise providing 25 to 40 per cent or more of sales. It goes further than a food-based superstore in appealing to one-stop shoppers and occupies 30 000 to 100 000 square feet or more. It lets a retailer operate efficiently, expand the number of people drawn to a store, raise impulse purchases and the size of the average transaction, sell both high-turnover/low-profit food items and lower-turnover/high-profit general merchandise, and offer fair prices. A **supercentre** is a combination store that integrates an economy supermarket with a discount department store, with at least 40 per cent of sales from nonfood items. It is 75 000 to 150 000 square feet in size, and carries 50 000 or more items. Among the firms with combination stores are Loblaws Superstore Atlantic, Real Canadian Superstore, Price/Costco warehouse, and France's Carrefour.

A **specialty store** concentrates on one product line, such as stereo equipment or hair-care services. Consumers like these stores since they are not faced with racks of unrelated products, do not have to search through several departments, are apt to find informed salespeople, can select from tailored assortments, and may avoid crowding. Specialty stores are quite successful with apparel, appliances, toys, electronics, furniture, personal care products, and personal services. Specialty stores include Tip Top Tailors, LensCrafters, and The Body Shop. See Figure 10-3.

A rather new type of specialty store—the category killer—is now gaining strength. The **category killer** is an especially large specialty store. It features an enormous selection in its product category and relatively low prices; and consumers are drawn from wide geographic areas. Toys "Я" Us and Staples/Business Depot are among the many specialty store chains that are opening new category killer stores to complement their existing stores. Blockbuster Video, the Sports Authority, and The Home Depot are among the chains fully based on the category killer store concept.

A **variety store** sells a wide assortment of inexpensive and popularly priced merchandise. It features stationery, gift items, women's accessories, toiletries, light hardware, toys, housewares, and confectionery items. With the growth of other retail store strategy mixes, variety stores have lost a lot of ground in recent years. BiWay Stores and Army and Navy Stores are examples of this type of store.

A department store employs at least fifty people and usually sells a general line of apparel for the family, household linens and textile products, and some mix of furniture, home furnishings, appliances, and consumer electronics. It is organized into separate departments for purposes of buying, promotion, service, and control. There are two types of department store: the traditional department store and the full-line discount store.

A **traditional department store** has a great assortment of goods and services, provides many customer services, is a fashion leader, and often serves as an anchor store in a shopping district or shopping centre. Prices are average to above average. It has high name recognition and uses all forms of media in ads. In recent years, traditional department stores have set up more boutiques, theme displays, and designer departments to compete with other firms. They face intense competition from specialty stores and discounters and consequently annual sales in 1995 were $6.5 billion, down from a high of $7.1 billion in 1991. Canada has essentially three department store chains: Sears, The Bay, and Eaton's, with estimated market shares of 41 per cent, 31 per cent and 28 per cent respectively.[12]

A **full-line discount store** is a department store with lower prices, a broad product assortment, a lower-rent location, more emphasis on self-service, brand-name merchandise, wide aisles, shopping carts, and more goods displayed on the sales floor. In 1995 Canadian full-line discounters annually sold over $7 billion in goods and services. They are among the largest retailers of apparel, housewares, electronics, health and beauty aids, auto supplies, toys, sporting goods, photographic products, and jewellery. Wal-Mart, K mart, and Zellers are examples of these kinds of retail operations.[13]

With a **membership warehouse club**, final consumers and businesses pay small yearly dues for the right to shop in a huge, austere warehouse. Products are often displayed in their original boxes, large sizes are stocked, and some product lines vary by time period (since clubs purchase overruns and one-of-a-kind items that cannot always be replaced). Consumers buy items at deep discounts. In the United States, this retailing format, whose annual sales skyrocketed from U.S.$2.5 billion in 1985 to U.S.$20 billion (excluding sales to business customers) in 1995, was the fastest-growing form of retailing. The advent of the Canada–U.S. Free Trade Agreement in 1989 and a slowing of U.S. growth due to marketplace saturation and overexpansion led to the expansion of this format into Canada. And it seems that this approach is having the same kind of impact in Canada as in the United States. Presently, Canada's most significant retailer using the club format is Price/Costco, with estimated annual sales of $4.5 billion.[14]

In recent years, other forms of low-price retailing have also grown. Among them are warehouse-style food stores, off-price specialty chains, discount drugstore chains, and factory outlet stores. These retailers all hold their prices down by maximizing inventory turnover, using plain store fixtures, locating at inexpensive sites, running few ads, and offering less customer service. They appeal to price-sensitive consumers. Examples of these retailers include Loblaws-owned No Frills (a warehouse-style food store) and A Buck or Two (an off-price specialty chain).

Nonstore Operations

With **nonstore retailing**, a firm uses a strategy mix that is not store-based to reach consumers and complete transactions. It does not involve conventional store facilities.

A **vending machine** uses coin- or card-operated machinery to dispense goods (such as beverages) or services (such as video rentals). It eliminates the need for salespeople, allows 24-hour sales, and can be placed outside rather than inside a store. Its sales are concentrated in a few products—beverages, food items, and cigarettes yield 99 per cent of the Canadian total. Machines may need intensive servicing due to breakdowns, stock-outs, and vandalism. Improved technology lets vending machines make change for bills, "talk" to consumers, use video screens to show products, brew coffee, and so on. Canadian sales through vending machines were $391.4 million in 1995, a rise from $376.8 million in 1994.

A **traditional department store** *is a fashion leader with many customer services.*

A **full-line discount store** *has self-service and popular brands.*

A **membership warehouse club** *offers deep discounts to its member customers.*

Nonstore retailing *is nontraditional.*

Vending machines *allow 24-hour self-service sales.*

---

[12]Ian McGugan, "Eaton's on the Brink," *Canadian Business* (March 1996), pp. 38–73.
[13]Leonard Kubas, "Navigating the New Retail Landscape," *Marketing Magazine* (July 31–August 7, 1995) pp. 11–12.
[14]"Price Costco Gets Even Bigger," *Marketing Magazine* (September 11, 1995), p. 3.

Direct selling *encompasses personal contacts with consumers in nonstore settings.*

In direct marketing, *a seller first communicates with consumers via nonpersonal media.*

LAND'S END
www.landsend.com/

L.L. BEAN
www.llbean.com/

Coffee accounted for 34 per cent of the total sales, soft drinks accounted for another 29 per cent of the total sales, and confectionaries comprised a further 17 per cent of the total.[15]

Direct selling involves personal contact with consumers in their homes (and other nonstore locations) and phone solicitations initiated by the retailer. Cosmetics, vacuum cleaners, household services (like carpet cleaning), dairy products, and newspapers are sometimes marketed via direct selling. In a cold canvass, a salesperson calls people or knocks on doors to find customers. With referrals, past buyers recommend friends to the salesperson. In the party method, one consumer acts as host and invites people to a sales demonstration in his or her home (or other nonstore site). To some consumers, direct selling has a poor image. In addition, sales force turnover is high and many people are not home during the day. To increase business, salespeople for firms such as Avon now target working women using office presentations during breaks and lunch hours. Direct selling has yearly revenues of $3.4 billion.[16] Avon, Tupperware, and Kids Only Clothing are direct selling organizations.

Direct marketing occurs when a consumer is first exposed to a good or service by a nonpersonal medium (such as direct mail, TV, radio, magazine, newspaper, or PC) and then orders by mail, phone, or PC. Many people find this a convenient way to shop because they do not have to leave their home. Although they do have to wait to receive their goods, express transportation services have offset some of the delay in delivery and made this form of retailing even more attractive.

In the U.S. more than one-half of households make such purchases each year but the Canadian market is less responsive with only 15 per cent of Canadians ordering every year. Despite the low level of response in Canada compared with the U.S., the sales growth in direct marketing is from 7 to 10 per cent each year in Canada and it is one of the faster growing sectors of Canadian retailing. Its growth is being fuelled by the popularity of both manufacturer brands and the private brands of many direct marketing firms (and consumer confidence in them), the large number of working women, and the belief that direct marketing is a good way to shop.[17]

For retailers, direct marketing offers low operating costs, coverage of a wide geographic area, and new market segments. Direct marketing is used by specialized firms, as well as store retailers that apply it to supplement their regular business. Among the most popular direct-marketing items are books; tapes and CDs; clothing; magazines; insurance; home accessories; and sports equipment. Yearly Canadian direct-marketing retail sales are about $3.2 billion, with about $1.8 billion of that in catalogue sales. Some examples of Canadian direct marketers include: Sears Canada (with half of Canadian catalogue sales), Regal Greetings & Gifts, and the Winnipeg Fur Exchange. See Figure 10-4. Hoping to expand their sales, a large number of American catalogue direct marketers have been servicing the Canadian market, including: Land's End, L.L. Bean, Victoria's Secret, Walt Disney, and the most recent entrant, Spiegel.[18]

Globally, the United States, Europe, and Japan account for 95 per cent of the world's mail-order business. The United States alone is responsible for 47 per cent of the total. These global markets represent excellent opportunities for sales growth of Canadian direct marketers. Curiously, despite its size and a favourable exchange rate, Canadian catalogue retailers have not focused on the the U.S. market because they believe it is overexposed and too competitive. For this reason many Canadian catalogue marketers are looking to Japan, an underexposed market with a favourable exchange rate. In March 1996, catalogue retailers Regal Greetings & Gifts, Kindred Spirits of Prince Edward Island, the Winnipeg Fur Exchange, Canadian Geographic Enterprises, B.C. Placings of Vancouver, and Cows Prince Edward Island of Charlottetown promoted themselves at the Tokyo Convention

[15]Statistics Canada, "Vending Machine Operators," *The Daily* (May 1, 1997).

[16]Statistics Canada, "Direct Selling, 1994," *The Daily* (August 19, 1996).

[17]Lara Mills, "Foreign Cataloguers Still Puzzling Over Canada," *Marketing Magazine* (June 12, 1995), p. 8; and David Napier, "Northern Exposure: Why Competing Cataloguers Are Welcoming Spiegel's Entry Into Canada," *Marketing Magazine* (April 29, 1996), pp. 12–13.

[18]James Pollock, "Lists of Opportunity," *Marketing Magazine* (May 22, 1995), pp. 14–15; James Pollock, "Pushing the Envelope," *Marketing Magazine* (November 20, 1995), pp. 14–15; and "Mail-Order Shopping: Which Catalogs Are Best?" *Consumer Reports* (October 1994), p. 621.

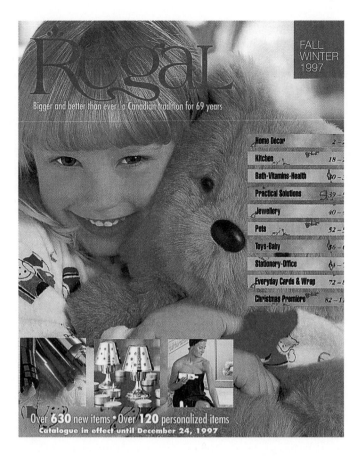

FIGURE 10-4
Regal Greetings & Gifts: A Canadian Tradition of Catalogue Retailing for Seventy Years
Reprinted with permission of REGAL Greetings & Gifts Inc.

Centre in hopes of getting a piece of the U.S.$1 billion dollar foreign-catalogue sales market in Japan.[19]

Considerations in Retail Planning

There are many factors for retailers to weigh in devising marketing plans—and for manufacturers, service providers, and wholesalers to keep in mind. Five key factors are store location, atmosphere, scrambled merchandising, the wheel of retailing, and technological advances.

Store Location

Store location is meaningful because it helps determine the customer mix and competition faced. Once selected, it is also inflexible. The basic forms of store location are the isolated store, the unplanned business district, and the planned shopping centre.

An **isolated store** is a freestanding retail outlet located on a highway or street. There are no adjacent stores with which the firm competes; but, there are also no stores to help draw shoppers. Customers may hesitate to travel to an isolated store unless it has a good product assortment and an established image. This site may be used by discount stores due to low rent and to accommodate suppliers who prefer them to be far enough away from stores selling goods and services at full prices. Some K mart and 7-Eleven stores are isolated.

An **unplanned business district** exists where multiple stores are located close to one another without prior planning as to the number and composition of stores. The four

*An **isolated store** is a freestanding outlet on a highway or side street.*

*In an **unplanned business district**, stores locate together with no prior planning.*

---

[19]James Pollock, "Eastward Ho!" *Marketing Magazine* (April 29, 1996), pp. 12–14; For an in-depth look at the global opportunities available to direct marketers, see Richard Miller, *Multinational Direct Marketing: The Methods and the Markets* (New York: McGraw-Hill, 1995).

unplanned sites are central business district, secondary business district, neighbourhood business district, and string.

A **central business district (CBD)** is the hub of retailing in a city and is sometimes called "downtown." It has the most commercial, employment, cultural, entertainment, and shopping facilities in a city—with at least one major department store and a broad grouping of specialty and convenience stores.

A **secondary business district (SBD)** is a shopping area bounded by the intersection of two major streets. Cities tend to have several SBDs, each with at least one branch department store, a variety store, and/or some larger specialty stores, as well as several smaller shops.

A **neighbourhood business district (NBD)** satisfies the convenience-shopping and service needs of a neighbourhood. It has a number of small stores, with the major retailer being a supermarket, a large drugstore, or a variety store.

A **string** is ordinarily composed of a group of stores with similar or compatible product lines that situate along a street or highway. Because this location is unplanned, various store combinations are possible. Car dealers, antique stores, and clothing stores often locate in strings.

*A **planned shopping centre** is centrally planned and has balanced tenancy.*

A **planned shopping centre** has centrally owned or managed facilities; it is planned and operated as an entity, ringed by parking, and based on balanced tenancy. With balanced tenancy, the number and composition of stores are related to overall shopper needs—stores complement each other in the variety and quality of their offerings. To ensure balance, a centre may limit the products a store carries.

Atmosphere

__Atmosphere__ consists of a store's exterior, general interior, layout, and displays.

Atmosphere is the sum total of the physical attributes of a retail store or group of stores that are used to develop an image and draw customers. It affects the target market attracted, the customer's shopping mood and time spent in the store, impulse purchases, and store positioning; and is related to the strategy chosen. As was shown in Table 10-7, a discount store would have simple fixtures, linoleum floors, and crowded displays. A full-service store would have elaborate fixtures, carpeted floors, and attractive displays.

There are four basic components of a store's atmosphere:

- *Exterior*—elements such as the storefront, the marquee, entrances, display windows, store visibility, store design, the surrounding area, and traffic congestion.

- *General interior*—elements such as flooring, colours, scents, lighting, fixtures, wall textures, temperature, aisle width, vertical transportation, personnel, cash register placement, and overall cleanliness.

- *Store layout*—elements such as the floor space allotted for customers, selling, and storage; product groupings; and department locations.

- *Interior (point-of-sale) displays*—elements such as merchandise cases and racks, mobiles, in-store ads, posters, and mannequins.

Canada's West Edmonton Mall—the world's largest planned shopping centre—uses an innovative atmosphere to draw millions of people annually, some from over 1200 kilometres away. It has eleven department stores, more than 800 other shops, a mile-long concourse, and fifty-eight entrances. Its size equals 115 football fields. The mall contains an amusement park, an ice-skating rink, a miniature golf course, and other attractions. It has parking for 20 000 vehicles. Total construction costs exceeded $700 million and the mall is estimated to bring $1.2 billion into Alberta each year.[20] See Figure 10-5.

WEST EDMONTON MALL
www.westedmall.com/

Scrambled Merchandising

*In **scrambled merchandising**, a retailer adds items to obtain one-stop shopping, higher margins, and impulse purchases.*

Scrambled merchandising occurs when a retailer adds goods and services that are unrelated to each other and to the firm's original business. Examples are supermarkets adding

---

[20]Brian Hutchinson, "Trouble in Big Mall Country," *Canadian Business* (September 1994), pp. 68–76; and Triple Five Corporation Ltd. correspondence.

FIGURE 10-5
The World's Largest Mall
Canada's West Edmonton Mall is the world's largest planned shopping centre.
Photo courtesy of West Edmonton Mall.

videocassette rentals, department stores offering theatre ticket services, restaurants carrying newspapers, and car washes stocking postcards.

There are limits to how far a firm should go with scrambled merchandising, especially if adding unrelated items would reduce buying, selling, and service effectiveness. Furthermore, stock turnover might be low for certain product lines should a retailer enter too many diverse product categories. Finally, scrambled merchandising may make a firm's image fuzzy to consumers.

The Wheel of Retailing

The **wheel of retailing** describes how low-end (discount) strategies can evolve into high-end (full-service, high-price) strategies and thus provide opportunities for new firms to enter as discounters. Retail innovators often first appear as low-price operators with low profit-margin requirements and low costs. As time passes, the innovators look to increase their sales and customer base. They upgrade product offerings, facilities, and services and turn into more traditional retailers. They may expand the sales force, move to better sites, and usher in delivery, credit, and alterations. The improvements lead to higher costs, which in turn cause higher prices. This creates openings for a new generation of retailers to emerge by appealing to the price-conscious shoppers who are left behind as existing firms move along the wheel. Figure 10-6 shows the wheel in action.

*The **wheel of retailing** shows how strategies change, leaving opportunities for new firms.*

There are some limitations in applying the wheel-of-retailing theory too literally. In particular, many retailers do not follow the pattern suggested, and trying to move along the wheel may cause a firm to lose its loyal customers. The best use of the wheel is in understanding that retailers can pursue distinct low-end, medium, and high-end strategies.

Technological Advances

Over the last several years, a number of technological advances related to retailing have emerged. The most dramatic are the computerized checkout system, video shopping services, data warehousing, computer-aided site selection, electronic banking, and operating efficiency.

Technological advances range from computerized checkout systems to enhanced operating efficiency.

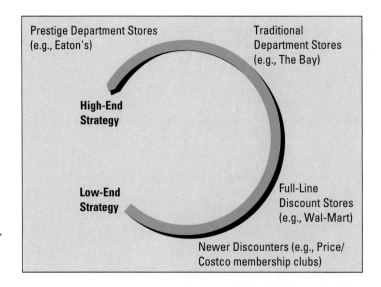

Prestige Department Stores
(e.g., Eaton's)

Traditional
Department Stores
(e.g., The Bay)

**High-End
Strategy**

**Low-End
Strategy**

Full-Line
Discount Stores
(e.g., Wal-Mart)

Newer Discounters (e.g., Price/
Costco membership clubs)

FIGURE 10-6
The Wheel of Retailing in Action

In a computerized checkout (electronic point-of-sale) system, a cashier manually rings up a sale or passes an item over or past an optical scanner; a computerized register instantly records and displays a sale. The customer gets a receipt, and inventory data are stored in the computer's memory bank. Such a system reduces checkout time, employee training, misrings, and the need for price marking on all products. It also generates a current listing of the merchandise in stock without taking a physical inventory, improves inventory control, reduces spoilage, and aids ordering.

Video shopping services let retailers efficiently, conveniently, and promptly present information, receive orders, and process transactions. These services can be divided into two basic categories: merchandise catalogues, and in-store and in-home ordering systems.

Video catalogues (shown on special monitors or via disc players/VCRs using conventional TV sets) allow consumers to view pre-recorded product and sales presentations in store and nonstore settings without the seller having to set up costly displays. With such catalogues (sometimes called kiosks), supermarkets can market appliances, airports can market watches, department stores can market gourmet foods, and mail-order firms can make their offerings come to life.

With an in-store video-ordering system, a consumer orders products by entering data into a self-prompting computer, which processes the order. After placing the order, the consumer usually goes to a checkout area where the item can be picked up and an invoice received. The consumer then pays a cashier. For an in-home system, goods and services are listed or displayed and then consumers order directly on special toll-free 800 phone numbers or through their PCs. To date, most in-home ordering has been from consumer phone responses to TV shows offered by such firms as the Canadian Home Shopping Network.

Cybermalls *are one of the new forms of retailing spawned by the computer age.*

One area of massive retail growth is expected to be shopping on the Internet in **cybermalls**. Many retailers have set up independent Internet Web sites and e-mail sites (e.g., Toronto's Cookbook Store), but a cybermall is a shared Web site. The Malls of Canada shopping site has ninety storefronts including firms such as: Bell Mobility, Carnival Cruiselines, and The Jewellery Archives. Growth of these malls had been expected to accelerate at a tremendous rate, but online sales have been disappointing. This is because only an estimated 8 per cent of Canadians are using online shopping. A major concern for consumers is the security of transactions and currency exchanges on the Internet when credit cards or bank debit cards are used for payment.[21]

Through "data warehousing," more retailers are embracing database marketing. For example:

Regal Greetings & Gifts of Toronto acquired a new catalogue entitled the *Jacarandra Tree*. Regal then used two years' worth of purchase behaviour information from its Disney Catalogue to

[21]Deborah Stokes, "Take Two for Cybermalls," *Marketing Magazine* (June 10, 1996), pp. 16, 19.

match up buyers from this list with potential buyers for items from the *Jacarandra Tree*. Keeping detailed information on customers enables Regal's managers to find and analyze data by customer, product, and transaction. The transaction information available to Regal includes not only purchases, but also requests for catalogues, shipping dates, and orders for merchandise that was not in stock.[22]

The availability of inexpensive computerized site-selection software is so prevalent that retailers of any size and type can now use it. For as little as U.S.$500, a retailer can buy geographic information systems (GIS) software that graphically depicts population characteristics, location attributes, roadways, and so on—for numerous potential or existing store sites. Canadian retail firms interested in locating in the U.S. can buy a CD-ROM diskette that lists 400 000 retail tenants in 34 000 U.S. shopping centres for U.S.$1795.[23]

Electronic banking involves the use of automatic teller machines (ATMs) and the instant processing of purchases. It provides central record keeping and lets customers conduct transactions twenty-four hours a day, seven days a week at many locations (such as banks and supermarkets). Deposits, withdrawals, and other banking and retailing tasks can be completed. ATMs are widely available in Canadian banks and trust companies, shopping centres, stores, airports, and other sites. To allow customers to make financial transactions over wider geographic areas, many banks have formed ATM networks. In North America there are hundreds of local and regional networks and half a dozen national (international) systems. The Cirrus and Plus networks allow customers to make transactions at tens of thousands of ATMs throughout North America and the world. There are 100 000 ATMs respectively in each of North America, Japan, and Europe.

As electronic banking spreads, more firms will participate in **debit transactions**, in which the amount of a sale is immediately charged against a buyer's bank account at the point of sale. A debit card system is different from current credit card policy, whereby consumers are sent bills and then remit payment. Debit cards will receive wide acceptance as a substitute for cheques. In 1995, approximately 7.5 per cent of all retail purchases were made with debit cards, compared to 3.5 per cent in 1994. One of the well-known brands of debit cards used in Canada is Interac.[24]

With **debit transactions**, *payments are immediately deducted from customers' accounts.*

Technological advances are also leading to greater retailer efficiency by:

- Increasing the use of self-service operations by firms marketing gasoline, airline tickets, and rental cars, and for hotel registrations and payment.

- Linking manufacturers, warehouses, and transportation firms.

- Introducing anti-shoplifting tags that set off an alarm if not properly removed by employees.

- Automating energy-control systems to monitor store temperature carefully and reduce fuel costs.

- Computerizing order entry in restaurants.

Furthermore, "The good news is that small retailers can also use technology as a tool in achieving greater efficiency. And the technology that's used doesn't have to be the highly complicated or expensive *Star Wars* variety."[25] It is essentially the same technology found in the home computers owned by millions of Canadians.

Recent Trends in Retailing

Retailing is in a great state of flux, particularly in Canada, as firms strive to defend or expand their positions in the marketplace. Many consumers no longer want to spend as much time shopping as they once did, various retail sectors have become saturated, a num-

This is a tough period for many retailers, due to changing consumer lifestyles, competition, and other factors.

[22]James Pollock, "Lists of Opportunity," *Marketing Magazine* (May 22, 1995), pp. 14–15.
[23]See Greg Hano, "Back to Basics," *Marketing Tools* (October 1995), pp. 10–15; and Michael Hartnett, "New Technologies Simplify Retail Site Selection," *Stores* (October 1995), pp. 45–46.
[24]"Interac Promotion to Boost Debit Cards," *Marketing Magazine* (October 9, 1995), p. 3.
[25]"Using Technology to Achieve Critical Success Factors," *Chain Store Age* (October 1995), Section Three, p. 8A.

ber of large retailers are operating under high levels of debt (typically caused by leveraged buyouts or overexpansion), and some retailers—after running frequent sales—have found it difficult to maintain regular prices. Here's what has been happening:

> The new rules of retailing include coping with nonstore competition, technology, and consolidation, as well as entertaining customers. Traditional jewellers are increasingly threatened by TV home shopping and catalogues. Hosiery manufacturers may sell pantyhose and socks on the Internet; perfumers are already doing so with scents. Small family nurseries are giving way to conglomerates in the bulb-and-seed business. Shoppers will soon see entertainment-retail destinations at which they can play tennis before buying a racquet or see a show about Julius Caesar's coronation. Virtually every retail business is involved with at least one of these issues.[26]

To succeed in the long run, Canadian retailers must respond to the trends they are facing. Among the most prominent are those relating to consumer demographics and lifestyles, competitive forces, operating costs, the labour force, and opportunities in foreign markets. Here is how various retailers are dealing with them.

The aging Canadian population, the increasing size of ethnic markets, and the saturation of many prime markets have resulted in various innovative retailing strategies. Club Monaco, a youth-oriented clothier owned by Dylex of Toronto, has chosen to expand by opening outlets in Japan, Korea, and Thailand where the youth markets are larger and growing much faster than in Canada. Leon's Furniture of Toronto has targeted the multicultural population of Toronto with specially designed ads for the Chinese, Italian, and Portuguese communities. Locations that have been underserved are being used—Price/Costco opened up a store in Moncton, New Brunswick, a relatively small population centre, in hopes of drawing customers from all of New Brunswick and the neighbouring Atlantic provinces.[27]

Retailers are adapting to the shopping needs and time constraints of working women and dual-earner households, and the increased consumer interest in quality and customer service. They are stocking such labour-saving products as ready-to-eat foods and pre-loaded PCs; lengthening store hours and opening additional days; expanding catalogue and phone sales efforts; re-emphasising personal selling; pre-wrapping gift items to eliminate waiting lines; setting up comprehensive specialty boutiques to minimize the number of departments a consumer must visit; adding special services, such as fashion coordinators; marketing high-quality private brands; and creating more attractive displays.

Retailing's intense competition has led to a wide spectrum of company responses. These are two illustrations: Market analysts believed that Canadian Tire would become a retail casualty as a result of the entrance of Wal-Mart and The Home Depot into Canada. Canadian Tire chose to respond by expanding and modernizing stores in small and mid-size Canadian markets. In addition, it improved customer service with a no-hassle returns policy, a frequent purchaser points program for credit card users and more training for sales staff. And it focused on its three core product areas of autos, housewares, and sports and leisure.

Building customer loyalty is the philosophy of Co-op Atlantic stores. Co-op Atlantic operates member-only stores, which have two approaches to building customer loyalty. Some stores charge weekly fees of $3 to $5 no matter how much a member spends. After paying their fee, members can then make their purchases at essentially no markup. A second approach allows both members and nonmembers to shop at the store. At the end of the year, members receive a dividend cheque. Developing a loyal customer franchise ensures the stores operating profits and efficiency, while the consumers benefit from low prices.[28]

CLUB MONACO
www.clubmonaco.com

---

[26]Fanglan Du and Ira Apfel, "The Future of Retailing," *American Demographics* (September 1995), p. 28.

[27]James Pollock, "Club Monaco Continues Asian Expansion," *Marketing Magazine* (November 13, 1995), p. 7; Andrea Haman, "Chinese Market: Leon's Furniture's TV Spots," *Marketing Magazine* (November 6, 1995), p. 21; and Mark Higgins, "Price Club Opens Two Atlantic Warehouse Stores," *Marketing Magazine* (November 6, 1995), p. 15.

[28]John Lorinc, "Road Warriors," *Canadian Business* (October 1995), pp. 26–43; and Mark Higgins, "Owners and Consumers," *Marketing Magazine* (November 6, 1995), pp. 14–15.

Because of the level of competition in many sectors of retailing, the price sensitivity of a large segment of consumers, and their general interest in improving efficiency (and profit margins), retailers are more concerned with cost control than ever before. For instance, several fast-food companies now use a format whereby different outlets occupy the same building (as food courts have done for years in shopping malls). This format lets them share common costs and even some employees. Most small hardware stores participate in buying cooperatives that enable them to secure quantity discounts and "buy smarter." Many supermarkets have increased their use of bulk selling, by which consumers select exact quantities of items such as candy and dried fruit from open displays. A number of mail-order firms are better targeting customers and containing their catalogue costs. United Furniture Warehouse of Coquitlam, B.C., has chosen a no-frills approach to keep costs down. United Furniture's strategy is to sell at warehouse prices, operate without commission sales staff, and finally, "We keep the overhead down." Literally. "We don't even have ceilings—just rafters like in a regular warehouse."[29]

Some Canadian retailers are having trouble attracting and retaining a quality labour force. According to surveys, retailers rank the labour shortage as one of the most crucial issues for them to address. Among the reasons why the shortage exists are that the number of available young people has declined; full-time career opportunities in other industries have attracted a number of part-time retail workers; many retail workers are inexperienced and have overly high job expectations, leading to employee dissatisfaction and turnover; hours can be long and irregular; some people do not like the pressure of interacting with customers on a regular basis; and the pay in other industries has been relatively higher.

A few of the actions retailers are taking to resolve the labour shortage are to recruit more at high schools, community colleges and universities, hire retired persons, offer child-care services for working mothers, raise starting salaries (sometimes to double the minimum wage or more), rotate employees among tasks to reduce boredom, reward good performance with bonuses, and encourage the best employees to pursue full-time career paths in retailing.

The Importance of Wholesaling

Wholesaling is an important aspect of distribution because of its impact on the economy, its functions in the distribution channel, and its relationships with suppliers and customers.

Wholesaling's Impact on the Economy

In Canada, there are about 65 000 wholesale merchant establishments with total annual sales exceeding $250 billion. There are about 1700 agents and brokers who function as wholesalers with annual sales near $40 billion. These revenues are higher than retail revenues, yet there are three times as many retail establishments (206 000) as wholesale.[30]

Wholesale sales are high, and wholesalers greatly affect final prices.

Revenues are high because wholesaling involves any purchases made by organizational consumers. Some products also move through multiple levels of wholesalers (e.g., regional, then local); an item can be sold twice or more at the wholesale level. There are more retailers because they serve individual, geographically dispersed final consumers; wholesalers handle fewer, larger, more concentrated customers.

From a cost perspective, wholesalers have a great impact on prices. Table 10-2 shows the per cent of wholesale selling prices that go to selected wholesalers to cover their operating expenses and pre-tax profits. For example, 31 per cent of the price that a general merchandise wholesaler charges its retailers covers that wholesaler's operating and other expenses (29 per cent) and pre-tax profit (2 per cent). Operating costs include inventory charges, sales force salaries, advertising, and rent.

Wholesaler costs and profits depend on inventory turnover, the dollar value of products, the functions performed, efficiency, and competition.

[29]Katrina Onstad, "Armchair Quarterback," *Canadian Business* (December 1995), pp. 80–81.
[30]Statistics Canada, *1995 Market Research Handbook* (Ottawa: Minister of Supply and Services Canada), pp. 95–96; and Statistics Canada, "Wholesale Trade," *The Daily* (Thursday, September 18, 1997).

Table 10-2

Selected Performance Data for Wholesalers by Product Category[a]

PRODUCT CATEGORY OF WHOLESALER	GROSS PROFIT (AS PER CENT OF SALES)[b]	OPERATING EXPENSES (AS PER CENT OF SALES)	ALL OTHER EXPENSES (AS PER CENT OF SALES)	PROFIT BEFORE TAXES (AS PER CENT OF SALES)
Building materials	25.3	22.5	0.4	2.3
Chemicals and allied products	28.8	25.7	0.3	2.8
Coffee, tea, and spices	29.0	25.4	1.1	2.5
Drugs, drug proprietaries, and druggists' supplies	29.3	25.0	0.5	3.8
Electronic parts and equipment	29.7	26.5	0.5	2.6
Fish and seafoods	15.2	12.9	0.4	1.8
Flowers, nursery stock, and florists' supplies	33.7	30.3	0.9	2.4
General groceries	18.2	16.4	0.4	1.5
General merchandise	31.3	28.4	0.7	2.2
Hardware and paints	29.9	26.8	0.6	2.4
Jewellery	28.2	24.6	0.9	2.7
Motor vehicle supplies and new parts	30.9	27.3	0.7	2.9
Petroleum bulk stations and terminals	14.8	13.7	0.0	1.2
Wine, liquor, and beer	23.7	20	0.4	2.4

[a] In interpreting these data, RMA cautions that the Studies be regarded only as a general guideline and not as an absolute industry norm. This is due to limited samples within categories, the categorization of firms by their primary Standard Industrial Classification (SIC) number only, and different methods of operations by firms within the same industry. For these reasons, RMA recommends that the figures be used only as general guidelines in addition to other methods of financial analysis.
[b] Total costs of wholesaling, which include expenses and profit. There are some rounding errors.

Source: Adapted from *RMA Annual Statement Studies 1995* (Philadelphia: Robert Morris Associates, 1995). Copyright © 1995, Robert Morris Associates; reprinted by permission.

The Functions of Wholesalers

Wholesalers perform tasks ranging from distribution to risk taking.

With regard to functions performed, wholesalers can:

- Enable manufacturers and service providers to distribute locally without making customer contacts.
- Provide a trained sales force.
- Provide marketing and research assistance for manufacturers, service providers, and retail or institutional consumers.
- Gather assortments for customers and let them make fewer transactions.
- Purchase large quantities, thus reducing total physical distribution costs.
- Provide warehousing and delivery facilities.
- Offer financing for manufacturers and service providers (by paying for products when they are shipped, not when they are sold) and retail or institutional consumers (by granting credit).

- Handle financial records.
- Process returns and make adjustments for defective merchandise.
- Take risks by being responsible for theft, deterioration, and obsolescence of inventory.[31]

Wholesalers that take title to and possession of products usually perform several or all of these tasks. Agents and brokers that facilitate sales, but do not take title or possession, tend to concentrate on more limited duties.

The use of independent wholesalers varies by industry. Most consumer products, food items, replacement parts, and office supplies are sold through independent wholesalers. In other industries, including heavy equipment, mainframe computers, gasoline, and temporary employment, manufacturers and service providers may bypass independent resellers.

Without independent wholesalers, organizational consumers would have to develop supplier contacts, deal with a number of suppliers and coordinate shipments, do more distribution functions, stock greater quantities, and place more emphasis on an internal purchasing agent or department. Many small retailers and other firms might be avoided as customers because they might not be profitably reached by a manufacturer or service provider; and they might not be able to buy necessary items elsewhere.

An illustration of the value of wholesaling is found in the North American auto parts industry, in which there used to be thousands of firms making a wide range of products and marketing them through a multitude of sales organizations. At that time, customers (mostly specialty stores and service stations) faced constant interruptions by salespeople; and manufacturers' sales costs were high. A better system exists today, with the organized use of a moderate number of independent distributors.

Wholesalers' Relationships with Suppliers and Customers

Independent wholesalers are often very much "in the middle," unsure whether their allegiance should be to manufacturers/service providers or their own customers. These comments show the dilemma many wholesalers face:

Wholesalers have obligations to both suppliers and customers.

> The challenge is to find ways individually, and as an industry, to show our customers and manufacturers exactly where and how we do and can add value. Our roles and performance are in a state of flux. The new theory is to cut out the wholesaler to reduce costs.[32]

Many wholesalers feel they get scant support from manufacturers/service providers. They desire training, technical assistance, product literature, and advertising. They dislike it when vendors alter territory assignments, shrink territory size, add new distributors to cover an existing geographic area, or decide to change to a direct channel and perform wholesale tasks themselves. Wholesalers want manufacturers/service providers to sell to them and not through them. Selling to the wholesaler means a distributor is viewed as a customer to be researched and satisfied. Selling through the wholesaler means retailers or final consumers are objects of manufacturers'/service providers' interest and wholesaler needs are less important. See Figure 10-7.

To remedy the situation, this is how many wholesalers are reacting:

> Wholesalers have traditionally viewed themselves as extensions of either their suppliers or customers. Wholesalers that saw themselves as extensions of suppliers adopted the mind set of their suppliers, structured operations to best assist suppliers, and viewed customers as "outside" this relationship. And wholesalers that saw their role as extensions of their customers adopted that mind set and business structure and viewed the supplier as "outside." In short, wholesalers have typically viewed themselves as "distributors."

[31]Adapted by the authors from Walters and Bergiel, *Marketing Channels*, p. 109; and Louis W. Stern, Adel L. El-Ansary, and James R. Brown, *Management in Marketing Channels* (Englewood Cliffs, N.J.: Prentice Hall, 1989), pp. 98–99.

[32]Craig MacClaren, "Squeezed Brokers Position for Value-Added Services," *Promo* (February 1995), p. 36; and Stephen Bennett, "Working the Middle Ground," *Progressive Grocer* (August 1995), p. 147.

Selling to the wholesaler

Manufacturer/Service Provider → Wholesaler → Retailer

The wholesaler is viewed as a customer who is researched and satisfied.

Selling through the wholesaler

Manufacturer/Service Provider → Wholesaler → Retailer

The retailer (or final customer) is the object of the manufacturer's/service provider's interests. The needs of the wholesaler are considered unimportant.

FIGURE 10-7
Selling to Versus Selling Through the Wholesaler

Today, more wholesalers feel they are in the "marketing support business." They view themselves as marketing *with* their suppliers and customers, not just being distributors. They recognize their primary role is to help both suppliers and customers devise better marketing programs. The marketing-support oriented wholesaler is willing to perform any task, activity, or function for either suppliers or customers that will result in more effective and efficient marketing for the entire channel.[33]

Types of Wholesaling

The three broad categories of wholesaling are outlined in Figure 10-8: manufacturer/service provider wholesaling, merchant wholesaling, and agents and brokers. Table 10-3 contains detailed descriptions of every type of independent wholesaler and shows their functions and special features.

Manufacturer/Service Provider Wholesaling

In **manufacturer/service provider wholesaling**, *a firm acts via its own sales or branch offices.*

In **manufacturer/service provider wholesaling**, a producer does all wholesaling functions itself. This occurs if a firm feels it is best able to reach retailers or other organizational customers by being responsible for wholesaling tasks itself. Manufacturer/service provider wholesalers include General Motors, IBM, Frito-Lay, Pitney Bowes, Prudential, and public utilities.

Wholesale activities by a manufacturer or service provider may be carried out via sales offices and/or branch offices. A sales office is located at a firm's production facilities or a site close to the market. No inventory is carried there. In contrast, a branch office has facilities for warehousing products, as well as for selling them.

Manufacturer/service provider wholesaling is most likely if independent intermediaries are unavailable, existing intermediaries are unacceptable to the manufacturer or service provider, the manufacturer or service provider wants control over marketing, customers are relatively few in number and each is a key account, customers desire personal service from the producer, customers are near to the firm or clustered, a computerized

[33]Robert F. Lusch, Deborah Zizzo, and James M. Kenderdine, "Strategic Renewal in Distribution," *Marketing Management*, Vol. 2 (Number 2, 1993), p. 25.

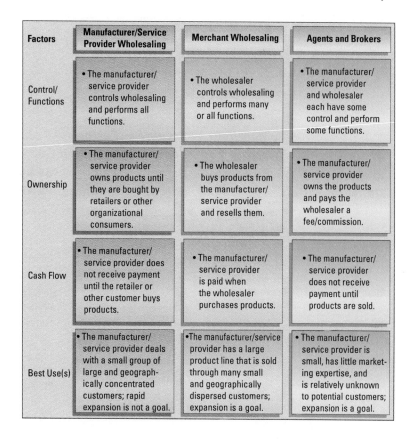

Factors	Manufacturer/Service Provider Wholesaling	Merchant Wholesaling	Agents and Brokers
Control/Functions	• The manufacturer/service provider controls wholesaling and performs all functions.	• The wholesaler controls wholesaling and performs many or all functions.	• The manufacturer/service provider and wholesaler each have some control and perform some functions.
Ownership	• The manufacturer/service provider owns products until they are bought by retailers or other organizational consumers.	• The wholesaler buys products from the manufacturer/service provider and resells them.	• The manufacturer/service provider owns the products and pays the wholesaler a fee/commission.
Cash Flow	• The manufacturer/service provider does not receive payment until the retailer or other customer buys products.	• The manufacturer/service provider is paid when the wholesaler purchases products.	• The manufacturer/service provider does not receive payment until products are sold.
Best Use(s)	• The manufacturer/service provider deals with a small group of large and geographically concentrated customers; rapid expansion is not a goal.	• The manufacturer/service provider has a large product line that is sold through many small and geographically dispersed customers; expansion is a goal.	• The manufacturer/service provider is small, has little marketing expertise, and is relatively unknown to potential customers; expansion is a goal.

FIGURE 10-8
The Broad Categories of Wholesaling

order system links a firm with customers, and/or laws (particularly in foreign markets) limit arrangements with independent resellers.

For instance, because Boeing makes multimillion-dollar aircraft and individual customer orders can be in the billions of dollars, manufacturer wholesaling is a must. When Boeing recently sold $3 billion in jets to General Electric, the complex negotiations took over a year.[34] And at Chrysler, manufacturer wholesaling means closer relationships with its auto dealers. Chrysler distributes its Mopar brand replacement parts directly to the retailers and works with them to market the parts.

BOEING
www.boeing.com/

Wholesale Merchants

Wholesale merchants buy, take title, and take possession of products for further resale. This is the largest wholesale category in sales—over $240 billion per year in Canada. As an example, Sysco is a merchant wholesaler that buys and handles 150 000 products from 3000 producers of food and related products from around the world. It resells these products and offers many customer services to its 250 000 clients—restaurants, hotels, schools, hospitals, fast-food chains, and other organizations in both Canada and the United States.[35]

Full-service merchant wholesalers perform a full range of distribution tasks. They provide credit, store and deliver products, offer merchandising and promotion assistance, have a personal sales force, offer research and planning support, pass along information to suppliers and customers, and provide installation and repair services. They are frequently used for grocery products, pharmaceuticals, hardware, plumbing equipment, tobacco, alcoholic beverages, and television program syndication.

Limited-service merchant wholesalers do not perform all the functions of full-service merchant wholesalers. For instance, they may not provide credit, merchandising assis-

*Wholesale merchants buy products and may offer **full** or **limited** service.*

---

[34]Jeff Cole and Susan Carey, "Boeing Co. to Get GE Job Valued at Over $3 Billion," *Wall Street Journal* (January 8, 1996), pp. A3–A4.

[35]Gary Hoover, Alta Campbell, and Patrick J. Spain (Eds.), *Hoover's Handbook of American Business 1995* (Austin, Texas: Reference Press, 1994), pp. 1004–1005.

Table 10-3
Characteristics of Independent Wholesalers

WHOLESALER TYPE	Provides Credit	Stores and Delivers	Takes Title	Provides Merchandising and Promotion Assistance	Provides Personal Sales Force	Performs Research and Planning	SPECIAL FEATURES
MAJOR FUNCTIONS							
I. Merchant wholesaler							
A. Full service							
1. General merchandise	Yes	Yes	Yes	Yes	Yes	Yes	Carries nearly all items a customer normally needs.
2. Specialty	Yes	Yes	Yes	Yes	Yes	Yes	Specializes in a narrow product range
3. Rack jobber	Yes	Yes	Yes	Yes	Yes	Yes	Furnishes racks and shelves, consignment sales
4. Franchise	Yes	Yes	Yes	Yes	Yes	Yes	Use of common business format, extensive management services
5. Cooperative							
a. Producer-owned	Yes	Yes	Yes	Yes	Yes	Yes	Farmer controlled, profits divided among members
b. Retailer-owned	Yes	Yes	Yes	Yes	Yes	Yes	Wholesaler owned by several retailers
B. Limited service							
1. Cash and carry	No	Stores, no delivery	Yes	No	No	No	No outside sales force, wholesale store for business needs
2. Drop shipper	Yes	Delivers, no storage	Yes	No	Yes	Sometimes	Ships items without physically handling them
3. Truck/wagon	Rarely	Yes	Yes	Yes	Yes	Sometimes	Sales and delivery on same call
4. Mail order	Sometimes	Yes	Yes	No	No	Sometimes	Catalogues used as sole promotion tool
II. Agents and brokers							
A. Agents							
1. Manufacturers' (service providers')	No	Sometimes	No	Yes	Yes	Sometimes	Sells selected items for several firms
2. Selling	Sometimes	Yes	No	Yes	Yes	Yes	Markets all the items of a firm
3. Commission (factor) merchants	Sometimes	Yes	No	No	Yes	Yes	Handles items on a consignment basis
B. Brokers							
1. Food	No	Sometimes	No	Yes	Yes	Yes	Brings together buyers and sellers
2. Stock	Sometimes	Sometimes	No	Yes	Yes	Yes	Brings together buyers and sellers

tance, or marketing research data. They are popular for construction materials, coal, lumber, perishables, equipment rentals, and specialty foods.

On average, full-service merchant wholesalers require more compensation than limited-service ones because they perform more functions.

FULL-SERVICE MERCHANT WHOLESALERS Full-service merchant wholesalers can be divided into general merchandise, specialty merchandise, rack jobber, franchise, and cooperative types.

General-merchandise (full-line) wholesalers carry a wide product assortment—nearly all the items needed by their customers. Thus, some general-merchandise hardware, drug, and clothing wholesalers stock many products, but not much depth in any one line. They seek to sell their retailers or other organizational customers all or most of their products and develop strong loyalty and exclusivity with them.

Specialty-merchandise (limited-line) wholesalers concentrate on a rather narrow product range and have an extensive selection in that range. They offer many sizes, colours, and models—and provide functions similar to other full-service merchant wholesalers. They are popular for health foods, seafood, retail store displays, frozen foods, and video rentals.

Rack jobbers furnish the racks or shelves on which products are displayed. They own the products on the racks, selling them on a consignment basis—so their clients pay after goods are resold. Unsold items are taken back. Jobbers set up displays, refill shelves, price mark goods, maintain inventory records, and compute the amount due from their customers. Rack jobbers usually handle heavily advertised, branded merchandise that is sold on a self-service basis. Included are magazines, health and beauty aids, cosmetics, drugs, hand tools, toys, housewares, and stationery.

In **franchise wholesaling**, independent retailers affiliate with an existing wholesaler to use a standardized storefront design, business format, name, and purchase system. Many times, suppliers produce goods and services according to specifications set by the franchise wholesaler. This form of wholesaling is utilized for hardware, auto parts, and groceries. Franchise wholesalers include Independent Grocers Alliance (IGA), Independent Druggists Association (IDA), Western Auto, and Home Hardware Stores. At IGA, affiliated retailers are supplied with such services as site selection, store engineering, interior design, and merchandising assistance.

Wholesale cooperatives are owned by member firms to economize functions and provide broad support. Producer-owned cooperatives are popular in farming. They market, transport, and process farm products—as well as make and distribute farm supplies. These cooperatives often sell to stores under their own names, such as Blue Diamond, Ocean Spray, Sunkist, and Welch's. With retailer-owned cooperatives, independent retailers form associations that purchase, lease, or build wholesale facilities. The cooperatives take title to merchandise, handle cooperative advertising, and negotiate with suppliers. They are used by hardware and grocery stores.

LIMITED-SERVICE MERCHANT WHOLESALERS Limited-service merchant wholesalers can be divided into cash-and-carry, drop shipper, truck/wagon, and mail-order types.

In **cash-and-carry wholesaling**, people from small businesses drive to wholesalers, order products, and take them back to a store or business. These wholesalers offer no credit or delivery, no merchandising and promotion help, no outside sales force, and no research or planning assistance. They are good for fill-in items, have low prices, and allow immediate product use. They are common for construction materials, electrical supplies, office supplies, auto supplies, hardware products, and groceries.

Drop shippers (desk jobbers) buy goods from manufacturers or suppliers and arrange for their shipment to retailers or industrial users. They have legal ownership, but do not take physical possession of products and have no storage facilities. They purchase items, leave them at manufacturers' plants, contact customers by phone, set up and coordinate carload shipments from manufacturers directly to customers, and are responsible for items that cannot be sold. Trade credit, a personal sales force, and some research and planning

General-merchandise wholesalers *sell a range of items.*

Specialty-merchandise wholesalers *sell a narrow line of products.*

Rack jobbers *set up displays and are paid after sales.*

With **franchise wholesaling**, *retailers join with a wholesaler.*

INDEPENDENT GROCERS ALLIANCE (IGA) INC.
www.igainc.com/

HOME HARDWARE
www.pagemaker.com/~home/overview.html

Producers or retailers can set up **wholesale cooperatives**.

In **cash-and-carry wholesaling**, *the customer drives to a wholesaler.*

Drop shippers *buy goods, but do not take possession.*

International Marketing in *Action*

Malofilm: International Distributor of Canadian Entertainment

Malofilm Distribution, a unit of Malofilm Communications Inc., is one of Canada's leading distributors of Canadian films and videocassettes. Its parent firm, Malofilm Communications, is an integrated entertainment company with average annual sales between $30 to $40 million and earnings between $2 to $3 million. Pure distribution accounts for about 95 per cent of the firm's revenues. Aside from domestic and international distribution, Malofilm's business consists of development and production of programming for theatre, video, television, and multimedia (such as video games for the Sony Playstation). Malofilm is also one of Canada's largest distributors of home videos and has an investment in TotalNet, one of the nation's largest providers of Internet services.

In the past, the main source of products and income for Malofilm has been the distribution of foreign-made films (mostly U.S. productions) in Canada. Malofilm has been very successful in this regard, acquiring the rights to distribute and sell entertainment titles such as: *Braveheart* (Best Picture Winner at the 1996 Academy Awards), *Highlander 3*, and *Margaret's Museum*.

However, for real growth and diversity, Malofilm needs access to markets much larger than Canada. This means controlling the rights to worldwide distribution of original productions. According to René Malo, CEO of Malofilm Communications Inc., the company plans to make production and international distribution account for more of the firm's revenue in the future. Malofilm plans to produce four feature films in 1996 (*J'en Suis*, *Scanners IV*, *Turning Blue*, and *The Last Chocolate Maker*), along with its involvement in the production of children's television programs (*Little Star*, *Mighty Machines*, and *Turtle Island*) and interactive digital media ("Jersey Devil" Game for Sony's Playstation, and the Montreal Canadiens 1909–1995 CD-ROM). The future in entertainment will quite likely be linked to Internet distribution, so Malofilm is looking ahead there as well.

In early 1996, Malofilm distribution began the process of expanding international distribution by becoming the international distributor for Toronto-based Associated Producers, a firm known for making award-winning and hard-hitting documentaries.

MALOFILM

www.malo.com/

TOTALNET

www.infobahnos.com/beta/francais/english.html

Truck/wagon wholesalers *offer products on a sales route.*

Mail-order wholesalers *sell through catalogues.*

are provided; merchandising and promotion support are not. Drop shippers are often used for coal, coke, and building materials. These goods have high freight costs, in relation to their value, because of their weight. Thus, direct shipments from suppliers to customers are needed.

Truck/wagon wholesalers generally have a regular sales route, offer items from a truck or wagon, and deliver goods at the same time as they sell them. They do provide merchandising and promotion support; however, they are considered limited service because they usually do not extend credit and offer little research and planning help. Operating costs are high due to the services performed and low average sales. These wholesalers often deal with goods requiring special handling or with perishables—such as bakery products, tobacco, meat, candy, potato chips, and dairy products.

Mail-order wholesalers use catalogues, instead of a personal sales force, to promote products and communicate with customers. They may provide credit but do not generally give merchandising and promotion support. They store and deliver goods, and offer

International Marketing in

Malofilm: International Distributor of Canadian Entertainment (continued)

President of Malofilm Distribution, Yves Dion, believes the worldwide explosion of news and information programming such as CNN (Cable News Network) and Headline News will lead to greater interest in documentary-type products.

Malofilm also distributes internationally the firm's own productions, like *Mojave Frankenstein*, a family film starring Burt Reynolds. To promote the film and get international distribution, Malofilm had Burt Reynolds interviewed on the syndicated TV show "Entertainment Tonight." Malofilm International is also handling world rights for the family film, *Kids of the Round Table*, which they have sold to over thirty countries, including the key market, the United States.

The control of all worldwide distribution rights is critical to international sales success. With control, Malofilm has the ability to allocate the rights on a nation-by-nation basis and in all media. Being able to subdivide rights by broadcast, theatrical release, and videocassette distribution allows Malofilm to maximize the revenue from film distribution. For example, the television rights for *Kids of the Round Table* in the U.S. were sold to The Disney Channel, while the U.S. video distribution rights were sold to Cabin Fever. In another example, Malofilm acquired international sales rights in all media to two movies launched at the 1996 Cannes Film Festival. One of the films, entitled *Sous-sol*, was produced in Quebec; the second, *The Interview*, was a combined Brazilian and American production. However, the Canadian production's domestic distribution rights were sold to another distributor, not Malofilm.

As a market analyst, discuss Malofilm's strategy and plans for sales growth based on international distribution.

Sources: "Malofilm Communications Inc. Picks Up International Sales Rights To Hard-Hitting, Controversial Documentaries From Award-Winning Associated Producers," *Canada NewsWire* (February 19, 1996), http://www.newswire.ca:80; "Malofilm Distribution Inc. Executive Producer And Foreign Distributor of 'Mojave Frankenstein'; Entertainment Tonight to Interview Burt Reynolds," *Canada NewsWire* (August 9, 1995); "Second Quarter Profit Up 59 Per Cent at Malofilm Communications Inc.," *Canada NewsWire* (May 27, 1996); and "Feature Film, Children's TV, And Multimedia Production Spur Growth Strategy at Malofilm Communications Inc.," *Canada NewsWire* (March 20, 1996).

---

some research and planning assistance. These wholesalers are found with jewellery, cosmetics, auto parts, specialty food product lines, business supplies, and small office equipment.

Agents and Brokers

Agents and **brokers** perform various wholesale tasks, but do not take title to products. Unlike merchant wholesalers, which make profits on the sales of products they own, agents and brokers work for commissions or fees as payment for their services. In Canada there are about 1700 brokers and agents and these account for almost $40 billion in sales each year. The main difference between agents and brokers is that agents are more apt to be used on a permanent basis.[36]

> **Agents** *and* **brokers** *do not take title to products.*

[36]Statistics Canada, *1995 Market Research Handbook* (Ottawa: Minister of Supply and Services Canada), p. 96.

Agents and brokers let a manufacturer or service provider expand sales volume despite limited resources. Their selling costs are a predetermined per cent of sales; and they have trained salespeople. There are manufacturers'/service providers' agents, selling agents, and commission (factor) merchants.

Manufacturers'/service providers' agents *work for many firms and carry noncompeting items.*

Manufacturers'/service providers' agents work for several manufacturers or service providers and carry noncompetitive, complementary products in exclusive territories. By selling noncompetitive items, the agents eliminate conflict-of-interest situations. By selling complementary products, they stock a fairly complete line of products for their market areas. They do not offer credit but may store and deliver products and give limited research and planning aid. Merchandising and promotional support are provided. These agents may supplement the sales efforts of their clients, help introduce new products, enter dispersed markets, and handle items with low average sales. They may carry only some of a firm's products; a manufacturer or service provider may hire many agents; larger firms may hire a separate one for every product line. Agents have little say on marketing and pricing. They earn commissions of 5 to 10 per cent of sales, and are popular for auto products, iron, steel, footwear, textiles, and commercial real estate and insurance.

Selling agents *market all the products of a manufacturer or service provider.*

Selling agents are responsible for marketing the entire output of a manufacturer/ service provider under a contractual agreement. They become the marketing departments for their clients and can negotiate price and other conditions of sale, such as credit and delivery. They perform all wholesale tasks except taking title. While a firm may use several manufacturers'/service providers' agents, it may employ only one sales agent. These agents are more apt to work for small firms than large ones. They are common for textile manufacturing, canned foods, metals, home furnishings, apparel, lumber, and metal products. Because they perform more tasks, they often get higher commissions than manufacturers'/service providers' representatives.

Commission merchants *assemble goods from local markets.*

Commission (factor) merchants receive goods on consignment, accumulate them from local markets, and arrange for their sale in a central location. They may offer credit; they do store and deliver goods, provide a sales force, and offer research and planning help. They normally do not assist in merchandising and promotion; but, they can negotiate prices with buyers, provided the prices are not below sellers' stated minimums. They may act in an auction setting; commissions vary. These wholesalers are used for agricultural and seafood products, furniture, and art.

Brokers are common for food and financial services. They are well informed about market conditions, terms of sale, sources of credit, price setting, potential buyers and sellers, and the art of negotiating. They do not take title and usually are not allowed to complete a transaction without approval.

Food brokers *and* **commercial stock brokers** *unite buyers and sellers to conclude sales.*

Food brokers introduce buyers and sellers of food and related general-merchandise items to one another and bring them together to complete a sale. They operate in specific locales and work for a limited number of food producers. Their sales forces call on chain-store buyers, store managers, and purchasing agents. Food brokers work closely with ad agencies. They generally represent the seller, who pays the commission; they do not actually provide credit but may store and deliver. Commissions are 3 to 5 per cent of sales.

Commercial stock brokers are licensed sales representatives who advise business clients, take orders, and then acquire stocks and/or bonds for the clients. They may aid the firms selling the stocks or bonds, represent either buyers or sellers (with both buyers and sellers paying commissions), and offer some credit. Although operating in particular areas, they typically sell the stocks and bonds of firms from throughout Canada, the United States, and around the world. They deal a lot over the phone and may help publicize new stock or bond offerings. The average commission for commercial stock brokers is 1 to 10 per cent of sales, depending on volume and stock prices.

Recent Trends in Wholesaling

Firms are becoming larger and more productive.

During the last fifteen years, wholesaling has changed dramatically, with independent wholesalers striving to protect their place in the channel. Among the key trends are those related to the evolving wholesaler mix, productivity, customer service, international opportunities, and target markets.

Since the early 1980s, the proportion of total sales volume contributed by merchant wholesaling, agents, and brokers has remained steady. However, there are fewer agent and broker wholesaler establishments and more merchant wholesaler establishments. The most recent Statistics Canada Census Data (1992) estimates that 63 000 companies engaged in merchant wholesaling in 1992, up from 49 000 in 1982. The average annual sales of these wholesalers was $3.9 million in 1992 compared to $2.9 million in 1982. In that same year, an estimated 5015 brokers and agents had average sales of $5.4 million, compared to 1758 agents and brokers in 1992 with average sales of $22 million. In the wholesaling business an astonishing 0.6 per cent of the firms accounted for 44 per cent of the sales.[37]

Since wholesalers' profit margins are small (1.5 per cent of sales for food wholesalers and less than 3 per cent of sales for general merchandise wholesalers), they are constantly seeking gains in productivity. For example, VWD Distributors, a Western Canadian pharmaceutical wholesaler, installed a $400 000 electronic carousel order-filling system, the first of its kind in Canada, in their Burnaby, B.C., facility. The new system allows one person to fill fourteen orders simultaneously. The system holds almost 80 per cent of VWD's inventory and the company hopes the new system will reduce handling and shipping errors, provide better inventory control, and reduce labour expenses.[38]

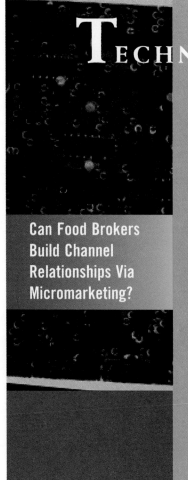

TECHNOLOGY & MARKETING

Can Food Brokers Build Channel Relationships Via Micromarketing?

The micromarketing approach recognizes that different marketing strategies may be necessary on a store-by-store basis to maximize a reseller's sales and profitability. Micromarketing opportunities are facilitated when retailers and suppliers are able to share vital information. This process increases trust between both parties. According to Ed Fargo, a vice-president of Eisenhart & Associates, a food brokerage firm, "When we can show a food retailer what's selling, who's buying, where those buyers live and what they like, we have won that food retailer's attention."

As a service to customers, Eisenhart & Associates compiles and evaluates research data on product sales, consumer demographics, lifestyles, and local advertising expenditures. Eisenhart's analysis relies on its computer-generated profiles of the typical users and heavy users of each account's product line. Thus, it can estimate a chain's market share in selected merchandise categories as compared with local supermarkets, mass merchandisers, and drug stores. Although a chain can develop similar analyses, Fargo realizes that "not all retailers can afford the time and effort to analyze hundreds of categories in this manner."

On the basis of this analysis, Eisenhart & Associates determines which stores in a chain would most benefit from special displays and in-store demonstrations, and which ones should be sold together using joint promotions. In many cases, Eisenhart is able to show that a product's contribution to sales and profits is greater than its proportionate use of shelf space.

Eisenhart & Associates then seeks to increase product positions on shelves (from ankle to eye level) or to add new items to a product line. For example, in one case, Fargo was able to convince a supermarket to add seven new items to a line of light yogurt.

As a food broker, what other opportunities exist for the building of channel relationships via micromarketing?

Source: Based on material in "Building Bridges," *Promo/ Progressive Grocer Special Report* (October 1994), **p. 9.**

[37]Industry Canada, "Wholesale Trade-Industry Profile, 1992," Industry Canada *Strategis* Web site (1994), http://www.ic.gc.ca/strategis.

[38]"VWD Installs Canada's First Computerized Carousel System For Wholesale Drug Operations," *Canada NewsWire* (August 9, 1995), http://www.newswire.ca:80.

Wholesalers are emphasizing customer service and looking to international markets.

WW GRAINGER
www.grainger.com/

FINNING LTD.
www.finning.ca/

Target market strategies are more complex.

Wholesalers have learned that customer service is extremely important in securing a competitive advantage, developing client loyalty, and attaining acceptable profit margins. For example, W.W. Grainger, a wholesaler of maintenance, repair, and operating supplies—offers a "value package" that includes electronic ordering and payment, cost-reduction consulting services, and so forth. As a Grainger vice-president says, "On sales calls these days, we seldom talk about why the motor we sell is better than someone else's motor; we talk about value-added services."[39]

And the Canadian Council of Grocery Distributors is trying to anticipate the needs of shoppers in the future. The Council expects that soon we will not have to shop during store hours, or even step into a store. Instead, we will visit virtual supermarkets, which retailers will present along with physical supermarkets. A pilot project of grocery shopping on the Web has already been launched.[40]

More wholesalers are turning to foreign markets for growth. Finning Ltd., a British Columbia-based wholesaler of Caterpillar and allied equipment, is concentrating on international expansion. Finning sells, finances, and provides customer service for this equipment. The company serves geographic markets in Western Canada, Britain, Poland, and Chile. The firm has over 4000 employees in its worldwide operations and sells heavy equipment to industry market segments such as mining, agricultural, petroleum, construction, and forestry. To service this equipment Finning has a hydraulic rebuild company and a component remanufacturing centre, both located in Edmonton. In order to be accepted more readily by international customers, Finning has sought and received certification under International Quality Standard ISO 9002.

Finning's efforts to improve international sales have paid off: international business accounted for 44 per cent of their 1996 sales of $1.87 billion and a total profit of $88.1 million or 4.7 per cent. European sales accounted for 24 per cent and Chilean sales represented 22 per cent of this total. In contrast, in 1994 Canadian sales represented 60 per cent of the company's total $1.46 billion in sales, while European sales accounted for 23 per cent and Chilean sales for 17 per cent. An important factor to consider is that European profit margins were 5.8 per cent of sales in 1996 and 4.6 per cent in 1994. In contrast, Canadian profit margins were lower, at 4.3 per cent in 1996 and 4.1 per cent in 1994. Chilean sales had the greatest increase, and the associated profit margins were the same as those in Canada with 1996 profit margins of 4.3 per cent compared to 1994 profit margins of 3.9 per cent. Still, international sales increased at a rate of 12.5 per cent, while Canadian sales increased at only 2.8 per cent, indicating the best growth potential for Finning is in international markets.[41]

In large numbers, wholesalers are diversifying the markets they serve or the products they carry: Farm and garden machinery wholesalers now sell to florists, hardware dealers, and garden supply stores. Plumbing wholesalers have added industrial accounts, contractors, and builders. Grocery wholesalers deal with hotels, airlines, hospitals, schools, and restaurants. Some food wholesalers have moved into apparel retailing and opened auto-parts stores.

Yet, some wholesalers are taking the opposite approach and seeking to appeal to one customer niche or need. Thus, Prudential Steel focuses on supplying line pipe for the oil and gas industry in Western Canada through its wholesale operation, Oil Country Tubular Goods. Like all wholesalers, Prudential has to manage its incoming goods costs carefully while remaining price competitive on outgoing goods. The price of steel has a major impact on acquisition costs and Prudential cannot control this cost. Likewise, the price of oil and gas affect exploration and oil and gas well operations and these greatly affect

---

[39]Thomas A. Stewart, "The Information Wars: What You Don't Know Will Hurt You," *Fortune* (June 12, 1995), pp. 120–121.

[40]Canadian Council of Grocery Distributors, "Grocery Shopping From Your Own Home," *Canada NewsWire* (May 27, 1996), http://www.newswire.ca.

[41]"Finning Ltd.: Fourth Quarter 1996 Press Release," *Canada NewsWire* (February 3, 1997); "Finning Ltd. Reports Record Revenue and Net Income," *Canada NewsWire* (February 1, 1996); and "Finning Ltd: New Chairman," *Canada NewsWire* (April 19, 1996).

Prudential's demand. Prudential had sales of $177 million in 1995, down from 1994 sales of $215 million because of low prices for oil and gas in 1995. Despite this, the firm is committed to its niche as a supplier of steel line pipes, which carry the products of oil and gas producers. In fact, Prudential management feels customer service is so critical that despite a fall in sales, the company kept a large inventory of finished goods on hand in 1995. This decision anticipated expanding sales in 1996 as oil and gas prices were rebounding and this resulted in sales of $161 million in the first nine months of 1996.[42]

MARKETING IN A CHANGING WORLD

Invasion of the U.S. Retailers[43]

Recently, many large U.S. retail operations, many of them category killers, have entered into Canada. From the consumer's perspective, selection has never been so good while prices have never seemed so low. But for thousands of retailers competing against U.S. invaders, the news is not so good. Take Wal-Mart, for example. In the U.S. Wal-Mart seems virtually unstoppable with its low prices and large assortments. Wal-Mart stores and Sam's Clubs blanket the United States. In addition to its rapid expansion into Canada with the acquisition of 122 Woolco stores from Woolworth, Wal-Mart is also expanding into Mexico, Hong Kong, and elsewhere. In its wake, vulnerable (unprepared) retailers have been falling by the wayside. Category killers such as The Home Depot, Price/Costco, and Business Depot are wiping out smaller independent businesses that once thrived as small specialists competing against department stores.

The current American invasion has not had its full impact yet, and it is expected that more foreign retail competition from both the United States and Europe will arise. Wal-Mart's entry has had an effect on retailers that are not positioned against it. For example, Eaton's Department Store has filed for bankruptcy protection from its creditors and is trying to remake itself by downsizing. After the entry of Spiegel on the heels of a number of other U.S. catalogue retailers, Sears Canada says its catalogue operations were no longer particularly profitable.

However, U.S. retailers have not steamrolled into Canada without trouble. Wal-Mart became embroiled in a trademark suit over its name with Wool-mart. Home Depot purchased Aikenhead's from Molson Cos. Ltd. but slowed the pace of its store openings. Borders books had its entry stalled by the Canadian government, responding to lobbying efforts by Canadian booksellers. Finally, Target Stores of Minneapolis decided not to enter at all given the size of the Canadian market and the level of competition that was being demonstrated.

Price/Costco's focus on the food market has caused expansion and repositioning of grocery retailers throughout Canada. For example, Sobey's, an Atlantic Canada-based retailer, has opened some stores in Ontario and has plans to enter the Quebec market. Meanwhile, A&P has opened some Food Basics stores in southern Ontario, which emphasize low prices. These stores are smaller than traditional grocery stores, do not have delis or bakeries, ask consumers to bag their own groceries, and carry more private labels.

Add the unknown impact of cybermalls and marketing on the Internet to the American invasion and one thing is clear: the Canadian retail market is, and will remain, a highly contested and unstable retailing environment. Nonetheless, as we have noted throughout *Marketing Essentials*, when companies follow sound marketing principles, they greatly increase their chances of success. And this is just as true of retailers in the age of the U.S. invasion.

[42]"Prudential Steel Ltd. Second Quarter Results Reflect More Normal Seasonal Downturn in Oil Patch Activity," *Canada NewsWire* (July 27 1995), http://www.newswire.ca:80; "Prudential Reports Strong Fourth Quarter," *Canada NewsWire* (February 21, 1996); and "Industry Drilling Strength Provides Prudential with Record Quarter," *Canada NewsWire* (October 24, 1996).

[43]James Pollock, "Canada Tougher Than U.S. Stores Thought," *Marketing Magazine* (July 3–10, 1995), p. 4; Andrea Haman, "By the Book," *Marketing Magazine* (November 27, 1995), pp. 9–10; Leonard Kubas, "Navigating the New Retail Landscape," *Marketing Magazine* (July 31–August 7, 1995), pp. 11–12; Eric Swetsky, "Wool-Mart versus Wal-Mart," *Marketing Magazine* (June 24, 1996), p. 20; and James Pollock, "A&P Expands No-frills Food Basics Division," *Marketing Magazine* (November 27, 1995), p. 2.

S U M M A R Y

1. *To define retailing and show its importance* Retailing encompasses those business activities involved with the sale of goods and services to the final consumer for personal, family, or household use. It is the final stage in a distribution channel. Average retail sales are small, yet the use of credit is widespread. Final consumers generally visit a retail store to make a purchase and they also make many unplanned purchases.

Retailing has an impact on the economy because of its total sales and the number of people employed. Retailers provide a variety of functions, including gathering a product assortment, providing information, handling merchandise, and completing transactions. Retailers deal with suppliers that sell products the retailers use in operating their businesses as well as suppliers selling items the retailers will resell.

2. *To discuss the different types of retailers, in terms of ownership, store strategy mix, and nonstore operations* Retailers may be categorized in several ways. The basic ownership formats are independent—a retailer operating only one outlet; chain—a retailer operating two or more outlets; franchise—a contractual arrangement between a franchiser and a franchisee to conduct a certain business; leased department—a department in a store that is leased to an outside party; and retail cooperative—an enterprise shared by retail owners. The ease of entry into retailing fosters competition and results in many new firms failing.

Different strategy mixes are used by convenience stores—well-situated, food-oriented retailers; conventional supermarkets—departmentalized food stores with minimum annual sales of $2 million; food-based superstores—diversified supermarkets that sell a broad range of food and nonfood items; combination stores (including supercentres)—outlets that go further than food-based superstores in carrying both food and general merchandise; specialty stores (including category killers)—outlets that concentrate on one merchandise or service line; variety stores—outlets selling a wide assortment of inexpensive and popularly priced merchandise; traditional department stores—outlets that have a great assortment, provide customer services, are fashion leaders, often dominate surrounding stores, and have average to above-average prices; full-line discount stores—department stores with a low-price, moderate-service orientation; membership warehouse clubs—stores that offer very low prices in austere settings; and other discounters—including limited-line stores and off-price chains.

Nonstore retailing occurs when a firm uses a strategy mix that is not store-based. Vending machines use coin- or card-operated machinery to dispense goods and services. Direct selling involves both personal contact with consumers in their homes (or other places) and phone solicitations initiated by retailers. Direct marketing occurs when consumers are exposed to goods and services through nonpersonal media and then order by mail, phone, or computer. Cybermalls and sales through Web sites are among the newest approaches to direct marketing. Nonstore retailing is now a large part of retailing.

3. *To explore five aspects of retail planning: store location, atmosphere, scrambled merchandising, the wheel of retailing, and technological advances* A firm may select from among three forms of store location: an isolated store—a freestanding outlet located on a highway or street; an unplanned business district—in which two or more stores locate close to one another without prior planning as to the number and composition of stores; and a planned shopping centre—which is centrally managed, as well as planned and operated as an entity. Only planned shopping centres utilize balanced tenancy, thus relating the store mix to consumer needs.

Atmosphere is the sum total of a store's physical characteristics that help develop an image and attract customers. It depends on the store's exterior, general interior, layout, and interior displays.

Scrambled merchandising occurs when a retailer adds products unrelated to its original business. The goals of scrambled merchandising are to encourage customer one-stop shopping, increase sales of high-profit items and impulse purchases, attract different target markets, and balance sales throughout the year.

The wheel of retailing explains low-end and high-end retail strategies and how they emerge. As low-cost, low-price innovators move along the wheel, they leave opportunities for newer, more cost-conscious firms to enter the market.

A number of technological advances have emerged over the past several years. These include computerized checkouts, video shopping services, data warehousing, computerized site selection, electronic banking, and techniques to improve operating efficiency.

4. *To define wholesaling and show its importance, and to describe the three broad categories of wholesaling (manufacturer/service provider wholesaling, merchant wholesaling, and agents and brokers)* Wholesaling involves the buying and/or handling of goods and services and their resale to organizational users, retailers, and/or other wholesalers but not the sale of significant volume to final consumers. In Canada, about 65 000 wholesale establishments distribute over $280 billion in goods and services annually.

Wholesale functions encompass distribution, personal selling, marketing and research assistance, gathering assortments, cost reductions, warehousing, financing, returns, and risk taking. These functions may be assumed by manufacturers/service providers or shared with independent wholesalers. The latter are sometimes in a precarious position because they are located between manufacturers/service providers and customers and must determine their responsibilities to each.

In manufacturer/service provider wholesaling, a producer undertakes all wholesaling functions itself. This form of wholesaling can be conducted through sales or branch offices. The sales office carries no inventory.

Merchant wholesalers buy, take title, and possess products for further resale. Full-service merchant wholesalers gather assortments of products, provide trade credit, store and deliver products, offer merchandising and promotion assistance, provide a personal sales force, offer research and planning support, and complete other functions as well. Limited-service merchant wholesalers take title to products but do not provide all wholesale functions.

Agents and brokers provide various wholesale tasks, such as negotiating purchases and expediting sales; but, they

do not take title. They are paid commissions or fees. Agents are used on a more permanent basis than brokers.

5. *To examine recent trends in retailing* The nature of retailing has changed dramatically in recent years. Among the key trends retailers are adapting to are those relating to consumer demographics and lifestyles, competitive forces, operating costs, the labour force, and international opportunities.

The nature of wholesaling has changed over the last several years. Trends involve the evolving wholesaler mix, productivity, customer service, international openings, and target markets.

KEY TERMS

retailing (p. 271)
wholesaling (p. 272)
independent retailer (p. 275)
retail chain (p. 275)
retail franchising (p. 275)
leased department (p. 275)
retail cooperative (p. 275)
retail store strategy mix (p. 276)
convenience store (p. 276)
conventional supermarket (p. 276)
food-based superstore (p. 277)
combination store (p. 278)
supercentre (p. 278)
specialty store (p. 278)
category killer (p. 278)
variety store (p. 278)
traditional department store (p. 279)

full-line discount store (p. 279)
membership warehouse club (p. 279)
nonstore retailing (p. 279)
vending machine (p. 279)
direct selling (p. 280)
direct marketing (p. 280)
isolated store (p. 281)
unplanned business district (p. 281)
planned shopping centre (p. 282)
atmosphere (p. 282)
scrambled merchandising (p. 282)
wheel of retailing (p. 283)
cybermalls (p. 284)
debit transactions (p. 285)
manufacturer/service provider wholesaling (p. 290)
wholesale merchants (p. 291)
full-service merchant wholesalers (p. 291)

limited-service merchant wholesalers (p. 291)
general-merchandise (full-line) wholesalers (p. 293)
specialty-merchandise (limited-line) wholesalers (p. 293)
rack jobbers (p. 293)
franchise wholesaling (p. 293)
wholesale cooperatives (p. 293)
cash-and-carry wholesaling (p. 293)
drop shippers (desk jobbers) (p. 293)
truck/wagon wholesalers (p. 294)
mail-order wholesalers (p. 294)
agents (p. 295)
brokers (p. 295)
manufacturers'/service providers' agents (p. 296)
selling agents (p. 296)
commission (factor) merchants (p. 296)
food brokers (p. 296)
commercial stock brokers (p. 296)

Review Questions

1. Describe the four basic functions performed by retailers.
2. Differentiate between selling to a wholesaler and selling through a wholesaler.
3. What are the benefits of retail franchising to the franchisee? To the franchiser?
4. Why would a store want to have leased shoe departments rather than operate these departments itself?
5. Under what circumstances should a manufacturer or service provider undertake wholesaling?
6. Distinguish between direct marketing and direct selling. Which has greater sales? Why?

7. Distinguish between limited-service merchant wholesalers and full-service merchant wholesalers.
8. Explain the wheel of retailing from the perspective of the battle between traditional department stores and full-line discount stores for market share.
9. How do manufacturers'/service providers' agents and selling agents differ?
10. Why is attracting and retaining a quality labour force so difficult for many Canadian retailers?

Discussion Questions

1. The typical retailer earns a profit of three per cent or less on its sales revenues. How can this amount be so low if 38 to 40 cents of every customer dollar spent in department stores and specialty stores go to the retailers?

2. As a prospective franchisee for a Robin's Donuts outlet, what criteria would you use in deciding whether Robin's Donuts is right for you? What criteria do you think Robin's Donuts should use in assessing potential franchisees? Explain the differences in your answers to these two questions.

3. "Wholesalers are very much in the middle, often not fully knowing whether their first allegiance should be to the manufacturer/service provider or the customer." Comment on this statement. Can wholesalers rectify this situation? Why or why not?

4. Develop a short checklist that Malofilm Communications Inc. (see the *International Marketing* box in this chapter) could use in determining whether to use merchant wholesalers or agents/brokers in different countries around the world to distribute its videocassette movies intended for retail sale.

5. Select a planned shopping centre near your college or university and evaluate it with respect to its size and the size of its trading area. (Note that the term "size" can have several definitions—take as many of them into account as possible when answering this question.)

PROMOTION

PLANNING

Part 5 covers the third major element of the marketing mix, promotion.

11 Promotion Planning and Personal Selling

Here, we broadly discuss promotion planning, which involves all communication used to inform, persuade, and/or remind people about an organization's or individual's goods, services, image, ideas, community involvement, or impact on society. We describe the basic types of promotion and the stages in a channel of communication. Next, we present the steps in developing an overall promotion plan, international promotion considerations, the legal environment, and criticisms of promotion. We also focus on personal selling, one of the four types of promotion. We define personal selling as oral communication with one or more prospective buyers by paid representatives for the purpose of making sales. We describe the scope, characteristics, and stages of planning for personal selling.

12 Advertising, Public Relations and Sales Promotion

In this chapter, we examine three of the four types of promotion: advertising, public relations, and sales promotion. We define advertising as paid, nonpersonal communication by an identified sponsor; public relations as any form of image-directed communication by an identified sponsor or the independent media; and sales promotion as the paid marketing communication activities (other than advertising, publicity, or personal selling) that stimulate consumer purchases and dealer effectiveness. We detail the scope of advertising, public relations, and sales promotion and their attributes. We discuss the development of advertising, public relations, and sales promotion plans in depth.

Part 5 Vignette
Promotion: Stimulating Marketplace Demand with Information

Promotion involves communicating information to help people find goods and help marketers find customers. In addition, it establishes and reinforces the product positioning image that has been selected for a good or service. In Part 5 you will be introduced to the four basic types of promotion: personal selling, advertising, public relations, and sales promotion. Chapter 11 deals with promotion theory, such as the use of promotion in image positioning. Image positioning is being employed by Canadian banks, which have been enjoying record profits throughout the mid-1990s. The Canadian public views this negatively given that these profits have occurred at a time when banks have been instituting transaction fees, paying low deposit interest rates, and charging high interest rates on credit cards. As a result, a lot of people feel that banks are greedy and untrustworthy. Aware of their image problems, Canadian banks have been employing public relations and advertising campaigns, and changing their way of doing business, to be more customer oriented. The Bank of Montreal took one of the most innovative approaches with their campaign slogan of "It Is Possible."™

Chapter 11 also introduces us to one of the four types of promotion, personal selling. The nature of the selling task is exemplified by Craig Procter, a RE/MAX real estate agent in Newmarket, Ontario. A top performing salesperson, Procter exemplifies how real estate agents work to create both ends of a home sale transaction. Agents must find sellers, who pay their commissions, and buyers, from whose proceeds the seller pays the agent. Procter believes that the first key to success in real estate sales involves creating awareness and interest in the agent's name. To make his name and real estate synonymous, Procter puts his name on billboards, bus shelters and bus stop benches, and on special promotional materials such as key chains, pens, pencils, business cards, and even plastic milk jugs! He also provides people in Newmarket with a toll free line to make personal calls to Toronto. The "catch" in this goodwill freebie is that before the call can be completed, the caller must listen to a Craig Procter phone pitch. The second key to his successful selling involves a "team" approach. Procter hires telemarketers and door-knockers who call people to see if they are thinking of selling their homes. When he gets a listing, Procter has a customer-service agent contact sellers and let them know how their homes are being perceived by potential buyers. Finally, Procter hires associate agents who work for him and do the basic tasks so he can be free to sign up new listings and present offers on homes. A salesperson functions as a source of personal communication of information, but the basic objective of helping customers find goods that fulfil their needs and wants remains, regardless of the form of communication.

Chapter 12 presents the three other types of promotion: advertising, public relations, and sales promotion. Creating advertising commercials as part of an advertising campaign is one of the topics featured in this chapter. Recently, Radio Shack developed a Canadian television campaign based on the theme "'This Place Is Completely Wired." Advertising agent Vaughan Weilland was hired to create a high-impact, humorous campaign as part of a pre-Christmas promotional effort. Weilland believes that effective advertising involves using humorous ads that cut through the clutter and command attention among an overexposed audience. For the Radio Shack ads, Weilland had comedian Peter McCormick create impromptu humorous situation ads built around the slogan "This Place Is Completely Wired." The use of improvisation and on-site filming is an extremely risky approach to take in advertising, and resulted in some very unusual circumstances for McCormick and Weilland. However, this approach also produced entertaining advertising.

> *Communicating information to help customers find goods and help marketers find customers is what promotion is all about.*

 CBC "Craig Procter"

CHAPTER 11

Promotion Planning and Personal Selling

Chapter Objectives

1 To define promotion planning and show its importance

2 To describe the general characteristics of advertising, public relations, personal selling, and sales promotion

3 To explain the channel of communication and how it functions

4 To examine the components of a promotion plan, international promotion considerations, the legal environment, and criticisms and defences of promotion

5 To examine the scope, importance, and characteristics of personal selling

6 To study the elements in a personal selling plan

{ *You have to have something that sets you apart from the competition— whether it be a particular product, quality, or service. And, burned by the foibles of human celebrity spokespeople, more and more companies are turning their corporate images (and fortunes) over to animated characters. After all, you have almost no chance of being embarrassed by Fred Flintstone, the Pink Panther, or Snoopy. These characters can help you maintain visibility, to stay favourably in the public eye.* }

Reprinted by permission.

OWENS-CORNING

www.owenscorning.com/

In particular, says John Lister (chief executive officer of Lister Butler, a corporate and brand identity consultant), animated characters can bring warmth and feeling to an otherwise boring category of products: "The goal of using a cartoon is to complement the product, not eclipse it, take top billing, or conflict with the intended message." Let's look at how Owens-Corning and Metropolitan Life use animated characters—the Pink Panther and the *Peanuts* group of figures—in their advertising programs.

For a decade and a half, Owens-Corning has utilized the Pink Panther in ads for its insulation products. The character is especially effective in reassuring people that insulating their attics is a task they can easily accomplish. This is an important message since marketing research studies have found that many consumers view this project as too difficult for the typical do-it-yourselfer.

The Pink Panther is a natural communicator because of its affable nature and colour. And Owens-Corning is the only firm that markets a pink-coloured insulation. The Pink Panther-based campaign is instrumental in allowing Owens-Corning to maintain an eight-to-one brand preference over its closest competitor. According to John Lister, Owens-Corning's success is due to the "masterful job of integrating the character into the product's identity."

In the mid-1980s, Metropolitan Life Insurance chose to hire *Peanuts* characters to help generate more warmth and feeling toward the company and its products. As a Metropolitan Life account executive noted, "We wanted to convey a warm and friendly personality, which we think we have. The characters convey a kind of trust and goodwill."

The MetLife *Peanuts* campaign continues to this day, with the characters used in everything from print media to TV ads. The firm believes the feelings that the *Peanuts* characters engender, "particularly of security," are a part of the insurance firm's solid positioning in the marketplace.

As with live actors, a company using animated characters as endorsers needs to safeguard its interests. A major concern is that a popular character could be used in so many product categories that its image becomes blurry. To avert this potential problem, MetLife has "an exclusive in the financial services market." According to a senior vice-president at Young & Rubicam, the advertising agency that handles the MetLife account, "We have an equity in the characters, and we can't afford to have that equity diluted."[1]

In this chapter, we will study many dimensions of promotion planning, including the usefulness of celebrities (human or animated) as sources in the channel of communication. Our discussion will also cover how the channel of communication works and the roles of the source, encoding, the message, the media, decoding, the audience, and feedback. Finally, we will study personal selling, which is one of the four basic types of promotion marketers can employ.

Overview

Promotion is any communication used to inform, persuade, and/or remind people about an organization's or individual's goods, services, image, ideas, community involvement, or impact on society. **Promotion planning** is systematic decision making relating to all aspects of an organization's or individual's communications efforts.

Communication occurs through brand names, packaging, company marquees and displays, personal selling, customer service, trade shows, sweepstakes, and messages in mass media (such as newspapers, television, radio, direct mail, billboards, magazines, and transit). It can be company sponsored or controlled by independent media. Messages may emphasize information, persuasion, fear, sociability, product performance, humour, and/or comparisons with competitors.

In this chapter, the context of promotion planning is provided. Included are discussions on promotion's importance, the basic promotion types, the channel of communication, promotion planning, international considerations, the legal environment, and general criticisms and defences of promotion. This chapter also looks at one of the major promotion forms: personal selling. Personal selling involves oral communication with one or more prospective buyers by paid representatives for the purpose of making sales. It relies on personal contact, unlike advertising and the publicity aspect of public relations. Its goals are similar to other promotion forms: informing, persuading, and/or reminding. Chapter 12 covers advertising, public relations, and sales promotion.

*Promotion planning focuses on a total **promotion** effort—informing, persuading, and reminding.*

Personal selling is one-on-one with buyers. Sales promotion includes paid supplemental efforts.

The Importance of Promotion

Promotion is a key element of the marketing mix. For new products, people must be informed about items and their features before they can develop favourable attitudes toward them. For products with some consumer awareness, the focus is on persuasion: converting knowledge to preference. For very popular products, the focus is on reminding: reinforcing existing consumer beliefs.

The people and/or organizations to whom a firm's promotional efforts are aimed may fall into various categories: consumers, shareholders, consumer advocacy groups, government, channel members, employees, competitors, and the general public. Firms often communicate with each of these audiences, not just with consumers. In addition, communication with each may be different because each category has distinct goals, knowledge, and needs.

Within an audience category (like consumers), a firm needs to identify and appeal to opinion leaders—those who influence others' decisions. It also should understand **word-of-mouth communication**, the process by which people express opinions and product-related experiences to one another. Unless a product or service has a sustained positive word-of-mouth reputation, it is hard to succeed.[2]

Word-of-mouth communication *occurs as people state opinions to others.*

[1]Christine Unruh, "Snap, Crackle, Pop," *Journal of Business Strategy*, Vol. 16 (March–April 1995), pp. 39–43.
[2]See Paula Fitzgerald Bone, "Word-of-Mouth Effects on Short-Term and Long-Term Product Judgments," *Journal of Business Research*, Vol. 32 (March 1995), pp. 213–223; and Chip Walker, "Word of Mouth," *American Demographics* (July 1995), pp. 38–44.

T a b l e 1 1 - 1

The Value of Promotion

PROMOTION

- Establishes an image for a company and its goods and services.
- Communicates features of goods and services.
- Creates awareness for new goods and services.
- Keeps existing goods and services popular.
- Can reposition the images or uses of faltering goods and services.
- Generates enthusiasm from channel members.
- Notes where goods and services can be purchased.
- Can persuade consumers to trade up from one product to a more expensive one.
- Alerts consumers to sales.
- Justifies (rationalizes) the prices of goods and services.
- Answers consumer questions.
- Closes transactions.
- Provides service for consumers after transactions are completed.
- Reinforces loyal consumers.
- Places the firm and its goods and services in a favourable light, relative to competitors.

A company's promotion plan usually stresses individual goods and services, with the intent of moving people from awareness to purchase. Yet the firm may also convey its overall image (industry innovator), views on ideas (nuclear energy), community service (funding a new hospital), or impact on society (the size of its workforce). Table 11-1 shows many valuable promotion functions.

A good promotion plan complements the product, distribution, and price aspects of the marketing mix. For example, Waterman—a maker of pens—distributes its products to finer stores and sets premium prices. It advertises in magazines such as *Canadian Business*, and expects retailers to provide first-rate personal selling. Ads are in colour and refer to product features, not prices. See Figure 11-1.

Well-conceived promotion plans are feasible even if companies have limited resources. For instance:

> Until 1989, Straight Arrow Products, a twenty-five-year old company, couldn't afford to do much marketing. Sales at the time were only $675 000 annually. Fast-forward five years: Sales reached $67 million and current owner W. Roger Dunavant was running a $4.8 million ad campaign. What happened? During 1989, without a bundle to spend on advertising, Dunavant (then the firm's director of sales and marketing) began to hit the road to sell the company's wares. The goods: grooming products that horse owners use on their animals—and themselves. The strategy: play up the novelty for all it was worth. Dunavant attended horse shows and handed out samples of Mane 'n Tail shampoo and conditioner and a cream called Hoofmaker (for equestrians' hands, not feet). He encouraged horse owners to use Mane 'n Tail on both themselves and their horses. One person he met at a show turned out to be a radio announcer who invited him for an interview. Once the show aired, other journalists from print and radio began calling. Dunavant bought Straight Arrow in 1993. He handled his own bookings until that year, when he hired a public relations firm. In 1994 alone, he gave 140 radio interviews. The result: skyrocketing sales and *Wall Street Journal* coverage.[3]

INTERNATIONAL ADVERTISING ASSOCIATION

www.iaaglobal.org

Promotion's importance is also evident from the expenditures and jobs it generates. The world's fifty largest advertising agencies have overall annual billings of U.S.$20 billion. The International Advertising Association's thousands of members are from ninety nations. In Canada alone, each year, business firms spend about $9 billion on media adver-

---

[3]Jeffrey A. Tannenbaum, "Priceless Promotions," *Wall Street Journal* (May 22, 1995), p. R20.

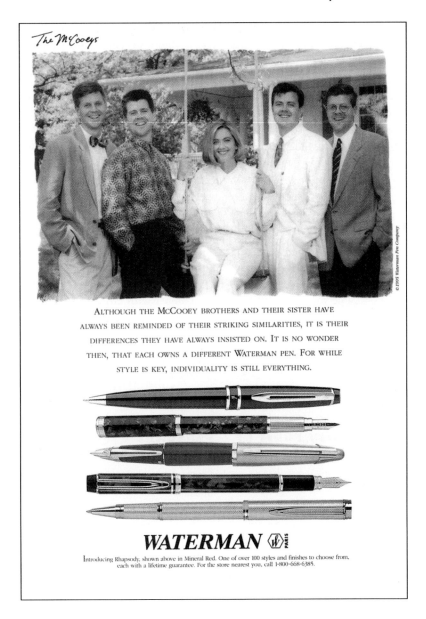

FIGURE 11-1
The Consistent, High-Quality Promotional Emphasis of Waterman Pens
Reprinted by permission of Waterman.

tising; 1.3 million people work in sales; 17.1 billion coupons are given out; and Canadian firms participate in the 4000 North American trade shows.[4]

Types of Promotion

In their communications programs, organizations use one or more of four basic types of promotion:

- **Advertising** is paid, nonpersonal communication regarding goods, services, organizations, people, places, and ideas that is transmitted through various media by business firms, government, and other nonprofit organizations, and individuals who are identified in the advertising message as the sponsor. The message is generally controlled by the sponsor.

Advertising, public relations (publicity), personal selling, *and* **sales promotion** *are the four key promotion types.*

[4]Statistics Canada, *1995 Market Research Handbook* (Ottawa: Minister of Supply and Services Canada), p. 164; Jim McElgunn, "CARD Releases New Figures on Ad Spending," *Marketing Magazine* (September 25, 1995), p. 6; Lara Mills, "In-ad Promos Lift Total Coupon Distribution," *Marketing Magazine* (February 12, 1996), p. 2; "The 1995 Annual Report on the Promotion Industry," *Promo Magazine's SourceBook '96*, p. 15; and Srinath Gopalakrishna, Gary L. Lilien, Jerome D. Williams, and Ian K. Sequeira, "Do Trade Shows Pay Off?" *Journal of Marketing*, Vol. 59 (July 1995), p. 75.

- **Public relations** includes any communication to foster a favourable image for goods, services, organizations, people, places, and ideas among their publics—such as consumers, investors, government, channel members, employees, and the general public. It may be nonpersonal or personal, paid or nonpaid, and sponsor controlled or not controlled. **Publicity** is the form of public relations that entails nonpersonal communication passed on through various media but not paid for by an identified sponsor. Wording and placement of publicity messages are generally media controlled.

- **Personal selling** involves oral communication with one or more prospective buyers by paid representatives for the purpose of making sales.

- **Sales promotion** involves paid marketing communication activities (other than advertising, publicity, or personal selling) that are intended to stimulate consumer purchases and dealer effectiveness. Included are trade shows, premiums, incentives, giveaways, demonstrations, and various other efforts not in the ordinary promotion routine.[5]

The general characteristics of each type of promotion are shown in Table 11-2. As discussed later in the chapter, many firms in some way combine them into an integrated promotional blend. This lets them reach their entire target market, present both persuasive and believable messages, have personal contact with customers, sponsor special events, and balance the promotional budget.

T a b l e   1 1 - 2
Characteristics of Promotional Types

FACTOR	ADVERTISING	PUBLICITY FORM OF PUBLIC RELATIONS[a]	PERSONAL SELLING	SALES PROMOTION
Audience	Mass	Mass	Small (one-to-one)	Varies
Message	Uniform	Uniform	Specific	Varies
Cost	Low per viewer or reader	None for media space and time; can be some costs for media releases and publicity materials	High per customer	Moderate per customer
Sponsor	Company	No formal sponsor in that media are not paid	Company	Company
Flexibility	Low	Low	High	Moderate
Control over content and placement	High	None (controlled by media)	High	High
Credibility	Moderate	High	Moderate	Moderate
Major goal	To appeal to a mass audience at a reasonable cost, and to create awareness and favourable attitudes	To reach a mass audience with an independently reported message	To deal with individual consumers, to resolve questions, to close sales	To stimulate short-run sales, to increase impulse purchases
Example	Television ad for a Sony CD player for use in cars	Magazine article describing the unique features of a Sony CD player for cars	Retail sales personnel explaining how a Sony CD player for cars works	A Sony CD player for cars exhibited at trade shows

[a] When public relations embodies advertising (an image-related message), personal selling (a salesperson describing the firm's public service efforts to college students), and/or sales promotion (distributing special discount coupons to low-income consumers), it takes on the characteristics of those promotional types. However, the goal would be more image-related than sales-related.

[5]Adapted by the authors from Peter D. Bennett (Ed.) *Dictionary of Marketing Terms*, Second Edition (Chicago: American Marketing Association, 1995), pp. 6, 206, 231, 232, and 253.

The Channel of Communication

To develop a proper promotion mix and interact effectively with a target audience, the **channel of communication (communication process)** shown in Figure 11-2 must be understood. Through such a channel, a source develops a message, transmits it to an audience by some medium, and gets feedback from the audience. The components of a communication channel are discussed next.

A message is sent to an audience through a **channel of communication**.

The Source

The **source** of communication is usually a company, an independent institution, or an opinion leader seeking to present a message to an audience. A firm communicates through a spokesperson, celebrity, actor playing a role, representative consumer, and/or salesperson.

A **source** *presents a message.*

A company spokesperson is typically a long-time employee who represents the firm in communications. The spokesperson has an aura of sincerity, commitment, and expertise. Sometimes, the spokesperson is a top executive, such as Loblaws' Dave Nichol, who pitched President's Choice products for years. Other times, front-line employees are used, such as a Shoppers Drug Mart pharmacist or a sales clerk from the Subway Sandwich shop. In general, this source has been quite effective.

A celebrity is used when the goal is to gain the audience's attention and improve product awareness. Problems can arise if the celebrity is perceived as insincere or unknowledgeable. Popular celebrities include hockey player Wayne Gretzky for Sharp, basketball player Michael Jordan for Nike, singer Céline Dion for the Bay, sprinter Donovan Bailey for Air Canada, and Snoopy and other *Peanuts* characters for Metropolitan Life Insurance.

Many ads have actors playing roles rather than celebrity spokespeople. In these commercials, the emphasis is on presenting a message about a good, service, or idea—rather than on the consumer recognizing a celebrity. The hope is that the consumer will learn more about product attributes.

A representative consumer is one who likes a product and recommends it in an ad. The person is shown with his or her name and hometown. The intent is to present a real consumer in an actual situation. A hidden camera or blind taste test is often used with this source. Today, viewers are more skeptical about how representative the endorser is.

Finally, a firm may use a salesperson to communicate with consumers. Many salespeople are knowledgeable, assertive, and persuasive. However, consumers may doubt their objectivity and tactics. Auto salespeople rate particularly low in consumer surveys.

An independent institution is not controlled by the firms on which it reports. It presents information in a professional, nonpaid (by the firms) manner. The Canadian Automobile Association and the local newspaper restaurant critic are examples of independent sources. They have great credibility for their readers because they discuss both good and bad points, but some segments of the population may not be exposed to these sources. The information presented may differ from that contained in a firm's commercials or sales-force presentations.

HUDSON'S BAY COMPANY

www.sd35.bc.ca/schools/ae/FL/hbc.html

CANADIAN AUTOMOBILE ASSOCIATION (BC)

www.caa.ca

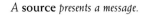

FIGURE 11-2
A Channel of Communication

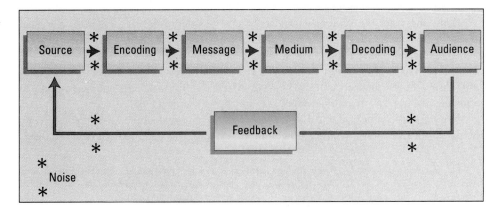

An opinion leader is a person who has face-to-face contact with and influences other potential consumers. Because he or she deals on a personal level, an opinion leader often has strong persuasive impact and believability; and he or she can offer social acceptance for followers. Thus, firms often address initial messages to opinion leaders, who then provide word-of-mouth communication to others. Many marketers believe opinion leaders not only influence, but also are influenced by, others (opinion receivers); even opinion leaders need approval for their choices.

In assessing a source, these questions are critical:

- Is the source believable?
- Is the source convincing?
- Does the source present an image consistent with the firm?
- Do consumers value the message of the source?
- Is the source seen as knowledgeable?
- Does the source complement the product he/she communicates about—or overwhelm it?
- Do significant parts of the market dislike the source?

Encoding

In **encoding**, *a source translates a thought into a message.*

Encoding is the process whereby a thought or idea is translated into a message by the source. At this stage, preliminary decisions are made as to message content, such as the use of symbolism and wording. It is vital that the thought or idea be translated exactly as the source intends. For example, a firm wanting to stress its product's prestige would include the concepts of status, exclusive ownership, and special features in a message. It would not emphasize a price lower than competitors, availability in discount stores, or the millions of people who have already purchased.

The Message

A **message** *combines words and symbols.*

A **message** is a combination of words and symbols transmitted to an audience. Its thrust depends on whether a firm's goal is to inform, persuade, or remind its audience. Almost all messages include some information on the company name, the product name, the desired image, differential advantages, and product attributes. A firm would also give information about availability and price at some point during the consumer's decision process.

Most communication involves one-sided messages, in which only the benefits of a good, service, or idea are cited. Fewer firms use two-sided messages, in which both benefits and limitations are noted. Firms are not anxious to point out their shortcomings, although consumer perceptions of honesty may be improved by two-sided messages. For example, in June 1996, Standard Life ran an ad in *Canadian Business* admitting they were headquartered in Scotland and had not been listed as one of the top insurance companies in Canada. However, the ad pointed out that the rankings of Canadian firms included worldwide assets, while foreign firms were ranked only by their Canadian assets. Standard Life's ad stated they had $90 billion in assets and that Canadian policyholders were fully protected.[6]

Many messages use symbolism and try to relate safety, social acceptance, or sexual appeal to a purchase. In symbolic messages, a firm stresses psychological benefits rather than tangible product performance. Clothing ads may offer acceptance by peers; and toothpaste may brighten teeth and make a person more sexually attractive. One type of symbolism, the use of fear appeals, has had mixed results. Although people respond to moderate fear appeals, strong messages may not be as well received:

Fear appeals can be useful. Ads alerting people to potential natural resource depletion, the danger of forest fires, ramifications of drunk driving, and the potential health hazards

---

[6]Ayn E. Crowley and Wayne D. Hoyer, "An Integrative Framework for Understanding Two-Sided Persuasion," *Journal of Consumer Research*, Vol. 20 (March 1994), p. 561; and Advertisement for Standard Life, "We're All For Comparisons . . . But Not of Apples and Oranges," *Canadian Business* (June 1996), p. 147.

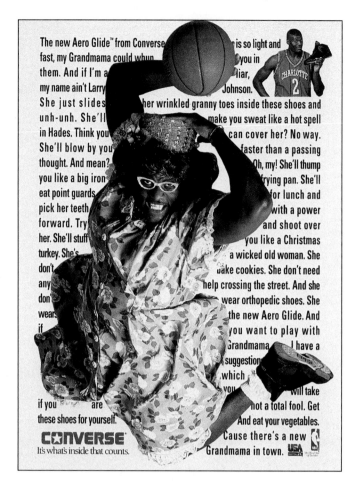

of permissive sexual behaviour are examples. The public good and advertisers' self-interest are compatible. In addition, these ads have an educational value that may prove useful over an extended period. However, marketers must avoid creating too much anxiety or discomfort among recipients, or the message may backfire.[7]

Humour is sometimes used to gain audience attention and retain it. Two popular examples are the Leon's Furniture "Ho, Ho, Hold The Payments" commercials and NBA basketball player Larry Johnson as "Grandma" in Converse shoe ads. However, a firm needs to be careful to get across the intended message when using humour—which should not make fun of the company, its goods, or its services; and humour should not dominate a message so the brand name or product's attributes go unnoticed. Figure 11-3 shows a Larry Johnson ad. Figure 11-4 is a Netherlands Vegetarian Council ad. Because humour has cultural underpinnings, the Dutch ad would probably not work well in North America, and it is likely that the Larry Johnson ad would not be appreciated in the Netherlands.

Comparative messages implicitly or explicitly contrast a firm's offerings with those of competitors. Implicit comparisons use an indirect brand X or leading brand approach ("Our industrial glues are more effective than other leading brands"). Explicit comparisons use a direct approach (such as the Nissan print ad, "We can see by your face that you've priced the new Camry from Toyota"). Comparative messages, in one form or another, are used in various TV and radio commercials, print ads, and other media. In addition, sales-

Comparative messages *position a firm in relation to its competitors.*

[7]Michael S. LaTour and Shaker A. Zahra, "Fear Appeals as Advertising Strategy: Should They Be Used?" *Journal of Consumer Marketing*, Vol. 6 (Spring 1989), p. 67. See also Tony L. Henthorne, Michael S. LaTour, and Rajan Nataraajan, "Fear Appeals in Print Advertising: An Analysis of Arousal and Ad Response," *Journal of Advertising*, Vol. 22 (June 1993), pp. 59–69; and James B. Hunt, John F. Tanner, Jr., and David P. Eppright, "Forty Years of Fear Appeal Research: Support for the Ordered Protection Motivation Model," in David W. Stewart and Naufel J. Vilcassim (Eds.), *1995 AMA Winter Educators' Proceedings* (Chicago: American Marketing Association, 1995), pp. 147–153.

FIGURE 11-4
A Humorous Dutch Ad: Feel Human Again, Eat Vegetarian
Reprinted by permission.

people often compare their products' attributes with competitors'. When using comparative messages, a firm has to be quite careful not to turn off consumers, place too much emphasis on a competitor's brand, or lose sight of its own differential advantages that should be promoted.

A message must be presented in a desirable, exclusive, and believable way. The good, service, or idea must be perceived as something worth buying or accepting. It also must be seen as unique to the seller—that is, it cannot be gotten elsewhere. Finally, the message must make believable claims.

Massed *or* distributed promotion *and the* **wearout rate** *must be carefully planned.*

Message timing must also be carefully planned. First, during what times of the year should a firm advertise, seek publicity, add salespeople, or run sales promotions? In **massed promotion**, communication efforts are concentrated in peak periods, like holidays. In **distributed promotion**, communication efforts are spread throughout the year. Figure 11-5 compares massed and distributed promotion.

Second, the **wearout rate**—the time it takes for a message to lose its effectiveness—must be determined. Some messages wear out quickly; others last for years. The wearout rate depends on the frequency of communications, message quality, the number of different messages used by a firm, and other factors. Ford has done such a good job with its "Quality is Job 1" message that it is still strong after many years.

The Medium

A medium *is a personal or nonpersonal channel for a message.*

The **medium** is the personal or nonpersonal means used to send a message. Personal media are company salespeople and other representatives, as well as opinion leaders. Nonpersonal (mass) media include newspapers, television, radio, direct mail, billboards, magazines, and transit.

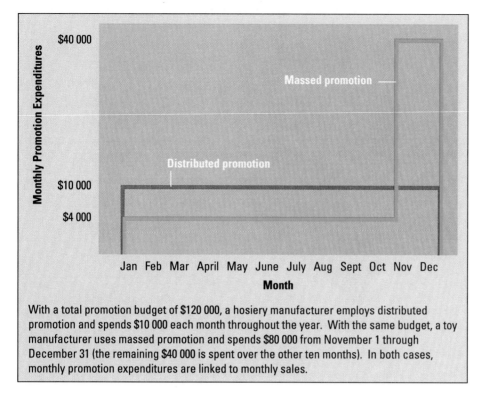

With a total promotion budget of $120 000, a hosiery manufacturer employs distributed promotion and spends $10 000 each month throughout the year. With the same budget, a toy manufacturer uses massed promotion and spends $80 000 from November 1 through December 31 (the remaining $40 000 is spent over the other ten months). In both cases, monthly promotion expenditures are linked to monthly sales.

FIGURE 11-5
Massed Versus Distributed Promotion

Personal media offer one-to-one audience contact. They are flexible, can adapt messages to individual needs, and can answer questions. They appeal to a small audience and are best with a concentrated market. Nonpersonal media have a large audience and low per-customer costs. They are not as flexible and dynamic as one-to-one contacts. They work best with a dispersed target market.

In deciding between personal and nonpersonal media, a firm should consider both total and per-unit costs, product complexity, audience attributes, and communication goals. The two kinds of media go well together since nonpersonal media generate consumer interest and personal media help close sales.

Decoding

Decoding is the process by which a message sent by a source is interpreted by an audience. The interpretation is based on the audience's background, and on the clarity and complexity of the message. For example, a woman who works in the home and a woman who works in an office might have different interpretations of a message on the value of child-care centres. Usually, as symbolism and complexity increase, clarity decreases. "*National Geographic*: Connect. Convince." is not as understandable a message as "Yellow Pages. It Pays. We'll Prove It." As noted earlier, it is essential that a message be decoded in the manner intended by the source (encoding = decoding). Is the business-to-business ad depicted in Figure 11-6 too provocative or merely attention grabbing? Is the serious message buried in the imagery or quite clear to the targeted audience?

Subliminal advertising is a highly controversial kind of promotion because it does not enable the audience to consciously decode a message. Instead, visual or verbal messages are presented so quickly that people do not see, hear, or remember them. Yet, the assumption is that they will buy goods and services because of subconscious impulses stimulated by these messages. The overwhelming evidence shows that subliminal ads cannot get people to buy things they do not want. In addition, subliminal ads are often misinterpreted; clear, well-labelled ads are much more effective. In Canada subliminal advertising is illegal.[8]

*In **decoding**, the audience translates the message sent by the source.*

Subliminal advertising *aims at a consumer's subconscious.*

[8] See Carl L. Witte, Madhavan Parthasarathy, and James W. Gentry, "Subliminal Perception Versus Subliminal Persuasion: A Re-Examination of the Basic Issues," in Barbara B. Stern and George M. Zinkham (Eds.), *1995 AMA Educators' Proceedings* (Chicago: American Marketing Association, 1995), pp. 133–138.

TAKE TWO AND CALL US IN THE MORNING. Healthcare professionals take

Polaroid photos with healthy results. Our GridFilm is used to measure and enhance written descriptions

of wounds. Our MicroCam instantly records microscopic specimens. We've even created an imaging

system that's revolutionizing radiology departments. If your business needs to document information stat,

call 1-800-348-5287, ext.793 for a free brochure. Until you know what we can

do for your business, you haven't seen the whole picture. **Polaroid**

FIGURE 11-6
Is This Business-to-Business Ad Easily Decoded?
Reprinted by permission.

The Audience

The **audience** *is usually the target market, but it can also include others.*

An **audience** is the object of a source's message. In most marketing situations, it is the target market. However, a source may also want to communicate an idea, build an image, or give information to shareholders, independent media, the public, government officials, and others.

The way a communication channel is used by a firm depends on the size and dispersion of the audience, demographic and lifestyle audience traits, and the availability of appropriate media. Because the communication process should be keyed to the audience, AIDS prevention groups have had a tough time getting their message across to teens and young adults:

> Past AIDS-related public service announcements have defined the problem as one of HIV/AIDS awareness, the assumption being that once young people are aware of AIDS, they will be motivated to practice APBs (AIDS preventive behaviours). However, this definition is outdated. It is now evident that AIDS awareness has been accomplished among teens and young adults. They are already aware that sexual intercourse and IV drug use represent the major modes of AIDS transmission. The challenge facing communicators is how to convert AIDS awareness into APBs. Although there is some need to keep generic AIDS messages before the public, rudimentary information/awareness-based appeals are of little use to a market that knows the elementary facts or when there is little evidence that basic knowledge leads to adoption of APBs.[9]

And to make matters still tougher for marketers, a recent global consumer survey found that people are rather down on promotion messages:

- 72 per cent believe marketers exaggerate health benefits.
- 70 per cent do not believe marketers respect consumers' intelligence.

[9]Kristina D. Frankenberger and Ajay S. Sukhdial, "Segmenting Teens for AIDS Preventive Behaviors with Implications for Marketing Communications," *Journal of Public Policy & Marketing*, Vol. 13 (Spring 1994), p. 134.

- 70 per cent believe marketers brainwash children.
- 62 per cent do not believe marketers give accurate information.
- 55 per cent do not believe marketers sponsor worthwhile events.
- 40 per cent do not believe ads are creative and entertaining.[10]

Feedback

Feedback is the response an audience has to a message. It may be a purchase, an attitude change, or a nonpurchase. A firm must understand that each of these responses is possible and devise a way of monitoring them.

The most desirable kind of feedback occurs if a consumer buys a good or service (or accepts an idea) after communication with or from the firm. This means a message is effective enough to stimulate a transaction.

A second type of feedback takes place if a firm finds its promotion efforts elicit a favourable audience attitude toward it or its offerings. For new goods or services, positive attitudes must usually be formed before purchases (awareness → favourable attitude → purchase). With existing products, people may have bought another brand just before receiving a message or be temporarily out of funds; generating their favourable attitudes may lead to future purchases.

The least desirable feedback is if the audience neither makes a purchase nor develops a favourable attitude. This may happen for one of several reasons: The audience does not recall the message; the audience is content with another brand; the audience did not believe the message; or no differential advantage is perceived.

Feedback consists of purchase, attitude, or nonpurchase responses to a message.

Noise

Noise is interference at any point along a channel of communication. Because of it, messages are sometimes encoded or decoded incorrectly or weak audience responses are made. Examples of noise are:

Noise may interfere with the communication process at any stage.

- A phone call interrupting a company's marketing manager while he or she is developing a promotional theme.
- A salesperson misidentifying a product and giving incorrect information.
- An impatient customer interrupting a sales presentation.
- A conversation between two consumers during a TV commercial.
- A direct-mail ad being opened by the wrong person.
- A consumer seeing a sale on a competitor's item while waiting at an office-supply store's checkout counter.

Promotion Planning

After a firm gains an understanding of the communication process, it is ready to develop an overall promotion plan. Such a plan consists of three parts: objectives, budgeting, and the promotion mix.

Objectives

Promotion objectives can be divided into two main categories: stimulating demand and enhancing company image.

In setting demand goals, the **hierarchy-of-effects model** should be used. It outlines the sequential short-term, intermediate, and long-term promotion goals for a firm to pursue—and works in conjunction with the consumer's decision process that was discussed in Chapter 4:

*The **hierarchy-of-effects model** outlines demand goals.*

[10]Roper Starch, "The World's View of Marketers," *Advertising Age* (January 15, 1996), pp. I–10.

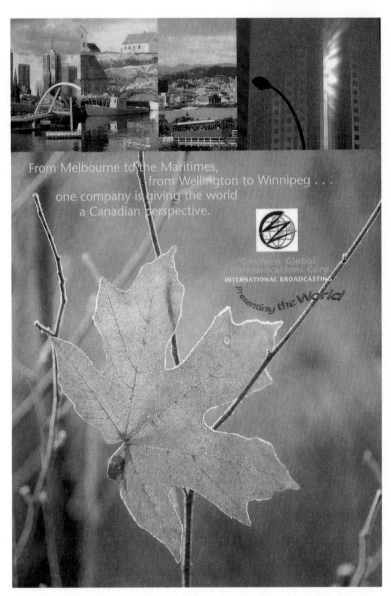

From Melbourne to the Maritimes, from Wellington to Winnipeg . . . one company is giving the world a Canadian perspective.

CanWest Global Communications Corp.
INTERNATIONAL BROADCASTING
Presenting the World

FIGURE 11-7
Institutional Advertising by CanWest Global Communications
Reprinted with permission of CanWest Global Communications Corp.

1. *Provide information*—Obtain consumer product recognition, then gain consumer knowledge of product attributes.
2. *Develop positive attitudes and feelings*—Obtain favourable attitudes, then gain preference for the company's brand(s) over those of competitors.
3. *Stimulate purchases and retain desires*—Obtain strong consumer preference, gain purchase of good or service, encourage continued purchases (brand loyalty).

By applying the hierarchy-of-effects model, a company can move from informing to persuading and then to reminding consumers about its offerings. At the early stages of the model, when a good or service is little known, **primary demand** should be sought. This is consumer demand for a product category. At later stages, with preference the goal, **selective demand** should be sought. This is consumer demand for a particular brand. Sometimes, organizations may try to sustain or revitalize interest in mature products and revert to a primary demand orientation. If promotion goals are image-oriented, a firm engages in public relations efforts—using suitable advertising, publicity, personal selling, and/or sales promotion (as noted in Table 11-2). **Institutional advertising** is used when the advertising goal is to enhance company image—and not to sell goods or services. This is illustrated in Figure 11-7, an ad for CanWest Global. Many of the leading advertisers in Canada run institutional ads.

Primary demand *is for a product category;* **selective demand** *is for a brand.*

Institutional advertising *is involved with image goals.*

International Marketing in

What Kind of Communication Strategy Should Be Used in Tanzania?

Tanzania, located in the southern tier of Africa, has a population of 30 million people. After years of socialism, high import restrictions, and very low per-capita income, conditions in Tanzania have recently improved. Several large firms have recently been drawn to Tanzania (such as PepsiCo, Coca-Cola, and Sterling Health)—based on the country's good resource base, stable political government, and fast-growing economy.

According to the executive chairman of ScanAd, Tanzania's largest advertising agency, when the company opened in 1990, "The Tanzanian population was literally starved of basic consumer needs. In the rural areas, people didn't know how to use toothpaste and they ate their bread dry."

Despite the recent growth, marketers in Tanzania still face various challenges. Tanzania's annual per-capita GDP is around U.S.$600. Total yearly advertising expenditures are currently under U.S.$3 million (versus U.S.$32 million in Kenya with a population of 26 million, and U.S.$30 million in Zimbabwe with a population of 14 million).

Promotional media are also very limited. For example, Radio Tanzania is the only real national medium because the country's two television stations only reach the two million inhabitants of Dar es Salaam. And though Tanzania's national literacy rate is about 45 per cent, its national newspaper's sales are hampered by its basic printing techniques and by road conditions so poor that newspapers can take four days to arrive. Even the most popular English-language daily newspaper, *The Daily News*, sells only 22 000 copies per day.

ScanAd does business in Tanzania with such large international clients as Swiss-Air, Toyota, and Sterling Health—while other agencies are content to plan advertising campaigns from nearby Nairobi, Kenya.

As the advertising manager for SwissAir (the international airline), develop a communication strategy to be used for the Tanzanian market.

Source: Based on material in Karen Yates, "Advertising's Heart of Darkness," *Advertising Age* (May 15, 1995), pp. I-10–I-15.

Budgeting

There are five basic ways to set a total promotion budget: all you can afford, incremental, competitive parity, percentage of sales, and objective and task. The choice depends on the requirements of the individual firm. Budgets can range from 1 to 5 per cent of sales for industrial-products firms to up to 20 to 30 per cent of sales for consumer-products firms.[11]

In the **all-you-can-afford method**, a firm first allots funds for other elements of marketing; any remaining marketing funds then go to the promotion budget. It is the weakest technique and used most often by small, production-oriented firms. It gives little importance to promotion, spending is not linked to goals, and there is a risk of having no promotion budget if finances are low.

With the **incremental method**, a company bases its new promotion budget on the previous one. A percentage is added to or subtracted from this year's budget to determine next year's. The technique is also used by small firms. It has these advantages: it gives the firm

Budgeting methods are **all you can afford, incremental, competitive parity, percentage of sales,** *and* **objective and task.**

[11]See Cyndee Miller, "Marketing Industry Report: Who's Spending What on Biz-to-Biz Marketing," *Marketing News* (January 1, 1996), pp. 1, 7.

a reference point, it bases the budget on a firm's feelings about past performance and future trends, and it is easy to calculate. Important disadvantages do exist: budget size is rarely tied to goals, "gut feelings" are overemphasized, and it is hard to evaluate success or failure.

In the **competitive parity method**, a firm's promotion budget is raised or lowered according to competitors' actions. It is useful to both large and small firms. The benefits are that it is keyed to a reference point, market-oriented, and conservative. The shortcomings are that it is a follower and not a leadership approach, it is difficult to get competitors' promotion data, and it assumes a similarity between the firm and its competitors (as to years in business, goods or services, image, prices, and so on) that may not exist.

With the **percentage-of-sales method**, a firm ties its promotion budget to sales revenue. In the first year, a promotion-to-sales ratio is set. During succeeding years, the ratio of promotion to sales dollars is constant. The benefits of this method are that it uses sales as a base, it is adaptable, and it links revenues and promotion. However, it bears no relation to promotion goals; promotion is a sales follower, not a sales leader; and promotion cuts occur in poor sales periods (when increases could help). The technique yields too large a budget in high sales periods and too small a budget in low sales periods.

Under the **objective-and-task method**, a firm sets promotion goals, determines the activities needed to satisfy them, and then establishes the proper budget. This is the best method. The advantages are that goals are clearly stated, spending is related to goal-oriented tasks, adaptability is offered, and it is easy to evaluate performance. The major weakness of objective and task is the complexity of setting goals and specific tasks, especially for small firms. Most large companies use some form of objective-and-task technique.

During promotional budgeting, a firm should keep the concept of marginal return in mind. The **marginal return** is the amount of sales each increment of promotion spending will generate. When a product is new, the marginal return is high because the market is expanding. When a product is established, the marginal return is lower because each additional increment of promotion has less of an impact on sales (due to a saturated target market).

The **marginal return** *is the sales generated by incremental promotional spending.*

The Promotion Mix

A **promotion mix** *somehow combines advertising, public relations, personal selling, and/or sales promotion. When done well,* **integrated marketing communications** *results.*

After establishing a total promotion budget, a company must determine its **promotion mix**. This is the firm's overall and specific communication program, including its involvement with advertising, public relations (publicity), personal selling, and/or sales promotion. Seldom does a company use just one type of promotion—such as a mail-order firm relying on ads, a hospital on publicity, or a flea-market vendor on selling. Typically, a promotion mix is used.

When a well-coordinated promotion mix is involved, a firm is undertaking **integrated marketing communications (IMC)**. An IMC program would be defined as one that "recognizes the value of a comprehensive plan that evaluates the strategic roles of a variety of communication disciplines—advertising, public relations, personal selling, and sales promotion—and combines them to provide clarity, consistency, and maximum communication impact."[12] For example, Frito-Lay has a sales force that visits every store stocking its products, advertises in papers and magazines and on TV, and distributes cents-off coupons. Hitachi has a large technical sales force, advertises in business and trade publications, and sends representatives to trade shows.

Each type of promotion has a distinct function and complements the other types. Ads appeal to big audiences and create awareness; without them, selling is more difficult, time-consuming, and costly. The publicity aspect of public relations provides credible information to a wide audience, but content and timing cannot be controlled. Selling has one-to-one contact, flexibility, and the ability to close sales; without it, the interest caused by ads might be wasted. Sales promotion spurs short-run sales and supplements ads and selling.

[12]Adapted by the authors from Janet Smith, "Integrated Marketing," *Marketing Tools* (November–December 1995), p. 64.

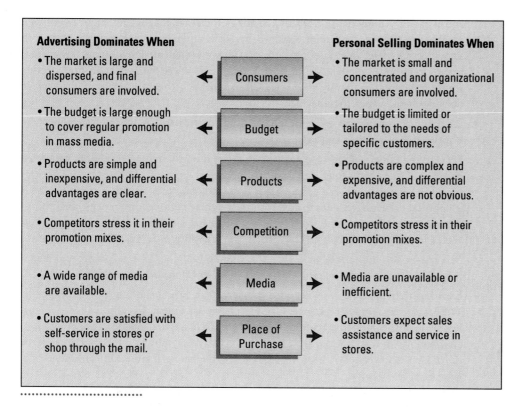

Advertising Dominates When		**Personal Selling Dominates When**
• The market is large and dispersed, and final consumers are involved.	Consumers	• The market is small and concentrated and organizational consumers are involved.
• The budget is large enough to cover regular promotion in mass media.	Budget	• The budget is limited or tailored to the needs of specific customers.
• Products are simple and inexpensive, and differential advantages are clear.	Products	• Products are complex and expensive, and differential advantages are not obvious.
• Competitors stress it in their promotion mixes.	Competition	• Competitors stress it in their promotion mixes.
• A wide range of media are available.	Media	• Media are unavailable or inefficient.
• Customers are satisfied with self-service in stores or shop through the mail.	Place of Purchase	• Customers expect sales assistance and service in stores.

FIGURE 11-8
Contrasting Promotion Mixes

The selection of a promotion mix depends on company attributes, the product life cycle, media access, and channel members. A small firm is limited in the kinds of ads it can afford or use efficiently; it may have to stress personal selling and a few sales promotions. A large firm covering a sizable geographic area could combine many ads, personal selling, and frequent sales promotions. As products move through the life cycle, promotion emphasis goes from information to persuasion to reinforcement; different media and messages are needed at each stage. Some media may not be accessible (no cigarette ads on TV) or require lengthy lead time (Yellow Pages). In addition, channel members may demand special promotions, sales support, and/or cooperative advertising allowances.

It is the job of a firm's marketing director (or vice-president) to set up a promotion budget and a promotion mix, as well as to allocate resources to each aspect of promotion. In large firms, there may be separate managers for advertising, public relations, personal selling, and sales promotion. They report to, and have their efforts coordinated by, the marketing director.

Figure 11-8 contrasts promotion mixes in which advertising and personal selling would dominate.

International Promotion Considerations

International promotion decisions should not be made until each market is carefully studied.

While preparing a promotion strategy for foreign nations, the channel of communication, promotion goals, budgeting, and the promotion mix should be carefully reviewed as they pertain to each market.

With regard to the channel of communication, a firm should recognize that:

- Source recognition and credibility vary by nation or region. In Canada, celebrities who are popular in English Canada may not be popular in Quebec. For example, Sprint Canada was using Candace Bergen as their advertising spokesperson in both languages. Candace Bergen was married to the late French film director Louis Malle and is fluently bilingual in both of Canada's official languages. Yet she was not well received in Quebec so Sprint replaced her with three spokespersons who are well known in Quebec: Jean-Luc Brassard, an Olympic gold medal-winning aerial skier; actor Dominique Michel; and Jacques Languirand, a well-known radio host. Actors from Hollywood are rarely received well in Quebec: "they always look like they've been dubbed, even if they haven't."[13]

- Encoding messages can be quite challenging, particularly if the messages must be translated into another language.

- Because the effects of message symbolism depend on the nation or region, care must be taken if fear, humorous, and/or sexual messages are used. Themes have to correspond to local customs. For example, for firms targeting the Canadian youth market it is important that approaches to advertising recognize regional differences. "In Toronto there's more stress on uniformity. A key to teens is 'Let's be different together,' but there's less of that in Quebec. You'll see more flexibility in terms of being unique."[14]

- In some locales, few residents have TVs, a limited number of newspapers and magazines are printed, and programs (channels) limit or do not accept ads.

- Ensuring that messages are decoded properly can be demanding: "To promote its Wash & Go shampoo, Procter & Gamble blanketed Polish TV and mailed samples. Poles found the dubbed ad culturally out of touch: It showed a woman popping out of a swimming pool and into a shower. 'We don't have swimming pools, and most of us don't have showers. We have baths,' sniffed Eugeniusz Smilowski, president of a Warsaw research group."[15]

- Making assumptions about audience traits in foreign markets without adequate research may lead to wrong assumptions: Western marketers entered the Indian market believing well-known brands would be accepted in India just like they had been accepted elsewhere. What they found out was that in India, "the consumer does not buy a global brand just because it is global. . . International brands have to be relevant in terms of perceived image, performance, and value if they are to succeed locally."[16]

- Global techniques for measuring promotion effectiveness are emerging.

In terms of promotion goals, budgeting, and the promotion mix, these points should be considered:

- For nations where a firm and its brands are unknown, a firm should have a series of promotion goals to lead people through the hierarchy-of-effects model. For nations in which a product category is new, primary demand must be created before selective demand is gained. To show goodwill, image ads may be even more important in foreign than in domestic markets.

- The promotion budgets in foreign countries must be keyed to the size of the markets and the activities required to succeed there. The objective-and-task method is highly recommended in setting international promotion budgets.

- Due to cultural, socioeconomic, infrastructure, and other differences, promotion mixes must be consistent with the countries served. In Western Europe, Germans listen to the radio most; the Dutch and British watch the most TV. And when Procter & Gamble mailed free samples (a form of sales promotion) of Wash & Go shampoo to people's homes in Poland, thieves broke into mailboxes to get the samples—which

[13]"Sprint Uses Local Stars in New Quebec Effort," *Marketing Magazine* (March 27, 1995), p. 3; and George Morris, "Homegrown Icons," *Marketing Magazine* (June 3, 1996), p. 14.

[14]Gail Chiasson, "Quebec 13 to 24," *Marketing Magazine* (February 20, 1995), p. 13.

[15]Gail E. Schares, "Colgate-Palmolive Is Really Cleaning Up in Poland," *Business Week* (March 15, 1993), p. 56.

[16]Tom Duncan, "Standardized Global Marketing Communication Campaigns Are Possible, They're Just Hard to Do," in Robert P. Leone and V. Kumar (Eds.), *1992 AMA Educators' Proceedings* (Chicago: American Marketing Association, 1992), p. 355; and Dilip Subramanian, "Western Marketers Join India's Economic Boom," *Marketing Magazine* (March 11, 1996), p. 5.

Table 11-3
Selected Canadian Regulations (Federal & Provincial) Affecting Promotion

MARKETING PRACTICE	LEGAL CONSIDERATIONS
Access to media	Cigarette, liquor, and drug manufacturers have restricted access.
Deception	It is illegal to make false statements or use messages that would mislead reasonable consumers and potentially harm them.
Bait-and-switch	It is illegal to lure a customer with an ad for a low-priced item and then, once the customer talks to a salesperson, to use a strong sales pitch intended to switch the shopper to a more expensive item.
Door-to-door selling	Many locales restrict door-to-door sales practices. A cooling-off period allows a person to cancel an in-home sale up to seven days after an agreement is reached.
Promotional allowances	Such allowances must be available to channel members in a fair and equitable manner.
Comparative advertisements	Claims must be substantiated. Federal and provincial regulators favour naming competitors in ads (not citing a competitor as brand X).
Testimonials or endorsements	A celebrity or expert endorser must actually use a product if he or she makes such a claim.
Contests	Advertisers must disclose the chances of winning and the manner in which prizes are to be distributed.

Source: Ed Ratushny, Q.C., "Report of the Consultative Panel on Amendments to the Competition Act," *Strategis*, Industry Canada, http://strategis.ic.gc.ca. Ottawa: Competition Bureau (April 15, 1996); and Keith J. Tuckwell, *Canadian Advertising, Third Edition*, Prentice-Hall: Scarborough, Ontario, (1995), pp. 20, 635–654.

they resold. As a Procter & Gamble manager said, "The tools we were using were new to that area."[17]

The Legal Environment of Promotion

Federal, provincial, and local governmental bodies in Canada—and similar bodies in other nations around the globe—have laws and rules regarding promotion practices. These regulations range from banning billboards in some locales to requiring celebrity endorsers to use products if they say they do. The Canadian federal agencies most involved with promotion are Industry Canada's Competition Bureau and the Canadian Radio-television and Telecommunications Commission (CRTC). Table 11-3 shows selected promotional practices that are subject to regulation.

The CRTC regulates all broadcast advertising but delegates some of this authority to other governmental bodies responsible for specific products. For example, Health Canada's Health Protection Branch regulates promotion for the Canadian pharmaceutical and cosmetic industry. Five regulatory tools are available to protect consumers and competing firms from undesirable promotion practices: full disclosure, substantiation, cease-and-desist orders, corrective advertising, and fines.

CRTC

www.crtc.gc.ca/

[17]"Data Watch," *Advertising Age* (October 26, 1992), p. I-10; and E. S. Browning, "Eastern Europe Poses Obstacles for Ads," *Wall Street Journal* (July 30, 1992), p. B6.

TECHNOLOGY & MARKETING

How Do You Avoid the Legal Pitfalls of Promoting in Cyberspace?

According to experts in the field, there are many legal risks associated with using the Internet for promotions. They advise marketers to keep this seven-point checklist in mind when planning and evaluating Internet-based promotions:

1. All Internet domain names and e-mail addresses are trademarks that must be cleared to ensure they are not owned by others and then legally protected.
2. A firm operating a bulletin board may be liable for the information showing up there. In a case involving slanderous information, Prodigy was held responsible for the same standards as traditional publishers.
3. The Screen Actors Guild claims jurisdiction over the employment of actors used in the production of online and CD-ROM programs. This affects videos that were initially made for television that are now used on the Internet.
4. As with other media, an individual's name, photograph, or likeness cannot be used in connection with any promotion, without his or her written permission.
5. Because the Internet is worldwide in terms of distribution, its use is subject to the laws in countries where the messages are reproduced.
6. The rights of photographers and freelance photographers may be affected by use of their materials on the Internet.
7. Marketers should reserve the right to cancel any Internet-based promotion in the event it is infected with a virus or otherwise cannot properly run.

As the advertising manager for Aiwa, you are responsible for devising an Internet-based promotion for a new line of surround-sound stereo receivers. How can you best assure that your promotion meets the above legal guidelines?

Source: Based on material in Douglas J. Wood and Linda A. Goldstein, "Seven Legal Pitfalls of Promoting in Cyberspace," *Promo* (July 1995), p. 21.

Full disclosure, substantiation, cease-and-desist orders, corrective advertising, *and* **fines** *are major governmental limits on promotion activities.*

Full disclosure requires that all data necessary for a consumer to make a safe and informed decision be provided in a promotion message. That is why Alka-Seltzer must mention that its regular version contains aspirin, and diet products must note how many calories they contain. In this way, consumers can assess the overall benefits and risks of a purchase.

Substantiation requires that a firm be able to prove all the claims it makes in promotion messages. This means thorough testing and evidence of performance are needed before making claims. In a recent Ontario court case, Unilever, maker of Dove soap, sued Procter & Gamble, maker of Oil of Olay, for an injunction against their comparative ads. Procter & Gamble ran an ad claiming Oil of Olay helped retain more skin moisture than Dove soap. The case hinged on the ability of Procter & Gamble to prove their claim with verifiable test results. Because they were able to do so, Unilever was denied an injunction.[18]

Under a **cease-and-desist order**, a firm must discontinue a promotion practice that is deemed deceptive and modify a message accordingly. The firm is usually not forced to admit guilt or pay fines, as long as it obeys the order.

Corrective advertising requires a firm to run new ads to correct the false impressions left by previous ones. Several years ago, Listerine was told to spend U.S.$10.2 million on ads in Canada and the U.S. to correct prior messages claiming it was a cold remedy. Listerine decided to run the ads (with the phrase "Listerine will not help prevent colds or sore throats or lessen their severity") after learning it would not otherwise be permitted to continue any advertising.

The last major remedy is **fines**, which are dollar penalties for deceptive promotion. A company may have to pay a sum to the government, as when K mart was fined $200 000

---

[18]Angela Di Padova, "Moisture and Misleading Advertising," *Marketing Magazine* (March 18, 1996), p. 20.

for misleading advertising related to advertised sale prices of mattresses. K mart promoted a sale on mattresses by claiming the price during the sale was 50 per cent less than the price would be *after* the sale. The advertising was judged to be misleading because the mattresses had been specially purchased for the sale, and would not be available afterwards. Therefore, promoting a discount price based on an after-the-sale price was misleading.[19]

In addition to government legislation, trade and professional associations often have rules or guidelines governing the use of promotion by their members. The International Advertising Association sets guidelines for the self-regulation of promotion throughout the world. Within Canada, marketers are asked to voluntarily abide by the Canadian Code of Advertising Standards, which is administered by the Canadian Advertising Foundation (CAF). The CAF delegates its responsibilities to various bodies in each of the provinces. For example, in Ontario, the Standards Division of the Canadian Advertising Foundation handles all English-language complaints about national advertising in Canada and any complaints in Ontario, while le Conseil des Normes de la Publicité handles all of the complaints on national advertising in French and all complaints in Quebec. In the Atlantic provinces and the Western provinces there are regional councils that handle complaints on advertising in these regions.[20]

Some cities have their own advertising councils to handle complaints. For example, the Windsor Media Council (Windsor, Ontario) places ads in the local media informing the community where they can register complaints and seek resolution concerning local advertising and media programming. Another important local body involved in self-regulation is the Better Business Bureau. The Better Business Bureau usually deals with more product and service complaints but complaints about promotional practices are handled as well.

BETTER BUSINESS BUREAU

www.bbb.org

Criticisms and Defences of Promotion

For many years, various industry trade groups have campaigned to improve the overall image of promotion. According to the general director of the International Advertising Association, "There's been enough talk about the bad—the clutter, the obtrusiveness, the stuffed mailboxes. It's time that people know about the good."[21]

Nonetheless, promotion is the most heavily criticized area of marketing. Here are a number of criticisms and the defences of marketers to them:

Promotion controversies centre on materialism, honesty, prices, symbolism, and consumer expectations.

DETRACTORS FEEL THAT PROMOTION:	MARKETING PROFESSIONALS ANSWER THAT PROMOTION:
Creates an obsession with material possessions.	Responds to consumer desires for material possessions. In affluent societies, these items are plentiful and paid for with discretionary earnings.
Is basically dishonest.	Is basically honest. The great majority of companies abide by all laws and set strict self-regulations. A few dishonest firms give a bad name to all.
Raises the prices of consumer goods and services.	Holds down prices. By increasing demand, promotion enables firms to use mass production and mass distribution and reduce per-unit costs. Employment is higher when demand is stimulated.
Overemphasizes symbolism and status.	Differentiates goods and services through symbolic and status appeals. Consumers desire distinctiveness and product benefits.
Causes excessively high expectations.	Keeps expectations high; it thereby sustains consumer motivation and worker productivity in order to satisfy expectations.

[19]Industry Canada, "K-mart Canada Limited Fined $200 000 for One Count of Misleading Advertising Under the Competition Act," Industry Canada *Strategis* Web site (April 13, 1995).

[20]Keith J. Tuckwell, *Canadian Advertising in Action, Third Edition*, Prentice Hall Canada: Scarborough, Ontario (1995), pp. 20, 635–654.

[21]Cyndee Miller, "The Marketing of Advertising," *Marketing News* (December 7, 1992), p. 2.

The Scope and Importance of Personal Selling

In Canada, 1.3 million people work in sales positions. In addition, 15 million people work in sales in the United States and millions more in other nations are also employed in sales jobs. Professional salespeople generate new customer accounts, ascertain needs, interact with consumers, emphasize knowledge and persuasion, and offer substantial service. They include stockbrokers, insurance agents, manufacturer sales representatives, and real estate brokers. Top salespeople can earn $100 000+ per year. Clerical salespeople answer simple queries, retrieve stock from inventory, recommend the best brand in a product category, and complete transactions by receiving payments and packing products. They include retail, wholesale, and manufacturer sales clerks.

From a marketing perspective, personal selling really goes far beyond the people in identified sales positions because every contact between a company representative and a customer entails some personal interaction. Lawyers, plumbers, hairdressers, and cashiers are not defined as salespeople, yet each comes in contact with the customer.

Selling is stressed when orders are large, consumers are concentrated, items are expensive, and service is required.

In some situations, a strong personal-selling emphasis may be needed. Large-volume customers require special attention. Geographically concentrated consumers may be more efficiently served by a sales force than by ads in mass media. Custom-made, expensive, and complex goods or services require in-depth consumer information, demonstrations, and follow-up calls. Tangential sales services—like gift wrapping and delivery—may be requested. If ads are not informative enough, questions can be resolved only by personal selling. New products may need personal selling to gain reseller acceptance. Entering a foreign market may best be achieved by personal contact with prospective resellers and/or consumers. Finally, many organizational customers expect a lot of personal contact. Generally, a decision to stress personal selling depends on such factors as cost, audience and needs, and a desire for flexibility.

Selling costs are often greater than advertising costs. For example, Fuller Brush sales commissions range up to 50 per cent of sales and auto parts firms, office and equipment firms, and appliance makers all spend far more on selling than on ads. The average cost of a single business-to-business field sales call is several hundred dollars; and it may take several visits to make a sale.[22]

High selling costs have led to a concern for efficiency. In telemarketing, phone calls initiate sales or set up sales appointments.

A number of strategies have been devised to keep selling costs down and improve the efficiency of the sales force, as these examples show:

- Many firms are routing salespeople more effectively to minimize travel time and expenses. Some firms are bypassing smaller customers in their personal selling efforts and specifying minimum order sizes for personalized service. This means opportunities for sellers willing to serve small accounts.

- With **telemarketing**, telephone communications are used to sell or solicit business or to set up an appointment for a salesperson to sell or solicit business. By using it, salespeople can talk to several consumers per hour, centralize operations and lower expenses, screen prospects, process orders and arrange shipments, provide customer service, assist the field sales staff, speed communications, and increase repeat business. A lot of companies rely on telephone personnel to contact customers; outside sales personnel (who actually call on customers) are then more involved with customer service and technical assistance. A broad range of both small and large firms use some form of telemarketing.

- Computerization is improving sales efficiency by providing salespeople with detailed—and speedy—data, making ordering easier, coordinating orders by various salespeople, and identifying the best prospects and their desires (such as preferred brands)—based on prior purchases. Thousands of Canadian salespeople now have

[22]Allison Lucas, "Portrait of a Salesperson," *Sales & Marketing Management* (June 1995), p. 13; and Richard T. Hise and Edward L. Reid, "Improving the Performance of the Industrial Sales Force in the 1990s," *Industrial Marketing Management*, Vol. 23 (October 1994), pp. 273–279.

FIGURE 11-9
The Buyer-Seller Dyad

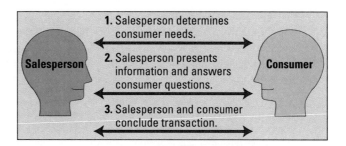

1. Salesperson determines consumer needs.
2. Salesperson presents information and answers consumer questions.
3. Salesperson and consumer conclude transaction.

Salesperson — Consumer

notebook PCs: "Anything that allows reps to squeeze a couple more hours out of their day has great benefits."[23]

- A lot of firms now view computerized customer databases as among their most valuable sales resources. These databases enable the firms to focus their efforts better, make sure their key accounts are regularly serviced, and use direct mailings to complement telephone calls and salesperson visits.

The Characteristics of Personal Selling

On the positive side, personal selling provides individual attention for each consumer and passes on a lot of information. There is a dynamic interplay between buyer and seller. This lets a firm use a **buyer-seller dyad**, the two-way flow of communication between both parties (see Figure 11-9.) That is not possible with advertising. Thus, personal selling can be flexible and adapted to specific consumer needs. For example, a real estate broker can use one sales presentation with a first-time buyer and another with a person who has already bought a home. A salesperson can also apply as much persuasion as needed and balance it against the need for information. Furthermore, through the buyer-seller dyad, a "relationship selling" approach is possible, whereby customer friendships may be developed.[24]

Personal selling targets a more defined and concentrated audience, which means less waste than with advertising. In addition, people who enter a store or who are contacted by a salesperson are more apt to buy a product than those watching an ad on TV. Because ads stimulate interest, those who make it to the personal selling stage are often key members of the target market. When unsolicited, direct selling has the most waste in personal selling.

Personal selling often clinches a sale and is usually conducted during the purchase stage of the consumer's decision process, taking place after an information search and exposure to ads. It holds repeat customers and those already convinced by advertising— and resolves any concerns of undecided consumers by answering questions about price, warranty, and other factors. It settles service issues, like delivery and installation. Feedback is immediate and clear-cut: Consumers may be asked their feelings about product features or they may complain; and salespeople may unearth a marketing program's strengths and weaknesses.

On the negative side, selling is ineffective for generating awareness because salespeople can handle only a limited number of consumers. A retail furniture salesperson may be able to talk to fewer than twenty people per day if the average length of a customer contact is fifteen minutes to a half hour. Sales personnel who call on customers can handle even fewer accounts, due to travel time. In addition, many consumers drawn by advertising may want self-service. This is discouraged by some aggressive salespeople.

Personal selling costs per customer can be very high due to the one-on-one nature of selling. An in-store furniture salesperson who talks to twenty customers daily might cost a firm $7 per presentation ($140/day compensation divided by 20), an amount much higher

Selling uses a **buyer-seller dyad** *and is flexible and efficient, closes sales, and provides feedback.*

---

[23]Tom Dellecave, Jr., "Getting the Bugs Out," *Sales & Marketing Management* (December 1995), Part 2, p. 27.
[24]See John J. Withey and Eric Panitz, "Face-to-Face Selling: Making It More Effective," *Industrial Marketing Management*, Vol. 24 (August 1995), pp. 239–246.

Selling has a limited audience, high costs per customer, and a poor image.

than an ad's cost per customer contact. For outside salespeople, hotel stays, meals, and transportation can amount to $250 or more daily per salesperson, and compensation must be added to these costs.

Finally, personal selling, especially among final consumers, has a poor image. It is criticized for a lack of honesty and pressure tactics:

> The public's consistent interpretation of the term *salesperson* has provided fodder for many dramatic works, anecdotes, and jokes that reflect the widely held negative stereotype of salespeople. As a result, people may avoid them deliberately. The consumer practice of visiting car dealerships after business hours [indicates the common distrust] of salespeople. This practice may be due to beliefs that consumers can evaluate alternative cars better in the absence of the "dreaded" salesperson. Sometimes, salespeople may even inhibit, rather than facilitate, mutually satisfying exchanges.[25]

The situation can be improved by better sales-force training and the use of consumer-oriented rather than seller-oriented practices.

Developing a Personal Selling Plan

A personal selling plan can be divided into the seven steps shown in Figure 11-10 and highlighted here.

Setting Objectives

Selling goals can be demand- and/or image-oriented. When image-oriented, they involve public relations. Although many firms have some interest in information, reminder, and image goals, the major goal usually is persuasion: converting consumer interest into a sale. Examples appear in Table 11-4.

Assigning Responsibility

A manager must oversee selling functions.

The personal selling function may be assigned to a marketing or sales manager who oversees all areas of selling, from planning to sales-force management. A small or specialized firm is likely to have its marketing manager oversee selling or use one general sales manager. A large or diversified firm may have multiple sales managers—assigned by product line, customer type, and/or region.

FIGURE 11-10
Developing a Personal Selling Plan

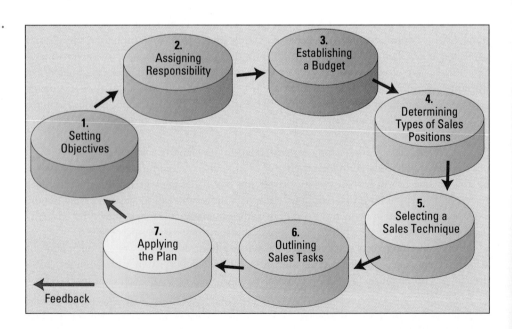

[25]Barry J. Babin, James S. Boles, and William R. Darden, "Salesperson Stereotypes, Consumer Emotions, and Their Impact on Information Processing," *Journal of the Academy of Marketing Science*, Vol. 23 (Spring 1995), p. 94.

T a b l e 1 1 - 4
Specific Personal Selling Objectives

....

TYPE OF OBJECTIVE	ILLUSTRATIONS
Demand-Oriented	
Information	To fully explain all attributes of goods and services
	To answer any questions
	To probe for any further questions
Persuasion	To distinguish attributes of goods or services from those of competitors
	To maximize the number of purchases relative to the presentations made
	To convert undecided consumers into buyers
	To sell complementary items—e.g., a telephoto lens with a camera
	To placate dissatisfied customers
Reminding	To ensure delivery, installation, etc.
	To follow-up after a good or service has been purchased
	To follow-up when a repurchase is near
	To reassure previous customers as they make a new purchase
Image-Oriented	
Industry and company	To have a good appearance for all personnel having customer contact
	To follow acceptable (ethical) sales practices
	To be respected by customers, employees, and other publics

....

These are the basic responsibilities of a sales manager:

- To understand the firm's goals, strategies, market position, and basic marketing plan and to convey them to the sales force.
- To determine and outline a sales philosophy, sales-force characteristics, selling tasks, a sales organization, and methods of customer contact.
- To prepare and update sales forecasts.
- To allocate selling resources based on sales forecasts and customer needs.
- To select, train, assign, compensate, and supervise sales personnel.
- To synchronize selling tasks with advertising, product planning, distribution, marketing research, production, and other activities.
- To assess sales performance by salesperson, product, product line, customer, customer group, and geographic area.
- To continuously monitor competitors' actions.
- To make sure the sales force acts in an ethical manner.
- To convey the image sought by the company.

Establishing a Budget

A **sales-expense budget** allots selling costs among salespeople, products, customers, and geographic areas for a given period. It is usually tied to a sales forecast and relates selling tasks to sales goals. It should be somewhat flexible in case expected sales are not reached or are exceeded.

These items should be covered in a budget: sales forecasts, overhead (manager's compensation, office costs), sales-force compensation, sales expenses (travel, lodging, meals,

*A **sales-expense budget** assigns spending for a specific time.*

Table 11-5

A Sales-Expense Budget for a Small Manufacturer Specializing in Business Machinery, 1997

ITEM	ESTIMATED ANNUAL COSTS (REVENUES)
Sales forecast	$1 950 000
Overhead (1 sales manager, 1 office)	$ 100 000
Sales-force compensation (2 salespeople)	90 000
Sales expenses	40 000
Sales meetings	5 000
Selling aids	15 000
Sales management costs	10 000
Total personal selling budget	$ 260 000
Personal selling costs as a percentage of sales forecast	13.3

entertainment), sales meetings, selling aids (including computer equipment), and sales management (employee selection and training) costs. Table 11-5 shows a budget for a small maker of business machinery.

The budget will be larger if customers are geographically dispersed and a lot of travel is required. Complex products need costly, time-consuming sales presentations and result in fewer calls per salesperson. An expanding sales force needs expenditures for recruiting and training salespeople.

Determining the Type(s) of Sales Positions

Salespeople can be broadly classed as order takers, order getters, or support personnel. Some firms employ one type of salesperson, others a combination.

*An **order taker** handles routine orders and sells items that are pre-sold.*

An **order taker** processes routine orders and reorders. This person is involved more with clerical than creative selling, typically for pre-sold goods or services. He or she arranges displays, restocks items, answers simple questions, writes up orders, and completes transactions. He or she may work in a warehouse (manufacturer clerk) or store (retail clerk) or call on customers (a field salesperson). An order taker has these advantages: compensation is rather low, little training is required, both selling and nonselling tasks are performed, and a sales force can be expanded or contracted quickly. However, an order taker is improper for goods and services that need creative selling, or where extensive information must be available for customers. Personnel turnover is high and enthusiasm may be limited due to the low salary and routine tasks.

*An **order getter** obtains leads, provides information, persuades customers, and closes sales.*

An **order getter** generates customer leads, provides information, persuades customers, and closes sales. He or she is the creative salesperson used for high-priced, complex, and/or new products. There is less emphasis on clerical work. The person may be inside (jewellery store salesperson) or outside (photocopier salesperson).[26] He or she is expert and enthusiastic, expands sales, and can convince undecided customers to buy or decided customers to add peripheral items—such as carpeting and appliances along with a newly built house. Yet, for many people, the order getter has a high-pressure image. He or she may also need expensive training. Such nonsales tasks as writing reports may be avoided because they take away from a seller's time with customers and are seldom rewarded. Compensation can be very high for salespersons who are effective order getters. Figure 11-11 contrasts order takers and order getters.

[26]See Kris Frieswick, "Inside Sales Takes Centre Stage," *Industrial Distribution* (October 1995), pp. 24–27.

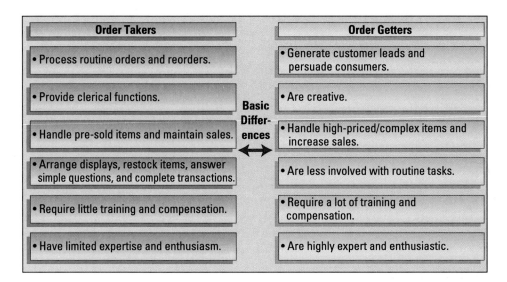

FIGURE 11-11
Contrasting Order Takers and Order Getters

Support personnel supplement a sales force. A **missionary salesperson** gives out information on new goods or services. He or she does not close sales but describes items' attributes, answers questions, and leaves written matter. This paves the way for later sales and is commonly used with prescription drugs. A **sales engineer** accompanies an order getter if a very technical or complex item is involved. He or she discusses specifications and long-range uses, while the order getter makes customer contacts and closes sales. A **service salesperson** ordinarily deals with customers after sales. Delivery, installation, and other follow-up tasks are done.

Missionary salespersons, sales engineers, and service salespersons are support personnel.

Selecting a Sales Technique

The two basic techniques for selling are the canned sales presentation and the need-satisfaction approach. The **canned sales presentation** is a memorized, repetitive presentation given to all customers interested in a given item. It does not adapt to customer needs or traits but presumes a general presentation will appeal to everyone. Although criticized for its inflexibility and nonmarketing orientation, it does have some value:

*The **canned sales presentation** is memorized and nonadaptive.*

> Inexperienced salespeople who are lacking in selling instinct and confidence will benefit from the professionalism, anticipation of questions and objections, and other fail-safe mechanisms often inherent in a company-prepared, memorized, audiovisual or flip-chart presentation. Consequently, this method should be considered when qualified new salespeople are scarce and when brevity of training is essential.[27]

The **need-satisfaction approach** is a high-level selling method based on the principle that each customer has different attributes and wants, and therefore the sales presentation should be adapted to the individual consumer. With this technique, a salesperson first asks such questions of the consumer as: What type of product are you looking for? Have you ever purchased this product before? What price range are you considering? Then the sales presentation is more responsive to the particular person; and a new shopper is treated quite differently from an experienced one. The need-satisfaction approach is more popular and customer-oriented; however, it requires better training and skilled sales personnel. This approach includes:

*The **need-satisfaction approach** adapts to individual consumers.*

- Using the buyer-seller dyad to generate two-way respect.
- Listening well.
- Making presentations based on a good grasp of the facts.

[27]Marvin A. Jolson, "The Underestimated Potential of the Canned Sales Presentation," *Journal of Marketing*, Vol. 39 (January 1975), p. 78.

- Spending time on pre-sales research ("homework").
- Being punctual for appointments (and willing to leave when the allotted time is over).
- Allowing the customer to talk.
- Offering "solutions," not goods and services.
- Showing competence.
- Acknowledging if a question cannot be answered, but getting back to the customer immediately with the correct answer.
- Not wasting a prospect's time.
- Providing superior service after the sale.[28]

The canned sales presentation works best with inexpensive, routine items that are heavily advertised and relatively pre-sold. The need-satisfaction approach works best with more expensive, more complex items that have moderate advertising and require substantial additional information for consumers.

Outlining Sales Tasks

*The **selling process** consists of seven steps.*

Thc tasks to be performed by the personal sales force need to be outlined. The **selling process** consists of prospecting for leads, approaching customers, determining consumer wants, giving a sales presentation, handling objections, closing the sale, and following up. See Figure 11-12.

Prospecting *creates customer leads.*

Outside selling requires a procedure, known as **prospecting**, to generate a list of customer leads. Blind prospecting uses phone directories and other general listings of potential customers; a small percentage of those contacted will be interested in a firm's offering. Lead prospecting depends on past customers and others for referrals; thus, a greater percentage of people will be interested because of the referral from someone they know. Inside selling does not involve prospecting because customers have already been drawn to a store or office through ads or prior purchase experience.

*The pre-approach and greeting are part of **approaching customers**.*

Approaching customers is a two-stage procedure: pre-approach and greeting. During pre-approach, a salesperson tries to get information about the customer from the firm's database, census materials, and/or other secondary data—as well as from referrals. The salesperson is then better equipped to interact with that customer. Inside retail salespeople may be unable to use a pre-approach; they often know nothing about a consumer until he or she enters the store. During the greeting, a salesperson begins a conversation. The intention is to put the customer at ease and build rapport.

The next step is to ascertain customer wants by asking the person a variety of questions regarding past experience, price, product features, intended uses, and the kinds of information still needed.

FIGURE 11-12
The Selling Process

[28]Adapted by the authors from James E. Lukaszewski and Paul Ridgeway, "To Put Your Best Foot Forward, Start by Taking These 21 Simple Steps," *Sales & Marketing Management* (June 1990), pp. 84–86. See also Fiona Gibb, "The New Sales Basics," *Sales & Marketing Management* (April 1995), p. 81.

The **sales presentation** includes a verbal description of a product, its benefits, options and models, price, associated services like delivery and warranty, and a demonstration (if needed). A canned sales presentation or need-satisfaction method may be used. The purpose of a sales presentation is to convert an undecided consumer into a purchaser.

The **sales presentation** *converts an uncertain consumer.*

After a presentation, the salesperson usually must handle objections from the consumer. Objections are of two kinds: the first kind request more information; the second kind raise issues that must be settled before a sale is made.

Once any objections have been settled, a salesperson is ready for **closing the sale**. This means getting a person to agree to a purchase. The salesperson must be sure no major objections remain before trying to close a sale. In addition, a salesperson must not argue with a consumer.

The **closing** *clinches a sale.*

For a large purchase, the salesperson should follow up after the sale to make sure the customer is pleased. Doing so achieves three goals: the customer is better satisfied; referrals are stimulated; and, repurchases are more likely. "Relationship selling is not about getting an order; it is about convincing customers that you will be there after an order, no matter what. Relationships are based on doing what is right, not doing what you can get away with."[29]

Besides the tasks in the selling process, a firm must clearly enumerate the nonselling tasks it wants sales personnel to perform. Among the nonselling tasks that may be assigned are setting up displays, writing up information sheets, marking prices on products, checking competitors' strategies, doing test-marketing analysis and consumer surveys, and training new employees.

Applying the Plan

Sales management—planning, implementing, and controlling the personal sales function—should be used in applying a personal selling plan. Sales management covers employee selection, training, territory allocation, compensation, and supervision.

Sales management *tasks range from employee selection to supervision.*

In selecting sales personnel, a combination of personal attributes should be assessed: mental (intelligence, ability to plan), physical (appearance, speaking ability), experiential (education, sales/business background), environmental (group memberships, social influences), personality (ambition, enthusiasm, tact, resourcefulness, stability), and willingness to be trained and to follow instructions.[30] Contrary to earlier beliefs, it is now pretty much accepted that good salespeople are not necessarily born; they are carefully selected and trained: "How would you describe the ideal salesperson? Extroverted, aggressive? Quick to develop a rapport? A good sense of humour, a competitive spirit, charisma? This has been a popular stereotype, to be sure, and no doubt there are some excellent sales professionals out there who actually do possess these qualities. On the other hand, it's also a popular misconception. The truth is, these factors aren't always the most important ones to consider when selecting and training top salespeople."[31]

The traits of potential salespeople must be compatible with the customers with whom they will interact and the requirements of the good or service being sold. The buyer-seller dyad operates better when there are some similarities in salesperson and customer characteristics. And certain product categories require much different education, technical training, and sales activities than others (such as jewellery versus computer sales).

Once these factors are studied, the firm would develop a formal selection procedure that specifies the personal attributes sought, sources of employees (such as colleges and employment agencies), and methods for selection (such as interviews and testing). It would be based on the firm's overall selling plan.

Salesperson training may take one or a combination of forms. A formal program uses a trainer, a classroom setting, lectures, and printed materials. It may also include role play-

[29]Michael Collins, "Breaking into the Big Leagues," *Marketing Tools* (January–February 1996), p. 28.

[30]Adapted by the authors from William J. Stanton, Richard H. Buskirk, and Rosann L. Spiro, *Management of a Sales Force*, Ninth Edition (Homewood, Ill.: Richard D. Irwin, 1995).

[31]Thomas Rollins, "How to Tell Competent Salespeople from the Other Kind," *Sales & Marketing Management* (September 1990), p. 116.

ing (in which trainees act out parts) and case analysis. Field trips take trainees out on actual calls so they can observe skilled salespeople in action. On-the-job training places trainees in their own selling situations under the close supervision of the trainer or a senior salesperson. Training often covers a range of topics; it should teach selling skills and include information on the firm and its offerings, the industry, and employee duties. At Caterpillar (the industrial and farm equipment manufacturer), "We train our sales force to understand why our customers buy our products, what their needs are, the importance of follow-up, the need to let a customer vent his/her anger, and how to help a customer resolve problems without passing the responsibility on to someone else in the company."[32] Besides initial training, continuous training or retraining of sales personnel may teach new techniques, explain new products, or improve performance.

*A **sales territory** contains the area, customers, and/or products assigned to a salesperson.*

Territory size and salesperson allocation are decided next. A **sales territory** consists of the geographic area, customers, and/or product lines assigned to a salesperson. If territories are assigned by customer type or product category, two or more salespeople may cover the same geographic area. Territory size depends on customer locations, order size, travel time and expenses, the time per sales call, the yearly visits for each account, and the amount of hours per year each salesperson has for selling tasks. The mix of established versus new customer accounts must also be considered. Allocating salespeople to specific territories depends on their ability, the buyer-seller dyad, the mix of selling and nonselling functions (such as one salesperson training new employees), and seniority. Proper territory size and allocation provide adequate coverage of customers, minimize territory overlap, recognize geographic boundaries, minimize travel expenses, encourage solicitation of new accounts, provide enough sales potential for good salespeople to be well rewarded, and are fair to the whole sales force.

*Sales compensation may be **straight salary**, **straight commission**, or a **combination** of the two.*

Salespeople can be compensated by straight salary, straight commission, or a combination of salary and commission or bonus. With a **straight salary plan**, a salesperson is paid a flat amount per time period. Earnings are not tied to sales. The advantages are that both selling and nonselling tasks can be specified and controlled, salespeople have security, and expenses are known in advance. The disadvantages are the low incentive to increase sales, expenses not being tied to productivity, and the continuing costs even if there are low sales. Order takers are usually paid straight salaries.

With a **straight commission plan**, a salesperson's earnings are directly related to sales, profits, customer satisfaction, or some other type of performance. The commission rate is often keyed to a quota, which is a productivity standard. The advantages of this plan are the motivated salespeople, the elimination of fixed sales compensation costs, and the fact that expenses are tied to productivity. The disadvantages are the firm's lack of control over nonselling tasks, the instability of a firm's expenses, and salesperson risks due to variable pay. Insurance, real estate, and direct-selling order getters often earn straight commissions. Typically, Canadian real estate salespersons receive a 6 per cent commission of $9000 for selling a $150 000 house.

To gain the advantages of both salary- and commission-oriented methods, many firms use elements of each in a **combination compensation plan**. Such plans balance company control, flexibility, and employee incentives; and some award bonuses for superior individual or company performance. All types of order getters work on a combination basis. According to various studies, about two-thirds of North American firms compensate sales personnel via some form of combination plan, one-fifth use a straight salary plan, and the rest use straight commissions. Smaller firms are more apt to use a straight salary plan and less apt to use a combination plan.

Supervision involves motivation, performance measures, nonselling tasks, and behaviour modification.

Supervision encompasses four aspects of sales management:

1. Sales personnel must be motivated. Their motivation depends on such factors as the clarity of the job (what tasks must be performed), the salesperson's desire to achieve, the variety of tasks performed, the incentives for undertaking each task, the style of the sales manager, flexibility, and recognition.

[32]Geoffrey Brewer, "Caterpillar Inc.: Industrial & Farm Equipment," *Sales & Marketing Management* (September 1993), p. 61.

Ethics AND TODAY'S MARKETER

Do Life Insurance Agents "Churn" So Much to Earn So Much?

Prudential and other agents have recently been scrutinized for "churning" insurance policies. Under this practice, agents recommend that customers use the built-in cash value from old policies to purchase new ones. Churning is often practised by agents as a way of increasing their commission income from loyal accounts. Because a new policy often generates a sales commission equal to half of the first year's premium, churning is highly profitable to agents.

Unfortunately, people are often not fully briefed about the consequences of switching policies. In one instance, a unsuspecting consumer was advised by an agent to borrow against the cash value in an existing policy so that the customer could purchase more insurance coverage. However, in such instances, the cash value of the old policy could run out, while the interest on the loan increases. The customer would then be forced to pay off the debt.

Churning is also generally not profitable for the insurance company. It often takes at least six years of payments for a new policy to be profitable due to the company's cost of sales commissions, administrative costs, and medical testing fees.

Despite these problems, it is hard to reduce churning activity. In many sales offices, monitoring this activity falls under the jurisdiction of junior managers. Because these managers are evaluated on the basis of the sales revenues of their agents, churning increases their income. In addition, many insurance agents represent multiple firms. An independent agent can easily churn a policyholder from one insurance provider to another. Finally, many insurance firms do not want to come down too hard on productive independent agents, since they can easily switch their loyalty from one insurance company to another.

As a Prudential marketing executive, how would you discourage independent agents from churning?

Source: Based on material in Leslie Scism, "Some Agents Churn Life-Insurance Policies, Hurt Their Customers," *Wall Street Journal* (January 3, 1995), pp. 1, 4.

2. Performance must be measured. To do this, achievements must be gauged against such goals as sales and calls per day. The analysis should take into account territory size, travel time, and experience. The failure of a salesperson is often related to poor listening skills, a lack of concentration on priorities, a lack of effort, the inability to determine customer needs, a lack of planning for presentations, overpromising on product performance, and inadequate knowledge.

3. The sales manager must ensure that all nonselling tasks are completed, even if sales personnel are not rewarded for them.

4. If a salesperson's performance does not meet expectations, then some action may be needed to modify behaviour.[33]

In sales management, these key factors should also be taken into account: the evolving role of women in selling and the special nature of selling in foreign markets.

PRUDENTIAL INSURANCE CO.
www.prudential.com/

[33]Thomas N. Ingram, Charles H. Schwepker, Jr., and Don Hutson, "Why Salespeople Fail," *Industrial Marketing Management*, Vol. 21 (August 1992), pp. 225–230; and "Pipe Down," *Sales & Marketing Management* (January 1994), p. 22. See also Goutam N. Challagalla and Tasadduq A. Shervani, "Dimensions and Types of Supervisory Control: Effects on Salesperson Performance and Satisfaction," *Journal of Marketing*, Vol. 60 (January 1996), pp. 89–105.

There are more women in sales than ever before, and international markets require special decisions.

One of the major changes in industrial sales forces over the last twenty years is "the accelerated recruitment of women into traditionally male-dominated sales positions."[34] According to Statistics Canada[35], women hold 46 per cent of the sales positions in Canada and industry observers expect that even more women will be recruited into sales forces in the future. Two researchers have noted:

> Sales managers do not have to provide special considerations or training programs for female salespersons to facilitate their socialization into the industrial sales force. Consequently, sales managers should not be concerned with incurring additional training expenses for females, nor do they need to behave more solicitously in their management practices toward women than men. To do otherwise will probably result in the demotivation of male salespersons, and will probably handicap females by intimating that they are deficient in some way and require additional assistance. Instead, sales managers should include women equally in all sales training, motivation, and socialization activities, just as these opportunities are extended to men.[36]

When firms go international, "they are faced with the task of establishing and managing sales forces in foreign markets. Once in place, they must decide how much home-office influence to exert on subsidiary sales policies. When faced with the diversity of the international marketplace, top marketing management is often uncertain about how much it should influence its overseas sales forces. Management benefits from knowing which sales decisions are suited to home-office input and, just as important, which are not."[37] In particular, the attributes of salespeople; salesperson training, compensation, and supervision; the dynamics of the buyer-seller dyad; and the selling process may need to be tailored to different foreign markets. For example, in many Arab countries, negotiations—particularly bargaining—are viewed as an enjoyable activity or even as a social event. Foreign salespeople need to respect the religious traditions of their Arab customers and recognize that Arab personnel may not be available at all times. In addition, they are known to refrain from saying "no" and to engage in contract renegotiations if the need arises. Arabs end negotiations by orally committing themselves, rather than doing so in writing.

MARKETING IN A CHANGING WORLD

Sales Training the 3M Way[38]

3M is taking a very novel approach to sales training for its veteran salespeople, and others can learn from its experiences. As one observer noted, "While innovation was long a part of the research, product development, and manufacturing processes at 3M, it wasn't as conspicuous in sales. 3M sales training, although always high-quality, was not focused as well as it might have been on customer needs. That's changed. Three years ago, innovation struck sales training: the firm started asking customers to tell it where salespeople needed to improve skills or get additional training."

The new sales-training approach is a big departure from prior 3M practice, when the company relied on broad customer satisfaction surveys rather than specific measures of salesperson performance. 3M now surveys customers to determine how its sales representatives are performing in terms of specific skills. In a typical year, 1000 or so business customers are surveyed.

The new program is called A.C.T.—assessment and analysis, curriculum content, and training transfer. It provides "customer-focused, just-in-time, on-demand sales training." This is how A.C.T. works:

---

[34]Patrick L. Schul and Brent M. Wren, "The Emerging Role of Women in Industrial Selling: A Decade of Change," *Journal of Marketing*, Vol. 56 (July 1992), p. 38.

[35]Statistics Canada, *1995 Market Research Handbook* (Ottawa: Minister of Supply Services), p. 164.

[36]Judy A. Siguaw and Earl D. Honeycutt, Jr., "An Examination of Gender Differences in Selling Behaviors and Job Attitudes," *Industrial Marketing Management*, Vol. 24 (January 1995), p. 51. See also Nancy Arnott, "It's a Woman's World," *Sales & Marketing Management* (March 1995), pp. 54–59.

[37]John S. Hill, Richard R. Still, and Onal O. Boya, "Managing the Multinational Sales Force," *International Marketing Review*, Vol. 8 (Number 1, 1991), pp. 19–31. See also Earl D. Honeycutt and John B. Ford, "Guidelines for Managing an International Sales Force," *Industrial Marketing Management*, Vol. 24 (March 1995), pp. 135–144.

[38]The material in this section is based on William Keenan, Jr., "Getting Customers into the A.C.T.," *Sales & Marketing Management* (February 1995), pp. 58–63.

- A written questionnaire assesses selling skills in six areas: knowledge of products and services, strategic skills critical to best using the time spent with the customer, interpersonal selling, sales negotiation, internal influence and teamwork, and customer-focused quality.
- Each participating salesperson personally gives the questionnaire to a select group of about six customers. The customers then rate the importance of each of the skill areas, and how well the salesperson is performing them.
- Completed questionnaires go to an outside tabulation firm. (Sales managers only receive composite scores for their salespeople, but not the results of individual salespeople.) Results are computed and the gaps in salesperson performance are derived.
- Each salesperson works with his or her sales manager to set up a training curriculum to correct key weaknesses, and to undergo appropriate training.
- The last step is transfer, whereby each salesperson applies what he or she has learned to actual customer situations.

SUMMARY

1. *To define promotion planning and show its importance* Promotion involves any communication that informs, persuades, and/or reminds people about an organization's or individual's goods, services, ideas, community involvement, or impact on society. Promotion planning is systematic and relates to all aspects of communication.

Promotion efforts are needed for both new products and existing ones. The audience for promotion may be consumers, shareholders, consumer advocacy groups, government, channel members, employees, competitors, and the public. With word-of-mouth communication, people express opinions and product-related experiences to one another. A firm may communicate its image, views on ideas, community involvement, or impact on society—as well as persuade people to buy. Good promotion enhances the other elements of the marketing mix. Promotion is a major activity around the world.

2. *To describe the general characteristics of advertising, public relations, personal selling, and sales promotion* Advertising is paid, nonpersonal communication transmitted through various media by organizations and individuals who are in some way identified as the sponsor. Public relations includes any communication (paid or nonpaid, nonpersonal or personal, sponsored by a firm or reported by an independent medium) designed to foster a favourable image. Publicity is the nonpaid, nonpersonal, nonsponsored form of public relations. Personal selling involves oral communication with one or more prospective buyers by paid representatives for the purpose of making sales. Sales promotion involves paid marketing activities to stimulate consumer purchases and dealers.

3. *To explain the channel of communication and how it functions* A source sends a message to its audience through a channel of communication. A channel consists of a source, encoding, the message, the medium, decoding, the audience, feedback, and noise.

A source is a company, an independent institution, or an opinion leader that seeks to present a message to an audience. Encoding is the process by which a thought or an idea is translated into a message by the source. A message is a combination of words and symbols transmitted to the audience. A medium is a personal or nonpersonal channel used to convey a message. Decoding is the process by which a message sent by a source is translated by the audience. The audience is the object of a source's message. Feedback is the response the audience makes to a message: purchase, attitude change, or nonpurchase. Noise is interference at any stage.

4. *To examine the components of a promotion plan, international promotion considerations, the legal environment, and criticisms and defences of promotion* Promotion goals may be demand- or image-oriented. Demand goals should correspond to the hierarchy-of-effects model, moving a consumer from awareness to purchase. Primary demand is total consumer demand for a product category; selective demand refers to consumer interest in a particular brand. Institutional advertising is used to enhance company image.

Five ways to set a promotion budget are: all you can afford (the weakest method), incremental, competitive parity, percentage of sales, and objective and task (the best method). Marginal return should be considered when budgeting.

A promotion mix is the overall and specific communication program of a firm, including its use of advertising, public relations (publicity), personal selling, and/or sales promotion. The mix can be well-rounded through integrated marketing communications. Many factors need to be considered in developing a promotion mix.

When devising an international promotion plan, the channel of communication, promotion goals, budgeting, and promotion mix should be studied for and applied to each market.

There are many laws and rules affecting promotion. The major ways to guard against undesirable promotion are full disclosure, substantiation, cease-and-desist orders, corrective advertising, and fines.

Critics are strong in their complaints about promotion practices and their effects. Marketers are equally firm in their defences.

5. To examine the scope, importance, and characteristics of personal selling Personal selling involves oral communication with one or more prospective buyers by paid representatives for the purpose of making sales. About 1.3 million Canadians work in selling jobs; millions more work in sales jobs throughout the world. Yet these numbers understate the value of personal selling because every contact between a company employee and a customer involves some degree of selling.

Selling is emphasized with high-volume clients, geographically concentrated customers, expensive and/or complex products, customers wanting sales services, and entries into foreign markets. Selling also handles objections and addresses other issues. Selling costs are higher than advertising costs at many firms. An average business-to-business sales call costs several hundred dollars. Thus, efficiency is important.

Selling fosters a buyer-seller dyad (a two-way communication flow), offers flexibility and adaptability, adds to relationships with customers, results in less audience waste, clinches sales, and provides immediate feedback. Yet, personal selling can handle only a limited number of customers, is rather ineffective for creating consumer awareness, has high costs per customer, and has a poor image for some consumers.

6. To study the elements in a personal selling plan A selling plan has seven steps: setting goals—demand- and/or image-related; assigning responsibility—to one manager or to several managers; setting a budget; choosing the type(s) of sales positions—order takers, order getters, and/or support salespeople; selecting a sales technique—the canned sales presentation or the need-satisfaction approach; outlining tasks—including each of the relevant steps in the selling process and nonselling tasks; and applying the plan—which centres on sales management.

KEY TERMS

promotion (p. 307)
promotion planning (p. 307)
word-of-mouth communication (p. 307)
advertising (p. 309)
public relations (p. 309)
publicity (p. 309)
personal selling (p. 309)
sales promotion (p. 309)
channel of communication (communication
    process) (p. 311)
source (p. 311)
encoding (p. 312)
message (p. 312)
comparative messages (p. 313)
massed promotion (p. 313)
distributed promotion (p. 314)
wearout rate (p. 314)
medium (p. 314)
decoding (p. 315)
subliminal advertising (p. 315)

audience (p. 316)
feedback (p. 317)
noise (p. 317)
hierarchy-of-effects model (p. 317)
primary demand (p. 318)
selective demand (p. 318)
institutional advertising (p. 318)
all-you-can-afford method (p. 319)
incremental method (p. 319)
competitive parity method (p. 319)
percentage-of-sales method (p. 319)
objective-and-task method (p. 319)
marginal return (p. 320)
promotion mix (p. 320)
integrated marketing communications (IMC) (p. 320)
full disclosure (p. 324)
substantiation (p. 324)
cease-and-desist order (p. 324)
corrective advertising (p. 324)
fines (p. 324)

telemarketing (p. 326)
buyer-seller dyad (p. 327)
sales-expense budget (p. 329)
order taker (p. 330)
order getter (p. 330)
missionary salesperson (p. 331)
sales engineer (p. 331)
service salesperson (p. 331)
canned sales presentation (p. 331)
need-satisfaction approach (p. 331)
selling process (p. 332)
prospecting (p. 332)
approaching customers (p. 332)
sales presentation (p. 333)
closing the sale (p. 333)
sales management (p. 333)
sales territory (p. 334)
straight salary plan (p. 334)
straight commission plan (p. 334)
combination compensation plan (p. 334)

Review Questions

1. Why is promotion planning important?
2. Distinguish among advertising, public relations, personal selling, and sales promotion.
3. What is the role of an opinion leader in a channel of communication?
4. Explain the hierarchy-of-effects model. How is it related to demand objectives?
5. Describe each of the methods of promotional budgeting.
6. State the basic criticisms and defences of promotion.

7. Statistics Canada lists 1.3 million people in sales positions in Canada. Why does this figure understate the importance of personal selling?
8. Under what circumstances should personal selling be emphasized? Why?
9. Distinguish among order-taker, order-getter, and support sales personnel.
10. When is a canned sales presentation appropriate? When is it inappropriate?

Discussion Questions

1. What are the advantages and disadvantages of changing messages (themes) infrequently?
2. As the marketing manager for a small Canadian-based Portuguese book publisher that is entering the Brazilian market for the first time, devise a promotion budget relying on the objective-and-task method.
3. Develop a promotion mix for:
   a. A global restaurant chain.
   b. A small janitorial service.
   c. A four-person dental practice.
   d. A medium-sized sporting-goods manufacturer.
4. Comment on this statement: "Although its role may differ, telemarketing may be successfully used during the selling process for any type of good or service."
5. How would you handle these objections raised at the end of a sales presentation?
   a. "I saw the price of the same item at a competing store for 10 per cent less than what you are asking."
   b. "Your warranty period is much too short."
   c. "None of the alternatives you showed me is satisfactory."

CHAPTER 12
Advertising, Public Relations, and Sales Promotion

Chapter Objectives

1. To examine the scope, importance, and characteristics of advertising

2. To study the elements in an advertising plan

3. To examine the scope, importance, and characteristics of public relations

4. To study the elements in a public relations plan

5. To examine the scope, importance, and characteristics of sales promotion

6. To study the elements in a sales promotion plan

Electro-Power Mixer

} *Infomercials represent a powerful marketing vehicle that is not limited by geographic borders. New cable and distribution systems are exploding around the globe. The kinds of products that sell on TV appeal to a mass market and fall into categories that many cultures buy, such as cosmetics, personal care items, fitness equipment, and kitchen supplies.* }

An infomercial is a full-length TV advertising program (typically thirty minutes) that airs on cable television—or on broadcast media at a fringe time. While watching infomercials, consumers call in orders and items are then delivered directly to their homes or offices. An infomercial is especially useful for products requiring demonstrations to show their benefits.

Infomercials are successfully promoting a variety of goods and services— including food preparation devices (such as juice preparation machines and pasta makers), cosmetics, exercise equipment, instructional videos on computer software, and car waxes. Through a French-language infomercial running twice a day on Infopub, an infomercial channel which is part of Le Groupe Vidéotron Ltée of Montreal, Royal Diamond Cookware received 2000 calls and generated $200 000 in sales in less than three weeks.

There are several factors behind a good infomercial. They relate to the use of testimonials, program length, product pricing, two-step offers, and production considerations. Let's now review each.

A key to the success of any infomercial is the proper use of testimonials. A testimonial is particularly important with two types of infomercials—those that sell a product replacing an "earlier generation" item and the "I made a ton of money and so can you" types of programs. Testimonials do not have to come from a celebrity; they can come from satisfied customers. Some celebrity testimonials can be very effective; however, celebrities can also double an infomercial's production cost.

Even though most infomercials are thirty minutes long, most viewers watch only part of a show. Therefore, infomercial sponsors often divide their programs into self-sustaining parts (such as three ten-minute segments) and give people a chance to order merchandise during each portion of the program.

According to one industry expert, the price of a product appearing on an infomercial should exceed $40 to $50, due to the high production costs and media expenditures. If an appropriate item is priced at a lower amount, sponsors may sell the product as a package of three for $49.95 or as part of a "buy two for $49.95, get one free" promotion.

Some products require a two-step offer, in which a sponsor first generates a list of prospects from an infomercial and then makes separate calls to try to close sales. Two-step offers are appropriate to screen prospects by getting additional information about the prospects' needs, product use, or company size. A negative element of the two-step approach is that the sponsor needs to sell the potential consumer twice, on both the initial inquiry and close.

Producers must include several production considerations in planning and implementing infomercials: The offer should be listed as available for a limited time only to increase sales responses. A toll-free number should be clearly listed. Humour can be used in establishing rapport with the customer, but infomercial experts warn against using humour when promoting a product. And lastly, the qualifications of an "expert host" should be mentioned in the infomercial to enhance credibility.[1]

In this chapter, we will study the advertising, public relations, and sales promotion aspects of promotion.

---

[1]Andrea Haman, "Powerful Pitches," *Marketing Magazine* (December 4, 1995), p. 14; Kim Cleland, "Infomercial Audience Crosses Over Cultures," *Advertising Age* (January 15, 1996), p. I–8; Hershell Gordon Lewis, "Information on Infomercials," *Direct Marketing* (March 1995), pp. 30–32; and Zachary Schiller and Ron Grover, "And Now, A Show from Your Sponsor," *Business Week* (May 22, 1995), pp. 100–104.

Overview

Advertising and public relations are two of the major forms of promotion.

This chapter covers three promotion forms: advertising, public relations, and sales promotions. As defined in Chapter 11, advertising is paid, nonpersonal communication regarding goods, services, organizations, people, places, and ideas; it may be used by businesses, government, and other nonprofit organizations, and individuals. Its distinguishing features are that a sponsor pays for its message, a set format is sent to an entire audience through mass media, the sponsor's name is clearly presented, and the sponsor controls the message.

In contrast, public relations involves communication that fosters a favourable image for goods, services, organizations, people, places, and ideas among their various publics. Its unique features are that it is more image- than sales-oriented; it includes image-oriented advertising, personal selling, and sales promotion; and it often seeks favourable publicity for a firm. As an aspect of public relations, publicity entails nonpersonal communication that is transmitted via mass media but not paid for by an identified sponsor. The media usually control the wording and placement of publicity messages.

The distinctions between advertising and publicity are in part revealed by this statement: "Advertising is paid for, publicity is prayed for."

Sales promotion involves paid marketing communication activities (other than advertising, publicity, or personal selling) that stimulate consumers and dealers. Among the kinds of promotions classed as sales promotions are coupons, trade shows, contests and sweepstakes, and point-of-purchase displays.

The scope and importance, characteristics, and planning considerations for advertising, public relations, and sales promotions are examined in this chapter.

The Scope and Importance of Advertising

In 1996 alone, it is estimated that U.S.$375 billion was spent on advertising around the world—U.S.$6.7 billion in Canada (equivalent to about $9 billion in Canadian funds); nearly U.S.$175 billion in the United States, and just about U.S.$200 billion outside North America (half in Western Europe).[2] Table 12-1 shows per cent of expenditures by medium for Canada, the United States, and Western Europe. In Canada, catalogues and direct mail command the largest expenditure while newspapers and television are the next most used media. In the United States and Western Europe, newspapers and TV are the preferred media; but, newspapers are more popular for Western European advertisers, partly due to greater vehicle choice relative to television. Direct mail is also a key and growing medium in all three areas. The largest media difference between Canada, the U.S., and Western Europe is with magazines, which are more popular in Western Europe.

Three-quarters of North American firms spend less than 4 per cent of sales on advertising. Ads are most important for standardized products aimed at large markets.

ZURICH CANADA
www.zurcan.com/

The per cent of sales devoted to advertising varies by industry and firm; and company advertising as a per cent of sales is usually very low. During 1995, expenditures were less than 2.0 per cent of sales in 40 per cent of North American industries; 2.0 to 3.9 per cent of sales in 35 per cent of North American industries; and at least 4.0 per cent of sales in 25 per cent of North American industries.[3] Among the leading advertisers in the world, such as Procter & Gamble, which spends about U.S.$5 billion annually, the percentages often far exceed industry averages.

An advertising emphasis is most likely if products are standardized, have easily communicated features, appeal to a large market, have low prices, are marketed through independent resellers, and/or are new. Leading brands often get large ad budgets to hold their positions. For example, Zurich Canada, a large insurance company, runs ads positioning itself with two themes: customer-focused and responsive. Zurich believes people see insurance companies as cold and impersonal and wants to change this perception for their firm.

---

[2]Jim McElgunn,"CARD Releases New Figures on Ad Spending," *Marketing Magazine* (September 25, 1995), p. 6; Stuart Elliott, "Advertising," *New York Times* (December 5, 1995), p. D10; and Sally Goll Beatty, "Agencies See Record Ad Spending in '96, Slowing Growth Thereafter," *Wall Street Journal* (December 5, 1995), p. B12.

[3]Computed by the authors from Schonfeld & Associates, "1995 Advertising to Sales Ratios for the 200 Largest Ad Spending Industries," *Advertising Age* (August 14, 1995), p. 26.

Table 12-1

Advertising Expenditures by Medium: Canada, the United States, and Western Europe

MEDIA	Canada[a]	PER CENT OF TOTAL EXPENDITURES United States[a]	Western Europe[a]
Direct Mail Catalogue	22.6	19.7	16.2
Newspapers	20.0	22.9	32.0
Television	19.2	22.8	25.0
Magazines	9.5	5.3	17.4
Yellow Pages	9.2	6.6	—
Outdoor	8.6	0.8	4.7
Radio	8.1	7.0	3.5
Business publications	1.8	2.2	—
Cinema	—	—	0.7
Farm publications	—	0.2	—
Miscellaneous	1.0	12.5	0.5
Total	100.0	100.0	100.0

[a]The media designations in the three areas differ because the sources for the Canadian, U.S., and European data are different.

Sources: Estimated by the authors from data reported in various issues of *Advertising Age;* and Jim McElgunn, "CARD Releases New Figures on Ad Spending," *Marketing Magazine* (September 25, 1995), p. 6.

To fulfil this positioning change the firm has set up Zurich-Assist, a 24-hour help line to deliver advice and guidance to Zurich policy holders, and is advertising this fact. Zurich uses an external advertising agency and its ads are placed on television and in maga-zines; in addition, Zurich has paid to have its logo displayed at Maple Leaf Gardens in Toronto. Through advertising, Zurich wants to be seen as a different kind of insurance company that is there to help.[4]

As a senior executive at the J. Walter Thompson advertising agency once noted, "Advertising works on television and it works in print. What's more, it especially pays to advertise during recessions. All too often, by focusing on the bottom line, firms sacrifice the long-term, brand-building gains advertising makes possible. In our view, this is a serious mistake."[5]

Due to low-involvement purchases, consumer behaviour may be easier to change than attitudes. One ad can have a strong effect on brand awareness. By advertising, it is easier to raise people's opinions of a little-known product than a well-known one. Ad effectiveness often rises over long-term campaigns.

The Characteristics of Advertising

On the positive side, advertising reaches a large, geographically dispersed market; and, for print media, circulation is supplemented by the passing of a copy from one reader to another. The costs per viewer or listener are low. For example, a single TV ad may cost $25 000 to air on the CBC network and reach 2 million people—a cost of $0.0125 per

J. WALTER THOMPSON COMPANY
www.jwtworld.com/

Advertising attracts an audience, has low per-customer costs, offers varied media, is surrounded by information, and aids selling.

[4]News Line, "Zurich Backs Help Line with TV Campaign," *Marketing Magazine* (February 26, 1996), p. 1.
[5]Peter Kim, "Does Advertising Work: A Review of the Evidence," *Journal of Consumer Marketing*, Vol. 9 (Fall 1992), p. 5.

International Marketing in *Action*

Which Soft Drink Is the Real Thing in Brazil?

With U.S.$6 billion in annual sales, Brazil has the world's fourth-largest soft-drink consumption after the United States, Mexico, and Germany. About 45 million of the country's residents are aged 10 to 24, the prime soda-drinking age group. Brazil's average per capita consumption is about twenty-four litres.

In a effort to gain additional market share in the Brazilian market, PepsiCo has invested more than U.S.$500 million in advertising and distribution facilities since 1994. Because of this initiative, Pepsi has increased its overall market share of the Brazilian soda market from 5 per cent to 6 per cent. During the same period Coca-Cola's overall soda market share has dropped by 1.5 per cent—to 38 per cent. In the cola segment, Pepsi has a 7 per cent share; Coca-Cola's is nearly 88 per cent share.

Pepsi has devised twenty different TV commercials targeted specifically at the Brazilian market. One of these commercials shows Coca-Cola executives worrying about Pepsi's revised look, reformulated taste, and new distribution prowess. In response, Coca-Cola is increasing its advertising budget and running a new campaign—with a photocopy salesperson, who while demonstrating the world's most advanced copy machine, says that no one can copy Coca-Cola.

Royal Crown Cola (RC), owned by Cott Corporation of Canada, is entering the Brazilian market in alliance with a local distributor. Using the firm's "Shake things up" international advertising slogan, RC invested U.S.$750 000 in a promotional campaign aimed at three Brazilian test market areas. After a national rollout, RC hopes to go from 0 per cent to 3 per cent market share in the cola segment by the end of 1997.

As the advertising manager for RC, what would you do to compete with Coke and Pepsi in Brazil?

Source: Based on material in Claudia Penteado, "Pepsi Challenges Coke in Brazil," *Advertising Age* (January 16, 1995), p. 12.

---

person (for media time). A broad range of media is available: from national (international) television to local newspapers and even the Internet. Thus, a firm's goals and resources may be matched with the most appropriate medium.

A sponsor has control over message content, graphics, timing, and size or length, as well as the audience targeted. A uniform message is sent to the whole audience. With print media, people can study and restudy messages. Editorial content (a news story or segment of a broadcast show) often borders an ad. This can raise readership or viewing/listening, enhance an image, and create the proper mood for an ad. A firm may even seek specialized media or sections of media (like a paper's sports section for a sports equipment ad).

Ads ease the way for personal selling by creating audience awareness and liking for brands. They also enable self-service wholesalers and retailers to operate, and they sustain an industry—mail order. With a pulling strategy, advertising enables a firm to show its resellers that consumer demand exists.

Advertising is inflexible and can be wasteful, costly, and limit information and feedback.

On the negative side, because messages are standardized, they are rather inflexible and not responsive to consumer questions. This makes it hard to satisfy the needs of a diverse audience. And since many media appeal to broad audiences, a large portion of viewers or readers may be wasted for a sponsor. For instance, a single-unit health spa or a local roofing-materials firm might find that only one-fifth of a newspaper's readers live in its shopping area.

Advertising sometimes requires high total expenditures, although costs per viewer or reader are low. This may keep smaller firms from using some media. In the example earlier in this section, it was said that a TV ad might cost only $0.0125 per viewer. Yet, media time alone for that ad would be $25 000— for one ad, placed once. Also, because high costs lead to brief messages, most ads do not provide much information. TV commercials are very short, averaging 30 seconds or less; few are as long as one minute. Further, because ads are impersonal, feedback is harder to get and it may not be immediately available.

Mass media are used by many people who do not view or listen to ads. They watch TV, read print media, and so on, but ignore ads and discard direct mail. Of concern to television advertisers is "zapping," whereby a viewer uses a remote-control device to switch programs when an ad comes on.

Developing an Advertising Plan

The process of developing an advertising plan consists of the nine steps shown in Figure 12-1 and discussed below.

Setting Objectives

An organization's advertising goals relate either to the demand for its product or service or to its image, with image-oriented ads being part of the firm's public relations effort. Table 12-2 cites several possible goals. Usually, a number of them are pursued in an advertising plan.

As an example, in late 1995 and early 1996 the Bank of Montreal decided to run an image-oriented ad campaign with very clear goals: to allay consumer concerns and to reduce anti-bank sentiments. Anti-bank sentiments were strong because bank profits were at record levels in 1994 and 1995, just after banks had significantly raised existing transaction fees and imposed new ones on their customers. In addition, bank credit card interest rates were very high at a time when prime interest rates were falling to twenty-five-year lows. One of the concerns expressed by consumers was that banks did not appear to be changing in response to the social and economic changes occurring around them. To tap into these sentiments, the Bank of Montreal decide to run an "It is possible"™ campaign.

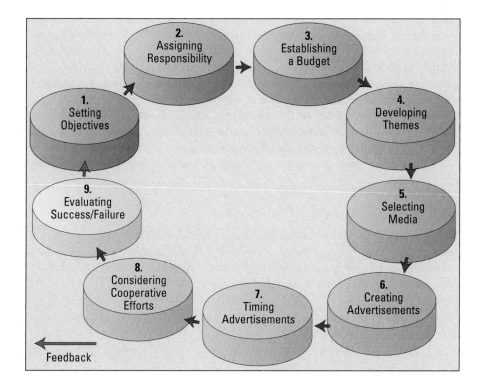

FIGURE 12-1
Developing an Advertising Plan

Table 12-2

Illustrations of Specific Advertising Objectives

TYPE OF OBJECTIVE	ILLUSTRATIONS
Demand-Oriented	
Information	To create target market awareness for a new brand
	To acquaint consumers with new business or store hours
	To reduce the time salespeople take to answer basic questions
Persuasion	To gain brand preference
	To increase store traffic
	To achieve brand loyalty
Reminding (retention)	To stabilize sales
	To maintain brand loyalty
	To sustain brand recognition and image
Image-Oriented	
Industry	To develop and maintain a favourable industry image
	To generate primary demand
Company	To develop and maintain a favourable company image
	To generate selective demand

The campaign featured black and white ads of Canadians holding up signs with statements like: "I'm buying mutual funds" and "This year I'm going to retire" and questions like "Will I ever own my own home?" and "Can a bank help?". The ending line for these ads is "It is possible,"™ the idea being that with the help of the Bank of Montreal the consumers' financial situation would be all right.[6]

Assigning Responsibility

In assigning advertising responsibility, a firm can rely on its internal personnel involved with marketing functions, use an in-house advertising department, or hire an outside advertising agency. Although many firms use internal personnel or in-house departments, most involved with advertising on a regular or sizable basis employ outside agencies (some in addition to their own personnel or departments). Diversified firms may hire a different agency for each product line. A firm's decision to use an outside agency depends on its own expertise and resources and on the role of advertising for the firm.

An **advertising agency** is an organization that provides a variety of advertising-related services to client firms. It often works with clients in devising their advertising plans—including themes, media choice, copywriting, and other tasks. A large agency may also offer market research, product planning, consumer research, public relations, and other services.

*An **advertising agency** may work with a firm to develop its ad plan, conduct research, or provide other services.*

Establishing a Budget

After figuring its overall advertising spending by the all-you-can-afford, incremental, competitive parity, percentage-of-sales, or objective-and-task method, a firm sets a detailed ad budget—to specify the funds for each type of advertising (such as product and institutional messages) and each medium (such as newspapers and radio). Because demand-oriented ads generate revenues, firms should be cautious about reducing these budgets. A better campaign, not a lower budget, may be the answer if performance does not reach goals.

[6]Laura Medcalf, "It's even possible at BMO," *Marketing Magazine* (October 23, 1995), p. 4; Michael Valpy, "Yours Sincerely, Your Soothing Bank," *Marketing Magazine* (March 25, 1996), p. 8.

These points should be addressed: What do various alternatives cost for time or space (a thirty-second TV spot versus a full-page magazine ad)? How many placements are needed for an ad to be effective? (If it takes four telecasts of a single ad to make an impact, a budget must allow four placements.) Have media prices risen recently? How should a firm react during an industry sales slump? What channel members are assigned to which promotion tasks? Do channel members require contributions toward advertising? What does it cost to produce an ad? How should a budget be allocated for domestic versus international ads?

According to a recent survey of international advertising executives, 28 per cent of firms allow personnel in each pan-geographic region to determine their own needs and then petition headquarters for a budget; 28 per cent allow each individual market to have its own advertising strategy and budget; and 20 per cent control budgeting decisions from their world headquarters. Airlines are most likely to use the pan-geographic approach. Consumer products and high-tech companies are most apt to have individual market budgeting.[7]

Developing Themes

A firm next develops **advertising themes**, the overall appeals for its campaign. A good or service appeal centres on the item and its attributes. A consumer appeal describes a product in terms of consumer benefits rather than features. An institutional appeal deals with a firm's image. Table 12-3 presents a full range of advertising themes from which a firm may select. Figure 12-2 shows a thematic ad from The Canadian Dairy Bureau.

*Basic **advertising themes** are product, consumer, and/or institutional appeals.*

Table 12-3
Advertising Themes

THEME	EXAMPLE
Good- or Service-Related	
Dominant features described	Maytag washers emphasize dependability and durability.
Competitive advantages cited	Aiwa stresses the superior quality of its portable stereos.
Price used as dominant feature	Suave beauty products advertise low prices.
News or information domination	New-model laser printers point out enhancements in colour and fonts.
Size of market detailed	Chrysler emphasizes its leading position as a mini-van maker.
Primary demand sought	The Dairy Bureau, Canadian Dairy Product symbol.
Consumer-Related	
Good or service uses explained	Pillsbury ads have cake recipes.
Cost benefits of good or service shown	Owens-Corning states how consumers reduce heating bills with Fiberglas insulation.
Emphasis on how good or service helps consumer	Canadian Pacific Hotels mentions how its rooms are set to accommodate all the needs of business travellers with new work centres.
Threatening situation	Ombrelle sunscreen talks about the threat of skin cancer and how the product can help reduce the risk.
Incentives given to encourage purchases	An ad mentions $1 off the purchase as an introductory offer for a new brand of coffee.
Institutional-Related	
Favourable image sought	The Bank of Montreal talks about how a bank can help Canadians plan their future with their "It is possible"™ campaign.
Growth, profits, and potential described to attract investors	Companies regularly take out full-page ads in business sections of major newspapers.

[7]Jan Jaben, "Ad Decision Makers Favor Regional Angle," *Advertising Age* (May 15, 1995), pp. I-3, I-16.

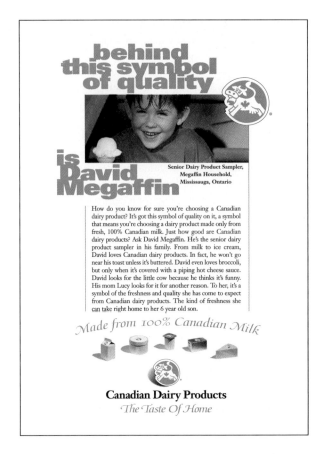

FIGURE 12-2
The Canadian Dairy Bureau: Seeking Primary Demand
Reprinted with permission of Dairy Farmers of Canada.

Selecting Media

There are many media available, as noted in Table 12-4. In selecting them, costs, reach, waste, narrowcasting, frequency, message permanence, persuasive impact, clutter, lead time, and media innovations should be reviewed.

Advertising media costs *are total and per person.*

Advertising media costs are outlays for media time or space. They are related to ad length or size, as well as media attributes. First, the total cost to place an ad in a given medium should be computed—for example, $30 000 for a full-page colour ad in a magazine. Second, per-reader or -viewer costs should be derived (stated on a per-thousand basis). If a $30 000 ad goes in a magazine with a 500 000 circulation, the cost per thousand is $60.

Reach *includes circulation and passalongs.*

Reach refers to the number of viewers, readers, or listeners in a medium's audience. For TV and radio, it is the total number of people who watch or listen to an ad. For print media, it has two aspects: circulation and passalong rate. Circulation is the number of copies sold or distributed to people. The passalong rate is the number of times each copy is read by another reader. For instance, each copy of *Maclean's* is read by several people. The magazine passalong rate is much higher than that for daily papers.

Waste *is the audience segment not in the target market.*

Waste is the part of a medium's audience not in a firm's target market. Because media appeal to mass audiences, it can be a big factor. This can be shown by continuing the magazine example noted in media costs. If the magazine is a special-interest one for amateur photographers, a film producer would know that 450 000 readers might have an interest in a new fast-speed film; 50 000 would have no interest. The latter represents the wasted audience for its ad. So, the real cost is $66.67 ($30 000/450 000 × 1000 = $66.67) per thousand circulation. The firm also knows a general-interest magazine runs ads for film. That magazine sells one million copies and a full-page ad costs $40 000—$40 per thousand. Yet, the firm expects only 200 000 people to have an interest in photography. Thus, the real cost is $200 ($40 000/200 000 × 1000 = $200) per thousand circulation. See Figure 12-3.

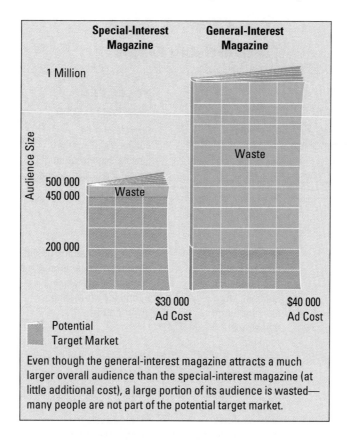

Special-Interest Magazine

General-Interest Magazine

1 Million

Audience Size

Waste

500 000
450 000

Waste

200 000

$30 000
Ad Cost

$40 000
Ad Cost

Potential Target Market

Even though the general-interest magazine attracts a much larger overall audience than the special-interest magazine (at little additional cost), a large portion of its audience is wasted—many people are not part of the potential target market.

FIGURE 12-3
Waste in Advertising

Narrowcasting, which presents advertising messages to rather limited and well-defined audiences, is a way to reduce the audience waste with mass media. It may be achieved using direct mail, local cable TV, specialty magazines, and other targeted media. In narrowcasting, a firm gets less waste in return for a smaller reach. Given that 74.1 per cent of Canadian homes get cable TV programs, this medium has great potential for local narrowcasting.[8]

Frequency is how often a medium can be used. It is greatest for papers, radio, and TV. Different ads may appear daily and a strategy may be easily changed. Phone directories, outdoor ads, and magazines have the poorest frequency. A Yellow Pages ad may be placed only once per year.

Message permanence refers to the number of exposures one ad generates (repetition) and how long it remains available to the audience. Outdoor ads, transit ads, and phone directories yield many exposures per message; and many magazines are retained by consumers for long periods. On the other hand, radio and TV ads last only 5 to 60 seconds.

Persuasive impact is the ability of a medium to stimulate consumers. Television often has the highest persuasive impact because it is able to combine audio, video, colour, and animation. Magazines also have high persuasive impact. Many newspapers are improving their technology in order to feature colour ads and increase their persuasive impact.

Clutter involves the number of ads found in a single program, issue, and so forth of a medium. It is low when few ads are presented, such as Hallmark placing only scattered commercials on the TV specials for which it is the exclusive sponsor. It is high when there are many ads, such as the large amount of supermarket ads in a newspaper's Wednesday issue. Overall, magazines have the highest clutter. And TV is criticized for allowing too much clutter, particularly for assigning more time per hour to commercials and for letting

In **narrowcasting**, *advertisers seek to reduce waste.*

Frequency *is highest for daily media.*

Message permanence *refers to exposures per ad.*

Persuasive impact *is highest for TV.*

Clutter *occurs when there are many ads.*

[8]Statistics Canada, *1995 Market Research Handbook* (Ottawa: Minister of Supply Services), p. 229.

Table 12-4

Advertising Media

MEDIUM	MARKET COVERAGE	BEST USES	SELECTED ADVANTAGES	SELECTED DISADVANTAGES
Daily newspaper	Entire metropolitan area; local editions used sometimes	Medium and large firms	Short lead time, concentrated market, flexible, high frequency, passalongs, surrounded by content	General audience, heavy ad competition, limited colour, limited creativity
Weekly newspaper	One community	Local firms	Same as daily	Heavy ad competition, very limited colour, limited creativity, small market
Commercial television	Regional, national, or international	Regional manufacturers and large retailers; national, large manufacturers and largest retailers	Reach, low cost per viewer, persuasive impact, creative options, flexible, high frequency, surrounded by programs	High minimum total costs, general audience, lead time for popular shows, short messages, limited availability
Cable television	Local, regional, national, or international	Local, regional, and national manufacturers and retailers	More precise audience and more creative than commercial television	Not all consumers hooked up; ads not yet fully accepted on programs
Direct mail	Advertiser selects market	New products, book clubs, financial services, catalogue sales	Precise audience, flexible, personal approach, less clutter from other messages	High throwaway rate, receipt by wrong person, low credibility
Magazines	Local, national, or international (with regional issues)	Local service retailers and mail-order firms; major manufacturers and retailers	Colour, creative options, affluent audience, permanence of messages, passalongs, flexible, surrounded by content	Long lead time, poor frequency (if monthly), ad clutter, geographically dispersed audience
Radio	Entire metropolitan area	Local or regional firms	Low costs, selective market, high frequency, immediacy of messages surrounded by content	No visual impact, commercial clutter, channel switching, consumer distractions

firms show very brief messages (e.g., 15 seconds or shorter). About one-third of all television ads are 15-second spots.[9]

Lead time *is needed for placing an* *ad.*

AMERICA ONLINE
www.aol.com/

COMPUSERVE
www.compuserve.com/

Lead time is the period required by a medium for placing an ad. It is shortest for newspapers and longest for magazines and phone directories. Popular TV shows may also require a lengthy lead time since the number of ads they can carry is limited. With a long lead time, because a firm must place ads well in advance, it risks improper themes in a changing environment.

There have been many media innovations in advertising in recent years. These include commercial online computer services such as Compuserve, America Online Canada, and the other fast-emerging services that let people "surf the Web"; regional editions and special one-sponsor issues ("advertorials") to revitalize magazines; specialized Yellow Pages;

[9]Robert J. Kent, "Competitive Clutter in Network Television Advertising: Current Levels and Advertiser Responses," *Journal of Advertising Research*, Vol. 35 (January–February 1995), pp. 49–57.

Table 12-4 (Cont'd)

MEDIUM	MARKET COVERAGE	BEST USES	SELECTED ADVANTAGES	SELECTED DISADVANTAGES
Business publications	National, regional, or international	Corporate advertising, industrial firms	Selective market, high readability, surrounded by content, message permanence, passalongs	Restricted product applications, may not be read by proper decision maker, not final-consumer oriented
Outdoor	Entire metro-politan area or one location	Brand-name products, nearby retailers, reminder ads	Large size, colour, creative options, repetition, less clutter, message permanence	Legal restrictions, consumer distrac-tions, general audience, inflexible, limited content, long lead time
Transit	Urban community with a transit system	Firms located along transit route	Concentrated market, message permanence, repetition, action-oriented messages, colour, creative options	Clutter of ads, consumer distractions, geographically limited audience
Telephone directories	Entire metro-politan area (with local supplements)	All types of retailers, professionals, service companies	Low costs, perma-nence of messages, repetition, cover-age of market, specialized listings, action-oriented messages	Clutter of ads, limited creativity, very long lead time, low appeal to passive consumers
Internet	Local, national, or international	All types and sizes of firms	Low costs, huge potential audience, vast geographic coverage and amount of information conveyed, interactivity	Clutter of ads, viewed as a novelty by some, goals unclear (advertising vs. entertainment and education), no set rate structure
Flyers	Single neighbourhood	Local firms	Low costs, market coverage, little waste, flexible	High throwaway rate, poor image

televised ads in supermarkets, movie theatres, and aircraft; more radio stations handling ads in stereo; better quality in outdoor signs; full-length televised advertising programs (infomercials); and direct-mail ads with CD-ROM diskettes.

Creating Advertisements

There are four fundamental decisions that the advertiser must make when creating adver-tisements:

Ad creation involves content, schedul-ing, media placement, and variations.

1. Determining the message content and devising the ads. Each ad needs a headline or opening to create consumer interest and copy that presents the message. Content decisions also involve the use of colour and illustrations, ad size or length, the source, the use of symbolism, and the adaptations needed for foreign markets. The role of these factors depends on a firm's goals and resources.

2. Outlining a promotion schedule. This should allow for all copy and artwork and be based on the lead time needed for the chosen media.

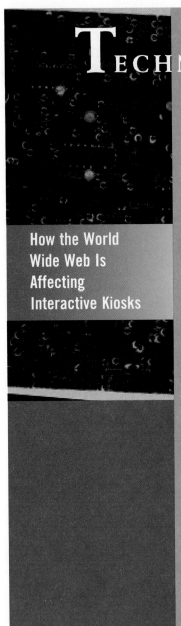

TECHNOLOGY & MARKETING

How the World Wide Web Is Affecting Interactive Kiosks

Prior to the ascension of the World Wide Web as an interactive medium between marketers and consumers, a different interactive technology was being embraced. Interactive kiosks were seen as having tremendous potential. Kiosks are machines that stand alone, usually in a business location, and allow users to interact with them for specific purposes, such as providing information, processing transactions, and collecting information. Kiosks usually have "touch" screens, which make them very easy to use.

Many firms that have experimented with kiosks are financial institutions. Customers could use them to apply for loans, check their credit card or account balances, and look up information. For example, Toronto Dominion tested kiosks in some of their bank branches. Although a large number of people used the kiosks for information, very few completed transactions on them. Now with the wider access of the World Wide Web, firms are not spending much on kiosk development for mass customer use, preferring instead to spend money on development of Web sites.

However, the kiosk has not died. Toronto Dominion uses kiosks at trade shows to promote their services and interact with customers. Kiosks are always open and ready to interact with customers, unlike people, who take breaks or get tied up doing many different tasks. In addition, kiosks can collect information at trade shows in a less intrusive manner than direct interaction involves. People feel less rushed and less self-conscious answering questions from a machine than they do answering questions from a person.

Canadian Tire is a retailer who has set up kiosks in its stores. The kiosks are designed as merchandise directories. Shoppers Drug Mart has used kiosks as part of a cross promotion to allow customers to select seats and dates for NBA tickets purchased for the Toronto Raptors or Vancouver Grizzlies. Another use involves placing kiosks in places where people are normally waiting for service and they can serve as an amusement and information gathering device at the same time. Hotel lobbies are seen as a good place for having interactive kiosks.

Finally, kiosks could be set up to interact with and display elaborate Web sites and thus provide users with a more delightful experience of using the World Wide Web.

As the marketing manager of a Canadian hotel chain, discuss the various ways your firm could employ kiosks to serve your guests more effectively.

Source: Based on material in Anita Lahey, "Life After the Web," *Marketing Magazine* (March 18, 1996), p. 19.

3. Specifying each ad's location in a broadcast program or print medium. As costs have risen, more firms have become concerned about ad placement.

4. Choosing how many variations of a basic message to use. This depends on the frequency of presentations and the ad quality. Sony has been able to run its "There's Nothing Like a Real Trinitron" message for years (see Figure 12-4).

Timing Advertisements

Timing refers to how often an ad is shown and when to advertise during the year.

Potential advertisers must make two major decisions about the timing of advertisements: how often a given ad will be shown and when to advertise during the year. First, a firm must balance audience awareness and knowledge with the danger of irritating the audience if it places an ad a number of times in a short period. Thus, McDonald's runs its ads repeatedly, but changes them often. Second, a firm must choose whether to advertise throughout the year or in concentrated periods. Distributed ads maintain brand recognition and

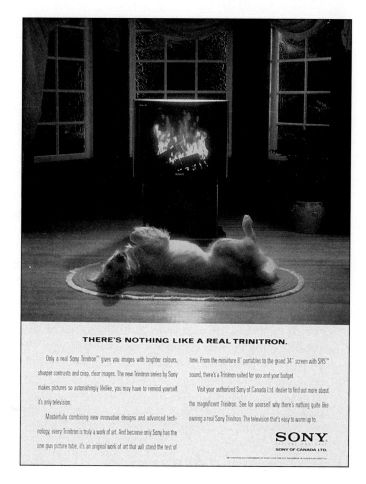

increase sales in nonpeak periods. They are used by most manufacturers and general-merchandise retailers. Massed ads are concentrated in peak periods to generate short-run consumer enthusiasm; they ignore sales in nonpeak periods. Specialty manufacturers and retailers use this method.

Other timing considerations include when to advertise new products, when to stop advertising existing products, how to coordinate advertising and other promotional tools, when to change basic themes, and how to space messages during the hierarchy-of-effects process.

Considering Cooperative Efforts

To stimulate advertising by channel members and/or to hold down its own ad budget, a firm may consider cooperative efforts. With **cooperative advertising**, two or more firms share some advertising costs. In a vertical cooperative-advertising agreement, firms at different stages in a distribution channel (such as a manufacturer and a wholesaler) share costs. In a horizontal cooperative-advertising agreement, two or more independent firms at the same stage in a distribution channel share costs (such as retailers in a mall).

In **cooperative advertising**, *costs are shared by multiple parties.*

Good cooperative agreements state the share of costs paid by each party, the functions and responsibilities of each party, the advertisements to be covered, and the basis for termination. They also benefit each participant.

Each year, manufacturers offer millions of dollars in vertical cooperative-advertising support in Canada. Yet distribution intermediaries typically use only about two-thirds of the money offered. The nonuse by so many resellers is due to their perceptions of manufacturer inflexibility involving messages and media, the costs of cooperative advertising to the resellers, restrictive provisions (such as high minimum purchases to be eligible), and the emphasis on the manufacturer's name in ads. To remedy this, more manufacturers are now flexible as to the messages and media they will support, pay a larger share of advertising costs, have eased restrictive provisions, and feature reseller names more prominently in ads.

Evaluating Success or Failure

Advertising's success or failure depends on how well it helps an organization to achieve promotion goals. Creating customer awareness and increasing sales are distinct goals; success or failure in reaching them must be measured differently. In addition, advertising can be quite difficult to isolate as the single factor leading to a certain image or sales level.

Here are various examples dealing with the evaluation of advertising's success or failure:

- The typical consumer is bombarded with 300 advertising messages each day—about 110 000 per year. According to one major research study, two-thirds of people believe a nationally advertised brand creates the perception that it is of better quality than brands that are not heavily advertised; and in choosing among two unfamiliar brands, two-thirds of people will select the one that is advertised most.[10]

- A survey of consumers in twenty-two nations found that advertising is favourably regarded, although opinions differ by country: "Individuals in former Communist nations are among the most enthusiastic supporters of advertising, apparently reflecting their current desire to embrace consumer-oriented Western capitalism. Egypt was the only market where respondents were consistently anti-advertising."[11]

- Young adults (those 18 to 34) account for one-third of all Yellow Pages use. They are more apt than older adults to rely on information in display ads and less likely to have a specific company name in mind when consulting the Yellow Pages.[12]

The Scope and Importance of Public Relations

Public relations efforts can have a major impact.

Each firm would like to foster the best possible relations with its publics and to receive favourable publicity about its offerings or the firm itself. Sometimes, as with restaurant or theatre reviews, publicity can greatly increase sales or virtually put a firm out of business. For example, Tout Sweet Chocolates went bankrupt when letters were sent to some of the retailers carrying its products claiming they had been poisoned. Retailers pulled all of the products off their shelves and consumers balked at buying any newly produced chocolates even though no tampering was discovered in any of the recalled products. The negative publicity associated with this incident undermined Tout Sweet with its creditors and they put the firm into receivership despite the fact that Tout Sweet chocolate products were of the highest quality.[13]

In Canada, The Canadian Public Relations Society has 1600 members, and many of the larger business firms in Canada and trade associations have their own public relations departments. Worldwide, the International Public Relations Association has 1000 members from sixty nations; yet, the role of public relations varies greatly by nation: "In many foreign areas, the term *public relations* really means *press relations*. Working with the press abroad is not easy; there may be a language barrier, and many times, government controls the media."[14]

CANADIAN PUBLIC RELATIONS SOCIETY
www.cprs.ca/

[10]Michael J. McCarthy, "Mind Probe," *Wall Street Journal* (March 22, 1991), p. B3; and "Advertising Makes the Difference," *Advertising Age* (January 15, 1996), p. 30.

[11]Laurel Wentz, "Major Global Study Finds Consumers Support Ads," *Advertising Age* (October 11, 1993), pp. I-1, I-21.

[12]Jeffrey Casey, "How Do We Get Into This Person's Head?" *Link* (October–November 1995), pp. 37–45.

[13]Michael McCullough, "Poison Threat Sinks Tout Sweet Chocolates," *Marketing Magazine* (May 6, 1996), p. 4.

[14]Nancy Boomer, "CPRS Toughens Up Accreditation Standards," *Marketing Magazine* (June 17, 1996), p. 4; and Fraser P. Seitel, *The Practice of Public Relations*, Sixth Ed. (Englewood Cliffs, New Jersey: Prentice Hall, 1995), various pages.

Table 12-5

Public Relations-Related Situations and How a Firm Could Respond to Them

SITUATION	POOR RESPONSE	GOOD RESPONSE
Fire breaks out in a company plant	Requests for information by media are ignored.	Company spokesperson explains the fire's causes and the precautions to avoid it and answers questions.
New product introduced	Advertising is used without publicity.	Pre-introduction news releases, product samples, and testimonials are used.
News story about product defects	Media requests for information are ignored, blanket denials are issued, and there is hostility to reporters.	Company spokesperson says tests are being done, describes the procedure for handling defects, and takes questions.
Competitor introduces new product	A demand-oriented advertising campaign is stepped up.	Extensive news releases, statistics, and spokespeople are made available to media to present firm's competitive features.
High profits reported	Profits are justified and positive effects on the economy are cited.	Profits are explained, comparative data are provided, and profit uses are noted: research and community development.
Overall view of public relations	There is an infrequent need for public relations; crisis fighting is used when bad reports are circulated.	There is an ongoing need for public relations, strong planning, and plans to counter bad reports.

The competition to gain media attention for publicity is intense. After all, in Canada, television broadcasting is done on only two national television networks, with fourteen regional commercial networks and twenty-one cable specialty networks available as well. In terms of print media there are only fourteen consumer magazines with circulations of 500 000 or more. Nonetheless, there are many opportunities for publicity—with 350 AM radio stations, 517 FM radio stations, 131 originating commercial television stations covering 43 television markets, 110 daily newspapers, and 900 community newspapers around Canada.[15]

Some firms have poor policies to deal with their publics and the media, and fail to develop a sustained public relations effort. Table 12-5 shows several public relations-related situations and how a firm could deal with them. Since unfavourable publicity can occur, a firm must be ready to deal with it in the best way possible. Negative publicity can happen to any firm; a successful one will have a plan to handle it. A firm may get the media on its side by being candid and acting promptly; media may be used to help explain complex issues; and by cooperating with reporters, preconceived notions may be dispelled.

The interrelationship of public relations and other promotion forms must be understood. If advertising, personal selling, and sales promotion are image-oriented, public relations is involved. If they are demand-oriented, it is not. Figure 12-5 shows the interface

Public relations encompasses image-directed ads, selling, and sales promotion—as well as publicity.

[15]Canadian Media Directors' Council, *Media Digest 1997-98*, (Toronto, Ontario: Marketing Magazine), various pages.

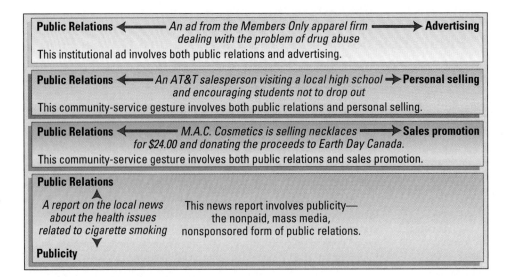

FIGURE 12-5
The Relationship Between Public Relations and the Other Elements of the Promotion Mix

between public relations and other promotion tools. Figure 12-6 shows an effective institutional ad.

> For organizations of all sizes and types, public relations is a necessary part of the marketing mix. This is as true for the two-person SOHO (small office/home office) operation as it is for the multinational corporation. Lack of a big budget for PR is no excuse: Public relations has been called the last free thing in Canada, and that's very nearly true. It's possible to run a whole PR campaign with a pen, a fax machine, and a little brainpower. A lot of PR has to do with timing. The real name of the game in public relations is contacts—the editors, reporters, and other media people you need to get your story out.[16]

FIGURE 12-6
A Socially Responsible Public Relations Campaign
Reprinted by permission.

[16]Gene Koprowski, "Extra: Smart Companies Use Public Relations Tactics to Get Good Ink," *Marketing Tools* (October 1995), p. 48.

The Characteristics of Public Relations

Public relations offers several benefits. Since it is image-oriented, good feelings toward a firm by its external publics can be fostered. In addition, employee morale (pride) is enhanced if the firm is community and civic minded.

When publicity is involved, there are no costs for message time or space. A prime-time television ad may cost $50 000 to $80 000 or more per minute of media time; a five-minute report on a network newscast does not cost anything for media time. However, there are costs for news releases, a public relations department, and so on. As with advertising, publicity reaches a mass audience. In a short time, new products or company policies are well known.

Message believability is higher with publicity because stories appear in independent media. A newspaper's movie review is more credible than an ad in the same paper—the reader links independence with objectivity. Similarly, people may pay more attention to news than to ads. *Canadian Living* has both cooking advice and food ads; people read the stories, but flip through ads. There are a dozen or more ads in a half-hour TV show and hundreds of them in a typical magazine; feature stories are fewer in number and stand out more.

Public relations also has limitations, compared to other promotion forms. Some firms question the value of image-oriented communications and are disinterested in activities not directly tied to sales and profits. They may give the poor responses that were indicated in Table 12-5.

With publicity, a firm has less control over messages and their timing, placement, and coverage by the media. It may issue detailed press releases and find only parts cited in the media; and media may be more critical than a firm would like. Media tend to find disasters, scandals, and product recalls more newsworthy than press releases. And the accessibility of the Internet for disgruntled consumers provides another outlet for bad publicity. This shows how bad publicity can be intense and spread quickly:

> When Rich Koch, a computer salesperson from Florida, bought a new U.S.$13 000 Dodge Neon, it quickly developed glitches. The driver's door latch sometimes refused to release, the plastic liners inside both fenders rattled, and sealant oozed from around the rear window. So, Koch posted an electronic memo on Prodigy detailing his car's woes for the online service's 1.2 million subscribers. "I'd never buy another," he wrote in disgust. Unfortunately for Chrysler, Koch wasn't the only one taking aim at its quality problems. In its annual survey of auto quality, J.D. Power & Associates ranked Chrysler cars below industry averages. And *Consumer Reports* warned readers to be wary of the Dodge Intrepid, Jeep Cherokee pickup, and Dodge Ram pickup—which all had above-average chances of landing in the repair shop.[17]

A firm may want publicity during certain periods, such as when a new product is introduced or a new store opened, but the media may not provide coverage until much later. Similarly, the media determine a story's placement; it may follow a crime or sports report. Finally, the media choose whether to cover a story at all and the amount of coverage devoted to it. A firm-sponsored jobs program might go unreported or get three-sentence coverage in a local paper.

Publicity may be hard to plan in advance because newsworthy events occur quickly and unexpectedly. Thus, short-run and long-run public relations plans should differ in approach. Publicity must complement advertising and not be a substitute. The assets of each (credibility and low costs for publicity, control and coverage for ads) are needed for a good communications program.

To optimize their public relations efforts, at many companies:

- Public relations personnel have regular access to senior executives.

- The publicity value of annual reports is recognized.

- Public relations messages are professionally prepared (with the same care used in writing ad copy) and continuously given to media.

Public relations engenders good feelings; publicity has no time costs, a large audience, high credibility, and attentiveness.

Public relations may be downplayed by some firms; publicity cannot be controlled or timed accurately by a company.

[17]David Woodruff, "An Embarrassment of Glitches Galvanizes Chrysler," *Business Week* (April 17, 1995), p. 76.

- Internal personnel and media personnel interaction is fostered.
- Public-service events are planned to obtain maximum media coverage.
- Part of the promotion budget goes to publicity-generating tasks.
- There is a better understanding of the kinds of stories the media are apt to cover and how to present stories to the media.

Developing a Public Relations Plan

Developing a public relations plan is much like devising an advertising plan. It involves the seven steps shown in Figure 12-7, and which are described next.

Setting Objectives

Public relations goals are image-oriented (firm and/or industry). The choice of goals guides the entire public relations plan.

These are some goals that could be set:

- To gain placement for news releases and coverage of company spokespersons with a variety of media.
- To have the media report on the accomplishments of the company.
- To have the company's position presented when controversy arises.
- To coordinate publicity with advertising.
- To gain more media coverage than competitors.
- To sustain favourable publicity as long as possible.
- To reach out to community groups.
- To have publics view the firm and its industry favourably.

While setting goals, this truism should be kept in mind: "PR involves both *performance* and *recognition*. It is possible to boast excellent performance without being properly recognized, but it is not possible to earn recognition that is not based on solid performance. Woe to the firm that tries to get the R (recognition) without the P (performance)."[18]

FIGURE 12-7
Developing a Public Relations Plan

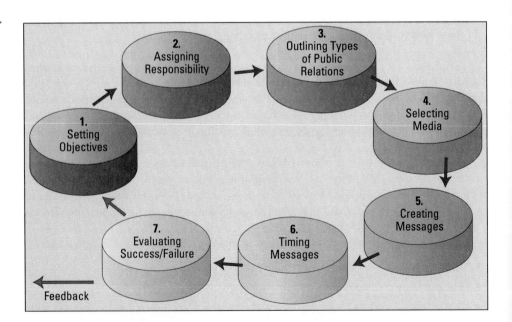

[18]Nat B. Read, "Sears PR Debacle Shows How Not to Handle a Crisis," *Wall Street Journal* (January 11, 1993), p. A16.

AND TODAY'S MARKETER

Is It Getting Harder to Tell the TV Programs from the Ads?

A product placement occurs when a branded product is shown during a TV show or movie, often being used by an actor—such as when James Bond (Pierce Brosnan) drove a new BMW Z3 roadster in the movie *GoldenEye*.

It is important to note that if a program is going to air in the United States, a frequently sought market for Canadian entertainment vehicles, the U.S. Federal Communications Commission requires full disclosure of all product placement fees that are paid directly by companies to TV show producers. However, companies can bypass this provision by paying product placement firms, instead. To protect themselves from legal action, all TV networks require producers to sign a statement indicating that they have not received a product placement fee.

Marketers favouring the use of product placements feel this is a relatively inexpensive way of gaining recognition for a new product or reinforcement for an existing one. A $20 000 product placement, for example, can reach more people for a longer time period than a $250 000, thirty-second commercial. Networks also benefit from product placements by getting free props.

Those that question the use of product placements cite both implementation and societal concerns. On an implementation level, product placements can be hit or miss. Product visibility can be poor if a camera pans too quickly or if a brand name is out of focus. Like publicity, a firm cannot overly rely on product placement. There are also concerns when too many brands are placed on the same show.

On a societal level, product placements can blur the distinction between advertising and program content. According to the executive director of the Center for Science in the Public Interest, "You can zap a commercial. But you can't zap something that's on a program."

As an advertising consultant, give a strategy for using product placements on *Seinfeld*, the popular TV comedy. In the past, Snapple iced tea, Rold Gold pretzels, Diet Coke, and Columbo frozen yogurt were featured on the show.

Sources: Based on material in Fara Warner, "Why It's Getting Harder to Tell the Shows From the Ads," *Wall Street Journal* (June 15, 1995), pp. B1, B11; and Daniel Shannon, "Nobody Does It Better," *Promo* (January 1996), p. 10.

Assigning Responsibility

A firm has three options in assigning public relations responsibility: it may use its existing marketing personnel, an in-house public relations department, or an in-house publicity department; it may have an outside advertising agency handle public relations; or it may hire a specialized public relations firm. Internal personnel or an in-house department ensure more control and secrecy. An outside firm often has better contacts and expertise. Each approach is popular; and they may be combined.[19]

A firm can use an in-house department, hire an outside ad agency, or hire a specialist.

[19]See Gene Koprowski, "Hiring an Agency," *Marketing Tools* (October 1995), pp. 48–49.

Procter & Gamble has an in-house publicity department and several outside public relations agencies. In contrast, some smaller firms rely on the services of specialists, which may charge retainer fees of $25 000 to $50 000 per year. Computer software, such as PRpower, can also let smaller firms easily set up media mailing lists.

Outlining the Types of Public Relations to Be Used

In this step, a firm first chooses the mix of institutional advertising, image-oriented personal selling, image-oriented sales promotion, and publicity to incorporate into an overall promotion plan. Next, public relations efforts must be coordinated with the demand-oriented promotion activities of the firm.

Finally, the general **publicity types** must be understood and envisioned. Each can play a role in an integrated public relations program:

Publicity types *involve news, features, releases, background material, and emergency information.*

- *News publicity* deals with international, national, regional, or local events. Planned releases can be prepared and regularly given out by a firm.
- *Business feature articles* are detailed stories about a company or its offerings that are given to business media.
- *Service feature articles* are lighter stories focusing on personal care, household items, and similar topics, and are sent to newspapers, cable TV stations, and magazines.
- *Finance releases* are stories aimed at the business sections of newspapers, TV news shows, and magazines.
- *Product releases* deal with new products and product improvements; they aim at all media forms.
- *Pictorial releases* are illustrations or pictures sent to the media.
- *Video news releases* are videotaped segments supplied to the media.
- *Background editorial material* is extra information given to media writers and editors; it enhances standard releases and provides filler for stories (like the biography of the chief executive of a company).
- *Emergency publicity* consists of special spontaneous news releases keyed to unexpected events.[20]

Selecting the Media for Public Relations Efforts

For institutional ads, personal selling, and sales promotion, traditional nonpersonal and/or personal media would be used. For publicity, a firm would typically focus on newspapers, television, magazines, radio, and business publications. Due to the infrequent publication schedule of many magazines and some business publications, publicity-seeking efforts may be aimed at daily or weekly media.

Public relations executives rank newspapers and business publications the highest. *The Globe and Mail, The Toronto Star, The Vancouver Sun,* and *Le Journal de Montreal* are preferred newspapers. *Canadian Business, The Financial Post,* and *En Route* are preferred business publications. *Maclean's* and *Time* magazine are preferred general news magazines.

FINANCIAL POST
www.canoe.ca/FP/

⚹ Creating Messages

The creation of public relations messages involves the same factors as other promotion forms—deciding on content and variations, and drawing up a production schedule. Messages can be conveyed in one or a combination of forms, such as news conferences, media releases, phone calls or personal contacts, media kits (a combination of materials on a story), special events (the Molson Grand Prix in Toronto), or videos.

Because it is essential that the media find a firm's publicity messages to be useful, these points need to be kept in mind:

---

[20]H. Frazier Moore, *Public Relations: Principles, Cases, and Problems,* Eighth Ed. (Homewood, Ill.: Richard D. Irwin, 1981), pp. 163–167.

1. Messages should be newsworthy.
2. Reporter deadlines should be respected.
3. Appropriate company representatives should be accessible to reporters.
4. "Mind-fogging" jargon should be avoided.
5. The phrase "no comment" should not be used.
6. Attribution rules (making the source and the content of a story "on" or "off" the record) should be set in advance.
7. A reporter should not be asked to kill a story.
8. Releases should be both easy to read (or view or hear), and easy to use.
9. There should be no hesitancy to volunteer a "bad" story (it will probably get out anyway).
10. Attention should be paid to the needs of each type of medium.[21]

Timing Messages

Public relations efforts should precede new-product introductions and generate excitement for them. For emergencies, media releases and spokespeople should be made available immediately. For ongoing public relations, messages should be properly spaced through the year. As already noted, a firm may find it hard to anticipate media coverage for both unexpected and planned publicity because the media control the timing.

Evaluating Success or Failure

There are several straightforward ways to rate a public relations campaign's success or failure. With institutional ads, image-oriented personal selling, and image-oriented sales promotion, a firm can conduct simple surveys to see how well these communications are received and their impact on its image. With publicity, a firm can count the stories about it, analyze coverage length and placement, review desired with actual timing of stories, evaluate audience reactions, and/or compute the cost of comparable advertising.

Here are some measures of public relations' success:

- Labatt ran a print campaign offering their thoughts on beer and asking readers to share some of theirs. Respondents were offered a free bottle opener for responding. In a two-week period almost 100 000 letters and phone calls came in. The information from these letters and calls provided Labatt with insights into their customers and the perception of beer marketing.[22]

- Wal-Mart now tracks the *quality*, as well as the quantity of their media coverage. It classifies items as news stories, letters to the editor, editorials, or opinion articles—for each market area.[23]

- According to various surveys, many chief executive officers feel effective public relations contribute to profits.[24]

The Scope and Importance of Sales Promotion

Due to intense competition in their industries, numerous firms are aggressively seeking every marketing edge possible. Thus, sales promotion activities worldwide are at their highest level. In the Canadian food and beverage industry, sales promotion expenditures

Sales promotion efforts are now quite extensive.

[21]Christel K. Beard and H. J. Dalton, Jr., "The Power of Positive Press," *Sales & Marketing Management* (January 1991), pp. 37–43. See also Daniel P. Dern, "News That's Fit to Print," *Marketing Tools* (October 1995), pp. 52–53.
[22]Terry Zuk, "Closing in on the Customer," *Marketing Magazine* (February 13, 1995), p. 14.
[23]Don E. Shinkle, "PR Measurement Is the Answer," *Public Relations Quarterly*, Vol. 39 (Fall 1994), pp. 16–17.
[24]Bristol Voss, "Measuring the Effectiveness of Advertising and PR," *Sales & Marketing Management* (October 1992), p. 123; Catherine B. Campbell, "Does Public Relations Affect the Bottom Line?" *Public Relations Journal*, Vol. 49 (October 1993), pp. 14–17; and Koprowski, "Extra: Smart Companies Use Public Relations Tactics to Get Good Ink," pp. 46–53.

are estimated to be $6.7 for every $1 spent on advertising. In comparison, in the United States the ratio is $2.57 for every $1 spent on advertising.[25]

The extent of sales promotion activities are illustrated in the following examples:

- In Canada, households receive about 400 coupons every year—a drop in the bucket compared to the U.S., where each household receives an average of 3000 coupons per year! Virtually all coupons have an expiry date to encourage faster redemption and to allow marketers to evaluate their effectiveness. In a typical year, most Canadian households use coupons, half on a regular basis. Yet, all told people redeem only two per cent of distributed coupons.[26]

- Business-to-business firms spend about 13 per cent of their marketing budgets on trade shows and exhibits. Fifty per cent of industrial trade show attendees report signing a purchase order as a result of a trade show visit.[27]

- According to International Events Group, North American firms spend U.S.$4.5 billion annually to sponsor special events—two-thirds on sports-related events. For example, Air Canada spent $8 million to be a sponsor of the 1996 Olympics in Atlanta, and agreed to be a sponsor for the 1998 Winter Olympics. A promotion related to their sponsorship was a special "Go Canada Go" promotion, which involved a chance for participants to win one of six private jet flights with 39 of their friends to the Olympics.[28]

- Zellers has been operating a frequent shopper program for over 10 years called Club Z. Currently, there are over 9.4 million members, 7.6 million of which make purchases on a monthly basis and are considered active. Club Z allows customers to build up points that can be redeemed for merchandise from a special catalogue, and in some cases, merchandise in the Zellers stores themselves. Customers get rewarded with special discounts and Zellers is able to build its customer database.[29]

- Point-of-purchase displays (P.O.Ps) are categorized as in-store media and are estimated to represent about $150 million in spending each year in Canada.[30] These displays stimulate impulse purchases and provide information. Besides traditional cardboard, metal, and plastic displays, more stores are now using digital electronic signs and video displays.

- In rural India (with its 650 million population), fewer than 15 per cent of the people use toothpaste. So, Colgate-Palmolive hires "video vans" to regularly visit local villages. The vans show a 27-minute infomercial on the value of toothpaste; free samples are then given out and tooth brushing demonstrations are provided.[31]

COLGATE-PALMOLIVE
www.colgate.com/

Several factors account for the strength of sales promotion as a marketing tool. As noted at the beginning of this section, firms are looking for any competitive edge they can get and this often involves some kind of sales promotion; sales promotions are more acceptable to firms and consumers than in the past; many firms want to improve short-run profits, and promotions allow for quick returns; more consumers look for promotions before buying (especially in economic downturns) and resellers put pressure on manufacturers to provide them; advertising and personal selling have become more expensive relative to sales promotion; and technology advances make aspects of sales promotion, like coupon redemption, easier to administer.

[25]Andrea Haman, "Causes of the Conundrum," *Marketing Magazine* (August 21–28, 1995), p. S7.

[26]Lara Mills, "1995 Coupon Calendar," *Marketing Magazine* (August 21–28, 1995), p. 12; and "The 1995 Annual Report on the Promotion Industry," *Promo* (July 1995), p. 38.

[27]Cyndee Miller, "Marketing Industry Report: Who's Spending What on Biz-to-Biz Marketing," *Marketing News* (January 1, 1996), p. 1; and John F. Tanner, Jr. and Lawrence B. Chonko, "Trade Show Objectives," *Industrial Marketing Management*, Vol. 24 (August 1995), pp. 257–264.

[28]"The 1995 Annual Report on the Promotion Industry," p. 40; and News Line, "Air Canada launches Atlanta promotion," *Marketing Magazine* (May 6, 1996), p. 1.

[29] News Line, "CIBC and Zellers launch Club Z Visa card," *Marketing Magazine* (October 23, 1995), p. 1.

[30]Lara Mills, "The Biggest Fish," *Marketing Magazine* (April 8, 1996), p. 9.

[31]Miriam Jordan, "In Rural India, Video Vans Sell Toothpaste and Shampoo," *Wall Street Journal* (January 10, 1996), pp. B1, B5.

The Characteristics of Sales Promotion

Sales promotion has many advantages. It helps attract customer traffic, for example, with new-product samples and trial offers, and it helps keep brand or company loyalty. A manufacturer can retain brand loyalty by giving gifts to regular customers and coupons for its brands. A reseller can retain loyal customers by offering incentives to frequent shoppers and using store coupons.

Rapid results can be gained from some promotions. Calendars, matchbooks, T-shirts, pens, and posters with the firm's name provide consumer value and are retained; thus, they remind the consumer of the company name every time they are used. Impulse purchases can be stimulated by in-store displays. For example, an attractive supermarket display for batteries can dramatically raise sales. In addition, a good display may lead a shopper to a bigger purchase than originally intended.

Excitement can be created by short-run promotions involving gifts, contests, or sweepstakes; and high-value items or high payoffs encourage consumers to participate. Contests offer the further benefit of customer involvement (through the completion of some skill-oriented activity). Many promotions are keyed to customer patronage—with the awarding of coupons, frequent shopper gifts, and referral gifts directly related to purchases. In these cases, promotions can be a fixed percentage of sales and their costs not incurred until transactions are completed. And resellers may be stimulated if sales promotion support is provided in the form of displays, manufacturer coupons, manufacturer rebates, and trade allowances.

Sales promotion lures customers, maintains loyalty, creates excitement, is often keyed to patronage, and appeals to channel members.

Sales promotion also has limitations. A firm's image may be tarnished if it always runs promotions. People may view discounts as representing a decline in product quality and believe a firm could not sell its offerings without them. Profit margins are often lower for a firm if sales promotion is used. When coupons, rebates, or other special deals are employed frequently, people may not buy when products are offered at regular prices; they will stock up each time there is a promotion. Some consumers may even interpret a regular price as an increase for items that are heavily promoted.

Sales promotion may hurt image, cause consumers to wait for special offers, and shift the focus from the product.

Some promotions shift the marketing focus away from the product itself to secondary factors. People may be lured by calendars and sweepstakes instead of product quality and features. In the short run, this generates consumer enthusiasm. In the long run, it may adversely affect a brand's image and sales because a product-related advantage has not been communicated. Sales promotion can enhance—not replace—advertising, personal selling, and public relations.

Developing a Sales Promotion Plan

A sales promotion plan consists of the steps shown in Figure 12-8 and explained next.

Setting Objectives

Sales promotion goals are usually demand-oriented. They may be related to channel members and to consumers.

Objectives associated with channel-member sales promotions include gaining distribution, receiving adequate shelf space, increasing dealer enthusiasm, raising sales, and getting cooperation in sales promotion expenditures. Objectives pertaining to consumer sales promotions include boosting brand awareness, increasing product trials, hiking average purchases, encouraging repurchases, obtaining impulse sales, emphasizing novelty, and supplementing other promotional tools.

Assigning Responsibility

Sales promotion duties are often shared by advertising and sales managers, with each directing the promotions in his or her area. Thus, an advertising manager would work on coupons, customer contests, calendars, and other mass promotions. A sales manager would work on trade shows, cooperative promotions, special events, demonstrations, and other efforts involving individualized attention directed at channel members or consumers.

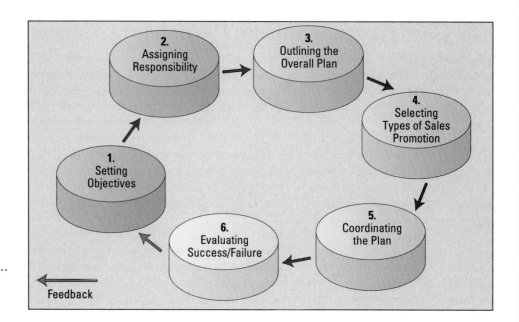

FIGURE 12-8
Developing a Sales Promotion Plan

Some companies have their own specialized sales promotion departments or hire out-side promotion firms. Outside sales promotion firms tend to operate in narrow areas—such as coupons, contests, or gifts—and generally can develop a sales promotion campaign at less expense than the user company could. These firms offer expertise, swift service, flexibility, and, when requested, distribution.

Outlining the Overall Plan

Next, a sales promotion plan should be outlined and include a budget, an orientation, conditions, media, duration and timing, and cooperative efforts. In setting a sales promotion budget, it is important to include all costs. For example, the average face value of a grocery coupon is over 65 cents; supermarkets receive a handling fee for each coupon they redeem; and there are costs for printing, mailing, and advertising coupons.

Sales promotion orientation refers to the focus of the promotion—channel members or consumers—and its theme. Promotions for channel members should raise their product knowledge, provide sales support, offer rewards for selling a promoted product, and seek better cooperation and efficiency. Promotions for consumers should induce impulse and larger-volume sales, sustain brand-name recognition, and gain participation. A promotion theme refers to its underlying channel-member or consumer message—such as a special sale, store opening, new-product introduction, holiday celebration, or customer recruitment. See Figure 12-9.

Sales promotion conditions are requirements channel members or consumers must meet to be eligible for a specific sales promotion. These may include minimum purchases, performance provisions, and/or minimum age. A channel member may have to stock a certain amount of merchandise to receive a free display case from a manufacturer. A consumer may have to send in proofs of purchase to get a refund or gift. In some cases, strict time limits are set as to the closing dates for participation in a sales promotion.

The media are the vehicles through which sales promotions reach channel members or consumers. They include direct mail, newspapers, magazines, television, the personal sales force, trade shows, and group meetings.

A promotion's duration may be short or long, depending on its goals. Coupons usually have quick closing dates because they are used to increase store traffic. Frequent shopper points often can be redeemed for at least one year; their goal is to maintain loyalty. As noted earlier, if promotions are lengthy or offered frequently, consumers may come to expect them as part of a purchase. Some promotions are seasonal, and for these timing

Sales promotion orientation may be toward channel members and/or final consumers.

Sales promotion conditions are eligibility requirements.

FIGURE 12-9
Happy Father's Day
Reprinted by permission.

is crucial. They must be tied to such events as fall school openings or model or style changes.

Finally, the use of shared promotions should be decided. With cooperative efforts, each party pays some costs and gets benefits. These promotions can be sponsored by industry trade associations, manufacturers and/or service firms, wholesalers, and retailers. For example, "McDonald's realizes the strength of the Walt Disney Co. and its strength with animated films, and Disney made a conscious decision to work with us, to our mutual advantage. So, in March 1996, McDonald's headlined a two-tier promotion that included an instant-win trivia game for adults and a kid-targeted Happy Meals promotion. The entire effort surrounded Walt Disney Home Video's top-selling Masterpiece Collection of thirteen videos, including *The Lion King* and *Pocahontas*."[32]

Selecting the Types of Sales Promotion

There is a wide range of sales promotion tools available. The attributes of several promotion tools oriented to channel members are shown in Table 12-6. The attributes of several consumer-oriented sales promotion tools are noted in Table 12-7. Examples for each tool are also provided in these tables.

The selection of sales promotions should be based on such factors as company image, company goals, costs, participation requirements, and the enthusiasm of channel members or customers.

Coordinating the Plan

It is essential that sales promotion activities be well coordinated with other elements of the promotion mix. In particular:

Advertising and sales promotion should be integrated.

- Advertising and sales promotion plans should be integrated.
- The sales force should be notified of all promotions well in advance and trained to implement them.

---

[32]Kate Fitzgerald, "McDonald's Scores Big Promo Role with Disney," *Advertising Age* (January 8, 1996), p. 8.

Table   12 - 6

Selected Types of Sales Promotion Directed at Channel Members

TYPE	CHARACTERISTICS	ILLUSTRATION
Trade shows or meetings	One or a group of manufacturers invites channel members to attend sessions where products are displayed and explained.	The annual National Home Centre Show attracts more than one 1000 exhibitors and tens of thousands of attendees.
Training	The manufacturer provides training for personnel of channel members.	Compaq trains retail salespeople in how to operate and use its computers.
Trade allowances or special offers	Channel members are given discounts or rebates for performing specified functions or purchasing during certain time periods.	A local distributor receives a discount for running its own promotion for GE light bulbs.
Point-of-purchase displays	The manufacturer or wholesaler gives channel members fully equipped displays for its products and sets them up.	Coca-Cola provides refrigerators with its name on them to retailers carrying minimum quantities of Coca-Cola products.
Push money	Channel members' salespeople are given bonuses for pushing the brand of a certain manufacturer. Channel members may not like this if their salespeople shift loyalty to the manufacturer.	A salesperson in an office-equipment store is paid an extra $50 for every desk of a particular brand that is sold.
Sales contests	Prizes or bonuses are distributed if certain performance levels are met.	A wholesaler receives $2500 for selling 1000 microchips in a month.
Free merchandise	Discounts or allowances are provided in the form of merchandise.	A retailer gets one case of ballpoint pens free for every 10 cases purchased.
Demonstration	Free items are given to channel members for demonstration purposes.	A hospital-bed manufacturer offers demonstrator models to its distributors.
Gifts	Channel members are given gifts for carrying items or performing functions.	During one three-month period, a book publisher gives computerized cash registers to bookstores that agree to purchase a specified quantity of its books.
Cooperative	Two or more channel members share the cost of a promotion.	A manufacturer and retailer each pay part of the cost for T-shirts with the manufacturer's and retailer's names embossed.

- Publicity should be generated for special events, such as the appearance of a major celebrity.
- Sales promotions should be consistent with channel members' activities.

Evaluating Success or Failure

The success or failure of some sales promotions is simple to measure.

Measuring the success or failure of many types of sales promotions is straightforward, since the promotions are so closely linked to performance or sales. By analyzing before-and-after data, the impact of these promotions is clear. Trade show effectiveness can be gauged by counting the number of leads generated from a show, examining the sales from those leads and the cost per lead, getting customer feedback about a show from the sales force, and determining the amount of literature given out at a show. Companies can verify changes in sales as a result of dealer-training programs. Firms using coupons can review sales and compare redemption rates with industry averages. Surveys of channel members and consumers can indicate satisfaction with promotions, suggestions for improvements, and the effect of promotions on image.

Some sales promotions—such as event sponsorships and T-shirt giveaways—are more difficult to evaluate. Objectives are less definitive.

Table 12-7
Selected Types of Sales Promotion Directed at Consumers

TYPE	CHARACTERISTICS	ILLUSTRATION
Coupons	Manufacturers or channel members advertise special discounts for customers who redeem coupons.	P&G mails consumers a 50-cents-off coupon for Sure deodorant, which can be redeemed at any supermarket.
Refunds or rebates	Consumers submit proofs of purchase (usually to the manufacturer) and receive extra discount.	First Alert provides rebates to consumers submitting proofs of purchase for its fire alarms.
Samples	Free merchandise or services are given to consumers, generally for new items.	Health clubs offer a free one-month trial.
Contests or sweepstakes	Consumers compete for prizes by answering questions (contests) or filling out forms for random drawings of prizes (sweepstakes).	Publishers Clearing House sponsors annual sweepstakes and awards cash and other prizes.
Bonus packs or multipacks	Consumers receive discounts for purchasing in quantity.	An office-supply store runs a "buy one, get one free" sale on desk lamps.
Shows or exhibits	Many firms co-sponsor exhibitions for consumers.	The Canadian National Exhibition is annually scheduled for the public in Toronto.
Point-of-purchase displays	In-store displays remind customers and generate impulse purchases.	*TV Guide* sales in supermarkets are high because displays are placed at checkout counters.
Special events	Firms sponsor the Olympics, fashion shows, and other activities.	Air Canada is a worldwide sponsor of the Olympics.
Product placements	Branded goods and services depicted in movies and TV shows.	Nike sneakers appear in the movie *Forrest Gump*.
Gifts	Consumers get gifts for making a purchase or opening a new account.	Banks offer a range of gifts for consumers opening new accounts or expanding existing ones.
Frequent shopper	Consumers get gifts or special discounts, based on cumulative purchases. Points are amassed and exchanged for gifts or money.	Airline travellers can accumulate gifts and receive free trips or mileage gifts when enough miles have been earned.
Referral gifts	Existing customers are given gifts for referring their friends to the company.	Tupperware awards gifts to the hosts of their Tupperware parties.
Demonstrations	Goods or services are shown in action.	Different models of Apple computers are demonstrated in a complimentary lesson.

Here are three examples relating to the effectiveness of sales promotion:

- About two-thirds of supermarket shoppers say that end-aisle displays and circular coupons "frequently" catch their attention.[33]

- BMW received 6000 pre-orders for its Z3 roadster after it was seen in the James Bond thriller *GoldenEye*. The car wasn't commercially available until several months after the movie opened.[34]

- A study by the Canadian Congress of Advertising indicated that for nonpersonal sources of purchase information, 42 per cent of Canadians would rely on flyers and circulars as a source of information. This rating was barely behind newspapers, which were mentioned by 44 per cent of Canadians, and way ahead of the third-ranked source of information, television, which was mentioned by 35 per cent of respondents.[35]

[33]"Impact in the Aisles: The Marketer's Last Best Chance," *Promo* (January 1996), p. 26.
[34]Blair R. Fischer, "Making Your Product the Star Attraction," *Promo* (January 1996), p. 88.
[35]Jim McElgunn, "Study Says Nothing Beats Word of Mouth," *Marketing Magazine* (May 1, 1995), p. 9.

MARKETING IN A CHANGING WORLD

Dos and Don'ts for Using the Web[36]

Since October 1994, HotWired has operated a Web site—complete with advertising—on the Internet. These are some of the lessons it has learned and wants to pass along:

> *The most important decision.* A company must be clear about why it wants to be on the Web. Is the goal brand building, publicity, selling products, giving information, customer service, or order tracking?

- *The only valid measure is response.* An actual customer has much more value than an anonymous impression.

- *Bandwidth is still limited.* Because so many people are joining the Web, the average access speed is slowing. Thus, a company should keep its image, video, and text files small—and not waste customers' time.

- *Bigger is not always better.* A 1000-page Web site may not be better than a one-page site. The best Web sites are quick, personalized, and user-friendly.

- *Static sites are toxic.* The easiest way to lose traffic is to set up a site and not change its look often enough.

- *It's more than advertising.* "Marketing on the Web is about providing information and entertainment, and about fostering community. Many companies have also discovered that Web-based customer service functions are improving customer relations and saving money.

- *If it's not part of your media mix, you lose.* To succeed, a company must commit itself to the Web as an integral part of its media mix.

- *Don't ignore demographics or lifestyles.* "All sites are not equal, any more than all magazines or TV shows are equal."

- *No "Under Construction" signs.* "Vaporware is not appreciated. Don't open your site until it's ready."

- *No shovelware.* "TV isn't just radio with pictures, and the Net isn't just a brochure with buttons. It's a whole new medium, with a whole new dynamic."

SUMMARY

1. *To examine the scope, importance, and characteristics of advertising* Advertising is paid, nonpersonal communication sent through various media by identified sponsors. Canadian ad spending is $9 billion annually and non-Canadian spending exceeds U.S.$375 billion per year in such media as newspapers, TV, direct mail, Yellow Pages, radio, magazines, business publications, and outdoor ads. In many industries, advertising is under 2.0 per cent of sales.

It is most apt with standardized products and when features are easy to communicate, the market is large, prices are low, resellers are used in distribution, and/or products are new. In general, behaviour is easier to change than attitudes; one ad can have an impact; ads do well with little-known products; and effectiveness rises during extended campaigns.

Among advertising's advantages are its appeal to a geographically dispersed audience, low per-customer costs, the availability of a broad variety of media, the firm's control over all aspects of a message, the surrounding editorial content, and how it complements personal selling. Disadvantages include message inflexibility, the fact that some viewers or readers are not in the target audience, high media costs, limited information provided, difficulty in getting audience feedback, and low audience involvement.

2. *To study the elements in an advertising plan* An advertising plan has nine steps: setting goals—demand and image types; assigning duties—internal and/or external; setting a budget; developing themes—good/service, consumer, and institutional; selecting media—based on costs, reach, waste, narrowcasting, frequency, message permanence, persuasive

[36]The material in this section is based on HotWired, "How *Not* to Advertise on the Web," *Advertising Age* (December 4, 1995), p. 17.

impact, clutter, lead time, and media innovations; creating ads—including content, placement, and variations; timing ads; considering cooperative efforts—both vertical and horizontal; and evaluating success or failure.

3. *To examine the scope, importance, and characteristics of public relations* Public relations includes any communication that fosters a favourable image among a firm's various publics. It is more image- than sales-oriented; embodies image-oriented ads, personal selling, and sales promotion; and seeks favourable publicity—the nonpersonal communication sent via various media but not paid for by identified sponsors. There are thousands of companies with their own public relations departments and many specialized public relations firms. Companies try to get positive publicity and to avoid negative publicity. Competition is intense for placing publicity releases. Some firms have ineffective policies to deal with independent media or develop a sustained publicity campaign.

Among its advantages are its image orientation, its positive effects on employee morale, and—for publicity—its lack of cost for message time, its high credibility, and audience attentiveness. The disadvantages of public relations—compared with other promotion forms—include the lack of interest by some firms in image-oriented communications and the lack of control over publicity placements by the firm, the media's interest in negative events, and the difficulty in planning publicity in advance.

4. *To study the elements in a public relations plan* A public relations plan has seven steps: setting goals—company and/or industry; assigning duties—internal and/or external; outlining types of public relations—the mix of image-oriented promotion forms and the categories of publicity (news publicity, business and service feature articles, finance releases, product and pictorial releases, video news releases, background editorial releases,

and emergency publicity); choosing media; creating messages; timing messages; and weighing success or failure.

5. *To examine the scope, importance, and characteristics of sales promotion* Sales promotion encompasses paid marketing communication activities (other than advertising, publicity, or personal selling) that stimulate consumer purchases and dealer effectiveness. In the Canadian food and beverage industry, sales promotion expenditures are estimated to be $6.7 for every $1 spent on advertising.

The rapid growth of sales promotion is due to firms aggressively looking for a competitive edge, the greater acceptance of sales promotion tools by both firms and consumers, quick returns, the pressure by consumers and channel members for promotions and their popularity during economic downturns, the high costs of other promotional forms, and technological advances that make them easier to administer.

A sales promotion helps attract customer traffic and loyalty, provides value and may be retained by consumers, increases impulse purchases, creates excitement, is keyed to patronage, and improves reseller cooperation. However, sales promotions may also hurt a firm's image, encourage consumers to wait for promotions before making purchases, and shift the focus away from product attributes. Sales promotion cannot replace other forms of promotion.

6. *To study the elements in a sales promotion plan* A promotion plan has six steps: setting goals—ordinarily demand-oriented; assigning responsibility—to advertising and sales managers, company departments, and/or outside specialists; outlining the overall plan—including orientation, conditions, and other factors; selecting the types of sales promotion; coordinating the plan with the other elements of the promotion mix; and evaluating its success or failure.

KEY TERMS

advertising agency (p. 346)
advertising themes (p. 347)
advertising media costs (p. 348)
reach (p. 348)
waste (p. 348)

narrowcasting (p. 349)
frequency (p. 349)
message permanence (p. 349)
persuasive impact (p. 349)
clutter (p. 349)

lead time (p. 350)
cooperative advertising (p. 353)
publicity types (p. 360)
sales promotion orientation (p. 364)
sales promotion conditions (p. 364)

Review Questions

1. Explain the statement "Advertising is paid for, publicity is prayed for."

2. List five objectives of advertising and give an example of how each may be accomplished.

3. A small firm has an overall annual budget of $50 000 for advertising. What specific decisions must it make in allocating the budget?

4. Differentiate among these advertising concepts: reach, narrowcasting, waste, clutter, and frequency.

5. What are the pros and cons of cooperative advertising?

6. Explain several ways that public relations as practised in both Canada and the U.S. may differ from public relations in other countries.

7. According to public relations executives, which are the two most preferred media for receiving publicity?

8. State three ways for a firm to evaluate the success or failure of its public relations efforts.

9. What are the limitations associated with sales promotion?

10. Why is the success or failure of many types of sales promotion relatively easy to measure?

Discussion Questions

1. Devise an advertising plan for generating primary demand for domestically made TVs.

2. A hotel chain knows a full-page ad in a general-interest magazine like *Maclean's* would cost $25 000; the magazine's total audience is 550 000, 200 000 of whom are part of the chain's target market. A full-page ad in *Ski Canada* magazine would cost $5000; its total audience is 50 000, 40 000 of whom are part of the chain's target market. Which magazine should the hotel chain select? Why?

3. Present and evaluate current examples of companies using institutional advertising, image-oriented personal selling, image-oriented sales promotion, and publicity.

4. Why do you think so many firms handle public relations-related situations poorly?

5. List several sales promotion techniques that would be appropriate for a university. List several that would be appropriate for a minor league baseball team. Explain the differences in your two lists.

PRICE PLANNING

Part 6 covers the fourth and final element of the marketing mix, pricing.

13 Price Planning and Strategy

In this chapter, we study the role of price, its importance in transactions, and its interrelationship with other marketing variables. We contrast price-based and nonprice-based approaches. We also look at each of the factors affecting price decisions in depth: consumers, costs, government, channel members, and competition. Next, we explain how to construct and enact a pricing strategy. First, we distinguish among sales, profit, and status quo objectives. We discuss the role of a broad price policy. Then, we introduce three approaches to pricing (cost-, demand-, and competition-based) and show how they may be applied. We also explain why these three pricing methods should be integrated. We examine a number of pricing tactics, such as customary and odd pricing. We conclude the chapter by noting methods for adjusting prices.

Part 6 Vignette
Pricing for Competition

For marketers, the value of goods and services is created by the choice of target market combined with the product, promotion, and distribution decisions. Capturing the value created and recovering the costs incurred from being in business is an objective of the pricing strategy. Marketers must ensure that the marketplace confers greater value to their offerings than it costs to provide them. Price planning and strategy as presented in Chapter 13 will look at the issues associated with pricing decisions.

Marketers can base their pricing strategies on their costs or on market responsiveness. Ontario Hydro and Hydro-Québec have been using cost-based pricing for their exports but now they find themselves facing price-based competition in a commodity market. A rapid expansion in the need for energy in the 1970s, coupled with an oil embargo by Middle Eastern oil producers, spawned strong government support for innovative approaches to new energy development in Canada and, simultaneously, a strong impetus toward energy conservation and efficiency. Consequently, Ontario Hydro and Hydro-Québec, government-regulated and -supported electricity producers, embarked on a number of "mega-projects" to supply more energy. At the same time, the marketplace responded with energy conservation behaviour and electrical appliances were redesigned to become more energy efficient. Ontario Hydro and Hydro Québec went to considerable expense to develop facilities that turned out be excessive for their markets. The solution seemed simple: sell the surplus power to the U.S. where there was a big market and a "shortage" of electrical power.

> *Price planning means ensuring that the marketplace values a firm's offerings at a price that is greater than the costs of providing them.*

Then the price of fossil fuels began to fall. Canadian natural gas producers had been very actively developing natural gas wells and building pipelines to eastern markets in both Canada and the United States. Consequently, gas-based power plants with lower costs of operation, low capital startup costs, and better transmission efficiency sprang up all over the eastern seaboard of the United States and began providing electricity for one-third of the price of electricity provided by Ontario Hydro and Hydro-Québec. Many U.S. customers defected to the lower-price providers, forcing Ontario Hydro and Hydro Québec, who wished to maintain their revenue, to raise prices for their current customers, thus encouraging more customers to consider alternative suppliers. The vicious pricing cycle that Ontario Hydro and Hydro-Québec find themselves in is now threatening their very survival.

When it comes to market competition, price can be one of the toughest ways to compete for customers, especially when your competitors undersell you. So why would any organization choose this approach? Businesses compete on price because it is the easiest way to differentiate products in the marketplace. WestJet and Greyhound Air chose to enter the airline business using price competition in 1996. The reason: if one air carrier can transport a person from Vancouver to Toronto for a lower fare than another, people will choose the carrier with the lower fare since the distance between Vancouver and Toronto remains the same no matter who does the flying.

The trick in the airline business is to offer lower fares than the competition while remaining profitable. That's not easy, since no domestic discount airline in Canada has been able to survive trying this trick. In fact, very few of the world's airlines are profitable, even without using discount pricing. The one exception has been Southwest Airlines in the United States. Southwest has been able to combine a low-cost structure with high-capacity utilization of its aircraft. WestJet and Greyhound Air were planning to try to duplicate Southwest's formula for success. Both firms had excellent plans and prospects for achieving the low-cost approach. However, Greyhound failed in the summer of 1997 while WestJet was marginally profitable in its first year.

CHAPTER 13
Price Planning and Strategy

Chapter Objectives

1. To define the terms price and price planning

2. To demonstrate the importance of price and study its relationship with other marketing variables

3. To differentiate between price-based and nonprice-based approaches

4. To present an overall framework for developing and applying a pricing strategy

5. To analyze sales-based, profit-based, and status quo-based pricing objectives, and to describe the role of a broad price policy

6. To discuss several specific decisions that must be made in implementing a pricing strategy

{
Recent growth in the music business has been set off by an explosion of new recording talent, the coming of age of Walkman-toting Generation Xers, and ever more ways to deliver tunes. "Music is a more important part of more people's lives than ever before," explains David Geffen, billionaire record impresario and co-founder of DreamWorks SKG. "Young people listen to more music than [baby boomers] did. They buy more music than we did. And we're still buying it, too."
}

Reprinted by permission.

The total sales of pre-recorded music in Canada, the United States, and around the world have increased dramatically in recent years. Globally, annual pre-recorded music sales are approaching U.S.$40 billion. In Canada the music retail business is worth $1.5 billion (Canadian). In 1994, Canadian pre-recorded music sales rose by 19.6 per cent and were on track for a 23 per cent growth rate in 1995.

The largest firm in the recording business is Warner Brothers, with over 22 per cent market share. Warner has many established recording artists, as well as such newer stars as Hootie & the Blowfish and Green Day.

Although close to 80 per cent of new releases fail, successful recordings are *very* profitable. A CD is relatively inexpensive to produce, usually costing less than U.S.$500 000. And besides the profits from CD sales, there are proceeds from catalogue and music publishing sales.

It once took a group several years—and many road tours—to obtain a following. But now, through rock videos on Much Music and the Internet, a group can receive incredible recognition and sales from its first recorded effort. The debut albums *Dookie* and *Cracked Rear View*, from Green Day and Hootie & the Blowfish, respectively, each sold more than six million copies. *Cracked Rear View* remained on the music charts for well over a year.

The high sales and profit potential have generated increased attention for the CD business. Both the News Corporation and Viacom have been looking at opportunities in the recording industry. Existing recording companies such as MCA and Warner Bros. are also launching new labels—at a cost of U.S.$50 million to U.S.$100 million per label (the same amount needed to bankroll a major action movie).

Let's look at the economics of producing and marketing a typical CD. A CD usually sells for $15.98 to $16.98 at retail. Since the standard wholesale cost for a major release is $10.00, the retailer's markup (at retail selling price) is as high as 40 per cent [($16.98 − $10.00)/$16.98)]. The $10.00 wholesale price represents the sales revenue to a recording company per CD.

From its $10.00, the recording company must pay for overhead and profits, artist royalties and copyright fees, marketing expenses, and CD manufacturing costs. Of these items, overhead (comprising record company administration expenses, recording costs,

MUCH MUSIC
www.muchmusic.com/

VIACOM
www.viacom.com/

MCA
www.mca.com/

returns, and profits) is the largest category, amounting to $4.25 to $5.25 per CD. The next largest expense, artist royalties and copyright fees, is $2.00 to $3.00 per CD. Marketing expenses for advertising, public relations, and physical distribution activities total $1.45. Lastly, manufacturing costs are $1.30; this consists of CD production ($0.75), the jewel box container ($0.30), and the printed booklet ($0.25) that accompany the CD.[1]

Overview

A **price** represents the value of a good or service for both the seller and the buyer. **Price planning** is systematic decision making by an organization regarding all aspects of pricing.

Through **price planning***, each* **price** *places a value on a good or service.*

The value of a good or service can involve both tangible and intangible factors. An example of a tangible factor is the cost saving to a soda distributor from buying a new bottling machine; and an example of an intangible factor is a consumer's pride in owning a Porsche rather than another brand of car.

For an exchange to take place, both buyer and seller must feel that the price of a good or service provides an equitable ("fair") value. To the buyer, the payment of a price reduces the purchasing power available for other items. To the seller, the receipt of a price is a source of revenue and a key determinant of sales and profit levels.

Many words are substitutes for the term *price*, including admission fee, membership fee, rate, tuition, service charge, donation, rent, salary, interest, retainer, and assessment. No matter what it is called, a price refers to all the terms of purchase: monetary and nonmonetary charges, discounts, handling and shipping fees, credit charges and other forms of interest, and late-payment penalties.

A nonmonetary exchange would be a department store awarding a gift to a person who gets a friend to shop at that store, or an airline offering tickets as payment for advertising space and time. Monetary and nonmonetary exchanges may be combined. This is common with autos, where the buyer gives the seller money plus a trade-in. That combination leads to a lower monetary price.

From a broader perspective, price is the mechanism for allocating goods and services among potential buyers and for ensuring competition among sellers in an open marketplace. If demand exceeds supply, prices are usually bid up by consumers. If supply exceeds demand, prices are usually reduced by sellers. See Figure 13-1.

In this chapter, the importance of price and its relationship to other marketing variables, price-based and nonprice-based approaches, and the factors affecting price decisions are studied. Next, we will look at the overall process of developing and applying a pricing strategy—including the setting of pricing objectives, the use of various pricing approaches, how a pricing strategy is implemented, and how prices can be adjusted.

The Importance of Price and Its Relationship to Other Marketing Variables

The importance of price decisions has risen considerably over the last thirty years. First, because price in a monetary or nonmonetary form is a component of the exchange process, it appears in every marketing transaction. More firms now realize the impact of price on image, sales, and profits. Second, deregulation in several industries has led to more price competition among firms. Third, in the 1970s and early 1980s, Canadian costs and prices rose rapidly—leading both firms and consumers to be price-conscious. In some other nations, costs and prices continue to escalate very quickly. Fourth, in the 1970s through the mid-1980s, a strong Canadian dollar with respect to other currencies gave foreign competitors a price advantage in Canadian markets. Today, the Canadian dollar is much weaker relative to such currencies as the U.S. dollar and the Japanese yen; and a larger

The stature of price decisions has risen because more firms recognize their far-reaching impact.

[1]Thom Geier, Betsy Streisand, and Kevin Whitelaw, "Recording Sound Sales," *U.S. News & World Report* (September 25, 1995), pp. 67–72; and Christian Allard, "Loony Tunes," *Canadian Business* (August 1995), pp. 73–74.

FIGURE 13-1
The Role of Price in Balancing Supply and Demand

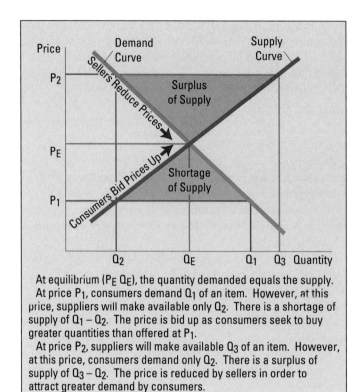

At equilibrium (P_E Q_E), the quantity demanded equals the supply. At price P_1, consumers demand Q_1 of an item. However, at this price, suppliers will make available only Q_2. There is a shortage of supply of $Q_1 - Q_2$. The price is bid up as consumers seek to buy greater quantities than offered at P_1.

At price P_2, suppliers will make available Q_3 of an item. However, at this price, consumers demand only Q_2. There is a surplus of supply of $Q_3 - Q_2$. The price is reduced by sellers in order to attract greater demand by consumers.

number of firms monitor international currency fluctuations and adapt their marketing strategies accordingly. Fifth, the rapid pace of technological advances has caused intense price competition for such products as PCs, CD players, and VCRs. Sixth, service-based firms are placing more emphasis on how they set prices. Seventh, in slow economic times, it is hard for firms to raise prices.

Many marketers share this view:

> Pricing is a manager's biggest marketing headache. It's where they feel the most pressure to perform and the least certain that they are doing a good job. The pressure is intensified because, for the most part, managers believe they don't have control over price: It is dictated by the market. Moreover, pricing is often seen as a difficult area in which to set goals and measure results. Ask managers to define the firm's manufacturing function, and they will cite a concrete goal, such as output and cost. Ask for a measure of productivity, and they will refer to cycle times. But pricing is hard to pin down. High unit sales and increased market share sound promising, but they may in fact mean a price is too low. And foregone profits do not appear on any scorecard.[2]

Inasmuch as a price places a value on the overall marketing mix offered to consumers (such as product features, product image, store location, and customer service), pricing decisions must be made in conjunction with product, distribution, and promotion plans. For instance, Parfums de Coeur makes imitations of expensive perfumes from Chanel, Estée Lauder, and Giorgio and sells them for one-third to one-fifth the price of those perfumes. It uses similar ingredients but saves on packaging, advertising, and personal selling costs. It distributes through such mass merchandisers as K mart.

These are some basic ways in which pricing is related to other marketing and company variables:

- Prices ordinarily vary over the life of a product category, from high prices to gain status-conscious innovators to lower prices to lure the mass market.

- Customer service is affected since low prices are often associated with less customer service.

[2]Robert J. Dolan, "How Do You Know When the Price Is Right?" *Harvard Business Review*, Vol. 73 (September–October 1995), p. 174.

- From a distribution perspective, the prices charged to resellers must adequately compensate them for their functions, yet be low enough to compete with other brands at the wholesale or retail level.

- There may be conflict in a distribution channel if a manufacturer tries to control or suggest final prices.

- Product lines with different features—and different prices—can attract different market segments.

- A sales force may need some flexibility in negotiating prices and terms, particularly with large business accounts.

- The roles of marketing and finance personnel must be coordinated. Marketers often begin with the prices that people are willing to pay and work backward to ascertain acceptable company costs. Finance people typically start with costs and add desired profits to set prices.

- As costs change, the firm must decide whether to pass these changes on to consumers, absorb them, or modify product features.

For firms marketing products in foreign countries, "One of the most significant and perplexing of decisions has to do with pricing. Determining what prices to charge and when to change those prices are almost always tough decisions, but they become even more complicated when a company begins offering products to customers in several international markets." The greater complexity is typically due to the divergent company goals in different markets, the varying attributes of each market, and other factors. Furthermore, the ability to set prices in foreign markets may be affected by variations in government rules, competition, currency exchange rates, anti-dumping laws, operating costs, the rate of inflation, the standard of living, and so on.[3]

Pricing internationally can be quite complicated.

Price-Based and Nonprice-Based Approaches

With a **price-based approach**, sellers influence consumer demand primarily through changes in price levels. With a **nonprice-based approach**, sellers downplay price as a factor in consumer demand by creating a distinctive good or service by means of promotion, packaging, delivery, customer service, availability, and other marketing factors. The more unique a product offering is perceived to be by consumers, the greater a firm's freedom to set prices above competitors'. See Figure 13-2.

*A **price-based approach** occurs when sellers stress low prices; a **nonprice-based approach** emphasizes factors other than price.*

FIGURE 13-2
Price-Based and Nonprice-Based Approaches

Price | **Price-Based Approach** | Price | **Nonprice-Based Approach**

P_1
P_2
Demand Curve
Q_1 Q_2 Quantity

A company operating at P_1 Q_1 may increase sales by lowering its price to P_2. This increases demand to Q_2.
A firm relying on a price-based approach must lower its prices to increase sales.

P_2
P_1
Differentiated Product
Undifferentiated Product
Q_1 Q_2 Quantity

Through a nonprice-based approach, the firm shifts the consumer demand curve to the right by successfully differentiating its products from competitors. This enables the firm to:
(a) increase demand from Q_1 to Q_2 at price P_1, or
(b) raise the price from P_1 to P_2 while maintaining a demand of Q_1.

[3]James K. Weekly, "Pricing in Foreign Markets: Pitfalls and Opportunities," *Industrial Marketing Management*, Vol. 21 (May 1992), pp. 173–179.

In a price-based approach, sellers move along a demand curve by raising or lowering prices. This is a flexible marketing technique because prices can be adjusted quickly and easily to reflect demand, cost, or competitive factors. Yet, of all the controllable marketing variables, price is the easiest for a competitor to copy. This may result in "me-too" strategies or even in price wars. Furthermore, the government may monitor anti-competitive aspects of price-based strategies.

In a nonprice-based approach, sellers shift consumer demand curves by stressing the distinctive attributes of their products. This lets firms increase unit sales at a given price or sell their original supply at a higher price. The risk with a nonprice strategy is that consumers may not perceive a seller's product as better than a competitor's. People would then buy the lower-priced item.

These are examples of price- and nonprice-oriented strategies:

- It was called "Grape Nuts Monday," April 15, 1996, the day that Post cereals in the United States rolled back the retail prices of its cereals by 20 per cent in response to severe price competition from private-label brands. Canadian consumers were anxiously awaiting a similar move in Canada but were disappointed. When asked about the situation, one manager said, "we have no plans to reduce prices. In fact, the U.S. reduction, generally speaking, brings U.S. list prices in line with (ours)." An independent industry observer supported this statement by commenting that U.S. price points are now comparable to Canadian price points. Private-label competition has always been strong in Canada, holding about 10 per cent of the market; consequently the market impact on prices had already been registered here.[4]

- Gucci is the Italian designer/manufacturer of upscale fashion accessories. ("Everyone in Hollywood has to have Gucci's velvet hip-huggers—and the suede loafers with the classic horse's bit on top of a lug sole are selling as fast as Gucci can deliver them.") Its shoes are priced from $160 to $1050, handbags go for $335 to $8995, and women's apparel prices are $110 to $9000. The company recently scrapped some of its cheaper items, such as canvas and plastic handbags.[5]

Factors Affecting Pricing Decisions

Before a firm develops a pricing strategy it should analyze the outside factors affecting decisions. Like distribution planning, pricing depends heavily on elements external to the firm. This contrasts with product and promotion decisions, which, with the exception of publicity, are more controlled by a firm. Sometimes, outside elements greatly influence the firm's ability to set prices; in other cases, they have little impact. Figure 13-3 outlines the major factors, which are discussed next.

Consumers

Company personnel involved with pricing decisions must understand the relationship between price and consumer purchases and perceptions. This relationship is explained by

FIGURE 13-3
Factors Affecting Price Decisions

[4]James Pollock, "Canada Skips Cereal Cuts," *Marketing Magazine* (April 29, 1996), p. 6.
[5]John Tagliabue, "Gucci Gains Ground with Revival of Style," *New York Times* (December 14, 1995), pp. D1, D6.

two economic principles—the law of demand and the price elasticity of demand—and by market segmentation.

The **law of demand** states that consumers usually purchase more units at a low price than at a high price. The **price elasticity of demand** indicates the sensitivity of buyers to price changes in terms of the quantities they will purchase.[6]

Price elasticity represents the percentage change in the quantity demanded relative to a specific percentage change in the price charged. This formula shows the percentage change in demand for each one per cent change in price:

$$\text{Price elasticity} = \frac{\dfrac{\text{Quantity 1} - \text{Quantity 2}}{\text{Quantity 1} + \text{Quantity 2}}}{\dfrac{\text{Price 1} - \text{Price 2}}{\text{Price 1} + \text{Price 2}}}$$

Because the quantity demanded usually falls as price rises, elasticity is a negative number. However, for purposes of simplicity, elasticity calculations are usually expressed as positive numbers.

Elastic demand occurs if relatively small changes in price result in large changes in quantity demanded. Numerically, price elasticity is greater than 1. With elastic demand, total revenue goes up when prices are decreased and goes down when prices rise. **Inelastic demand** takes place if price changes have little impact on the quantity demanded. Price elasticity is less than 1. With inelastic demand, total revenue goes up when prices are raised and goes down when prices decline. **Unitary demand** exists if price changes are exactly offset by changes in the quantity demanded, so total sales revenue remains constant. Price elasticity is 1.

Demand elasticity is based mostly on two criteria: availability of substitutes and urgency of need. If people *believe* there are many similar goods or services from which to choose or have no urgency to buy, demand is elastic and greatly influenced by price changes: Price increases lead to purchases of substitutes or delayed purchases, and decreases expand sales as people are drawn from competitors or move up the date of their purchases. For some people, the airfare for a vacation is highly elastic. If prices go up, they may travel to a nearer location by car or postpone a trip.

If consumers believe a firm's offering is unique or there is an urgency to buy, demand is inelastic and little influenced by price changes: neither price increases nor declines will have much impact on demand. In most locales, when heating oil prices go up or down, demand remains relatively constant because there is often no feasible substitute—and homes and offices must be properly heated. Brand loyalty also generates inelastic demand; consumers then feel their brands are distinctive and do not accept substitutes. Finally, emergency conditions increase demand inelasticity. A truck driver with a flat tire would pay more for a replacement than a driver with time to shop around.

It should be noted that demand elasticity usually varies over a wide range of prices for the same good or service. At very high prices, even revenues for essential goods and services may fall (mass-transit ridership would drop a lot if fares rose from $1.50 to $3; driving would become a more reasonable substitute). At very low prices, demand cannot be stimulated further; market saturation is reached and consumers may begin to perceive quality as inferior.

Price sensitivity varies by market segment because all people are not equally price-conscious. Consumers can be divided into such segments as these:

- *Price shoppers*—They are interested in the "best deal" for a product.
- *Brand-loyal customers*—They believe their current brands are better than others and will pay "fair" prices for those products.

According to the **law of demand***, more is bought at low prices;* **price elasticity** *explains reactions to changes.*

Demand may be **elastic***,* **inelastic***, or* **unitary** *depending on the availability of substitutes and urgency of need.*

Consumers can be segmented in terms of their price orientation.

---

[6]See N. Carroll Mohn, "Price Research for Decision Making," *Marketing Research* (Winter 1995), pp. 11–19; Stephen J. Hoch, Byung-Do Kim, Alan L. Montgomery, and Peter E. Rossi, "Determinants of Store-Level Price Elasticity," *Journal of Marketing Research*, Vol. 32 (February 1995), pp. 17–29; and Francis J. Mulhern and Robert P. Leone, "Measuring Market Response to Price Changes: A Classification Approach," *Journal of Business Research*, Vol. 33 (July 1995), pp. 197–205.

- *Status seekers*—They buy prestigious brands and product categories and will pay whatever prices are set; higher prices signify greater status.
- *Service/features shoppers*—They place a great value on customer service and/or product features and will pay for them.
- *Convenience shoppers*—They value ease of shopping, nearby locations, long hours by sellers, and other approaches that make shopping simple; they will pay above-average prices.

A firm must determine which segment or segments are represented by its target market and plan accordingly.

The consumer's (market segment's) perception of the price of a good or service as being high, fair, or low—its **subjective price**—may be more important than its actual price. For example, a consumer may feel a low price represents a good buy or inferior quality—or a high price represents status or poor value.

The following factors affect a consumer's (market segment's) subjective price:

- *Purchase experience with a particular good or service*—"How much have I paid in the past?"
- *Purchase experience with other, similar goods or services*—"What's a fair price for an item in the same or adjacent product category that I bought before?"
- *Self-image*—"How much should a person like me pay for something like this?"
- *Social situation*—"How much do the people around me expect me to pay for something like this?"
- *Context of the purchase*—"What should this cost in these circumstances?"[7]

Consumers have generally perceived cellular phones as expensive luxury items. To change this perception Cantel has promoted its "Amigo" brand phone with 10-cents-a-minute calling during off-peak phone hours. The idea is to make consumers perceive cellular phones as being more affordable. In fact, Cantel and Bell Mobility have been hammering the affordability point so hard that people can now get the actual cellular phones for "free" with 100 minutes of free air time. With the phone in hand customers need only pay monthly charges and for any calling time after the first 100 minutes.[8]

Costs

The costs of raw materials, supplies, labour, transportation, and other items are commonly beyond a firm's control. Yet, they have a great impact on prices.

In Canada, from the early 1970s into the 1980s, many costs rose rapidly and pushed prices to high levels, before levelling off. For example:

- The federal minimum wage rose from $2.00 per hour in 1972 to $4.00 per hour in 1996 (although 1996 provincial minimum wages range from a low of $4.75 in Newfoundland to a high of $6.85 in Ontario). Minimum wage rates have their greatest impact on fast-food retailers and other firms relying on semiskilled and unskilled labour.
- Mortgage interest rates more than doubled between 1977 and 1981, severely dampening the housing market, before starting to decline in 1983. Since 1993, they have been at twenty-five-year lows.
- The cost of prime-time TV ads has gone up dramatically. For example, the most expensive commercial broadcast time on earth is an ad on the NFL's championship, the Super Bowl. A 30-second ad on the 1972 Super Bowl cost U.S.$100 000. In 1997, the cost was U.S.$1.2 million.

*A consumer's perception of a price level is the **subjective price**.*

CANTEL
www.rogers.com/

---

[7]Ray Funkhouser, "Using Consumer Expectations as an Input to Pricing Decisions," *Journal of Product & Brand Management*, Vol. 1 (Spring 1992), p. 48. See also Richard W. Olshavsky, Andrew B. Aylesworth, and DeAnna S. Kempf, "The Price-Choice Relationship: A Contingent Processing Approach," *Industrial Marketing Management*, Vol. 33 (July 1995), pp. 207–218; and John R. Johnson, "How Valuable Is Value Added?" *Industrial Distribution* (May 1995), pp. 35–38.

[8]News Line, "Cantel Plays Up Affordability in Promo," *Marketing Magazine* (April 17, 1995), p. 3.

Over the past fifteen years, overall Canadian cost increases have been rather low. Although the 1980 inflation rate was 15 per cent, the 1996 rate was under 5 per cent. This means better cost control and more stable prices for most firms. Yet, unexpected events can still strike specific industries. As an example, a few years ago, the price of rhodium, a precious metal used to make catalytic converters for cars, rose rapidly from U.S.$1750 to U.S.$7000 per ounce due to problems at a refinery. Rhodium's cost per car went from U.S.$15 to U.S.$60.[9]

During periods of rapidly rising costs, firms can react in several ways: they can leave products unchanged and pass along all of their cost increases to consumers; leave products unchanged and pass along part of the cost increases and absorb part of them; modify products to hold down costs and maintain prices (by reducing size, using lesser-quality materials, or offering fewer options); modify products to gain consumer support for higher prices (by increasing size, using better-quality materials, offering more options, or upgrading customer service); and/or abandon unprofitable products. For instance, in response to a 50 to 60 per cent increase in the cost of pulp paper, Scott decided to reduce the number of sheets in the smallest roll of Scott Clean paper towels from 96 to 60—and *lower* the price by 10 per cent.[10]

When costs rise, companies pass along increases, alter products, or delete some items.

Despite a firm's or an industry's best efforts, it sometimes takes years to get runaway costs (and prices) under control. A good illustration is the North American auto industry, where costs and prices have risen substantially since 1970. The average new car had a retail price of under U.S.$3500 then; the average price now is over U.S.$17 000. Among the costs that auto executives have had to deal with are billions of dollars in retooling from large to small cars; high fixed costs for plant, equipment, and unionized labour; hundreds of millions of dollars for anti-pollution and safety devices; and investments of up to U.S.$1 billion or more to develop each major new model. Therefore, pricing decisions have to be made far in advance; and flexibility is limited.

If costs decline, firms can drop selling prices or raise profit margins, as these examples show: the use of microchips has reduced PC costs by requiring less wiring and assembly time in production, improving durability, and enlarging information-processing capability. PC prices have gone down steadily, thus expanding the market. On the other hand, low sugar prices let candy makers increase package size (and profits) without raising prices.

Cost decreases have mostly positive benefits for marketing strategies.

Sometimes, low costs can actually have a negative long-run impact:

> Since the oil price collapse of 1986, years of relatively cheap energy prices have brought the march toward greater efficiency to a virtual halt. And that has stymied the efforts to temper the indirect social and economic costs associated with energy use: increased dependence on foreign oil, which retards progress in cutting the trade deficit, and pollution and environmental damage— including the uncertain but potentially catastrophic effects of global warming.[11]

Government[12]

Canadian federal government actions related to pricing are set out in the Competition Act and fall into two major areas: criminal provisions and non-criminal provisions, as shown in Figure 13-4. The Competition Act became law in June 1986 and replaced the former Combines Investigation Act. Criminal provisions related to pricing include: conspiracy, bid-rigging, discriminatory and predatory pricing, price maintenance, and misleading advertising (with respect to price). Non-criminal matters include: refusal to deal, consignment selling, exclusive dealing, tied selling, and delivered pricing. Criminal provisions mean that matters with respect to these practices are normally dealt with through the court system. Non-criminal matters go before the Competition Tribunal, which is empowered to issue injunctions. Finally, individuals or firms can file civil suits if they have suffered damages due to anti-competitive behaviour in the marketplace.

Canada's Competition Act regulates pricing behaviour with criminal and non-criminal provisions.

[9]"Scarce Metal Hits $7000 an Ounce," *New York Times* (July 4, 1990), pp. 43, 48.

[10]Chad Rubel, "Marketers Try to Ease Sting of Price Increases," *Marketing News* (October 9, 1995), pp. 5–6.

[11]"Why Lower Energy Prices Can Be a Mixed Blessing," *Business Week* (February 8, 1993), p. 16.

[12]Unless otherwise stated, information in this section is based on: Industry Canada, "Canada's Competition Act: An Overview," Industry Canada *Strategis* Web site (1996), http://strategis.ic.gc.ca/sc_mrksv/competit/ engdoc/homepage.html.

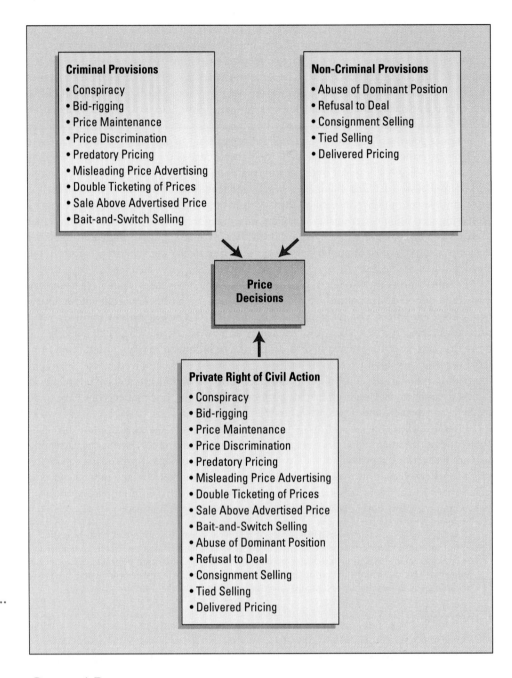

FIGURE 13-4
Canadian Legislative Regulations Affecting Price Decisions

Criminal Provisions

Conspiracy to price fix results from agreements among companies at the same stage in a channel to control resale prices.

CONSPIRACY TO PRICE FIX There are restrictions on price fixing among competitors. Often referred to as horizontal price fixing, it results from agreements among manufacturers, among wholesalers, or among retailers to set prices at a given stage in a channel of distribution. Such agreements are illegal according to the Competition Act, regardless of how "reasonable" prices are.

When violations are found, federal penalties can be severe: For example the legislation allows maximum penalties of fines as high as $10 million or imprisonment of up to five years, or both. In practice the penalties are usually less. For example, in 1994–95 the average fine for violations of the Competition Act was $61 191 per case, or $39 094 for each person accused. These fines were twice the level of those levied in the previous five years.[13]

---

[13]Industry Canada, "Strategic Approach to Marketing Practices Matters Yields Results," Industry Canada *Strategis* Web site (July 12, 1996), http://strategis.ic.gc.ca/sc_mrksv/competit/engdoc/homepage.html; and Industry Canada, "Canada's Competition Act: An Overview," Industry Canada *Strategis* Web site (June 12, 1996), http://strategis.ic.gc.ca/sc_mrksv/competit/engdoc/homepage.html.

In January 1996, thirteen individuals and ten companies in Edmonton were charged with price fixing on real estate property reports for resale homes. These reports were required before real estate transactions could be completed and prior to the price fixing arrangement the base price was $250 and negotiable. It was alleged that after the price fixing agreement, prices rose to $325 for these reports and they were not negotiated.[14]

To avoid price fixing charges, a firm must be careful not to:

- Coordinate discounts, credit terms, or conditions of sale with competitors.
- Talk about price levels, markups, and costs at trade association meetings.
- Plan with competitors to issue new price lists on the same date.
- Plan with competitors to rotate low bids on contracts.
- Agree with competitors to limit production to keep high prices.
- Exchange information with competitors, even informally.

Bid-rigging is very much akin to conspiracy. Bidders collude together or collude with the party offering the bid tender to restrain competition or to inflate bids. It may result in some competitors not submitting bids or in one competitor being given preferential bid treatment.

*With **bid-rigging**, bidders collude with tendering parties to inflate bids.*

Price maintenance occurs when manufacturers or wholesalers seek to control the final selling prices of their goods or services. Price maintenance is also known as fair trade, re-sale price maintenance, and vertical price fixing. It originated out of a desire by manufacturers and wholesalers to protect small resellers and maintain brand images by forcing all resellers within a given area to charge the same price for affected products. Price maintenance was criticized by consumer groups and many resellers and manufacturers as being noncompetitive, keeping prices too high, and rewarding reseller inefficiency.

Price maintenance occurs when manufacturers or wholesalers seek to control final retail selling prices.

The use of price maintenance has been illegal in Canada since 1951. Under the Competition Act, resellers cannot be forced to adhere to manufacturer or wholesaler list prices.

Manufacturers or wholesalers may only control final prices by one of these methods:

- Manufacturer or wholesaler ownership of sales facilities.
- Consignment selling. The manufacturer or wholesaler owns items until they are sold and assumes costs normally associated with the reseller, such as advertising and selling.
- Careful screening of the channel members that sell goods or services. A supplier can bypass or drop distributors if they are not living up to the supplier's performance standards, as long as there is no collusion between the supplier and other distributors. (A firm must be careful not to threaten channel members that do not adhere to suggested prices).
- Suggesting realistic selling prices.
- Pre-printing prices on products.
- Establishing customary prices (such as 50 cents for a newspaper) that are accepted by consumers.

PRICE DISCRIMINATION The Competition Act prohibits manufacturers and wholesalers from **price discrimination** when dealing with different channel-member purchasers. It is illegal to charge different prices for products with "like quality" if the effect of such discrimination is to injure competition. Price practices that can fall under the price discrimination portion of the Act include: differential prices, discounts, rebates, premiums, coupons, guarantees, delivery, warehousing, and credit rates. Terms and conditions of sale must be made available to all competing channel-member customers on a proportionately equal basis.

Price discrimination involves charging different prices to different channel members for products of "like quality."

---

[14]Industry Canada, "Enforcement: Current Activities," Industry Canada *Strategis* Web site (May 22, 1996), http://strategis.ic.gc.ca/sc_mrksv/competit/engdoc/homepage.html.

The price discrimination prohibitions of the Competition Act were originally intended to protect small retailers from unfair price competition by large chains. It was feared that small firms would be driven out of business due to the superior bargaining power (and the resultant lower selling prices) of chains. However, the price discrimination prohibitions of the Competition Act are applicable at all levels of the channel of distribution—including the retail level. Under the Competition Act price differences charged to competing purchasers (whether resellers or consumers) are limited to quantity or volume discounts or when products are of different quality. There are no other bases upon which a price differential can be legally granted and this includes so-called "functional discounts," which are legal in the United States.

Predatory pricing is of two types. The first involves selling products in different regions at different prices (not due to transportation costs) for the express purpose of eliminating existing competitors or lessening competition—such as preventing market entry of competitors. The second involves selling products at unreasonably low prices (essentially at cost or below cost) with the same purpose.

> *Predatory pricing involves setting low prices with the purpose of driving competitors out of business.*

DOUBLE PRICE TICKETING The **double ticketing** provision states that when two prices are marked on an item (as often occurs with sale products) it is illegal to charge the higher price.

> *Regulations on **double ticketing** ensure that when a product has two different prices, consumers pay the lowest price.*

SALE ABOVE ADVERTISED PRICE When an item is advertised in the media at a special price (assuming the price was not a misprint), the marketer is obliged to honour that price according to the terms of the advertising. Charging higher prices to individuals who have not heard of the sale or refusing to honour the price for individuals who have heard of the sale is a violation of the Competition Act.

> *Marketers are not allowed to make **sales above advertised prices**.*

Bait-and-switch selling is the intended practice of advertising a bargain price on a sale item and then not carrying a sufficient supply to satisfy the created demand. The intention is to "switch" customers to other, higher priced items. Signs of bait-and-switch are a refusal to demonstrate sale items, the belittling of sale items, inadequate quantities of sale items on hand, a refusal to take orders, demonstrations of defective items, and the use of compensation plans encouraging salespeople to use the tactic. However, advertisers can avoid violating this regulation by stating the quantity available, offering rainchecks during the sale, or making a reasonable attempt to obtain a large enough quantity.

> *Under **bait-and-switch selling**, sellers illegally draw customers by deceptive pricing.*

MISLEADING PRICE ADVERTISING For consumers, the Competition Act has its most visible impact with respect to **misleading price advertising**. In particular, regulating advertising with respect to regular prices is a key consideration in the Competition Act.

The Competition Bureau offers a Program of Advisory Opinions from which marketers can receive advice on their approach to pricing and price advertising. In addition, price advertising guidelines have been developed by various trade associations, such as the Better Business Bureau. Here are some price advertising guidelines that a firm could follow to avoid contravening the Competition Act:

> *Regulation of **misleading price advertising** is one of the most frequently enforced provisions of the Competition Act.*
>
> *The Program of Advisory Opinions provides advice to marketers on pricing and price advertising.*

- Do not claim or imply that a price has been reduced from a former level unless the original price was offered to the public on a regular basis during a reasonable, recent period of time.

- Do not claim a price is lower than that of competitors or the manufacturer's list price without verifying, through price comparisons involving large quantities of merchandise, that an item's price at other companies in the same trading area is in fact higher.

- A suggested list price or a pre-marked price cannot be advertised as a reference point for a sale or a comparison with other products unless the advertised product has really been sold at that price.

- Bargain offers (such as "free," "buy one, get one free," and "half-price sale") are considered deceptive if their terms are not disclosed at the beginning of a sales presentation or in an ad, the stated regular price of an item is inflated to create an impression of savings, or the quality or quantity of a product is lessened without informing the consumer. A firm may not continuously advertise the same product as being on sale.

Complaints about pricing are normally made to the Competition Bureau. The Director of the Competition Bureau determines whether a suspected violation of the Competition Act has occurred. The Director then decides whether the suspected violation involves criminal or non-criminal provisions. Violations of any of the previously discussed criminal provisions are referred to the Attorney General of Canada for prosecution under the Act. Prosecution of firms and individuals under the criminal provisions require that strict rules of evidence be applied and cases proved beyond a reasonable doubt. However, the suspected violation may be considered under one of the non-criminal provisions that will now be discussed.

NON-CRIMINAL PROVISIONS Non-criminal matters go before the Competition Tribunal, which is empowered to issue injunctions to stop the practices. The normal rules of evidence that apply in court cases do not apply in proceedings undertaken by the Competition Tribunal, although firms do have recourse through the court system if they so desire. Let's look at some of the pricing practices subject to the non-criminal provisions of the Competition Act.

ABUSE OF DOMINANT POSITION The competitive actions of firms who have a dominant position in sectors of the Canadian marketplace can adversely affect their competitors and lessen competition in the marketplace. Pricing considerations that involve **abuse of dominant position** include purchasing products to prevent the reduction of existing price levels and selling articles at a price lower than the acquisition cost to discipline or eliminate a competitor. When this practice involves a sale to a foreign market, it is referred to as product dumping. Before this provision can be enacted, it must be established that an individual or a firm does have substantial control of a class of business in Canada.

*Large firms who sell products below cost to eliminate competition are guilty of **abuse of dominant position**.*

The Competition Tribunal can recommend almost any remedy that can restore the level of competition to the marketplace, including prohibiting any actions that have been lessening competition and divesting a firm of its assets to reduce its market power.

REFUSAL TO DEAL Retailers or wholesalers might encounter a situation where a supplier will refuse to supply a product to them even though they are willing to deal under the supplier's usual trade terms and the supplier has an ample amount of products. If this **refusal to deal** is related to a dispute between the supplier and the retailer or wholesaler over price maintenance it is a violation of the Competition Act. In this case, the Competition Tribunal can order the supplier to accept the customer under the usual trade terms.

Refusal to deal is an illegal practice that may be used to force channel members to maintain prices.

Consignment selling occurs when a dealer is supplied products and only pays for what is sold, when it is sold. The dealer can return unsold goods to the supplier without any penalty. If the practice is undertaken so the supplier is able to price discriminate between consignees and other dealers or to ensure price maintenance, then it is a violation of the Competition Act. The Competition Tribunal can make an order to force the supplier to discontinue the practice.

Consignment selling is a way of ensuring price maintenance and can be used to practice price discrimination.

Tied sales occur when a supplier will only provide a product wanted by a customer on the condition that the customer agrees to purchase another type of product or refrain from purchasing a second product from another firm—in effect, tying one transaction to a second. If the tying results in less competition the Competition Tribunal can issue a prohibition order to stop the practice. Tied selling is a common approach in marketing and usually only becomes a problem when the tie is "unwanted." In this case, a firm may want only one product and find their supplier refuses to deal unless the firm accepts or rejects a second product too.

Tied sales are a problem when the "tied" product is unwanted.

A recent case of tied selling in Canada occurred in 1992, when Digital Equipment of Canada Ltd. came under investigation by the Competition Bureau. Digital Equipment presented a stated policy that buyers could obtain lower hardware and software prices if they used the company as their sole computer service provider. The reason the situation became a tied selling case was that many of the buyers had no recourse but to use Digital because of the proprietary nature of their equipment. As such, the policy had the effect of lessening competition, particularly when competing service providers had "lower" prices for maintenance services. Digital agreed to stop the practice and since it was a matter

DIGITAL EQUIPMENT OF CANADA LTD.
www.digital.ca/

involving a non-criminal provision, there was no admission of guilt and no further action on the part of the Competition Bureau.[15]

DELIVERED PRICING The practice of refusing a customer delivery on the same trade terms as similar customers in essentially the same location is a violation of **delivered pricing**. This regulation applies only if the customers have a comparable ability to receive delivery. For example, if a supplier had to make major capital investments or other accommodations to serve a customer, they could legitimately demand different trade terms. Another situation might involve products that are customarily supplied in bulk quantities on skids and off-loaded with a forklift truck to save labour. If a customer required that the product be broken down from the skids and handled manually, differential trade terms could be applied. Once again, the Competition Tribunal would make an order prohibiting the practice.

Channel Members

Each channel member seeks to play a significant role in setting prices so as to generate sales volume, obtain adequate profit margins, create a suitable image, ensure repeat purchases, and meet specific goals.

A manufacturer can gain greater control over prices by using an exclusive distribution system or avoiding price-oriented resellers; pre-marking prices on products; owning sales outlets; offering products on consignment; providing adequate margins to resellers; and, most importantly, by having strong brands to which people are brand loyal and for which they will pay premium prices.

A wholesaler or retailer can gain better control over prices by stressing its importance as a customer to the supplier, linking resale support to the profit margins allowed by the supplier, refusing to carry unprofitable items, stocking competing items, having strong private brands so people are loyal to the seller and not the supplier, and purchasing outside traditional channels.

Wholesalers and retailers may engage in **selling against the brand**, whereby they stock well-known brands at high prices, and then sell other brands for lower prices to increase sales of their private brands. This practice is disliked by manufacturers since sales of their brands decline.

Sometimes, wholesalers and retailers go outside traditional distribution channels and buy **grey market goods**—foreign-made products imported by distributors (suppliers) that are not authorized by the products' manufacturers. Personal stereos, VCRs, car stereos, watches, and cameras are just some of the items handled in this way.

If wholesalers and retailers buy grey market goods, their purchase prices are less than they would be otherwise and they have greater control over their own selling prices. The result is often discounted prices for consumers, which may be upsetting to manufacturers and authorized dealers.[16]

To maximize channel-member cooperation on pricing decisions, these factors should be considered: channel-member profit margins, price guarantees, special deals, and the impact of price increases. Wholesalers and retailers require appropriate profit margins to cover their costs (such as shipping, storage, credit, and advertising) and earn reasonable profits. Thus, the prices that are charged to them must take these profit margins into account. An attempt to reduce traditional margins for channel members may lose their cooperation and perhaps make them unwilling to carry a product. Pricing through a distribution channel is discussed later in the chapter.

Channel members may seek price guarantees to maintain inventory values and profit. **Price guarantees** assure resellers that the prices they pay are the lowest available. Any discount given to competitors will also be given to the original purchasers. Guarantees are most frequently requested for new firms or new products that want to gain entry into an established channel.

Delivered pricing means that customers in the same geographic area should be charged the same price.

To increase private-brand sales, some channel members sell against the brand.

Grey market goods bypass authorized channels.

Price guarantees reassure channel members.

---

[15]"Digital Agrees to Change Its Ways: Government Alleges 'Tied Selling'," *Globe & Mail* (October 31, 1992), p. B5.
[16]See Gert Assmus and Carsten Wiese, "How to Address the Gray Market Threat Using Price Coordination," *Sloan Management Review*, Vol. 36 (Spring 1995), pp. 31–41.

Special deals—consisting of limited-time discounts and/or free products—are often used to stimulate purchases by resellers. The deals may require channel members to share their savings with final consumers to increase the latter's demand. For example, soda bottlers normally give retailers large price discounts on new products to encourage them to make purchases and then offer low introductory prices to consumers.

The effects of price increases on channel members' behaviour must also be assessed. When firms raise prices to resellers, these increases tend to be passed along to consumers. This practice is more difficult for items with customary prices, such as candy, where small cost rises may be absorbed by the resellers. In any event, cooperation depends on an equitable distribution of costs and profit within the channel.

Competition

Another factor contributing to the degree of control a firm has over prices is the competitive environment within which it operates.

A **market-controlled price environment** is characterized by a high level of competition, similar goods and services, and little control over prices by individual firms. Those trying to charge much more than the going price would attract few customers because demand for any single firm is weak enough that customers would switch to competitors. There would similarly be little gained by selling for less because competitors would match price cuts.

A **company-controlled price environment** is characterized by moderate competition, well-differentiated goods and services, and strong control over prices by individual firms. Companies can succeed with above-average prices because people view their offerings as unique. Differentiation may be based on brand image, features, associated services, assortment, or other elements. Discounters also can carve out a niche in this environment by attracting consumers interested in low prices.

A **government-controlled price environment** is characterized by prices being set or strongly influenced by some level of government. Examples are public utilities, mass transit, insurance, and publicly funded colleges and universities. In each case, government bodies determine or affect prices after obtaining input from the relevant companies, institutions, and/or trade associations, as well as other interested parties (such as consumer groups).

Companies may have to adapt to a changing competitive environment in their industries. Firms in the transportation, telecommunications, and financial industries have seen their price environment shift from government- to market-controlled—although some strong firms in these industries have managed to develop a company-controlled price environment.

Price strategies are easy and quick to copy, so marketers must view price from both short- and long-run perspectives. Excessive price competition may lead to lengthy and costly **price wars**, in which various firms continually try to undercut each other's prices to draw customers. These wars often result in low profits or even losses for the participants, and in some companies being forced out of business.

In recent years, there have been price wars among some car-rental firms, airlines, blank videocassette tape manufacturers, PC makers, semiconductor manufacturers, supermarkets, insurance companies, and others. Although price wars have been more common in Canada and the United States (due to fierce competition in some industries), they are now spreading overseas—particularly to Europe and, to a lesser extent, Japan.

*A firm may face a **market-controlled, company-controlled,** or **government-controlled** price environment.*

Price wars occur when competitors constantly lower prices.

Developing and Applying a Pricing Strategy

As Figure 13-5 shows, a pricing strategy has five steps: objectives, broad policy, strategy, implementation, and adjustments. All of them are affected by the outside factors noted earlier in the chapter. Like any planning activity, a pricing strategy begins with a clear statement of goals and ends with an adaptive or corrective mechanism. Pricing decisions are integrated with the firm's overall marketing program during the broad price-policy step.

The development of a pricing strategy is not a one-time occurrence. It needs to be reviewed when a new product is introduced, an existing product is revised, the competitive

Factors Affecting Price Decisions

Objectives

Broad Price Policy

Pricing Strategy

Implementation of Pricing Strategy

Price Adjustments

• Consumers

• Costs

• Government

• Channel Members

• Competition

◄—— Feedback

FIGURE 13-5
A Framework for Developing and Applying a Pricing Strategy

environment changes, a product moves through its life cycle, a competitor initiates a price change, costs rise or fall, the firm's prices come under government scrutiny, and other events take place.

These are some indications a pricing strategy may be performing poorly:

- Prices are changed too frequently.
- Pricing policy is difficult to explain to consumers.
- Channel members complain that profit margins are inadequate.
- Price decisions are made without adequate marketing-research information.
- Too many different price options are available.
- Too much sales personnel time is spent in bargaining.
- Prices are inconsistent with the target market.
- A high percentage of goods is marked down or discounted late in the selling season to clear out surplus inventory.
- Too high a proportion of customers is price-sensitive and attracted by competitors' discounts. Demand is elastic.
- The firm has problems conforming with pricing legislation.

The rest of this chapter describes in detail the pricing framework outlined in Figure 13-5.

Pricing Objectives

A pricing strategy should be consistent with and reflect overall company goals. It is possible for different firms in the same industry to have dissimilar objectives and, therefore, distinct pricing strategies.

There are three general pricing objectives from which a firm may select: sales-based, profit-based, and status quo-based. With sales-based goals, a firm is interested in sales growth and/or maximizing market share. With profit-based goals, it is interested in maximizing profit, earning a satisfactory profit, optimizing the return on investment, and/or securing an early recovery of cash. With status quo-based goals, it seeks to avoid unfavourable government actions, minimize the effects of competitor actions, maintain good channel relations, discourage the entry of competitors, reduce demands from suppliers, and/or stabilize prices.

A company may pursue more than one pricing goal at the same time, such as increasing sales by 5 to 10 per cent each year, achieving a 15 per cent return on capital investments, and keeping prices near those of competitors. It may also set distinct short- and long-run goals. In the short run, it may seek high profit margins on new products; in the long run, these profit margins would drop to discourage potential competitors.

Sales-Based Objectives

A firm with **sales-based pricing objectives** is oriented toward high sales volume and/or expanding its share of sales relative to competitors. The company focuses on sales-based goals for either (or all) of three reasons: It sees market saturation or sales growth as a major step leading to market control and sustained profits. It wants to maximize unit sales and will trade low per-unit profits for larger total profits. It assumes greater sales will enable it to have lower per-unit costs.

> **Sales-based objectives** *seek high volume or market share.*

To gain high sales volume, **penetration pricing** is often employed—whereby low prices are used to capture the mass market for a good or service. It is a proper approach if customers are highly sensitive to price, low prices discourage actual and potential competitors, there are economies of scale (per-unit production and distribution costs fall as sales rise), and a large consumer market exists. Penetration pricing also recognizes that a high price may leave a product vulnerable to competition.

> **Penetration pricing** *aims at the mass market.*

WAL-MART
www.wal-mart.com/

Penetration pricing is used by such companies as Wal-Mart and Malt-O-Meal. At Wal-Mart the slogan is "watch for falling prices" and this retailer concentrates on "everyday low pricing" instead of running frequent sales. Malt-O-Meal makes no-frills cereals and sells them in bags rather than boxes. Its prices are half those of better-known brands.[17]

Penetration pricing may even tap markets not originally anticipated. For example, few people forecast that cordless phones would reach the sales volume attained during their peak. The market expanded rapidly after prices fell below $100. It grew again as new models were introduced for $60 and less.

Profit-Based Objectives

A company with **profit-based pricing objectives** orients its strategy toward some type of profit goals. With profit-maximization goals, high dollar profits are sought. With satisfactory-profit goals, stability over time is desired; rather than maximize profits in a given year (which could result in declines in nonpeak years), steady profits for a number of years are sought. With return-on-investment goals, profits are related to investment costs; these goals are often pursued by regulated utilities as a way of justifying rate increases. With early-recovery-of-cash goals, high initial profits are sought because firms are short of funds or uncertain about their future.

> **Profit-based objectives** *range from maximization to recovery of cash. Goals can be per unit or total.*

---

[17]Sean Silcoff, "The Price Is (Rarely) Right," *Canadian Business* (February 1997), pp. 62–66; Richard Gibson, "Quaker Oats Co. Will Begin Marketing Value-Priced Cereals Under Its Brand," *Wall Street Journal* (January 23, 1995), pp. 88, 90.

Profit may be expressed in per-unit or total terms. Per-unit profit equals the revenue a seller receives for one unit sold minus its costs. A product like custom-made furniture has a high unit profit. Total profit equals the revenue a seller receives for all items sold minus total costs. It is computed by multiplying per-unit profit times the number of units sold. A product like mass-marketed furniture has a low unit profit; success is based on the number of units sold (turnover). Products with high per-unit profits may have lower total profits than ones with low per-unit profits if the discount prices of the latter generate a much greater level of consumer demand. However, this depends on the elasticity of demand.

Skimming pricing uses high prices to attract the market segment more concerned with product quality, uniqueness, or status than price. It is proper if competition can be minimized (by means of patent protection, brand loyalty, raw material control, or high capital requirements), funds are needed for early cash recovery or further expansion, consumers are insensitive to price or willing to pay a high initial price, and unit costs remain equal or rise as sales increase (economies of scale are absent).

Skimming prices are used by such firms as Genentech, Canondale, and British Airways. Genentech is the maker of Activase, a patented brand of TPA (tissue plasminogen activator), a product that quickly clears the blood clots associated with heart attacks and effectively treats certain kinds of strokes. It sells Activase for about $1500 per dose. Canondale's Super V bikes retail for $3500 each. They have rear shock absorbers to boost comfort, rear frames that pivot vertically to keep the back wheels in constant contact with bumpy roads, light aluminium frames to maximize pedalling efficiency, and front suspensions that ease steering and ensure smoother rides. British Airways recently overhauled its first-class cabins to provide passengers with fully reclining seats, greater privacy, and more room. It is targeting those willing to pay U.S.$6600 for a round trip ticket between London and New York.[18]

Firms sometimes first employ skimming pricing and then penetration pricing, or they market both a premium brand and a value brand. High prices may be charged when competition is limited, or when a product is new. The first group of customers to buy a new product is usually less price sensitive than later groups. High initial prices may also be used to portray a high-quality image. Another advantage of starting a product off with high prices is the fact that it is always easier to lower prices than it is to raise them. After the initial market segment is saturated, penetration pricing can be used to appeal to the mass market and expand total sales volume. Thus, multiple segments can be reached with one product simply by altering pricing strategy.

Status Quo-Based Objectives

Status quo-based pricing objectives are sought by a firm interested in continuing a favourable or stable business climate for its operations.

The pricing strategy is used to minimize the impact of such outside parties as government, competitors, and channel members—and to avoid sales declines.

One should not infer that status quo goals require no effort. A firm must instruct salespeople not to offer different terms to competing channel members or else the government may accuse it of a Competition Act violation. It may have to match competitors' price cuts to keep customers—while striving to avoid price wars. It may have to accept lower profit margins in the face of rising costs to hold channel cooperation. It may have to charge penetration prices to discourage competitors from also marketing certain product lines.

Broad Price Policy

A **broad price policy** sets the overall direction (and tone) for a firm's pricing efforts and makes sure pricing decisions are coordinated with the firm's choices as to a target market,

---

Skimming pricing is aimed at the segment interested in quality or status.

BRITISH AIRWAYS
www.british-airways.com/bans/
checkin.htm

GENENTECH
www.gene.com/

Status quo-based objectives seek good business conditions and stability.

*A **broad price policy** links prices with the target market, image, and other marketing elements.*

---

[18]Ralph T. King, Jr., "TPA Scores Big in Treatment of Stroke," *Wall Street Journal* (December 14, 1995), p. 8; Ron Stodghill II, "Joe Montgomery's Wild Ride," *Business Week* (April 19, 1993), pp. 50, 52; and Charles Goldsmith, "Jet Ahoy! First-Class Fliers Go 'Yachting'," *Wall Street Journal* (December 4, 1995), pp. B1, B10.

International
Marketing in

Can Reebok's Global Hopscotching Pay Off in Lower Costs?

Ten years ago, most of Reebok's shoes and sneakers were produced in South Korea and Taiwan. However, as labour costs in these nations rose, Reebok sought new production facilities. Now, China and Indonesia account for 60 per cent of Reebok's annual worldwide production. That is almost 170 million pairs of sneakers and shoes. Only 9 per cent of Reebok footwear is still produced in South Korea.

Reebok is not alone in changing production sites on the basis of costs. According to the Athletic Footwear Association, a pair of sneakers costs about $27 to manufacture in East Asia and sells for $96 in North America. Nonetheless, after deducting operating expenses, a sneaker manufacturer is left with an average profit of just over $8 per pair. Thus, most manufacturers play a game of global hopscotching in their vendor sourcing.

Different parts of the same shoe are often produced in different countries. For Reebok's Kamikaze II sneaker, a basketball high top, cushioning materials are made in Southern California and then shipped along with moulded shoes to Reebok plants in South Korea and China for final assembly. Different types of sneakers are also made in different countries. Generally, a new production facility first produces a simple version of a running shoe or an aerobic shoe. After workers perfect their skills, more costly lines of shoes are manufactured there.

All of its Asian factories are evaluated through the six-point Reebok Supplier Certification Program that ranks suppliers on the basis of such attributes as the number of defective sneakers returned by retailers and on-time delivery. In addition, suppliers must comply with the firm's human-rights production standards.

As a consultant to Reebok, discuss the pros and cons of its global hopscotching approach.

Source: Based on material in David Fischer, "Global Hopscotch," *U.S. News & World Report* (June 5, 1995), pp. 43–45.

---

an image, and other marketing-mix factors. It incorporates short- and long-term pricing goals, as well as the role of pricing. Pricing can play a passive role—with customer purchases based on superior service, convenience, and quality—or it can play an active role—with purchases based on discount prices. Thus, a high-income segment buying status brands at upscale stores would expect premium prices. A moderate-income segment buying private brands at flea markets would expect low prices.

A firm outlines a broad price policy by placing individual decisions into an integrated format. It then decides on the interrelationship of prices for items within a product line, how often special discounts are used, how prices compare to competition, the frequency of price changes, and the method for setting new-product prices. As such, "marketing strategies attempt to define where the firm wants to be in the marketplace, and how it plans to get there. They provide the larger framework within which pricing and other programs are developed. Correspondingly, there should be a clear link between strategies and individual programs."[19]

---

[19]Michael H. Morris and Roger J. Calantone, "Four Components of Effective Pricing," *Industrial Marketing Management*, Vol. 19 (November 1990), p. 327.

Pricing Strategy

A pricing strategy may be cost-, demand-, and/or competition-based. When the three approaches are integrated, combination pricing is involved. See Figure 13-6.

Cost-Based Pricing

Under **cost-based pricing**, *expenses are computed, profit is projected, and a* **price floor** *set.*

In **cost-based pricing**, a firm sets prices by computing merchandise, service, and overhead costs and then adding an amount to cover its profit goal. Table 13-1 defines the key concepts in cost-based pricing and how they may be applied to big-screen television sets.

Cost-based prices are rather easy to derive because there is no need to estimate elasticity of demand or competitive reactions to price changes. There is also greater certainty about costs than demand or competitor responses to prices. Finally, cost-based pricing seeks reasonable profits since it is geared to covering all types of costs. It is often used by firms whose goals are stated in terms of profit or return on investment. A **price floor** is the lowest acceptable price a firm can charge and attain its profit goal.

When used by itself, cost-based pricing does have some significant limitations. It does not consider market conditions, the full effects of excess plant capacity, competitive prices, the product's phase in its life cycle, market share goals, consumers' ability to pay, and other factors.

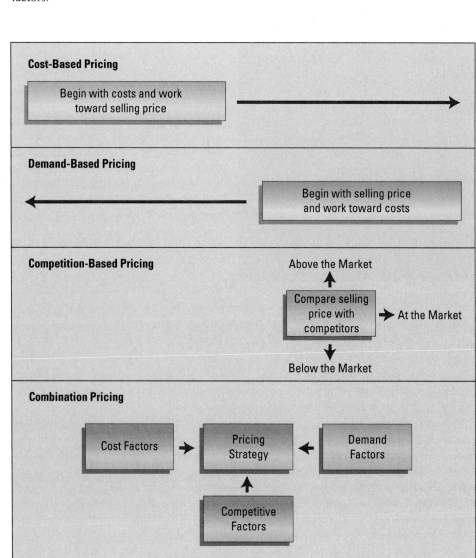

FIGURE 13-6
Ways of Developing a Pricing Strategy

Table 13-1

Key Cost Concepts and their Application to Big-Screen Television Sets

COST CONCEPT	DEFINITION	EXAMPLES[a]	SOURCES OF INFORMATION	METHOD OF COMPUTATION
Total fixed costs	Ongoing costs not related to volume. They are usually constant over a given range of output for a specified time.	Rent, salaries, electricity, real estate taxes, and plant and equipment.	Accounting data, bills, cost estimates.	Addition of all fixed cost components.
Total variable costs	Costs that change with increases or decreases in output (volume).	Parts (such as tuners and speakers), hourly employees who assemble sets, and sales commissions.	Cost data from suppliers, estimates of labour productivity, sales estimates.	Addition of all variable cost components.
Total costs	Sum of total fixed and total variable costs.	See above.	See above.	Addition of all fixed and variable cost components.
Average fixed costs	Average fixed costs per unit.	See above under total fixed costs.	Total fixed costs and production estimates.	Total fixed costs/ Quantity produced in units.
Average variable costs	Average variable costs per unit.	See above under total variable costs.	Total variable costs and production estimates.	Total variable costs/ Quantity produced in units.
Average total costs	Sum of average fixed costs and average variable costs.	See above under total fixed and total variable costs.	Total costs and production estimates.	Average fixed costs + Average variable costs or Total costs/Quantity produced in units.
Marginal costs	Costs of making an additional unit.	See above under total fixed and total variable costs.	Accounting data, bills, cost estimates of labour and materials.	(Total costs of producing current quantity + one unit) − (Total costs of producing current quantity).

[a]Such marketing costs as advertising and distribution are often broken down into both fixed and variable components.

Sometimes, it is hard to figure how such overhead costs as rent, lighting, personnel, and other general expenses should be allocated to each product. These costs are often assigned on the basis of product sales or the personnel time associated with each item. For instance, if product A accounts for 10 per cent of sales, it might be allotted 10 per cent of overhead costs. If product B receives 20 per cent of personnel time, it might be allotted 20 per cent of overhead costs. Yet, problems may arise since different methods for assigning costs may yield different results: How would costs be allocated if product A yields 10 per cent of sales and requires 20 per cent of personnel time?

In the following subsections, five cost-based pricing techniques are covered: cost-plus, markup, target, price-floor, and traditional break-even analysis. Figure 13-7 gives a synopsis of each technique. And Table 13-2 contains numerical examples of each.

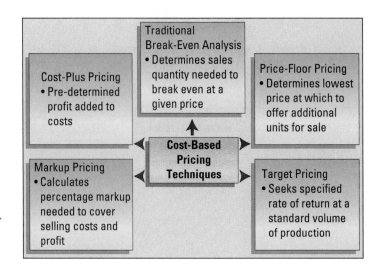

FIGURE 13-7
Cost-Based Pricing Techniques

Cost-plus pricing *is the easiest form of pricing, based on units produced, total costs, and profit.*

COST-PLUS PRICING For **cost-plus pricing**, prices are set by adding a predetermined profit to costs. It is the simplest form of cost-based pricing.

Generally, the steps for computing cost-plus prices are to estimate the number of units to be produced, calculate fixed and variable costs, and add a desired profit to costs. The formula for cost-plus pricing is:

$$\text{Price} = \frac{\text{Total fixed costs} + \text{Total variable costs} + \text{Projected profit}}{\text{Units produced}}$$

This method is easy to compute; yet, it has shortcomings. Profit is not expressed in relation to sales but in relation to costs, and price is not tied to consumer demand. Adjustments for rising costs are poorly conceived, and there are no plans for using excess capacity. There is little incentive to improve efficiency to hold down costs, and marginal costs are rarely analyzed.

Cost-plus pricing is most effective when price fluctuations have little influence on sales and when a firm is able to control prices. For example, the prices of custom-made furniture, ships, heavy machinery, and extracted minerals typically depend on the costs incurred in producing these items; thus, companies set prices by computing costs and adding a reasonable profit. Cost-plus pricing often allows firms to get consumer orders, produce items, and then derive prices after total costs are known. This protects sellers.

Markup pricing *considers per-unit product costs and the markups required to cover selling costs and profits. Markups should be expressed in terms of price rather than cost.*

MARKUP PRICING In **markup pricing**, a firm sets prices by computing the per-unit costs of producing (buying) goods and/or services and then determining the markup percentages needed to cover selling costs and profit. It is most commonly used by wholesalers and retailers, although it is employed by all types of organizations. The formula for markup pricing is:[20]

$$\text{Price} = \frac{\text{Product cost}}{(100 - \text{Markup per cent})/100}$$

There are several reasons why markups are commonly stated in terms of selling price instead of cost. One, since expenses, markdowns, and profits are computed as percentages of sales, citing markups as percentages of sales also aids in profit planning. Two, firms quote their selling prices and trade discounts to channel members as percentage reductions from final list prices. Three, competitive price data are more readily available than cost data. Four, profitability appears smaller if based on price rather than cost. This can be useful in avoiding criticism over high earnings.

---

[20]Markup can be calculated by transposing the formula above into:

$$\text{Markup per cent} = \frac{\text{Price} - \text{Product cost}}{\text{Price}} \times 100$$

Table 13-2

Examples of Cost-Based Pricing Techniques

....

Cost-Plus Pricing—A custom-sofa maker has total fixed costs of $50 000, variable costs of $500 per sofa, desires $10 000 in profits, and plans to produce 100 couches. What is the selling price per couch?

$$Price = \frac{Total\ fixed\ costs + Total\ variable\ costs + Projected\ profit}{Units\ produced}$$

$$= \frac{\$50\ 000 + \$500(100) + \$10\ 000}{100} = \underline{\$1100}$$

Markup Pricing—A retailer pays $30 for touch-tone phones and wants a markup on selling price of 40 per cent (30 per cent for selling costs and 10 per cent for profit). What is the final selling price?

$$Price = \frac{Merchandise\ costs}{(100 - Markup\ per\ cent)/100} = \frac{\$30}{(100-40)/100} = \underline{\$50}$$

Target Pricing—A specialty auto maker has spent $160 million for a new plant. It has a 25 per cent target return on investment. Standard production volume for the year is 5000 units. Average total costs, excluding the new plant, are $14 000 for each car (at a production level of 5000 cars). What is the selling price to the firm's retail dealers?

$$Price = \frac{Investment\ costs \times Target\ return\ on\ investment\ (\%)}{Standard\ volume}$$

$$+ \ Average\ total\ costs\ (at\ standard\ volume)$$

$$= \frac{\$160\ 000\ 000 \times .25}{5000} + \$14\ 000 = \underline{\$22\ 000}$$

Price-Floor Pricing—A big-screen TV manufacturer's plant capacity is 1000 units. Its total fixed costs are $500 000 and variable costs are $375 per unit. At full production, average fixed costs are $500 per unit. The firm sets a price of $1 100 to retailers and gets orders for 800 TVs at that price. It must operate at 80 per cent of capacity, unless it re-evaluates its pricing strategy. With price-floor pricing, it can sell the 200 additional sets to retailers. How?

The firm could let resellers buy one TV at $425 for every four they buy at $1100. Then, it earns a profit of $90 000 [revenues of ($1100 × 800) + ($425 × 200) less costs of ($875 × 1000)]. If it just makes and sells 800 TVs at full price, it earns $80 000 [revenues of ($1100 × 800) less variable costs of ($375 × 800) and fixed costs of $500 000]. The higher profits are due to the fact that marginal revenue > marginal cost.

Traditional Break-Even Analysis—A small candy maker has total fixed costs of $150 000 and variable costs per unit of $0.25. It sells to retailers for $0.40 per bar. What is the break-even point in units? In sales dollars?

$$\frac{Break\text{-}even\ point}{(units)} = \frac{Total\ fixed\ costs}{Price - Variable\ costs\ (per\ unit)} = \frac{\$150\ 000}{\$0.40 - \$0.25} = \underline{1\ 000\ 000}$$

$$\frac{Break\text{-}even\ point}{(sales\ dollars)} = \frac{Total\ fixed\ costs}{1 - \dfrac{Variable\ costs\ (per\ unit)}{Price}} = \frac{\$150\ 000}{1 - \dfrac{\$0.25}{\$0.40}} = \underline{\$250\ 000}$$

....

Markup size depends on traditional profit margins, company selling and operating expenses, suggested list prices, inventory turnover, competition, the extent to which products must be serviced, and the effort needed to complete transactions. Due to differences in selling costs among products, some firms use a **variable markup policy**, whereby separate categories of goods and services receive different percentage markups. Variable markups recognize that some items require greater personal selling, customer service, alterations, and end-of-season markdowns than others. For example, expensive cosmetics need

A variable markup policy responds to differences in selling costs among products.

more personal selling and customer service than paperback books, suits need greater custom alterations than shirts, and fashion items are marked down more than basic clothing late in the selling season.

Markup pricing, while having many of cost-plus pricing's limitations, is popular. It is fairly simple, especially for firms with uniform markups for several items. Channel members get fair profits. Price competition is less if firms have similar markups. Resellers can show their actual prices compared to suggested prices. Adjustments can be made as costs rise. Variable markups are responsive to selling-cost differences among products or channel members.

Target pricing *enables a rate of return on investment to be earned for a standard volume of production.*

TARGET PRICING In **target pricing**, prices are set to provide a particular rate of return on investment for a standard volume of production—the level of production a firm anticipates achieving. For example, in the paper industry, the standard volume of production is usually set at around 90 to 92 per cent of plant capacity.[21] For target pricing to operate properly, a company must sell its entire standard volume at specified prices.

Target pricing is used by capital-intensive firms (like auto makers) and public utilities (like water companies). The prices charged by utilities are based on fair rates of return on invested assets and must be approved by regulatory commissions. Mathematically, a target price is computed as:

$$\text{Price} = \frac{\text{Investment costs} \times \text{Target return on investment (\%)}}{\text{Standard volume}}$$
$$+ \text{ Average total costs (at standard volume)}$$

Target pricing has five major shortcomings. First, it is not useful for firms with low capital investments; it understates selling price. Second, because prices are not keyed to demand, the entire standard volume may not be sold at the target price. Third, production problems may hamper output and standard volume may not be attained. Fourth, price cuts to handle overstocked inventory are not planned under this approach. Fifth, if the standard volume is reduced due to expected poor sales performance, the price would have to be raised under a target-pricing calculation.

Price-floor pricing *may be used if there is excess capacity.*

PRICE-FLOOR PRICING A firm's usual goal is to set prices to cover the sum of average fixed costs, average variable costs, and profit per unit. But, when a firm has excess (unused) capacity, it may use **price-floor pricing** to determine the lowest price at which it is worthwhile to increase the amount of goods or services it makes available for sale.

The general principle in price-floor pricing is that the sale of additional units can be used to increase profits or help pay for fixed costs (which exist whether or not these items are made), as long as marginal revenues are greater than marginal costs. Although a firm cannot survive in the long run unless its average total costs are covered by prices, it may improve performance through price-floor pricing. The formula is:

$$\text{Price-floor price} = \text{Marginal revenue per unit} > \text{Marginal cost per unit}$$

Traditional break-even analysis *computes the sales needed to break even at a specific price.*

TRADITIONAL BREAK-EVEN ANALYSIS Like target pricing, **traditional break-even analysis** looks at the relationship among costs, revenues, and profits. While target pricing yields the price that results in a specified return on investment, traditional break-even analysis finds the sales quantity in units or dollars that is needed for total revenues (price × units sold) to equal total costs (fixed and variable) at a given price. If sales exceed the break-even quantity, a firm earns a profit. If sales are less than the break-even quantity, it loses money. Traditional break-even analysis does not consider return on investment, but can be extended to take profit planning into account. It is used by all kinds of sellers.

[21]*Industrial Outlook 1994* (Washington, D.C.: U.S. Department of Commerce, 1994), pp. 10-1–10-2.

The break-even point can be computed in terms of units or sales dollars:

$$\text{Break-even point (units)} = \frac{\text{Total fixed costs}}{\text{Price} - \text{Variable costs (per unit)}}$$

$$\text{Break-even point (sales dollars)} = \frac{\text{Total fixed costs}}{1 - \dfrac{\text{Variable costs (per unit)}}{\text{Price}}}$$

These formulas are derived from the equation: Price $\times$ Quantity = Total fixed costs + (Variable costs per unit $\times$ Quantity).

Break-even analysis can be adjusted to take into account the profit sought by a firm:

$$\text{Break-even point (units)} = \frac{\text{Total fixed costs} + \text{Projected profit}}{\text{Price} - \text{Variable costs (per unit)}}$$

$$\text{Break-even point (sales dollars)} = \frac{\text{Total fixed costs} + \text{Projected profit}}{1 - \dfrac{\text{Variable costs (per unit)}}{\text{Price}}}$$

There are limitations to traditional break-even analysis. First, as with all forms of cost-based pricing, demand is not considered. The presumption is that wide variations in quantity can be sold at the same price; this is highly unlikely. Second, it is assumed that all costs can be divided into fixed and variable categories. Yet, some, like advertising, are difficult to define; advertising can be fixed or a per cent of sales. Third, it is assumed that variable costs per unit are constant over a range of quantities. However, purchase discounts or overtime wages may alter these costs. Fourth, it is assumed that fixed costs remain constant; but increases in production may lead to higher costs for new equipment, new full-time employees, and other items.

By including demand considerations, each of the cost-based techniques can be improved. Demand-based pricing techniques are discussed next.

Demand-Based Pricing

With **demand-based pricing**, a firm sets prices after studying consumer desires and ascertaining the range of prices acceptable to the target market. This approach is used by companies that believe price is a key factor in consumer decision making. These companies identify a **price ceiling**, which is the maximum amount consumers will pay for a given good or service. If the ceiling is exceeded, consumers will not make purchases. Its level depends on the elasticity of demand (availability of substitutes and urgency of need) and consumers' subjective price regarding the particular good or service.

Demand-based techniques require that the firm research the quantities that consumers will purchase at various prices, sensitivity to price changes, the existence of market segments, and consumers' ability to pay. Demand estimates tend to be less precise than cost estimates. Also, firms that do inadequate cost analysis and rely on demand data may end up losing money if they make unrealistically low cost assumptions.

Under demand-based pricing, very competitive situations may lead to small markups and lower prices because consumers will purchase substitutes. In these cases, costs must be held down or prices will be too high—as might occur with cost-based pricing. For noncompetitive situations, firms can set large markups and high prices since demand is rather inelastic. There is less emphasis on costs when setting prices in these situations. With cost-based pricing, firms are more apt to set overly low prices in noncompetitive markets.

Four demand-based pricing techniques are reviewed next: demand-minus, chain-markup, modified break-even, and price discrimination. Figure 13-8 gives a synopsis of each technique, and Table 13-3 contains numerical examples of each.

Two aspects of competition-based pricing are discussed in the following subsections: price leadership and competitive bidding.

Under **demand-based pricing,** *consumers are researched and a* **price ceiling** *set.*

FIGURE 13-8
Demand-Based Pricing Techniques

T a b l e   1 3 - 3

Examples of Demand-Based Pricing Techniques

Demand-Minus Pricing—A mail-order CD-ROM encyclopedia publisher has done consumer research and found people are willing to spend $60.00 for its brand. Its selling expenses and profits are expected to be 35 per cent of the selling price. What is the maximum it can spend to develop and produce each CD-ROM encyclopedia?

$$\text{Maximum merchandise costs} = \text{Price} \times [(100 - \text{Markup per cent})/100]$$
$$= \$60.00 \times [(100 - 35)/100] = \underline{\$39.00}$$

Chain-Markup Pricing—A ladies' shoe maker knows women will pay $50.00 for a pair of its shoes. It sells via wholesalers and retailers. Each requires a markup of 30 per cent; the manufacturer wants a 25 per cent markup. (a) What is the maximum price that retailers and wholesalers will spend for a pair of shoes? (b) What is the maximum the manufacturer can spend to make each pair of shoes?

(a) $$\text{Maximum selling price to retailer} = \text{Final selling price} \times [(100 - \text{Retailer's markup})/100]$$
$$= \$50.00 \times [(100 - 30)/100] = \underline{\$35.00}$$

$$\text{Maximum selling price to wholesaler} = \text{Selling price to retailer} \times [(100 - \text{Wholesaler's markup})/100]$$
$$= \$35.00 \times [(100 - 30)/100] = \underline{\$24.50}$$

(b) $$\text{Maximum merchandise costs to manufacturer} = \text{Selling price to wholesaler} \times [(100 - \text{Manufacturer's markup})/100]$$
$$= \$24.50 \times [(100 - 25)/100] = \underline{\$18.38}$$

Modified Break-Even Analysis—An aspirin maker has total fixed costs of $2 000 000 and variable costs of $1.50 per bottle. Research shows the following demand schedule. At what price should the company sell its aspirin?

Selling Price	Quantity Demanded	Total Revenue	Total Cost	Total Profit (Loss)	
$3.00	2 000 000	$ 6 000 000	$5 000 000	$1 000 000	Maximum
2.50	3 200 000	8 000 000	6 800 000	1 200 000 ←———	profit at
2.00	5 000 000	10 000 000	9 500 000	500 000	price of $2.50

Price Discrimination—A sports team knows people will pay different prices for tickets, based on location. It offers 10 000 tickets at $30 each, 25 000 at $20 each, and 20 000 at $12 each. What are profits if total costs per game are $750 000?

$$\text{Profit} = (\text{Revenues from Segment A} + \text{Segment B} + \text{Segment C}) - \text{Total costs}$$
$$= (\$300\ 000 + \$500\ 000 + \$240\ 000) - \$750\ 000 = \underline{\$290\ 000}$$

DEMAND-MINUS PRICING Through **demand-minus (demand-backward) pricing**, a firm finds the proper selling price and works backward to compute costs. This approach stipulates that price decisions revolve around consumer demand rather than company operations. It is used by firms selling directly to consumers.

In demand-minus pricing, selling price, then markup, and finally maximum product costs are computed.

Demand-minus pricing has three steps: first the selling price is determined by consumer surveys or other research; then the required markup percentage is set, based on selling expenses and desired profits; finally, the maximum acceptable per-unit cost for making or buying a product is computed. This formula is used:

$$\text{Maximum product cost} = \text{Price} \times [(100 - \text{Markup per cent})/100]$$

It shows that product cost is derived after selling price and markup are set.

The difficulty in demand-minus pricing is that marketing research may be time-consuming or complex, particularly if many items are involved. Also, new-product pricing research may be particularly inaccurate.

CHAIN-MARKUP PRICING **Chain-markup pricing** extends demand-minus calculations all the way from resellers back to suppliers (manufacturers): the final selling price is determined, markups for each channel member are examined, and the maximum acceptable costs to each member are computed.

Chain-markup pricing *traces demand-minus calculations from channel members to suppliers.*

In a traditional consumer-goods channel, the markup chain is composed of:

1. $\text{Maximum selling price to retailer} = \text{Final selling price} \times [(100 - \text{retailer's markup})/100]$

2. $\text{Maximum selling price to wholesaler} = \text{Selling price to retailer} \times [(100 - \text{wholesaler's markup})/100]$

3. $\text{Maximum product cost to manufacturer} = \text{Selling price to wholesaler} \times [100 - \text{manufacturer's markup})/100]$

By using chain-markup pricing, price decisions can be related to consumer demand and each reseller is able to see the effects of price changes on the total distribution channel. The interdependence of firms becomes more clear; they cannot set prices independently of one another.

MODIFIED BREAK-EVEN ANALYSIS **Modified break-even analysis** combines traditional break-even analysis with an evaluation of demand at various levels of price. Traditional analysis focuses on the sales needed to break even at a given price. It does not indicate the likely level of demand at that price, examine how consumers respond to different levels of price, consider that the break-even point can vary greatly depending on the price the firm happens to select, or calculate the price that maximizes profits.

Melding traditional break-even analysis with demand evaluation at various prices is **modified break-even analysis**.

Modified analysis reveals the price-quantity mix that maximizes profits. It shows that profits do not inevitably rise as the quantity sold increases because lower prices may be needed to expand demand. It also verifies that a firm should examine various price levels and select the one with the greatest profits. Finally, it relates demand to price, rather than assuming that the same volume could be sold at any price.

PRICE DISCRIMINATION With a **price discrimination** approach, a firm sets two or more distinct prices for a product so as to appeal to different final consumer or organizational consumer segments. Higher prices are offered to inelastic segments and lower prices to elastic ones. Price discrimination can be customer-based, product-based, time-based, or place-based.

Setting distinct prices to reach different market segments is **price discrimination**.

In customer-based price discrimination, prices differ by customer category for the same good or service. Price differentials may relate to a consumer's ability to pay (lawyers and accountants partially set prices in this manner), negotiating ability (the price of an office building is usually set by bargaining), or buying power (discounts are given for volume purchases).

Through product-based price discrimination, a firm markets a number of features, styles, qualities, brands, or sizes of a product and sets a different price for each product ver-

Ethics AND TODAY'S MARKETER

When Is a Sale Price Really a Sale Price?

In 1995, the Retail Council of Canada expressed concern over how the Competition Bureau was interpreting the regulations of misleading advertising with respect to sale prices. Regulation of misleading advertising is a criminal provision of the Competition Act so violations must be referred to the Attorney General of Canada and prosecuted through the court system. Many of the prominent members of the council had either been convicted, or were facing charges of misleading advertising related to prices, including K mart Canada, which had a conviction over a mattress sale, and Hudson's Bay Company, which was facing seventeen separate charges related to activities in 1994

The contention of the Retail Council is that the law does not reflect the current state of retail competition in the marketplace and needs to be changed. The focus of changes of interest to the Retail Council is on the definition of a "sale" price in relation to what constitutes a "regular" price. Under the current definition used by the Competition Bureau, the price at which 51 per cent of the volume of goods is sold is considered the regular price. However, when products go on sale, the intention of retailers is to make volume sales, and it is hard to predict what these volumes will be. The retailers would like the interpretation of regular price to be: the price set for 51 per cent of the time for which the item is available. Retailers contend that they cannot control sales volumes but they can control the amount of time for which a product is offered for sale at a specific price.

According to the Retail Council of Canada, when the Competition Act was written, most retailers held sales for the purpose of inventory clearance so the 51 per cent volume rule was quite reasonable. In today's competitive environment, sales are used to create in-store traffic and to introduce new products. Pricing "new" products is particularly troublesome for retailers when they have to establish a "regular" price using the 51 per cent volume rule.

One other part of the argument for change presented by the Retail Council is based on a market research survey that was undertaken by Thompson Lightstone & Company Ltd. of Toronto. A key finding of the survey was that consumers are generally very skeptical about sale prices. This finding would imply that in practice, using the term "sale" is less likely to be misleading since consumers are skeptical. This argument could be used to ask legislators to ease up a bit. However, the survey also noted that consumers are also strongly attracted to sales. This finding would support the contention that regulators should remain vigilant with respect to retail activity in the marketplace to protect consumers from unscrupulous and manipulative pricing practices.

As a consultant to the Director of the Competition Bureau, debate the merits of the Retail Council of Canada's argument and make a policy recommendation on how the Bureau should define a "regular" price.

Sources: Based on material in James Pollock, "RCC Wants Law Changed," *Marketing Magazine* (June 19, 1995), p. 3.

sion. Price differentials are greater than cost differentials for the various versions. For example, a dishwasher may be priced at $400 in white and $450 in brown, although the brown colour costs the manufacturer only $10 more. There is inelastic demand by customers desiring the special colour, and product versions are priced accordingly.

Under time-based price discrimination, a firm varies prices for day versus evening (movie theatre tickets), peak versus off-peak hours (telephone and utility rates), or season (hotel rates). Consumers who insist on prime-time use pay higher prices than those who are willing to make their purchases at other times.

For place-based price discrimination, prices differ by seat location (sports and entertainment events), floor location (office buildings, hotels), or geographic location (resort cities). The demand for locations near the stage, elevators, or warm climates drives the prices of these locations up. General admission tickets, basement offices, and moderate-temperature resorts are priced lower to attract consumers to otherwise less desirable purchases.

When a firm engages in price discrimination, it should use **yield management pricing**— whereby it determines the mix of price–quantity combinations that generates the highest level of revenues for a given period. A company wants to make sure that it gives itself every opportunity to sell as many goods and services at full price as possible, while also seeking to sell as many units as it can. It does not want to sell so many low-price items that it jeopardizes full-price sales. Thus, a 1000-seat theatre offering first-run plays must determine how many tickets to sell as orchestra (at $50 each) and how many to sell as general admission (at $25 each). If it tries to sell too many orchestra tickets, there may be empty seats during a performance. If it looks to sell too many general admission tickets, the theatre may be full—but total revenues may be unsatisfactory.[22]

Before using price discrimination, a firm should consider these questions: Are there distinct market segments? Do people communicate with each other about product features and prices? Can product versions be differentiated? Will some consumers choose low-priced models when they might otherwise buy high-priced models if they are the only ones available? How do the marginal costs of adding product alternatives compare with marginal revenues? Will channel members stock all models? How difficult is it to explain product differences to consumers? Under what conditions is price discrimination legal?

Yield management pricing *lets firms optimize price discrimination efforts.*

Competition-Based Pricing

In **competition-based pricing**, a firm uses competitors' prices rather than demand or cost considerations as its primary pricing guideposts. The company may not respond to changes in demand or costs unless they also have an effect on competitors' prices. It can set prices below the market, at the market, or above the market, depending on its customers, image, marketing mix, consumer loyalty, and other factors. This approach is applied by firms contending with others selling similar items (or those perceived as similar).

Competition-based pricing is popular. It is simple, with no reliance on demand curves, price elasticity, or costs per unit. The ongoing market price level is assumed to be fair for both consumers and companies. Pricing at the market level does not disrupt competition, and therefore does not lead to retaliation. However, it may lead to complacency; and different firms may not have the same demand and cost structures.

Competition-based pricing *is setting prices relative to other firms.*

PRICE LEADERSHIP Price leadership exists in situations where one firm (or a few firms) is usually the first to announce price changes and others in the industry follow. The price leader's role is to set prices that reflect market conditions, without disrupting the marketplace—it must not turn off consumers with price increases perceived as too large or precipitate a price war with competitors by excessive price cuts.

Price leaders are generally firms that have significant market shares, well-established positions, respect from competitors, and the desire to initiate price changes. As an illustration, a frequent price leader in the newsprint industry has been Canada's Abitibi-Price. It is the world's largest newsprint maker, has the largest production capacity, and has the dominant market share. Because over one-half of its revenues are in newsprint, the firm has a strong commitment to maintain stable prices.

Over the last several years, the role of price leaders has been greatly reduced in many industries, including steel, chemical, glass container, and newsprint, as many smaller firms have sought to act more independently. Even Abitibi-Price has been affected by this trend. At various times, it has announced higher newsprint prices and then has had to backtrack after competitors decided not to go along.

Price leadership *occurs when one or a few firms initiate price changes in an industry; they are effective when others follow.*

[22]See Edwin McDowell, "His Goal: No Room at the Inns," *New York Times* (November 23, 1995), pp. D1, D8.

Announcements of price changes by industry leaders must be communicated through the media. It is illegal for firms in the same industry or in competing ones to confer with one another regarding the setting of prices.

COMPETITIVE BIDDING Through competitive bidding (discussed in Chapter 5), two or more firms independently submit prices to a customer for a specific good, project, and/or service. Sealed bids may be requested by some government or organizational consumers; each seller then has one chance to make its best offer.

Various mathematical models have been applied to competitive bidding. All use the expected profit concept, which states that as the bid price increases, the profit to a firm increases but the probability of its winning a contract decreases. Although a firm's potential profit (loss) at a given bid amount can usually be estimated accurately, the probability of getting a contract (underbidding all other qualified competitors) can be hard to determine.

Combination Pricing

It is essential that companies integrate cost, demand, and competitive pricing techniques through combination pricing.

Although cost-, demand-, and competition-based pricing methods have been discussed separately, aspects of the three approaches are usually integrated into a **combination pricing** approach. A cost-based approach sets a price floor and outlines the various costs incurred in doing business. It establishes profit margins, target prices, and/or break-even quantities. A demand-based approach finds out the prices consumers will pay and the ceiling prices for each channel member. It develops the price–quantity mix that maximizes profits and allows a firm to reach different market segments (if it so desires). A competition-based approach examines the proper price level for the firm in relation to competitors.

Unless the approaches are integrated, critical issues may be overlooked. Table 13-4 shows a list of questions a firm should consider in setting prices.

Table 13-4

Selected Issues to Consider When Combining Pricing Techniques

....

Cost-Based
What profit margin does a price level permit?

Do markups allow for differences in product investments, installation and servicing, and selling effort and merchandising skills?

Are there accurate and timely cost data by good, service, project, process, and/or store?

Are cost changes monitored and prices adjusted accordingly?

Are there specific profit or return-on-investment goals?

What is the price-floor price for each good, service, project, process, and/or store?

What are the break-even points for each good, service, project, process, and/or store?

Demand-Based
What type of demand does each good, service, project, process, and/or store face?

Have price elasticities been estimated for various price levels?

Are demand-minus, chain-markup, and modified break-even analyses utilized?

Has price discrimination been considered?

How loyal are customers?

Competition-Based
How do prices compare with those of competitors?

Is price leadership used in the industry? By whom?

How do competitors react to price changes?

How are competitive bids determined?

Is the long-run expected profit concept used in competitive bidding?

....

Implementing a Pricing Strategy

Implementing a pricing strategy involves a wide variety of separate but related specific decisions, besides the broader concepts just discussed. The decisions involve whether and how to use customary versus variable pricing, a one-price policy versus flexible pricing, odd pricing, the price–quality association, leader pricing, multiple-unit pricing, price lining, price bundling, geographic pricing, and purchase terms.

Customary Versus Variable Pricing

Customary pricing occurs when a firm sets prices and seeks to maintain them for an extended time. Prices are not changed during this period. Customary pricing is used for items like candy, gum, magazines, restaurant food, and mass transit. Rather than modify prices to reflect cost increases, firms may reduce package size, change ingredients, or have a more restrictive transfer policy among bus lines. The assumption is that consumers prefer one of these alternatives to a price hike.

*With **customary pricing**, one price is maintained over an extended period. Under **variable pricing**, prices reflect costs or differences in demand.*

Variable pricing allows a firm to intentionally alter prices in response to cost fluctuations or differences in consumer demand. When costs change, prices are lowered or raised accordingly; the fluctuations are not absorbed and product quality is not modified to maintain customary prices. Through price discrimination, a firm can offer distinct prices to appeal to different market segments. In this way, the prices charged to diverse consumers are not based on costs, but on consumer sensitivity to price. Many firms use some form of variable pricing.

It is possible to combine customary and variable pricing. For example, a magazine may be $3 per single copy and $24 per year's subscription ($2 an issue)—two customary prices are charged; and the consumer selects the offer he or she finds most attractive.

A One-Price Policy Versus Flexible Pricing

A **one-price policy** lets a firm charge the same price to all customers seeking to purchase a good or service under similar conditions. Prices may differ according to the quantity bought, time of purchase, and services obtained (such as delivery and installation); but all consumers are given the opportunity to pay the same price for the same combinations of goods and services. This builds consumer confidence, is easy to administer, eliminates bargaining, and permits self-service and catalogue sales. Today, throughout Canada, one-price policies are the rule for most retailers. In industrial marketing, a firm with a one-price policy would not allow sales personnel to deviate from a published price list.

*All buying the same product pay the same price under a **one-price policy**. Different customers may pay different prices with **flexible pricing**.*

With **flexible pricing**, a firm sets prices based on the consumer's ability to negotiate or on the buying power of a large customer. For instance, people who are knowledgeable or are good bargainers would pay lower prices than those who are not knowledgeable or are weaker bargainers. Jewellery stores, car dealers, flea markets, real estate brokers, antique shops, and many types of industrial marketers frequently use flexible pricing. In some cases, salesperson commissions are keyed to the profitability of orders; this encourages salespeople to solicit higher prices. Flexible prices to resellers are subject to the Competition Act restrictions explained earlier. Flexible pricing is much more prevalent outside North America, where this practice (sometimes known as "haggling") may be culturally ingrained.

One result of flexible pricing is the practice whereby consumers gather information from full-service sellers, shop around for the best available price, and then challenge discount sellers to "beat the lowest price." This practice is detrimental to full-service firms and allows discounters to hold down selling costs (and encourage further bargaining).

Odd Pricing

Odd pricing is used when selling prices are set at levels below even dollar values, such as 49 cents, $4.95, and $199. It has proven popular for several reasons. For one thing, people like getting change. Because the cashier must make change, employers ensure that transactions are properly recorded and money is placed in the cash register. Consumers gain the

Odd prices are those set below even-dollar values.

impression that a firm thinks carefully about its prices and sets them as low as possible. They may also believe that odd prices represent price reductions; a price of $8.95 may be viewed as a discount from $10.

Odd prices one or two cents below the next even price (29 cents, $2.98) are common up to $4 or $5. Beyond that point and up to $50 or so, five-cent reductions from the highest even price ($19.95, $49.95) are more usual. For expensive items, odd endings are in dollars ($499, $5995).

Odd prices may help consumers stay within their price limits and still buy the best items available. A shopper willing to spend "less than $20" for a tie will be attracted to a $19.95 tie and might be as likely to purchase it as a $17 tie because it is within the defined price range. Yet, the imposition of the federal Goods and Services Tax combined with provincial sales taxes in nine Canadian provinces has the effect of raising odd prices into higher dollar levels and may reduce the impact of odd pricing as a selling tool.

The Price–Quality Association

The **price–quality association** *deals with perceptions.* **Prestige pricing** *indicates that consumers may not buy when a price is too low.*

According to the **price–quality association**, consumers may believe high prices represent high quality and low prices represent low quality. This association tends to be most valid when quality is difficult to judge on bases other than price, buyers perceive large differences in quality among brands, buyers have little experience or confidence in assessing quality (as with a new product), high prices are used to exclude the mass market, brand names are unknown, or brand names require certain price levels to sustain their images.

If brand names are well-known and/or people are confident of their ability to compare different brands in terms of nonprice factors, the price–quality association may be less valid. Then, many consumers may be more interested in the perceived value they receive for their money—and not necessarily believe a higher price represents better quality. It is essential that prices properly reflect both the quality and the image a firm seeks for its offerings.

With **prestige pricing**, a theory drawn from the price–quality association, it is assumed that consumers will not buy goods or services at prices they consider to be too low. Most people set their own price floors and will not purchase at prices below those floors—because they feel quality and status would be inferior at extremely low prices. Most people also set ceilings with regard to the prices they consider acceptable for particular goods or services. Above those ceilings, items would be seen as too expensive. For each good or service, a firm should set its prices in the target market's acceptable range between the floor and ceiling. See Figure 13-9 for an example using designer jeans.

Leader Pricing

Leader pricing *is used to attract customers to low prices.*

With **leader pricing**, a firm advertises and sells key items in its product assortment at less than their usual profit margins. For a wholesaler or retailer, the goal is to increase customer traffic. For a manufacturer, the goal is to gain greater consumer interest in its overall product line. In both cases, it is hoped that consumers will buy regularly priced merchandise in addition to the specially priced items that attract them.

Leader pricing is most used with well-known, high-turnover, frequently bought products. For example, in some drugstores, one of the best-selling items in terms of dollar sales is Kodak film. To stimulate customer traffic into these stores, film may be priced very low; in some cases, it is sold at close to cost. Film is a good item for leader pricing because consumers are able to detect low prices and they are attracted into a store by a discount on the item, which regularly sells for several dollars.

There are two kinds of leader pricing: loss leaders and prices higher than cost but lower than regular prices. The use of loss leaders must be undertaken carefully to avoid violating the Competition Act.

Multiple-Unit Pricing

With **multiple-unit pricing,** *quantity discounts are intended to result in higher sales volume.*

Multiple-unit pricing is a practice whereby a firm offers discounts to consumers to encourage them to buy in quantity, so as to increase overall sales volume. By offering

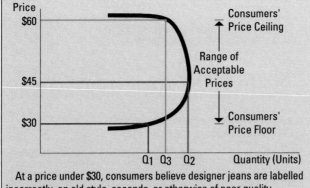

At a price under $30, consumers believe designer jeans are labelled incorrectly, an old style, seconds, or otherwise of poor quality. Demand is negligible.

At $30, consumer demand is Q_1. A small group of discount-oriented consumers will buy the jeans. This is the minimum price they will pay for a good pair of designer jeans.

As the price goes from $30 to $45, demand rises continuously as more consumers perceive the jeans as a high-quality, status product. At $45, sales peak at Q_2.

As the price goes from $45 to $60, consumer demand drops gradually to Q_3. Within this range, some consumers begin to see the jeans as too expensive. But many will buy the jeans until they reach $60, their ceiling price.

At a price over $60, consumers believe designer jeans are too expensive. Demand is negligible.

FIGURE 13-9
Demand for Designer Jeans under Prestige Pricing

items at two for 89 cents or six for $139, a firm attempts to sell more units than at 50 cents or $25 each.

There are four major benefits from multiple-unit pricing: customers may increase their immediate purchases if they feel they get a bargain; they may boost long-term consumption if they make larger purchases, as occurs with soda pop; competitors' customers may be attracted by the discounts; and a firm may be able to clear out slow-moving and end-of-season merchandise.

Multiple-unit pricing will not be successful if consumers merely shift their purchases and do not hike their consumption. For example, multiple-unit pricing for Heinz ketchup may not result in consumers using more ketchup with their meals. Thus, it would not raise total dollar sales; consumers would simply buy ketchup less frequently because it can be stored. However, it does have the benefit of protecting against competitive activity because consumers are carrying an inventory of ketchup and although they are not buying more Heinz ketchup, they are also not in the market for the competitor's ketchup either.

Price Lining

Price lining involves selling products at a range of prices, with each representing a distinct level of quality (or features). Instead of setting one price for a single version of a good or service, a firm sells two or more versions (with different levels of quality or features) at different prices. Price lining involves two decisions: prescribing the price range (floor and ceiling) and setting specific price points in that range.

A price range may be low, intermediate, or high. For example, inexpensive radios may be priced from $8 to $20, moderately priced radios from $22 to $50, and expensive radios from $55 to $120. After the range is chosen, a limited number of price points is set. The price points must be distinct and not too close together. Inexpensive radios could be priced at $8, $12, and $20. They would not be priced at $8, $9, $10, $11, $12, $13, $14, $15, $16, $17, $18, $19, and $20. This would confuse consumers and be inefficient for the firm. Figure 13-10 illustrates how MacWarehouse uses price lining to sell its Apple Computers.

When price lining, a firm must consider these factors: Price points must be spaced far enough apart so customers perceive differences among product versions—otherwise, consumers might view the price floor as the price they should pay and believe there is no

Price lining *sets a range of selling prices and price points within that range.*

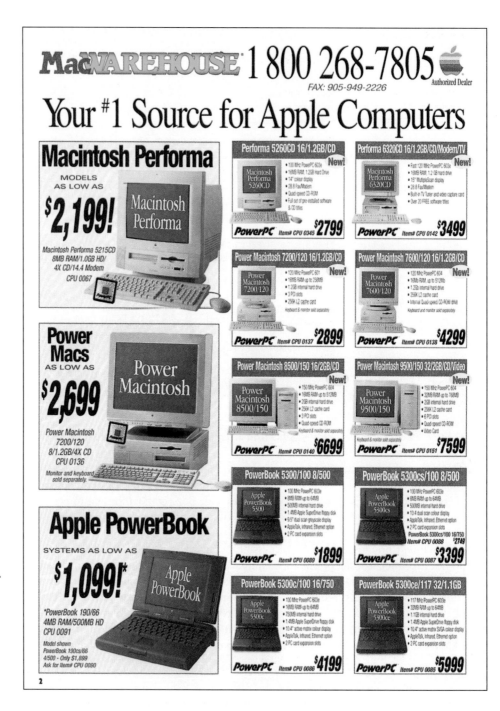

difference among models. Price points should be spaced farther apart at higher prices because consumer demand becomes more inelastic. Relationships among price points must be kept when costs rise, so clear differences are retained. If radio costs rise 25 per cent, prices should be set at $10, $15, and $25 (up from $8, $12, and $20).

Price lining offers benefits for both sellers and consumers. Sellers can offer a product assortment, attract market segments, trade up shoppers within a price range, control inventory by price point, reduce competition by having versions over a price range, and increase overall sales volume. Consumers gain because choices are greater, confusion is lessened, comparisons are easier, and quality options are available within a given price range.

Price lining does have constraints. Consumers may feel price gaps are too large—a $25 handbag may appear cheap, while the next price point of $100 may be too expensive. Rising costs may squeeze individual prices and make it hard for a firm to keep the proper relationships in its line. And markdowns or special sales may disrupt the balance in a price line, unless all items in the line are proportionately reduced in price.

Price Bundling

Some form of price bundling can be used in a strategy. With **bundled pricing**, a firm sells a basic product, options, and customer service for one total price. An industrial-equipment manufacturer may have a single price for a drill press, its delivery, its installation, and a service contract. Individual items, such as the drill press, would not be sold separately.

With **unbundled pricing**, a firm breaks down prices by individual components and allows the consumer to decide what to purchase. A discount appliance store may have separate prices for a refrigerator, its delivery, its installation, and a service contract.

Many companies choose to offer consumers both pricing options and allow a slight discount for bundled pricing.

*A firm can use **bundled** or **unbundled** pricing.*

Geographic Pricing

Geographic pricing outlines responsibility for transportation charges. Many times, it is not negotiated but depends on the traditional practices in the industry in which the firm operates; and all companies in the industry normally conform to the same geographic pricing format. Geographic pricing often involves industrial marketing situations.

These are the most common methods of geographic pricing:

*   *FOB mill (factory) pricing*—The buyer picks a transportation form and pays all freight charges, the seller pays the costs of loading the goods (hence, "free on board"), and the delivered price to the buyer depends on freight charges.
*   *Uniform delivered pricing*—All buyers pay the same delivered price for the same quantity of goods, regardless of their location; the seller pays for shipping.
*   *Zone pricing*—It provides for a uniform delivered price to all buyers within a geographic zone; through a multiple-zone system, delivered prices vary by zone.
*   *Base-point pricing*—Firms in an industry establish basing points from which the costs of shipping are computed; the delivered price to a buyer reflects the cost of transporting goods from the basing point nearest to the buyer, regardless of the actual site of supply.

Geographic pricing *alternatives are FOB mill (factory), uniform delivered, zone, and base-point pricing.*

Purchase Terms

Purchase terms are the provisions of price agreements. They include discounts, the timing of payments, and credit arrangements.

Discounts are the reductions from final selling prices that are available to resellers and consumers for performing certain functions, paying cash, buying large amounts, buying in off-seasons, or enhancing promotions. As an example, a wholesaler may buy goods at 40 per cent off the manufacturer's suggested final list selling price. This 40 per cent covers the wholesaler's expenses, profit, and discount to the retailer. The retailer could buy goods for 25 per cent off list (the wholesaler keeping 15 per cent for its costs and profit). In giving discounts, firms must make them proportionately available to all competing channel members, to avoid violating the Competition Act.

Payment timing must be specified in a purchase agreement. Final consumers may pay immediately or after delivery. In credit transactions, payments are not made until bills are received; they may be made over time. Organizational consumers are also quite interested in the timing of payments and negotiate for the best terms. For example, terms of net 30 mean products do not have to be paid for until 30 days after receipt. They must then be paid for in full. Terms of 2/10, net 30 mean a buyer receives a 2 per cent discount if the full bill is paid within 10 days after merchandise receipt. The buyer must pay the face value of a bill within 30 days after the receipt of products. Various time terms are available.

When marketing internationally, sellers must sometimes be prepared to wait an extended period to receive payments. At one time, it took North American firms an average of 337 days to get paid by Iranian businesses, 129 days to get paid by Kenyan businesses, 123 days to get paid by Argentine businesses, and 119 days to get paid by Brazilian clients.[23]

Purchase terms *outline pricing provisions.*

---

[23]"Your Check Is in the Mail," *Wall Street Journal* (December 8, 1992), p. 2.

TECHNOLOGY & MARKETING

Will Paper Prices Force Magazines to Go "Online"?

It almost seems like the industry is committing economic suicide but in the last couple of years paper prices have been escalating at unprecedented rates. World prices for paper have nearly doubled since 1994. This makes it very hard on firms in the printing and publishing industry. To stay in business media publishers are forced to hike advertising rates and newsstand prices while book publishers are forced to hike trade prices. All of these increases make their way to consumers, who pay more for their reading material and more for the products advertised in the media.

Curiously, these price hikes are coming at a time when demand for paper could well undergo a major decline due to increased use of electronic publishing and electronic media through home computers and the Internet. It is even conceivable that some paper producers are seeing the handwriting on the wall and the high prices are due to their desire to get some big profits before they are wiped out.

Traditional publishers have coped with the increases in a couple of basic ways. They have passed on some of the costs by raising product prices and in the case of paid media, raising advertising rates. In the newspaper industry one response has been a reduction in the actual size of the papers coupled with moderate price increases.

However, another response is to simply go "paperless." A large number of popular Canadian magazines have already established online electronic products. Magazines like *Maclean's, Canadian Business, L'actualité, Saturday Night,* and *Canadian Living* have online versions. Southam and Torstar have joined in a partnership to launch an online classified ad service. Even the government has reduced its dependence on paper by providing more online services and fewer print publications. For example, Statistics Canada no longer publishes its daily information release (appropriately called *The Daily*) on paper but offers it as a free online information service on the Statistics Canada Web site.

The longest running online magazine in Canada is *Vancouver Village*, which is found on the World Wide Web. Much of the content of *Vancouver Village* was culled from *Vancouver Magazine* and *Western Living Magazine*. Currently revenue for *Vancouver Village* is derived from sponsorships and classified advertising. The current thinking is that online publishing targeted at consumers will have to earn its revenues from the advertisers, while providing the consumers the information for free. The circulation potential for online publishing has tremendous potential and the cost of publishing will not be affected by "paper" prices.

As a consultant to the paper industry, what recommendations would you make concerning their current pricing strategies? Explain your answer.

Sources: Based on material in Jim McElgunn, "Paper Prices Still Rising," *Marketing Magazine* (January 29, 1996), p. 3; Jim McElgunn, "Southam, Torstar Join for Online Classifieds," *Marketing Magazine* (January 29, 1996), p. 3; Andrea Haman, "Surviving on Paper," *Marketing Magazine* (June 26, 1995), p. 16; and Michael McCullough, "The Tricky Jump to Cyberspace," *Marketing Magazine* (August 14, 1995), p. 20.

VANCOUVER VILLAGE
www.vanmag.com/Welcome.html

Open *and* **revolving credit accounts** *are possible.*

A firm that allows credit purchases may use open accounts or revolving accounts. With an **open credit account**, the buyer receives a monthly bill for the goods and services bought during the preceding month. The account must be paid in full each month. With a **revolving credit account**, the buyer agrees to make minimum monthly payments during an extended period of time and pays interest on outstanding balances. Today, various types of organizations (from Xerox to some physicians offering laser eye corrective surgery) offer some form of credit plan. Auto makers provide their own cut-rate financing programs to stimulate sales and leasing.

Price Adjustments

After a price strategy is enacted, it often requires continuous fine-tuning to reflect changes in costs, competitive conditions, and demand. Prices can be adjusted by alterations in list prices, escalator clauses and surcharges, added markups, markdowns, and rebates.

List prices are the regularly quoted prices provided to customers. They may be pre-printed on price tags, in catalogues, and in dealer purchase orders. Modifications in list prices are necessary if there are sustained changes in labour costs, raw material costs, and market segments and as a product moves through its life cycle. When these events are long term in nature, they enable customary prices to be revised, new catalogues to be printed, and adjustments to be completed in an orderly fashion.

Costs or economic conditions may sometimes be so volatile that revised list prices cannot be printed or distributed efficiently. Escalator clauses or surcharges can then be used. Both allow prices to be adjusted quickly. With **escalator clauses**, a firm is contractually allowed to raise the prices of items to reflect higher costs in those items' essential ingredients without changing printed list prices. It may even be able to set prices at the time of delivery. **Surcharges** are across-the-board published price increases that supplement list prices. These may be used with catalogues because of their simplicity; an insert is distributed with the catalogue.

When list prices are not involved, **additional markups** can be used to raise regular selling prices if demand is unexpectedly high or costs are rising. There is a risk to this. For example, supermarkets get bad publicity for relabelling low-cost existing items at higher prices so they match those of newer merchandise purchased at higher costs.

Markdowns are reductions from items' original selling prices. All types of sellers use them to meet the lower prices of competitors, counteract overstocking of merchandise, clear out shopworn merchandise, deplete assortments of odds and ends, and increase customer traffic.

Although manufacturers regularly give discounts to resellers, they may periodically offer cash **rebates** to customers to stimulate the purchase of an item or a group of items. Rebates are flexible, do not alter basic prices, involve direct communication between consumers and manufacturers (since rebates are usually sent to consumers by manufacturers), and do not affect resellers' profits (as regular price reductions do). Price cuts by individual resellers may not generate the same kind of consumer enthusiasm. Rebate popularity can be traced to their usage by the auto industry to help cut down on inventory surpluses. Rebates have also been offered by Canadian Tire, Sega, Gillette, Polaroid, Minolta, and a number of others. The major disadvantage is that so many firms have used rebates that their impact may be lessened.

Whenever adjustments are needed, channel members should cooperatively agree on their individual roles. Price hikes or cuts should not be unilateral.

List prices, escalator clauses, surcharges, additional markups, markdowns, and rebates are key pricing tools.

MARKETING IN A CHANGING WORLD

Dealing with Non-Paying Customers[24]

An interesting situation facing many business people today is when customers use services that are paid for by third parties, usually insurers. People have eyeglass plans, drug plans, medical plans, and other company benefits. Car warranty repairs and car insurance repairs are also situations where third-party payments occur. In these circumstances the exchange of value between the service provider, the customer, and the paying insuring party gets distorted because the benefit of the service is separated from the price of the service.

The interests of the three parties are all different in these exchanges. For example, the service provider is chiefly concerned with getting paid a fair value; the customer wants fast, efficient, and high-quality service; and finally, the third-party provider wants low costs but strong revenues. Problems can occur when the interests of the different parties come into conflict as a result of the exchange, which they often do. And when competition gets added to the mix, the situation can get very confused.

[24]The material in this section is based on Gail Chiasson, "Quebec Drug Marketers Take the Offensive," *Marketing Magazine* (September 25, 1995), p. 6; and the experiences of author William J. Wellington as a pharmaceutical representative.

Take the case of pharmaceutical marketing in Canada. In most provinces, senior citizens and welfare recipients are covered by provincial drug plans. Unlike private drug plans, which are profit-making enterprises, provincial drug plans are operated on a cost-recovery basis. Consequently, provincial drug plans have tended to focus on providing medications at the lowest possible cost. This means patients are often given generic drugs as opposed to name-brand drugs. In some cases, the patients and physicians have expressed concern that the generics were not up to the quality standards of name-brand medications. And many patients are not even aware of the fact that they may not be receiving the "best" quality product on the market, because by law, pharmacies are required to fill prescriptions with the lowest cost medication to keep costs down and save patients money.

The distortion in values has another unfortunate aspect. Physicians prescribe medications that are very expensive, knowing that the patient will not have to pay for them directly. Patients have prescriptions filled knowing they will not have to pay directly for the medication and then decide not to take the medication. Because the monetary exchange of values has been separated, this situation ends up costing the system a lot of money and the users are none the wiser.

As one pharmacist commented, "I once had a patient receive three prescriptions worth $200 and then had to listen to a complaint about how his insurance company had raised his co-pay from 35¢ a prescription to $1. Later he returned one of the prescriptions, valued at $100, and asked for $1 back, saying he decided not to take it. When I told him that I could not give him a refund because of the risk of product tampering he became so angry I was afraid of violence and my staff were about to call the police. He eventually calmed down but insisted I transfer his medical file to one of my competitors. All of this, over one lousy dollar. I shudder to think how he would have behaved if he had paid the full price!"

One way of bringing the exchange of values back into focus is to have co-pay and reimbursement types of insurance plans. In these instances, the consumer pays a portion of the cost of the service directly or pays for the complete service and then receives a reimbursement from the insurance company. The value of the service is duly registered by the consumer and the risk of loss if there is no reimbursement is also borne by the consumer. In this way, the balance in the exchange of values gets returned and all of the parties tend to act more responsibly toward one another.

SUMMARY

1. *To define the terms price and price planning* A price represents the value of a product for both the seller and the buyer. Price planning is systematic decision making relating to all aspects of pricing by a firm; it involves both tangible and intangible factors, purchase terms, and the nonmonetary exchange of goods and services. Exchange does not take place unless the buyer and seller agree a price represents an equitable value. Price also balances supply and demand.

2. *To demonstrate the importance of price and study its relationship with other marketing variables* Price (monetary or nonmonetary) is part of every type of exchange. During the last three decades, price decisions have become more important to business executives. This is due to factors such as deregulation, cost increases, currency rates, technological advances, the greater price emphasis by service companies, and periodic economic slowdowns.

Price decisions must be made in conjunction with other marketing-mix elements. And pricing is often related to the product life cycle, customer service levels, and other specific marketing and company variables. Setting prices for international markets can be complex and influenced by factors specific to the country.

3. *To differentiate between price-based and nonprice-based approaches* Under a price-based approach, sellers influence demand primarily by means of changes in price levels; they move consumers along a demand curve by raising or lowering prices. With a nonprice-based approach, sellers downplay price and emphasize such marketing attributes as image, packaging, and features; they shift the demand curves of consumers by stressing product distinctiveness.

4. *To present an overall framework for developing and applying a pricing strategy* A pricing strategy has five stages: objectives, broad policy, strategy, implementation, and adjustments. The stages are affected by outside factors and must be integrated with a firm's marketing mix.

5. *To analyze sales-based, profit-based, and status quo-based pricing objectives, and to describe the role of a broad price policy* Sales goals centre on volume and/or market share. In penetration pricing, a company sets low prices to capture a mass market. Profit goals focus on profit maximization, satisfactory profits, optimum return on investment, and/or early cash recovery. In skimming pricing, a firm seeks to capture the segment less concerned with price than with quality or status. Status quo goals are geared toward minimizing the impact of outside parties and ensuring stability. Two or more pricing objectives may be combined.

A broad price policy sets the overall direction for a firm's pricing efforts. Through it, a firm decides if it is price- or nonprice-oriented.

6. *To discuss several specific decisions that must be made in implementing a pricing strategy* Enacting a price strategy involves a variety of interlocking specific decisions. Customary pricing is employed when a firm sets prices for an extended period. With variable pricing, a firm alters prices to coincide with cost or consumer demand fluctuations.

In a one-price policy, all consumers purchasing under similar conditions pay the same price. Flexible pricing allows a firm to vary prices based on a shopper's ability to negotiate or the buying power of a large customer.

Odd-pricing is used if selling prices are set below even-dollar values. According to the price–quality association, consumers may believe there is a correlation between price and quality. With prestige pricing, it is assumed that con-

sumers do not buy products at prices that are considered too low. They set price floors, as well as price ceilings.

Under leader pricing, key items are sold at less than their usual profit margins to increase consumer traffic. Multiple-unit pricing is a practice in which a company offers discounts to consumers for buying in quantity.

Price lining involves the sale of goods and services at a range of prices, with each embodying a distinct level of quality (or features). In bundled pricing, a firm offers a basic product, options, and customer service for one total price; through unbundled pricing, it breaks down prices by individual components and lets consumers decide what to buy.

Geographic pricing outlines the responsibility for transportation. Purchase terms are the provisions of price agreements, including discounts, timing of payments, and credit.

Once a pricing strategy is implemented, it usually needs regular fine-tuning to reflect cost, competition, and demand changes. Prices can be adjusted by changing list prices, including escalator clauses and surcharges in contracts, marking prices up or down, and offering direct rebates.

KEY TERMS

Review Questions

1. Cite at least three reasons why price decisions are so important today.
2. What is the risk of using a nonprice-oriented strategy?
3. At a price of $40, a firm could sell 900 units. At a price of $25, it could sell 1200 units. Calculate the elasticity of demand and state what price the firm should charge—and why.
4. Is conspiracy to price fix always illegal? Explain your answer.
5. In what way are loss leaders different from bait-and-switch advertising?
6. When should a firm pursue penetration pricing? Skimming pricing?
7. Why are markups usually computed on the basis of selling price?
8. A firm requires a 14 per cent return on a $700 000 investment in order to produce a new electric garage-door opener. If the standard volume is 50 000 units, fixed costs are $500 000, and variable costs are $48 per unit, what is the target price?
9. A company making office desks has total fixed costs of $2 million per year and variable costs of $450 per desk. It sells the desks to retailers for $750 apiece. Compute the traditional break-even point in both units and dollars.
10. How does price lining benefit manufacturers? Retailers? Consumers?

Discussion Questions

1. How could a firm estimate price elasticity for a new industrial product? A mature industrial product?
2. Present five examples of price advertising for a hardware store that would violate the price advertising guidelines mentioned in the chapter.
3. A movie theatre has weekly fixed costs (land, building, and equipment) of $3500. Variable weekly costs (movie rental, electricity, ushers, etc.) are $1800. From a price-floor pricing perspective, how much revenue must a movie generate during a slow week for it to be worthwhile to open the theatre? Explain your answer.
4. A retailer determines that customers are willing to spend $27.95 on a new John Grisham (author of *The Client* and other best-sellers in the legal arena) novel. The publisher charges the retailer $22.50 for each copy. The retailer wants a 30 per cent markup. Comment on this situation.
5. a. A wholesaler of small industrial tools has fixed costs of $350 000, variable costs of $20 per tool, and faces this demand schedule from its hardware-store customers:

Price	Quantity Demanded
$24	100,000
$27	85,000
$30	65,000
$33	40,000

At what price is profit maximized?

b. If the company noted in Question 5a decides to sell 40 000 small tools at $33 and 45 000 of these tools at $27, what will its profit be? What are the risks of this approach?

MARKETING

MANAGEMENT

In Part 7, we tie together the concepts introduced in earlier chapters and discuss planning for the future.

14 ## Strategic Planning: A Marketing Perspective

Here we first distinguish between strategic business plans and strategic marketing plans, and describe the total quality approach to strategic planning. Next, we look at the different kinds of strategic plans and the relationship between marketing and other functional areas. We then present the steps in the strategic planning process in considerable detail. A sample outline of a strategic plan for a business firm is highlighted.

15 ## Pulling It All Together: Integrating and Analyzing the Marketing Plan

We first note the value of developing and analyzing integrated marketing plans. Next, we examine the elements in a well-integrated marketing plan: clear organizational mission, long-term competitive advantages, precisely defined target market, compatible subplans, coordination among SBUs, coordination of the marketing mix, and stability over time. Then, we study five types of marketing plan analysis: benchmarking, customer satisfaction research, marketing cost analysis, sales analysis, and the marketing audit. These are important tools for evaluating the success or failure of marketing plans. We conclude with a look at why and how firms should anticipate and plan for the future.

Part 7 Vignette
Integrated Marketing Plans

Marketing involves putting together component parts to produce a result. Marketers, therefore, need to realize that optimization of any particular element of the marketing mix may not work well and that weakness in a particular element does not have to lead to disaster; in short, marketers must try to see the big picture. Refer back to Figure 1-3 for the marketing concept, which includes these elements: a consumer orientation, a market-driven approach, a value-based philosophy, a goal orientation, and an integrated marketing focus. Throughout the preceding six parts of the book we have focused on a number of organizations that, to varying degrees, have implemented the marketing concept in their lines of business. When we looked at these organizations, we focused on a particular element of marketing. However, to assume that these firms were ignoring the other elements of the marketing mix would be a mistake. In fact, in most instances, other elements of the marketing mix were discussed in relation to the element of focus, and often the overall strategy of the organization was considered as well.

In Part 7 we will consider how a firm's strategic marketing planning and its marketing mix are related. Chapter 14 introduces us to strategic marketing plans that must be made so that marketing activity can be coordinated with other functional activities of business firms. Chapter 15 introduces us to the importance of developing and evaluating integrated marketing plans.

> *Marketers who view the marketing mix as a totality know that it usually is not beneficial to optimize particular elements.*

 "M.A.C."

As surprising as it may seem, a firm may have an overall marketing strategy despite the fact that it does not have, or undertake, formal marketing planning. For example, Makeup Art Cosmetics (M.A.C.) is an innovative Canadian cosmetics firm that does not have a formal marketing plan, but does have an overall marketing strategy. The president, Frank Toskan, discusses the firm's strategy, which is a form of product differentiation combined with intuitive management. Although he indicates that decision making for M.A.C. has been based on "what feels good," this approach has produced a company that has an articulated segmentation, target market, and positioning strategy for its products. In terms of M.A.C.'s marketing mix, there are clear product, distribution, promotion, and pricing strategies. The long term outlook for M.A.C. is also fairly clear since its acquisition by Estée Lauder, one of the world's largest cosmetic companies. M.A.C. was added to Estée Lauder's portfolio of firms because it was a case of Estée Lauder either owning M.A.C. or creating a firm to compete with it. M.A.C.'s success to date has stemmed from using a push marketing strategy in an industry where the standard approach to marketing has been the use of strong pull strategies for products with well-established brand images.

In terms of Estée Lauder's marketing strategy, M.A.C. is one brand name in a portfolio that includes the Estée Lauder, Aramis, Clinique and Prescriptives cosmetic product lines. The need for a comprehensive integrated marketing plan on the part of Estée Lauder to manage all of these brands is paramount. At the moment, this plan allows M.A.C. to continue to act freely even as Estée Lauder controls the activities of its other divisions. Whether M.A.C. will continue to have this freedom will depend on Estée Lauder's future plans.

14

Strategic Planning: A Marketing Perspective

Chapter Objectives

1 To define strategic planning and consider its importance for marketing

2 To describe the total quality approach to strategic planning and show its relevance to marketing

3 To look at the different kinds of strategic plans and the relationships between marketing and the other functional areas in an organization

4 To describe thoroughly each of the steps in the strategic planning process: defining organizational mission, establishing strategic business units, setting marketing objectives, performing situation analysis, developing marketing strategy, implementing tactics, and monitoring results

5 To show how a strategic plan may be devised and applied

{ *According to Roberto Goizueta, Coca-Cola's chair and chief executive officer, "You can't stumble if you're not moving. And if you stumble and make a decision that doesn't pan out, then you move quickly to change it. But it's better than standing still."* }

Reprinted by permission.

Although Coca-Cola has always had a reputation as a successful marketer, until recently its strategic planners were slow to respond to changes in the marketplace. Thus, the firm did not enter India until the late 1980s; at the same time, it was sluggish in dealing with the popularity of private-label soda in Great Britain; and in the early 1990s, it virtually ignored iced teas, new-age juices, and flavoured waters. By the time Coca-Cola responded in each of these instances, its competitors were able to garner a sizable market share.

Today, Coca-Cola uses a much quicker, more aggressive approach in its market-planning activities. For example, the firm now markets such new drinks as Mountain Blast, Surge, Powerade sports drink and Strawberry Passion Awareness Fruitopia fruit drink; and it has developed and introduced new packaging and promotions. Says Roberto Goizueta, "Nothing energizes an organization like speed."

In the not-too-distant past, some marketing analysts saw PepsiCo as the "hot" soft-drink company most likely to come out with new products and the best advertising campaigns. Now, they credit Coca-Cola with these qualities. Even arch-rival PepsiCo acknowledges Coca-Cola's new-found strength. PepsiCo's head of marketing states that "Coke has definitely raised the bar."

One good example of Coca-Cola's peppy approach to planning involves Japan, the firm's most profitable market. Japanese consumers are noted for demanding new products at breakneck speed; and while soda companies typically launch a total of 700 to 800 new drinks per year, few last for more than a month. Until 1993, Coca-Cola did not keep pace with its competitors. Then, it set up a product development centre that reduced the launch time for new drinks from 90 days to 30 days. Because of this, Coca-Cola now releases 50 new products per year in Japan—and its Japanese development centre serves all of Asia. A similar strategy is also being used for North America and Europe.

Coca-Cola's increased responsiveness applies equally to the withdrawal of slow-selling products. Formerly, the firm would take its time in discontinuing poor-sellers. Thus, ViProMin, a fortified tomato juice launched in the 1960s, was distributed by Coca-Cola for several years despite poor sales. Some analysts feel the slow-withdrawal strategy was caused by Coca-Cola's unwillingness to publicly acknowledge defeat. Now, Coca-Cola is better able to shrug off failure. That is why the firm's Japanese "lactic-based" drink was quickly pulled after the product's initial sales growth slowed.

Coca-Cola's superior planning is quite evident in Eastern Europe. When the Soviet Union collapsed, Coca-Cola rapidly built manufacturing, distribution, and marketing facilities from scratch. In contrast, PepsiCo kept using its old network of inefficient state-run bottlers. Furthermore, Coca-Cola's aggressive strategy has given its products the image as the "milk of capitalism," especially among the young. Not surprisingly, Coca-Cola's current sales in Eastern Europe greatly exceed those of Pepsi.[1]

In this chapter, we will consider strategic planning from a marketing perspective and review in depth each of the steps in the strategic planning process. We will also examine the use of strategic planning by both small and large firms.

Overview

As described earlier in Chapter 2, the environment within which marketing operates includes a number of factors directed by top management and others directed by marketing. To coordinate these factors and provide guidance for decision making, it is helpful to employ a formal strategic planning process. To marketers, such a process consists of two main components: a strategic business plan and a strategic marketing plan.

---

[1]Robert Frank, "Coca-Cola is Shedding Its Once-Stodgy Image with Swift Expansion," *Wall Street Journal* (August 22, 1995), pp. A1, A5.

A **strategic business plan** "describes the overall direction an organization will pursue within its chosen environment and guides the allocation of resources and effort. It also provides the logic that integrates the perspectives of functional departments and operating units, and points them all in the same direction." It has (1) an external orientation; (2) a process for formulating strategies; (3) methods for analyzing strategic situations and alternatives; and (4) a commitment to action.[2]

A **strategic marketing plan** outlines the marketing actions to undertake, why those actions are needed, who is responsible for carrying them out, when and where they will be completed, and how they will be coordinated. Thus, a marketing plan is carried out within the context of a firm's broader strategic plan.

Strategic planning involves both **strategic business plans** *and* **strategic marketing plans**.

There are a number of reasons why marketers need an appreciation of the relationship between strategic planning and marketing. One, strategic planning gives direction to a firm's efforts and better enables it to understand marketing research; consumer analysis; and product, distribution, promotion, and price planning. It is a hierarchical process, moving from company-wide guidelines down to specific marketing decisions. Two, a strategic plan ensures each company division has clear goals that are integrated with the firm's overall goals. Three, different functional areas are encouraged to coordinate efforts. Four, strategic planning forces a firm to assess its strengths and weaknesses and to consider environmental opportunities and threats. Five, the alternative actions or combinations of actions a firm can take are outlined. Six, a basis for allotting resources is set. Seven, the value of having a procedure for assessing performance can be shown.

Marketing's role in strategic planning is indeed a crucial one:

> In industry after industry, the opportunity today is clear. It is now possible for companies to focus directly on achieving the full potential of customer relationships. Doing so will require executives to abandon outdated management models. But, as with prior shifts in management thinking, those who act early will reap disproportionate rewards.[3]

> Strategic planning should stress market information, market-segment definition, and market targeting. All company activities should be built around the goal of creating the desired position with a well-defined set of customers. Separate market segments should be the subject of separate plans that focus on developing customer relationships that emphasize the firm's distinctive competence. [Marketing's] contribution to strategic planning and implementation begins with the analysis of market segments and an assessment of a firm's ability to satisfy customer needs. This includes analyzing demand trends, competition, and in industrial markets, competitive conditions. Marketing also plays a key role by working with top management to define business purpose in terms of customer-need satisfaction. In a market-oriented view of the strategic planning process, financial goals are seen as results and rewards, not the fundamental purpose of business.[4]

Marketing should have a key role in strategic planning.

In Chapter 14, we discuss a total quality approach to strategic planning, various kinds of strategic plans, relationships between marketing and other functional areas, and the strategic planning process—and show how strategic planning may be applied. Chapter 15, which concludes the text, deals with how marketing plans are integrated and analyzed using a total quality framework.

A Total Quality Approach to Strategic Planning

When devising strategic plans, any firm—small or large, domestic or international, manufacturing or services driven—should adopt a total quality perspective. **Total quality** is a process- and output-related philosophy, whereby a firm strives to fully satisfy customers in an effective and efficient manner. To flourish, a total quality program needs all of the following:

All firms should adopt a **total quality** *approach, thereby becoming more process- and output-oriented in satisfying consumers.*

---

[2]Peter D. Bennett (Ed.), *Dictionary of Marketing Terms*, Second Edition (Chicago: American Marketing Association, 1995), p. 276.

[3]Alan W. H. Grant and Leonard A. Schlesinger, "Realize Your Customers' Full Profit Potential," *Harvard Business Review*, Vol. 59 (September–October 1995), p. 72.

[4]Frederick E. Webster, Jr., "The Rediscovery of the Marketing Concept," *Business Horizons*, Vol. 31 (May–June 1988), pp. 37–38.

- *A process-related philosophy*—Total quality is based on all the activities undertaken to create, develop, market, and deliver a good or service to the customer. A firm gains a competitive advantage if it can offer the same quality good or service at a lower cost or if it can offer a better-quality good or service than other companies.

- *An output-related philosophy*—Although process-related activities give a good or service its value, usually the consumer can only judge the total quality of the finished product. Many consumers care about what they buy, rather than how it was made.

- *Customer satisfaction*—To the consumer, total quality refers to how well a good or service performs. Thus, customer service is a key element in a person's ultimate satisfaction, which is affected by the gap between that person's expectations of product performance and actual performance.

- *Effectiveness*—To a marketer, this means how well various marketing activities (such as adding new product features) are received by consumers.

- *Efficiency*—To a marketer, this involves the costs of various marketing activities. A firm is efficient when it holds down costs, while offering consumers the appropriate level of quality.

- *Customer focus*—From a total quality perspective, a firm views the consumer as a partner and seeks input from that partner as it creates, develops, markets, and delivers a good or service.

- *Top management commitment*—Because a total quality program must be believed in by everyone who works for and comes into contact with a firm, senior executives must be dedicated to making it work and make sure corners are not cut in an attempt to be more efficient. In the best firms, "total quality" becomes ingrained as part of the corporate culture.

- *Continuous improvement*—In most cases, today's total quality will become tomorrow's suboptimal quality; so, a firm must continuously improve. A complacent firm will be hurt by the dynamics of the marketplace and fast-paced technological and global trends.

- *Employee support and involvement*—For a total quality program to work, employees must buy into it. Empowering employees not only gets them involved in the total quality process, but it also assures that customer problems are promptly addressed and resolved in the customer's favour.

- *Supplier and distributor support and involvement*—Due to their involvement in creating total quality, both suppliers and resellers can have a dramatic effect on it. They too must buy into a firm's efforts at total quality.

For a total quality program to work, every party in the process must participate.

Figure 14-1 shows how a successful total quality program works. At the left are the participants in a total quality program, who together engage in the process of creating total quality. There is an interchange among the parties and between the parties and the process. A good's or service's effectiveness and efficiency both influence and are influenced by the total quality process, and the output of the process is total quality. Both process and outcome are regularly improved.

If consumers feel a good or service has superior quality, they will buy it; when the experience with a good or service is positive, the result is customer satisfaction, which is one measure of effectiveness. Finally, the level of customer satisfaction affects the consumer's future input into the total quality process, as represented by the feedback loop in the figure. The fact that the consumer appears three times in the diagram (consumer input, consumer purchase, and customer satisfaction) is evidence of the importance of the consumer in total quality.

As one expert notes, "To see things truly from the customer's perspective is to stand at the end of a long sequence of events, all of which have to mesh smoothly. Hotel clerks may be charming and attentive, but if the computer system is down, their courtesy isn't going to help much. Within any company, TQM theory holds, is a whole chain of 'internal customers' like the hotel clerk, ending with the person at the cash register, credit card in hand. The trick is to get everyone working together while keeping the ultimate cus-

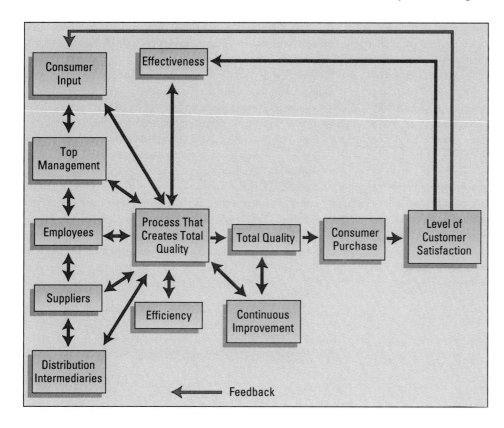

FIGURE 14-1
The Keys to a Successful Total Quality Program

tomer in focus." To Siemens (the German-based industrial firm), "Quality is when your customers come back and your products don't."[5]

Kinds of Strategic Plans

Strategic plans can be categorized by their duration, scope, and method of development. They range from short-run, specific, and department generated to long-run, broad, and management generated.

Plans may be short-run (typically one year), moderate in length (two to five years), or long-run (five to ten or even fifteen years). Many firms rely on a combination: Short-run and moderate-length plans are more detailed and operational in nature than long-run plans.

At Japan's Canon Corporation (which makes cameras, business machines, and optical products), short run plans show a "numerical expression of management activities during defined operating periods"; moderate-length plans "develop strategies to achieve the direction and goals defined by long-range plans, to provide guidelines for short-range plans, and to ensure optimum resource procurement and allocation"; and long-run plans are "more a vision or concept rather than plans, in the sense that they provide the direction and goals for a firm to pursue in a rapidly changing environment, and they lead to the achievement of qualitative innovations in every aspect of operations."[6]

The scope of strategic marketing plans also varies. There may be separate marketing plans for each of a firm's major products; a single, integrated marketing plan encompassing all products; or a broad business plan with a section devoted to marketing. Separate marketing plans by product line are often used by consumer-goods manufacturers; a single,

Short-run plans are precise; long-run plans outline needs.

CANON CORPORATION
www.canon.com/

Consumer-products firms often have plans for each line.

---

[5]Frank Rose, "Now Quality Means Service Too," *Fortune* (April 22, 1991), pp. 97–108; and Earl Naumann and Patrick Shannon, "What Is Customer-Driven Marketing?" *Business Horizons*, Vol. 35 (November–December 1992), p. 44. See also John Shea and David Gobeli, "TQM: The Experience of Ten Small Businesses," *Business Horizons*, Vol. 38 (January–February 1995), pp. 71–77.

[6]Toshio Nakahara and Yutaka Isono, "Strategic Planning for Canon; The Crisis and the New Vision," *Long Range Planning*, Vol. 25 (February 1992), p. 67.

integrated marketing plan is often employed by service firms; and a broad business plan is often utilized by industrial-goods manufacturers. A firm's diversity and the number of distinct market segments it seeks both have a strong influence here.

Last, strategic plans may be developed via a bottom-up, top-down, or combination approach. In bottom-up marketing planning, input from salespeople, product managers, advertising personnel, and other marketing areas is used to set objectives, budgets, forecasts, timetables, and marketing mixes. Bottom-up plans are realistic and good for morale. Yet it may be hard to coordinate each bottom-up plan and to include different assumptions about the same concept when setting an integrated, company-wide marketing plan.

Bottom-up plans foster employee input; top-down plans are set by top management.

The shortcomings of bottom-up plans are resolved in the top-down approach, whereby senior managers centrally direct and control planning activities. A top-down plan can use complex assumptions about competition or other external factors and provide a uniform direction for the marketing effort. Yet, if input from lower-level managers is not actively sought, morale may suffer.

The solution may be to use a combination of the two approaches, with senior executives setting overall goals and policy and marketing personnel forming plans for carrying out marketing policies. As the chief executive of one firm remarked:

> You can't have a workable strategy forced down from the top. Empowering middle managers is a necessity. They manage what we as a corporation want to accomplish. To make them think strategically comes from sharing the direction and from having a set of supportive organizational systems. So it's real work, not sermons, that makes us and our middle managers strategic thinkers.[7]

Strengthening Relationships Between Marketing and Other Functional Areas

The perspectives of marketing and other functional areas need to be reconciled.

An organization's strategic planning must accommodate the distinct needs of marketing and other functional areas. This is not always simple, due to the different orientations of each area. Marketing people may seek tailor-made products, flexible budgets, non-routine transactions, many product versions, frequent purchases, customer-driven new products, employee compensation incentives, and aggressive actions against competitors. These may conflict with the goals of other functional areas to seek mass production (production), well-established budgets (finance), routine transactions (accounting), limited models (engineering), infrequent orders (purchasing), technology-driven new products (research and development), fixed employee compensation (personnel), and passive actions against competitors (legal).

Top management makes sure every functional area sees the need for a balanced view in company decision making and has a say in the decisions that are made. Although some degree of tension among departments is inevitable, conflict can be lessened by encouraging interdepartmental contact; seeking employees with both technical and marketing expertise; forming multifunctional task forces, committees, and management-development programs; and setting goals for each department that take the other departments into account.[8]

The Strategic Planning Process

The strategic planning process includes steps from defining a mission to monitoring results.

As Figure 14-2 illustrates, the strategic planning process has seven interrelated steps: defining organizational mission, establishing strategic business units, setting marketing

[7]Manab Thakur and Luis Ma. R. Calingo, "Strategic Thinking Is Hip, But Does It Make a Difference?" *Business Horizons*, Vol. 35 (September–October 1992), p. 47.

[8]See Jeen-Su Lim, "Vital Cross-Functional Linkages with Marketing," *Industrial Marketing Management*, Vol. 21 (May 1992), pp. 159–165; Victoria L. Crittenden, "Close the Marketing/Manufacturing Gap," *Sloan Management Review*, Vol. 33 (Spring 1992), pp. 41–51; and Michael D. Hutt, Beth A. Walker, and Gary L. Frankwick, "Hurdle the Cross-Functional Barriers to Strategic Change," *Sloan Management Review*, Vol. 36 (Spring 1995), pp. 22–30.

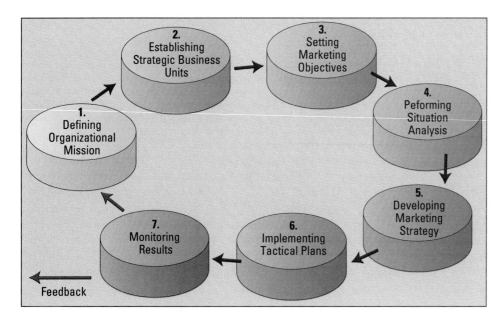

FIGURE 14-2
The Strategic Planning Process

objectives, performing situation analysis, developing marketing strategy, implementing tactics, and monitoring results. Because the process encompasses both strategic business planning and strategic marketing planning, it is usually conducted by a combination of senior company executives and marketers.

This process is applicable to small and large firms, consumer-products and industrial-products firms, goods- and services-based firms, domestic and international firms, and profit-oriented and nonprofit-oriented institutions. While planning at each step in the process may differ by type of organization, using a thorough strategic plan is beneficial for any organization.

The steps in strategic planning are discussed in the following sections.

Defining Organizational Mission

An **organizational mission** is a long-term commitment to a type of business and a place in the market. It "describes the scope of the firm and its dominant emphasis and values," based on that firm's history, current management preferences, resources, and distinctive competences, and on environmental factors.[9]

An organizational mission can be expressed in terms of the customer group(s) served, the goods and services offered, the functions performed, and/or the technologies utilized. It is more comprehensive than the line-of-business concept noted in Chapter 2. And it is considered implicitly whenever a firm seeks a new customer group or abandons an existing one, introduces a new product (good or service) category or deletes an old one, acquires another company or sells one of its own businesses, engages in more marketing functions (a wholesaler opening retail stores) or in fewer marketing functions (a small innovative toy maker licensing its inventions to an outside company that produces, distributes, and promotes them), or shifts its technological focus (a phone manufacturer placing more emphasis on cellular phones).

Here are two diverse illustrations of clear organizational missions:

Lands' End is a leading international direct merchant of traditionally styled, casual clothing for men, women, and children, accessories, shoes, and soft luggage. Its products are offered through regular mailings of a monthly catalogue and four specialty catalogues. Lands' End is

A firm sets its direction in an **organizational mission**.

[9]Bennett, *Dictionary of Marketing Terms*, p. 67. See also James Krobe Jr., "Do You Really Need a Mission Statement?" *Across the Board* (July–August 1995), pp. 17–21.

known for providing products of exceptional quality at prices representing honest value, enhanced by a commitment to excellence in customer service.[10]

B.C. Sugar Refinery Limited has decided that a "sugar diet" is just what it needs for success. It is Canada's largest sugar company and the third largest in North America. In 1990 B.C. Sugar had holdings in specialty chemicals and oil and natural gas. The firm decided to exit these ventures and proceeded to buy up 50 per cent of a larger competitor, Lantic Sugar of Montreal, followed by purchasing the remaining 50 per cent a year-and-a-half later. The firm believes that by sticking to its core business coupled with the reduction of trade barriers to the U.S. market they can enjoy something even sweeter than their product, success.[11]

JOSTENS LEARNING CORPORATION
www.jlc.com/

Organizations that diversify too much may lack a clear sense of direction. For example, Jostens—the maker of class rings, yearbooks, and other items targeted to high school and university students—was extremely profitable for four decades. Then, it launched Jostens Learning Corporation in 1989, even though its senior executives did not have expertise in educational software. Jostens' software business flopped, largely because of the high startup costs for clients and intense competition; and the firm lost $16 million in 1994. As one analyst observed, "Nobody was taking a hard look at what was going on—nobody seemed to be asking the right questions."[12]

Establishing Strategic Business Units

Strategic business units *are separate operating units in an organization.*

After defining its mission, a firm may form strategic business units. Each **strategic business unit (SBU)** is a self-contained division, product line, or product department in an organization with a specific market focus and a manager with complete responsibility for integrating all functions into a strategy.[13] An SBU may include all products with the same physical features or products bought for the same use by customers, depending on the mission of the organization. Each SBU has these general attributes:

- A specific target market.
- Its own senior marketing executive.
- Control over its resources.
- Its own marketing strategy.
- Clear-cut competitors.
- Distinct differential advantages.

The SBU concept lets companies identify those business units with the greatest earnings potential and allocate to them the resources needed for their growth. For instance, at General Electric, every SBU must have a unique purpose, identifiable competitors, and all its major business functions (manufacturing, finance, and marketing) within the control of that SBU's manager. Units not performing up to expectations are constantly reviewed and, if necessary, consolidated with other units, sold, or closed down.[14]

The proper number of SBUs depends on a firm's organizational mission, its resources, and the willingness of top management to delegate authority. A small or specialized firm can have as few as one SBU, a diversified one up to 100 or more. Thus, Johnson Controls has the four SBUs depicted in Figure 14-3; General Electric has 12 SBUs—ranging from aircraft engines to lighting to information services; Dover has 70 SBUs—ranging from elevators to garbage trucks to welding torches; and Johnson & Johnson has 165+ SBUs—related to consumer, pharmaceutical, and professional products.[15]

[10]*Lands' End 1995 Annual Report.*
[11]"The Top Ten Performers," *Canadian Business* (June 1994), p. 110.
[12]Kenneth Labich, "Why Companies Fail," *Fortune* (November 14, 1994), pp. 52–54.
[13]Subhash C. Jain, *Marketing Planning & Strategy*, Fourth Edition (Cincinnati: South-Western, 1993), pp. 15–19.
[14]Noel M. Tichy and Stratford Sherman, *Control Your Destiny or Someone Else Will* (New York: Doubleday, 1993).
[15]*General Electric 1995 Annual Report;* Phillip L. Zweig, "Who Says the Conglomerate Is Dead?" *Business Week* (January 23, 1995), pp. 92–93; and Brian O'Reilly, "J&J Is on a Roll," *Fortune* (December 26, 1994), pp. 178–192.

FIGURE 14-3
The SBUs of Johnson Controls
Reprinted by permission.

Setting Marketing Objectives

A firm needs overall marketing objectives, as well as goals for each SBU. Objectives are often described in both quantitative terms (dollar sales, percentage profit growth, market share, etc.) and qualitative terms (image, level of innovativeness, industry leadership role, etc.).

For example, Quaker Oats Company's eight key goals are: (1) "Provide total shareholder returns that exceed the cost of equity and the S&P 500 stock index over time." (2) "Maintain a robust financial position from strong operating cash flows, while generating economic value via the use of leverage." (3) "Aggressively market brands for leadership positions. We assess our strength by our ability to grow, acquire, or maintain brands that are number one or two in their categories." (4) "Profitably grow the volume of key brands at better-than-industry-average rates by offering greater value to the customer." (5) "Enhance productivity and efficiency in every element of our business." (6) "Develop mutually beneficial, interdependent relationships with our trade customers to improve the economic return of both parties." (7) "Build high-performance teams of resourceful, motivated, and productive employees." (8) "Raise the productivity of low-return businesses or divest them."[16]

Small firms' goals are often less ambitious, but no less important. For example, Upper Canada Brewing of Toronto is a small regional brewer in an industry dominated by the Labatt and Molson giants. Upper Canada has positioned itself as a Canadian and community brewery. One of their advertising themes is: "Think Globally, Drink Locally." Microbrewery operations by their very nature are small and local and the cost of going to the next level is often not worth the trouble to their owners.[17]

Marketing objectives may include quantitative and qualitative measures.

---

[16]*Quaker Oats Company 1995 Annual Report.*
[17]Sean Eckford, "Small Brewers Play Canadian-Ownership Card," *Marketing Magazine* (August 14, 1995), p 4.

International Marketing in Action

Understanding the Marketing Strategies of U.S. and South African Firms

To successfully compete in foreign markets, Canadian marketing managers must understand how businesses compete. Very often, the marketing approach of a nation will require adjustments in the way a firm does business. The United States and South Africa represent excellent market opportunities for Canadian firms since both countries do business in English, one of Canada's official languages. These are some of the ways in which the marketing strategies used in the United States and South Africa differed.

- U.S. firms focus more on competitive advantage and identifying target markets as key components in their strategies. In contrast, South African firms place more emphasis on company positioning and taking advantage of trends and opportunities as market strategy components.
- With regard to target marketing approaches, South African firms have a greater tendency to focus on the entire market (rather than individual customers or multiple segments).
- In terms of demand-based strategies, U.S. firms are more apt to try to take customers from competitors and attract new users to the market.
- In terms of pricing, U.S. firms engage in more penetration pricing (aimed at charging a lower price to capture the mass market) than South African firms.
- U.S. firms use market research and online databases more than their South African counterparts, while South African firms make greater use of product portfolio analysis and formal planning procedures.
- South African firms use more financial managers and external consultants.

As a marketing manager for a small Canadian manufacturer who wants to market internationally, what could you learn from the above findings?

Source: Based on material in Michael H. Morris and Leyland F. Pitt, "Implementing Marketing Strategies in the U.S. and South Africa," *Long Range Planning*, Vol. 27 (February 1994), pp. 56–71.

Performing Situation Analysis

Situation analysis *investigates a firm's strengths, weaknesses, opportunities, and threats.*

In **situation analysis**, also known as SWOT analysis, an organization identifies its internal strengths (S) and weaknesses (W), as well as external opportunities (O) and threats (T). Situation analysis seeks to answer: Where is a firm now? In what direction is it headed? Answers are derived by recognizing the company's strengths and weaknesses relative to its competitors, studying the environment for opportunities and threats, assessing the firm's ability to capitalize on opportunities and to minimize or avoid threats, and anticipating competitors' responses to company strategies.

Situation analysis can, and should be, conducted at any point in a firm's life. For instance, when Ann Bayley, President of Iceculture Inc., started her business it was to provide ice bowls as a free add-on to her husband's catering business. Ann has been quick to recognize opportunities and Iceculture is now a $100 000 business going beyond weddings and hospitality events to include winter carnival displays. Iceculture got into the winter carnival business when Ann offered to supply ice carving as a backup to worried Winter Carnival organizers in Grand Bend, Ontario, who had planned a carnival but did not plan on a lack of snow. Winter carnivals have now become a major growth market for

Iceculture. Of course, the product does have one important problem, customers complain that it melts. Ann plans to seize this opportunity by launching fake ice.[18]

Sometimes, situation analysis reveals weaknesses or threats that cannot be overcome, and a company opts to drop or sell a product line or division. Thus, in 1995, General Mills sold its restaurant division—comprised of the Red Lobster, Olive Garden, and China Coast chains. Why? Fifty-five per cent of General Mills' food profits were being used to fund the restaurant business; and the firm decided to focus instead on its leading food brands: Wheaties, Cheerios, Betty Crocker baking products, Yoplait yogurt, and others.[19]

Developing Marketing Strategy

A **marketing strategy** outlines the way in which the marketing mix is used to attract and satisfy the target market(s) and achieve an organization's goals. Marketing-mix decisions centre on product, distribution, promotion, and price plans. A separate strategy is necessary for each SBU in an organization; these strategies must be coordinated.

A good **marketing strategy** *provides a framework for marketing activities.*

A marketing strategy should be explicit to provide proper guidance. It should take into account a firm's mission, resources, abilities, and standing in the marketplace; the status of the firm's industry and the product groups in it (such as light versus ice beer); domestic and international competitive forces; such environmental factors as the economy and population growth; and the best opportunities for growth—and the threats that could dampen it.

Four strategic planning approaches are presented next: the product/market opportunity matrix, the Boston Consulting Group matrix, the General Electric business screen, and the Porter generic strategy model.

THE PRODUCT/MARKET OPPORTUNITY MATRIX The **product/market opportunity matrix** identifies four alternative marketing strategies to maintain and/or increase sales of business units and products: market penetration, market development, product development, and diversification (see Figure 14-4).[20] The choice of an alternative depends on the market saturation of an SBU or product and the firm's ability to introduce new products. Two or more alternatives may be combined.

The **product/market opportunity matrix** *involves* **market penetration, market development, product development,** *and* **diversification** *options.*

Market penetration is effective when the market is growing or not yet saturated. A firm seeks to expand the sales of its present products in its present markets through more intensive distribution, aggressive promotion, and competitive pricing. Sales are increased by attracting non-users and competitors' customers and raising the usage rate among current customers. United Parcel Service is a good example of a firm that has pursued a market penetration strategy. UPS (see Figure 14-5) is the world's largest package-delivery firm.

FIGURE 14-4
The Product/Market Opportunity Matrix

Source: Adapted from H. Igor Ansoff, "Strateges for Diversification," *Harvard Business Review, Vol. 35* (September–October 1957), pp. 113–124.

[18]Tim Falconer, "Freeze Play," *Canadian Business* (September 1995), p. 100.

[19]Leah Rickard, "General Mills Gathers Rewards of Change," *Advertising Age* (July 10, 1995), p. 4; and Richard Gibson, "General Mills Gets in Shape for Turnaround," *Wall Street Journal* (September 26, 1995), pp. B1, B4.

[20]H. Igor Ansoff, "Strategies for Diversification," *Harvard Business Review*, Vol. 35 (September–October 1957), pp. 113–124.

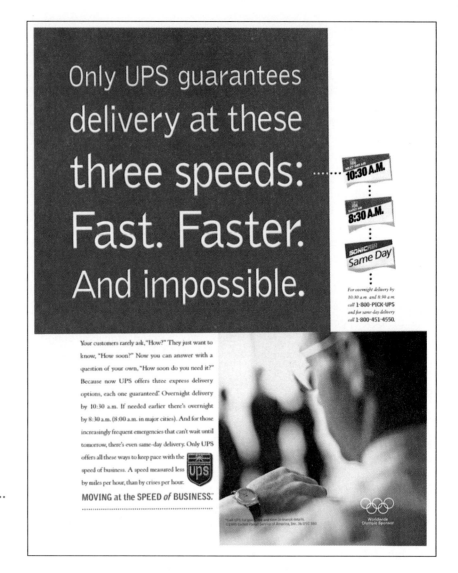

It advertises extensively on TV and in magazines. Low prices and extensive distribution are centrepieces of its strategy.

Market development is effective when a local or regional business looks to widen its market, new market segments are emerging due to changes in consumer lifestyles and demographics, and innovative uses are discovered for a mature product. A firm seeks greater sales of present products from new markets or new product uses. It can enter new geographic markets, appeal to market segments it is not yet satisfying, and reposition existing products. New distribution methods may be tried; promotion efforts are more descriptive. For example, UPS is stepping up efforts around the world, where client use of delivery services tends to be much less frequent than in North America.

Product development is effective when an SBU has a core of strong brands and a sizable consumer following. A firm develops new or modified products to appeal to present markets. It stresses new models, better quality, and other minor innovations closely related to entrenched products—and markets them to loyal customers. Traditional distribution methods are used; promotion stresses that the new product is made by a well-established firm. For example, UPS now offers more shipping choices than ever before, including GroundSaver, GroundTrac, 3 Day Select, Next Day Air, 2nd Day Air, and Worldwide Expedited Package services.

Diversification is used so a firm does not become too dependent on one SBU or product line. The firm becomes involved with new products aimed at new markets. These prod-

Relative Market Share

High | Low

High

SBU
Designation: Star

Marketing Strategy: Large marketing efforts to maintain or increase market share

SBU
Designation: Question Mark

Marketing Strategy: Intensify marketing efforts or leave the market

Industry Growth Rate

Low

SBU
Designation: Cash Cow

Marketing Strategy: Use profits to aid growing SBUs, maintain position

SBU
Designation: Dog

Marketing Strategy: Reduce efforts or divest

Relative market share is an SBU's market share in comparison to the leading competitors in the industry. Industry growth rate is the annual growth of all similar businesses in the market (such as sugarless gum).

FIGURE 14-6
The Boston Consulting Group Matrix

Source: Adapted from Bruce D. Henderson, "The Experience Curve Reviewed: 1V. The Growth Share Matrix of the Product Portfolio" (Boston: Boston Consulting Group, 1973). *Perspectives* No. 135.

ucts may be new to the industry or new only to the company. Distribution and promotion orientations are both different from those usually followed by the firm. UPS has diversified by gaining a 15 per cent stake in Mail Boxes Etc., the leading North American neighbourhood mailing and business service-centre franchiser.[21]

THE BOSTON CONSULTING GROUP MATRIX The **Boston Consulting Group matrix** lets a firm classify each SBU in terms of its market share relative to major competitors and annual industry growth (see Figure 14-6). A firm can see which SBUs are dominant—compared to competitors—and whether the industries in which it operates are growing, stable, or declining. The matrix identifies four types of SBUs: star, cash cow, question mark, and dog, and offers strategies for each of them.[22]

The assumption is that the higher an SBU's market share, the better its long-run marketplace position because of rather low per-unit costs and high profitability. This is due to economies of scale (larger firms can automate or standardize production, service tasks, distribution, promotion, and so on), experience (as operations are repeated, a firm becomes more effective), and better bargaining power. At the same time, the industry growth rate indicates a firm's need to invest. A high growth rate means a big investment will be needed to maintain or expand the firm's position in a growing market.

A **star** is a leading SBU (high market share) in an expanding industry (high growth). The main goal is to sustain differential advantages in the face of rising competition. A star can generate substantial profits but requires financing for continued growth. Market share can be kept or increased through intensive advertising, product introductions, greater distribution, and/or price reductions. As industry growth slows, a star becomes a cash cow.

A **cash cow** is a leading SBU (high market share) in a mature or declining industry (low growth). It often has loyal customers, making it hard for competitors to woo them. Since sales are steady, without high costs for product development and the like, a cash cow produces more cash (profit) than needed to keep its market share. Profits support the growth of other company SBUs. Marketing is oriented to reminder ads, periodic price dis-

The **Boston Consulting Group** matrix *uses market share and industry growth to describe* **stars**, **cash cows**, **question marks**, *and* **dogs**.

[21]Gary Hoover, Alta Campbell, and Patrick J. Spain (Eds.), *Hoover's Handbook of American Business 1995* (Austin, Texas: Reference Press, 1994), pp. 1062–1063.

[22]See *Perspectives on Experience* (Boston: Boston Consulting Group, 1972); and D. Sudharshan, *Marketing Strategy: Relationships, Offerings, Timing & Resource Allocation* (Englewood Cliffs, N.J.: Prentice Hall, 1995), pp. 244–253.

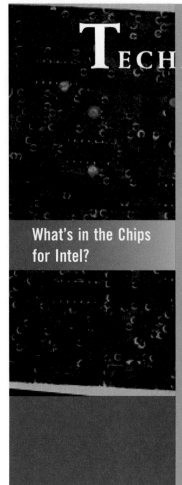

TECHNOLOGY & MARKETING

What's in the Chips for Intel?

Due to its estimated 75 per cent of the microprocessor chip market, Intel Corporation has the advantage of economies of scale (lower per-unit costs than competitors) and high profits. As a result, the firm regularly generates all the cash it needs for new-product development. And because the investment required to develop new microprocessor chips is growing quite rapidly, this places a tough burden on Intel's competitors. According to industry experts, the capital spending needed to devise the Pentium chip was U.S.$5 billion. This was five times the amount needed for the 486 chip and 50 times that for the 386 chip. In general, plant and equipment costs double every four years.

Some analysts say that Intel will become the world's most profitable company by the year 2000. They estimate that Intel's annual earnings may reach U.S.$8 billion to U.S.$11 billion in that year. Few large firms have been able to match Intel's recent five-year average earnings growth rate of 37 per cent. In addition, company executives suggest that microprocessor chips are less vulnerable than other products to the business cycle.

Much of Intel's strategy revolves around an observation made in 1965 by Intel's then chairman, Gordon E. Moore. This observation, now known as Moore's Law, states that the number of transistors that can be placed on a chip doubles every 18 months or so. Making smaller circuits also means that chips get faster, consume less energy, become more reliable, and cost less. For example, Intel's new P6 chip has 254 times more computing power per U.S.$100 in cost than the Intel 8086 chip used by IBM in its initial PC sold in 1981.

As a marketing analyst, what do you think Intel must do to meet the year 2000 profit goals noted above?

Source: Based on material in Don Clark, "A Big Bet Made Intel What It Is Today: Now, It Wagers Again," *Wall Street Journal* (July 7, 1995), pp. A1, A6; and Brent Schlender, "Why Andy Grove Can't Stop," *Fortune* (July 10, 1995), pp. 88–98.

counts, keeping up distribution channels, and offering new styles or options to encourage repurchases.

A **question mark** is an SBU that has had little impact (low market share) in an expanding industry (high growth). There is low consumer support, differential advantages are weak, and competitors are leaders. To improve, a big marketing investment is needed in the face of strong competition. A firm must decide whether to beef up promotion, add distributors, improve product attributes, and cut prices—or to abandon the market. The choice depends on whether a firm believes the SBU can compete successfully with more support and what that support will cost.

A **dog** is an SBU with limited sales (low market share) in a mature or declining industry (low growth). Despite time in the marketplace, a dog has a small customer following—and lags behind competitors in sales, image, and so on. A dog usually has cost disadvantages and few growth opportunities. A firm with such an SBU can appeal to a specialized market, harvest profits by cutting support services, or exit the market.

Dylex Ltd. was the parent firm of the women's fashion clothiers Fairweather and Braemar and men's clothiers Tip Top and Harry Rosen, as well as Bi-Way and Thrifty's. It also has a holding in Club Monaco. Dylex's most recent strategy has been to build market share for their stores by maintaining customer loyalty and emphasizing store branding. Dylex is the kind of firm to which the Boston Consulting Group matrix can be applied. For example, Braemar and Fairweather have been treated as "Cash Cow SBUs." To sustain growth in their retail business Dylex is considering developing products for an aging population and capitalizing on the casual-business attire market. Dylex is planning to go after the upscale men's attire market by repositioning the Tip Top division, thus making it a "Question Mark SBU." The firm is also considering the acquisition of competing clothier Mark's Work Wearhouse to add a "Star SBU" to their portfolio. Dylex divested the "Dog

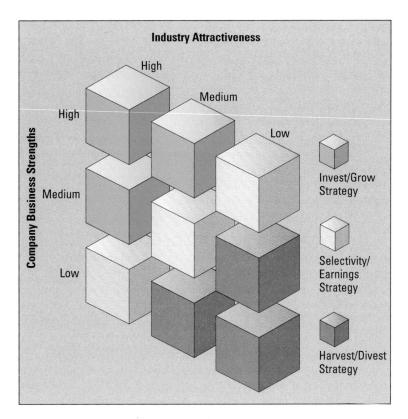

FIGURE 14-7
The General Electric Business Screen
Source: Maintaining Strategies for the Future Through Current Crises (Fairfield, Ct.: General Electric, 1975).

SBU" of Harry Rosen but still has its Bi-Way stores whose image the firm is planning to change. The focus on growth and market share for Dylex falls right in line with the principles suggested by the Boston Consulting Group matrix. Dylex is seeking growth opportunities to "build on the diversity of the Dylex portfolio.[23]

THE GENERAL ELECTRIC BUSINESS SCREEN The **General Electric business screen** categorizes SBUs and products in terms of industry attractiveness and company business strengths. It involves more variables than the product/market opportunity matrix or the Boston Consulting Group matrix. Industry attractiveness factors include market size and growth, competition, technological advances, and the social/legal environment. Company business strength is measured according to differential advantages, market share, patent protection, marketing effectiveness, control over prices, and economies of scale. An SBU may have high, medium, or low industry attractiveness, as well as high, medium, or low company business strengths; it would be positioned accordingly on the business screen in Figure 14-7.[24]

SBUs in green are investment/growth areas. They are in strong industries and performing well. They are similar to stars in the Boston Consulting Group matrix. Full marketing resources are proper, and high profits are expected. Innovations, product-line extensions, product and image ads, distribution intensity, and solid price margins are pursued.

SBUs in yellow are selectivity/earnings areas. They are not positioned as well as investment/growth ones. An SBU may be strong in a weak industry (like a cash cow), okay in a somewhat attractive industry, or weak in an attractive industry (like a question mark). A firm wants to hold the earnings and strength of cash cows, and use marketing to maintain customer loyalty and distribution support. For question marks, a firm must decide whether to raise its marketing investment, focus on a specialized market niche, acquire

The **General Electric business screen** *measures industry attractiveness and company business strengths.*

[23]James Pollock, "At Bat for Dylex," *Marketing Magazine* (November 13, 1995), pp. 1, 12; and "Dylex to Unload Rosen and Braemar Stakes," *Marketing Magazine* (February 19, 1996), p. 1; Leslie McNob, "Climbing Out of the Bargain Basement," *Marketing Magazine* (September 8, 1997), p. 4; and Beth Mitchell, "Retailers Optimistic about Menswear Rebound," *Marketing Magazine* (September 8, 1997), p. 2.
[24]See Derek F. Abell and John S. Hammond, *Strategic Market Planning* (Englewood Cliffs, N.J.: Prentice-Hall, 1979), pp. 211–227; and David A. Aaker, *Strategic Market Management* (New York: Wiley, 1995), pp. 164–167.

another business in the industry, or trim product lines. The medium/medium SBU is an opportunity to appeal to under-served segments and to selectively invest in marketing.

SBUs in red represent harvest/divest areas. They are similar to dogs in the Boston Consulting Group matrix. A firm can minimize its marketing effort, concentrate on a few products rather than a product line, divest, or close down the SBU. Profits are harvested because investments are minimal.

Bausch & Lomb applies the fundamentals of the business screen: It has "a heritage of technical achievement and product excellence dating to 1853. The company markets personal health, medical, biomedical, and optics products on the basis of quality and differentiated benefits. Its strategic focus is on selected segments of global health care and optical markets where it is advantaged with superior technology, low production costs, and established brand names. Products have earned worldwide consumer recognition and are frequently recommended by health-care professionals."[25]

The **Porter generic strategy model** *distinguishes among cost leadership, differentiation, and focus strategies.*

THE PORTER GENERIC STRATEGY MODEL The **Porter generic strategy model** identifies two key marketing planning concepts and the options available for each: competitive scope (broad or narrow target) and competitive advantage (lower cost or differentiation). The model, shown in Figure 14-8, pinpoints these basic strategies: cost leadership, differentiation, and focus.[26]

With a cost leadership strategy, an SBU aims at a broad market and offers goods or services in large quantities. Due to economies of scale, a firm can reduce per-unit costs and have low prices. This gives it higher profit margins than competitors, better response to cost rises, and/or the ability to attract price-conscious consumers. Among those using cost leadership is Royal Airlines. The latter has been called Canada's most efficient carrier. Royal began operations in 1992 and is fanatically dedicated to keeping overhead low and revenue and profits high. In fact, its managers speak with pride as they mention how they have borrowed heavily from management approaches developed by famous cost controlling firms like Wal-Mart. To keep revenues high, Royal focuses on international flights to the Caribbean and other warm-weather destinations in the winter, and serves European and cross-Canada destinations in the summer. This focus on the tourist segment at peak flying times allows them to have fully booked flights and flexible scheduling, which keep costs down and revenues high.[27]

In a differentiation strategy, an SBU aims at a large market by offering goods or services that are viewed as distinctive. The goods or services have a broad appeal, yet are per-

FIGURE 14-8
The Porter Generic Strategy Model

Source: Michael E. Porter, *Competitive Advantage: Creating and Sustaining Superior Performance* (New York: Free Press, 1985), p. 12. Reprinted with the permission of The Free Press, a division of Macmillan Inc. Copyright © 1985 by Michael E. Porter.

[25]*Bausch & Lomb 1992 Annual Report;* and *Bausch & Lomb 1994 Annual Report.*

[26]Michael E. Porter, *Competitive Advantage: Creating and Sustaining Superior Performance* (New York: Free Press, 1985), pp. 11–26; and Michael E. Porter, *Competitive Strategy: Techniques for Analyzing Industries and Competitors* (New York: Free Press, 1980), pp. 34–46. See also Steven P. Schnaars, *Marketing Strategy: A Customer-Driven Approach* (New York: Free Press, 1991), pp. 112–131.

[27]Tamsen Tillson, "On a Wing and a Prayer," *Canadian Business* (October 1995), pp. 90–100.

ceived by consumers as unique by virtue of features, availability, reliability, etc.; price is less important. Among those using differentiation are Federal Express, Seiko, Caterpillar Tractor, and Harry Rosen's menswear stores.[28]

With a focus strategy, an SBU (which could be a small firm) seeks a narrow market segment by offering low prices or a unique product. It can control costs by concentrating on a few key products aimed at specific consumers or by having a specialist reputation and serving a market unsatisfied by competitors. Samsung is a South Korean producer of inexpensive consumer electronics; James Izatt of Vancouver develops turf-growing systems for golf courses and sports fields, which he then licenses.[29]

The Porter model shows that a small firm can profit by concentrating on one competitive niche, even though its total market share may be low. A firm does not have to be large to do well.

EVALUATION OF STRATEGIC PLANNING APPROACHES The strategic planning approaches just discussed are widely used—at least informally. Many firms assess alternative market opportunities; know which products are stars, cash cows, question marks, and dogs; recognize what factors affect performance; understand their industries; and realize they can target broad or narrow customer bases. Formally, strategic planning models are most apt to be used by larger firms; and the models are adapted to the needs of the specific firm employing them.

The major strengths of these approaches are that they let a firm analyze all SBUs and products, study the effects of various strategies, learn the opportunities to pursue and the threats to avoid, compute marketing and other resource needs, focus on meaningful differential advantages, compare performance against designated goals, and discover principles for improving. Competitors' actions and long-term trends can also be followed.

The major weaknesses of these approaches are that they may be hard to use (particularly by a small firm), may be too simplistic and omit key factors, are somewhat arbitrary in defining SBUs and evaluative criteria (like relative market share), may not be applicable to all companies and situations (a dog SBU may actually be profitable and generate cash), do not adequately account for environmental conditions (like the economy), may overvalue market share, and are often used by staff planners rather than line managers.

These techniques only aid planning. They do not replace the need for managers to study each situation and base marketing strategies on the unique aspects of their industry, firm, and SBUs.

Strategic models have pros and cons, and should be only part of planning.

Implementing Tactical Plans

A **tactical plan** specifies the short-run actions (tactics) that a firm undertakes in implementing a given marketing strategy. A tactical plan has three basic elements: specific tasks, a time frame, and resource allocation.

The specific tasks relate to the marketing mix and may be aimed at creating a variety of combinations, from high quality, high service, low distribution intensity, personal-selling emphasis, and above-average prices to low quality, low service, high distribution intensity, advertising emphasis, and low prices. Each SBU has a distinct marketing mix, based on its target market and strategic emphasis. The individual mix elements must be coordinated for each SBU and conflicts among SBUs minimized.

The time frame may mean being the first to introduce a product, bringing out a product when the market is most receptive, or quickly reacting to a competitor's strategy to catch it off guard. A firm must balance its desire to be an industry leader with clear-cut competitive advantages against its concern for the risks of innovation. Marketing opportunities exist for limited periods of time, and the firm needs to act quickly.

Resource allocation (or marketing investments) can be classed as order processing or order generating. Order-processing costs are associated with recording and handling

A marketing strategy is enacted using **tactical plans**.

[28]James Pollock, "At Bat for Dylex."
[29]Kerry Banks, "Blade Runner," *Canadian Business* (February 1996), p. 104.

orders, such as order entry, computer-data handling, and merchandise handling. The goal is to minimize those costs, subject to a given level of service. Order-generating costs, such as advertising and personal selling, produce revenues. Reducing them may have a harmful effect on sales and profits. Thus, a firm should estimate sales at various levels of costs and for various combinations of marketing functions. Maximum profit rarely occurs at the lowest level of expenditure on order-generating costs.

Tactical decisions differ from strategic decisions in several key ways:

- They are less complex and more structured.
- They have a much shorter time horizon.
- They require a considerably lower resource commitment.
- They are enacted and adjusted more often.

At Frito-Lay, tactical planning means preparing its delivery people and its retailers for new product introductions, aggressively promoting its products, maintaining its profit margins—while not giving competitors any opportunities to win market share through lower prices, and servicing its retail accounts very well. How do Frito-Lay personnel avoid complacency in light of such a strong position? As its chief executive says, "I wake up every morning thinking, I haven't sold one bag of Fritos yet. We're always raising the bar on ourselves and our future."[30]

Monitoring Results

Performance is evaluated by **monitoring results**.

Monitoring results involves comparing the actual performance of a firm, business unit, or product against planned performance for a specified period. Actual performance data are then fed back into the strategic planning process. Budgets, timetables, sales and profit statistics, cost analyses, and image studies are just some measures that can be used to assess results.

When actual performance lags behind plans, corrective action is taken. For instance, "if implementation problems persist, it is not (in most instances) because employees mean to do the wrong thing. It is because they do not know the right thing to do. The first task in making strategy work, then, is to identify the right behaviour—that is, behaviour that reduces costs, improves quality, pleases customers, and adds to profitability."[31]

Some plans must be revised due to the impact of uncontrollable factors on sales and costs. Many far-sighted firms develop contingency plans to outline their responses in advance, should unfavourable conditions arise. (Techniques for evaluating marketing effectiveness are covered in Chapter 15.)

Devising a Strategic Plan

Written documents aid strategic planning and are useful for all sorts of firms.

Having a written strategic plan encourages executives to carefully think out and coordinate each step in the planning process, pinpoint problem areas, be consistent, tie the plan to goals and resources, measure performance, and send a clear message to employees and others. A sample outline for a written strategic plan and an application of strategic planning by a small firm are presented next.

Sample Outline for a Written Strategic Plan

What are the ingredients of a good strategic plan? Here is a brief list:

- It should affect the consideration of strategic choices.
- It should force a long-range view.
- It should make the resource allocation system visible.
- It should provide methods to help strategic analysis and decision making.

---

[30]Robert Frank, "Frito-Lay Devours Snack-Food Business," *New York Times* (October 27, 1995), pp. B1, B4.
[31]Steven J. Heyer and Reginald Van Lee, "Rewiring the Corporation," *Business Horizons*, Vol. 35 (May–June 1992), p. 21.

Ethics AND TODAY'S MARKETER

Is Genentech Too Aggressive with Its Marketing?

Genentech, a biotechnology company, has always been an aggressive marketer. Some observers feel that it may be *too* aggressive. One industry expert familiar with G. Kirk Raab, Genentech's chief executive officer, says "Within the law, Kirk will take it as close to the edge as he can." As a result, the U.S. Food and Drug Administration has been investigating Genentech's marketing practices, particularly its sale of approved drugs for non-approved uses or at higher-than-approved dosage levels.

An example of a questionable Genentech strategy is its use of a database of patients who have particular illnesses. Genentech pays nurses and doctors' assistants as much as $50 per patient for information on the person's illness, current treatment, and outcome. Its heart attack registry, for instance, includes detailed questions about Genentech's clot-buster for heart attack patients (TPA), but not about those patients who are receiving other medicines or treatments. According to sources critical of Genentech, the firm has used this database to exaggerate the effectiveness of TPA and understate its drawbacks (which include the increased likelihood of a stroke and high drug costs). Genentech even promoted a seminar with a malpractice attorney to warn doctors of the liability associated with using an inferior substitute product.

Perhaps the greatest source of controversy concerns Genentech's marketing of Protropin, its growth hormone product. In an indictment, a Genentech executive was accused of providing a $224 000 research grant and consulting fee to a doctor who prescribed high doses of Protroprin. And while Genentech has also funded charities that screen school-aged children who are very short, Genentech does not disclose its funding to either the schools or parents. Critics say Genentech is selling its growth hormone to about twice the number of children that would benefit from the product.

As a marketing manager for Protropin, where do you draw the line between ethical and unethical behaviour?

Source: Based on material in Ralph T. King, "In Marketing of Drugs, Genentech Tests Limits of What Is Acceptable," *Wall Street Journal* (January 10, 1995), pp. A1, A6.

- It should be a basis for managing a firm or SBU strategically.
- It should provide a communication and coordination system both horizontally (between SBUs and departments) and vertically (from senior executives to front-line employees).
- It should help a firm and its SBUs cope with change.[32]

Table 14-1 presents a sample outline for a written strategic plan from a marketing perspective. This outline may be used by firms of any size or type.

Labatt: Dealing with a Changing Brewing Market

Labatt Brewing Company has the reputation in Canada as "the savviest marketer in sudsland." Earning and keeping this reputation has not been easy and will not get any easier.

Labatt's reputation as a "savvy" brewer comes from having a detailed strategic plan.

[32]Aaker, *Strategic Market Management*, pp. 17–18.

T a b l e   1 4 – 1

A Sample Outline for a Written Strategic Plan—From a Marketing Perspective

Using as much detail as possible, please address each of these points for your firm:

1. Organizational Mission
   (a) In 50 words or less, describe the current mission of your organization.
   (b) In 50 words or less, describe how you would like your organizational mission to evolve over the next five years. The next ten years.
   (c) Is your firm on track regarding the mission statements in (a) and (b)? Explain your answer.
   (d) Discuss the organizational mission in terms of your target market(s), your functions performed, and your overall style of marketing.
   (e) Discuss the organizational mission in terms of company diversification.
   (f) How is the organizational mission communicated to employees?

2. Strategic Business Units
   (a) State the present organizational structure of your firm.
   (b) Assess the present organizational structure.
   (c) How would you expect the organizational structure to evolve over the next five years? The next ten years?
   (d) Does your firm have strategic business units? If yes, describe them. If no, why not?
   (e) Does your firm have a separate marketing plan for each target market, major product, and so on? Explain your answer and relate it to (d).
   (f) Does each product or business unit in your firm have a marketing manager, proper resources, and clear competitors? Explain your answer.

3. Marketing Objectives
   (a) Cite your organization's overall marketing goals for the next one, three, five, and ten years.
   (b) Cite your organization's specific marketing goals by target market and product for the next one, five, and ten years:
      • Sales.
      • Market share.
      • Profit.
      • Image.
      • Customer loyalty.
   (c) What criteria will be used to determine whether goals have been fully, partially, or unsatisfactorily reached?

4. Situation Analysis
   (a) Describe the present overall strengths, weaknesses, opportunities, and threats (SWOT) facing your organization.
   (b) How do you expect the factors noted in your answer (a) to change over the next five to ten years?

Labatt has been brewing beer in Canada since 1847. It brews and markets a number of well-known national brands of beer including: Cold-Filtered Genuine Draft, Labatt Ice, Labatt 50, Labatt Blue, Blue Light, Labatt Extra Dry, Labatt Lite, John Labatt Classic, Wildcat, Labatt 0.5, Kokanee, Kokanee Gold, Kokanee Light, and Labatt Copper. In addition, Labatt also brews and markets Budweiser, Bud Light, Carlsberg, and Carlsberg Light brands of beer under licence. Labatt's main competitor and the market leader is Molson Brewery, which is owned by the U.S.-based Miller Brewing Company. Labatt and Molson comprise 90 per cent of the Canadian brewing industry.

Aside from battling each other, both these companies must prepare to handle major upheavals in their competitive environment caused by expected changes in interprovincial trade barriers for beer, a ruling by GATT (General Agreement on Tariffs and Trade) that trade barriers to beer from the United States be removed, and the emergence of microbrewing and home brewing. In the face of competition from Molson and the expected changes, Labatt's strategic planning will be very important to its future.

Table 14-1 (continued)

....

(c) For each of the key products or businesses of your firm, describe the present strengths, weaknesses, opportunities, and threats.

(d) How do you expect the factors noted in your answer to (c) to change over the next five to ten years?

(e) How will your firm respond to the factors mentioned in the answers for (a) to (d)?

5. Developing Strategy
   (a) Describe the target market, marketing mix, and differential advantages for each of your products or businesses.
   (b) Does your firm have sufficient resources and capabilities to carry out its marketing strategy? Explain your answer.
   (c) Compare your firm's strategy with those of leading competitors.
   (d) Describe your use of these strategic approaches: market penetration, market development, product development, and diversification.
   (e) For each product or business, detail the characteristics of your firm's present customers, as well as those who should be sought in the future.
   (f) Categorize each of your products or businesses as a star, cash cow, question mark, or dog. Explain your reasoning.
   (g) What is the impact of the categorization cited in (f) on your strategy?
   (h) For each product or business, which of these approaches is most apt: invest/grow, selectivity/earnings, or harvest/divest? Explain your reasoning.
   (i) For each of your products or businesses, which of these approaches is most appropriate: cost leadership, differentiation, cost focus, or differentiation focus? Explain your reasoning.
   (j) Describe how the plans for all of your firm's products or businesses are coordinated.

6. Implementation
   (a) Describe the procedures to activate your firm's strategy.
   (b) For each product or business, how does your firm ensure that the strategy is implemented as intended with regard to the target market and marketing mix?
   (c) Do marketing personnel have appropriate authority (i.e., are they empowered) and resources to implement plans? Explain your answer.
   (d) Are ongoing marketing budgets sufficient? Does your organization differentiate between order-generating and order-processing costs? Explain your answers.
   (e) How do you expect competitors to react as you implement your strategy?
   (f) Are there contingency plans in case of unexpected results?

7. Monitoring Results
   (a) Describe the procedures used by your firm to monitor steps 1 to 6.
   (b) For each company product or business, is planned performance compared with actual performance on a regular basis? Explain your answer.
   (c) Is a SWOT analysis conducted regularly? Explain your answer.
   (d) How are performance results communicated through the organization?
   (e) What procedures do you use to respond to the findings of performance reviews?

....

ORGANIZATIONAL MISSION In June of 1995 Labatt was acquired in a friendly takeover by Interbrew S.A., a Belgian brewing conglomerate. This acquisition has resulted in the company returning to its 1847 roots: Interbrew S.A. was quite specific in stating that they wanted no part of any of the other businesses Labatt was involved in, and let it be known that companies in the entertainment division were for sale.

ESTABLISHING STRATEGIC BUSINESS UNITS In 1993, Labatt was a multinational conglomerate with annual sales of $2.135 billion and 5700 employees in its two main businesses of brewing and entertainment. Labatt had a strong sales base in Canada, which accounted for 84 per cent of company revenues, while the brewing operations accounted for 84 per cent of Labatt's total sales as well. One of two large brewers in Canada, Labatt operated 10 breweries and marketed 36 brands of ale and lager while holding a

44.5 per cent share of the Canadian market as of March 1994. Molson held a market share of just under 50 per cent at that time. Labatt also exports beer to 20 other countries including the United States. However, with the takeover by Interbrew S.A. in June 1995, the plan is for Labatt to have one main SBU: brewing.

SETTING MARKETING OBJECTIVES Labatt has a number of marketing goals but their main objective is to overtake Molson to become the number one brewer in Canada. As of March 1997, Molson's market share of the Canadian beer market was 46.1 per cent while Labatt's share was 44.1 per cent. To achieve this main objective Labatt has set two secondary objectives for themselves. The first is to hold on to the market share of their flagship brand, Labatt Blue. The second objective is to introduce new products to quickly gain market share and then hold onto the gains.

PERFORMING SITUATION ANALYSIS Beer distribution in Canada is unique in that each of the ten provinces has independent control over beer distribution. The two major markets for beer, Quebec and Ontario, have very diverse distribution channels. In Quebec, beer is sold through company-owned and independent beer distributors, while in Ontario, all beer is sold through Brewers Warehousing Corporation, which is owned by the brewers themselves. The distribution of beer in the remaining provinces of Canada is through outlets owned and operated by the provincial governments—except in Alberta where distribution is similar to that in Quebec. In Ontario, the largest beer market, there is virtually no price competition between brands of beer so that nonprice factors have become critical to marketing beer in this province.

MOOSEHEAD
www.moosehead.ca/

Across Canada several microbreweries have been asserting themselves in the large metropolitan markets, and brew-your-own-beer operations are also growing into a significant competitive threat through their low price positioning. The microbreweries are growing at a tremendous rate; Sleeman Brewery of Guelph, Ontario, recently merged with Okanagan Spring Brewery of Vernon, British Columbia. Moosehead Breweries from Dartmouth, Nova Scotia, is competing aggressively while identifying itself as the only "Canadian" brewery left since Interbrew S.A.'s takeover of Labatt.

One microbrewery, Pacific Western Brewery in Prince George, British Columbia, has even had the audacity to market its products in Japan. Japanese consumers are well disposed toward Canadian beers and Pacific Western is the number three export in Japan, trailing only Heineken and Budweiser!

The Canadian beer market itself has been experiencing no volume growth in consumption. Labatt and Molson have been looking at foreign markets for their growth potential and have made strong inroads in the United States and Japan. However, the competition in Canada is expected to be fierce when Canada complies with a GATT ruling to eliminate trade barriers to American beer. In order for the Canadian brewing industry to compete against foreign beers there needs to be a level playing field for brewers within Canada, which means that interprovincial trade barriers for beer will have to be eliminated too.

DEVELOPING MARKETING STRATEGY In order to accomplish the objective of becoming number one in market share in Canada, Labatt's CEO Hugo Powell is employing a number of approaches. In the past five years, Labatt and Molson have combined to introduce 40 new products or line extensions. Labatt has been very successful with this strategy: 25 per cent of its current sales are from products introduced since 1992.

The marketing strategy Labatt has been pursuing is to offer unique products to gain market share, which must then be held. Labatt has presented innovative new products while holding the number one beer brand position with Labatt Blue. However, Blue's market share recently fell to 12.3 per cent from its peak of 19 per cent in the late 1980s. Brand loyalty to beer can be very strong, particularly in the 19- to 29-year-old age group, which is influenced heavily by advertising. A new advertising campaign aimed at this group is designed to reverse Blue's falling market share.

Labatt is preparing to meet the expected environmental changes through product innovations based on research on consumer wants and needs and cost-cutting measures.

IMPLEMENTING TACTICAL PLANS To strengthen Labatt's flagship brand, Blue, and introduce new products, the critical marketing tools are advertising, sales promotion, public relations, and personal selling. Labatt's is marketing internationally with a great deal of success by concentrating on innovative products like Labatt Ice Beer. The latter made the strongest market-share gains in the Japanese market recently and the Labatt method of brewing ice beer has been licensed to several foreign breweries in the South American market. In the summer of 1997 Labatt used the fruits of previous cost-cutting measures such as standardizing bottles and reducing administrative staff to implement a series of weekend $2/case price reductions in the Ontario market.

MONITORING RESULTS Every quarter, Hugo Powell goes before the board of directors of Labatt to give a report. He describes the company's position at the time and provides targets to meet in the next two quarters. One board member has described Powell as a very focused individual who provides specific targets, specific reasons for the targets, and the specific means of accomplishing these targets. Given Labatt's commitment to planning, involvement with sound marketing principles, and its reputation as "the savviest marketer in sudsland," it is a good bet that the company will handle changes to its industry quite well.[33]

MARKETING IN A CHANGING WORLD

What Business Are We In?[34]

According to Peter Drucker, the long-time management guru, "What to do" (organizational mission) is the main challenge now facing top management. The story is a familiar one: A firm that was a superstar only yesterday finds it is stagnant, frustrated, and in trouble. This phenomenon is not confined to Canadian and American firms. It is common in Japan and Germany, the Netherlands and France, Italy and Sweden. The root cause of nearly every one of these crises is not that things are being done poorly. It is not even that the wrong things are being done. Usually, the right things are being done—but fruitlessly.

This occurs when the assumptions that a firm makes about its mission no longer fit reality. These are assumptions that shape its behaviour, dictate its decisions about what to do and what not to do, and define what a firm deems meaningful results. The assumptions relate to markets; customer and competitor values and behaviour; technology and its dynamics; and company strengths and weaknesses. They are what Drucker calls a company's "theory of the business."

[33]"Historical Report, John Labatt Ltd.," *Financial Post Datagroup* (Nov. 5, 1993); Conference Board of Canada, *The Canadian Brewing Industry: An Assessment of the Impacts of Liberalized Interprovincial Trade in Canada* (June 1990), pp. 1–32; "How U.S. Beer Will Uncap the Canadian Market," *Financial Times of Canada*, Vol. 80 (November 11–17, 1991), pp. 1, 4; "Labatt's Blues: Can the Savviest Marketer in Sudsland Revive the Flagging Fortunes of Canada's Top Brew?," *Report on Business Magazine*, Vol. 7 (June 1991), pp. 40–48; "Labatt Could Cut 100 Managers, Sources Say," *Financial Post*, Vol. 3 (January 16, 1991), p. 3; Douglas Faulkner, "Powell's Big Picture," *Marketing Magazine* (November 20, 1995), pp. 12–13; Stan Sutter, "Labatt Deal Gives Interbrew a North American Beachhead," *Marketing Magazine* (June 19, 1995), p. 6; James Pollock, "Labatt Stronger After Buyout by Interbrew," *Marketing Magazine* (June 19, 1995), p. 3; David Menzies, "Molson Muscle," *Marketing Magazine* (August 18/25, 1997), pp. 11–13; Report on Market Share, "Who's Got What," *Marketing Magazine* (May 26, 1997), p. 11; Eve Lazurus, "Pacific Western Beer Finds Niche in Japan," *Marketing Magazine* (May 19, 1997), p. 3; and Lara Mills, "Breweries Summer Price Wars End in Tie," *Marketing Magazine* (September 29, 1997), p. 2.

[34]The material in this section is based on Peter F. Drucker, "The Theory of the Business," *Harvard Business Review*, Vol. 72 (September–October 1994), pp. 95–104.

To remedy the situation, Drucker suggests that a company needs to assess its current business [organizational mission] regularly—and decide what it really should be. Here is how a firm can do this:

- "Every three years, an organization should challenge every product, every service, every policy, every distribution channel with the question, 'If we were not in it already, would we be going into it now?'"
- The firm should "study what goes on outside the business, especially with regard to non customers. The first signs of fundamental change rarely appear within one's own organization or among one's own customers. Almost always they show up first among one's non customers."
- "To diagnose problems early, managers must pay attention to warning signs. A theory of the business always becomes obsolete when a firm attains its original goals. Attaining one's objectives is not cause for celebration; it is cause for new thinking."
- To establish, maintain, or reorient an organizational mission does not require genius, but hard work. "It is not being clever; it is being conscientious. It is what CEOs are paid for."

SUMMARY

1. *To define strategic planning and consider its importance for marketing* Strategic planning encompasses both strategic business plans and strategic marketing plans. Strategic business plans describe the overall direction firms will pursue within their chosen environment and guide the allocation of resources and effort. Strategic marketing plans outline what marketing actions to undertake, why those actions are needed, who is responsible for carrying them out, when and where they will be completed, and how they will be coordinated.

Strategic planning provides guidance via a hierarchical process, clarifies goals, encourages cooperation among departments, focuses on strengths and weaknesses (as well as opportunities and threats), examines alternatives, helps allocate resources, and points up the value of monitoring results.

2. *To describe the total quality approach to strategic planning and its relevance to marketing* A total quality approach should be used while devising and enacting business and marketing plans. With this approach, a firm adopts a process- and output-related philosophy, by which it strives to fully satisfy consumers in an effective and efficient manner. There is a customer focus; a top management commitment; emphasis on continuous improvement; and support and involvement from employees, suppliers, and channel members.

3. *To look at the different kinds of strategic plans and the relationships between marketing and other functional areas in an organization* A firm's strategic plans may be short-run, moderate in length, or long-run. Strategic marketing plans may be for each major product, presented as one company-wide marketing plan, or considered part of an overall business plan. A bottom-up, top-down, or combined management approach may be used.

The interests of marketing and the other key functional areas in a firm need to be accommodated in a strategic plan. Departmental conflict can be reduced by improving communications, employing personnel with broad backgrounds, establishing interdepartmental development programs, and blending departmental goals.

4. *To describe thoroughly each of the steps in the strategic planning process* First, a firm defines its organizational mission—the long-term commitment to a type of business and a place in the market. Second, it establishes strategic business units (SBUs), which are self-contained divisions, product lines, or product departments with specific market focuses and separate managers. Third, quantitative and qualitative marketing objectives are set. Fourth, through situation analysis, a firm identifies its internal strengths and weaknesses, as well as external opportunities and threats.

Fifth, a firm develops a marketing strategy—to outline the way in which the marketing mix is used to attract and satisfy the target market(s) and accomplish organizational goals. Every SBU has its own marketing mix. The approaches to strategy planning include the product/market opportunity matrix, the Boston Consulting Group matrix, the General Electric business screen, and the Porter generic strategy model. They should be viewed as planning tools that aid decision making; they do not replace the need for executives to engage in hands-on planning for each situation.

Sixth, a firm uses tactical plans to specify the short-run actions necessary to implement a given marketing strategy. At this stage, specific tasks, a time horizon, and resource allocation are operationalized. Seventh, a firm monitors results by comparing actual performance against planned performance; and this information is fed back into the strategic planning process. Adjustments in strategy are made as needed.

5. *To show how a strategic plan may be devised and applied* Strategic planning works best when it is done systematically and comprehensively. This is exemplified by Labatt Brewing Company, one of Canada's finest brewers.

KEY TERMS

strategic business plan (p. 417)
strategic marketing plan (p. 417)
total quality (p. 417)
strategic planning process (p. 424)
organizational mission (p. 425)
strategic business unit (SBU) (p. 426)
situation analysis (p. 424)
marketing strategy (p. 425)

product/market opportunity matrix (p. 425)
market penetration (p. 425)
market development (p. 425)
product development (p. 425)
diversification (p. 425)
Boston Consulting Group matrix (p. 427)
star (p. 427)

cash cow (p. 427)
question mark (p. 427)
dog (p. 427)
General Electric business screen (p. 429)
Porter generic strategy model (p. 430)
tactical plan (p. 431)
monitoring results (p. 432)

Review Questions

1. What are the benefits of strategic planning?
2. Explain Figure 14-2, which deals with the total quality approach.
3. Distinguish between bottom-up and top-down strategic plans. What are the pros and cons of each?
4. Why are conflicts between marketing and other functional areas inevitable? How can these conflicts be reduced or avoided?
5. Under what circumstances should a company consider reappraising its organizational mission?

6. What is a strategic business unit? Why is this concept so important for strategic planning?
7. In situation analysis, what is the distinction between strengths and opportunities and between weaknesses and threats? How should a firm react to each of these factors?
8. Compare the BCG matrix, the General Electric business screen, and the Porter generic strategy models.
9. Explain how tactical decisions differ from strategic decisions.
10. What are the ingredients of a good strategic plan?

Discussion Questions

1. Do you think your college or university is following a total quality approach? Why or why not? What total quality recommendations would you make for your school?
2. Comment on this statement: "In the market-oriented view of the strategic planning process, financial goals are seen as results and rewards, not the fundamental purpose of business."
3. What issues should a small airline study during situation analysis? How could it react to them?

4. Give a current example of each of these strategic approaches: market development, product development, market penetration, and diversification. Evaluate the strategies.
5. Develop a rating scale to use in analyzing the industry attractiveness and company business strengths of a small stock brokerage firm, a medium-sized management consulting firm, or a large auto supplies manufacturer.

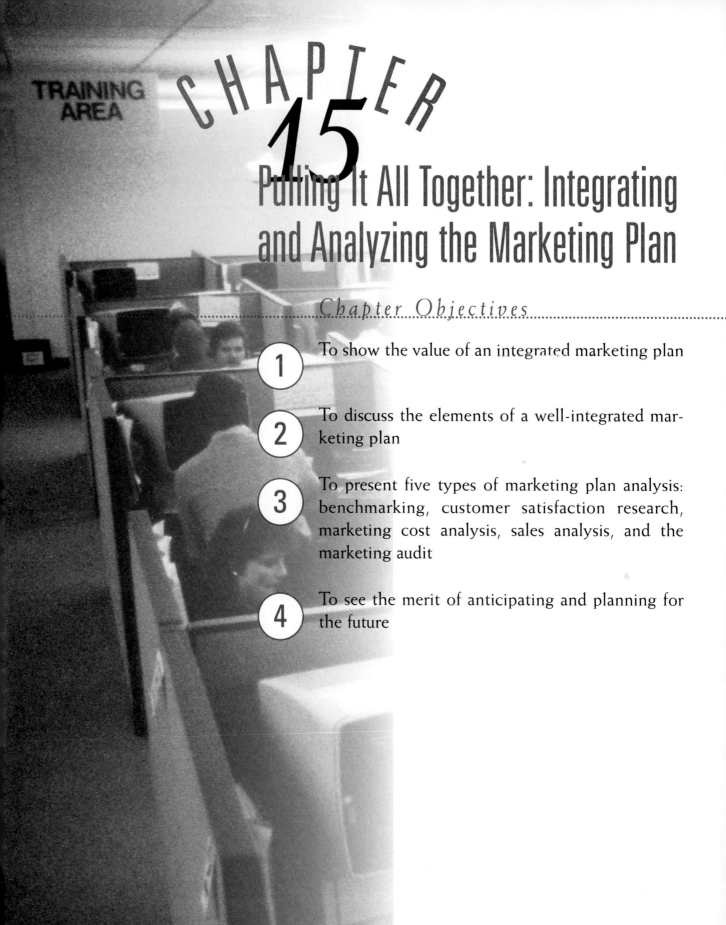

TRAINING AREA

CHAPTER 15

Putting It All Together: Integrating and Analyzing the Marketing Plan

Chapter Objectives

1 To show the value of an integrated marketing plan

2 To discuss the elements of a well-integrated marketing plan

3 To present five types of marketing plan analysis: benchmarking, customer satisfaction research, marketing cost analysis, sales analysis, and the marketing audit

4 To see the merit of anticipating and planning for the future

> *Today's Canadian corporate planners, ravaged by the modern scourges of globalization, downsizing, and technological change, look for solutions and security at the American firms of Motorola, Microsoft, and Springfield ReManufacturing (the guru of open book management). Some 2000 devotees stream through AT&T Universal Card's super-efficient telephone customer service centre in Jacksonville, Florida, every year, at U.S.$375 a pop. More than 5000 supplicants have sojourned at Federal Express' expansive overnight package facility in Memphis for a U.S.$250 midnight hub tour and all-day seminar. USAA, the San Antonio-based insurer, has drawn more than 2100 seekers to its monthly program from such far-flung locales as Australia, Italy, Japan, South Korea, and South Africa.*

Firms such as Motorola, AT&T, and Federal Express are now viewed as "management meccas." And business visitors are drawn to these meccas to gain benchmarking insights, so they can better set performance standards for their own organizations. Benchmarking is becoming a more widely recognized component of a firm's integrated marketing program.

Each mecca company has been publicly recognized for its excellence in a specific aspect of business—by winning the Baldridge Award for quality in the U.S., by being lauded in the media, and/or by constantly increasing sales and profits:

MOTOROLA
www.mot.com/

AT&T
www.att.com/

- Motorola offers an eight-hour seminar on its famed "six sigma" quality program, which aims for only one defect per 1 000 000-unit production run. The seminar also includes material on how to reduce the time from when a new product idea is approved to when the product is commercialized, as well as Motorola's total customer satisfaction philosophy.

- AT&T's Universal Card walks executives through its customer service centre, which handles 1.5 million calls per month. A standout portion of its session features the high-technology system that lets AT&T employees retrieve a customer's bill and payment record even before the phone is picked up.

- Federal Express' session features a full tour of its package-handling facility, a discussion of its customer service policies, and its measurement of service quality.

Visits to management meccas are growing, since more management consulting firms are including them as part of their client training. In contrast to other techniques, such visits enable managers to see how concepts are really enacted, instead of evaluating different theories. "You get a real sense for the culture of the company, for what the people are like, and what the place looks like," says Jay Michaud, a vice-president with CSC Consulting. It also allows executives to talk with others who have had similar experiences.

By visiting such management meccas as General Electric, Lands' End, and Fidelity Investments, GTE found a better way to handle customer service—based on the technology these three firms were utilizing. As a result of its new methods, GTE can now complete a customer order in less than two hours, versus the three to four days it took using the previous technology. And the student has become the professor, as hundreds of managers from other firms visit GTE each year to learn about its high-tech customer service methods.[1]

In this chapter, we will study how a firm can integrate and analyze its marketing plan—and see the value of developing and implementing a clear, forward-looking, cohesive, and adaptable strategy.

Overview

Chapters 1 and 2 introduced basic marketing concepts and described the marketing environment. Chapter 3 the role of marketing information systems and marketing research. Chapters 4 to 13 centred on specific aspects of marketing: describing and selecting target markets, and the marketing mix (product, distribution, promotion, and price planning). Chapter 14 presented the strategic planning process as it applies to marketing.

This chapter ties things together, and describes how a marketing plan can be integrated and evaluated. It builds on the discussion of strategic planning in Chapter 14—particularly, the total quality approach (whereby a firm strives to fully satisfy customers in an effective and efficient manner). With an integrated marketing effort, individual marketing components are synchronized and everyone is "on the same page." And when an organization wants to appraise performance, capitalize on strengths, minimize weaknesses, and plan for the future, marketing analysis (including benchmarking and customer satisfaction) is necessary.

This is the challenge, as one expert sees it:

> Do you know where your marketing plan is? In a world where competitors observe and rapidly imitate each other's advancements in product development, pricing, packaging, and distribution, internal and external communication is more important than ever as a way of differentiating your business from those of competitors. At its most basic level, a marketing plan defines a business niche, summarizes objectives, and presents strategies for getting from point A to point B. But roadmaps need constant updating to reflect the addition of new routes. Likewise, in a decade in which technology, international relations, and the competitive landscape are constantly changing, the concept of a static marketing plan has to be reassessed.
>
> Two of today's hottest buzzwords are "interactive" and "integrated." A successful marketing plan has to be both. "Interactive" means your marketing plan should be a conversation between your business and your customers. It's your chance to tell customers about your business and to listen and act on their responses. "Integrative" means the message in your marketing is consistently reinforced by every department within your company. Marketing is as much a function of the finance and manufacturing areas as it is the advertising and public relations areas.[2]

Wal-Mart's ten basic rules are applied to a wide range of firms.

Thus, every organization can learn from the focused management rules of Wal-Mart, the world's leading retailer. These principles were developed by the late Sam Walton, the firm's founder, and are in his words:

1. "Commit to your business. Believe in it more than anybody else."

2. "Share your profits with all your associates [workers] and treat them as partners. In turn, they will treat you as a partner."

3. "Motivate your partners [workers]. Constantly, day by day, think of new and more interesting ways to motivate and challenge. Set high goals, encourage competition, and keep score."

[1]John A. Byrne, "Management Meccas," *Business Week* (September 18, 1995), pp. 122–132.
[2]Shelly Reese, "The Very Model of a Modern Marketing Plan," *Marketing Tools* (January–February 1996), pp. 56–59.

4. "Communicate everything you possibly can to your partners [workers]. The more they know, the more they'll understand. The more they understand, the more they'll care. Once they care, there's no stopping them."

5. "Appreciate everything your associates do for the business. Nothing else can quite substitute for a few well-chosen, well-timed, sincere words of praise. They're absolutely free and worth a fortune."

6. "Celebrate your successes. Find humour in your failures. Don't take yourself so seriously. Loosen up and everybody around you will loosen up."

7. "Listen to everyone in your company. The folks on the front lines—the ones who actually talk to the customer—are the only ones who really know what's going on out there. You'd better find out what they know. This is really what total quality is all about."

8. "Exceed your customers' expectations. If you do, they'll come back over and over. Make good on all your mistakes, and don't make excuses—apologize. The two most important words I ever wrote were on the first Wal-Mart sign: SATISFACTION GUARANTEED."

9. "Control your expenses better than your competition. This is where you can always find the competitive advantage. You can make a lot of different mistakes and still recover if you run an efficient operation. Or you can be brilliant and still go out of business if you're inefficient."

10. "Swim upstream. Ignore the conventional wisdom. If everybody else is doing it one way, there's a good chance you can find your niche by going in exactly the opposite direction."[3]

Integrating the Marketing Plan

When a marketing plan is properly integrated, all of its various parts are unified, consistent, and coordinated; and a total quality approach can be followed. Although this appears a simple task, it is important to recall that a firm may have long-run, moderate-length, and short-run plans; the different strategic business units in an organization may require separate marketing plans; and each aspect of the marketing mix requires planning. For example:

From a total quality perspective, the many parts of a marketing plan should be unified, consistent, and coordinated.

- An overall plan is poorly integrated if short-run profits are earned at the expense of moderate- or long-run profits. This could occur if marketing research or new-product planning expenditures are reduced to raise profits temporarily. A firm could also encounter difficulties if plans are changed too frequently, leading to a blurred image for consumers and a lack of focus for executives.

- Resources need to be allocated among SBUs, so funds are given to those with high potential. The target markets, product images, price levels, and so on, of each SBU must be distinctive—yet not in conflict with one another. Physical distribution efforts and channel member arrangements need to be timed so the system and its role in a total quality program are not strained by two or more SBUs making costly demands simultaneously.

- Even though a promotion plan primarily deals with one strategic element, it must also be integrated with product, distribution, and pricing plans. It must reflect the proper image for a firm's products, encourage channel cooperation, and demonstrate that products are worth the prices set.

[3]Sam Walton and John Huey, *Made in America* (New York: Doubleday, 1992).

FIGURE 15-1
Elements Leading to a Well-Integrated Marketing Plan

A well-integrated marketing plan incorporates the elements shown in Figure 15-1. These elements are explained next.

Clear Organizational Mission

The organizational mission should be clear and directive.

A clear organizational mission outlines a firm's commitment to a type of business and a place in the market. It directs the company's total quality efforts. The organizational mission is involved whenever a firm seeks new customer groups or abandons existing ones, adds or deletes product lines, acquires other firms or sells part of its own business, performs different marketing functions, and/or shifts technological focus (as noted in Chapter 14). Both top management and marketing personnel must be committed to an organizational mission for it to be achieved; and the mission must be communicated to customers, company employees, suppliers, and distribution intermediaries. For example, PHH has a directive yet flexible organizational mission with a total quality approach:

> PHH is in the service business. We don't make cars. We don't own real-estate companies. We aren't a traditional bank. We specialize in business processes that are not an organization's primary focus, but are essential to top performance.
> *Vehicle Management Services*—Companies which operate fleets of vehicles turn to PHH for expert assistance in selecting, purchasing, managing, and remarketing their cars, vans, and trucks. Our consultative, information, and administrative services, as well as our extensive national networks of suppliers, help keep a client's drivers safely and productively on the road, while efficiently managing expenses through process improvements and valuable information. And PHH's fuel and service cards mean added driver convenience and client cost-savings through the world's largest fuel, vehicle repair, and maintenance network.
> *Relocation and Real-Estate Services*—Mobility for organizations and their employees is a critical factor in business success. PHH companies are dedicated to helping clients manage the complex process of relocating employees where they can be most effective. With comprehensive high-quality services and extensive real estate-related supplier networks, PHH facilitates the process of home selling, home finding, moving, and settling into the new area for the relocating family. PHH also provides property management and marketing services to financial institutions, and location planning and strategic management consulting to businesses and municipalities.
> *Mortgage Banking Services*—Finding the right home financing is a complicated business. PHH works with corporations, credit unions, real-estate brokers, and affinity groups to provide a full range of residential first mortgages and casualty insurance-related products. Via customer-focused services, centralized management, and extensive telecommunications and computer capabilities, PHH has grown into one of the top 20 mortgage originators in [North America].[4]

Many experts believe a firm should reappraise its organizational mission if the company has values that do not fit a changing environment, its industry undergoes rapid changes, its performance is average or worse, it is changing size (from small to large or large to small), or opportunities unrelated to its original mission arise.

[4]*PHH Corporation: Your Connection to Quality Business Services* (n.d.).

Long-Term Competitive Advantages

Long-term competitive advantages are company, product, and marketing attributes whose distinctiveness and appeal to consumers can be maintained over an extended period of time. A firm must capitalize on the attributes that are most important to consumers and prepare competitive advantages accordingly. For competitive advantages to be sustainable, consumers must perceive a consistent positive difference in key attributes between the company's offerings and those of competitors; that difference must be linked to a capability gap that competitors will have difficulty in closing (due to patents, superior marketing skills, customer loyalty, and other factors); and the company's offerings must appeal to some enduring consumer need. While concentrating on its competitive advantages, a company should not lose sight of the importance of customer service and its role in a total quality program.

As Michael Treacy and Fred Wiersema say in their best-selling book, *The Discipline of Market Leaders*:

> Today's market leaders understand the battle they're in. They know they have to redefine value by raising customer expectations in the one component of value they choose to highlight. Casio, for instance, establishes new affordability levels for familiar products such as calculators; Hertz makes car rental nearly as convenient as taking a cab; Lands' End shows individuals that they're not just a number; and Home Depot proves that old-fashioned, knowledgeable advice hasn't gone the way of trading stamps.
>
> But wait a minute. These companies don't shine in every way. A successful company like Wal-Mart doesn't peddle haute couture; Lands' End doesn't sell clothing for the lowest possible cost; and Starbucks, the Seattle coffee chain, doesn't slide a cup of java under your nose any faster or more conveniently than anyone else. Yet, all of these companies are thriving because they shine in a way their customers care most about. They have honed at least one component of value to a level of excellence that puts all competitors to shame. Our research shows that no company can succeed today by trying to be all things to all people. It must instead find the unique value that it alone can deliver to a chosen market.[5]

Because smaller firms often cannot compete on the basis of low prices, they tend to concentrate on other competitive advantages, such as:

- Targeting underserved market niches, including international ones.

- Having unique offerings through specialization. Firms can be innovative, process customized orders, or otherwise adapt products for particular customers.

- Stressing product quality and reliability. "The more crucial the performance of a product to customer needs, the lower will be the concern with pricing."

- Engaging in extra efforts to gain customer loyalty by making the purchase process easy, giving superior service, and promising the long-term availability of goods and services. As one small-firm manager said, "We know our products are reliable and do not require visits. But when our clients see us physically inspecting machines, sometimes merely dusting them, they have a sense of security and comfort." This is a total quality approach.

- Emphasizing relationship marketing, whereby personal relationships with their suppliers are viewed as important by customers.[6]

When implementing a marketing strategy, a firm should note that its competitive advantages may not apply in all situations. For instance, an advantage can lose its value when transferred to another nation. This can occur because an advantage is not relevant in a different context or because it can easily be countered by local competitors: "Products that are superior in the home market may not offer customer-perceived value in the target

Competitive advantages should centre on company, product, and marketing attributes with long-range distinctiveness.

STARBUCKS
www.occ.com/starbucks/history.html

---

[5]Michael Treacy and Fred Wiersema, *The Discipline of Market Leaders* (Reading, Mass.: Addison-Wesley, 1995).

[6]Peter Wright, "Competitive Strategies for Small Business," *Collegiate Forum* (Spring 1983), pp. 3–4; Steven P. Galante, "More Firms Quiz Customers for Clues about Competition," *Wall Street Journal* (March 3, 1986), p. 21; "Hot Growth Companies," *Business Week* (May 27, 1991), pp. 78–84; and Donna Fenn, "Leader of the Pack," *Inc.* (February 1996), pp. 31–38.

International Marketing in *Action*

Does Korea's Samsung Represent the Conglomerate of the Future?

Under chair Lee Kun, Samsung is expanding from its traditional businesses—electronics, chemicals, finance, and heavy machinery—into autos, aerospace, transportation, and entertainment. It has also begun to negotiate strategic alliances with such firms as Boeing, Walt Disney, and Nissan. According to its chair, Samsung Group plans to more than quadruple its 1994 sales level to reach U.S.$200 billion in annual sales as of 2001.

More than one-half of its expansion projects are being financed through Samsung Electronics, the firm's semiconductor manufacturing division. If the worldwide demand for memory chips continues, Samsung can become a major conglomerate, on the level of a General Electric. If not, Samsung could be remembered as a firm that gambled with large stakes but lost.

In the past, Samsung's success confounded some critics. For instance, it became the world's top producer of semiconductors in just ten years. However, Samsung now plans on being a major player in some of the world's most competitive and capital-intensive industries. Among its planned projects are:

- A U.S.$4.5 billion investment over a three-year period to develop a new line of cars with Nissan.

- A U.S.$3 billion investment for three more semiconductor plants (one in North America and two in Europe and Southeast Asia).

- A U.S.$150 million investment as a partner in a Sino-Korean venture to build a 100-seat jetliner.

Besides being successful in these ventures, some analysts believe Samsung needs to move away from its present discount image. In some markets, Samsung products sell for as much as 30 per cent less than other brands; this reduces the firm's overall profitability.

As a marketing consultant to Samsung, evaluate its strategic plan.

Sources: Based on material in Steve Glain, "Korea's Samsung Plans Very Rapid Expansion into Autos, Other Lines," *Wall Street Journal* (March 2, 1995), pp. A1, A5; and Laxmi Nakami, Kevin Kelly, and Larry Armstrong, "Look Out World—Samsung is Coming," *Business Week* (July 10, 1995), pp. 52–53.

country because the price is too high or the degree of sophistication is excessive. The value of well-known brand names and trademarks can be reduced by piracy and imitation. Technological advantages can be neutralized by the weakness of intellectual property law and laxity in enforcing the law. Whether an advantage retains its value depends on the fit between conditions in the target country and the nature of the advantage."[7]

Precisely Defined Target Market(s)

The target market(s) should be identified precisely.

By precisely defining its target market(s), a firm identifies the specific customers to be addressed in its marketing plans. This guides the firm's current marketing efforts and future direction. For example, as noted in Figure 15-2, IBM is focused on business customers

[7]Yao-Su Hu, "The International Transferability of the Firm's Advantages," *California Management Review*, Vol. 37 (Summer 1995), p. 83.

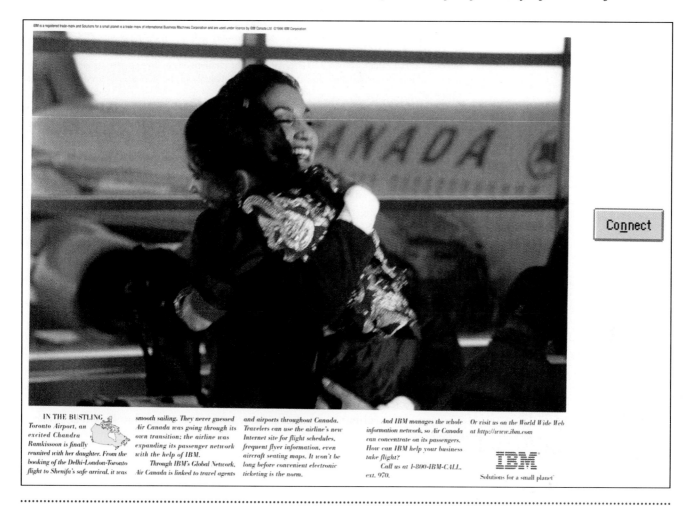

FIGURE 15-2
Target Marketing and IBM
IBM is targeting businesses by positioning itself as a firm that provides expertise for networking around the world.
Reprinted with permission of IBM Canada Ltd.

interested in computer networking. IBM has been repositioning its image away from being a company that provides "hardware" to businesses to being a company that provides "expertise" to businesses on a global basis. The "Solutions for a small planet™" slogan is so critical to this new positioning that IBM has trademarked it. The theme in this ad is "Connect," but IBM runs a number of ads with different themes to appeal to different business needs. In one ad the theme is "Secure" and the focus of the ad is how IBM can help protect businesses who have system networks from hackers and other people who might break in. Another ad uses the theme "Merge" and talks about how IBM can help a firm's various offices around the world work as a team even if the various offices have different computer platforms such as :"Windows, UNIX, Mac or OS/2."[8] Whenever a firm such as IBM engages in differentiated marketing (multiple segmentation), it is essential that each segment be described fully.

A firm's target market approach may have to be fine-tuned due to changing demographics and lifestyles—or falling sales. Today, a lot of consumers are more demanding:

> The balance of power between producers and buyers has shifted to the latter. Most industries today are no longer constrained by supply. In fact, an overabundance of suppliers is crowding

---

[8]IBM Advertisement, "Timbuktu," *Canadian Business Technology* (Spring 1996), p. 1; IBM Advertisement, "Connect," *Canadian Business* (August 1996), pp. 34–35; and IBM Advertisement, "Hacker," *Canadian Business Technology* (Summer 1996), p. 1.

every part of the market. Customers, who are becoming more astute in their buying practices every day, have tremendous choice in deciding who will get their business. The 1990s have become the "value decade"; buyers carefully examine total offerings to find out which one yields the best overall value compared to alternatives. The challenge is to give customers all of what they want, and none of what they don't want: the best quality *and* the best prices, served quickly *and* with a smile![9]

In this context, a total quality approach is especially crucial in attracting and retaining consumers.

Compatible Long-, Moderate-, and Short-Term Subplans

Long-, moderate-, and short-term subplans must be compatible.

The long-, moderate-, and short-term marketing subplans of a firm need to be compatible with one another. Long-term plans are the most general and set a broad framework for moderate-term plans. Short-term plans are the most specific; but they need to be derived from both moderate- and long-term plans. At Motorola, this means "placing farsighted bets on a wide array of technologies while expanding in fast-growing, developing markets. We think we're making balanced investments for the future."[10]

Unfortunately, adequate plans and subplans are not always set—or are not communicated to employees. According to one study of employees at small and midsized firms, 77 per cent say their firms have a clear organizational mission; 55 per cent feel top management actions support the organizational mission; 57 per cent believe all departments, branches, and divisions have specific and measurable goals; 38 per cent feel all employees understand what is expected of them; and 22 per cent say all employees are held accountable for daily performance.[11] For a total quality program to work, these percentages must be considerably higher.

One important current trend among many companies is the shrinking time frame of marketing plans:

> Because customer priorities are constantly changing, a marketing plan should change with them. For years, conventional wisdom was "prepare a five-year marketing plan and review it every year." But change happens a lot faster than it did twenty or even ten years ago. For that reason, Bob Dawson of The Business Group, a consulting firm, recommends that firms prepare three-year plans and review them every quarter. Frequent reviews enable companies to identify potential problems and opportunities before the competition does. "Preventative maintenance for a company is as important as putting oil in a car," Dawson says. "You don't wait a whole year to do it. You can't change history, but you can anticipate what's going to happen."[12]

Coordination Among SBUs

SBUs should be coordinated.

Coordination among an organization's SBUs is enhanced when the functions, strategies, and resources allocated to each are described in long-term, moderate-term, and short-term plans. For instance, at GE (General Electric), the firm from which the SBU concept was first derived, there are now twelve SBUs (in technology, services, and manufacturing)— down from 350 several years ago: "Only businesses that were number one or number two in their markets could win in the increasingly global arena. Those that were not leaders were fixed, closed, or sold." Today, GE's goal is to "attain competitive advantages that let it rank first or second in every market it serves." And its planning and resource allocation are structured accordingly.

Virtually all of GE's SBUs are market leaders, including aircraft engines, circuit breakers, electric motors, engineering plastics, industrial and power systems, nonbank financial services, major appliances, lighting, locomotives, and medical diagnostic imaging. Problematic SBUs are singled out for special attention by top management, which coordinates plans and assigns resources. Thus, when GE decided to hold onto its broadcasting SBU (even though the NBC TV network had fallen to a weak third in audience ratings as

[9]William A. Band, "Customer-Accelerated Change," *Marketing Management* (Winter 1995), pp. 47–48.
[10]Peter Coy and Ron Stodghill II, "Is Motorola a Bit Too Patient?" *Business Week* (February 5, 1996), pp. 150–151.
[11]Oechsli Institute, "Reality Check," *Inc.* (March 1993), p. 34.
[12]Reese, "The Very Model of a Modern Marketing Plan," pp. 60–61.

of 1993), a renewed commitment was pledged. By 1996, NBC was again number one with such popular shows as *ER*, *Seinfeld*, and *Friends*.[13]

The coordination of SBUs by large multinational firms can be particularly complex. For example, ABB (Asea Brown Boveri) has 175 global managers at its Swiss headquarters. They oversee 200 000 employees and 1000+ companies that operate in 140 countries around the globe: "ABB isn't Japanese, nor is it Swiss or Swedish. It is a global firm without a national identity, though its mailing address is in Zurich. The company's top thirteen managers hold frequent meetings in different countries. Since they share no common first language, they speak only English, a foreign tongue to all but one."[14]

Coordination of the Marketing Mix

The components of the marketing mix (product, distribution, promotion, and price) need to be coordinated and consistent with a firm's organizational mission. As an example, Intuit Inc. is a computer software maker, founded in 1984. It specializes in user-friendly personal-finance programs for PCs. From 1984 to 1986, sales were very low—due to a lack of startup capital: "Without money, there were no distribution channels and no customers. What computer store would carry an unknown software product, unsupported by advertising?" The firm then invested $170 000 in advertising and sales took off. By 1996, Intuit products were carried by virtually every type of computer software store and it had 1.7 million loyal customers.[15] Its current marketing mix is outstanding and adheres to a total quality philosophy:

The marketing mix within each SBU has to be coordinated.

- *Product*—Intuit's Quicken software is the leading personal-finance program on the market. It helps consumers balance their chequebooks, set up budgets, and monitor investments. Quicken has been upgraded and improved a number of times. New programs, such as QuickBooks bookkeeping software, are heavily tested before they are introduced.

- *Distribution*—Intuit products are sold by all types of retailers across North America and a number of other countries, including Wal-Mart, major computer chains, a number of bookstores, and mail-order firms. Some of Intuit's software is even bundled with computer hardware; for example, the Quicken program is often included with the Macintosh Performa line of computers.

- *Promotion*—Although ad expenditures are modest, Intuit runs ads in such magazines as *PC* and *ComputerLife*, and it seeks out publicity. The firm is also quite clever. In one recent ad campaign, it used this approach: "Stop Cheating—yourself out of legitimate, money-saving tax deductions. That's why you need TurboTax . . . Complete Satisfaction—We guarantee you'll be satisfied with TurboTax or your money back." The firm does spend about 10 per cent of revenues on customer service personnel, including technical-support people who handle 800-number telephone calls.

- *Price*—Quicken, Quicken for Windows, TurboTax, and MacIn-Tax have "street prices" (the discounted prices offered by resellers) of $40 to $45. Included in purchases are a detailed owner's manual, the right to upgrades at a modest price, and telephone support service. Most competing programs are much more expensive than Quicken.

Stability Over Time

A marketing plan must have a certain degree of stability over time for it to be implemented and evaluated properly. This does not mean a plan should be inflexible and therefore unable to adjust to a dynamic environment. Rather, it means a broad marketing plan,

The stability of the basic plan should be maintained over time.

---

[13]Stephen W. Quickel, "CEO of the Year: Welch on Welch," *Financial World* (April 3, 1990), p. 62; Al Ries, "The Discipline of the Narrow Focus," *Journal of Business Strategy*, Vol. 13 (November–December 1992), p. 5; Noel M. Tichy and Stratford P. Sherman, *Control Your Own Destiny or Someone Else Will* (New York: Doubleday, 1993); and Gary Hoover, Alta Campbell, and Patrick J. Spain (Eds.), *Hoover's Handbook of American Business 1996* (Austin, Texas: Reference Press, 1996), pp. 544–545.

[14]Carla Rappoport, "A Tough Swede Invades the U.S.," *Fortune* (June 29, 1992), p. 76; Rich Karlgaard, "Percy Barnevik," *Forbes ASAP* (January 2, 1995), pp. 65–68; and Patrick J. Spain and James R. Talbot (Eds.), *Hoover's Handbook of World Business 1995-1996* (Austin, Texas: Reference Press, 1995), pp. 94–95.

[15]John Case, "Customer Service: The Last Word," *Inc.* (April 1991), pp. 88–93; and Intuit advertisement, *ComputerLife* (January 1996).

consistent with a firm's organizational mission and total quality approach, should guide long-term efforts and be fine-tuned regularly; the basic plan should remain in effect for a number of years. Short-run marketing plans can be much more flexible, as long as they conform to long-term goals and the organizational mission. Thus, low prices might be part of a long-term marketing plan, but in any particular year, prices might have to be raised in response to environmental forces.

An example of a firm striving to maintain a stable—but flexible—approach is Bell Canada. It has been serving Canadians since the 1880s and up until July 1994, when it faced full competition in the long distance phone market, it was "the" phone company. Today, Bell is in a battle to hold its customer base in the face of severe competition, which has seen its market share fall from 100 per cent to 73 per cent in two years. Despite this rapid fall, Bell has been stemming the tide of defections and hopes to stabilize the market.

Where AT&T Canada and Sprint, Bell's competitors, use price as their main weapon to attract customers, Bell focuses on service, support, and reliability. In addition, Bell has been appealing to the business market with affordable 1-800 and 1-888 toll-free numbers to expand their market. Bell Canada set its corporate mission in its 1995 annual report as follows: "To be a pivotal player in the global economy, helping people and organizations realize their potential by connecting them with ease and imagination to the individuals and ideas that they need to grow and prosper."

To fulfil this corporate mission Bell Canada has chosen to embark on what they term an "aggressive three-year business plan." The goals of the plan are threefold: to make sure Bell Canada "survives, thrives and meets customers' needs in an increasingly competitive environment." The plan recognizes the firm's loss of revenues (estimated at $700 million), market share, and net income and the need to invest in new technologies to fight competition and to maintain Bell's place in the market. In light of these changes, according to John McLennan, Bell's CEO, the specific objective is to return Bell Canada to historic levels of financial performance by the end of 1997 and then maintain them. The plan put forward is designed to have a combined operating impact of $1 billion in terms of increased revenues and decreased costs.

The activities that will be undertaken in the plan include the following:

- Investment in technology, including a broadband network.
- Increasing revenues through price increases on local rates and adding new services such as interactive multimedia, personal communications services, Internet access, and cable television.
- Business transformation in terms of how Bell does business. This will involve an initial investment of $1.7 billion. The outcome of this investment will be improved customer service with fewer resources. Employee training will be undertaken to make sure Bell employees have the skills to compete in the marketplace. New revenue-generating opportunities will be researched.
- Workforce downsizing of 10 000 employees.
- Priority placed on marketing and sales.[16]

Analyzing the Marketing Plan

Marketing plan analysis *compares actual and targeted achievements.*

Marketing plan analysis involves comparing actual performance with planned or expected performance for a specified period of time. If actual performance is unsatisfactory, corrective action may be needed. Also, plans must sometimes be revised because of the impact of uncontrollable variables.

Five techniques used to analyze marketing plans are discussed in the following sections: benchmarking, customer satisfaction research, marketing cost analysis, sales analy-

---

[16]*Bell Canada 1995 Annual Report;* Harvey Schachter, "Ma Bell, Femme Fatale," *Canadian Business* (June 1996), pp. 121–124; and Bell Canada, "Overview," Bell Canada Web site, http://www.bell.ca.

DIRECT ACCESS TO MUTUAL FUNDS.
DIRECT ACCESS TO COMPARISON.

Compare the long and short term performance numbers of Canada's ten most popular equity funds.

10 LARGEST CANADIAN EQUITY FUNDS ranked by one year returns*						
Fund	Load	1 year	3 years	5 years	10 years	Assets (,000)
Altamira Equity	N	24.4%	15.1%	24.7%	n/a	2,516,842
Investors Retirement Mutual	Y	19.7%	11.9%	9.5%	8.2%	2,258,800
Industrial Growth	Y	19.5%	11.7%	9.5%	8.1%	1,366,001
Investors Canadian Equity	Y	19.2%	11.9%	12.2%	8.3%	2,555,400
Investors Retirement Gth Portfolio	Y	19.1%	11.6%	9.9%	n/a	1,489,400
Ivy Canadian	Y	18.3%	12.1%	n/a	n/a	1,373,735
Trimark Canadian	Y	18.2%	13.8%	13.6%	11.2%	1,461,911
Trimark RSP Equity	Y	16.6%	12.6%	11.8%	n/a	2,726,997
Trimark Select Canadian Growth	Y	15.9%	12.4%	n/a	n/a	2,757,447
MD Equity	N	15.4%	11.1%	10.3%	8.9%	1,465,555

Funds shown represent 46.4% of all Canadian equity funds.

Now to make the comparison even more impressive, remember that because you can access Altamira's No-Load Mutual Funds directly, you pay no commission, only a one time forty dollar set up fee. Once you make the comparison, the phone call is that much easier.

**Call and ask for a free information kit,
or if you have any specific questions, ask to speak to
one of Altamira's Mutual Fund Specialists.**

Altamira
Helping you take control

Call 1-800-263-7396, ext. 55
e-mail: advice@altamira.com   net: http://www.altamira.com

The rates of return are the historical annual compounded returns for the periods ended April 30, 1996, including changes in unit value and reinvestment of all distributions and do not take into account any optional charges payable by any unitholder which would have reduced returns. Past performance is not necessarily indicative of future performance. Mutual Funds are sold by prospectus only. The simplified prospectus contains important information which you should read carefully before investing, also note pages two and three of our prospectus for all fees pertaining to our funds. As with all Altamira Mutual Funds there is no front or back-end load; only a one time forty dollar set up fee. *Source: Globe Information Services, using Globe HySales. The information shown compares the performance of the ten largest Canadian equity funds by one year returns.

**FIGURE 15-3
Altamira: Benchmarking Versus the Competition**
Reprinted with permission of Altamira Investment Services Inc.

sis, and the marketing audit. Though our discussion of these tools is limited to their utility in evaluating marketing plans, they may also be employed when developing and modifying these plans.

Benchmarking

For a firm to properly assess the effectiveness of its marketing plans, it must set performance standards. That is, it must specify exactly what constitutes "success." One way to do this is to utilize **benchmarking**, whereby a firm sets its own marketing performance standards based on the competence of the best companies in its industry, innovative companies in other industries anywhere around the world, the prowess of direct competitors, and/or prior actions by the firm itself. Xerox, a leader in this area, uses benchmarking to

*In **benchmarking**, specific points of comparison are set so performance can be measured.*

measure its goods, services, and practices "against the toughest competitors or those recognized as industry leaders."[17] Among the growing number of other firms now using benchmarking are Bell Canada, DuPont, Ford, IBM, Kodak, Marriott, Motorola, and Altamira Mutual Funds. As Figure 15-3 illustrates, the benchmark for Altamira Mutual Funds is the "10 largest Canadian equity funds."

Benchmarking may be divided into two main categories:

> Strategic benchmarks for business performance are measures which set overall direction, and show managers how others have succeeded in similar circumstances. Process benchmarks, in contrast, usually indicate standards which should be achievable in day-to-day operations, given the willingness to learn.[18]

According to one worldwide study of over 580 companies in four industries (computer, auto, health care, and banking), a greater percentage of North American firms regularly engage in benchmarking than their Japanese and German counterparts. Nonetheless, there are some universal truths about total quality that can aid any firm. Those that do best communicate the corporate strategic plan to employees, customers, suppliers, and channel members; upgrade and simplify development and production processes; set up formal practices to certify suppliers; and scrutinize and reduce cycle time (how long it takes a firm to get from designing to delivering a good or service).[19]

There are three steps in the benchmarking ladder: novice, journeyman, and master.

The sponsors of the just-mentioned study, Ernst & Young and the American Quality Foundation, recommend that a benchmarking program be approached in three stages. Firms can hurt themselves by setting unrealistic goals if they compare themselves to those at a later stage:

- *Novice*—A firm in this category should strive to emulate direct competitors, not world-class companies. It should rely on customers for new-product ideas and choose suppliers mostly on price and reliability criteria. There should be a focus on cost-reduction potential, with a "don't develop it, buy it" thrust. Workers should be rewarded for teamwork and quality. The firm should identify processes that add value, simplify those processes, and move faster in responding to the marketplace.

- *Journeyman*—A firm in this category should encourage workers to find ways to do their jobs better and to simplify operations. It should strive to emulate market leaders and selected world-class companies. Consumer input, formal marketing research, and internal ideas should be used in generating new products. The firm should select suppliers having good quality, and then look at their prices. Compensation for both workers and managers should be linked to teamwork and quality. The firm should refine practices to improve the value added per employee, the time to market, and customer satisfaction.

- *Master*—A firm in this category relies on self-managed, multiskilled teams that emphasize horizontal processes (like product development and logistics). It measures its product development, distribution, and customer service against the world's best. Consumer input, benchmarking, and internal research and development should be used in generating new products. The firm should select suppliers that are technologically advanced and offer superior quality. Strategic partnerships are employed to diversify production. Compensation for senior executives should be linked to teamwork and quality. The firm should continue to refine its practices to improve the value added per employee, the time to market, and customer satisfaction.[20]

---

[17]Beth Enslow, "The Benchmarking Bonanza," *Across the Board* (April 1992), p. 17. See also Thomas C. Powell, "Total Quality Management as Competitive Advantage: A Review and Empirical Study," *Strategic Management Journal*, Vol. 16 (January 1995), pp. 15–37; and Roland T. Rust, Anthony J. Zahorik, and Timothy L. Keiningham, "Return on Quality (ROQ): Making Service Quality Financially Accountable," *Journal of Marketing*, Vol. 59 (April 1995), pp. 58–70.

[18]Tony Clayton and Bob Luchs, "Strategic Benchmarking at ICI Fibres," *Long Range Planning*, Vol. 27 (June 1994), p. 56.

[19]Jeremy Main, "How to Steal the Best Ideas Around," *Fortune* (October 1992), pp. 102–106; Cyndee Miller, "TQM's Value Criticized in New Report," *Marketing News* (November 9, 1992), pp. 1, 16; and Gilbert Fuchsberg, " 'Total Quality' Is Termed Only a Partial Success," *Wall Street Journal* (October 1, 1992), pp. B1, B7.

[20]Otis Port, John Carey, Kevin Kelly, and Stephanie Anderson Forest, "Quality: Small and Midsize Companies Seize the Challenge—Not a Moment Too Soon," *Business Week* (November 30, 1992), pp. 66–72.

Some useful benchmarks for Canadian firms are award achievements like the Canada Export Awards, the Entrepreneur of the Year Award, and The Award for Canadian-American Business Achievement. For Canadian firms who do business in the United States, the Malcolm Baldridge National Quality Award criteria and Fortune's Corporate Reputations survey criteria are good benchmarks.

Every year the Department of Foreign Affairs and International Trade sponsors a set of Export Awards for the Canadian firms who are the leading exporters in their industries in terms of growth. In 1995 the Export Development Corporation and the Canadian Imperial Bank of Commerce became official sponsors too.

The Entrepreneur of the Year Award is sponsored by Air Canada, The Bank of Montreal, Ernst & Young, Nesbitt Burns, McCarthy Tetrault Law Firm, and *Canadian Business* magazine. It is granted to firms in five regions in Canada (Pacific Canada, the Prairies, Ontario, Quebec, and Atlantic Canada). Within each of these regions, an entrepreneur of the year is chosen and then the best entrepreneurs in ten business categories are identified. The categories are manufacturing, agriculture and food, retailing, services, emerging entrepreneurs, turnaround entrepreneurs, master entrepreneurs, high technology, supporters of entrepreneurship, and socially responsible entrepreneurs.

The award for Canadian-American Business Achievement is sponsored by Nortel (Northern Telecom), FHS International, The Canadian-American Business Council, *Profit* magazine, and *Canadian Business* magazine. This award is focused on rewarding cooperative ventures between a Canadian and American firm that "demonstrate business success, innovation, and community contribution."[21]

A firm does not have to actually participate in any of these competitions to benefit from the benchmarks. Any organization can assess itself and compare its results with others. Canadian firms can benchmark themselves against competitors by applying the criteria used for the various awards.

For example, the criteria used for the Baldridge Award involve rating companies in seven areas: leadership; information and analysis (such as competitive comparisons and benchmarks); strategic quality planning; human resource development and management; management of process quality; quality and operational results; and customer focus and satisfaction. Of the maximum 1000 points a company can score, 300 are for customer focus and satisfaction. Fortune's Corporate Reputations survey rates companies in eight areas: quality of management; quality of goods or services; innovativeness; long-term investment value; financial soundness; the ability to attract, develop, and keep talented people; responsibility to the community and the environment; and wise use of corporate resources. Companies are rated within their own industry.

Customer Satisfaction Research

As defined in Chapter 1, **customer satisfaction** is the degree to which there is a match between a customer's expectations of a good or service and the actual performance of that good or service, including customer service. Today more than ever, companies realize they must measure the level of customer satisfaction through regular research:

Research is needed to gauge customer satisfaction. ACSI is a broad project that is doing so.

How little we know about these indispensable strangers, our customers. Are they happy? Restless? Was it good for them, too? Will they come back tomorrow? The answers to these questions profoundly affect any business. Indeed, one could say they define a business. They also define the meaning of economic activity, for in the largest sense an economy cannot be described by adding up how many passenger-miles of air travel it logs or how much wood its woodchucks chuck per hour. All these count (and we count them). But in the final analysis, what matters is how well an economy satisfies its customers' needs and wants.[22]

---

[21]"Mohawk Oil Honored in Vancouver," *Marketing Magazine* (March 20, 1995), p. 3; "Entrepreneur of the Year," *Canadian Business*, advertising feature (June 1996), p. 95; "Once Again A Pair of Winners," *Canadian Business*, advertising feature (June 1996), p. 111; and "The 1995 Canada Export Awards," *Canadian Business*, advertising supplement (November 1995), pp. 69–76.

[22]Thomas A. Stewart, "After All You've Done for Your Customers, Why Are They Still Not Happy?" *Fortune* (December 11, 1995), p. 179.

The largest ongoing research project on customer satisfaction in the world is undertaken annually in the United States. The American Customer Satisfaction Index (ACSI) is a joint effort by the University of Michigan and the American Society for Quality Control. To compute ACSI, 30 000 consumers are surveyed about 3900 goods and services. The surveys cover "perceptions of service, quality, value, how well the good or service lived up to expectations, how it compared to an ideal, and how willing people were to pay more for it." With a maximum score of 100, these were the highest-rated firms in 1996: H.J. Heinz (90), Hershey Foods (88), Cadillac (88), Coca-Cola (87), UPS (87), Pillsbury (87), Mercedes-Benz (87), PepsiCo (86), Cadbury Schweppes (86), Federal Express (86), Mars (86), and General Mills (86). The average score for all companies was 72.2.[23]

Any firm can measure its own customer satisfaction. Here is an eight-step procedure to do so:

1. "Institute a process to tap management, employees, outside consultants, and industry sources for input on the dimensions critical to customer satisfaction. Environmental scanning of trade publications and competitors and a regular program of internal focus groups can accomplish this."

2. "Use this feedback to develop an ongoing program of customer focus groups and personal interviews to identify critical customer satisfaction dimensions."

3. "Work with a professional staff to develop telephone and/or mail survey instruments to reliably and validly incorporate identified dimensions."

4. "Regardless of whether the people developing the survey are internal or external, make sure they understand the theoretical basis of the instruments and are familiar with standard procedures for developing and testing reliable, valid items. Keep in mind that customer satisfaction survey results that simply describe what was found provide no guidance for developing an action plan to improve satisfaction."

5. "Regularly do surveys and re-evaluate their reliability and validity."

6. "From these data, develop a customer satisfaction metric that not only relates the level of satisfaction of your customers, but also analyzes the importance of the various dimensions of that satisfaction."

7. "Use the dimensional information to develop an action plan for improving each dimension and communicating these improvements to customers. Remember: delivery of customer satisfaction is not a reality if the customer does not notice it."

8. "Tie the performance evaluation and compensation of each employee involved in the action plan to its accomplishment. This will ensure that the customers' goals match employees' goals. Remember: what gets measured gets rewarded, and what gets rewarded gets done."[24]

[23]Joyce E. Davis, "Americans Are More Finicky Than Ever," *Fortune* (February 3, 1997), pp. 108–110.

[24]John T. Mentzer, Carol C. Bienstock, and Kenneth B. Kahn, "Benchmarking Satisfaction," *Marketing Management* (Summer 1995), pp. 41–46. See also Dominique V. Turpin, "Japanese Approaches to Customer Satisfaction: Some Best Practices," *Long Range Planning*, Vol. 28 (June 1995), pp. 84–90; Abbie Griffin, Greg Gleason, Rick Preiss, and Dave Shevenaugh, "Best Practice for Customer Satisfaction in Manufacturing Firms," *Sloan Management Review*, Vol. 36 (Winter 1995), pp. 87–98; and William Keenan, Jr., "Customer Service," *Sales & Marketing Management* (January 1996), pp. 63–66.

Ethics AND TODAY'S MARKETER

How Far Should Customer Satisfaction Guarantees Go?

A money-back guarantee can be an especially strong competitive advantage in attracting skeptical customers. It can also function as an early warning system about potential problems and serve as a motivator to employees. For example, after studying its returns, mail-order retailer L.L. Bean found that "the wrong size" was the most frequent reason for returns. As a result, it revised the size information in all of its catalogues. And besides providing information to correct its operations, the president of Hampton Inns believes the hotel's service guarantee motivates its maids to be sure rooms are especially clean.

An example of an effective satisfaction guarantee is Xerox's "Total Satisfaction Guarantee." It covers the firm's equipment for three years from the date of purchase. Says a Xerox spokesperson, "We're putting the customer in charge. The customer is the sole arbiter and decision maker." Crest toothpaste also offers consumers their money back if they are not satisfied with the results of their dental examinations after six months of use.

Yet, not all companies openly embrace guarantees as a means of building customer loyalty. Some fear that too many customers will ask for a refund on the basis of a trivial complaint. And some companies that promote guarantees extensively in their advertising make it difficult to collect: "A guarantee program can either be the centrepiece of a service company's entire operation or simply a promotional tool. Many businesses continue to make shallow promises with slogans because they are not prepared to guarantee what their customers want, or because the process for getting the company to make good on its offer is overly complicated."

As a marketing manager for a leading hotel chain, develop a money-back guarantee policy that is designed both to reimburse dissatisfied guests and to reduce lost revenues due to trivial complaints.

Source: Based on material in Jonathan Barsky, "Guarantee; Warranty; Loyalty," *Marketing Tools* (September 1995), pp. 72–75.

Marketing Cost Analysis

Marketing cost analysis is used to evaluate the cost efficiency of various marketing factors, such as different total quality configurations, product lines, order sizes, distribution methods, sales territories, channel members, salespersons, advertising media, and customer types. Although a firm may be very profitable, it is highly unlikely that all of its products, distribution methods, and so on are equally cost efficient (or profitable).

Cost efficiency is measured in **marketing cost analysis**.

With marketing cost analysis, a firm can determine which factors (classifications) are the most efficient and which are the least efficient, and make appropriate adjustments. It can also generate information that may be needed to substantiate price compliance with the Competition Act.

For this type of analysis to work properly, a firm needs to obtain and to use continuous and accurate cost data. Table 15-1 presents several examples of marketing cost analysis.

Table 15-1

Examples of Marketing Cost Analysis

MARKETING FACTOR	STRATEGY/TACTICS STUDIED	PROBLEM/OPPORTUNITY DISCOVERED	ACTION APPLIED
Customer type	What are the relative costs of selling X-rays to dentists, doctors, and hospitals?	Per-unit costs of hospital sales are lowest (as are prices); per-unit costs of dentist and doctor sales are highest (as are prices).	Current efforts are maintained. Each customer is serviced.
Product	Should a manufacturer accept a retailer's proposal that the firm make 700 000 private-label sneakers?	Substantial excess capacity exists; the private label would require no additional fixed costs.	A contract is signed. Different features for private and manufacturer labels are planned.
Distribution	Should a men's suit maker sell directly to consumers, as well as through normal channels?	Startup and personal selling costs would be high. Additional sales would be minimal.	Direct sales are not undertaken.
Order size	What is the minimum order size a hardware manufacturer should accept?	Orders below $30 do not have positive profit margins; they are too costly to process.	Small orders are discouraged through surcharges and minimum order size.
Advertising media	Which is more effective, TV or magazine advertising?	TV ads cost $0.05 for every potential customer reached; magazine ads cost $0.07.	TV ads are increased.
Personal selling	What are the costs of making a sale?	15 per cent of sales covers compensation and selling expenses, 2 per cent above the industry average.	Sales personnel are encouraged to phone customers before visiting them, to confirm appointments.

Table 15-2

A Natural-Account Expense Classification

Net sales (after returns and discounts)	$1 000 000	
Less: Costs of goods sold	450 000	
Gross profit		$550 000
Less: Operating expenses (natural account expenses)		
Salaries and fringe benefits	220 000	
Rent	40 000	
Advertising	30 000	
Supplies	6 100	
Insurance	2 500	
Interest expense	1 400	
Total operating expenses		300 000
Net profit before taxes		$250 000

Marketing cost analysis consists of three steps: studying natural account expenses, reclassifying natural accounts into functional ones, and allocating functional accounts by marketing classification.

Table 15-3
Reclassifying Natural Accounts into Functional Accounts

NATURAL ACCOUNTS	TOTAL	FUNCTIONAL ACCOUNTS						
		Marketing Adminis-tration	Personal Selling	Adver-tising	Transpor-tation	Ware-housing	Marketing Research	General Adminis-tration
Salaries and fringe benefits	$220 000	$30 000	$50 000	$15 000	$10 000	$20 000	$30 000	$65 000
Rent	40 000	3 000	7 000	3 000	2 000	10 000	5 000	10 000
Advertising	30 000			30 000				
Supplies	6 100	500	1 000	500			1 100	3 000
Insurance	2 500		1 000			1 200		300
Interest expense	1 400							1 400
Total	$300 000	$33 500	$59 000	$48 500	$12 000	$31 200	$36 100	$79 700

STUDYING NATURAL ACCOUNT EXPENSES The first step is to determine the level of expenses for all **natural accounts**, which report costs by the names of the expenses and not by their purposes. Such expense categories include salaries, rent, advertising, supplies, insurance, and interest. These are the names most often entered in accounting records. Table 15-2 shows a natural-account expense classification.

Natural accounts are reported as salaries, rent, and insurance.

RECLASSIFYING NATURAL ACCOUNTS INTO FUNCTIONAL ACCOUNTS Natural accounts are then reclassified into **functional accounts**, which indicate the purposes or activities for which expenditures have been made. Included as functional expenses are marketing administration, personal selling, advertising, transportation, warehousing, marketing research, and general administration. Table 15-3 reclassifies the natural accounts of Table 15-2 into functional accounts.

Functional accounts denote the purpose or activity of expenditures.

Once functional accounts are established, cost analysis becomes clearer. For instance, if salaries and fringe benefits increase by $25 000 over the prior year, natural account analysis cannot allocate the rise to a functional area. Functional account analysis can pinpoint the areas of marketing that have higher personnel costs.

ALLOCATING FUNCTIONAL ACCOUNTS BY MARKETING CLASSIFICATION The third step assigns functional costs by product, distribution method, customer, or another marketing classification. This reports each classification as a profit centre. Table 15-4 shows how costs can be allocated among different products, using the data in Tables 15-2 and 15-3. From Table 15-4, it is clear that product A has the highest sales and highest total profit. However, product C has the greatest profit as a per cent of sales.

Functional costs are assigned with each marketing classification becoming a profit centre.

In assigning functional costs, these points should be kept in mind. One, assigning some costs—such as marketing administration—to different products, customers, or other classifications is usually somewhat arbitrary. Two, the elimination of a poorly performing classification would lead to overhead costs—such as general administration—being allotted among the remaining product or customer categories. This may actually result in lower overall total profit. Thus, a firm should distinguish between those separable expenses that are directly associated with a given classification category and can be eliminated if a category is dropped, and those common expenses that are shared by various categories and cannot be eliminated if one is dropped.[25]

[25]See Joseph A. Ness and Thomas G. Cucuzza, "Tapping the Full Potential of ABC," *Harvard Business Review*, Vol. 73 (July–August 1995), pp. 130–138.

Table 15-4

Allocating Functional Expenses by Product

	TOTAL		PRODUCT A		PRODUCT B		PRODUCT C
Net sales	$1 000 000		$500 000		$300 000		$200 000
Less: Cost of goods sold	450 000		250 000		120 000		80 000
Gross profit		$550 000		$250 000		$180 000		$120 000
Less: Operating expenses (functional account expenses)							
Marketing administration	33 500		16 000		10 000		7 500
Personal selling	59 000		30 000		17 100		11 900
Advertising	48 500		20 000		18 000		10 500
Transportation	12 000		5 000		5 000		2 000
Warehousing	31 200		20 000		7 000		4 200
Marketing research	36 100		18 000		11 000		7 100
General administration	79 700		40 000		23 000		16 700
Total operating expenses		300 000		149 000		91 100		59 900
Net profit before taxes		$250 000		$101 000		$88 900		$60 100
Profit as per cent of sales		25.0		20.2		29.6		30.1

A firm must differentiate between order-generating and order-processing costs (described in Chapter 14) before making any strategic changes suggested by marketing cost analysis:

> After a decade of frantic cost-cutting, the downside of downsizing is beginning to take its toll: decimated sales staffs turn in lousy numbers. "Survivor syndrome" takes hold, and overburdened staffers just go through the motions of working. New-product ideas languish. Risk-taking dwindles because the culture of cost-cutting emphasizes the certainties of cutting costs over the uncertainties—and expense—of trying something new."[26]

In making cost cuts, a company must be especially sure to judge the effects of those cuts on the total quality of its goods and services.

Sales Analysis

Sales analysis *looks at sales data to assess the effectiveness of a marketing strategy.*

Sales analysis is the detailed study of sales data for the purpose of appraising the appropriateness and effectiveness of a marketing strategy. Without adequate sales analysis, a poor response to the total quality offered by a firm may not be seen early enough, the value of certain market segments and territories may be overlooked, sales effort may be poorly matched with market potential, trends may be missed, or support for sales personnel may not be forthcoming. Sales analysis enables plans to be set in terms of revenues by product, product line, salesperson, region, customer type, time period, price line, method of sale, and so on. It also compares actual sales against planned sales. More firms engage in sales analysis than in marketing cost analysis.

The main source of sales analysis data is the sales invoice, which may be written, typed, or computer generated. An invoice may contain such information as the customer's name and address, the quantity ordered, the price paid, purchase terms, all the different

---

[26]Bernard Wysocki, Jr., "Some Companies Cut Costs Too Far, Suffer 'Corporate Anorexia,'" *Wall Street Journal* (July 5, 1995), p. A1. See also Robin Cooper and W. Bruce Crew, "Control Tomorrow's Costs Through Today's Designs," *Harvard Business Review*, Vol. 74 (January–February 1996), pp. 88–97.

items bought at the same time, the order date, shipping arrangements, and the salesperson. Summary data are generated by adding invoices. The use of computerized marking, cash register, and inventory systems speeds data recording and improves their accuracy.

In conducting sales analysis, proper control units must be selected. **Control units** are the sales categories for which data are gathered, such as boys', men's, girls', and women's clothing. Although a marketing executive can broaden a control system by adding several sales categories together, wide categories cannot be broken down into components. Thus, a narrow sales category is preferable to one that is too wide. It is also helpful to select control units consistent with other company, trade association, and government data. A stable classification system is necessary to compare data from different time periods.

Control units *are an essential aspect of sales analysis.*

A key concept in undertaking sales analysis is that summary data, such as overall sales or market share, are usually insufficient to diagnose a firm's areas of strength and weakness. More intensive investigation is needed. Two sales analysis techniques that offer in-depth probing are the 80-20 principle and sales exception reporting.

According to the **80-20 principle**, in many organizations, a large proportion of total sales (profit) is likely to come from a small proportion of customers, products, or territories. Thus, to function as efficiently as possible, firms need to determine sales and profit by customer, product, or territory. Marketing efforts can then be allocated accordingly. Firms that do not isolate and categorize data are acting in error. Through faulty reasoning, they would place equal effort into each sale instead of concentrating on key accounts. These errors are due to a related concept, the **iceberg principle**, which states that superficial data are insufficient to make sound evaluations.

The **80-20 principle** *notes that a large share of sales (profits) often comes from few customers, products, or territories. Analysis errors may be due to the* **iceberg principle.**

This is how one firm is using the 80-20 principle in its sales analysis:

> In April 1996, Pepsi undertook a massive promotion to bolster youth loyalty and encourage frequent purchasing by young Canadians. At the time, the Pepsi "Get Stuff" promotion was described as "one of the largest consumer-loyalty programs ever run by a packaged-goods company in Canada." The approach of the campaign involved consumers collecting points off specially marked packages of Pepsi, Diet Pepsi, and Pepsi Max. The points could be collected and redeemed for merchandise from a Pepsi Get Stuff catalogue. Described as a consumer "outreach" campaign, the promotion was designed to help Pepsi identify the heaviest product users through point redemption. Furthermore, the product usage of these users could be assessed as Pepsi Points associated with different packages were slightly different too. For example, 7-Eleven has Pepsi points on their Big Gulp cups and these points are different in value and shape from the Pepsi points carried on other packages. Pepsi planned to run the promotion for a six-month period and distributed 460 million points on 175 million packages with $92 million in premiums available.[27]

Analysis can be further enhanced by **sales exception reporting**, which highlights situations where sales goals are not met or sales opportunities are present. A slow-selling item report cites products whose sales are below forecasts. It could suggest such corrective actions as price reductions, promotions, and sales incentives to increase unit sales. A fast-selling item report cites items whose sales exceed forecasts. It points out openings, as well as items that need more inventory on hand to prevent stockouts. Finally, sales exception reporting enables a firm to evaluate the validity of forecasts and make the proper modifications in them. Figure 15-4 presents examples of the 80-20 principle, the iceberg principle, and sales exception reporting.

Sales exception reporting *centres on unmet goals or special opportunities.*

Organizations also may use sales analysis to identify and monitor consumer buying patterns by answering such questions as these:

- Who purchases? Organizational vs. final consumer, geographic region, end use, purchase history, customer size, customer demographics.

- What is purchased? Product line, price category, brand, country of origin, package size, options purchased.

- Where are purchases made? Place of customer contact, purchase location, warehouse location.

---

[27]Jeff Lobb, "The Right (Pepsi) Stuff," *Marketing Magazine* (July 8, 1996), p. 15.

FIGURE 15-4
Sales Analysis Concepts

80-20 Principle				
	Annual Sales		Marketing Expenditures	
	$	%	$	%
Product A	1 000 000	50.0	200 000	44.4
Product B	750 000	37.5	150 000	33.3
Product C	250 000	12.5	100 000	22.2
Total	$2 000 000	100.0	$450 000	100.0*

*Rounding error.
Although a company gets only 12.5 per cent of total sales from Product C, it spends 22.2 per cent of its marketing budget on that product.

Sales Exception Reporting

SALES REPORT		
	Expected Sales	Actual Sales
Product 1	$50 000	$100 000
Product 2	$50 000	$50 000
Product 3	$75 000	$75 000
Product 4	$75 000	$50 000

A review of the sales report indicates that Product 1 has done much better than expected, while Product 4 has done much worse.

Iceberg Principle Only the tip of the iceberg is seen with superficial analysis (aggregate data).

The entire iceberg is seen with in-depth analysis (detailed, categorized data).

- How are items purchased? Form of payment, billing terms, delivery form, packaging technique.
- When are purchases heaviest and lightest? Season, day of week, time of day.
- How much is purchased? Unit sales volume, dollar sales volume, profit margin.
- What types of promotion get the best sales results? Advertising, personal selling, sales promotion.
- What prices are paid? List prices vs. discounted prices.

The Marketing Audit

*A **marketing audit** examines a firm in a systematic, critical, and unbiased manner.*

A **marketing audit** is a systematic, critical, impartial review and appraisal of the basic goals and policies of the marketing function, and of the organization, methods, procedures, and personnel employed to implement the policies and achieve the goals.[28] The purpose of a marketing audit is to determine how well a firm's marketing efforts are being conducted and how they can be improved. Audits should be conducted on a regular basis.

The marketing audit process involves the six steps shown in Figure 15-5:

1. A marketing audit may be conducted by company specialists, by company division or department managers, or by outside specialists. Expertise, access to information, costs, and potential biases are some of the factors to be considered when choosing audit personnel.

2. An audit may be undertaken at the end of a calendar year, at the end of a firm's annual reporting year, or when conducting a physical inventory. An audit should be performed at least annually, although some firms prefer more frequent analysis. It should be completed during the same time period each year to allow comparisons. In some cases, unannounced audits are useful to keep employees alert and to ensure spontaneous answers.

[28]Christopher H. Lovelock and Charles A. Weinberg, *Public & Nonprofit Marketing*, Second Edition (Redwood City, Calif.: Scientific Press, 1989), pp. 47–48. See also Peter Spillard, Matthew Moriarty, and John Woodthorpe, "The Role Matrix: A Diagnostic of Marketing Health," *European Journal of Marketing*, Vol. 28 (Number 7, 1994), pp. 55–76; and Robert S. Kaplan and David P. Norton, "Using the Balanced Scorecard as a Strategic Management System," *Harvard Business Review*, Vol. 74 (January–February 1996), pp. 75–85.

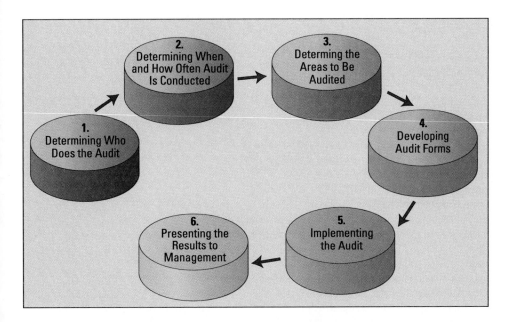

FIGURE 15-5
The Marketing Audit Process

A horizontal audit studies overall marketing performance; a vertical audit analyzes one aspect of marketing.

3. A **horizontal audit** (also known as a marketing-mix audit) studies the overall marketing performance of a firm with particular emphasis on the interrelationship of variables and their relative importance. A **vertical audit** (also known as a functional audit) is an in-depth analysis of one aspect of a firm's marketing strategy, such as product planning. The two audits should be used in conjunction with one another because a horizontal audit often reveals areas needing further study.

4. Audit forms list the topics to be examined and the exact information required to evaluate each topic. Forms usually resemble questionnaires, and they are completed by the auditor. Examples of audit forms are contained in Figures 15-6 and 15-7.

5. When implementing an audit, decisions need to be made with regard to its duration, whether employees are to be aware of the audit, whether the audit is performed while a firm is open or closed for business, and how the final report is to be prepared.

6. The last step in an audit is to present findings and recommendations to management. However, the auditing process is complete only after suitable responses are taken by management. It is the responsibility of management, not the auditor, to determine these responses.

Despite the merits, many firms still do not use formal marketing audits. Three factors mostly account for this. First, success or failure is difficult to establish in marketing. A firm may have poor performance despite the best planning if environmental factors intervene. On the other hand, good results may be based on a firm's being at the right place at the right time. Second, if marketing audits are completed by company personnel, they may not be comprehensive enough to be considered audits. Third, the pressures of other activities often mean that only a small part of a firm's marketing strategy is audited or that audits are done irregularly.

Anticipating and Planning for the Future

The next decade promises to be a complex one for marketers everywhere, as they try to anticipate trends and plan long-run strategies. On the positive side, this period should see increasing consumer affluence in many countries, improvements in technological capabilities, expanding worldwide markets, greater deregulation of industry, and other opportunities. On the negative side, the period will probably witness greater competition among firms based in different countries, relatively slow to moderate growth in North American and European markets, some resource instability, and an uncertain worldwide economy.

Does Your Department, Division, or Firm . . .	Answer Yes or No to Each Question
Planning, Organization, and Control	
1. Have specific objectives?	_ _ _ _ _ _ _ _
2. Devise objectives to meet changing conditions?	_ _ _ _ _ _ _ _
3. Study customer needs, attitudes, and behaviour?	_ _ _ _ _ _ _ _
4. Organize marketing efforts in a systematic way?	_ _ _ _ _ _ _ _
5. Have a market planning process?	_ _ _ _ _ _ _ _
6. Engage in comprehensive sales forecasting?	_ _ _ _ _ _ _ _
7. Integrate buyer behaviour research in market planning?	_ _ _ _ _ _ _ _
8. Have strategy and tactics within the marketing plan?	_ _ _ _ _ _ _ _
9. Have clearly stated contingency plans?	_ _ _ _ _ _ _ _
10. Monitor environmental changes?	_ _ _ _ _ _ _ _
11. Incorporate social responsibility as a criterion for decision making?	_ _ _ _ _ _ _ _
12. Control activities via marketing cost analysis, sales analysis, and the marketing audit?	_ _ _ _ _ _ _ _
Marketing Research	
13. Utilize marketing research for planning, as well as problem solving?	_ _ _ _ _ _ _ _
14. Have a marketing information system?	_ _ _ _ _ _ _ _
15. Give enough support to marketing research?	_ _ _ _ _ _ _ _
16. Have adequate communication between marketing research and line executives?	_ _ _ _ _ _ _ _
Products	
17. Utilize a systematic product-planning process?	_ _ _ _ _ _ _ _
18. Plan product policy relative to the product life-cycle concept?	_ _ _ _ _ _ _ _
19. Have a procedure for developing new products?	_ _ _ _ _ _ _ _
20. Periodically review all products?	_ _ _ _ _ _ _ _
21. Monitor competitive developments in product planning?	_ _ _ _ _ _ _ _
22. Revise mature products?	_ _ _ _ _ _ _ _
23. Phase out weak products?	_ _ _ _ _ _ _ _
Distribution	
24. Motivate channel members?	_ _ _ _ _ _ _ _
25. Have sufficient market coverage?	_ _ _ _ _ _ _ _
26. Periodically evaluate channel members?	_ _ _ _ _ _ _ _
27. Evaluate alternative shipping arrangements?	_ _ _ _ _ _ _ _
28. Study warehouse and facility locations?	_ _ _ _ _ _ _ _
29. Compute economic order quantities?	_ _ _ _ _ _ _ _
30. Modify channel decisions as conditions warrant?	_ _ _ _ _ _ _ _
Promotion	
31. Have an overall promotion plan?	_ _ _ _ _ _ _ _
32. Balance promotion components within the plan?	_ _ _ _ _ _ _ _
33. Measure the effectiveness of advertising?	_ _ _ _ _ _ _ _
34. Seek out favourable publicity?	_ _ _ _ _ _ _ _
35. Have a procedure for recruiting and retaining sales personnel?	_ _ _ _ _ _ _ _
36. Analyze the sales-force organization periodically?	_ _ _ _ _ _ _ _
37. Moderate the use of sales promotions?	_ _ _ _ _ _ _ _
Prices	
38. Have a pricing strategy that is in compliance with government regulations?	_ _ _ _ _ _ _ _
39. Have a pricing strategy that satisfies channel members?	_ _ _ _ _ _ _ _
40. Estimate demand and cost factors before setting prices?	_ _ _ _ _ _ _ _
41. Plan for competitive developments?	_ _ _ _ _ _ _ _
42. Set prices that are consistent with image?	_ _ _ _ _ _ _ _
43. Seek to maximize total profits?	_ _ _ _ _ _ _ _

FIGURE 15-6
A Horizontal Marketing Audit Form

**Total Quality
Health Check-up Questionnaire**

After filling out questionnaire, return to : _____

The purpose of this questionnaire is to provide a means for companies to conduct a study of their employees, to determine the degree of involvement and commitment to the principles and practices of Total Quality Management.

The questionnaire is based on the criteria embodied in the Baldridge Quality Award categories (Being employed by many companies as an integrated management system and to conform to requirements in attaining the award).

INDIVIDUAL INSTRUCTIONS

Identify your position title and company department in the spaces below, then respond to each of the following ten statements, indicating your personal opinion as to the degree of compliance with the criteria in company operations. When completed, return to the individual identified at the top of the sheet for tabulation and reporting of results.

Your Position: _____ Department: _____

QUALITY HEALTH CRITERIA (Circle numbers at right to indicate agreement)	HOW ARE WE DOING? Not true Very true
1. External customer expectations define the quality of our goods and services.	0 1 2 3 4 5
2. Cross-functional and inter-departmental cooperation are encouraged and supported.	0 1 2 3 4 5
3. There is active leadership for quality improvement at all levels of management.	0 1 2 3 4 5
4. Employees have the authority to act on goods and service quality problems.	0 1 2 3 4 5
5. A team approach is used to solve quality problems and to meet customer expectations.	0 1 2 3 4 5
6. Measures of internal and external customer expectations are well understood.	0 1 2 3 4 5
7. Employees are brought into decisions that affect the quality of their work.	0 1 2 3 4 5
8. There is major emphasis on the prevention and solving of quality problems.	0 1 2 3 4 5
9. Individuals and teams are given recognition for contributions to quality improvement.	0 1 2 3 4 5
10. Systems are in place to assess and respond to changing customer expectations and needs.	0 1 2 3 4 5

**FIGURE 15-7
A Total-Quality Vertical-Audit Form**

Source: Dick Berry, "How Healthy Is Your Company?" *Marketing News* (February 15, 1993), p. 2. Reprinted by permission of the American Marketing Association.

Long-range plans must take into account both the external variables facing a firm and its capacity for change. Specifically, what variables will affect the firm? What trends are forecast that might affect the firm? Is the firm able to respond to these trends (for example, does it have the necessary resources and lead time)? A firm that does not anticipate and respond to future trends has a good possibility of falling into Levitt's marketing myopia trap and losing ground to more farsighted competitors:

> Most managers manage for yesterday's conditions because yesterday is where they got their experiences and had their successes. But management is about tomorrow, not yesterday. Tomorrow concerns what should be done, not what has been done. "Should" is determined by the external environment—what competitors (old, new, and potential) can and might do, the

Planning efforts for the future must consider external factors and company abilities.

Technology & Marketing

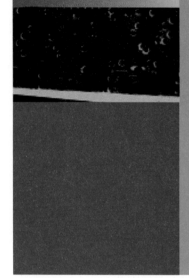

Can You Predict Where Communications Technology Is Heading?

According to many technology experts, new applications for the "boring" telephone are going to explode in the near future. Here are some predictions:

- Appliances will soon will be equipped with phones that are programmed to automatically dial a service centre when an internal sensor detects a malfunction.
- Air conditioners will have phones that let people turn them on or off from remote locations.
- Cars will have phones that automatically dial the police or an ambulance in the event an air bag is deployed.

One of the major reasons for the expected increase in phone applications is that through research, AT&T has been able to reduce the size of a phone to a computer chip that is the size of a finger nail. This unit can be mass produced at a cost of a few dollars. Accordingly, the small size and low cost will allow phones to be easily installed in household appliances, auto dashboards, and other places.

In the long term, Compaq envisions marketing a central personal computer for the home into which consumers could plug all of their major appliances. And the computer would be connected to a phone line. According to Compaq's vice-president of corporate development, "You might be able to call home and tell 'home' to turn on the oven or to change the code of the security system."

Some analysts caution that consumers may reject innovations that phone designers feel are the most promising. A vice-president at Sony Electronics says that avant garde prototypes become actual products "about as often as concept cars do—not never, but never often."

As vice-president of long-range planning for Camco Inc., a Canadian home appliance firm with $444 million in sales, plan a major appliance strategy based on the information just provided.

Source: Based on material in Bart Ziegler, "Anytime, Anywhere," *Wall Street Journal* (March 20, 1995), p. R18.

choices this will give customers and those who advise or direct customers, the rules constantly being made by governments and other players, demographic changes, advances in generalized knowledge and technology, changing ecology and public sentiments, and the like.

The most precious thing a manager brings to a job is the wisdom conferred by experience—precisely so that he or she can operate decisively and effectively with limited information, with dispatch and confidence. But when change accelerates, when it comes unexpectedly from constantly unexpected directions, when new technologies and social and environmental conditions occur so disjunctively, the wisdom conferred by experience needs help. That is one reason professional staffs and consultants proliferate. It is also why, in this age of rapid acceleration, this hazardous new age of fast history, managers must take time to carefully think for themselves.[29]

Many North American middle managers think they've beaten the Japanese. They think they've won. They think they're smarter. But they don't understand the nature of the competition. The Japanese have a proven ability to cope with crisis. Japanese companies are, of necessity, becom-

---

[29]Theodore Levitt, "The Thinking Manager," *Across the Board* (June 1992), pp. 11, 13.

ing world-class experts at managing through tough times. Today, their customers won't spend enough, their currency won't fall enough, and their government won't—or can't—do enough. So Japanese managers are going back to the drawing board, sometimes literally. They are redesigning products, redeploying workers, reconfiguring distribution systems, and generally retooling some of their most storied management practices—from just-in-time production to consensus decision-making, from flexible manufacturing to continuous improvement.[30]

3M illustrates what a firm can do to prepare for the uncertain future. It recently decided to divest itself of businesses with annual sales of U.S.$3 billion (including computer diskettes, videotape, and audiotape). 3M believed its long-term prospects in those businesses were not strong. The firm is expanding its efforts in "microreplication" technologies that can "refract light or transport it, strip adhesive from plastic film or serve as a fastener, reduce water drag on boat hulls or polish golf clubs." 3M is more aggressive in obtaining ideas from business customers; and it is extremely interested in gaining insights into the unarticulated needs of those customers. As 3M's chief executive says, "We're going to do two principal things: be very innovative and satisfy our customers in all respects."[31]

To prepare for the future, companies can do the following:

- *Company vision planning*—This articulates the firm's future mission.
- *Scenario planning*—This identifies the range of events that may occur in the future.
- *Contingency planning*—This prepares alternative strategies, each keyed to a specific scenario (such as a slow-growth economy).
- *Competitive positioning*—This outlines where a firm will be positioned in the future versus competitors.
- *Competitive benchmarking*—This keeps the firm focused on how well it is doing versus its competitors.
- *Ongoing marketing research*—This entails consumer and other relevant research.[32]

As we look ahead, it is clear that the role of marketing will take on greater importance at many companies. Here is why:

> Marketing is responsible for more than the sale, and its responsibilities differ depending on the level of organization and strategy. It is the management function responsible for making sure that every aspect of the business is focused on delivering superior value [total quality] to customers in the competitive marketplace. The business is increasingly likely to be a network of strategic partnerships among designers, technology providers, manufacturers, distributors, and information specialists. The business will be defined by its customers, not its products or factories or offices. This is a critical point: in network organizations, it is the ongoing relationship with a set of customers that represents the most important business asset. Marketing as a distinct management function will be responsible for being expert on the customer and keeping the rest of the network organization informed about the customer. At the corporate and business unit levels, marketing may merge with strategic planning or, more generally, the strategy development function, with shared responsibility for information, environmental scanning, and coordination of the network activities.[33]

---

[30]Ronald Henkoff, "New Management Secrets from Japan: Really," *Fortune* (November 27, 1995), p. 136.

[31]Thomas A. Stewart, "3M Fights Back," *Fortune* (February 5, 1996), pp. 94–99.

[32]Adapted by the authors from Bernard Taylor, "The New Strategic Leadership: Driving Change, Getting Results," *Long Range Planning*, Vol. 28 (October 1995), pp. 71–81.

[33]Frederick E. Webster, Jr., "The Changing Role of Marketing in the Corporation," *Journal of Marketing*, Vol. 56 (October 1992), p. 14.

MARKETING IN A CHANGING WORLD

Stemming the Tide of Customer Defections[34]

As discussed in this chapter, measuring customer satisfaction is a key task for marketing-oriented firms. Yet, too many companies assume that satisfied customers will automatically be loyal customers. What these companies fail to recognize is that other firms may offer better choices and lure "defectors."

For example, even if you are satisfied with Air Canada, might you fly with WestJet Airlines, a new no-frills airline that started up in Calgary in February 1996, promising fares 50 to 70 per cent lower than Air Canada's? Even if you are pleased with a Jeep Cherokee, might you still switch to the more luxurious Range Rover the next time you buy? Of course, the answer to both questions is yes. Customer defections are always possible, and companies must learn to deal with them.

These are among the mistaken impressions that some firms have:

> First, it is sufficient merely to satisfy a customer; as long as a customer responds with at least a satisfied rating, the company–customer relationship is strong. In other words, a level of satisfaction below complete or total satisfaction is acceptable. After all, this is the real world, where goods and services are rarely perfect and people are hard to please. Second, the investment required to change customers from satisfied to completely satisfied will not provide an attractive financial return and probably is not a wise use of resources. There may even be instances—most notably, when competing in a cut-throat commodity market—where it doesn't pay to try to satisfy any customers. Third, each division with a relatively high average rating should focus on the customers in the lowest-satisfaction categories. Striving to understand the causes of their dissatisfaction and concentrating efforts on addressing them is the best use of resources.

To stem the tide of customer defections, instead of relying on the preceding flawed assumptions, firms must see that:

- With rare exceptions, complete customer satisfaction is the key to gaining customer loyalty and superior long-term financial results.

- Even in relatively noncompetitive markets, providing customers with outstanding value may be the most reliable way to secure sustained customer satisfaction and loyalty.

- Very poor goods and services are not the sole cause—and may not even be the main one—of high customer dissatisfaction. A company may be attracting the wrong customers or have an inadequate process for turning around the right customers after they have bad experiences.

- Different satisfaction levels require different kinds of actions.

- Customer satisfaction surveys alone are insufficient marketing feedback.

[34]The material in this section is based on Terry Bullick, "No-Frills Airline Takes Flight in Western Canada," *Marketing Magazine* (February 19, 1996), p. 2; and Thomas O. Jones and W. Earl Sasser, Jr., "Why Satisfied Customers Defect," *Harvard Business Review*, Vol. 73 (November–December 1995), pp. 88–95.

SUMMARY

1. *To show the value of an integrated marketing plan* Integrated planning builds upon a firm's strategic planning efforts and its use of a total quality approach. In this way, everyone is "on the same page." An integrated marketing plan is one in which all of its various parts are unified, consistent, and coordinated.

2. *To discuss the elements of a well-integrated marketing plan* There are several major elements in an integrated marketing plan. A clear organizational mission outlines a firm's commitment to a type of business and a place in the market. Long-term competitive advantages are company, product, and marketing attributes—whose distinctiveness and appeal to consumers can be maintained over an extended period of time. A precisely defined target market enables a firm to identify the specific consumers it addresses in a marketing plan.

The long-, moderate-, and short-term marketing subplans of a firm need to be compatible with one another. Coordination among SBUs is enhanced when the functions, strategies, and resources of each are described and monitored by top management. The components of the marketing mix need to be coordinated within each SBU. The plan must have a certain degree of stability over time.

3. *To present five types of marketing plan analysis: benchmarking, customer satisfaction research, marketing cost analysis, sales analysis, and the marketing audit* Marketing plan analysis compares a firm's actual performance with its planned or expected performance for a specified period of time. If actual performance is unsatisfactory, corrective action may be needed. Plans may have to be revised because of the impact of uncontrollable variables.

Through benchmarking, a company can set its own marketing performance standards by studying the best firms in its industry, innovative firms in any industry, direct competitors, and/or the company itself. There are strategic benchmarks and process benchmarks. In general, firms progress through three stages as they engage in benchmarking: novice, journeyman, and master. Awards such as the Canada Export Awards, the Entrepreneur of the Year Award and The Award for Canadian-American Business Achievement are good benchmarks. Surveys using criteria such as those used to award the Malcolm Baldridge National Quality Award and measure Fortune's Corporate Reputations are good benchmarking tools.

In customer satisfaction research, a firm determines the degree to which customer expectations regarding a good or service are actually satisfied. The world's largest research project in this area is the American Customer Satisfaction Index (ACSI), which rates thousands of goods and services. In 1995, the average ACSI score for all companies was 73.7 (out of 100).

Marketing cost analysis evaluates the cost efficiency of various marketing factors, such as different total quality configurations, product lines, order sizes, distribution methods, sales territories, channel members, salespersons, advertising media, and customer types. Continuous and accurate cost data are needed. Marketing cost analysis involves studying natural account expenses, reclassifying natural accounts into functional accounts, and allocating accounts by marketing classification.

Sales analysis is the detailed study of sales data for the purpose of appraising the appropriateness and effectiveness of a marketing strategy. Sales analysis enables plans to be set in terms of revenues by product, product line, salesperson, region, customer type, time period, price line, or method of sale. It also monitors actual sales against planned sales. More firms use sales analysis than marketing cost analysis. The main source of sales data is the sales invoice; control units must be specified. Sales analysis should take the 80-20 principle, the iceberg principle, and sales exception reporting into account.

The marketing audit is a systematic, critical, impartial review and appraisal of a firm's marketing objectives, strategy, implementation, and organization. It contains six steps: determining who does the audit, establishing when and how often the audit is conducted, deciding what the audit covers, developing audit forms, implementing the audit, and presenting the results. A horizontal audit studies the overall marketing performance of a firm. A vertical audit is an in-depth analysis of one aspect of marketing strategy.

4. *To see the merit of anticipating and planning for the future* Long-range plans must take into account both the external variables facing a firm and its capacity for change. A firm that does not anticipate and respond to future trends has a good chance of falling into Levitt's marketing myopia trap—which should be avoided.

KEY TERMS

marketing plan analysis (p. 450)
benchmarking (p. 451)
customer satisfaction (p. 453)
marketing cost analysis (p. 455)
natural accounts (p. 457)

functional accounts (p. 457)
sales analysis (p. 458)
control units (p. 459)
80-20 principle (p. 459)
iceberg principle (p. 459)

sales exception reporting (p. 459)
marketing audit (p. 460)
horizontal audit (p. 461)
vertical audit (p. 461)

Review Questions

1. State five of Wal-Mart's ten focused management rules.
2. Explain Figure 15-1, which deals with a well-integrated marketing plan.
3. Why might competitive advantages not travel well internationally?
4. What is benchmarking? How should a novice firm use it differently from a master firm?
5. Discuss the value of measuring customer satisfaction with studies like the American Customer Satisfaction Index (ACSI).
6. Why is functional account cost analysis more useful than natural account analysis?
7. Distinguish between marketing cost analysis and sales analysis.
8. When conducting sales analysis, why is it necessary that control units not be too wide?
9. Differentiate between a vertical and a horizontal marketing audit.
10. What are some of the positive and negative trends firms are likely to face over the coming decade?

Discussion Questions

1. Do you think your college or university is applying an integrated marketing approach? Why or why not? What marketing recommendations would you make for your school?
2. Develop a customer satisfaction survey for your local bank. Discuss the kinds of information you are seeking.
3. What data could a manufacturer obtain from a monthly analysis of its sales to wholesalers? How could this information improve marketing plans?
4. Develop a vertical marketing audit form for Sony to appraise its relationship with the retailers that carry its products.
5. As the marketing vice-president for a small book publisher, how would you prepare for the future? What key trends do you foresee over the next decade? How would you address them?

Company and Name Index

Subject Index